HOLY BIBLE

NEW TESTAMENT

HOLY BIBLE

NEW TESTAMENT

REVISED STANDARD VERSION

Catholic Edition

Cenacle

CHARLOTTE, NC

Nihil Obstat
Thomas Hanlon, S.T.L., L.S.S, PH.L.

Imprimatur
+ Gordon Joseph
Archbishop of Saint Andrews and Edinburgh
Feast of Epiphany 1966

ISBN: 978-1-951739-06-5

This Bible is published exclusively for
CENACLE
Charlotte, NC

APOSTOLIC LETTER
ISSUED "MOTU PROPRIO"

BY THE SUPREME PONTIFF

FRANCIS

"*APERUIT ILLIS*"

INSTITUTING THE SUNDAY OF THE WORD OF GOD

1. "He opened their minds to understand the Scriptures" (*Lk* 24:45). This was one of the final acts of the risen Lord before his Ascension. Jesus appeared to the assembled disciples, broke bread with them and opened their minds to the understanding of the sacred Scriptures. To them, amid their fear and bewilderment, he unveiled the meaning of the paschal mystery: that in accordance with the Father's eternal plan he had to suffer and rise from the dead, in order to bring repentance and the forgiveness of sins (cf. *Lk* 24:26.46–47). He then promised to send the Holy Spirit, who would give them strength to be witnesses of this saving mystery (cf. *Lk* 24:49).

The relationship between the Risen Lord, the community of believers and sacred Scripture is essential to our identity as Christians. Without the Lord who opens our minds to them, it is impossible to understand the Scriptures in depth. Yet the contrary is equally true: without the Scriptures, the events of the mission of Jesus and of his Church in this world would remain incomprehensible. Hence, Saint Jerome could rightly claim: "Ignorance of the Scriptures is ignorance of Christ" (*Commentary on the Book of Isaiah*, Prologue: PL 24,17B).

2. At the conclusion of the Extraordinary Jubilee of Mercy, I proposed setting aside "a Sunday given over entirely to the word of God, so as to appreciate the inexhaustible riches contained in that constant dialogue between the Lord and his people" (*Misericordia et Misera*, 7). Devoting a specific Sunday of the liturgical year to the word of God can enable the Church to experience anew how the risen Lord opens up for us the treasury of his word and enables us to proclaim its unfathomable riches before the world. Here, we are reminded of the teaching of Saint Ephrem: "Who is able to understand, Lord, all the richness of even one of your words? There is more that eludes us than what we can understand. We are like the thirsty drinking from a fountain. Your word has as many aspects as the perspectives of those who study it. The Lord has coloured his word with diverse beauties, so that those who study it can contemplate what stirs them. He has hidden in his word all treasures, so that each of us may find a richness in what he or she contemplates" (*Commentary on the Diatessaron*, 1, 18).

With this Letter, I wish to respond to the many requests I have received from the people of God that the entire Church celebrate, in unity of purpose, a Sunday of the Word of God. It is now common for the Christian community to set aside moments to reflect on the great importance of the word of God for everyday living. The various local Churches have undertaken a wealth of initiatives to make the sacred Scripture more accessible to believers, to increase their gratitude for so great a gift, and to help them to strive daily to embody and bear witness to its teachings.

The Second Vatican Council gave great impulse to the rediscovery of the word of God, thanks to its Dogmatic Constitution *Dei Verbum*, a document that deserves to be read and appropriated ever anew. The Constitution clearly expounds the nature of sacred Scripture, its transmission from generation to generation (Chapter II), its divine inspiration (Chapter III) embracing the Old and New Testaments (Chapters IV and V), and the importance of Scripture for the life of the Church (Chapter VI). To advance this teaching, Pope Benedict XVI convoked an Assembly of the Synod of Bishops in 2008 on "The Word of God in the Life and Mission of the Church", and then issued the Apostolic Exhortation *Verbum Domini*, whose teaching remains fundamental for our communities.[1] That document emphasizes in particular the performative character of the Word of God, especially in the context of the liturgy, in which its distinctively sacramental character comes to the fore.[2]

It is fitting, then that the life of our people be constantly marked by this decisive relationship with the living word that the Lord never tires of speaking to his Bride, that she may grow in love and faithful witness.

3. Consequently, I hereby declare that the Third Sunday in Ordinary Time is to be devoted to the celebration, study and dissemination of the word of God. This *Sunday of the Word of God* will thus be a fitting part of that time of the year when we are encouraged to strengthen our bonds with the Jewish people and to pray for Christian unity. This is more than a temporal coincidence: the celebration of the *Sunday of the Word of God* has ecumenical value, since the Scriptures point out, for those who listen, the path to authentic and firm unity.

The various communities will find their own ways to mark this *Sunday* with a certain solemnity. It is important, however, that in the Eucharistic celebration the sacred text be enthroned, in order to focus the attention of the assembly on the normative value of God's word. On this Sunday, it would be particularly appropriate to highlight the proclamation of the word of the Lord and to emphasize in the homily the honour that it is due. Bishops could celebrate the Rite of Installation of Lectors or a similar commissioning of readers, in order to bring out the importance of the proclamation of God's word in the liturgy. In this regard, renewed efforts should be made to provide members of the faithful with the training needed to be genuine proclaimers of the word, as is already the practice in the case of acolytes or extraordinary ministers of Holy Communion. Pastors can also find ways of giving a Bible, or one of its books, to the entire assembly as a way of showing the importance of learning how to read, appreciate and pray daily with sacred Scripture, especially through the practice of *lectio divina*.

4. The return of the people of Israel to their homeland after the Babylonian exile was marked by the public reading of the book of the Law. In the book of Nehemiah, the Bible gives us a moving description of that moment. The people

[1]Cf. AAS 102 (2010), 692–787.

[2]"The sacramentality of the word can thus be understood by analogy with the real presence of Christ under the appearances of the consecrated bread and wine. By approaching the altar and partaking in the Eucharistic banquet we truly share in the body and blood of Christ. The proclamation of God's word at the celebration entails an acknowledgment that Christ himself is present, that he speaks to us, and that he wishes to be heard" (*Verbum Domini*, 56).

assembled in Jerusalem, in the square before the Water Gate, to listen to the Law. They had been scattered in exile, but now they found themselves gathered "as one" around the sacred Scripture (*Neh* 8:1). The people lent "attentive ears" (*Neh* 8:3) to the reading of the sacred book, realizing that in its words they would discover the meaning of their lived experience. The reaction to the proclamation of was one of great emotion and tears: "[The Levites] read from the book, from the law of God, clearly; and they gave the sense, so that the people understood the reading. And Nehemiah, who was the governor, and Ezra the priest and scribe, and the Levites who taught the people said to all the people, 'This day is holy to the Lord your God; do not mourn or weep'. For all the people wept when they heard the words of the law. Then he said to them, 'Go your way, eat the fat and drink sweet wine and send portions to him for whom nothing is prepared; for this day is holy to our Lord; and do not be grieved, for the joy of the Lord is your strength'" (*Neh* 8:8–10).

These words contain a great teaching. The Bible cannot be just the heritage of some, much less a collection of books for the benefit of a privileged few. It belongs above all to those called to hear its message and to recognize themselves in its words. At times, there can be a tendency to monopolize the sacred text by restricting it to certain circles or to select groups. It cannot be that way. The Bible is the book of the Lord's people, who, in listening to it, move from dispersion and division towards unity. The word of God unites believers and makes them one people.

5. In this unity born of listening, pastors are primarily responsible for explaining sacred Scripture and helping everyone to understand it. Since it is the people's book, those called to be ministers of the word must feel an urgent need to make it accessible to their community.

The homily, in particular, has a distinctive function, for it possesses "a quasi-sacramental character" (*Evangelii Gaudium*, 142). Helping people to enter more deeply into the word of God through simple and suitable language will allow priests themselves to discover the "beauty of the images used by the Lord to encourage the practice of the good" (ibid.). This is a pastoral opportunity that should not be wasted!

For many of our faithful, in fact, this is the only opportunity they have to grasp the beauty of God's word and to see it applied to their daily lives. Consequently, sufficient time must be devoted to the preparation of the homily. A commentary on the sacred readings cannot be improvised. Those of us who are preachers should not give long, pedantic homilies or wander off into unrelated topics. When we take time to pray and meditate on the sacred text, we can speak from the heart and thus reach the hearts of those who hear us, conveying what is essential and capable of bearing fruit. May we never tire of devoting time and prayer to Scripture, so that it may be received "not as a human word but as what it really is, the word of God" (*1 Thess* 2:13).

Catechists, too, in their ministry of helping people to grow in their faith, ought to feel an urgent need for personal renewal through familiarity with, and study of, the sacred Scriptures. This will help them foster in their hearers a true dialogue with the word of God.

6. Before encountering his disciples, gathered behind closed doors, and opening their minds to the understanding of the Scriptures (cf. *Lk* 24:44–45), the risen Lord appeared to two of them on the road to Emmaus from Jerusalem (cf. *Lk* 24:13–35). Saint Luke's account notes that this happened on the very day of his resurrection, a Sunday. The two disciples were discussing the recent events concerning Jesus' passion and death. Their

journey was marked by sorrow and disappointment at his tragic death. They had hoped that he would be the Messiah who would set them free, but they found themselves instead confronted with the scandal of the cross. The risen Lord himself gently draws near and walks with them, yet they do not recognize him (cf. v. 16). Along the way, he questions them, and, seeing that they have not grasped the meaning of his passion and death, he exclaims: "O foolish men, and slow of heart" (v. 25). Then, "beginning with Moses and all the prophets, he interpreted to them the things about himself in all the Scriptures" (v.27). Christ is the first exegete! Not only did the Old Testament foretell what he would accomplish, but he himself wished to be faithful to its words, in order to make manifest the one history of salvation whose fulfilment is found in Christ.

7. The Bible, as sacred Scripture, thus speaks of Christ and proclaims him as the one who had to endure suffering and then enter into his glory (cf. v. 26). Not simply a part, but the whole of Scripture speaks of Christ. Apart from the Scriptures, his death and resurrection cannot be rightly understood. That is why one of the most ancient confessions of faith stressed that "Christ died for our sins in accordance with the Scriptures, that he was buried, that he was raised on the third day in accordance with the Scriptures, and that he appeared to Cephas" (*1Cor*15:3–5). Since the Scriptures everywhere speak of Christ, they enable us to believe that his death and resurrection are not myth but history, and are central to the faith of his disciples.

A profound bond links sacred Scripture and the faith of believers. Since faith comes from hearing, and what is heard is based on the word of Christ (cf. *Rom* 10:17), believers are bound to listen attentively to the word of the Lord, both in the celebration of the liturgy and in their personal prayer and reflection.

8. The journey that the Risen Lord makes with the disciples of Emmaus ended with a meal. The mysterious wayfarer accepts their insistent request: "Stay with us, for it is almost evening and the day is now far spent" (*Lk* 24:29). They sit down at table, and Jesus takes the bread, blesses it, breaks it and offers it to them. At that moment, their eyes are opened, and they recognize him (cf. v. 31).

This scene clearly demonstrates the unbreakable bond between sacred Scripture and the Eucharist. As the Second Vatican Council teaches, "the Church has always venerated the divine Scriptures as she has venerated the Lord's body, in that she never ceases, above all in the sacred liturgy, to partake of the bread of life and to offer it to the faithful from the one table of the word of God and the body of Christ" (*Dei Verbum*, 21).

Regular reading of sacred Scripture and the celebration of the Eucharist make it possible for us to see ourselves as part of one another. As Christians, we are a single people, making our pilgrim way through history, sustained by the Lord, present in our midst, who speaks to us and nourishes us. A day devoted to the Bible should not be seen as a yearly event but rather a year-long event, for we urgently need to grow in our knowledge and love of the Scriptures and of the risen Lord, who continues to speak his word and to break bread in the community of believers. For this reason, we need to develop a closer relationship with sacred Scripture; otherwise, our hearts will remain cold and our eyes shut, struck as we are by so many forms of blindness.

Sacred Scripture and the sacraments are thus inseparable. When the sacraments are introduced and illumined by God's word, they become ever more clearly the goal of a process whereby Christ opens our minds and hearts to acknowledge his saving work. We should always keep in mind the teaching found in the Book of Revelation: the Lord is standing at the door and knocking. If anyone should hear his voice and open for him, he will come in and eat with them (cf. 3:20). Christ Jesus is knocking at our door in the words of sacred Scripture. If we hear his voice and open the doors of our minds and hearts, then he will enter our lives and remain ever with us.

9. In the Second Letter to Timothy, which is in some ways his spiritual testament, Saint Paul urges his faithful co-worker to have constant recourse to sacred Scripture. The Apostle is convinced that "all Scripture is inspired by God and profitable for teaching, for reproof, for correction, and for training in righteousness" (3:16). Paul's exhortation to Timothy is fundamental to the teaching of the conciliar Constitution *Dei Verbum* on the great theme of biblical inspiration, which emphasizes the Scriptures' *saving purpose*, *spiritual dimension* and inherent *incarnational principle*.

First, recalling Paul's encouragement to Timothy, *Dei Verbum* stresses that "we must acknowledge that the books of Scripture firmly, faithfully and without error, teach that truth which God, for the sake of our salvation, wished to see confided to the sacred Scriptures" (No. 11). Since the Scriptures teach with a view to salvation through faith in Christ (cf. *2 Tim* 3:15), the truths contained therein are profitable for our salvation. The Bible is not a collection of history books or a chronicle, but is aimed entirely at the integral salvation of the person. The evident historical setting of the books of the Bible should not make us overlook their primary goal, which is our salvation. Everything is directed to this purpose and essential to the very nature of the Bible, which takes shape as a history of salvation in which God speaks and acts in order to encounter all men and women and to save them from evil and death.

To achieve this saving purpose, sacred Scripture, by the working of the Holy Spirit, makes human words written in human fashion become the word of God (cf. *Dei Verbum*, 12). The role of the Holy Spirit in the Scriptures is primordial. Without the work of the Spirit, there would always be a risk of remaining limited to the written text alone. This would open the way to a fundamentalist reading, which needs to be avoided, lest we betray the inspired, dynamic and spiritual character of the sacred text. As the Apostle reminds us: "The letter kills, but the Spirit gives life" (*2 Cor* 3:6). The Holy Spirit, then, makes sacred Scripture the living word of God, experienced and handed down in the faith of his holy people.

10. The work of the Holy Spirit has to do not only with the formation of sacred Scripture; it is also operative in those who hear the word of God. The words of the Council Fathers are instructive: sacred Scripture is to be "read and interpreted in the light of the same Spirit through whom it was written" (*Dei Verbum*, 12). God's revelation attains its completion and fullness in Jesus Christ; nonetheless, the Holy Spirit does not cease to act. It would be reductive indeed to restrict the working of the Spirit to the divine inspiration of sacred Scripture and its various human authors. We need to have confidence in the working of the Holy Spirit as he continues in his own way to provide "inspiration" whenever the Church teaches the sacred Scriptures, whenever the Magisterium authentically interprets them (cf. ibid., 10), and whenever each believer makes them the norm of his or her spiritual life. In this sense, we can understand the words spoken by Jesus to his disciples when they told him that they now understood the meaning of his parables:

"Every scribe who has been trained for the kingdom of heaven is like a householder who brings out of his treasure what is new and what is old" (*Mt* 13:52).

11. Finally, *Dei Verbum* makes clear that "the words of God, expressed in human language, are in every way like human speech, just as the Word of the eternal Father, in taking upon himself the weak flesh of human beings, also took on their likeness" (No. 13). We can say that the incarnation of the eternal Word gives shape and meaning to the relationship between God's word and our human language, in all its historical and cultural contingency. This event gives rise to Tradition, which is also God's word (cf. ibid., 9). We frequently risk separating sacred Scripture and sacred Tradition, without understanding that together they are the one source of Revelation. The written character of the former takes nothing away from its being fully a living word; in the same way, the Church's living Tradition, which continually hands that word down over the centuries from one generation to the next, possesses that sacred book as the "supreme rule of her faith" (ibid., 21). Moreover, before becoming a written text, the word of God was handed down orally and kept alive by the faith of a people who, in the midst of many others, acknowledged it as their own history and the source of their identity. Biblical faith, then, is based on the living word, not on a book.

12. When sacred Scripture is read in the light of the same Spirit by whom it was written, it remains ever new. The Old Testament is never old once it is part of the New, since all has been transformed thanks to the one Spirit who inspired it. The sacred text as a whole serves a prophetic function regarding not the future but the present of whoever is nourished by this word. Jesus himself clearly stated this at the beginning of his ministry: "Today this Scripture has been fulfilled in your hearing" (*Lk* 4:21). Those who draw daily nourishment from God's word become, like Jesus, a contemporary of all those whom they encounter: they are not tempted to fall into sterile nostalgia for the past, or to dream of ethereal utopias yet to come.

Sacred Scripture accomplishes its prophetic work above all in those who listen to it. It proves both sweet and bitter. We are reminded of the words of the prophet Ezekiel when, commanded by the Lord to eat the scroll of the book, he tells us: "It was in my mouth as sweet as honey" (3:3). John the Evangelist too, on the island of Patmos, echoes Ezekiel's experience of eating the scroll, but goes on to add: "It was sweet as honey in my mouth, but when I had eaten it my stomach was made bitter" (*Rev* 10:10).

The sweetness of God's word leads us to share it with all those whom we encounter in this life and to proclaim the sure hope that it contains (cf. *1 Pet* 3:15–16). Its bitterness, in turn, often comes from our realization of how difficult it is to live that word consistently, or our personal experience of seeing it rejected as meaningless for life. We should never take God's word for granted, but instead let ourselves be nourished by it, in order to acknowledge and live fully our relationship with him and with our brothers and sisters.

13. Yet another challenge raised by sacred Scripture has to do with love. God's word constantly reminds us of the merciful love of the Father who calls his children to live in love. The life of Jesus is the full and perfect expression of this divine love, which holds nothing back but offers itself to all without reserve. In the parable of Lazarus, we find a valuable teaching. When both Lazarus and the rich man die, the latter, seeing the poor man Lazarus in Abraham's bosom, asks that Lazarus be sent to his brothers to warn them to love their neighbour, lest they

also experience his torment. Abraham's answer is biting: "They have Moses and the prophets; let them hear them" (*Lk* 16:29). To listen to sacred Scripture and then to practise mercy: this is the great challenge before us in life. God's word has the power to open our eyes and to enable us to renounce a stifling and barren individualism and instead to embark on a new path of sharing and solidarity.

14. One of the most significant moments in Jesus' relationship with his disciples is found in the account of the Transfiguration. He goes up the mountain with Peter, James and John to pray. The evangelists tell us that as Jesus' face and clothing became dazzlingly white, two men conversed with him: Moses and Elijah, representing respectively the Law and the Prophets; in other words, sacred Scripture. Peter's reaction to this sight is one of amazement and joy: "Master, it is well that we are here; let us make three tents, one for you and one for Moses and one for Elijah" (*Lk* 9:33). At that moment a cloud overshadows them, and the disciples are struck with fear.

The Transfiguration reminds us of the Feast of Tabernacles, when Ezra and Nehemiah read the sacred text to the people after their return from exile. At the same time, it foreshadows Jesus' glory, as a way of preparing the disciples for the scandal of the Passion: that divine glory is also evoked by the cloud enveloping the disciples as a symbol of God's presence. A similar transfiguration takes place with sacred Scripture, which transcends itself whenever it nourishes the lives of believers. As the Apostolic Exhortation *Verbum Domini* reminds us: "In rediscovering the interplay between the different senses of Scripture it becomes essential to grasp the *passage from letter to spirit*. This is not an automatic, spontaneous passage; rather, the letter needs to be transcended" (No. 38).

15. Along our path of welcoming God's word into our hearts, the Mother of the Lord accompanies us. She is the one who was called blessed because she believed in the fulfilment of what the Lord had spoken to her (cf. *Lk* 1:45). Mary's own beatitude is prior to all the beatitudes proclaimed by Jesus about the poor and those who mourn, the meek, the peacemakers and those who are persecuted, for it is the necessary condition for every other kind of beatitude. The poor are not blessed because they are poor; they become blessed if, like Mary, they believe in the fulfilment of God's word. A great disciple and master of sacred Scripture, Saint Augustine, once wrote: "Someone in the midst of the crowd, seized with enthusiasm, cried out: 'Blessed is the womb that bore you' and Jesus replied, 'Rather, blessed are they who hear the word of God and keep it'. As if to say: My mother, whom you call blessed, is indeed blessed, because she keeps the word of God. Not because in her the Word became flesh and dwelt among us, but because she keeps that same word of God by which she was made and which, in her womb, became flesh" (*Tractates on the Gospel of John*, 10, 3).

May the Sunday of the Word of God help his people to grow in religious and intimate familiarity with the sacred Scriptures. For as the sacred author taught of old: "This word is very near to you: it is in your mouth and in your heart for your observance" (*Dt* 30:14).

Given in Rome, at the Basilica of Saint John Lateran, on 30 September 2019, the liturgical Memorial of Saint Jerome, on the inauguration of the 1600th anniversary of his death.

FRANCISCUS

Table of Contents

Foreword

Despite the decline of religious practice, the appetite of English people for new versions of Scripture is, paradoxically, greater than ever. Educated people are still expected to have some acquaintance with the Bible even though religious convictions are no longer demanded. One does not need to be either a Christian or a scholar to recognize the Bible as great literature. With the growth of literacy greater numbers are able to enjoy the Bible's unique appeal. No other religious writing however exalted can compete with the inspired text.

We welcome a Catholic edition of the Revised Standard Version, not only because it will lead more of our people to read the Bible, but also because of its ecumenical value. May all who read it grow in the knowledge and love of God's own word.

✠ JOHN CARDINAL HEENAN
Archbishop of Westminster
December 1965

The Editors of this edition, Dom Bernard Orchard, O.S.B. and the Reverend R.C. Fuller, D.D.D., L.S.S., wish to express appreciation for permission to use, with authorized changes, the Revised Standard Version of the Bible, copyrighted, 1946, 1952, and 1957.

The Books of the Bible in Alphabetical Order and Abbreviations

Acts of the Apostles	Acts	Mark	Mk
Colossians	Col	Matthew	Mt
1 Corinthians	1 Cor	1 Peter	1 Pet
2 Corinthians	2 Cor	2 Peter	2 Pet
Ephesians	Eph	Philemon	Philem
Galatians	Gal	Philippians	Phil
Hebrews	Heb	Revelation	Rev
James	Jas	Romans	Rom
John	Jn	1 Thessalonians	1 Thess
1 John	1 Jn	2 Thessalonians	2 Thess
2 John	2 Jn	1 Timothy	1 Tim
3 John	3 Jn	2 Timothy	2 Tim
Jude	Jude	Titus	Titus
Luke	Lk		

The New Testament

The Gospel According to

MATTHEW

The Genealogy of Jesus the Messiah

1 The book of the genealogy of Jesus
Christ, the son of David, the son of
Abraham.
2 Abraham was the father of Isaac,
and Isaac the father of Jacob, and Ja-
cob the father of Judah and his broth-
ers, 3 and Judah the father of Perez and
Zerah by Tamar, and Perez the father of
Hezron, and Hezron the father of Ram,[a]
4 and Ram[b] the father of Ammin′adab,
and Ammin′adab the father of Nahshon,
and Nahshon the father of Salmon, 5 and
Salmon the father of Bo′az by Rahab, and
Bo′az the father of Obed by Ruth, and
Obed the father of Jesse, 6 and Jesse the
father of David the king.
And David was the father of Solomon
by the wife of Uri′ah, 7 and Solomon the
father of Rehobo′am, and Rehobo′am
the father of Abi′jah, and Abi′jah the fa-
ther of Asa,[c] 8 and Asa[d] the father of Je-
hosh′aphat, and Jehosh′aphat the father
of Joram, and Joram the father of Uzzi′ah,
9 and Uzzi′ah the father of Jotham, and
Jotham the father of Ahaz, and Ahaz
the father of Hezeki′ah, 10 and Hezeki′ah
the father of Manas′seh, and Manas′seh
the father of Amos,[e] and Amos[f] the fa-
ther of Josi′ah, 11 and Josi′ah the father of
Jechoni′ah and his brothers, at the time
of the deportation to Babylon.
12 And after the deportation to Bab-
ylon: Jechoni′ah was the father of She-
al′ti-el,[g] and She-al′ti-el[h] the father of
Zerub′babel, 13 and Zerub′babel the fa-
ther of Abi′ud, and Abi′ud the father of
Eli′akim, and Eli′akim the father of Azor,
14 and Azor the father of Zadok, and Za-
dok the father of Achim, and Achim the
father of Eli′ud, 15 and Eli′ud the father of
Elea′zar, and Elea′zar the father of Mat-
than, and Matthan the father of Jacob,
16 and Jacob the father of Joseph the hus-
band of Mary, of whom Jesus was born,
who is called Christ.
17 So all the generations from Abra-
ham to David were fourteen genera-
tions, and from David to the deportation
to Babylon fourteen generations, and
from the deportation to Babylon to the
Christ fourteen generations.

The Birth of Jesus the Messiah

18 Now the birth of Jesus Christ[i] took
place in this way. When his mother
Mary had been betrothed to Joseph, be-
fore they came together she was found
to be with child of the Holy Spirit; 19 and
her husband Joseph, being a just man
and unwilling to put her to shame, re-
solved to send her away quietly. 20 But
as he considered this, behold, an angel
of the Lord appeared to him in a dream,
saying, "Joseph, son of David, do not fear
to take Mary your wife, for that which
is conceived in her is of the Holy Spirit;
21 she will bear a son, and you shall call
his name Jesus, for he will save his peo-
ple from their sins." 22 All this took place
to fulfil what the Lord had spoken by the
prophet:
23 "Behold, a virgin shall conceive and
bear a son,
and his name shall be called
Emman′u-el"
(which means, God with us). 24 When Jo-
seph woke from sleep, he did as the an-
gel of the Lord commanded him; he took
his wife, 25 but knew her not until she
had borne a son; and he called his name
Jesus.

[a] **1.3** Greek *Aram* [b] **1.4** Greek *Aram* [c] **1.7** Greek *Asaph* [d] **1.8** Greek *Asaph* [e] **1.10** Other authorities read *Amon* [f] **1.10** Other authorities read *Amon* [g] **1.12** Greek *Salathiel* [h] **1.12** Greek *Salathiel* [i] **1.18** Other ancient authorities read *of the Christ*

The Visit of the Wise Men

2 Now when Jesus was born in Beth-
lehem of Judea in the days of Herod
the king, behold, wise men from the East
came to Jerusalem, saying, 2“Where is
he who has been born king of the Jews?
For we have seen his star in the East,
and have come to worship him.” 3When
Herod the king heard this, he was trou-
bled, and all Jerusalem with him; 4and as-
sembling all the chief priests and scribes
of the people, he inquired of them where
the Christ was to be born. 5They told him,
“In Bethlehem of Judea; for so it is writ-
ten by the prophet:
6 ‘And you, O Bethlehem, in the land
of Judah,
are by no means least among the
rulers of Judah;
for from you shall come a ruler
who will govern my people Israel.’ ”
7 Then Herod summoned the wise men
secretly and ascertained from them what
time the star appeared; 8and he sent them
to Bethlehem, saying, “Go and search dil-
igently for the child, and when you have
found him bring me word, that I too may
come and worship him.” 9When they had
heard the king they went their way; and
lo, the star which they had seen in the
East went before them, till it came to
rest over the place where the child was.
10When they saw the star, they rejoiced
exceedingly with great joy; 11and going
into the house they saw the child with
Mary his mother, and they fell down
and worshiped him. Then, opening their
treasures, they offered him gifts, gold
and frankincense and myrrh. 12And be-
ing warned in a dream not to return to
Herod, they departed to their own coun-
try by another way.

The Escape to Egypt

13 Now when they had departed, behold,
an angel of the Lord appeared to Joseph
in a dream and said, “Rise, take the child
and his mother, and flee to Egypt, and
remain there till I tell you; for Herod is
about to search for the child, to destroy
him.” 14And he rose and took the child
and his mother by night, and departed
to Egypt, 15and remained there until the
death of Herod. This was to fulfil what
the Lord had spoken by the prophet, “Out
of Egypt have I called my son.”

The Massacre of the Infants

16 Then Herod, when he saw that he had
been tricked by the wise men, was in a
furious rage, and he sent and killed all
the male children in Bethlehem and in
all that region who were two years old
or under, according to the time which
he had ascertained from the wise men.
17Then was fulfilled what was spoken by
the prophet Jeremiah:
18 “A voice was heard in Ramah,
wailing and loud lamentation,
Rachel weeping for her children;
she refused to be consoled,
because they were no more.”

The Return from Egypt

19 But when Herod died, behold, an angel
of the Lord appeared in a dream to Joseph
in Egypt, saying, 20“Rise, take the child
and his mother, and go to the land of Is-
rael, for those who sought the child’s life
are dead.” 21And he rose and took the child
and his mother, and went to the land of Is-
rael. 22But when he heard that Archela′us
reigned over Judea in place of his father
Herod, he was afraid to go there, and be-
ing warned in a dream he withdrew to
the district of Galilee. 23And he went and
dwelt in a city called Nazareth, that what
was spoken by the prophets might be ful-
filled, “He shall be called a Nazarene.”

The Proclamation of John the Baptist

3 In those days came John the Baptist,
preaching in the wilderness of Judea,
2“Repent, for the kingdom of heaven is at
hand.” 3For this is he who was spoken of
by the prophet Isaiah when he said,

"The voice of one crying in the
wilderness:
Prepare the way of the Lord,
make his paths straight."
[4]Now John wore a garment of camel's
hair, and a leather girdle around his
waist; and his food was locusts and wild
honey. [5]Then went out to him Jerusalem
and all Judea and all the region about the
Jordan, [6]and they were baptized by him
in the river Jordan, confessing their sins.
7 But when he saw many of the Phari-
sees and Sad'ducees coming for baptism,
he said to them, "You brood of vipers!
Who warned you to flee from the wrath to
come? [8]Bear fruit that befits repentance,
[9]and do not presume to say to yourselves,
'We have Abraham as our father'; for I
tell you, God is able from these stones to
raise up children to Abraham. [10]Even now
the axe is laid to the root of the trees; ev-
ery tree therefore that does not bear good
fruit is cut down and thrown into the fire.
11 "I baptize you with water for repen-
tance, but he who is coming after me is
mightier than I, whose sandals I am not
worthy to carry; he will baptize you with
the Holy Spirit and with fire. [12]His win-
nowing fork is in his hand, and he will
clear his threshing floor and gather his
wheat into the granary, but the chaff he
will burn with unquenchable fire."

The Baptism of Jesus

13 Then Jesus came from Galilee to the
Jordan to John, to be baptized by him.
[14]John would have prevented him, say-
ing, "I need to be baptized by you, and do
you come to me?" [15]But Jesus answered
him, "Let it be so now; for thus it is fit-
ting for us to fulfil all righteousness."
Then he consented. [16]And when Jesus
was baptized, he went up immediately
from the water, and behold, the heavens
were opened[j] and he saw the Spirit of
God descending like a dove, and alight-
ing on him; [17]and lo, a voice from heaven,
saying, "This is my beloved Son,[k] with
whom I am well pleased."

The Temptation of Jesus

4 Then Jesus was led up by the Spirit
into the wilderness to be tempted
by the devil. [2]And he fasted forty days
and forty nights, and afterward he was
hungry. [3]And the tempter came and said
to him, "If you are the Son of God, com-
mand these stones to become loaves of
bread." [4]But he answered, "It is written,
'Man shall not live by bread alone,
but by every word that proceeds
from the mouth of God.'"
[5]Then the devil took him to the holy city,
and set him on the pinnacle of the tem-
ple, [6]and said to him, "If you are the Son
of God, throw yourself down; for it is
written,
'He will give his angels charge of
you,'
and
'On their hands they will bear you up,
lest you strike your foot against a
stone.'"
[7]Jesus said to him, "Again it is written,
'You shall not tempt the Lord your God.'"
[8]Again, the devil took him to a very high
mountain, and showed him all the king-
doms of the world and the glory of them;
[9]and he said to him, "All these I will give
you, if you will fall down and worship
me." [10]Then Jesus said to him, "Begone,
Satan! for it is written,
'You shall worship the Lord your
God
and him only shall you serve.'"
[11]Then the devil left him, and behold, an-
gels came and ministered to him.

Jesus Begins His Ministry in Galilee

12 Now when he heard that John had been
arrested, he withdrew into Galilee; [13]and
leaving Nazareth he went and dwelt in
Caper'na-um by the sea, in the territory
of Zeb'ulun and Naph'tali, [14]that what was

[j] **3.16** Other ancient authorities add *to him*
[k] **3.17** Or *my Son, my* (or *the*) *Beloved*

spoken by the prophet Isaiah might be
fulfilled:

15 “The land of Zeb′ulun and the land
of Naph′tali,
toward the sea, across the Jordan,
Galilee of the Gentiles—
16 the people who sat in darkness
have seen a great light,
and for those who sat in the region
and shadow of death
light has dawned.”

17 From that time Jesus began to preach,
saying, “Repent, for the kingdom of
heaven is at hand.”

Jesus Calls the First Disciples

18 As he walked by the Sea of Galilee, he
saw two brothers, Simon who is called
Peter and Andrew his brother, casting a
net into the sea; for they were fishermen.
19 And he said to them, “Follow me, and I
will make you fishers of men.” 20 Imme-
diately they left their nets and followed
him. 21 And going on from there he saw
two other brothers, James the son of Ze-
b′edee and John his brother, in the boat
with Zeb′edee their father, mending
their nets, and he called them. 22 Immedi-
ately they left the boat and their father,
and followed him.

Jesus Ministers to Crowds of People

23 And he went about all Galilee, teach-
ing in their synagogues and preaching
the gospel of the kingdom and healing
every disease and every infirmity among
the people. 24 So his fame spread through-
out all Syria, and they brought him all
the sick, those afflicted with various
diseases and pains, demoniacs, epilep-
tics, and paralytics, and he healed them.
25 And great crowds followed him from
Galilee and the Decap′olis and Jerusalem
and Judea and from beyond the Jordan.

The Beatitudes

5 Seeing the crowds, he went up on the
mountain, and when he sat down his
disciples came to him. 2 And he opened
his mouth and taught them, saying:

3 “Blessed are the poor in spirit, for
theirs is the kingdom of heaven.

4 “Blessed are those who mourn, for
they shall be comforted.

5 “Blessed are the meek, for they shall
inherit the earth.

6 “Blessed are those who hunger and
thirst for righteousness, for they shall
be satisfied.

7 “Blessed are the merciful, for they
shall obtain mercy.

8 “Blessed are the pure in heart, for
they shall see God.

9 “Blessed are the peacemakers, for
they shall be called sons of God.

10 “Blessed are those who are perse-
cuted for righteousness’ sake, for theirs
is the kingdom of heaven.

11 “Blessed are you when men revile
you and persecute you and utter all
kinds of evil against you falsely on my
account. 12 Rejoice and be glad, for your
reward is great in heaven, for so men
persecuted the prophets who were be-
fore you.

Salt and Light

13 “You are the salt of the earth; but if salt
has lost its taste, how shall its saltness be
restored? It is no longer good for any-
thing except to be thrown out and trod-
den under foot by men.

14 “You are the light of the world. A city
set on a hill cannot be hid. 15 Nor do men
light a lamp and put it under a bushel,
but on a stand, and it gives light to all in
the house. 16 Let your light so shine be-
fore men, that they may see your good
works and give glory to your Father who
is in heaven.

The Law and the Prophets

17 “Think not that I have come to abolish
the law and the prophets; I have come not
to abolish them but to fulfil them. 18 For
truly, I say to you, till heaven and earth

pass away, not an iota, not a dot, will pass
from the law until all is accomplished.
[19]Whoever then relaxes one of the least
of these commandments and teaches
men so, shall be called least in the king-
dom of heaven; but he who does them
and teaches them shall be called great in
the kingdom of heaven. [20]For I tell you,
unless your righteousness exceeds that
of the scribes and Pharisees, you will
never enter the kingdom of heaven.

Concerning Anger

21 "You have heard that it was said to the
men of old, 'You shall not kill; and who-
ever kills shall be liable to judgment.'
[22]But I say to you that every one who is
angry with his brother[l] shall be liable to
judgment; whoever insults[m] his brother
shall be liable to the council, and who-
ever says, 'You fool!' shall be liable to the
hell[n] of fire. [23]So if you are offering your
gift at the altar, and there remember
that your brother has something against
you, [24]leave your gift there before the
altar and go; first be reconciled to your
brother, and then come and offer your
gift. [25]Make friends quickly with your
accuser, while you are going with him to
court, lest your accuser hand you over to
the judge, and the judge to the guard, and
you be put in prison; [26]truly, I say to you,
you will never get out till you have paid
the last penny.

Concerning Adultery

27 "You have heard that it was said, 'You
shall not commit adultery.' [28]But I say
to you that every one who looks at a
woman lustfully has already committed
adultery with her in his heart. [29]If your
right eye causes you to sin, pluck it out
and throw it away; it is better that you
lose one of your members than that your
whole body be thrown into hell.[o] [30]And if
your right hand causes you to sin, cut it
off and throw it away; it is better that you
lose one of your members than that your
whole body go into hell.[p]

Concerning Divorce

31 "It was also said, 'Whoever divorces
his wife, let him give her a certificate
of divorce.' [32]But I say to you that every
one who divorces his wife, except on the
ground of unchastity, makes her an adul-
teress; and whoever marries a divorced
woman commits adultery.

Concerning Oaths

33 "Again you have heard that it was said
to the men of old, 'You shall not swear
falsely, but shall perform to the Lord
what you have sworn.' [34]But I say to you,
Do not swear at all, either by heaven, for
it is the throne of God, [35]or by the earth,
for it is his footstool, or by Jerusalem, for
it is the city of the great King. [36]And do
not swear by your head, for you cannot
make one hair white or black. [37]Let what
you say be simply 'Yes' or 'No'; anything
more than this comes from evil.[q]

Concerning Retaliation

38 "You have heard that it was said, 'An
eye for an eye and a tooth for a tooth.'
[39]But I say to you, Do not resist one who
is evil. But if any one strikes you on the
right cheek, turn to him the other also;
[40]and if any one would sue you and take
your coat, let him have your cloak as
well; [41]and if any one forces you to go
one mile, go with him two miles. [42]Give
to him who begs from you, and do not
refuse him who would borrow from you.

Love for Enemies

43 "You have heard that it was said, 'You
shall love your neighbor and hate your
enemy.' [44]But I say to you, Love your

[l] **5.22** Other ancient authorities insert *without cause* [m] **5.22** Greek *says Raca to* (an obscure term of abuse) [n] **5.22** Greek *Gehenna* [o] **5.29** Greek *Gehenna* [p] **5.30** Greek *Gehenna*
[q] **5.37** Or *the evil one*

enemies and pray for those who per-
secute you, [45]so that you may be sons
of your Father who is in heaven; for he
makes his sun rise on the evil and on the
good, and sends rain on the just and on
the unjust. [46]For if you love those who
love you, what reward have you? Do
not even the tax collectors do the same?
[47]And if you salute only your brethren,
what more are you doing than others? Do
not even the Gentiles do the same? [48]You,
therefore, must be perfect, as your heav-
enly Father is perfect.

Concerning Almsgiving

6 "Beware of practicing your piety be-
fore men in order to be seen by them;
for then you will have no reward from
your Father who is in heaven.

2 "Thus, when you give alms, sound no
trumpet before you, as the hypocrites do
in the synagogues and in the streets, that
they may be praised by men. Truly, I say
to you, they have their reward. [3]But when
you give alms, do not let your left hand
know what your right hand is doing, [4]so
that your alms may be in secret; and your
Father who sees in secret will reward you.

Concerning Prayer

5 "And when you pray, you must not be
like the hypocrites; for they love to stand
and pray in the synagogues and at the
street corners, that they may be seen by
men. Truly, I say to you, they have their
reward. [6]But when you pray, go into your
room and shut the door and pray to your
Father who is in secret; and your Father
who sees in secret will reward you.

7 "And in praying do not heap up
empty phrases as the Gentiles do; for
they think that they will be heard for
their many words. [8]Do not be like them,
for your Father knows what you need
before you ask him. [9]Pray then like this:

Our Father who art in heaven,
Hallowed be thy name.
10 Thy kingdom come,
Thy will be done,
On earth as it is in heaven.
11 Give us this day our daily bread;[r]
12 And forgive us our debts,
As we also have forgiven our
debtors;
13 And lead us not into temptation,
But deliver us from evil.[s]

[14]For if you forgive men their trespasses,
your heavenly Father also will forgive
you; [15]but if you do not forgive men their
trespasses, neither will your Father for-
give your trespasses.

Concerning Fasting

16 "And when you fast, do not look dis-
mal, like the hypocrites, for they disfig-
ure their faces that their fasting may be
seen by men. Truly, I say to you, they have
their reward. [17]But when you fast, anoint
your head and wash your face, [18]that your
fasting may not be seen by men but by
your Father who is in secret; and your Fa-
ther who sees in secret will reward you.

Concerning Treasures

19 "Do not lay up for yourselves trea-
sures on earth, where moth and rust[t]
consume and where thieves break in and
steal, [20]but lay up for yourselves trea-
sures in heaven, where neither moth nor
rust[u] consumes and where thieves do not
break in and steal. [21]For where your trea-
sure is, there will your heart be also.

The Sound Eye

22 "The eye is the lamp of the body. So, if
your eye is sound, your whole body will
be full of light; [23]but if your eye is not
sound, your whole body will be full of
darkness. If then the light in you is dark-
ness, how great is the darkness!

[r] **6.11** Or *our bread for the morrow* [s] **6.13** Or *the evil one.* Other authorities, some ancient, add, in some form, *For thine is the kingdom and the power and the glory, for ever. Amen.* [t] **6.19** Or *worm* [u] **6.20** Or *worm*

Serving Two Masters

24 "No one can serve two masters; for
either he will hate the one and love the
other, or he will be devoted to the one
and despise the other. You cannot serve
God and mammon.

Do Not Worry

25 "Therefore I tell you, do not be anx-
ious about your life, what you shall eat
or what you shall drink, nor about your
body, what you shall put on. Is not life
more than food, and the body more than
clothing? 26Look at the birds of the air:
they neither sow nor reap nor gather
into barns, and yet your heavenly Father
feeds them. Are you not of more value
than they? 27And which of you by being
anxious can add one cubit to his span of
life?[v] 28And why are you anxious about
clothing? Consider the lilies of the field,
how they grow; they neither toil nor
spin; 29yet I tell you, even Solomon in
all his glory was not arrayed like one of
these. 30But if God so clothes the grass of
the field, which today is alive and tomor-
row is thrown into the oven, will he not
much more clothe you, O men of little
faith? 31Therefore do not be anxious, say-
ing, 'What shall we eat?' or 'What shall
we drink?' or 'What shall we wear?' 32For
the Gentiles seek all these things; and
your heavenly Father knows that you
need them all. 33But seek first his king-
dom and his righteousness, and all these
things shall be yours as well.

34 "Therefore do not be anxious about
tomorrow, for tomorrow will be anxious
for itself. Let the day's own trouble be
sufficient for the day.

Judging Others

7 "Judge not, that you be not judged.
2For with the judgment you pro-
nounce you will be judged, and the mea-
sure you give will be the measure you
get. 3Why do you see the speck that is
in your brother's eye, but do not notice
the log that is in your own eye? 4Or how
can you say to your brother, 'Let me take
the speck out of your eye,' when there is
the log in your own eye? 5You hypocrite,
first take the log out of your own eye,
and then you will see clearly to take the
speck out of your brother's eye.

Profaning the Holy

6 "Do not give dogs what is holy; and do
not throw your pearls before swine, lest
they trample them under foot and turn
to attack you.

Ask, Search, Knock

7 "Ask, and it will be given you; seek,
and you will find; knock, and it will be
opened to you. 8For every one who asks
receives, and he who seeks finds, and to
him who knocks it will be opened. 9Or
what man of you, if his son asks him for
bread, will give him a stone? 10Or if he
asks for a fish, will give him a serpent?
11If you then, who are evil, know how
to give good gifts to your children, how
much more will your Father who is in
heaven give good things to those who ask
him! 12So whatever you wish that men
would do to you, do so to them; for this is
the law and the prophets.

The Narrow Gate

13 "Enter by the narrow gate; for the gate
is wide and the way is easy,[w] that leads
to destruction, and those who enter by
it are many. 14For the gate is narrow and
the way is hard, that leads to life, and
those who find it are few.

A Tree and Its Fruit

15 "Beware of false prophets, who come
to you in sheep's clothing but inwardly
are ravenous wolves. 16You will know
them by their fruits. Are grapes gath-
ered from thorns, or figs from thistles?
17So, every sound tree bears good fruit,

[v] **6.27** Or *to his stature*
[w] **7.13** Other ancient authorities read *for the way is wide and easy*

but the bad tree bears evil fruit. 18A
sound tree cannot bear evil fruit, nor
can a bad tree bear good fruit. 19Every
tree that does not bear good fruit is cut
down and thrown into the fire. 20Thus
you will know them by their fruits.

Concerning Self-Deception

21 "Not every one who says to me, 'Lord,
Lord,' shall enter the kingdom of heaven,
but he who does the will of my Father
who is in heaven. 22On that day many will
say to me, 'Lord, Lord, did we not proph-
esy in your name, and cast out demons in
your name, and do many mighty works
in your name?' 23And then will I declare
to them, 'I never knew you; depart from
me, you evildoers.'

Hearers and Doers

24 "Every one then who hears these
words of mine and does them will be like
a wise man who built his house upon the
rock; 25and the rain fell, and the floods
came, and the winds blew and beat upon
that house, but it did not fall, because it
had been founded on the rock. 26And ev-
ery one who hears these words of mine
and does not do them will be like a foolish
man who built his house upon the sand;
27and the rain fell, and the floods came,
and the winds blew and beat against that
house, and it fell; and great was the fall
of it."

28 And when Jesus finished these
sayings, the crowds were astonished
at his teaching, 29for he taught them as
one who had authority, and not as their
scribes.

Jesus Cleanses a Leper

8 When he came down from the moun-
tain, great crowds followed him; 2and
behold, a leper came to him and knelt be-
fore him, saying, "Lord, if you will, you
can make me clean." 3And he stretched
out his hand and touched him, saying,
"I will; be clean." And immediately his
leprosy was cleansed. 4And Jesus said to
him, "See that you say nothing to any one;
but go, show yourself to the priest, and
offer the gift that Moses commanded, for
a proof to the people."[x]

Jesus Heals a Centurion's Servant

5 As he entered Caper'na-um, a centu-
rion came forward to him, beseeching
him 6and saying, "Lord, my servant is
lying paralyzed at home, in terrible dis-
tress." 7And he said to him, "I will come
and heal him." 8But the centurion an-
swered him, "Lord, I am not worthy to
have you come under my roof; but only
say the word, and my servant will be
healed. 9For I am a man under authority,
with soldiers under me; and I say to one,
'Go,' and he goes, and to another, 'Come,'
and he comes, and to my slave, 'Do this,'
and he does it." 10When Jesus heard him,
he marveled, and said to those who fol-
lowed him, "Truly, I say to you, not even[y]
in Israel have I found such faith. 11I tell
you, many will come from east and west
and sit at table with Abraham, Isaac, and
Jacob in the kingdom of heaven, 12while
the sons of the kingdom will be thrown
into the outer darkness; there men will
weep and gnash their teeth." 13And to the
centurion Jesus said, "Go; be it done for
you as you have believed." And the ser-
vant was healed at that very moment.

Jesus Heals Many at Peter's House

14 And when Jesus entered Peter's house,
he saw his mother-in-law lying sick with
a fever; 15he touched her hand, and the
fever left her, and she rose and served
him. 16That evening they brought to him
many who were possessed with demons;
and he cast out the spirits with a word,
and healed all who were sick. 17This was
to fulfil what was spoken by the prophet
Isaiah, "He took our infirmities and bore
our diseases."

[x]**8.4** Greek *to them* [y]**8.10** Other ancient authorities read *with no one*

Would-Be Followers of Jesus

18 Now when Jesus saw great crowds around him, he gave orders to go over to the other side. [19]And a scribe came up and said to him, "Teacher, I will follow you wherever you go." [20]And Jesus said to him, "Foxes have holes, and birds of the air have nests; but the Son of man has nowhere to lay his head." [21]Another of the disciples said to him, "Lord, let me first go and bury my father." [22]But Jesus said to him, "Follow me, and leave the dead to bury their own dead."

Jesus Stills the Storm

23 And when he got into the boat, his disciples followed him. [24]And behold, there arose a great storm on the sea, so that the boat was being swamped by the waves; but he was asleep. [25]And they went and woke him, saying, "Save, Lord; we are perishing." [26]And he said to them, "Why are you afraid, O men of little faith?" Then he rose and rebuked the winds and the sea; and there was a great calm. [27]And the men marveled, saying, "What sort of man is this, that even winds and sea obey him?"

Jesus Heals the Gadarene Demoniacs

28 And when he came to the other side, to the country of the Gadarenes,[z] two demoniacs met him, coming out of the tombs, so fierce that no one could pass that way. [29]And behold, they cried out, "What have you to do with us, O Son of God? Have you come here to torment us before the time?" [30]Now a herd of many swine was feeding at some distance from them. [31]And the demons begged him, "If you cast us out, send us away into the herd of swine." [32]And he said to them, "Go." So they came out and went into the swine; and behold, the whole herd rushed down the steep bank into the sea, and perished in the waters. [33]The herdsmen fled, and going into the city they told everything, and what had happened to the demoniacs. [34]And behold, all the city came out to meet Jesus; and when they saw him, they begged him to leave their neighborhood.

Jesus Heals a Paralytic

9 And getting into a boat he crossed over and came to his own city. [2]And behold, they brought to him a paralytic, lying on his bed; and when Jesus saw their faith he said to the paralytic, "Take heart, my son; your sins are forgiven." [3]And behold, some of the scribes said to themselves, "This man is blaspheming." [4]But Jesus, knowing[a] their thoughts, said, "Why do you think evil in your hearts? [5]For which is easier, to say, 'Your sins are forgiven,' or to say, 'Rise and walk'? [6]But that you may know that the Son of man has authority on earth to forgive sins"—he then said to the paralytic—"Rise, take up your bed and go home." [7]And he rose and went home. [8]When the crowds saw it, they were afraid, and they glorified God, who had given such authority to men.

The Call of Matthew

9 As Jesus passed on from there, he saw a man called Matthew sitting at the tax office; and he said to him, "Follow me." And he rose and followed him.

10 And as he sat at table[b] in the house, behold, many tax collectors and sinners came and sat down with Jesus and his disciples. [11]And when the Pharisees saw this, they said to his disciples, "Why does your teacher eat with tax collectors and sinners?" [12]But when he heard it, he said, "Those who are well have no need of a physician, but those who are sick. [13]Go and learn what this means, 'I desire mercy, and not sacrifice.' For I came not to call the righteous, but sinners."

[z] **8.28** Other ancient authorities read *Gergesenes*; some, *Gerasenes* [a] **9.4** Other ancient authorities read *seeing* [b] **9.10** Greek *reclined*

The Question about Fasting

14 Then the disciples of John came to
him, saying, "Why do we and the Phari-
sees fast,[c] but your disciples do not fast?"
15 And Jesus said to them, "Can the wed-
ding guests mourn as long as the bride-
groom is with them? The days will come,
when the bridegroom is taken away
from them, and then they will fast. 16 And
no one puts a piece of unshrunk cloth on
an old garment, for the patch tears away
from the garment, and a worse tear is
made. 17 Neither is new wine put into old
wineskins; if it is, the skins burst, and
the wine is spilled, and the skins are de-
stroyed; but new wine is put into fresh
wineskins, and so both are preserved."

A Girl Restored to Life and a Woman Healed

18 While he was thus speaking to them,
behold, a ruler came in and knelt before
him, saying, "My daughter has just died;
but come and lay your hand on her, and
she will live." 19 And Jesus rose and fol-
lowed him, with his disciples. 20 And be-
hold, a woman who had suffered from a
hemorrhage for twelve years came up
behind him and touched the fringe of
his garment; 21 for she said to herself, "If
I only touch his garment, I shall be made
well." 22 Jesus turned, and seeing her he
said, "Take heart, daughter; your faith
has made you well." And instantly the
woman was made well. 23 And when Jesus
came to the ruler's house, and saw the
flute players, and the crowd making a tu-
mult, 24 he said, "Depart; for the girl is not
dead but sleeping." And they laughed at
him. 25 But when the crowd had been put
outside, he went in and took her by the
hand, and the girl arose. 26 And the report
of this went through all that district.

Jesus Heals Two Blind Men

27 And as Jesus passed on from there,
two blind men followed him, crying
aloud, "Have mercy on us, Son of David."
28 When he entered the house, the blind
men came to him; and Jesus said to them,
"Do you believe that I am able to do this?"
They said to him, "Yes, Lord." 29 Then he
touched their eyes, saying, "According to
your faith be it done to you." 30 And their
eyes were opened. And Jesus sternly
charged them, "See that no one knows
it." 31 But they went away and spread his
fame through all that district.

Jesus Heals One Who Was Mute

32 As they were going away, behold, a
dumb demoniac was brought to him.
33 And when the demon had been cast out,
the dumb man spoke; and the crowds
marveled, saying, "Never was anything
like this seen in Israel." 34 But the Phar-
isees said, "He casts out demons by the
prince of demons."

The Harvest Is Great, the Laborers Few

35 And Jesus went about all the cities and
villages, teaching in their synagogues
and preaching the gospel of the kingdom,
and healing every disease and every in-
firmity. 36 When he saw the crowds, he
had compassion for them, because they
were harassed and helpless, like sheep
without a shepherd. 37 Then he said to his
disciples, "The harvest is plentiful, but
the laborers are few; 38 pray therefore the
Lord of the harvest to send out laborers
into his harvest."

The Twelve Apostles

10 And he called to him his twelve
disciples and gave them authority
over unclean spirits, to cast them out,
and to heal every disease and every in-
firmity. 2 The names of the twelve apos-
tles are these: first, Simon, who is called
Peter, and Andrew his brother; James
the son of Zeb'edee, and John his brother;
3 Philip and Bartholomew; Thomas and
Matthew the tax collector; James the son

[c] **9.14** Other ancient authorities add *much* or *often*

of Alphaeus, and Thaddaeus;[d] 4 Simon
the Cananaean, and Judas Iscariot, who
betrayed him.

The Mission of the Twelve

5 These twelve Jesus sent out, charging
them, "Go nowhere among the Gentiles,
and enter no town of the Samaritans, 6 but
go rather to the lost sheep of the house
of Israel. 7 And preach as you go, saying,
'The kingdom of heaven is at hand.' 8 Heal
the sick, raise the dead, cleanse lepers,
cast out demons. You received without
pay, give without pay. 9 Take no gold, nor
silver, nor copper in your belts, 10 no bag
for your journey, nor two tunics, nor
sandals, nor a staff; for the laborer de-
serves his food. 11 And whatever town or
village you enter, find out who is worthy
in it, and stay with him until you depart.
12 As you enter the house, salute it. 13 And
if the house is worthy, let your peace
come upon it; but if it is not worthy, let
your peace return to you. 14 And if any
one will not receive you or listen to your
words, shake off the dust from your feet
as you leave that house or town. 15 Truly,
I say to you, it shall be more tolerable on
the day of judgment for the land of So-
dom and Gomor'rah than for that town.

Coming Persecutions

16 "Behold, I send you out as sheep in the
midst of wolves; so be wise as serpents
and innocent as doves. 17 Beware of men;
for they will deliver you up to councils,
and flog you in their synagogues, 18 and
you will be dragged before governors
and kings for my sake, to bear testimony
before them and the Gentiles. 19 When
they deliver you up, do not be anxious
how you are to speak or what you are
to say; for what you are to say will be
given to you in that hour; 20 for it is not
you who speak, but the Spirit of your
Father speaking through you. 21 Brother
will deliver up brother to death, and the
father his child, and children will rise
against parents and have them put to
death; 22 and you will be hated by all for
my name's sake. But he who endures to
the end will be saved. 23 When they per-
secute you in one town, flee to the next;
for truly, I say to you, you will not have
gone through all the towns of Israel, be-
fore the Son of man comes.

24 "A disciple is not above his teacher,
nor a servant[e] above his master; 25 it is
enough for the disciple to be like his
teacher, and the servant[f] like his mas-
ter. If they have called the master of the
house Be-el'zebul, how much more will
they malign those of his household.

Whom to Fear

26 "So have no fear of them; for nothing
is covered that will not be revealed, or
hidden that will not be known. 27 What I
tell you in the dark, utter in the light; and
what you hear whispered, proclaim upon
the housetops. 28 And do not fear those
who kill the body but cannot kill the soul;
rather fear him who can destroy both soul
and body in hell.[g] 29 Are not two sparrows
sold for a penny? And not one of them will
fall to the ground without your Father's
will. 30 But even the hairs of your head
are all numbered. 31 Fear not, therefore;
you are of more value than many spar-
rows. 32 So every one who acknowledges
me before men, I also will acknowledge
before my Father who is in heaven; 33 but
whoever denies me before men, I also will
deny before my Father who is in heaven.

Not Peace, but a Sword

34 "Do not think that I have come to bring
peace on earth; I have not come to bring
peace, but a sword. 35 For I have come to
set a man against his father, and a daugh-
ter against her mother, and a daughter-
in-law against her mother-in-law; 36 and

[d] **10.3** Other ancient authorities read *Lebbaeus* or *Lebbaeus called Thaddaeus* [e] **10.24** Or *slave* [f] **10.25** Or *slave* [g] **10.28** Greek *Gehenna*

a man's foes will be those of his own household. [37]He who loves father or mother more than me is not worthy of me; and he who loves son or daughter more than me is not worthy of me; [38]and he who does not take his cross and follow me is not worthy of me. [39]He who finds his life will lose it, and he who loses his life for my sake will find it.

Rewards

40 "He who receives you receives me, and he who receives me receives him who sent me. [41]He who receives a prophet because he is a prophet shall receive a prophet's reward, and he who receives a righteous man because he is a righteous man shall receive a righteous man's reward. [42]And whoever gives to one of these little ones even a cup of cold water because he is a disciple, truly, I say to you, he shall not lose his reward."

11 And when Jesus had finished instructing his twelve disciples, he went on from there to teach and preach in their cities.

Messengers from John the Baptist

2 Now when John heard in prison about the deeds of the Christ, he sent word by his disciples [3]and said to him, "Are you he who is to come, or shall we look for another?" [4]And Jesus answered them, "Go and tell John what you hear and see: [5]the blind receive their sight and the lame walk, lepers are cleansed and the deaf hear, and the dead are raised up, and the poor have good news preached to them. [6]And blessed is he who takes no offense at me."

Jesus Praises John the Baptist

7 As they went away, Jesus began to speak to the crowds concerning John: "What did you go out into the wilderness to behold? A reed shaken by the wind? [8]Why then did you go out? To see a man[h] clothed in soft raiment? Behold, those who wear soft raiment are in kings' houses. [9]Why then did you go out? To see a prophet?[i] Yes, I tell you, and more than a prophet. [10]This is he of whom it is written,

'Behold, I send my messenger before
thy face,
who shall prepare thy way before
thee.'

[11]Truly, I say to you, among those born of women there has risen no one greater than John the Baptist; yet he who is least in the kingdom of heaven is greater than he. [12]From the days of John the Baptist until now the kingdom of heaven has suffered violence,[j] and men of violence take it by force. [13]For all the prophets and the law prophesied until John; [14]and if you are willing to accept it, he is Eli′jah who is to come. [15]He who has ears to hear,[k] let him hear.

16 "But to what shall I compare this generation? It is like children sitting in the market places and calling to their playmates,

17 'We piped to you, and you did not
dance;
we wailed, and you did not mourn.'

[18]For John came neither eating nor drinking, and they say, 'He has a demon'; [19]the Son of man came eating and drinking, and they say, 'Behold, a glutton and a drunkard, a friend of tax collectors and sinners!' Yet wisdom is justified by her deeds."[l]

Woes to Unrepentant Cities

20 Then he began to upbraid the cities where most of his mighty works had been done, because they did not repent. [21]"Woe to you, Chora′zin! woe to you,

[h] **11.8** Or *What then did you go out to see? A man . . .* [i] **11.9** Other ancient authorities read *What then did you go out to see? A prophet?* [j] **11.12** Or *has been coming violently* [k] **11.15** Other ancient authorities omit *to hear* [l] **11.19** Other ancient authorities read *children* (Lk 7.35)

Beth-sa'ida! for if the mighty works done
in you had been done in Tyre and Sidon,
they would have repented long ago in
sackcloth and ashes. 22But I tell you, it
shall be more tolerable on the day of
judgment for Tyre and Sidon than for
you. 23And you, Caper'na-um, will you be
exalted to heaven? You shall be brought
down to Hades. For if the mighty works
done in you had been done in Sodom,
it would have remained until this day.
24But I tell you that it shall be more toler-
able on the day of judgment for the land
of Sodom than for you."

Jesus Thanks His Father

25 At that time Jesus declared, "I thank
thee, Father, Lord of heaven and earth,
that thou hast hidden these things from
the wise and understanding and revealed
them to babes; 26yea, Father, for such was
thy gracious will.[m] 27All things have been
delivered to me by my Father; and no one
knows the Son except the Father, and no
one knows the Father except the Son and
any one to whom the Son chooses to re-
veal him. 28Come to me, all who labor and
are heavy laden, and I will give you rest.
29Take my yoke upon you, and learn from
me; for I am gentle and lowly in heart, and
you will find rest for your souls. 30For my
yoke is easy, and my burden is light."

Plucking Grain on the Sabbath

12 At that time Jesus went through
the grainfields on the sabbath; his
disciples were hungry, and they began
to pluck ears of grain and to eat. 2But
when the Pharisees saw it, they said to
him, "Look, your disciples are doing
what is not lawful to do on the sabbath."
3He said to them, "Have you not read
what David did, when he was hungry,
and those who were with him: 4how he
entered the house of God and ate the
bread of the Presence, which it was not
lawful for him to eat nor for those who
were with him, but only for the priests?
5Or have you not read in the law how on
the sabbath the priests in the temple pro-
fane the sabbath, and are guiltless? 6I tell
you, something greater than the temple
is here. 7And if you had known what this
means, 'I desire mercy, and not sacri-
fice,' you would not have condemned the
guiltless. 8For the Son of man is lord of
the sabbath."

The Man with a Withered Hand

9 And he went on from there, and en-
tered their synagogue. 10And behold,
there was a man with a withered hand.
And they asked him, "Is it lawful to heal
on the sabbath?" so that they might ac-
cuse him. 11He said to them, "What man
of you, if he has one sheep and it falls
into a pit on the sabbath, will not lay hold
of it and lift it out? 12Of how much more
value is a man than a sheep! So it is law-
ful to do good on the sabbath." 13Then he
said to the man, "Stretch out your hand."
And the man stretched it out, and it was
restored, whole like the other. 14But the
Pharisees went out and took counsel
against him, how to destroy him.

God's Chosen Servant

15 Jesus, aware of this, withdrew from
there. And many followed him, and he
healed them all, 16and ordered them not
to make him known. 17This was to fulfil
what was spoken by the prophet Isaiah:

18 "Behold, my servant whom I have
chosen,
my beloved with whom my soul is
well pleased.
I will put my Spirit upon him,
and he shall proclaim justice to
the Gentiles.
19 He will not wrangle or cry aloud,
nor will any one hear his voice in
the streets;
20 he will not break a bruised reed
or quench a smoldering wick,

[m]**11.26** Or *so it was well-pleasing before thee*

till he brings justice to victory;
21 and in his name will the Gentiles
hope."

Jesus and Beelzebul

22 Then a blind and dumb demoniac was
brought to him, and he healed him, so
that the dumb man spoke and saw. [23]And
all the people were amazed, and said,
"Can this be the Son of David?" [24]But
when the Pharisees heard it they said,
"It is only by Be-el'zebul, the prince of
demons, that this man casts out demons."
[25]Knowing their thoughts, he said to
them, "Every kingdom divided against
itself is laid waste, and no city or house
divided against itself will stand; [26]and
if Satan casts out Satan, he is divided
against himself; how then will his king-
dom stand? [27]And if I cast out demons
by Be-el'zebul, by whom do your sons
cast them out? Therefore they shall be
your judges. [28]But if it is by the Spirit
of God that I cast out demons, then the
kingdom of God has come upon you. [29]Or
how can one enter a strong man's house
and plunder his goods, unless he first
binds the strong man? Then indeed he
may plunder his house. [30]He who is not
with me is against me, and he who does
not gather with me scatters. [31]Therefore
I tell you, every sin and blasphemy will
be forgiven men, but the blasphemy
against the Spirit will not be forgiven.
[32]And whoever says a word against the
Son of man will be forgiven; but who-
ever speaks against the Holy Spirit will
not be forgiven, either in this age or in
the age to come.

A Tree and Its Fruit

33 "Either make the tree good, and its
fruit good; or make the tree bad, and its
fruit bad; for the tree is known by its
fruit. [34]You brood of vipers! how can you
speak good, when you are evil? For out
of the abundance of the heart the mouth
speaks. [35]The good man out of his good
treasure brings forth good, and the evil
man out of his evil treasure brings forth
evil. [36]I tell you, on the day of judgment
men will render account for every care-
less word they utter; [37]for by your words
you will be justified, and by your words
you will be condemned."

The Sign of Jonah

38 Then some of the scribes and Phari-
sees said to him, "Teacher, we wish to see
a sign from you." [39]But he answered them,
"An evil and adulterous generation seeks
for a sign; but no sign shall be given to it
except the sign of the prophet Jonah. [40]For
as Jonah was three days and three nights
in the belly of the whale, so will the Son
of man be three days and three nights
in the heart of the earth. [41]The men of
Nin'eveh will arise at the judgment with
this generation and condemn it; for they
repented at the preaching of Jonah, and
behold, something greater than Jonah is
here. [42]The queen of the South will arise
at the judgment with this generation and
condemn it; for she came from the ends
of the earth to hear the wisdom of Solo-
mon, and behold, something greater than
Solomon is here.

The Return of the Unclean Spirit

43 "When the unclean spirit has gone
out of a man, he passes through water-
less places seeking rest, but he finds
none. [44]Then he says, 'I will return to my
house from which I came.' And when he
comes he finds it empty, swept, and put
in order. [45]Then he goes and brings with
him seven other spirits more evil than
himself, and they enter and dwell there;
and the last state of that man becomes
worse than the first. So shall it be also
with this evil generation."

The True Kindred of Jesus

46 While he was still speaking to the
people, behold, his mother and his breth-
ren stood outside, asking to speak to

him.[n] 48But he replied to the man who told him, "Who is my mother, and who are my brethren?" 49And stretching out his hand toward his disciples, he said, "Here are my mother and my brethren! 50For whoever does the will of my Father in heaven is my brother, and sister, and mother."

The Parable of the Sower

13 That same day Jesus went out of the house and sat beside the sea. 2And great crowds gathered about him, so that he got into a boat and sat there; and the whole crowd stood on the beach. 3And he told them many things in parables, saying: "A sower went out to sow. 4And as he sowed, some seeds fell along the path, and the birds came and devoured them. 5Other seeds fell on rocky ground, where they had not much soil, and immediately they sprang up, since they had no depth of soil, 6but when the sun rose they were scorched; and since they had no root they withered away. 7Other seeds fell upon thorns, and the thorns grew up and choked them. 8Other seeds fell on good soil and brought forth grain, some a hundredfold, some sixty, some thirty. 9He who has ears,[o] let him hear."

The Purpose of the Parables

10 Then the disciples came and said to him, "Why do you speak to them in parables?" 11And he answered them, "To you it has been given to know the secrets of the kingdom of heaven, but to them it has not been given. 12For to him who has will more be given, and he will have abundance; but from him who has not, even what he has will be taken away. 13This is why I speak to them in parables, because seeing they do not see, and hearing they do not hear, nor do they understand. 14With them indeed is fulfilled the prophecy of Isaiah which says:

'You shall indeed hear but never understand,
and you shall indeed see but never perceive.
15 For this people's heart has grown dull,
and their ears are heavy of hearing,
and their eyes they have closed,
lest they should perceive with their eyes,
and hear with their ears,
and understand with their heart,
and turn for me to heal them.'

16But blessed are your eyes, for they see, and your ears, for they hear. 17Truly, I say to you, many prophets and righteous men longed to see what you see, and did not see it, and to hear what you hear, and did not hear it.

The Parable of the Sower Explained

18 "Hear then the parable of the sower. 19When any one hears the word of the kingdom and does not understand it, the evil one comes and snatches away what is sown in his heart; this is what was sown along the path. 20As for what was sown on rocky ground, this is he who hears the word and immediately receives it with joy; 21yet he has no root in himself, but endures for a while, and when tribulation or persecution arises on account of the word, immediately he falls away.[p] 22As for what was sown among thorns, this is he who hears the word, but the cares of the world and the delight in riches choke the word, and it proves unfruitful. 23As for what was sown on good soil, this is he who hears the word and understands it; he indeed bears fruit, and yields, in one case a hundredfold, in another sixty, and in another thirty."

[n]**12.46** Other ancient authorities insert verse 47, *Some one told him, "Your mother and your brethren are standing outside, asking to speak to you"* [o]**13.9** Other ancient authorities add here and in verse 43 *to hear* [p]**13.21** Or *stumbles*

The Parable of Weeds among the Wheat

24 Another parable he put before them,
saying, "The kingdom of heaven may be
compared to a man who sowed good seed in
his field; 25 but while men were sleeping, his
enemy came and sowed weeds among the
wheat, and went away. 26 So when the plants
came up and bore grain, then the weeds
appeared also. 27 And the servants[q] of the
householder came and said to him, 'Sir, did
you not sow good seed in your field? How
then has it weeds?' 28 He said to them, 'An
enemy has done this.' The servants[r] said to
him, 'Then do you want us to go and gather
them?' 29 But he said, 'No; lest in gathering
the weeds you root up the wheat along with
them. 30 Let both grow together until the
harvest; and at harvest time I will tell the
reapers, Gather the weeds first and bind
them in bundles to be burned, but gather
the wheat into my barn.'"

The Parable of the Mustard Seed

31 Another parable he put before them,
saying, "The kingdom of heaven is like a
grain of mustard seed which a man took
and sowed in his field; 32 it is the smallest
of all seeds, but when it has grown it is
the greatest of shrubs and becomes a
tree, so that the birds of the air come and
make nests in its branches."

The Parable of the Yeast

33 He told them another parable. "The
kingdom of heaven is like leaven which
a woman took and hid in three measures
of meal, till it was all leavened."

The Use of Parables

34 All this Jesus said to the crowds in
parables; indeed he said nothing to them
without a parable. 35 This was to fulfil
what was spoken by the prophet:[s]

> "I will open my mouth in parables,
> I will utter what has been hidden
> since the foundation of the
> world."

Jesus Explains the Parable of the Weeds

36 Then he left the crowds and went into
the house. And his disciples came to him,
saying, "Explain to us the parable of the
weeds of the field." 37 He answered, "He
who sows the good seed is the Son of
man; 38 the field is the world, and the good
seed means the sons of the kingdom; the
weeds are the sons of the evil one, 39 and
the enemy who sowed them is the devil;
the harvest is the close of the age, and the
reapers are angels. 40 Just as the weeds
are gathered and burned with fire, so
will it be at the close of the age. 41 The Son
of man will send his angels, and they will
gather out of his kingdom all causes of
sin and all evildoers, 42 and throw them
into the furnace of fire; there men will
weep and gnash their teeth. 43 Then the
righteous will shine like the sun in the
kingdom of their Father. He who has
ears, let him hear.

Three Parables

44 "The kingdom of heaven is like trea-
sure hidden in a field, which a man found
and covered up; then in his joy he goes
and sells all that he has and buys that field.

45 "Again, the kingdom of heaven is
like a merchant in search of fine pearls,
46 who, on finding one pearl of great
value, went and sold all that he had and
bought it.

47 "Again, the kingdom of heaven is like
a net which was thrown into the sea and
gathered fish of every kind; 48 when it was
full, men drew it ashore and sat down and
sorted the good into vessels but threw
away the bad. 49 So it will be at the close of
the age. The angels will come out and sep-
arate the evil from the righteous, 50 and
throw them into the furnace of fire; there
men will weep and gnash their teeth.

Treasures New and Old

51 "Have you understood all this?" They
said to him, "Yes." 52 And he said to them,

[q] **13.27** Or *slaves* [r] **13.28** Or *slaves* [s] **13.35** Other ancient authorities read *the prophet Isaiah*

"Therefore every scribe who has been trained for the kingdom of heaven is like a householder who brings out of his treasure what is new and what is old."

The Rejection of Jesus at Nazareth

53 And when Jesus had finished these parables, he went away from there, 54 and coming to his own country he taught them in their synagogue, so that they were astonished, and said, "Where did this man get this wisdom and these mighty works? 55 Is not this the carpenter's son? Is not his mother called Mary? And are not his brethren James and Joseph and Simon and Judas? 56 And are not all his sisters with us? Where then did this man get all this?" 57 And they took offense at him. But Jesus said to them, "A prophet is not without honor except in his own country and in his own house." 58 And he did not do many mighty works there, because of their unbelief.

The Death of John the Baptist

14 At that time Herod the tetrarch heard about the fame of Jesus; 2 and he said to his servants, "This is John the Baptist, he has been raised from the dead; that is why these powers are at work in him." 3 For Herod had seized John and bound him and put him in prison, for the sake of Hero′di-as, his brother Philip's wife;[t] 4 because John said to him, "It is not lawful for you to have her." 5 And though he wanted to put him to death, he feared the people, because they held him to be a prophet. 6 But when Herod's birthday came, the daughter of Hero′di-as danced before the company, and pleased Herod, 7 so that he promised with an oath to give her whatever she might ask. 8 Prompted by her mother, she said, "Give me the head of John the Baptist here on a platter." 9 And the king was sorry; but because of his oaths and his guests he commanded it to be given; 10 he sent and had John beheaded in the prison, 11 and his head was brought on a platter and given to the girl, and she brought it to her mother. 12 And his disciples came and took the body and buried it; and they went and told Jesus.

Feeding the Five Thousand

13 Now when Jesus heard this, he withdrew from there in a boat to a lonely place apart. But when the crowds heard it, they followed him on foot from the towns. 14 As he went ashore he saw a great throng; and he had compassion on them, and healed their sick. 15 When it was evening, the disciples came to him and said, "This is a lonely place, and the day is now over; send the crowds away to go into the villages and buy food for themselves." 16 Jesus said, "They need not go away; you give them something to eat." 17 They said to him, "We have only five loaves here and two fish." 18 And he said, "Bring them here to me." 19 Then he ordered the crowds to sit down on the grass; and taking the five loaves and the two fish he looked up to heaven, and blessed, and broke and gave the loaves to the disciples, and the disciples gave them to the crowds. 20 And they all ate and were satisfied. And they took up twelve baskets full of the broken pieces left over. 21 And those who ate were about five thousand men, besides women and children.

Jesus Walks on the Water

22 Then he made the disciples get into the boat and go before him to the other side, while he dismissed the crowds. 23 And after he had dismissed the crowds, he went up into the hills by himself to pray. When evening came, he was there alone, 24 but the boat by this time was many furlongs distant from the land,[u] beaten by the waves; for the wind was

[t] **14.3** Other ancient authorities read *his brother's wife*

[u] **14.24** Other ancient authorities read *was out on the sea*

against them. [25]And in the fourth watch
of the night he came to them, walking on
the sea. [26]But when the disciples saw him
walking on the sea, they were terrified,
saying, "It is a ghost!" And they cried out
for fear. [27]But immediately he spoke to
them, saying, "Take heart, it is I; have no
fear."

28 And Peter answered him, "Lord, if it
is you, bid me come to you on the water."
[29]He said, "Come." So Peter got out of the
boat and walked on the water and came
to Jesus; [30]but when he saw the wind,[v]
he was afraid, and beginning to sink he
cried out, "Lord, save me." [31]Jesus imme-
diately reached out his hand and caught
him, saying to him, "O man of little faith,
why did you doubt?" [32]And when they
got into the boat, the wind ceased. [33]And
those in the boat worshiped him, saying,
"Truly you are the Son of God."

Jesus Heals the Sick in Gennesaret

34 And when they had crossed over, they
came to land at Gennes'aret. [35]And when
the men of that place recognized him,
they sent round to all that region and
brought to him all that were sick, [36]and
besought him that they might only touch
the fringe of his garment; and as many as
touched it were made well.

The Tradition of the Elders

15 Then Pharisees and scribes came
to Jesus from Jerusalem and said,
[2]"Why do your disciples transgress the
tradition of the elders? For they do not
wash their hands when they eat." [3]He
answered them, "And why do you trans-
gress the commandment of God for the
sake of your tradition? [4]For God com-
manded, 'Honor your father and your
mother,' and, 'He who speaks evil of fa-
ther or mother, let him surely die.' [5]But
you say, 'If any one tells his father or his
mother, What you would have gained
from me is given to God,[w] he need not
honor his father.' [6]So, for the sake of your
tradition, you have made void the word[x]
of God. [7]You hypocrites! Well did Isaiah
prophesy of you, when he said:

8 'This people honors me with their
lips,
but their heart is far from me;
9 in vain do they worship me,
teaching as doctrines the precepts
of men.' "

Things That Defile

10 And he called the people to him and
said to them, "Hear and understand:
[11]not what goes into the mouth defiles a
man, but what comes out of the mouth,
this defiles a man." [12]Then the disciples
came and said to him, "Do you know
that the Pharisees were offended when
they heard this saying?" [13]He answered,
"Every plant which my heavenly Father
has not planted will be rooted up. [14]Let
them alone; they are blind guides. And if
a blind man leads a blind man, both will
fall into a pit." [15]But Peter said to him,
"Explain the parable to us." [16]And he said,
"Are you also still without understand-
ing? [17]Do you not see that whatever goes
into the mouth passes into the stomach,
and so passes on?[y] [18]But what comes out
of the mouth proceeds from the heart,
and this defiles a man. [19]For out of the
heart come evil thoughts, murder, adul-
tery, fornication, theft, false witness,
slander. [20]These are what defile a man;
but to eat with unwashed hands does not
defile a man."

The Canaanite Woman's Faith

21 And Jesus went away from there and
withdrew to the district of Tyre and
Sidon. [22]And behold, a Canaanite woman
from that region came out and cried,
"Have mercy on me, O Lord, Son of Da-
vid; my daughter is severely possessed

[v]**14.30** Other ancient authorities read *strong wind* [w]**15.5** Or *an offering* [x]**15.6** Other ancient authorities read *law* [y]**15.17** Or *is evacuated*

by a demon." 23But he did not answer
her a word. And his disciples came and
begged him, saying, "Send her away, for
she is crying after us." 24He answered,
"I was sent only to the lost sheep of the
house of Israel." 25But she came and knelt
before him, saying, "Lord, help me."
26And he answered, "It is not fair to take
the children's bread and throw it to the
dogs." 27She said, "Yes, Lord, yet even the
dogs eat the crumbs that fall from their
master's table." 28Then Jesus answered
her, "O woman, great is your faith! Be
it done for you as you desire." And her
daughter was healed instantly.

Jesus Cures Many People

29 And Jesus went on from there and
passed along the Sea of Galilee. And he
went up into the hills, and sat down there.
30And great crowds came to him, bring-
ing with them the lame, the maimed, the
blind, the dumb, and many others, and
they put them at his feet, and he healed
them, 31so that the throng wondered,
when they saw the dumb speaking, the
maimed whole, the lame walking, and
the blind seeing; and they glorified the
God of Israel.

Feeding the Four Thousand

32 Then Jesus called his disciples to
him and said, "I have compassion on
the crowd, because they have been with
me now three days, and have nothing
to eat; and I am unwilling to send them
away hungry, lest they faint on the way."
33And the disciples said to him, "Where
are we to get bread enough in the desert
to feed so great a crowd?" 34And Jesus
said to them, "How many loaves have
you?" They said, "Seven, and a few small
fish." 35And commanding the crowd to sit
down on the ground, 36he took the seven
loaves and the fish, and having given
thanks he broke them and gave them to
the disciples, and the disciples gave them
to the crowds. 37And they all ate and were
satisfied; and they took up seven bas-
kets full of the broken pieces left over.
38Those who ate were four thousand
men, besides women and children. 39And
sending away the crowds, he got into the
boat and went to the region of Mag'adan.

The Demand for a Sign

16 And the Pharisees and Sad'ducees
came, and to test him they asked
him to show them a sign from heaven.
2He answered them,[z] "When it is eve-
ning, you say, 'It will be fair weather;
for the sky is red.' 3And in the morning,
'It will be stormy today, for the sky is
red and threatening.' You know how to
interpret the appearance of the sky, but
you cannot interpret the signs of the
times. 4An evil and adulterous genera-
tion seeks for a sign, but no sign shall be
given to it except the sign of Jonah." So he
left them and departed.

The Yeast of the Pharisees and Sadducees

5 When the disciples reached the other
side, they had forgotten to bring any
bread. 6Jesus said to them, "Take heed
and beware of the leaven of the Pharisees
and Sad'ducees." 7And they discussed it
among themselves, saying, "We brought
no bread." 8But Jesus, aware of this, said,
"O men of little faith, why do you discuss
among yourselves the fact that you have
no bread? 9Do you not yet perceive? Do
you not remember the five loaves of the
five thousand, and how many baskets
you gathered? 10Or the seven loaves of
the four thousand, and how many bas-
kets you gathered? 11How is it that you
fail to perceive that I did not speak about
bread? Beware of the leaven of the Phari-
sees and Sad'ducees." 12Then they under-
stood that he did not tell them to beware
of the leaven of bread, but of the teaching
of the Pharisees and Sad'ducees.

[z] **16.2** Other ancient authorities omit the following words to the end of verse 3

Peter's Declaration about Jesus

13 Now when Jesus came into the district of Caesare′a Philippi, he asked his disciples, "Who do men say that the Son of man is?" 14 And they said, "Some say John the Baptist, others say Eli′jah, and others Jeremiah or one of the prophets." 15 He said to them, "But who do you say that I am?" 16 Simon Peter replied, "You are the Christ, the Son of the living God." 17 And Jesus answered him, "Blessed are you, Simon Bar-Jona! For flesh and blood has not revealed this to you, but my Father who is in heaven. 18 And I tell you, you are Peter,[a] and on this rock[b] I will build my church, and the powers of death[c] shall not prevail against it. 19 I will give you the keys of the kingdom of heaven, and whatever you bind on earth shall be bound in heaven, and whatever you loose on earth shall be loosed in heaven." 20 Then he strictly charged the disciples to tell no one that he was the Christ.

Jesus Foretells His Death and Resurrection

21 From that time Jesus began to show his disciples that he must go to Jerusalem and suffer many things from the elders and chief priests and scribes, and be killed, and on the third day be raised. 22 And Peter took him and began to rebuke him, saying, "God forbid, Lord! This shall never happen to you." 23 But he turned and said to Peter, "Get behind me, Satan! You are a hindrance[d] to me; for you are not on the side of God, but of men."

The Cross and Self-Denial

24 Then Jesus told his disciples, "If any man would come after me, let him deny himself and take up his cross and follow me. 25 For whoever would save his life will lose it, and whoever loses his life for my sake will find it. 26 For what will it profit a man, if he gains the whole world and forfeits his life? Or what shall a man give in return for his life? 27 For the Son of man is to come with his angels in the glory of his Father, and then he will repay every man for what he has done. 28 Truly, I say to you, there are some standing here who will not taste death before they see the Son of man coming in his kingdom."

The Transfiguration

17 And after six days Jesus took with him Peter and James and John his brother, and led them up a high mountain apart. 2 And he was transfigured before them, and his face shone like the sun, and his garments became white as light. 3 And behold, there appeared to them Moses and Eli′jah, talking with him. 4 And Peter said to Jesus, "Lord, it is well that we are here; if you wish, I will make three booths here, one for you and one for Moses and one for Eli′jah." 5 He was still speaking, when lo, a bright cloud overshadowed them, and a voice from the cloud said, "This is my beloved Son,[e] with whom I am well pleased; listen to him." 6 When the disciples heard this, they fell on their faces, and were filled with awe. 7 But Jesus came and touched them, saying, "Rise, and have no fear." 8 And when they lifted up their eyes, they saw no one but Jesus only.

9 And as they were coming down the mountain, Jesus commanded them, "Tell no one the vision, until the Son of man is raised from the dead." 10 And the disciples asked him, "Then why do the scribes say that first Eli′jah must come?" 11 He replied, "Eli′jah does come, and he is to restore all things; 12 but I tell you that Eli′jah has already come, and they did not know him, but did to him whatever they pleased. So also the Son of man will suffer at their hands." 13 Then the disciples understood that he was speaking to them of John the Baptist.

[a] **16.18** Greek *Petros* [b] **16.18** Greek *petra* [c] **16.18** Greek *the gates of Hades* [d] **16.23** Greek *stumbling block* [e] **17.5** Or *my Son, my* (or *the*) *Beloved*

Jesus Cures a Boy with a Demon

14 And when they came to the crowd, a
man came up to him and kneeling before
him said, 15“Lord, have mercy on my son,
for he is an epileptic and he suffers ter-
ribly; for often he falls into the fire, and
often into the water. 16And I brought him
to your disciples, and they could not heal
him.” 17And Jesus answered, “O faithless
and perverse generation, how long am
I to be with you? How long am I to bear
with you? Bring him here to me.” 18And
Jesus rebuked him, and the demon came
out of him, and the boy was cured in-
stantly. 19Then the disciples came to Jesus
privately and said, “Why could we not
cast it out?” 20He said to them, “Because of
your little faith. For truly, I say to you, if
you have faith as a grain of mustard seed,
you will say to this mountain, ‘Move from
hence to yonder place,’ and it will move;
and nothing will be impossible to you.”[f]

Jesus Again Foretells His Death and Resurrection

22 As they were gathering[g] in Galilee,
Jesus said to them, “The Son of man is to
be delivered into the hands of men, 23and
they will kill him, and he will be raised
on the third day.” And they were greatly
distressed.

Jesus and the Temple Tax

24 When they came to Caper′na-um, the
collectors of the half-shekel tax went up
to Peter and said, “Does not your teacher
pay the tax?” 25He said, “Yes.” And when
he came home, Jesus spoke to him first,
saying, “What do you think, Simon? From
whom do kings of the earth take toll or
tribute? From their sons or from oth-
ers?” 26And when he said, “From others,”
Jesus said to him, “Then the sons are free.
27However, not to give offense to them, go
to the sea and cast a hook, and take the first
fish that comes up, and when you open its
mouth you will find a shekel; take that and
give it to them for me and for yourself.”

True Greatness

18 At that time the disciples came to
Jesus, saying, “Who is the greatest
in the kingdom of heaven?” 2And calling
to him a child, he put him in the midst of
them, 3and said, “Truly, I say to you, unless
you turn and become like children, you
will never enter the kingdom of heaven.
4Whoever humbles himself like this child,
he is the greatest in the kingdom of heaven.

Temptations to Sin

5 “Whoever receives one such child in my
name receives me; 6but whoever causes
one of these little ones who believe in me
to sin,[h] it would be better for him to have
a great millstone fastened round his neck
and to be drowned in the depth of the sea.

7 “Woe to the world for temptations to
sin![i] For it is necessary that temptations
come, but woe to the man by whom the
temptation comes! 8And if your hand or
your foot causes you to sin,[j] cut it off and
throw it from you; it is better for you to
enter life maimed or lame than with two
hands or two feet to be thrown into the
eternal fire. 9And if your eye causes you
to sin,[k] pluck it out and throw it from
you; it is better for you to enter life with
one eye than with two eyes to be thrown
into the hell[l] of fire.

The Parable of the Lost Sheep

10 “See that you do not despise one of
these little ones; for I tell you that in
heaven their angels always behold the
face of my Father who is in heaven.[m]

[f] **17.20** Other ancient authorities insert verse 21, *“But this kind never comes out except by prayer and fasting”* [g] **17.22** Other ancient authorities read *abode* [h] **18.6** Greek *causes . . . to stumble* [i] **18.7** Greek *stumbling blocks* [j] **18.8** Greek *causes . . . to stumble* [k] **18.9** Greek *causes . . . to stumble* [l] **18.9** Greek *Gehenna* [m] **18.10** Other ancient authorities add verse 11, *For the Son of man came to save the lost*

[12]What do you think? If a man has a hun-
dred sheep, and one of them has gone
astray, does he not leave the ninety-
nine on the hills and go in search of the
one that went astray? [13]And if he finds
it, truly, I say to you, he rejoices over
it more than over the ninety-nine that
never went astray. [14]So it is not the will of
my[n] Father who is in heaven that one of
these little ones should perish.

Reproving Another Who Sins

15 "If your brother sins against you, go
and tell him his fault, between you and
him alone. If he listens to you, you have
gained your brother. [16]But if he does not
listen, take one or two others along with
you, that every word may be confirmed
by the evidence of two or three wit-
nesses. [17]If he refuses to listen to them,
tell it to the church; and if he refuses
to listen even to the church, let him be
to you as a Gentile and a tax collector.
[18]Truly, I say to you, whatever you bind
on earth shall be bound in heaven, and
whatever you loose on earth shall be
loosed in heaven. [19]Again I say to you,
if two of you agree on earth about any-
thing they ask, it will be done for them
by my Father in heaven. [20]For where two
or three are gathered in my name, there
am I in the midst of them."

Forgiveness

21 Then Peter came up and said to him,
"Lord, how often shall my brother sin
against me, and I forgive him? As many
as seven times?" [22]Jesus said to him, "I do
not say to you seven times, but seventy
times seven.[o]

The Parable of the Unforgiving Servant

23 "Therefore the kingdom of heaven
may be compared to a king who wished
to settle accounts with his servants.
[24]When he began the reckoning, one was
brought to him who owed him ten thou-
sand talents;[p] [25]and as he could not pay,
his lord ordered him to be sold, with his
wife and children and all that he had,
and payment to be made. [26]So the ser-
vant fell on his knees, imploring him,
'Lord, have patience with me, and I will
pay you everything.' [27]And out of pity
for him the lord of that servant released
him and forgave him the debt. [28]But that
same servant, as he went out, came upon
one of his fellow servants who owed him
a hundred denarii;[q] and seizing him by
the throat he said, 'Pay what you owe.'
[29]So his fellow servant fell down and be-
sought him, 'Have patience with me, and
I will pay you.' [30]He refused and went
and put him in prison till he should pay
the debt. [31]When his fellow servants saw
what had taken place, they were greatly
distressed, and they went and reported
to their lord all that had taken place.
[32]Then his lord summoned him and said
to him, 'You wicked servant! I forgave
you all that debt because you besought
me; [33]and should not you have had mercy
on your fellow servant, as I had mercy
on you?' [34]And in anger his lord deliv-
ered him to the jailers,[r] till he should pay
all his debt. [35]So also my heavenly Father
will do to every one of you, if you do not
forgive your brother from your heart."

Teaching about Divorce

19 Now when Jesus had finished these
sayings, he went away from Galilee
and entered the region of Judea beyond
the Jordan; [2]and large crowds followed
him, and he healed them there.

3 And Pharisees came up to him and
tested him by asking, "Is it lawful to di-
vorce one's wife for any cause?" [4]He an-
swered, "Have you not read that he who
made them from the beginning made

[n] **18.14** Other ancient authorities read *your*
[o] **18.22** Or *seventy-seven times*
[p] **18.24** This talent was more than fifteen years' wages of a laborer
[q] **18.28** The denarius was a day's wage for a laborer
[r] **18.34** Greek *torturers*

them male and female, 5 and said, 'For
this reason a man shall leave his father
and mother and be joined to his wife, and
the two shall become one'?[s] 6 So they are
no longer two but one.[t] What therefore
God has joined together, let not man put
asunder." 7 They said to him, "Why then
did Moses command one to give a certif-
icate of divorce, and to put her away?"
8 He said to them, "For your hardness of
heart Moses allowed you to divorce your
wives, but from the beginning it was not
so. 9 And I say to you: whoever divorces
his wife, except for unchastity,[u] and
marries another, commits adultery; and
he who marries a divorced woman, com-
mits adultery."[v]

10 The disciples said to him, "If such
is the case of a man with his wife, it is
not expedient to marry." 11 But he said to
them, "Not all men can receive this pre-
cept, but only those to whom it is given.
12 For there are eunuchs who have been
so from birth, and there are eunuchs
who have been made eunuchs by men,
and there are eunuchs who have made
themselves eunuchs for the sake of the
kingdom of heaven. He who is able to re-
ceive this, let him receive it."

Jesus Blesses Little Children

13 Then children were brought to him
that he might lay his hands on them and
pray. The disciples rebuked the people;
14 but Jesus said, "Let the children come to
me, and do not hinder them; for to such
belongs the kingdom of heaven." 15 And
he laid his hands on them and went away.

The Rich Young Man

16 And behold, one came up to him, say-
ing, "Teacher, what good deed must I
do, to have eternal life?" 17 And he said
to him, "Why do you ask me about what
is good? One there is who is good. If you
would enter life, keep the command-
ments." 18 He said to him, "Which?" And
Jesus said, "You shall not kill, You shall
not commit adultery, You shall not steal,
You shall not bear false witness, 19 Honor
your father and mother, and, You shall
love your neighbor as yourself." 20 The
young man said to him, "All these I have
observed; what do I still lack?" 21 Jesus
said to him, "If you would be perfect,
go, sell what you possess and give to
the poor, and you will have treasure in
heaven; and come, follow me." 22 When
the young man heard this he went away
sorrowful; for he had great possessions.

23 And Jesus said to his disciples,
"Truly, I say to you, it will be hard for a
rich man to enter the kingdom of heaven.
24 Again I tell you, it is easier for a camel
to go through the eye of a needle than for
a rich man to enter the kingdom of God."
25 When the disciples heard this they
were greatly astonished, saying, "Who
then can be saved?" 26 But Jesus looked at
them and said to them, "With men this is
impossible, but with God all things are
possible." 27 Then Peter said in reply, "Lo,
we have left everything and followed
you. What then shall we have?" 28 Jesus
said to them, "Truly, I say to you, in the
new world, when the Son of man shall sit
on his glorious throne, you who have fol-
lowed me will also sit on twelve thrones,
judging the twelve tribes of Israel. 29 And
every one who has left houses or broth-
ers or sisters or father or mother or chil-
dren or lands, for my name's sake, will
receive a hundredfold,[w] and inherit eter-
nal life. 30 But many that are first will be
last, and the last first.

The Laborers in the Vineyard

20 "For the kingdom of heaven is like
a householder who went out early
in the morning to hire laborers for his

[s] **19.5** Greek *one flesh* [t] **19.6** Greek *one flesh* [u] **19.9** Other ancient authorities, after *unchastity*, read *makes her commit adultery* [v] **19.9** Other ancient authorities omit *and he who marries a divorced woman, commits adultery* [w] **19.29** Other ancient authorities read *manifold*

vineyard. 2 After agreeing with the labor-
ers for a denarius[x] a day, he sent them
into his vineyard. 3 And going out about
the third hour he saw others standing
idle in the market place; 4 and to them
he said, 'You go into the vineyard too,
and whatever is right I will give you.' So
they went. 5 Going out again about the
sixth hour and the ninth hour, he did the
same. 6 And about the eleventh hour he
went out and found others standing; and
he said to them, 'Why do you stand here
idle all day?' 7 They said to him, 'Because
no one has hired us.' He said to them,
'You go into the vineyard too.' 8 And when
evening came, the owner of the vineyard
said to his steward, 'Call the laborers and
pay them their wages, beginning with
the last, up to the first.' 9 And when those
hired about the eleventh hour came, each
of them received a denarius. 10 Now when
the first came, they thought they would
receive more; but each of them also re-
ceived a denarius. 11 And on receiving it
they grumbled at the householder, 12 say-
ing, 'These last worked only one hour,
and you have made them equal to us who
have borne the burden of the day and the
scorching heat.' 13 But he replied to one of
them, 'Friend, I am doing you no wrong;
did you not agree with me for a denar-
ius? 14 Take what belongs to you, and go; I
choose to give to this last as I give to you.
15 Am I not allowed to do what I choose
with what belongs to me? Or do you be-
grudge my generosity?'[y] 16 So the last will
be first, and the first last."

A Third Time Jesus Foretells His Death and Resurrection

17 And as Jesus was going up to Jerusa-
lem, he took the twelve disciples aside,
and on the way he said to them, 18 "Be-
hold, we are going up to Jerusalem; and
the Son of man will be delivered to the
chief priests and scribes, and they will
condemn him to death, 19 and deliver
him to the Gentiles to be mocked and
scourged and crucified, and he will be
raised on the third day."

The Request of the Mother of James and John

20 Then the mother of the sons of Ze-
b'edee came up to him, with her sons, and
kneeling before him she asked him for
something. 21 And he said to her, "What do
you want?" She said to him, "Command
that these two sons of mine may sit, one
at your right hand and one at your left,
in your kingdom." 22 But Jesus answered,
"You do not know what you are asking.
Are you able to drink the cup that I am
to drink?" They said to him, "We are
able." 23 He said to them, "You will drink
my cup, but to sit at my right hand and at
my left is not mine to grant, but it is for
those for whom it has been prepared by
my Father." 24 And when the ten heard it,
they were indignant at the two brothers.
25 But Jesus called them to him and said,
"You know that the rulers of the Gentiles
lord it over them, and their great men ex-
ercise authority over them. 26 It shall not
be so among you; but whoever would be
great among you must be your servant,
27 and whoever would be first among you
must be your slave; 28 even as the Son of
man came not to be served but to serve,
and to give his life as a ransom for many."

Jesus Heals Two Blind Men

29 And as they went out of Jericho, a
great crowd followed him. 30 And behold,
two blind men sitting by the roadside,
when they heard that Jesus was passing
by, cried out,[z] "Have mercy on us, Son of
David!" 31 The crowd rebuked them, tell-
ing them to be silent; but they cried out
the more, "Lord, have mercy on us, Son
of David!" 32 And Jesus stopped and called
them, saying, "What do you want me to

[x] **20.2** The denarius was a day's wage for a laborer
[y] **20.15** Or *is your eye evil because I am good?*
[z] **20.30** Other ancient authorities insert *Lord*

do for you?" [33]They said to him, "Lord, let
our eyes be opened." [34]And Jesus in pity
touched their eyes, and immediately they
received their sight and followed him.

Jesus' Triumphal Entry into Jerusalem

21 And when they drew near to Jeru-
salem and came to Beth'phage, to
the Mount of Olives, then Jesus sent two
disciples, [2]saying to them, "Go into the
village opposite you, and immediately
you will find an ass tied, and a colt with
her; untie them and bring them to me. [3]If
any one says anything to you, you shall
say, 'The Lord has need of them,' and he
will send them immediately." [4]This took
place to fulfil what was spoken by the
prophet, saying,
5 "Tell the daughter of Zion,
Behold, your king is coming to
you,
humble, and mounted on an ass,
and on a colt, the foal of an ass."
[6]The disciples went and did as Jesus had
directed them; [7]they brought the ass and
the colt, and put their garments on them,
and he sat thereon. [8]Most of the crowd
spread their garments on the road,
and others cut branches from the trees
and spread them on the road. [9]And the
crowds that went before him and that fol-
lowed him shouted, "Hosanna to the Son
of David! Blessed is he who comes in the
name of the Lord! Hosanna in the high-
est!" [10]And when he entered Jerusalem,
all the city was stirred, saying, "Who is
this?" [11]And the crowds said, "This is the
prophet Jesus from Nazareth of Galilee."

Jesus Cleanses the Temple

12 And Jesus entered the temple of God[a]
and drove out all who sold and bought
in the temple, and he overturned the ta-
bles of the money-changers and the seats
of those who sold pigeons. [13]He said to
them, "It is written, 'My house shall be
called a house of prayer'; but you make it
a den of robbers."
14 And the blind and the lame came to
him in the temple, and he healed them.
[15]But when the chief priests and the
scribes saw the wonderful things that
he did, and the children crying out in the
temple, "Hosanna to the Son of David!"
they were indignant; [16]and they said to
him, "Do you hear what these are say-
ing?" And Jesus said to them, "Yes; have
you never read,
'Out of the mouth of babes and
sucklings
thou hast brought perfect praise'?"
[17]And leaving them, he went out of the
city to Bethany and lodged there.

Jesus Curses the Fig Tree

18 In the morning, as he was returning
to the city, he was hungry. [19]And seeing a
fig tree by the wayside he went to it, and
found nothing on it but leaves only. And
he said to it, "May no fruit ever come
from you again!" And the fig tree with-
ered at once. [20]When the disciples saw
it they marveled, saying, "How did the
fig tree wither at once?" [21]And Jesus an-
swered them, "Truly, I say to you, if you
have faith and never doubt, you will not
only do what has been done to the fig tree,
but even if you say to this mountain, 'Be
taken up and cast into the sea,' it will be
done. [22]And whatever you ask in prayer,
you will receive, if you have faith."

The Authority of Jesus Questioned

23 And when he entered the temple, the
chief priests and the elders of the peo-
ple came up to him as he was teaching,
and said, "By what authority are you do-
ing these things, and who gave you this
authority?" [24]Jesus answered them, "I
also will ask you a question; and if you
tell me the answer, then I also will tell
you by what authority I do these things.
[25]The baptism of John, whence was it?

[a] **21.12** Other ancient authorities omit *of God*

From heaven or from men?" And they
argued with one another, "If we say,
'From heaven,' he will say to us, 'Why
then did you not believe him?' 26 But if
we say, 'From men,' we are afraid of the
multitude; for all hold that John was a
prophet." 27 So they answered Jesus, "We
do not know." And he said to them, "Nei-
ther will I tell you by what authority I do
these things.

The Parable of the Two Sons

28 "What do you think? A man had two
sons; and he went to the first and said,
'Son, go and work in the vineyard to-
day.' 29 And he answered, 'I will not'; but
afterward he repented and went. 30 And
he went to the second and said the same;
and he answered, 'I go, sir,' but did not go.
31 Which of the two did the will of his fa-
ther?" They said, "The first." Jesus said to
them, "Truly, I say to you, the tax collec-
tors and the harlots go into the kingdom
of God before you. 32 For John came to you
in the way of righteousness, and you did
not believe him, but the tax collectors
and the harlots believed him; and even
when you saw it, you did not afterward
repent and believe him.

The Parable of the Wicked Tenants

33 "Hear another parable. There was a
householder who planted a vineyard,
and set a hedge around it, and dug a wine
press in it, and built a tower, and let it out
to tenants, and went into another coun-
try. 34 When the season of fruit drew
near, he sent his servants to the tenants,
to get his fruit; 35 and the tenants took his
servants and beat one, killed another,
and stoned another. 36 Again he sent
other servants, more than the first; and
they did the same to them. 37 Afterward he
sent his son to them, saying, 'They will re-
spect my son.' 38 But when the tenants saw
the son, they said to themselves, 'This is
the heir; come, let us kill him and have
his inheritance.' 39 And they took him and
cast him out of the vineyard, and killed
him. 40 When therefore the owner of the
vineyard comes, what will he do to those
tenants?" 41 They said to him, "He will put
those wretches to a miserable death, and
let out the vineyard to other tenants who
will give him the fruits in their seasons."

42 Jesus said to them, "Have you never
read in the scriptures:

> 'The very stone which the builders
> rejected
> has become the head of the corner;
> this was the Lord's doing,
> and it is marvelous in our eyes'?

43 Therefore I tell you, the kingdom of
God will be taken away from you and
given to a nation producing the fruits of
it. 44 And he who falls on this stone will be
broken to pieces; but when it falls on any
one, it will crush him."[b]

45 When the chief priests and the
Pharisees heard his parables, they per-
ceived that he was speaking about them.
46 But when they tried to arrest him, they
feared the multitudes, because they held
him to be a prophet.

The Parable of the Wedding Banquet

22 And again Jesus spoke to them in
parables, saying, 2 "The kingdom
of heaven may be compared to a king
who gave a marriage feast for his son,
3 and sent his servants to call those who
were invited to the marriage feast; but
they would not come. 4 Again he sent
other servants, saying, 'Tell those who
are invited, Behold, I have made ready
my dinner, my oxen and my fat calves
are killed, and everything is ready; come
to the marriage feast.' 5 But they made
light of it and went off, one to his farm,
another to his business, 6 while the rest
seized his servants, treated them shame-
fully, and killed them. 7 The king was an-
gry, and he sent his troops and destroyed
those murderers and burned their city.

[b] **21.44** Other ancient authorities omit verse 44

[8]Then he said to his servants, 'The wedding is ready, but those invited were not worthy. [9]Go therefore to the thoroughfares, and invite to the marriage feast as many as you find.' [10]And those servants went out into the streets and gathered all whom they found, both bad and good; so the wedding hall was filled with guests.

11 "But when the king came in to look at the guests, he saw there a man who had no wedding garment; [12]and he said to him, 'Friend, how did you get in here without a wedding garment?' And he was speechless. [13]Then the king said to the attendants, 'Bind him hand and foot, and cast him into the outer darkness; there men will weep and gnash their teeth.' [14]For many are called, but few are chosen."

The Question about Paying Taxes

15 Then the Pharisees went and took counsel how to entangle him in his talk. [16]And they sent their disciples to him, along with the Hero′di-ans, saying, "Teacher, we know that you are true, and teach the way of God truthfully, and care for no man; for you do not regard the position of men. [17]Tell us, then, what you think. Is it lawful to pay taxes to Caesar, or not?" [18]But Jesus, aware of their malice, said, "Why put me to the test, you hypocrites? [19]Show me the money for the tax." And they brought him a coin.[c] [20]And Jesus said to them, "Whose likeness and inscription is this?" [21]They said, "Caesar's." Then he said to them, "Render therefore to Caesar the things that are Caesar's, and to God the things that are God's." [22]When they heard it, they marveled; and they left him and went away.

The Question about the Resurrection

23 The same day Sad′ducees came to him, who say that there is no resurrection; and they asked him a question, [24]saying, "Teacher, Moses said, 'If a man dies, having no children, his brother must marry the widow, and raise up children for his brother.' [25]Now there were seven brothers among us; the first married, and died, and having no children left his wife to his brother. [26]So too the second and third, down to the seventh. [27]After them all, the woman died. [28]In the resurrection, therefore, to which of the seven will she be wife? For they all had her."

29 But Jesus answered them, "You are wrong, because you know neither the scriptures nor the power of God. [30]For in the resurrection they neither marry nor are given in marriage, but are like angels[d] in heaven. [31]And as for the resurrection of the dead, have you not read what was said to you by God, [32]'I am the God of Abraham, and the God of Isaac, and the God of Jacob'? He is not God of the dead, but of the living." [33]And when the crowd heard it, they were astonished at his teaching.

The Greatest Commandment

34 But when the Pharisees heard that he had silenced the Sad′ducees, they came together. [35]And one of them, a lawyer, asked him a question, to test him. [36]"Teacher, which is the great commandment in the law?" [37]And he said to him, "You shall love the Lord your God with all your heart, and with all your soul, and with all your mind. [38]This is the great and first commandment. [39]And a second is like it, You shall love your neighbor as yourself. [40]On these two commandments depend all the law and the prophets."

The Question about David's Son

41 Now while the Pharisees were gathered together, Jesus asked them a question, [42]saying, "What do you think of the Christ? Whose son is he?" They said to him, "The son of David." [43]He said to them, "How is it then that David, inspired by the Spirit,[e] calls him Lord, saying,

[c]**22.19** Greek *a denarius* [d]**22.30** Other ancient authorities add *of God* [e]**22.43** Or *David in the Spirit*

44 'The Lord said to my Lord,
Sit at my right hand,
till I put thy enemies under thy feet'?
45If David thus calls him Lord, how is he
his son?" 46And no one was able to answer
him a word, nor from that day did any
one dare to ask him any more questions.

Jesus Denounces Scribes and Pharisees

23 Then said Jesus to the crowds and
to his disciples, 2"The scribes and
the Pharisees sit on Moses' seat; 3so prac-
tice and observe whatever they tell you,
but not what they do; for they preach, but
do not practice. 4They bind heavy bur-
dens, hard to bear,[f] and lay them on men's
shoulders; but they themselves will not
move them with their finger. 5They do all
their deeds to be seen by men; for they
make their phylacteries broad and their
fringes long, 6and they love the place
of honor at feasts and the best seats in
the synagogues, 7and salutations in the
market places, and being called rabbi by
men. 8But you are not to be called rabbi,
for you have one teacher, and you are all
brethren. 9And call no man your father
on earth, for you have one Father, who
is in heaven. 10Neither be called masters,
for you have one master, the Christ. 11He
who is greatest among you shall be your
servant; 12whoever exalts himself will be
humbled, and whoever humbles himself
will be exalted.

13 "But woe to you, scribes and Phar-
isees, hypocrites! because you shut the
kingdom of heaven against men; for
you neither enter yourselves, nor allow
those who would enter to go in.[g] 15Woe to
you, scribes and Pharisees, hypocrites!
for you traverse sea and land to make a
single proselyte, and when he becomes a
proselyte, you make him twice as much a
child of hell[h] as yourselves.

16 "Woe to you, blind guides, who say,
'If any one swears by the temple, it is
nothing; but if any one swears by the gold
of the temple, he is bound by his oath.'
17You blind fools! For which is greater,
the gold or the temple that has made the
gold sacred? 18And you say, 'If any one
swears by the altar, it is nothing; but if
any one swears by the gift that is on the
altar, he is bound by his oath.' 19You blind
men! For which is greater, the gift or the
altar that makes the gift sacred? 20So he
who swears by the altar, swears by it and
by everything on it; 21and he who swears
by the temple, swears by it and by him
who dwells in it; 22and he who swears by
heaven, swears by the throne of God and
by him who sits upon it.

23 "Woe to you, scribes and Pharisees,
hypocrites! for you tithe mint and dill
and cummin, and have neglected the
weightier matters of the law, justice and
mercy and faith; these you ought to have
done, without neglecting the others.
24You blind guides, straining out a gnat
and swallowing a camel!

25 "Woe to you, scribes and Pharisees,
hypocrites! for you cleanse the outside
of the cup and of the plate, but inside
they are full of extortion and rapacity.
26You blind Pharisee! first cleanse the in-
side of the cup and of the plate, that the
outside also may be clean.

27 "Woe to you, scribes and Pharisees,
hypocrites! for you are like whitewashed
tombs, which outwardly appear beauti-
ful, but within they are full of dead men's
bones and all uncleanness. 28So you also
outwardly appear righteous to men,
but within you are full of hypocrisy and
iniquity.

29 "Woe to you, scribes and Pharisees,
hypocrites! for you build the tombs of
the prophets and adorn the monuments
of the righteous, 30saying, 'If we had lived

[f] **23.4** Other ancient authorities omit *hard to bear* [g] **23.13** Other authorities add here (or after verse 12) verse 14, *Woe to you, scribes and Pharisees, hypocrites! for you devour widows' houses and for a pretense you make long prayers; therefore you will receive the greater condemnation* [h] **23.15** Greek *Gehenna*

in the days of our fathers, we would not
have taken part with them in shedding
the blood of the prophets.' 31 Thus you
witness against yourselves, that you
are sons of those who murdered the
prophets. 32 Fill up, then, the measure of
your fathers. 33 You serpents, you brood
of vipers, how are you to escape being
sentenced to hell?[i] 34 Therefore I send
you prophets and wise men and scribes,
some of whom you will kill and crucify,
and some you will scourge in your syn-
agogues and persecute from town to
town, 35 that upon you may come all the
righteous blood shed on earth, from the
blood of innocent Abel to the blood of
Zechari'ah the son of Barachi'ah, whom
you murdered between the sanctuary
and the altar. 36 Truly, I say to you, all this
will come upon this generation.

The Lament over Jerusalem

37 "O Jerusalem, Jerusalem, killing the
prophets and stoning those who are sent
to you! How often would I have gath-
ered your children together as a hen
gathers her brood under her wings, and
you would not! 38 Behold, your house is
forsaken and desolate.[j] 39 For I tell you,
you will not see me again, until you say,
'Blessed is he who comes in the name of
the Lord.'"

The Destruction of the Temple Foretold

24 Jesus left the temple and was
going away, when his disciples
came to point out to him the buildings of
the temple. 2 But he answered them, "You
see all these, do you not? Truly, I say to
you, there will not be left here one stone
upon another, that will not be thrown
down."

Signs of the End of the Age

3 As he sat on the Mount of Olives, the
disciples came to him privately, saying,
"Tell us, when will this be, and what will
be the sign of your coming and of the
close of the age?" 4 And Jesus answered
them, "Take heed that no one leads you
astray. 5 For many will come in my name,
saying, 'I am the Christ,' and they will
lead many astray. 6 And you will hear of
wars and rumors of wars; see that you
are not alarmed; for this must take place,
but the end is not yet. 7 For nation will
rise against nation, and kingdom against
kingdom, and there will be famines and
earthquakes in various places: 8 all this is
but the beginning of the sufferings.

Persecutions Foretold

9 "Then they will deliver you up to
tribulation, and put you to death; and
you will be hated by all nations for my
name's sake. 10 And then many will fall
away,[k] and betray one another, and hate
one another. 11 And many false proph-
ets will arise and lead many astray.
12 And because wickedness is multiplied,
most men's love will grow cold. 13 But he
who endures to the end will be saved.
14 And this gospel of the kingdom will be
preached throughout the whole world,
as a testimony to all nations; and then the
end will come.

The Desolating Sacrilege

15 "So when you see the desolating sac-
rilege spoken of by the prophet Daniel,
standing in the holy place (let the reader
understand), 16 then let those who are
in Judea flee to the mountains; 17 let him
who is on the housetop not go down to
take what is in his house; 18 and let him
who is in the field not turn back to take
his mantle. 19 And alas for those who are
with child and for those who give suck
in those days! 20 Pray that your flight may
not be in winter or on a sabbath. 21 For
then there will be great tribulation, such
as has not been from the beginning of the
world until now, no, and never will be.

[i] **23.33** Greek *Gehenna* [j] **23.38** Other ancient authorities omit *and desolate* [k] **24.10** Or *stumble*

22 And if those days had not been short-
ened, no human being would be saved;
but for the sake of the elect those days
will be shortened. 23 Then if any one says
to you, ‘Lo, here is the Christ!’ or ‘There
he is!’ do not believe it. 24 For false Christs
and false prophets will arise and show
great signs and wonders, so as to lead
astray, if possible, even the elect. 25 Lo, I
have told you beforehand. 26 So, if they
say to you, ‘Lo, he is in the wilderness,’ do
not go out; if they say, ‘Lo, he is in the in-
ner rooms,’ do not believe it. 27 For as the
lightning comes from the east and shines
as far as the west, so will be the coming
of the Son of man. 28 Wherever the body
is, there the eagles[l] will be gathered
together.

The Coming of the Son of Man

29 “Immediately after the tribulation
of those days the sun will be darkened,
and the moon will not give its light, and
the stars will fall from heaven, and the
powers of the heavens will be shaken;
30 then will appear the sign of the Son of
man in heaven, and then all the tribes
of the earth will mourn, and they will
see the Son of man coming on the clouds
of heaven with power and great glory;
31 and he will send out his angels with a
loud trumpet call, and they will gather
his elect from the four winds, from one
end of heaven to the other.

The Lesson of the Fig Tree

32 “From the fig tree learn its lesson: as
soon as its branch becomes tender and
puts forth its leaves, you know that sum-
mer is near. 33 So also, when you see all
these things, you know that he is near,
at the very gates. 34 Truly, I say to you,
this generation will not pass away till
all these things take place. 35 Heaven and
earth will pass away, but my words will
not pass away.

The Necessity for Watchfulness

36 “But of that day and hour no one
knows, not even the angels of heaven,
nor the Son,[m] but the Father only. 37 As
were the days of Noah, so will be the com-
ing of the Son of man. 38 For as in those
days before the flood they were eating
and drinking, marrying and giving in
marriage, until the day when Noah en-
tered the ark, 39 and they did not know
until the flood came and swept them all
away, so will be the coming of the Son of
man. 40 Then two men will be in the field;
one is taken and one is left. 41 Two women
will be grinding at the mill; one is taken
and one is left. 42 Watch therefore, for
you do not know on what day your Lord
is coming. 43 But know this, that if the
householder had known in what part of
the night the thief was coming, he would
have watched and would not have let his
house be broken into. 44 Therefore you
also must be ready; for the Son of man is
coming at an hour you do not expect.

The Faithful or the Unfaithful Slave

45 “Who then is the faithful and wise
servant, whom his master has set over
his household, to give them their food
at the proper time? 46 Blessed is that ser-
vant whom his master when he comes
will find so doing. 47 Truly, I say to you,
he will set him over all his possessions.
48 But if that wicked servant says to him-
self, ‘My master is delayed,’ 49 and begins
to beat his fellow servants, and eats and
drinks with the drunken, 50 the master of
that servant will come on a day when he
does not expect him and at an hour he
does not know, 51 and will punish[n] him,
and put him with the hypocrites; there
men will weep and gnash their teeth.

The Parable of the Ten Bridesmaids

25 “Then the kingdom of heaven shall
be compared to ten maidens who

[l] **24.28** Or *vultures*

[m] **24.36** Other ancient authorities omit *nor the Son*

[n] **24.51** Or *cut him in pieces*

took their lamps and went to meet the
bridegroom.[o] 2 Five of them were foolish,
and five were wise. 3 For when the foolish
took their lamps, they took no oil with
them; 4 but the wise took flasks of oil with
their lamps. 5 As the bridegroom was de-
layed, they all slumbered and slept. 6 But
at midnight there was a cry, 'Behold, the
bridegroom! Come out to meet him.' 7 Then
all those maidens rose and trimmed their
lamps. 8 And the foolish said to the wise,
'Give us some of your oil, for our lamps
are going out.' 9 But the wise replied, 'Per-
haps there will not be enough for us and
for you; go rather to the dealers and buy
for yourselves.' 10 And while they went
to buy, the bridegroom came, and those
who were ready went in with him to the
marriage feast; and the door was shut.
11 Afterward the other maidens came also,
saying, 'Lord, lord, open to us.' 12 But he
replied, 'Truly, I say to you, I do not know
you.' 13 Watch therefore, for you know nei-
ther the day nor the hour.

The Parable of the Talents

14 "For it will be as when a man going
on a journey called his servants and en-
trusted to them his property; 15 to one
he gave five talents,[p] to another two, to
another one, to each according to his
ability. Then he went away. 16 He who had
received the five talents went at once and
traded with them; and he made five tal-
ents more. 17 So also, he who had the two
talents made two talents more. 18 But he
who had received the one talent went and
dug in the ground and hid his master's
money. 19 Now after a long time the mas-
ter of those servants came and settled
accounts with them. 20 And he who had
received the five talents came forward,
bringing five talents more, saying, 'Mas-
ter, you delivered to me five talents; here I
have made five talents more.' 21 His master
said to him, 'Well done, good and faithful
servant; you have been faithful over a
little, I will set you over much; enter into
the joy of your master.' 22 And he also who
had the two talents came forward, say-
ing, 'Master, you delivered to me two tal-
ents; here I have made two talents more.'
23 His master said to him, 'Well done,
good and faithful servant; you have been
faithful over a little, I will set you over
much; enter into the joy of your master.'
24 He also who had received the one talent
came forward, saying, 'Master, I knew
you to be a hard man, reaping where you
did not sow, and gathering where you did
not winnow; 25 so I was afraid, and I went
and hid your talent in the ground. Here
you have what is yours.' 26 But his master
answered him, 'You wicked and slothful
servant! You knew that I reap where I
have not sowed, and gather where I have
not winnowed? 27 Then you ought to have
invested my money with the bankers,
and at my coming I should have received
what was my own with interest. 28 So take
the talent from him, and give it to him
who has the ten talents. 29 For to every
one who has will more be given, and he
will have abundance; but from him who
has not, even what he has will be taken
away. 30 And cast the worthless servant
into the outer darkness; there men will
weep and gnash their teeth.'

The Judgment of the Nations

31 "When the Son of man comes in his
glory, and all the angels with him, then
he will sit on his glorious throne. 32 Be-
fore him will be gathered all the nations,
and he will separate them one from an-
other as a shepherd separates the sheep
from the goats, 33 and he will place the
sheep at his right hand, but the goats at
the left. 34 Then the King will say to those
at his right hand, 'Come, O blessed of my
Father, inherit the kingdom prepared
for you from the foundation of the world;

[o] **25.1** Other ancient authorities add *and the bride*

[p] **25.15** This talent was more than fifteen years' wages of a laborer

35 for I was hungry and you gave me food,
I was thirsty and you gave me drink, I
was a stranger and you welcomed me, 36 I
was naked and you clothed me, I was sick
and you visited me, I was in prison and
you came to me.' 37 Then the righteous
will answer him, 'Lord, when did we see
thee hungry and feed thee, or thirsty and
give thee drink? 38 And when did we see
thee a stranger and welcome thee, or na-
ked and clothe thee? 39 And when did we
see thee sick or in prison and visit thee?'
40 And the King will answer them, 'Truly,
I say to you, as you did it to one of the
least of these my brethren, you did it to
me.' 41 Then he will say to those at his left
hand, 'Depart from me, you cursed, into
the eternal fire prepared for the devil
and his angels; 42 for I was hungry and
you gave me no food, I was thirsty and
you gave me no drink, 43 I was a stranger
and you did not welcome me, naked and
you did not clothe me, sick and in prison
and you did not visit me.' 44 Then they
also will answer, 'Lord, when did we see
thee hungry or thirsty or a stranger or
naked or sick or in prison, and did not
minister to thee?' 45 Then he will answer
them, 'Truly, I say to you, as you did it not
to one of the least of these, you did it not
to me.' 46 And they will go away into eter-
nal punishment, but the righteous into
eternal life."

The Plot to Kill Jesus

26 When Jesus had finished all these
sayings, he said to his disciples,
2 "You know that after two days the Pass-
over is coming, and the Son of man will
be delivered up to be crucified."

3 Then the chief priests and the elders
of the people gathered in the palace of
the high priest, who was called Ca'iaphas,
4 and took counsel together in order to
arrest Jesus by stealth and kill him. 5 But
they said, "Not during the feast, lest
there be a tumult among the people."

The Anointing at Bethany

6 Now when Jesus was at Bethany in the
house of Simon the leper, 7 a woman came
up to him with an alabaster jar of very
expensive ointment, and she poured it
on his head, as he sat at table. 8 But when
the disciples saw it, they were indignant,
saying, "Why this waste? 9 For this oint-
ment might have been sold for a large
sum, and given to the poor." 10 But Jesus,
aware of this, said to them, "Why do you
trouble the woman? For she has done a
beautiful thing to me. 11 For you always
have the poor with you, but you will not
always have me. 12 In pouring this oint-
ment on my body she has done it to pre-
pare me for burial. 13 Truly, I say to you,
wherever this gospel is preached in the
whole world, what she has done will be
told in memory of her."

Judas Agrees to Betray Jesus

14 Then one of the twelve, who was called
Judas Iscariot, went to the chief priests
15 and said, "What will you give me if I
deliver him to you?" And they paid him
thirty pieces of silver. 16 And from that
moment he sought an opportunity to be-
tray him.

The Passover with the Disciples

17 Now on the first day of Unleavened
Bread the disciples came to Jesus, saying,
"Where will you have us prepare for you
to eat the passover?" 18 He said, "Go into
the city to such a one, and say to him,
'The Teacher says, My time is at hand;
I will keep the passover at your house
with my disciples.'" 19 And the disciples
did as Jesus had directed them, and they
prepared the passover.

20 When it was evening, he sat at table
with the twelve disciples;[q] 21 and as they
were eating, he said, "Truly, I say to you,
one of you will betray me." 22 And they
were very sorrowful, and began to say to
him one after another, "Is it I, Lord?" 23 He

[q] **26.20** Other authorities omit *disciples*

answered, “He who has dipped his hand in the dish with me, will betray me. 24 The Son of man goes as it is written of him, but woe to that man by whom the Son of man is betrayed! It would have been better for that man if he had not been born.” 25 Judas, who betrayed him, said, “Is it I, Master?”[r] He said to him, “You have said so.”

The Institution of the Lord’s Supper

26 Now as they were eating, Jesus took bread, and blessed, and broke it, and gave it to the disciples and said, “Take, eat; this is my body.” 27 And he took a cup, and when he had given thanks he gave it to them, saying, “Drink of it, all of you; 28 for this is my blood of the[s] covenant, which is poured out for many for the forgiveness of sins. 29 I tell you I shall not drink again of this fruit of the vine until that day when I drink it new with you in my Father’s kingdom.”

Peter’s Denial Foretold

30 And when they had sung a hymn, they went out to the Mount of Olives. 31 Then Jesus said to them, “You will all fall away because of me this night; for it is written, ‘I will strike the shepherd, and the sheep of the flock will be scattered.’ 32 But after I am raised up, I will go before you to Galilee.” 33 Peter declared to him, “Though they all fall away because of you, I will never fall away.” 34 Jesus said to him, “Truly, I say to you, this very night, before the cock crows, you will deny me three times.” 35 Peter said to him, “Even if I must die with you, I will not deny you.” And so said all the disciples.

Jesus Prays in Gethsemane

36 Then Jesus went with them to a place called Gethsem′ane, and he said to his disciples, “Sit here, while I go yonder and pray.” 37 And taking with him Peter and the two sons of Zeb′edee, he began to be sorrowful and troubled. 38 Then he said to them, “My soul is very sorrowful, even to death; remain here, and watch[t] with me.” 39 And going a little farther he fell on his face and prayed, “My Father, if it be possible, let this cup pass from me; nevertheless, not as I will, but as thou wilt.” 40 And he came to the disciples and found them sleeping; and he said to Peter, “So, could you not watch[u] with me one hour? 41 Watch[v] and pray that you may not enter into temptation; the spirit indeed is willing, but the flesh is weak.” 42 Again, for the second time, he went away and prayed, “My Father, if this cannot pass unless I drink it, thy will be done.” 43 And again he came and found them sleeping, for their eyes were heavy. 44 So, leaving them again, he went away and prayed for the third time, saying the same words. 45 Then he came to the disciples and said to them, “Are you still sleeping and taking your rest? Behold, the hour is at hand, and the Son of man is betrayed into the hands of sinners. 46 Rise, let us be going; see, my betrayer is at hand.”

The Betrayal and Arrest of Jesus

47 While he was still speaking, Judas came, one of the twelve, and with him a great crowd with swords and clubs, from the chief priests and the elders of the people. 48 Now the betrayer had given them a sign, saying, “The one I shall kiss is the man; seize him.” 49 And he came up to Jesus at once and said, “Hail, Master!”[w] And he kissed him. 50 Jesus said to him, “Friend, why are you here?”[x] Then they came up and laid hands on Jesus and seized him. 51 And behold, one of those who were with Jesus stretched out his hand and drew his sword, and struck the

[r] **26.25** Or *Rabbi* [s] **26.28** Other ancient authorities insert *new* [t] **26.38** Or *keep awake* [u] **26.40** Or *keep awake* [v] **26.41** Or *keep awake* [w] **26.49** Or *Rabbi* [x] **26.50** Or *do that for which you have come*

slave of the high priest, and cut off his ear. [52]Then Jesus said to him, "Put your sword back into its place; for all who take the sword will perish by the sword. [53]Do you think that I cannot appeal to my Father, and he will at once send me more than twelve legions of angels? [54]But how then should the scriptures be fulfilled, that it must be so?" [55]At that hour Jesus said to the crowds, "Have you come out as against a robber, with swords and clubs to capture me? Day after day I sat in the temple teaching, and you did not seize me. [56]But all this has taken place, that the scriptures of the prophets might be fulfilled." Then all the disciples forsook him and fled.

Jesus before the High Priest

57 Then those who had seized Jesus led him to Ca'iaphas the high priest, where the scribes and the elders had gathered. [58]But Peter followed him at a distance, as far as the courtyard of the high priest, and going inside he sat with the guards to see the end. [59]Now the chief priests and the whole council sought false testimony against Jesus that they might put him to death, [60]but they found none, though many false witnesses came forward. At last two came forward [61]and said, "This fellow said, 'I am able to destroy the temple of God, and to build it in three days.'" [62]And the high priest stood up and said, "Have you no answer to make? What is it that these men testify against you?" [63]But Jesus was silent. And the high priest said to him, "I adjure you by the living God, tell us if you are the Christ, the Son of God." [64]Jesus said to him, "You have said so. But I tell you, hereafter you will see the Son of man seated at the right hand of Power, and coming on the clouds of heaven." [65]Then the high priest tore his robes, and said, "He has uttered blasphemy. Why do we still need witnesses? You have now heard his blasphemy. [66]What is your judgment?" They answered, "He deserves death." [67]Then they spat in his face, and struck him; and some slapped him, [68]saying, "Prophesy to us, you Christ! Who is it that struck you?"

Peter's Denial of Jesus

69 Now Peter was sitting outside in the courtyard. And a maid came up to him, and said, "You also were with Jesus the Galilean." [70]But he denied it before them all, saying, "I do not know what you mean." [71]And when he went out to the porch, another maid saw him, and she said to the bystanders, "This man was with Jesus of Nazareth." [72]And again he denied it with an oath, "I do not know the man." [73]After a little while the bystanders came up and said to Peter, "Certainly you are also one of them, for your accent betrays you." [74]Then he began to invoke a curse on himself and to swear, "I do not know the man." And immediately the cock crowed. [75]And Peter remembered the saying of Jesus, "Before the cock crows, you will deny me three times." And he went out and wept bitterly.

Jesus Brought before Pilate

27 When morning came, all the chief priests and the elders of the people took counsel against Jesus to put him to death; [2]and they bound him and led him away and delivered him to Pilate the governor.

The Suicide of Judas

3 When Judas, his betrayer, saw that he was condemned, he repented and brought back the thirty pieces of silver to the chief priests and the elders, [4]saying, "I have sinned in betraying innocent blood." They said, "What is that to us? See to it yourself." [5]And throwing down the pieces of silver in the temple, he departed; and he went and hanged himself. [6]But the chief priests, taking the pieces of silver, said, "It is not lawful to put them into the treasury, since they are blood money." 7 So they took counsel, and bought with them the potter's field, to bury strangers in. 8 Therefore that field has been called the Field of Blood to this day. 9 Then was fulfilled what had been spoken by the prophet Jeremiah, saying, "And they took the thirty pieces of silver, the price of him on whom a price had been set by some of the sons of Israel, 10 and they gave them for the potter's field, as the Lord directed me."

Pilate Questions Jesus

11 Now Jesus stood before the governor; and the governor asked him, "Are you the King of the Jews?" Jesus said to him, "You have said so." 12 But when he was accused by the chief priests and elders, he made no answer. 13 Then Pilate said to him, "Do you not hear how many things they testify against you?" 14 But he gave him no answer, not even to a single charge; so that the governor wondered greatly.

Barabbas or Jesus?

15 Now at the feast the governor was accustomed to release for the crowd any one prisoner whom they wanted. 16 And they had then a notorious prisoner, called Barab'bas.[y] 17 So when they had gathered, Pilate said to them, "Whom do you want me to release for you, Barab'bas[z] or Jesus who is called Christ?" 18 For he knew that it was out of envy that they had delivered him up. 19 Besides, while he was sitting on the judgment seat, his wife sent word to him, "Have nothing to do with that righteous man, for I have suffered much over him today in a dream." 20 Now the chief priests and the elders persuaded the people to ask for Barab'bas and destroy Jesus. 21 The governor again said to them, "Which of the two do you want me to release for you?" And they said, "Barab'bas." 22 Pilate said to them, "Then what shall I do with Jesus who is called Christ?" They all said, "Let him be crucified." 23 And he said, "Why, what evil has he done?" But they shouted all the more, "Let him be crucified."

Pilate Hands Jesus over to Be Crucified

24 So when Pilate saw that he was gaining nothing, but rather that a riot was beginning, he took water and washed his hands before the crowd, saying, "I am innocent of this righteous man's blood;[a] see to it yourselves." 25 And all the people answered, "His blood be on us and on our children!" 26 Then he released for them Barab'bas, and having scourged Jesus, delivered him to be crucified.

The Soldiers Mock Jesus

27 Then the soldiers of the governor took Jesus into the praetorium, and they gathered the whole battalion before him. 28 And they stripped him and put a scarlet robe upon him, 29 and plaiting a crown of thorns they put it on his head, and put a reed in his right hand. And kneeling before him they mocked him, saying, "Hail, King of the Jews!" 30 And they spat upon him, and took the reed and struck him on the head. 31 And when they had mocked him, they stripped him of the robe, and put his own clothes on him, and led him away to crucify him.

The Crucifixion of Jesus

32 As they were marching out, they came upon a man of Cyre'ne, Simon by name; this man they compelled to carry his cross. 33 And when they came to a place called Gol'gotha (which means the place of a skull), 34 they offered him wine to drink, mingled with gall; but when he tasted it, he would not drink it. 35 And when they had crucified him, they divided his garments among them by casting lots; 36 then they sat down and kept

[y] **27.16** Other ancient authorities read *Jesus Barabbas* [z] **27.17** Other ancient authorities read *Jesus Barabbas* [a] **27.24** Other authorities omit *righteous* or *man's*

watch over him there. [37]And over his
head they put the charge against him,
which read, "This is Jesus the King of the
Jews." [38]Then two robbers were crucified
with him, one on the right and one on the
left. [39]And those who passed by derided
him, wagging their heads [40]and saying,
"You who would destroy the temple and
build it in three days, save yourself! If
you are the Son of God, come down from
the cross." [41]So also the chief priests, with
the scribes and elders, mocked him, say-
ing, [42]"He saved others; he cannot save
himself. He is the King of Israel; let him
come down now from the cross, and we
will believe in him. [43]He trusts in God; let
God deliver him now, if he desires him;
for he said, 'I am the Son of God.'" [44]And
the robbers who were crucified with him
also reviled him in the same way.

The Death of Jesus

45 Now from the sixth hour there was
darkness over all the land[b] until the ninth
hour. [46]And about the ninth hour Jesus
cried with a loud voice, "Eli, Eli, la'ma
sabach-tha'ni?" that is, "My God, my God,
why hast thou forsaken me?" [47]And some
of the bystanders hearing it said, "This
man is calling Eli'jah." [48]And one of them
at once ran and took a sponge, filled it with
vinegar, and put it on a reed, and gave it to
him to drink. [49]But the others said, "Wait,
let us see whether Eli'jah will come to save
him."[c] [50]And Jesus cried again with a loud
voice and yielded up his spirit.

51 And behold, the curtain of the tem-
ple was torn in two, from top to bottom;
and the earth shook, and the rocks were
split; [52]the tombs also were opened, and
many bodies of the saints who had fallen
asleep were raised, [53]and coming out of
the tombs after his resurrection they
went into the holy city and appeared to
many. [54]When the centurion and those
who were with him, keeping watch over
Jesus, saw the earthquake and what took
place, they were filled with awe, and said,
"Truly this was the Son[d] of God!"

55 There were also many women there,
looking on from afar, who had followed
Jesus from Galilee, ministering to him;
[56]among whom were Mary Mag'dalene,
and Mary the mother of James and Joseph,
and the mother of the sons of Zeb'edee.

The Burial of Jesus

57 When it was evening, there came a
rich man from Arimathe'a, named Joseph,
who also was a disciple of Jesus. [58]He went
to Pilate and asked for the body of Jesus.
Then Pilate ordered it to be given to him.
[59]And Joseph took the body, and wrapped
it in a clean linen shroud, [60]and laid it in
his own new tomb, which he had hewn in
the rock; and he rolled a great stone to the
door of the tomb, and departed. [61]Mary
Mag'dalene and the other Mary were
there, sitting opposite the sepulchre.

The Guard at the Tomb

62 Next day, that is, after the day of Prepa-
ration, the chief priests and the Pharisees
gathered before Pilate [63]and said, "Sir, we
remember how that imposter said, while
he was still alive, 'After three days I will
rise again.' [64]Therefore order the sepul-
chre to be made secure until the third
day, lest his disciples go and steal him
away, and tell the people, 'He has risen
from the dead,' and the last fraud will be
worse than the first." [65]Pilate said to them,
"You have a guard[e] of soldiers; go, make it
as secure as you can."[f] [66]So they went and
made the sepulchre secure by sealing the
stone and setting a guard.

The Resurrection of Jesus

28 Now after the sabbath, toward the
dawn of the first day of the week,
Mary Mag'dalene and the other Mary
went to see the sepulchre. [2]And behold,

[b]**27.45** Or *earth* [c]**27.49** Other ancient authorities insert *And another took a spear and pierced his side, and out came water and blood* [d]**27.54** Or *a son* [e]**27.65** Or *Take a guard* [f]**27.65** Greek *know*

there was a great earthquake; for an an-
gel of the Lord descended from heaven
and came and rolled back the stone, and
sat upon it. [3]His appearance was like
lightning, and his raiment white as snow.
[4]And for fear of him the guards trembled
and became like dead men. [5]But the angel
said to the women, "Do not be afraid; for
I know that you seek Jesus who was cru-
cified. [6]He is not here; for he has risen,
as he said. Come, see the place where he[g]
lay. [7]Then go quickly and tell his disciples
that he has risen from the dead, and be-
hold, he is going before you to Galilee;
there you will see him. Lo, I have told
you." [8]So they departed quickly from the
tomb with fear and great joy, and ran to
tell his disciples. [9]And behold, Jesus met
them and said, "Hail!" And they came up
and took hold of his feet and worshiped
him. [10]Then Jesus said to them, "Do not
be afraid; go and tell my brethren to go to
Galilee, and there they will see me."

The Report of the Guard

11 While they were going, behold, some
of the guard went into the city and told
the chief priests all that had taken place.
[12]And when they had assembled with
the elders and taken counsel, they gave
a sum of money to the soldiers [13]and
said, "Tell people, 'His disciples came by
night and stole him away while we were
asleep.' [14]And if this comes to the gover-
nor's ears, we will satisfy him and keep
you out of trouble." [15]So they took the
money and did as they were directed;
and this story has been spread among
the Jews to this day.

The Commissioning of the Disciples

16 Now the eleven disciples went to
Galilee, to the mountain to which Jesus
had directed them. [17]And when they
saw him they worshiped him; but some
doubted. [18]And Jesus came and said to
them, "All authority in heaven and on
earth has been given to me. [19]Go there-
fore and make disciples of all nations,
baptizing them in the name of the Father
and of the Son and of the Holy Spirit,
[20]teaching them to observe all that I have
commanded you; and lo, I am with you
always, to the close of the age."

[g] **28.6** Other ancient authorities read *the Lord*

MARK

The Proclamation of John the Baptist

1 The beginning of the gospel of Jesus
Christ, the Son of God.[a]
2 As it is written in Isaiah the prophet,[b]
"Behold, I send my messenger
before thy face,
who shall prepare thy way;
3 the voice of one crying in the
wilderness:
Prepare the way of the Lord,
make his paths straight—"
4John the baptizer appeared[c] in the wil-
derness, preaching a baptism of repen-
tance for the forgiveness of sins. 5And
there went out to him all the country of
Judea, and all the people of Jerusalem;
and they were baptized by him in the
river Jordan, confessing their sins. 6Now
John was clothed with camel's hair, and
had a leather girdle around his waist,
and ate locusts and wild honey. 7And
he preached, saying, "After me comes
he who is mightier than I, the thong of
whose sandals I am not worthy to stoop
down and untie. 8I have baptized you
with water; but he will baptize you with
the Holy Spirit."

The Baptism of Jesus

9 In those days Jesus came from Naza-
reth of Galilee and was baptized by John
in the Jordan. 10And when he came up
out of the water, immediately he saw the
heavens opened and the Spirit descend-
ing upon him like a dove; 11and a voice
came from heaven, "Thou art my beloved
Son;[d] with thee I am well pleased."

The Temptation of Jesus

12 The Spirit immediately drove him out
into the wilderness. 13And he was in the
wilderness forty days, tempted by Satan;
and he was with the wild beasts; and the
angels ministered to him.

The Beginning of the Galilean Ministry

14 Now after John was arrested, Jesus
came into Galilee, preaching the gospel
of God, 15and saying, "The time is ful-
filled, and the kingdom of God is at hand;
repent, and believe in the gospel."

Jesus Calls the First Disciples

16 And passing along by the Sea of Gal-
ilee, he saw Simon and Andrew the
brother of Simon casting a net in the sea;
for they were fishermen. 17And Jesus said
to them, "Follow me and I will make you
become fishers of men." 18And immedi-
ately they left their nets and followed
him. 19And going on a little farther, he
saw James the son of Zeb'edee and John
his brother, who were in their boat
mending the nets. 20And immediately
he called them; and they left their father
Zeb'edee in the boat with the hired ser-
vants, and followed him.

The Man with an Unclean Spirit

21 And they went into Caper'na-um; and
immediately on the sabbath he entered
the synagogue and taught. 22And they
were astonished at his teaching, for he
taught them as one who had authority,
and not as the scribes. 23And immedi-
ately there was in their synagogue a man
with an unclean spirit; 24and he cried
out, "What have you to do with us, Jesus
of Nazareth? Have you come to destroy
us? I know who you are, the Holy One of
God." 25But Jesus rebuked him, saying,
"Be silent, and come out of him!" 26And
the unclean spirit, convulsing him and

[a]**1.1** Other ancient authorities omit *the Son of God* [b]**1.2** Other ancient authorities read *in the prophets*
[c]**1.4** Other ancient authorities read *John was baptizing* [d]**1.11** Or *my Son, my* (or *the*) *Beloved*

crying with a loud voice, came out of him.
[27]And they were all amazed, so that they
questioned among themselves, saying,
"What is this? A new teaching! With au-
thority he commands even the unclean
spirits, and they obey him." [28]And at once
his fame spread everywhere throughout
all the surrounding region of Galilee.

Jesus Heals Many at Simon's House

29 And immediately he[e] left the syna-
gogue, and entered the house of Simon
and Andrew, with James and John. [30]Now
Simon's mother-in-law lay sick with a
fever, and immediately they told him of
her. [31]And he came and took her by the
hand and lifted her up, and the fever left
her; and she served them.

32 That evening, at sundown, they
brought to him all who were sick or pos-
sessed with demons. [33]And the whole
city was gathered together about the
door. [34]And he healed many who were
sick with various diseases, and cast out
many demons; and he would not permit
the demons to speak, because they knew
him.

A Preaching Tour in Galilee

35 And in the morning, a great while be-
fore day, he rose and went out to a lonely
place, and there he prayed. [36]And Simon
and those who were with him followed
him, [37]and they found him and said to
him, "Every one is searching for you."
[38]And he said to them, "Let us go on to
the next towns, that I may preach there
also; for that is why I came out." [39]And
he went throughout all Galilee, preach-
ing in their synagogues and casting out
demons.

Jesus Cleanses a Leper

40 And a leper came to him beseeching
him, and kneeling said to him, "If you
will, you can make me clean." [41]Moved
with pity, he stretched out his hand and
touched him, and said to him, "I will; be
clean." [42]And immediately the leprosy
left him, and he was made clean. [43]And
he sternly charged him, and sent him
away at once, [44]and said to him, "See that
you say nothing to any one; but go, show
yourself to the priest, and offer for your
cleansing what Moses commanded, for
a proof to the people."[f] [45]But he went out
and began to talk freely about it, and to
spread the news, so that Jesus[g] could no
longer openly enter a town, but was out
in the country; and people came to him
from every quarter.

Jesus Heals a Paralytic

2 And when he returned to Caper'-
na-um after some days, it was re-
ported that he was at home. [2]And many
were gathered together, so that there
was no longer room for them, not even
about the door; and he was preaching the
word to them. [3]And they came, bringing
to him a paralytic carried by four men.
[4]And when they could not get near him
because of the crowd, they removed the
roof above him; and when they had made
an opening, they let down the pallet on
which the paralytic lay. [5]And when Jesus
saw their faith, he said to the paralytic,
"My son, your sins are forgiven." [6]Now
some of the scribes were sitting there,
questioning in their hearts, [7]"Why does
this man speak thus? It is blasphemy!
Who can forgive sins but God alone?"
[8]And immediately Jesus, perceiving
in his spirit that they thus questioned
within themselves, said to them, "Why
do you question thus in your hearts?
[9]Which is easier, to say to the paralytic,
'Your sins are forgiven,' or to say, 'Rise,
take up your pallet and walk'? [10]But that
you may know that the Son of man has
authority on earth to forgive sins"—he
said to the paralytic— [11]"I say to you, rise,
take up your pallet and go home." [12]And
he rose, and immediately took up the

[e] **1.29** Other ancient authorities read *they* [f] **1.44** Greek *to them* [g] **1.45** Greek *he*

pallet and went out before them all; so
that they were all amazed and glorified
God, saying, "We never saw anything
like this!"

Jesus Calls Levi

13 He went out again beside the sea; and
all the crowd gathered about him, and he
taught them. 14 And as he passed on, he
saw Levi the son of Alphaeus sitting at
the tax office, and he said to him, "Follow
me." And he rose and followed him.

15 And as he sat at table in his house,
many tax collectors and sinners were
sitting with Jesus and his disciples; for
there were many who followed him.
16 And the scribes of[h] the Pharisees, when
they saw that he was eating with sinners
and tax collectors, said to his disciples,
"Why does he eat[i] with tax collectors and
sinners?" 17 And when Jesus heard it, he
said to them, "Those who are well have
no need of a physician, but those who are
sick; I came not to call the righteous, but
sinners."

The Question about Fasting

18 Now John's disciples and the Pharisees
were fasting; and people came and said
to him, "Why do John's disciples and the
disciples of the Pharisees fast, but your
disciples do not fast?" 19 And Jesus said to
them, "Can the wedding guests fast while
the bridegroom is with them? As long
as they have the bridegroom with them,
they cannot fast. 20 The days will come,
when the bridegroom is taken away from
them, and then they will fast in that day.
21 No one sews a piece of unshrunk cloth
on an old garment; if he does, the patch
tears away from it, the new from the old,
and a worse tear is made. 22 And no one
puts new wine into old wineskins; if he
does, the wine will burst the skins, and
the wine is lost, and so are the skins; but
new wine is for fresh skins."[j]

Pronouncement about the Sabbath

23 One sabbath he was going through
the grainfields; and as they made their
way his disciples began to pluck ears of
grain. 24 And the Pharisees said to him,
"Look, why are they doing what is not
lawful on the sabbath?" 25 And he said to
them, "Have you never read what David
did, when he was in need and was hun-
gry, he and those who were with him:
26 how he entered the house of God, when
Abi'athar was high priest, and ate the
bread of the Presence, which it is not
lawful for any but the priests to eat, and
also gave it to those who were with him?"
27 And he said to them, "The sabbath was
made for man, not man for the sabbath;
28 so the Son of man is lord even of the
sabbath."

The Man with a Withered Hand

3 Again he entered the synagogue, and
a man was there who had a withered
hand. 2 And they watched him, to see
whether he would heal him on the sab-
bath, so that they might accuse him. 3 And
he said to the man who had the withered
hand, "Come here." 4 And he said to them,
"Is it lawful on the sabbath to do good or
to do harm, to save life or to kill?" But
they were silent. 5 And he looked around
at them with anger, grieved at their
hardness of heart, and said to the man,
"Stretch out your hand." He stretched
it out, and his hand was restored. 6 The
Pharisees went out, and immediately
held counsel with the Hero'di-ans against
him, how to destroy him.

A Multitude at the Seaside

7 Jesus withdrew with his disciples to the
sea, and a great multitude from Galilee
followed; also from Judea 8 and Jerusa-
lem and Idume'a and from beyond the
Jordan and from about Tyre and Sidon a
great multitude, hearing all that he did,

[h] **2.16** Other ancient authorities read *and*
[i] **2.16** Other ancient authorities add *and drink*
[j] **2.22** Other ancient authorities omit *but new wine is for fresh skins*

came to him. 9And he told his disciples to
have a boat ready for him because of the
crowd, lest they should crush him; 10for
he had healed many, so that all who had
diseases pressed upon him to touch him.
11And whenever the unclean spirits be-
held him, they fell down before him and
cried out, "You are the Son of God." 12And
he strictly ordered them not to make him
known.

Jesus Appoints the Twelve

13 And he went up into the hills, and
called to him those whom he desired; and
they came to him. 14And he appointed
twelve,[k] to be with him, and to be sent
out to preach 15and have authority to
cast out demons: 16Simon whom he sur-
named Peter; 17James the son of Zeb'edee
and John the brother of James, whom he
surnamed Bo-aner'ges, that is, sons of
thunder; 18Andrew, and Philip, and Bar-
tholomew, and Matthew, and Thomas,
and James the son of Alphaeus, and
Thaddaeus, and Simon the Cananaean,
19and Judas Iscariot, who betrayed him.

Jesus and Beelzebul

Then he went home; 20and the crowd
came together again, so that they could
not even eat. 21And when his friends
heard it, they went out to seize him, for
they said, "He is beside himself." 22And
the scribes who came down from Jerusa-
lem said, "He is possessed by Be-el'zebul,
and by the prince of demons he casts
out the demons." 23And he called them to
him, and said to them in parables, "How
can Satan cast out Satan? 24If a kingdom
is divided against itself, that kingdom
cannot stand. 25And if a house is divided
against itself, that house will not be able
to stand. 26And if Satan has risen up
against himself and is divided, he cannot
stand, but is coming to an end. 27But no
one can enter a strong man's house and
plunder his goods, unless he first binds
the strong man; then indeed he may
plunder his house.

28 "Truly, I say to you, all sins will be
forgiven the sons of men, and whatever
blasphemies they utter; 29but whoever
blasphemes against the Holy Spirit
never has forgiveness, but is guilty of an
eternal sin"— 30for they had said, "He has
an unclean spirit."

The True Kindred of Jesus

31 And his mother and his brethren
came; and standing outside they sent
to him and called him. 32And a crowd
was sitting about him; and they said to
him, "Your mother and your brethren[l]
are outside, asking for you." 33And he
replied, "Who are my mother and my
brethren?" 34And looking around on
those who sat about him, he said, "Here
are my mother and my brethren! 35Who-
ever does the will of God is my brother,
and sister, and mother."

The Parable of the Sower

4 Again he began to teach beside the
sea. And a very large crowd gathered
about him, so that he got into a boat and
sat in it on the sea; and the whole crowd
was beside the sea on the land. 2And he
taught them many things in parables,
and in his teaching he said to them: 3"Lis-
ten! A sower went out to sow. 4And as
he sowed, some seed fell along the path,
and the birds came and devoured it.
5Other seed fell on rocky ground, where
it had not much soil, and immediately it
sprang up, since it had no depth of soil;
6and when the sun rose it was scorched,
and since it had no root it withered away.
7Other seed fell among thorns and the
thorns grew up and choked it, and it
yielded no grain. 8And other seeds fell
into good soil and brought forth grain,
growing up and increasing and yielding

[k] **3.14** Other ancient authorities add *whom also he named apostles*

[l] **3.32** Other early authorities add *and your sisters*

thirtyfold and sixtyfold and a hundred-
fold." [9]And he said, "He who has ears to
hear, let him hear."

The Purpose of the Parables

10 And when he was alone, those who
were about him with the twelve asked
him concerning the parables. [11]And he
said to them, "To you has been given
the secret of the kingdom of God, but
for those outside everything is in par-
ables; [12]so that they may indeed see but
not perceive, and may indeed hear but
not understand; lest they should turn
again, and be forgiven." [13]And he said to
them, "Do you not understand this par-
able? How then will you understand all
the parables? [14]The sower sows the word.
[15]And these are the ones along the path,
where the word is sown; when they hear,
Satan immediately comes and takes
away the word which is sown in them.
[16]And these in like manner are the ones
sown upon rocky ground, who, when
they hear the word, immediately receive
it with joy; [17]and they have no root in
themselves, but endure for a while; then,
when tribulation or persecution arises
on account of the word, immediately
they fall away.[m] [18]And others are the
ones sown among thorns; they are those
who hear the word, [19]but the cares of
the world, and the delight in riches, and
the desire for other things, enter in and
choke the word, and it proves unfruit-
ful. [20]But those that were sown upon the
good soil are the ones who hear the word
and accept it and bear fruit, thirtyfold
and sixtyfold and a hundredfold."

A Lamp under a Bushel Basket

21 And he said to them, "Is a lamp
brought in to be put under a bushel, or
under a bed, and not on a stand? [22]For
there is nothing hid, except to be made
manifest; nor is anything secret, except
to come to light. [23]If any man has ears to
hear, let him hear." [24]And he said to them,
"Take heed what you hear; the measure
you give will be the measure you get, and
still more will be given you. [25]For to him
who has will more be given; and from
him who has not, even what he has will
be taken away."

The Parable of the Growing Seed

26 And he said, "The kingdom of God is
as if a man should scatter seed upon the
ground, [27]and should sleep and rise night
and day, and the seed should sprout and
grow, he knows not how. [28]The earth pro-
duces of itself, first the blade, then the
ear, then the full grain in the ear. [29]But
when the grain is ripe, at once he puts in
the sickle, because the harvest has come."

The Parable of the Mustard Seed

30 And he said, "With what can we com-
pare the kingdom of God, or what para-
ble shall we use for it? [31]It is like a grain
of mustard seed, which, when sown
upon the ground, is the smallest of all the
seeds on earth; [32]yet when it is sown it
grows up and becomes the greatest of all
shrubs, and puts forth large branches, so
that the birds of the air can make nests in
its shade."

The Use of Parables

33 With many such parables he spoke
the word to them, as they were able to
hear it; [34]he did not speak to them with-
out a parable, but privately to his own
disciples he explained everything.

Jesus Stills a Storm

35 On that day, when evening had come,
he said to them, "Let us go across to the
other side." [36]And leaving the crowd,
they took him with them, just as he was,
in the boat. And other boats were with
him. [37]And a great storm of wind arose,
and the waves beat into the boat, so that
the boat was already filling. [38]But he was

[m] **4.17** Or *stumble*

in the stern, asleep on the cushion; and
they woke him and said to him, "Teacher,
do you not care if we perish?" 39 And he
awoke and rebuked the wind, and said
to the sea, "Peace! Be still!" And the wind
ceased, and there was a great calm. 40 He
said to them, "Why are you afraid? Have
you no faith?" 41 And they were filled
with awe, and said to one another, "Who
then is this, that even wind and sea obey
him?"

Jesus Heals the Gerasene Demoniac

5 They came to the other side of the
sea, to the country of the Ger′asenes.[n]
2 And when he had come out of the boat,
there met him out of the tombs a man
with an unclean spirit, 3 who lived among
the tombs; and no one could bind him any
more, even with a chain; 4 for he had of-
ten been bound with fetters and chains,
but the chains he wrenched apart, and
the fetters he broke in pieces; and no one
had the strength to subdue him. 5 Night
and day among the tombs and on the
mountains he was always crying out,
and bruising himself with stones. 6 And
when he saw Jesus from afar, he ran and
worshiped him; 7 and crying out with a
loud voice, he said, "What have you to
do with me, Jesus, Son of the Most High
God? I adjure you by God, do not torment
me." 8 For he had said to him, "Come out of
the man, you unclean spirit!" 9 And Jesus[o]
asked him, "What is your name?" He re-
plied, "My name is Legion; for we are
many." 10 And he begged him eagerly not
to send them out of the country. 11 Now a
great herd of swine was feeding there on
the hillside; 12 and they begged him, "Send
us to the swine, let us enter them." 13 So he
gave them leave. And the unclean spirits
came out, and entered the swine; and the
herd, numbering about two thousand,
rushed down the steep bank into the sea,
and were drowned in the sea.

14 The herdsmen fled, and told it in the
city and in the country. And people came
to see what it was that had happened.
15 And they came to Jesus, and saw the
demoniac sitting there, clothed and in
his right mind, the man who had had the
legion; and they were afraid. 16 And those
who had seen it told what had happened
to the demoniac and to the swine. 17 And
they began to beg Jesus[p] to depart from
their neighborhood. 18 And as he was
getting into the boat, the man who had
been possessed with demons begged him
that he might be with him. 19 But he re-
fused, and said to him, "Go home to your
friends, and tell them how much the
Lord has done for you, and how he has
had mercy on you." 20 And he went away
and began to proclaim in the Decap′olis
how much Jesus had done for him; and
all men marveled.

A Girl Restored to Life and a Woman Healed

21 And when Jesus had crossed again in
the boat to the other side, a great crowd
gathered about him; and he was beside
the sea. 22 Then came one of the rulers of
the synagogue, Ja′irus by name; and see-
ing him, he fell at his feet, 23 and besought
him, saying, "My little daughter is at the
point of death. Come and lay your hands
on her, so that she may be made well, and
live." 24 And he went with him.

And a great crowd followed him and
thronged about him. 25 And there was a
woman who had had a flow of blood for
twelve years, 26 and who had suffered
much under many physicians, and had
spent all that she had, and was no better
but rather grew worse. 27 She had heard
the reports about Jesus, and came up be-
hind him in the crowd and touched his
garment. 28 For she said, "If I touch even
his garments, I shall be made well." 29 And
immediately the hemorrhage ceased; and

[n] **5.1** Other ancient authorities read *Gergesenes*, some *Gadarenes*
[o] **5.9** Greek *he*
[p] **5.17** Greek *him*

she felt in her body that she was healed
of her disease. 30 And Jesus, perceiving in
himself that power had gone forth from
him, immediately turned about in the
crowd, and said, "Who touched my gar-
ments?" 31 And his disciples said to him,
"You see the crowd pressing around you,
and yet you say, 'Who touched me?' " 32 And
he looked around to see who had done it.
33 But the woman, knowing what had been
done to her, came in fear and trembling
and fell down before him, and told him the
whole truth. 34 And he said to her, "Daugh-
ter, your faith has made you well; go in
peace, and be healed of your disease."

35 While he was still speaking, there
came from the ruler's house some who
said, "Your daughter is dead. Why trou-
ble the Teacher any further?" 36 But ignor-
ing[q] what they said, Jesus said to the ruler
of the synagogue, "Do not fear, only be-
lieve." 37 And he allowed no one to follow
him except Peter and James and John the
brother of James. 38 When they came to
the house of the ruler of the synagogue,
he saw a tumult, and people weeping and
wailing loudly. 39 And when he had en-
tered, he said to them, "Why do you make
a tumult and weep? The child is not dead
but sleeping." 40 And they laughed at him.
But he put them all outside, and took the
child's father and mother and those who
were with him, and went in where the
child was. 41 Taking her by the hand he
said to her, "Tal'itha cu'mi"; which means,
"Little girl, I say to you, arise." 42 And im-
mediately the girl got up and walked; for
she was twelve years old. And immedi-
ately they were overcome with amaze-
ment. 43 And he strictly charged them that
no one should know this, and told them to
give her something to eat.

The Rejection of Jesus at Nazareth

6 He went away from there and came
to his own country; and his disciples
followed him. 2 And on the sabbath he be-
gan to teach in the synagogue; and many
who heard him were astonished, saying,
"Where did this man get all this? What is
the wisdom given to him? What mighty
works are wrought by his hands! 3 Is not
this the carpenter, the son of Mary and
brother of James and Joses and Judas and
Simon, and are not his sisters here with
us?" And they took offense[r] at him. 4 And
Jesus said to them, "A prophet is not with-
out honor, except in his own country,
and among his own kin, and in his own
house." 5 And he could do no mighty work
there, except that he laid his hands upon
a few sick people and healed them. 6 And
he marveled because of their unbelief.

And he went about among the villages
teaching.

The Mission of the Twelve

7 And he called to him the twelve, and
began to send them out two by two, and
gave them authority over the unclean
spirits. 8 He charged them to take noth-
ing for their journey except a staff; no
bread, no bag, no money in their belts;
9 but to wear sandals and not put on two
tunics. 10 And he said to them, "Where
you enter a house, stay there until you
leave the place. 11 And if any place will not
receive you and they refuse to hear you,
when you leave, shake off the dust that
is on your feet for a testimony against
them." 12 So they went out and preached
that men should repent. 13 And they cast
out many demons, and anointed with oil
many that were sick and healed them.

The Death of John the Baptist

14 King Herod heard of it; for Jesus's[s]
name had become known. Some[t] said,
"John the baptizer has been raised from
the dead; that is why these powers are at
work in him." 15 But others said, "It is Eli'-
jah." And others said, "It is a prophet, like

[q] **5.36** Or *overhearing*. Other ancient authorities read *hearing*
[r] **6.3** Or *stumbled*
[s] **6.14** Greek *his*
[t] **6.14** Other ancient authorities read *he*

one of the prophets of old." [16]But when
Herod heard of it he said, "John, whom I
beheaded, has been raised." [17]For Herod
had sent and seized John, and bound him
in prison for the sake of Hero'di-as, his
brother Philip's wife; because he had
married her. [18]For John said to Herod, "It
is not lawful for you to have your broth-
er's wife." [19]And Hero'di-as had a grudge
against him, and wanted to kill him. But
she could not, [20]for Herod feared John,
knowing that he was a righteous and
holy man, and kept him safe. When he
heard him, he was much perplexed; and
yet he heard him gladly. [21]But an oppor-
tunity came when Herod on his birthday
gave a banquet for his courtiers and of-
ficers and the leading men of Galilee.
[22]For when Hero'di-as' daughter came in
and danced, she pleased Herod and his
guests; and the king said to the girl, "Ask
me for whatever you wish, and I will
grant it." [23]And he vowed to her, "What-
ever you ask me, I will give you, even half
of my kingdom." [24]And she went out, and
said to her mother, "What shall I ask?"
And she said, "The head of John the bap-
tizer." [25]And she came in immediately
with haste to the king, and asked, saying,
"I want you to give me at once the head
of John the Baptist on a platter." [26]And the
king was exceedingly sorry; but because
of his oaths and his guests he did not
want to break his word to her. [27]And im-
mediately the king sent a soldier of the
guard and gave orders to bring his head.
He went and beheaded him in the prison,
[28]and brought his head on a platter, and
gave it to the girl; and the girl gave it to
her mother. [29]When his disciples heard
of it, they came and took his body, and
laid it in a tomb.

Feeding the Five Thousand

30 The apostles returned to Jesus, and
told him all that they had done and
taught. [31]And he said to them, "Come
away by yourselves to a lonely place, and
rest a while." For many were coming and
going, and they had no leisure even to
eat. [32]And they went away in the boat to a
lonely place by themselves. [33]Now many
saw them going, and knew them, and they
ran there on foot from all the towns, and
got there ahead of them. [34]As he landed
he saw a great throng, and he had com-
passion on them, because they were like
sheep without a shepherd; and he began
to teach them many things. [35]And when it
grew late, his disciples came to him and
said, "This is a lonely place, and the hour
is now late; [36]send them away, to go into
the country and villages round about
and buy themselves something to eat."
[37]But he answered them, "You give them
something to eat." And they said to him,
"Shall we go and buy two hundred dena-
rii[u] worth of bread, and give it to them to
eat?" [38]And he said to them, "How many
loaves have you? Go and see." And when
they had found out, they said, "Five, and
two fish." [39]Then he commanded them all
to sit down by companies upon the green
grass. [40]So they sat down in groups, by
hundreds and by fifties. [41]And taking the
five loaves and the two fish he looked up
to heaven, and blessed, and broke the
loaves, and gave them to the disciples to
set before the people; and he divided the
two fish among them all. [42]And they all
ate and were satisfied. [43]And they took
up twelve baskets full of broken pieces
and of the fish. [44]And those who ate the
loaves were five thousand men.

Jesus Walks on the Water

45 Immediately he made his disciples
get into the boat and go before him to
the other side, to Beth-sa'ida, while he
dismissed the crowd. [46]And after he had
taken leave of them, he went up into the
hills to pray. [47]And when evening came,
the boat was out on the sea, and he was
alone on the land. [48]And he saw that they

[u] **6.37** The denarius was a day's wage for a laborer

were distressed in rowing, for the wind
was against them. And about the fourth
watch of the night he came to them, walk-
ing on the sea. He meant to pass by them,
49 but when they saw him walking on the
sea they thought it was a ghost, and cried
out; 50 for they all saw him, and were ter-
rified. But immediately he spoke to them
and said, "Take heart, it is I; have no fear."
51 And he got into the boat with them and
the wind ceased. And they were utterly
astounded, 52 for they did not understand
about the loaves, but their hearts were
hardened.

Healing the Sick in Gennesaret

53 And when they had crossed over, they
came to land at Gennes'aret, and moored
to the shore. 54 And when they got out of
the boat, immediately the people rec-
ognized him, 55 and ran about the whole
neighborhood and began to bring sick
people on their pallets to any place where
they heard he was. 56 And wherever he
came, in villages, cities, or country, they
laid the sick in the market places, and be-
sought him that they might touch even
the fringe of his garment; and as many
as touched it were made well.

The Tradition of the Elders

7 Now when the Pharisees gathered
together to him, with some of the
scribes, who had come from Jerusalem,
2 they saw that some of his disciples ate
with hands defiled, that is, unwashed.
3 (For the Pharisees, and all the Jews, do
not eat unless they wash their hands,[v] ob-
serving the tradition of the elders; 4 and
when they come from the market place,
they do not eat unless they purify[w] them-
selves; and there are many other tradi-
tions which they observe, the washing
of cups and pots and vessels of bronze.[x])
5 And the Pharisees and the scribes asked
him, "Why do your disciples not live[y] ac-
cording to the tradition of the elders, but
eat with hands defiled?" 6 And he said to
them, "Well did Isaiah prophesy of you
hypocrites, as it is written,

'This people honors me with their lips,
but their heart is far from me;
7 in vain do they worship me,
teaching as doctrines the precepts of men.'

8 You leave the commandment of God,
and hold fast the tradition of men."

9 And he said to them, "You have a
fine way of rejecting the commandment
of God, in order to keep your tradition!
10 For Moses said, 'Honor your father and
your mother'; and, 'He who speaks evil
of father or mother, let him surely die';
11 but you say, 'If a man tells his father or
his mother, What you would have gained
from me is Corban' (that is, given to God)[z]—
12 then you no longer permit him to do
anything for his father or mother, 13 thus
making void the word of God through
your tradition which you hand on. And
many such things you do."

14 And he called the people to him
again, and said to them, "Hear me, all of
you, and understand: 15 there is nothing
outside a man which by going into him
can defile him; but the things which come
out of a man are what defile him."[a] 17 And
when he had entered the house, and left
the people, his disciples asked him about
the parable. 18 And he said to them, "Then
are you also without understanding?
Do you not see that whatever goes into
a man from outside cannot defile him,
19 since it enters, not his heart but his
stomach, and so passes on?"[b] (Thus he
declared all foods clean.) 20 And he said,
"What comes out of a man is what defiles

[v] **7.3** One Greek word is of uncertain meaning and is not translated [w] **7.4** Other ancient authorities read *baptize* [x] **7.4** Other ancient authorities add *and beds* [y] **7.5** Greek *walk* [z] **7.11** Or *an offering* [a] **7.15** Other ancient authorities add verse 16, *"If any man has ears to hear, let him hear"* [b] **7.19** Or *is evacuated*

a man. 21For from within, out of the heart
of man, come evil thoughts, fornication,
theft, murder, adultery, 22coveting, wick-
edness, deceit, licentiousness, envy,
slander, pride, foolishness. 23All these
evil things come from within, and they
defile a man."

The Syrophoenician Woman's Faith

24 And from there he arose and went
away to the region of Tyre and Sidon.[c]
And he entered a house, and would not
have any one know it; yet he could not be
hid. 25But immediately a woman, whose
little daughter was possessed by an un-
clean spirit, heard of him, and came and
fell down at his feet. 26Now the woman
was a Greek, a Syrophoeni'cian by birth.
And she begged him to cast the demon
out of her daughter. 27And he said to her,
"Let the children first be fed, for it is not
right to take the children's bread and
throw it to the dogs." 28But she answered
him, "Yes, Lord; yet even the dogs un-
der the table eat the children's crumbs."
29And he said to her, "For this saying you
may go your way; the demon has left
your daughter." 30And she went home,
and found the child lying in bed, and the
demon gone.

Jesus Cures a Deaf Man

31 Then he returned from the region of
Tyre, and went through Sidon to the Sea
of Galilee, through the region of the De-
cap'olis. 32And they brought to him a man
who was deaf and had an impediment
in his speech; and they besought him to
lay his hand upon him. 33And taking him
aside from the multitude privately, he
put his fingers into his ears, and he spat
and touched his tongue; 34and looking
up to heaven, he sighed, and said to him,
"Eph'phatha," that is, "Be opened." 35And
his ears were opened, his tongue was
released, and he spoke plainly. 36And he
charged them to tell no one; but the more
he charged them, the more zealously
they proclaimed it. 37And they were as-
tonished beyond measure, saying, "He
has done all things well; he even makes
the deaf hear and the dumb speak."

Feeding the Four Thousand

8 In those days, when again a great
crowd had gathered, and they had
nothing to eat, he called his disciples to
him, and said to them, 2"I have compas-
sion on the crowd, because they have
been with me now three days, and have
nothing to eat; 3and if I send them away
hungry to their homes, they will faint on
the way; and some of them have come a
long way." 4And his disciples answered
him, "How can one feed these men with
bread here in the desert?" 5And he asked
them, "How many loaves have you?" They
said, "Seven." 6And he commanded the
crowd to sit down on the ground; and he
took the seven loaves, and having given
thanks he broke them and gave them to
his disciples to set before the people; and
they set them before the crowd. 7And
they had a few small fish; and having
blessed them, he commanded that these
also should be set before them. 8And they
ate, and were satisfied; and they took up
the broken pieces left over, seven baskets
full. 9And there were about four thou-
sand people. 10And he sent them away;
and immediately he got into the boat
with his disciples, and went to the dis-
trict of Dalmanu'tha.[d]

The Demand for a Sign

11 The Pharisees came and began to ar-
gue with him, seeking from him a sign
from heaven, to test him. 12And he sighed
deeply in his spirit, and said, "Why does
this generation seek a sign? Truly, I say
to you, no sign shall be given to this gen-
eration." 13And he left them, and getting

[c] **7.24** Other ancient authorities omit *and Sidon*

[d] **8.10** Other ancient authorities read *Magadan* or *Magdala*

into the boat again he departed to the
other side.

The Yeast of the Pharisees and of Herod

14 Now they had forgotten to bring
bread; and they had only one loaf with
them in the boat. [15]And he cautioned
them, saying, "Take heed, beware of the
leaven of the Pharisees and the leaven
of Herod."[e] [16]And they discussed it with
one another, saying, "We have no bread."
[17]And being aware of it, Jesus said to
them, "Why do you discuss the fact that
you have no bread? Do you not yet per-
ceive or understand? Are your hearts
hardened? [18]Having eyes do you not see,
and having ears do you not hear? And
do you not remember? [19]When I broke
the five loaves for the five thousand, how
many baskets full of broken pieces did
you take up?" They said to him, "Twelve."
[20]"And the seven for the four thousand,
how many baskets full of broken pieces
did you take up?" And they said to him,
"Seven." [21]And he said to them, "Do you
not yet understand?"

Jesus Cures a Blind Man at Bethsaida

22 And they came to Beth-sa'ida. And
some people brought to him a blind man,
and begged him to touch him. [23]And he
took the blind man by the hand, and led
him out of the village; and when he had
spit on his eyes and laid his hands upon
him, he asked him, "Do you see any-
thing?" [24]And he looked up and said, "I
see men; but they look like trees, walk-
ing." [25]Then again he laid his hands upon
his eyes; and he looked intently and was
restored, and saw everything clearly.
[26]And he sent him away to his home, say-
ing, "Do not even enter the village."

Peter's Declaration about Jesus

27 And Jesus went on with his disciples,
to the villages of Caesare'a Philippi; and
on the way he asked his disciples, "Who
do men say that I am?" [28]And they told
him, "John the Baptist; and others say,
Eli'jah; and others one of the prophets."
[29]And he asked them, "But who do you
say that I am?" Peter answered him, "You
are the Christ." [30]And he charged them to
tell no one about him.

Jesus Foretells His Death and Resurrection

31 And he began to teach them that the
Son of man must suffer many things, and
be rejected by the elders and the chief
priests and the scribes, and be killed,
and after three days rise again. [32]And he
said this plainly. And Peter took him, and
began to rebuke him. [33]But turning and
seeing his disciples, he rebuked Peter,
and said, "Get behind me, Satan! For you
are not on the side of God, but of men."

34 And he called to him the multitude
with his disciples, and said to them, "If
any man would come after me, let him
deny himself and take up his cross and
follow me. [35]For whoever would save
his life will lose it; and whoever loses
his life for my sake and the gospel's will
save it. [36]For what does it profit a man, to
gain the whole world and forfeit his life?
[37]For what can a man give in return for
his life? [38]For whoever is ashamed of me
and of my words in this adulterous and
sinful generation, of him will the Son of
man also be ashamed, when he comes
in the glory of his Father with the holy
9 angels." [1]And he said to them, "Truly,
I say to you, there are some stand-
ing here who will not taste death before
they see the kingdom of God come with
power."

The Transfiguration

2 And after six days Jesus took with him
Peter and James and John, and led them
up a high mountain apart by themselves;
and he was transfigured before them,

[e]**8.15** Other ancient authorities read *the Herodians*

3 and his garments became glistening, intensely white, as no fuller on earth could bleach them. 4 And there appeared to them Eli'jah with Moses; and they were talking to Jesus. 5 And Peter said to Jesus, "Master,[f] it is well that we are here; let us make three booths, one for you and one for Moses and one for Eli'jah." 6 For he did not know what to say, for they were exceedingly afraid. 7 And a cloud overshadowed them, and a voice came out of the cloud, "This is my beloved Son;[g] listen to him." 8 And suddenly looking around they no longer saw any one with them but Jesus only.

The Coming of Elijah

9 And as they were coming down the mountain, he charged them to tell no one what they had seen, until the Son of man should have risen from the dead. 10 So they kept the matter to themselves, questioning what the rising from the dead meant. 11 And they asked him, "Why do the scribes say that first Eli'jah must come?" 12 And he said to them, "Eli'jah does come first to restore all things; and how is it written of the Son of man, that he should suffer many things and be treated with contempt? 13 But I tell you that Eli'jah has come, and they did to him whatever they pleased, as it is written of him."

The Healing of a Boy with a Spirit

14 And when they came to the disciples, they saw a great crowd about them, and scribes arguing with them. 15 And immediately all the crowd, when they saw him, were greatly amazed, and ran up to him and greeted him. 16 And he asked them, "What are you discussing with them?" 17 And one of the crowd answered him, "Teacher, I brought my son to you, for he has a dumb spirit; 18 and wherever it seizes him, it dashes him down; and he foams and grinds his teeth and becomes rigid; and I asked your disciples to cast it out, and they were not able." 19 And he answered them, "O faithless generation, how long am I to be with you? How long am I to bear with you? Bring him to me." 20 And they brought the boy to him; and when the spirit saw him, immediately it convulsed the boy, and he fell on the ground and rolled about, foaming at the mouth. 21 And Jesus[h] asked his father, "How long has he had this?" And he said, "From childhood. 22 And it has often cast him into the fire and into the water, to destroy him; but if you can do anything, have pity on us and help us." 23 And Jesus said to him, "If you can! All things are possible to him who believes." 24 Immediately the father of the child cried out[i] and said, "I believe; help my unbelief!" 25 And when Jesus saw that a crowd came running together, he rebuked the unclean spirit, saying to it, "You dumb and deaf spirit, I command you, come out of him, and never enter him again." 26 And after crying out and convulsing him terribly, it came out, and the boy was like a corpse; so that most of them said, "He is dead." 27 But Jesus took him by the hand and lifted him up, and he arose. 28 And when he had entered the house, his disciples asked him privately, "Why could we not cast it out?" 29 And he said to them, "This kind cannot be driven out by anything but prayer and fasting."[j]

Jesus Again Foretells His Death and Resurrection

30 They went on from there and passed through Galilee. And he would not have any one know it; 31 for he was teaching his disciples, saying to them, "The Son of man will be delivered into the hands of men, and they will kill him; and when he is killed, after three days he will rise." 32 But they did not understand the saying, and they were afraid to ask him.

[f] **9.5** Or *Rabbi* [g] **9.7** Or *my Son, my* (or *the*) *Beloved* [h] **9.21** Greek *he* [i] **9.24** Other ancient authorities add *with tears* [j] **9.29** Other ancient authorities omit *and fasting*

Who Is the Greatest?

33 And they came to Caper′na-um; and
when he was in the house he asked them,
"What were you discussing on the way?"
34 But they were silent; for on the way
they had discussed with one another
who was the greatest. 35 And he sat down
and called the twelve; and he said to
them, "If any one would be first, he must
be last of all and servant of all." 36 And he
took a child, and put him in the midst of
them; and taking him in his arms, he said
to them, 37 "Whoever receives one such
child in my name receives me; and who-
ever receives me, receives not me but
him who sent me."

Another Exorcist

38 John said to him, "Teacher, we saw a
man casting out demons in your name,[k]
and we forbade him, because he was
not following us." 39 But Jesus said, "Do
not forbid him; for no one who does a
mighty work in my name will be able
soon after to speak evil of me. 40 For
he that is not against us is for us. 41 For
truly, I say to you, whoever gives you a
cup of water to drink because you bear
the name of Christ, will by no means
lose his reward.

Temptations to Sin

42 "Whoever causes one of these little
ones who believe in me to sin,[l] it would
be better for him if a great millstone
were hung round his neck and he were
thrown into the sea. 43 And if your hand
causes you to sin,[m] cut it off; it is bet-
ter for you to enter life maimed than
with two hands to go to hell,[n] to the
unquenchable fire.[o] 45 And if your foot
causes you to sin,[p] cut it off; it is better
for you to enter life lame than with two
feet to be thrown into hell.[q,r] 47 And if
your eye causes you to sin,[s] pluck it out;
it is better for you to enter the kingdom
of God with one eye than with two eyes
to be thrown into hell,[t] 48 where their
worm does not die, and the fire is not
quenched. 49 For every one will be salted
with fire.[u] 50 Salt is good; but if the salt
has lost its saltness, how will you sea-
son it? Have salt in yourselves, and be at
peace with one another."

Teaching about Divorce

10 And he left there and went to the
region of Judea and beyond the
Jordan, and crowds gathered to him
again; and again, as his custom was, he
taught them.

2 And Pharisees came up and in or-
der to test him asked, "Is it lawful for a
man to divorce his wife?" 3 He answered
them, "What did Moses command you?"
4 They said, "Moses allowed a man to
write a certificate of divorce, and to put
her away." 5 But Jesus said to them, "For
your hardness of heart he wrote you this
commandment. 6 But from the beginning
of creation, 'God made them male and fe-
male.' 7 'For this reason a man shall leave
his father and mother and be joined to
his wife,[v] 8 and the two shall become one.'[w]
So they are no longer two but one.[x] 9 What
therefore God has joined together, let not
man put asunder."

10 And in the house the disciples asked
him again about this matter. 11 And he
said to them, "Whoever divorces his wife
and marries another, commits adultery
against her; 12 and if she divorces her hus-
band and marries another, she commits
adultery."

[k] **9.38** Other ancient authorities add *who does not follow us* [l] **9.42** Greek *stumble* [m] **9.43** Greek *stumble* [n] **9.43** Greek *Gehenna* [o] **9.43** Verses 44 and 46 (which are identical with verse 48) are omitted by the best ancient authorities [p] **9.45** Greek *stumble* [q] **9.45** Greek *Gehenna* [r] **9.45** Verses 44 and 46 (which are identical with verse 48) are omitted by the best ancient authorities [s] **9.47** Greek *stumble* [t] **9.47** Greek *Gehenna* [u] **9.49** Other ancient authorities add *and every sacrifice will be salted with salt* [v] **10.7** Other ancient authorities omit *and be joined to his wife* [w] **10.8** Greek *one flesh* [x] **10.8** Greek *one flesh*

Jesus Blesses Little Children

13 And they were bringing children
to him, that he might touch them; and
the disciples rebuked them. [14]But when
Jesus saw it he was indignant, and said
to them, "Let the children come to me,
do not hinder them; for to such belongs
the kingdom of God. [15]Truly, I say to you,
whoever does not receive the kingdom of
God like a child shall not enter it." [16]And
he took them in his arms and blessed
them, laying his hands upon them.

The Rich Man

17 And as he was setting out on his jour-
ney, a man ran up and knelt before him,
and asked him, "Good Teacher, what
must I do to inherit eternal life?" [18]And
Jesus said to him, "Why do you call me
good? No one is good but God alone. [19]You
know the commandments: 'Do not kill,
Do not commit adultery, Do not steal, Do
not bear false witness, Do not defraud,
Honor your father and mother.'" [20]And
he said to him, "Teacher, all these I have
observed from my youth." [21]And Jesus
looking upon him loved him, and said
to him, "You lack one thing; go, sell what
you have, and give to the poor, and you
will have treasure in heaven; and come,
follow me." [22]At that saying his counte-
nance fell, and he went away sorrowful;
for he had great possessions.

23 And Jesus looked around and said
to his disciples, "How hard it will be for
those who have riches to enter the king-
dom of God!" [24]And the disciples were
amazed at his words. But Jesus said to
them again, "Children, how hard it is
for those who trust in riches[y] to enter
the kingdom of God! [25]It is easier for a
camel to go through the eye of a needle
than for a rich man to enter the kingdom
of God." [26]And they were exceedingly
astonished, and said to him,[z] "Then who
can be saved?" [27]Jesus looked at them and
said, "With men it is impossible, but not
with God; for all things are possible with
God." [28]Peter began to say to him, "Lo, we
have left everything and followed you."
[29]Jesus said, "Truly, I say to you, there is
no one who has left house or brothers or
sisters or mother or father or children
or lands, for my sake and for the gospel,
[30]who will not receive a hundredfold
now in this time, houses and brothers
and sisters and mothers and children
and lands, with persecutions, and in the
age to come eternal life. [31]But many that
are first will be last, and the last first."

A Third Time Jesus Foretells His Death and Resurrection

32 And they were on the road, going up to
Jerusalem, and Jesus was walking ahead
of them; and they were amazed, and those
who followed were afraid. And taking the
twelve again, he began to tell them what
was to happen to him, [33]saying, "Behold,
we are going up to Jerusalem; and the
Son of man will be delivered to the chief
priests and the scribes, and they will con-
demn him to death, and deliver him to the
Gentiles; [34]and they will mock him, and
spit upon him, and scourge him, and kill
him; and after three days he will rise."

The Request of James and John

35 And James and John, the sons of Ze-
b'edee, came forward to him, and said to
him, "Teacher, we want you to do for us
whatever we ask of you." [36]And he said
to them, "What do you want me to do
for you?" [37]And they said to him, "Grant
us to sit, one at your right hand and one
at your left, in your glory." [38]But Jesus
said to them, "You do not know what
you are asking. Are you able to drink the
cup that I drink, or to be baptized with
the baptism with which I am baptized?"
[39]And they said to him, "We are able."
And Jesus said to them, "The cup that I

[y] **10.24** Other ancient authorities omit *for those who trust in riches*

[z] **10.26** Other ancient authorities read *to one another*

drink you will drink; and with the bap-
tism with which I am baptized, you will
be baptized; [40]but to sit at my right hand
or at my left is not mine to grant, but it
is for those for whom it has been pre-
pared." [41]And when the ten heard it, they
began to be indignant at James and John.
[42]And Jesus called them to him and said
to them, "You know that those who are
supposed to rule over the Gentiles lord it
over them, and their great men exercise
authority over them. [43]But it shall not
be so among you; but whoever would be
great among you must be your servant,
[44]and whoever would be first among you
must be slave of all. [45]For the Son of man
also came not to be served but to serve,
and to give his life as a ransom for many."

The Healing of Blind Bartimaeus

46 And they came to Jericho; and as he
was leaving Jericho with his disciples
and a great multitude, Bartimae'us, a
blind beggar, the son of Timae'us, was
sitting by the roadside. [47]And when he
heard that it was Jesus of Nazareth, he
began to cry out and say, "Jesus, Son of
David, have mercy on me!" [48]And many
rebuked him, telling him to be silent; but
he cried out all the more, "Son of David,
have mercy on me!" [49]And Jesus stopped
and said, "Call him." And they called the
blind man, saying to him, "Take heart;
rise, he is calling you." [50]And throwing
off his mantle he sprang up and came
to Jesus. [51]And Jesus said to him, "What
do you want me to do for you?" And the
blind man said to him, "Master,[a] let me
receive my sight." [52]And Jesus said to
him, "Go your way; your faith has made
you well." And immediately he received
his sight and followed him on the way.

Jesus' Triumphal Entry into Jerusalem

11 And when they drew near to Jeru-
salem, to Beth'phage and Bethany,
at the Mount of Olives, he sent two of his
disciples, [2]and said to them, "Go into the
village opposite you, and immediately as
you enter it you will find a colt tied, on
which no one has ever sat; untie it and
bring it. [3]If any one says to you, 'Why are
you doing this?' say, 'The Lord has need
of it and will send it back here immedi-
ately.'" [4]And they went away, and found
a colt tied at the door out in the open
street; and they untied it. [5]And those
who stood there said to them, "What are
you doing, untying the colt?" [6]And they
told them what Jesus had said; and they
let them go. [7]And they brought the colt
to Jesus, and threw their garments on
it; and he sat upon it. [8]And many spread
their garments on the road, and others
spread leafy branches which they had
cut from the fields. [9]And those who went
before and those who followed cried out,
"Hosanna! Blessed is he who comes in the
name of the Lord! [10]Blessed is the king-
dom of our father David that is coming!
Hosanna in the highest!"

11 And he entered Jerusalem, and went
into the temple; and when he had looked
round at everything, as it was already
late, he went out to Bethany with the
twelve.

Jesus Curses the Fig Tree

12 On the following day, when they came
from Bethany, he was hungry. [13]And see-
ing in the distance a fig tree in leaf, he
went to see if he could find anything on
it. When he came to it, he found nothing
but leaves, for it was not the season for
figs. [14]And he said to it, "May no one ever
eat fruit from you again." And his disci-
ples heard it.

Jesus Cleanses the Temple

15 And they came to Jerusalem. And he
entered the temple and began to drive out
those who sold and those who bought in
the temple, and he overturned the tables

[a] **10.51** Or *Rabbi*

of the money-changers and the seats of
those who sold pigeons; 16and he would
not allow any one to carry anything
through the temple. 17And he taught, and
said to them, "Is it not written, 'My house
shall be called a house of prayer for all
the nations'? But you have made it a den
of robbers." 18And the chief priests and
the scribes heard it and sought a way
to destroy him; for they feared him, be-
cause all the multitude was astonished at
his teaching. 19And when evening came
they[b] went out of the city.

The Lesson from the Withered Fig Tree

20 As they passed by in the morning,
they saw the fig tree withered away to
its roots. 21And Peter remembered and
said to him, "Master,[c] look! The fig tree
which you cursed has withered." 22And
Jesus answered them, "Have faith in
God. 23Truly, I say to you, whoever says
to this mountain, 'Be taken up and cast
into the sea,' and does not doubt in his
heart, but believes that what he says will
come to pass, it will be done for him.
24Therefore I tell you, whatever you ask
in prayer, believe that you receive it,
and you will. 25And whenever you stand
praying, forgive, if you have anything
against any one; so that your Father also
who is in heaven may forgive you your
trespasses."[d]

Jesus' Authority Is Questioned

27 And they came again to Jerusalem.
And as he was walking in the temple, the
chief priests and the scribes and the el-
ders came to him, 28and they said to him,
"By what authority are you doing these
things, or who gave you this authority
to do them?" 29Jesus said to them, "I will
ask you a question; answer me, and I
will tell you by what authority I do these
things. 30Was the baptism of John from
heaven or from men? Answer me." 31And
they argued with one another, "If we say,
'From heaven,' he will say, 'Why then did
you not believe him?' 32But shall we say,
'From men'?"—they were afraid of the
people, for all held that John was a real
prophet. 33So they answered Jesus, "We
do not know." And Jesus said to them,
"Neither will I tell you by what authority
I do these things."

The Parable of the Wicked Tenants

12 And he began to speak to them in
parables. "A man planted a vine-
yard, and set a hedge around it, and dug a
pit for the wine press, and built a tower,
and let it out to tenants, and went into an-
other country. 2When the time came, he
sent a servant to the tenants, to get from
them some of the fruit of the vineyard.
3And they took him and beat him, and
sent him away empty-handed. 4Again he
sent to them another servant, and they
wounded him in the head, and treated
him shamefully. 5And he sent another,
and him they killed; and so with many
others, some they beat and some they
killed. 6He had still one other, a beloved
son; finally he sent him to them, saying,
'They will respect my son.' 7But those ten-
ants said to one another, 'This is the heir;
come, let us kill him, and the inheritance
will be ours.' 8And they took him and
killed him, and cast him out of the vine-
yard. 9What will the owner of the vine-
yard do? He will come and destroy the
tenants, and give the vineyard to others.
10Have you not read this scripture:

'The very stone which the builders
rejected
has become the head of the corner;
11 this was the Lord's doing,
and it is marvelous in our eyes'?"

12 And they tried to arrest him, but
feared the multitude, for they perceived
that he had told the parable against them;
so they left him and went away.

[b]**11.19** Other ancient authorities read *he* [c]**11.21** Or *Rabbi* [d]**11.25** Other ancient authorities add verse 26, *"But if you do not forgive, neither will your Father who is in heaven forgive your trespasses"*

The Question about Paying Taxes

13 And they sent to him some of the Pharisees and some of the Hero´di-ans, to entrap him in his talk. [14]And they came and said to him, "Teacher, we know that you are true, and care for no man; for you do not regard the position of men, but truly teach the way of God. Is it lawful to pay taxes to Caesar, or not? [15]Should we pay them, or should we not?" But knowing their hypocrisy, he said to them, "Why put me to the test? Bring me a coin,[e] and let me look at it." [16]And they brought one. And he said to them, "Whose likeness and inscription is this?" They said to him, "Caesar's." [17]Jesus said to them, "Render to Caesar the things that are Caesar's, and to God the things that are God's." And they were amazed at him.

The Question about the Resurrection

18 And Sad´ducees came to him, who say that there is no resurrection; and they asked him a question, saying, [19]"Teacher, Moses wrote for us that if a man's brother dies and leaves a wife, but leaves no child, the man[f] must take the wife, and raise up children for his brother. [20]There were seven brothers; the first took a wife, and when he died left no children; [21]and the second took her, and died, leaving no children; and the third likewise; [22]and the seven left no children. Last of all the woman also died. [23]In the resurrection whose wife will she be? For the seven had her as wife."

24 Jesus said to them, "Is not this why you are wrong, that you know neither the scriptures nor the power of God? [25]For when they rise from the dead, they neither marry nor are given in marriage, but are like angels in heaven. [26]And as for the dead being raised, have you not read in the book of Moses, in the passage about the bush, how God said to him, 'I am the God of Abraham, and the God of Isaac, and the God of Jacob'? [27]He is not God of the dead, but of the living; you are quite wrong."

The First Commandment

28 And one of the scribes came up and heard them disputing with one another, and seeing that he answered them well, asked him, "Which commandment is the first of all?" [29]Jesus answered, "The first is, 'Hear, O Israel: The Lord our God, the Lord is one; [30]and you shall love the Lord your God with all your heart, and with all your soul, and with all your mind, and with all your strength.' [31]The second is this, 'You shall love your neighbor as yourself.' There is no other commandment greater than these." [32]And the scribe said to him, "You are right, Teacher; you have truly said that he is one, and there is no other but he; [33]and to love him with all the heart, and with all the understanding, and with all the strength, and to love one's neighbor as oneself, is much more than all whole burnt offerings and sacrifices." [34]And when Jesus saw that he answered wisely, he said to him, "You are not far from the kingdom of God." And after that no one dared to ask him any question.

The Question about David's Son

35 And as Jesus taught in the temple, he said, "How can the scribes say that the Christ is the son of David? [36]David himself, inspired by[g] the Holy Spirit, declared,

'The Lord said to my Lord,
Sit at my right hand,
till I put thy enemies under thy feet.'

[37]David himself calls him Lord; so how is he his son?" And the great throng heard him gladly.

Jesus Denounces the Scribes

38 And in his teaching he said, "Beware of the scribes, who like to go about in long robes, and to have salutations in the

[e] **12.15** Greek *a denarius* [f] **12.19** Greek *his brother* [g] **12.36** Or *himself, in*

market places [39]and the best seats in the
synagogues and the places of honor at
feasts, [40]who devour widows' houses and
for a pretense make long prayers. They
will receive the greater condemnation."

The Widow's Offering

41 And he sat down opposite the trea-
sury, and watched the multitude put-
ting money into the treasury. Many rich
people put in large sums. [42]And a poor
widow came, and put in two copper coins,
which make a penny. [43]And he called his
disciples to him, and said to them, "Truly,
I say to you, this poor widow has put in
more than all those who are contribut-
ing to the treasury. [44]For they all contrib-
uted out of their abundance; but she out
of her poverty has put in everything she
had, her whole living."

The Destruction of the Temple Foretold

13 And as he came out of the temple,
one of his disciples said to him,
"Look, Teacher, what wonderful stones
and what wonderful buildings!" [2]And
Jesus said to him, "Do you see these great
buildings? There will not be left here
one stone upon another, that will not be
thrown down."

3 And as he sat on the Mount of Olives
opposite the temple, Peter and James and
John and Andrew asked him privately,
[4]"Tell us, when will this be, and what will
be the sign when these things are all to
be accomplished?" [5]And Jesus began to
say to them, "Take heed that no one leads
you astray. [6]Many will come in my name,
saying, 'I am he!' and they will lead many
astray. [7]And when you hear of wars and
rumors of wars, do not be alarmed; this
must take place, but the end is not yet.
[8]For nation will rise against nation, and
kingdom against kingdom; there will be
earthquakes in various places, there will
be famines; this is but the beginning of
the sufferings.

Persecution Foretold

9 "But take heed to yourselves; for they
will deliver you up to councils; and you
will be beaten in synagogues; and you
will stand before governors and kings for
my sake, to bear testimony before them.
[10]And the gospel must first be preached
to all nations. [11]And when they bring
you to trial and deliver you up, do not
be anxious beforehand what you are to
say; but say whatever is given you in that
hour, for it is not you who speak, but the
Holy Spirit. [12]And brother will deliver up
brother to death, and the father his child,
and children will rise against parents and
have them put to death; [13]and you will be
hated by all for my name's sake. But he
who endures to the end will be saved.

The Desolating Sacrilege

14 "But when you see the desolating sac-
rilege set up where it ought not to be (let
the reader understand), then let those who
are in Judea flee to the mountains; [15]let him
who is on the housetop not go down, nor
enter his house, to take anything away;
[16]and let him who is in the field not turn
back to take his mantle. [17]And alas for those
who are with child and for those who give
suck in those days! [18]Pray that it may not
happen in winter. [19]For in those days there
will be such tribulation as has not been
from the beginning of the creation which
God created until now, and never will be.
[20]And if the Lord had not shortened the
days, no human being would be saved; but
for the sake of the elect, whom he chose, he
shortened the days. [21]And then if any one
says to you, 'Look, here is the Christ!' or
'Look, there he is!' do not believe it. [22]False
Christs and false prophets will arise and
show signs and wonders, to lead astray, if
possible, the elect. [23]But take heed; I have
told you all things beforehand.

The Coming of the Son of Man

24 "But in those days, after that tribula-
tion, the sun will be darkened, and the

moon will not give its light, [25]and the
stars will be falling from heaven, and the
powers in the heavens will be shaken.
[26]And then they will see the Son of man
coming in clouds with great power and
glory. [27]And then he will send out the an-
gels, and gather his elect from the four
winds, from the ends of the earth to the
ends of heaven.

The Lesson of the Fig Tree

28 "From the fig tree learn its lesson:
as soon as its branch becomes tender
and puts forth its leaves, you know that
summer is near. [29]So also, when you see
these things taking place, you know that
he is near, at the very gates. [30]Truly, I
say to you, this generation will not pass
away before all these things take place.
[31]Heaven and earth will pass away, but
my words will not pass away.

The Necessity for Watchfulness

32 "But of that day or that hour no one
knows, not even the angels in heaven,
nor the Son, but only the Father. [33]Take
heed, watch and pray;[h] for you do not
know when the time will come. [34]It is like
a man going on a journey, when he leaves
home and puts his servants in charge,
each with his work, and commands the
doorkeeper to be on the watch. [35]Watch
therefore—for you do not know when
the master of the house will come, in the
evening, or at midnight, or at cockcrow,
or in the morning— [36]lest he come sud-
denly and find you asleep. [37]And what I
say to you I say to all: Watch."

The Plot to Kill Jesus

14 It was now two days before the
Passover and the feast of Unleav-
ened Bread. And the chief priests and the
scribes were seeking how to arrest him
by stealth, and kill him; [2]for they said,
"Not during the feast, lest there be a tu-
mult of the people."

The Anointing at Bethany

3 And while he was at Bethany in the
house of Simon the leper, as he sat at
table, a woman came with an alabas-
ter jar of ointment of pure nard, very
costly, and she broke the jar and poured
it over his head. [4]But there were some
who said to themselves indignantly,
"Why was the ointment thus wasted?
[5]For this ointment might have been
sold for more than three hundred de-
narii,[i] and given to the poor." And they
reproached her. [6]But Jesus said, "Let
her alone; why do you trouble her? She
has done a beautiful thing to me. [7]For
you always have the poor with you, and
whenever you will, you can do good
to them; but you will not always have
me. [8]She has done what she could; she
has anointed my body beforehand for
burying. [9]And truly, I say to you, wher-
ever the gospel is preached in the whole
world, what she has done will be told in
memory of her."

Judas Agrees to Betray Jesus

10 Then Judas Iscariot, who was one of
the twelve, went to the chief priests in
order to betray him to them. [11]And when
they heard it they were glad, and prom-
ised to give him money. And he sought
an opportunity to betray him.

The Passover with the Disciples

12 And on the first day of Unleavened
Bread, when they sacrificed the passover
lamb, his disciples said to him, "Where
will you have us go and prepare for you
to eat the passover?" [13]And he sent two
of his disciples, and said to them, "Go
into the city, and a man carrying a jar of
water will meet you; follow him, [14]and
wherever he enters, say to the house-
holder, 'The Teacher says, Where is my
guest room, where I am to eat the pass-
over with my disciples?' [15]And he will
show you a large upper room furnished

[h] **13.33** Other ancient authorities omit *and pray*

[i] **14.5** The denarius was a day's wage for a laborer

and ready; there prepare for us." 16 And
the disciples set out and went to the city,
and found it as he had told them; and
they prepared the passover.
17 And when it was evening he came
with the twelve. 18 And as they were at ta-
ble eating, Jesus said, "Truly, I say to you,
one of you will betray me, one who is eat-
ing with me." 19 They began to be sorrow-
ful, and to say to him one after another,
"Is it I?" 20 He said to them, "It is one of the
twelve, one who is dipping bread in the
same dish with me. 21 For the Son of man
goes as it is written of him, but woe to
that man by whom the Son of man is be-
trayed! It would have been better for that
man if he had not been born."

The Institution of the Lord's Supper

22 And as they were eating, he took
bread, and blessed, and broke it, and
gave it to them, and said, "Take; this is my
body." 23 And he took a cup, and when he
had given thanks he gave it to them, and
they all drank of it. 24 And he said to them,
"This is my blood of the[j] covenant, which
is poured out for many. 25 Truly, I say to
you, I shall not drink again of the fruit
of the vine until that day when I drink it
new in the kingdom of God."

Peter's Denial Foretold

26 And when they had sung a hymn,
they went out to the Mount of Olives.
27 And Jesus said to them, "You will all
fall away; for it is written, 'I will strike
the shepherd, and the sheep will be scat-
tered.' 28 But after I am raised up, I will
go before you to Galilee." 29 Peter said to
him, "Even though they all fall away, I
will not." 30 And Jesus said to him, "Truly,
I say to you, this very night, before the
cock crows twice, you will deny me three
times." 31 But he said vehemently, "If I
must die with you, I will not deny you."
And they all said the same.

Jesus Prays in Gethsemane

32 And they went to a place which was
called Gethsem'ane; and he said to his dis-
ciples, "Sit here, while I pray." 33 And he
took with him Peter and James and John,
and began to be greatly distressed and
troubled. 34 And he said to them, "My soul
is very sorrowful, even to death; remain
here, and watch."[k] 35 And going a little far-
ther, he fell on the ground and prayed that,
if it were possible, the hour might pass
from him. 36 And he said, "Abba, Father,
all things are possible to thee; remove this
cup from me; yet not what I will, but what
thou wilt." 37 And he came and found them
sleeping, and he said to Peter, "Simon,
are you asleep? Could you not watch[l] one
hour? 38 Watch[m] and pray that you may not
enter into temptation; the spirit indeed
is willing, but the flesh is weak." 39 And
again he went away and prayed, saying
the same words. 40 And again he came and
found them sleeping, for their eyes were
very heavy; and they did not know what
to answer him. 41 And he came the third
time, and said to them, "Are you still sleep-
ing and taking your rest? It is enough; the
hour has come; the Son of man is betrayed
into the hands of sinners. 42 Rise, let us be
going; see, my betrayer is at hand."

The Betrayal and Arrest of Jesus

43 And immediately, while he was still
speaking, Judas came, one of the twelve,
and with him a crowd with swords and
clubs, from the chief priests and the
scribes and the elders. 44 Now the be-
trayer had given them a sign, saying,
"The one I shall kiss is the man; seize him
and lead him away safely." 45 And when
he came, he went up to him at once, and
said, "Master!"[n] And he kissed him. 46 And
they laid hands on him and seized him.
47 But one of those who stood by drew his
sword, and struck the slave of the high
priest and cut off his ear. 48 And Jesus said

[j] **14.24** Other ancient authorities insert *new*
[k] **14.34** Or *keep awake*
[l] **14.37** Or *keep awake*
[m] **14.38** Or *keep awake*
[n] **14.45** Or *Rabbi*

to them, "Have you come out as against a
robber, with swords and clubs to capture
me? 49 Day after day I was with you in the
temple teaching, and you did not seize
me. But let the scriptures be fulfilled."
50 And they all forsook him, and fled.
51 And a young man followed him,
with nothing but a linen cloth about his
body; and they seized him, 52 but he left
the linen cloth and ran away naked.

Jesus before the Council

53 And they led Jesus to the high priest;
and all the chief priests and the elders and
the scribes were assembled. 54 And Peter
had followed him at a distance, right into
the courtyard of the high priest; and he
was sitting with the guards, and warming
himself at the fire. 55 Now the chief priests
and the whole council sought testimony
against Jesus to put him to death; but they
found none. 56 For many bore false wit-
ness against him, and their witness did
not agree. 57 And some stood up and bore
false witness against him, saying, 58 "We
heard him say, 'I will destroy this tem-
ple that is made with hands, and in three
days I will build another, not made with
hands.'" 59 Yet not even so did their testi-
mony agree. 60 And the high priest stood
up in the midst, and asked Jesus, "Have
you no answer to make? What is it that
these men testify against you?" 61 But he
was silent and made no answer. Again the
high priest asked him, "Are you the Christ,
the Son of the Blessed?" 62 And Jesus said, "I
am; and you will see the Son of man sitting
at the right hand of Power, and coming
with the clouds of heaven." 63 And the high
priest tore his mantle, and said, "Why do
we still need witnesses? 64 You have heard
his blasphemy. What is your decision?"
And they all condemned him as deserving
death. 65 And some began to spit on him,
and to cover his face, and to strike him,
saying to him, "Prophesy!" And the guards
received him with blows.

Peter Denies Jesus

66 And as Peter was below in the court-
yard, one of the maids of the high priest
came; 67 and seeing Peter warming himself,
she looked at him, and said, "You also were
with the Nazarene, Jesus." 68 But he denied
it, saying, "I neither know nor understand
what you mean." And he went out into the
gateway.[o] 69 And the maid saw him, and be-
gan again to say to the bystanders, "This
man is one of them." 70 But again he denied
it. And after a little while again the by-
standers said to Peter, "Certainly you are
one of them; for you are a Galilean." 71 But
he began to invoke a curse on himself and
to swear, "I do not know this man of whom
you speak." 72 And immediately the cock
crowed a second time. And Peter remem-
bered how Jesus had said to him, "Before
the cock crows twice, you will deny me
three times." And he broke down and wept.

Jesus before Pilate

15 And as soon as it was morning the
chief priests, with the elders and
scribes, and the whole council held a
consultation; and they bound Jesus and
led him away and delivered him to Pi-
late. 2 And Pilate asked him, "Are you the
King of the Jews?" And he answered him,
"You have said so." 3 And the chief priests
accused him of many things. 4 And Pilate
again asked him, "Have you no answer to
make? See how many charges they bring
against you." 5 But Jesus made no further
answer, so that Pilate wondered.

Pilate Hands Jesus over to Be Crucified

6 Now at the feast he used to release for
them one prisoner whom they asked.
7 And among the rebels in prison, who
had committed murder in the insurrec-
tion, there was a man called Barab'bas.
8 And the crowd came up and began to
ask Pilate to do as he was wont to do for
them. 9 And he answered them, "Do you
want me to release for you the King of the

[o] **14.68** Or *fore-court.* Other ancient authorities add *and the cock crowed*

Jews?" 10For he perceived that it was out of
envy that the chief priests had delivered
him up. 11But the chief priests stirred up
the crowd to have him release for them
Barab′bas instead. 12And Pilate again said
to them, "Then what shall I do with the
man whom you call the King of the Jews?"
13And they cried out again, "Crucify him."
14And Pilate said to them, "Why, what evil
has he done?" But they shouted all the
more, "Crucify him." 15So Pilate, wishing
to satisfy the crowd, released for them
Barab′bas; and having scourged Jesus, he
delivered him to be crucified.

The Soldiers Mock Jesus

16 And the soldiers led him away inside
the palace (that is, the praetorium); and
they called together the whole battalion.
17And they clothed him in a purple cloak,
and plaiting a crown of thorns they put
it on him. 18And they began to salute
him, "Hail, King of the Jews!" 19And they
struck his head with a reed, and spat
upon him, and they knelt down in hom-
age to him. 20And when they had mocked
him, they stripped him of the purple
cloak, and put his own clothes on him.
And they led him out to crucify him.

The Crucifixion of Jesus

21 And they compelled a passer-by, Simon
of Cyre′ne, who was coming in from the
country, the father of Alexander and Ru-
fus, to carry his cross. 22And they brought
him to the place called Gol′gotha (which
means the place of a skull). 23And they of-
fered him wine mingled with myrrh; but
he did not take it. 24And they crucified
him, and divided his garments among
them, casting lots for them, to decide what
each should take. 25And it was the third
hour, when they crucified him. 26And
the inscription of the charge against him
read, "The King of the Jews." 27And with
him they crucified two robbers, one on his
right and one on his left.[p] 29And those who
passed by derided him, wagging their
heads, and saying, "Aha! You who would
destroy the temple and build it in three
days, 30save yourself, and come down
from the cross!" 31So also the chief priests
mocked him to one another with the
scribes, saying, "He saved others; he can-
not save himself. 32Let the Christ, the King
of Israel, come down now from the cross,
that we may see and believe." Those who
were crucified with him also reviled him.

The Death of Jesus

33 And when the sixth hour had come,
there was darkness over the whole land[q]
until the ninth hour. 34And at the ninth
hour Jesus cried with a loud voice, "E′lo-i,
E′lo-i, la′ma sabach-tha′ni?" which means,
"My God, my God, why hast thou forsaken
me?" 35And some of the bystanders hear-
ing it said, "Behold, he is calling Eli′jah."
36And one ran and, filling a sponge full of
vinegar, put it on a reed and gave it to him
to drink, saying, "Wait, let us see whether
Eli′jah will come to take him down." 37And
Jesus uttered a loud cry, and breathed his
last. 38And the curtain of the temple was
torn in two, from top to bottom. 39And
when the centurion, who stood facing
him, saw that he thus[r] breathed his last, he
said, "Truly this man was the Son[s] of God!"

40 There were also women looking
on from afar, among whom were Mary
Mag′dalene, and Mary the mother of
James the younger and of Joses, and Sa-
lo′me, 41who, when he was in Galilee, fol-
lowed him, and ministered to him; and
also many other women who came up
with him to Jerusalem.

The Burial of Jesus

42 And when evening had come, since
it was the day of Preparation, that is, the

[p] **15.27** Other ancient authorities insert verse 28, *And the scripture was fulfilled which says, "He was reckoned with the transgressors"* [q] **15.33** Or *earth* [r] **15.39** Other ancient authorities insert *cried out and* [s] **15.39** Or *a son*

day before the sabbath, 43 Joseph of Ari-
mathe'a, a respected member of the coun-
cil, who was also himself looking for the
kingdom of God, took courage and went
to Pilate, and asked for the body of Jesus.
44 And Pilate wondered if he were already
dead; and summoning the centurion, he
asked him whether he was already dead.[t]
45 And when he learned from the centu-
rion that he was dead, he granted the body
to Joseph. 46 And he bought a linen shroud,
and taking him down, wrapped him in
the linen shroud, and laid him in a tomb
which had been hewn out of the rock; and
he rolled a stone against the door of the
tomb. 47 Mary Mag'dalene and Mary the
mother of Joses saw where he was laid.

The Resurrection of Jesus

16 And when the sabbath was past,
Mary Mag'dalene, and Mary the
mother of James, and Salo'me, bought
spices, so that they might go and anoint
him. 2 And very early on the first day of
the week they went to the tomb when
the sun had risen. 3 And they were say-
ing to one another, "Who will roll away
the stone for us from the door of the
tomb?" 4 And looking up, they saw that
the stone was rolled back; for it was very
large. 5 And entering the tomb, they saw
a young man sitting on the right side,
dressed in a white robe; and they were
amazed. 6 And he said to them, "Do not
be amazed; you seek Jesus of Nazareth,
who was crucified. He has risen, he is not
here; see the place where they laid him.
7 But go, tell his disciples and Peter that
he is going before you to Galilee; there
you will see him, as he told you." 8 And
they went out and fled from the tomb; for
trembling and astonishment had come
upon them; and they said nothing to any
one, for they were afraid.

Jesus Appears to Mary Magdalene

9 Now when he rose early on the first day
of the week, he appeared first to Mary
Mag'dalene, from whom he had cast out
seven demons. 10 She went out and told
those who had been with him, as they
mourned and wept. 11 But when they
heard that he was alive and had been
seen by her, they would not believe it.

Jesus Appears to Two Disciples

12 After this he appeared in another
form to two of them, as they were walk-
ing into the country. 13 And they went
back and told the rest, but they did not
believe them.

Jesus Commissions the Disciples

14 Afterward he appeared to the eleven
themselves as they sat at table; and he
upbraided them for their unbelief and
hardness of heart, because they had not
believed those who saw him after he had
risen. 15 And he said to them, "Go into all
the world and preach the gospel to the
whole creation. 16 He who believes and is
baptized will be saved; but he who does
not believe will be condemned. 17 And
these signs will accompany those who
believe: in my name they will cast out
demons; they will speak in new tongues;
18 they will pick up serpents, and if they
drink any deadly thing, it will not hurt
them; they will lay their hands on the
sick, and they will recover."

The Ascension of Jesus

19 So then the Lord Jesus, after he had
spoken to them, was taken up into
heaven, and sat down at the right hand of
God. 20 And they went forth and preached
everywhere, while the Lord worked with
them and confirmed the message by the
signs that attended it. Amen.[u]

[t] **15.44** Other ancient authorities read *whether he had been some time dead* [u] **16.20** Other ancient authorities omit verses 9–20. Some ancient authorities conclude Mark instead with the following: *But they reported briefly to Peter and those with him all that they had been told. And after this, Jesus himself sent out by means of them, from east to west, the sacred and imperishable proclamation of eternal salvation.*

The Gospel According to

LUKE

Dedication to Theophilus

1 Inasmuch as many have undertaken to compile a narrative of the things which have been accomplished among us, [2]just as they were delivered to us by those who from the beginning were eyewitnesses and ministers of the word, [3]it seemed good to me also, having followed all things closely[a] for some time past, to write an orderly account for you, most excellent Theoph'ilus, [4]that you may know the truth concerning the things of which you have been informed.

The Birth of John the Baptist Foretold

5 In the days of Herod, king of Judea, there was a priest named Zechari'ah,[b] of the division of Abi'jah; and he had a wife of the daughters of Aaron, and her name was Elizabeth. [6]And they were both righteous before God, walking in all the commandments and ordinances of the Lord blameless. [7]But they had no child, because Elizabeth was barren, and both were advanced in years.

8 Now while he was serving as priest before God when his division was on duty, [9]according to the custom of the priesthood, it fell to him by lot to enter the temple of the Lord and burn incense. [10]And the whole multitude of the people were praying outside at the hour of incense. [11]And there appeared to him an angel of the Lord standing on the right side of the altar of incense. [12]And Zechari'ah was troubled when he saw him, and fear fell upon him. [13]But the angel said to him, "Do not be afraid, Zechari'ah, for your prayer is heard, and your wife Elizabeth will bear you a son, and you shall call his name John.

14 And you will have joy and gladness,
and many will rejoice at his birth;
15 for he will be great before the
Lord,
and he shall drink no wine nor
strong drink,
and he will be filled with the Holy
Spirit,
even from his mother's womb.
16 And he will turn many of the sons of
Israel to the Lord their God,
17 and he will go before him in the
spirit and power of Eli'jah,
to turn the hearts of the fathers to
the children,
and the disobedient to the wisdom
of the just,
to make ready for the Lord a people
prepared."

[18]And Zechari'ah said to the angel, "How shall I know this? For I am an old man, and my wife is advanced in years." [19]And the angel answered him, "I am Gabriel, who stand in the presence of God; and I was sent to speak to you, and to bring you this good news. [20]And behold, you will be silent and unable to speak until the day that these things come to pass, because you did not believe my words, which will be fulfilled in their time." [21]And the people were waiting for Zechari'ah, and they wondered at his delay in the temple. [22]And when he came out, he could not speak to them, and they perceived that he had seen a vision in the temple; and he made signs to them and remained dumb. [23]And when his time of service was ended, he went to his home.

24 After these days his wife Elizabeth conceived, and for five months she hid herself, saying, [25]"Thus the Lord has done to me in the days when he looked on me, to take away my reproach among men."

[a]**1.3** Or *accurately* [b]**1.5** Greek *Zacharias*

The Birth of Jesus Foretold

26 In the sixth month the angel Gabriel
was sent from God to a city of Galilee
named Nazareth, 27 to a virgin betrothed
to a man whose name was Joseph, of the
house of David; and the virgin's name
was Mary. 28 And he came to her and
said, "Hail, full of grace,[c] the Lord is with
you!"[d] 29 But she was greatly troubled at
the saying, and considered in her mind
what sort of greeting this might be. 30 And
the angel said to her, "Do not be afraid,
Mary, for you have found favor with
God. 31 And behold, you will conceive in
your womb and bear a son, and you shall
call his name Jesus.

32 He will be great, and will be called
the Son of the Most High;
and the Lord God will give to him
the throne of his father David,
33 and he will reign over the house of
Jacob for ever;
and of his kingdom there will be no
end."

34 And Mary said to the angel, "How can
this be, since I have no husband?" 35 And
the angel said to her,

"The Holy Spirit will come upon you,
and the power of the Most High will
overshadow you;
therefore the child to be born[e] will
be called holy,
the Son of God.

36 And behold, your kinswoman Eliza-
beth in her old age has also conceived a
son; and this is the sixth month with her
who was called barren. 37 For with God
nothing will be impossible." 38 And Mary
said, "Behold, I am the handmaid of the
Lord; let it be to me according to your
word." And the angel departed from her.

Mary Visits Elizabeth

39 In those days Mary arose and went
with haste into the hill country, to a city
of Judah, 40 and she entered the house of
Zechari'ah and greeted Elizabeth. 41 And
when Elizabeth heard the greeting of
Mary, the babe leaped in her womb;
and Elizabeth was filled with the Holy
Spirit 42 and she exclaimed with a loud
cry, "Blessed are you among women, and
blessed is the fruit of your womb! 43 And
why is this granted me, that the mother
of my Lord should come to me? 44 For
behold, when the voice of your greeting
came to my ears, the babe in my womb
leaped for joy. 45 And blessed is she who
believed that there would be[f] a fulfil-
ment of what was spoken to her from the
Lord." 46 And Mary said,

Mary's Song of Praise

"My soul magnifies the Lord,
47 and my spirit rejoices in God my
Savior,
48 for he has regarded the low estate of
his handmaiden.
For behold, henceforth all
generations will call me blessed;
49 for he who is mighty has done great
things for me,
and holy is his name.
50 And his mercy is on those who fear
him
from generation to generation.
51 He has shown strength with his arm,
he has scattered the proud in the
imagination of their hearts,
52 he has put down the mighty from
their thrones,
and exalted those of low degree;
53 he has filled the hungry with good
things,
and the rich he has sent empty away.
54 He has helped his servant Israel,
in remembrance of his mercy,
55 as he spoke to our fathers,
to Abraham and to his posterity for
ever."

56 And Mary remained with her about
three months, and returned to her home.

[c] **1.28** Or *O favored one* [d] **1.28** Other ancient authorities add *"Blessed are you among women!"*
[e] **1.35** Other ancient authorities add *of you* [f] **1.45** Or *believed, for there will be*

The Birth of John the Baptist

57 Now the time came for Elizabeth to
be delivered, and she gave birth to a son.
[58]And her neighbors and kinsfolk heard
that the Lord had shown great mercy to
her, and they rejoiced with her. [59]And
on the eighth day they came to circum-
cise the child; and they would have
named him Zechari'ah after his father,
[60]but his mother said, "Not so; he shall
be called John." [61]And they said to her,
"None of your kindred is called by this
name." [62]And they made signs to his fa-
ther, inquiring what he would have him
called. [63]And he asked for a writing tab-
let, and wrote, "His name is John." And
they all marveled. [64]And immediately
his mouth was opened and his tongue
loosed, and he spoke, blessing God.
[65]And fear came on all their neighbors.
And all these things were talked about
through all the hill country of Judea;
[66]and all who heard them laid them up
in their hearts, saying, "What then will
this child be?" For the hand of the Lord
was with him.

Zechariah's Prophecy

67 And his father Zechari'ah was filled
with the Holy Spirit, and prophesied,
saying,

68 "Blessed be the Lord God of Israel,
for he has visited and redeemed his
people,
69 and has raised up a horn of
salvation for us
in the house of his servant David,
70 as he spoke by the mouth of his holy
prophets from of old,
71 that we should be saved from our
enemies,
and from the hand of all who hate
us;
72 to perform the mercy promised to
our fathers,
and to remember his holy
covenant,
73 the oath which he swore to our
father Abraham, [74]to grant us
that we, being delivered from the
hand of our enemies,
might serve him without fear,
75 in holiness and righteousness
before him all the days of our
life.
76 And you, child, will be called the
prophet of the Most High;
for you will go before the Lord to
prepare his ways,
77 to give knowledge of salvation to his
people
in the forgiveness of their sins,
78 through the tender mercy of our
God,
when the day shall dawn upon[g] us
from on high
79 to give light to those who sit in
darkness and in the shadow of
death,
to guide our feet into the way of
peace."

[80]And the child grew and became strong
in spirit, and he was in the wilderness
till the day of his manifestation to Israel.

The Birth of Jesus

2 In those days a decree went out from
Caesar Augustus that all the world
should be enrolled. [2]This was the first
enrollment, when Quirin'i-us was gov-
ernor of Syria. [3]And all went to be en-
rolled, each to his own city. [4]And Joseph
also went up from Galilee, from the city
of Nazareth, to Judea, to the city of Da-
vid, which is called Bethlehem, because
he was of the house and lineage of Da-
vid, [5]to be enrolled with Mary, his be-
trothed, who was with child. [6]And while
they were there, the time came for her to
be delivered. [7]And she gave birth to her
first-born son and wrapped him in swad-
dling cloths, and laid him in a manger,
because there was no place for them in
the inn.

[g] **1.78** Or *whereby the dayspring will visit.* Other ancient authorities read *since the dayspring has visited*

The Shepherds and the Angels

8 And in that region there were shep-
herds out in the field, keeping watch
over their flock by night. 9 And an angel
of the Lord appeared to them, and the
glory of the Lord shone around them,
and they were filled with fear. 10 And the
angel said to them, "Be not afraid; for be-
hold, I bring you good news of a great joy
which will come to all the people; 11 for to
you is born this day in the city of David a
Savior, who is Christ the Lord. 12 And this
will be a sign for you: you will find a babe
wrapped in swaddling cloths and lying
in a manger." 13 And suddenly there was
with the angel a multitude of the heav-
enly host praising God and saying,

14 "Glory to God in the highest,
and on earth peace among men with
whom he is pleased!"[h]

15 When the angels went away from
them into heaven, the shepherds said
to one another, "Let us go over to Beth-
lehem and see this thing that has hap-
pened, which the Lord has made known
to us." 16 And they went with haste, and
found Mary and Joseph, and the babe ly-
ing in a manger. 17 And when they saw it
they made known the saying which had
been told them concerning this child;
18 and all who heard it wondered at what
the shepherds told them. 19 But Mary kept
all these things, pondering them in her
heart. 20 And the shepherds returned, glo-
rifying and praising God for all they had
heard and seen, as it had been told them.

Jesus Is Named

21 And at the end of eight days, when he
was circumcised, he was called Jesus, the
name given by the angel before he was
conceived in the womb.

Jesus Is Presented in the Temple

22 And when the time came for their pu-
rification according to the law of Moses,
they brought him up to Jerusalem to
present him to the Lord 23 (as it is writ-
ten in the law of the Lord, "Every male
that opens the womb shall be called holy
to the Lord") 24 and to offer a sacrifice
according to what is said in the law of
the Lord, "a pair of turtledoves, or two
young pigeons." 25 Now there was a man
in Jerusalem, whose name was Simeon,
and this man was righteous and devout,
looking for the consolation of Israel, and
the Holy Spirit was upon him. 26 And it
had been revealed to him by the Holy
Spirit that he should not see death be-
fore he had seen the Lord's Christ. 27 And
inspired by the Spirit[i] he came into the
temple; and when the parents brought in
the child Jesus, to do for him according
to the custom of the law, 28 he took him up
in his arms and blessed God and said,

29 "Lord, now lettest thou thy servant
depart in peace,
according to thy word;
30 for mine eyes have seen thy
salvation
31 which thou hast prepared in the
presence of all peoples,
32 a light for revelation to the Gentiles,
and for glory to thy people Israel."

33 And his father and his mother mar-
veled at what was said about him; 34 and
Simeon blessed them and said to Mary
his mother,

"Behold, this child is set for the fall
and rising of many in Israel,
and for a sign that is spoken
against
35 (and a sword will pierce through
your own soul also),
that thoughts out of many hearts
may be revealed."

36 And there was a prophetess, Anna,
the daughter of Phan'u-el, of the tribe
of Asher; she was of a great age, having
lived with her husband seven years from
her virginity, 37 and as a widow till she
was eighty-four. She did not depart from
the temple, worshiping with fasting and

[h] **2.14** Other ancient authorities read *peace, good will among men*

[i] **2.27** Or *in the Spirit*

prayer night and day. 38 And coming up at that very hour she gave thanks to God, and spoke of him to all who were looking for the redemption of Jerusalem.

The Return to Nazareth

39 And when they had performed everything according to the law of the Lord, they returned into Galilee, to their own city, Nazareth. 40 And the child grew and became strong, filled with wisdom; and the favor of God was upon him.

The Boy Jesus in the Temple

41 Now his parents went to Jerusalem every year at the feast of the Passover. 42 And when he was twelve years old, they went up according to custom; 43 and when the feast was ended, as they were returning, the boy Jesus stayed behind in Jerusalem. His parents did not know it, 44 but supposing him to be in the company they went a day's journey, and they sought him among their kinsfolk and acquaintances; 45 and when they did not find him, they returned to Jerusalem, seeking him. 46 After three days they found him in the temple, sitting among the teachers, listening to them and asking them questions; 47 and all who heard him were amazed at his understanding and his answers. 48 And when they saw him they were astonished; and his mother said to him, "Son, why have you treated us so? Behold, your father and I have been looking for you anxiously." 49 And he said to them, "How is it that you sought me? Did you not know that I must be in my Father's house?" 50 And they did not understand the saying which he spoke to them. 51 And he went down with them and came to Nazareth, and was obedient to them; and his mother kept all these things in her heart.

52 And Jesus increased in wisdom and in stature,[j] and in favor with God and man.

[j] **2.52** Or *years*

The Proclamation of John the Baptist

3 In the fifteenth year of the reign of Tibe'ri-us Caesar, Pontius Pilate being governor of Judea, and Herod being tetrarch of Galilee, and his brother Philip tetrarch of the region of Iturae'a and Trachoni'tis, and Lysa'ni-as tetrarch of Abile'ne, 2 in the high-priesthood of Annas and Ca'iaphas, the word of God came to John the son of Zechari'ah in the wilderness; 3 and he went into all the region about the Jordan, preaching a baptism of repentance for the forgiveness of sins. 4 As it is written in the book of the words of Isaiah the prophet,

"The voice of one crying in the
wilderness:
Prepare the way of the Lord,
make his paths straight.
5 Every valley shall be filled,
and every mountain and hill shall
be brought low,
and the crooked shall be made
straight,
and the rough ways shall be made
smooth;
6 and all flesh shall see the salvation
of God."

7 He said therefore to the multitudes that came out to be baptized by him, "You brood of vipers! Who warned you to flee from the wrath to come? 8 Bear fruits that befit repentance, and do not begin to say to yourselves, 'We have Abraham as our father'; for I tell you, God is able from these stones to raise up children to Abraham. 9 Even now the axe is laid to the root of the trees; every tree therefore that does not bear good fruit is cut down and thrown into the fire."

10 And the multitudes asked him, "What then shall we do?" 11 And he answered them, "He who has two coats, let him share with him who has none; and he who has food, let him do likewise." 12 Tax collectors also came to be baptized, and said to him, "Teacher, what shall we

do?" 13 And he said to them, "Collect no
more than is appointed you." 14 Soldiers
also asked him, "And we, what shall we
do?" And he said to them, "Rob no one by
violence or by false accusation, and be
content with your wages."
15 As the people were in expectation,
and all men questioned in their hearts
concerning John, whether perhaps he
were the Christ, 16 John answered them
all, "I baptize you with water; but he who
is mightier than I is coming, the thong of
whose sandals I am not worthy to untie;
he will baptize you with the Holy Spirit
and with fire. 17 His winnowing fork is in
his hand, to clear his threshing floor, and
to gather the wheat into his granary, but
the chaff he will burn with unquench-
able fire."
18 So, with many other exhortations,
he preached good news to the people.
19 But Herod the tetrarch, who had been
reproved by him for Hero'di-as, his
brother's wife, and for all the evil things
that Herod had done, 20 added this to them
all, that he shut up John in prison.

The Baptism of Jesus

21 Now when all the people were bap-
tized, and when Jesus also had been bap-
tized and was praying, the heaven was
opened, 22 and the Holy Spirit descended
upon him in bodily form, as a dove, and
a voice came from heaven, "Thou art
my beloved Son;[k] with thee I am well
pleased."[l]

The Ancestors of Jesus

23 Jesus, when he began his ministry,
was about thirty years of age, being the
son (as was supposed) of Joseph, the son
of Heli, 24 the son of Matthat, the son of
Levi, the son of Melchi, the son of Jan'-
na-i, the son of Joseph, 25 the son of Matta-
thi'as, the son of Amos, the son of Nahum,
the son of Esli, the son of Nag'ga-i, 26 the
son of Ma'ath, the son of Mattathi'as,
the son of Sem'e-in, the son of Josech,
the son of Joda, 27 the son of Jo-an'an, the
son of Rhesa, the son of Zerub'babel, the
son of She-al'ti-el,[m] the son of Neri, 28 the
son of Melchi, the son of Addi, the son of
Cosam, the son of Elma'dam, the son of
Er, 29 the son of Joshua, the son of Elie'zer,
the son of Jorim, the son of Matthat,
the son of Levi, 30 the son of Simeon, the
son of Judah, the son of Joseph, the son
of Jonam, the son of Eli'akim, 31 the son
of Me'le-a, the son of Menna, the son of
Mat'tatha, the son of Nathan, the son of
David, 32 the son of Jesse, the son of Obed,
the son of Bo'az, the son of Sala, the son
of Nahshon, 33 the son of Ammin'adab, the
son of Admin, the son of Arni, the son of
Hezron, the son of Perez, the son of Ju-
dah, 34 the son of Jacob, the son of Isaac,
the son of Abraham, the son of Terah,
the son of Nahor, 35 the son of Serug, the
son of Re'u, the son of Peleg, the son of
Eber, the son of Shelah, 36 the son of Ca-
i'nan, the son of Arphax'ad, the son of
Shem, the son of Noah, the son of Lamech,
37 the son of Methu'selah, the son of Enoch,
the son of Jared, the son of Maha'lale-el,
the son of Ca-i'nan, 38 the son of Enos, the
son of Seth, the son of Adam, the son of
God.

The Temptation of Jesus

4 And Jesus, full of the Holy Spirit, re-
turned from the Jordan, and was led
by the Spirit 2 for forty days in the wil-
derness, tempted by the devil. And he
ate nothing in those days; and when they
were ended, he was hungry. 3 The devil
said to him, "If you are the Son of God,
command this stone to become bread."
4 And Jesus answered him, "It is written,
'Man shall not live by bread alone.'" 5 And
the devil took him up, and showed him all
the kingdoms of the world in a moment
of time, 6 and said to him, "To you I will

[k] **3.22** Or *my Son, my* (or *the*) *Beloved* [l] **3.22** Other ancient authorities read *today I have begotten thee*
[m] **3.27** Greek *Salathiel*

give all this authority and their glory;
for it has been delivered to me, and I give
it to whom I will. 7If you, then, will wor-
ship me, it shall all be yours." 8And Jesus
answered him, "It is written,

'You shall worship the Lord your
God,
and him only shall you serve.'"

9And he took him to Jerusalem, and set
him on the pinnacle of the temple, and
said to him, "If you are the Son of God,
throw yourself down from here; 10for it
is written,

'He will give his angels charge of
you, to guard you,'

11and

'On their hands they will bear you up,
lest you strike your foot against a
stone.'"

12And Jesus answered him, "It is said,
'You shall not tempt the Lord your God.'"
13And when the devil had ended every
temptation, he departed from him until
an opportune time.

The Beginning of the Galilean Ministry

14 And Jesus returned in the power of
the Spirit into Galilee, and a report con-
cerning him went out through all the
surrounding country. 15And he taught in
their synagogues, being glorified by all.

The Rejection of Jesus at Nazareth

16 And he came to Nazareth, where he
had been brought up; and he went to the
synagogue, as his custom was, on the sab-
bath day. And he stood up to read; 17and
there was given to him the book of the
prophet Isaiah. He opened the book and
found the place where it was written,

18 "The Spirit of the Lord is upon me,
because he has anointed me to
preach good news to the poor.
He has sent me to proclaim release
to the captives
and recovering of sight to the blind,
to set at liberty those who are
oppressed,
19 to proclaim the acceptable year of
the Lord."

20And he closed the book, and gave it back
to the attendant, and sat down; and the
eyes of all in the synagogue were fixed
on him. 21And he began to say to them,
"Today this scripture has been fulfilled
in your hearing." 22And all spoke well of
him, and wondered at the gracious words
which proceeded out of his mouth; and
they said, "Is not this Joseph's son?" 23And
he said to them, "Doubtless you will
quote to me this proverb, 'Physician, heal
yourself; what we have heard you did at
Caper'na-um, do here also in your own
country.'" 24And he said, "Truly, I say to
you, no prophet is acceptable in his own
country. 25But in truth, I tell you, there
were many widows in Israel in the days
of Eli'jah, when the heaven was shut up
three years and six months, when there
came a great famine over all the land;
26and Eli'jah was sent to none of them but
only to Zar'ephath, in the land of Sidon, to
a woman who was a widow. 27And there
were many lepers in Israel in the time of
the prophet Eli'sha; and none of them was
cleansed, but only Na'aman the Syrian."
28When they heard this, all in the syna-
gogue were filled with wrath. 29And they
rose up and put him out of the city, and
led him to the brow of the hill on which
their city was built, that they might
throw him down headlong. 30But passing
through the midst of them he went away.

The Man with an Unclean Spirit

31 And he went down to Caper'na-um, a
city of Galilee. And he was teaching them
on the sabbath; 32and they were aston-
ished at his teaching, for his word was
with authority. 33And in the synagogue
there was a man who had the spirit of an
unclean demon; and he cried out with
a loud voice, 34"Ah![n] What have you to

[n] **4.34** Or *Let us alone*

do with us, Jesus of Nazareth? Have you
come to destroy us? I know who you
are, the Holy One of God." 35 But Jesus re-
buked him, saying, "Be silent, and come
out of him!" And when the demon had
thrown him down in the midst, he came
out of him, having done him no harm.
36 And they were all amazed and said to
one another, "What is this word? For
with authority and power he commands
the unclean spirits, and they come out."
37 And reports of him went out into every
place in the surrounding region.

Healings at Simon's House

38 And he arose and left the synagogue,
and entered Simon's house. Now Simon's
mother-in-law was ill with a high fever,
and they besought him for her. 39 And he
stood over her and rebuked the fever,
and it left her; and immediately she rose
and served them.

40 Now when the sun was setting, all
those who had any that were sick with
various diseases brought them to him;
and he laid his hands on every one of
them and healed them. 41 And demons
also came out of many, crying, "You are
the Son of God!" But he rebuked them,
and would not allow them to speak, be-
cause they knew that he was the Christ.

Jesus Preaches in the Synagogues

42 And when it was day he departed and
went into a lonely place. And the people
sought him and came to him, and would
have kept him from leaving them; 43 but
he said to them, "I must preach the good
news of the kingdom of God to the other
cities also; for I was sent for this pur-
pose." 44 And he was preaching in the
synagogues of Judea.[o]

Jesus Calls the First Disciples

5 While the people pressed upon him
to hear the word of God, he was stand-
ing by the lake of Gennes'aret. 2 And he
saw two boats by the lake; but the fish-
ermen had gone out of them and were
washing their nets. 3 Getting into one of
the boats, which was Simon's, he asked
him to put out a little from the land.
And he sat down and taught the people
from the boat. 4 And when he had ceased
speaking, he said to Simon, "Put out into
the deep and let down your nets for a
catch." 5 And Simon answered, "Master,
we toiled all night and took nothing! But
at your word I will let down the nets."
6 And when they had done this, they en-
closed a great shoal of fish; and as their
nets were breaking, 7 they beckoned to
their partners in the other boat to come
and help them. And they came and filled
both the boats, so that they began to sink.
8 But when Simon Peter saw it, he fell
down at Jesus' knees, saying, "Depart
from me, for I am a sinful man, O Lord."
9 For he was astonished, and all that were
with him, at the catch of fish which they
had taken; 10 and so also were James and
John, sons of Zeb'edee, who were part-
ners with Simon. And Jesus said to Si-
mon, "Do not be afraid; henceforth you
will be catching men." 11 And when they
had brought their boats to land, they left
everything and followed him.

Jesus Cleanses a Leper

12 While he was in one of the cities,
there came a man full of leprosy; and
when he saw Jesus, he fell on his face
and besought him, "Lord, if you will, you
can make me clean." 13 And he stretched
out his hand, and touched him, saying,
"I will; be clean." And immediately the
leprosy left him. 14 And he charged him
to tell no one; but "go and show yourself
to the priest, and make an offering for
your cleansing, as Moses commanded,
for a proof to the people."[p] 15 But so much
the more the report went abroad con-
cerning him; and great multitudes gath-
ered to hear and to be healed of their

[o] **4.44** Other ancient authorities read *Galilee*

[p] **5.14** Greek *to them*

infirmities. 16 But he withdrew to the wil-
derness and prayed.

Jesus Heals a Paralytic

17 On one of those days, as he was teach-
ing, there were Pharisees and teachers
of the law sitting by, who had come from
every village of Galilee and Judea and
from Jerusalem; and the power of the
Lord was with him to heal.[q] 18 And be-
hold, men were bringing on a bed a man
who was paralyzed, and they sought to
bring him in and lay him before Jesus;[r]
19 but finding no way to bring him in,
because of the crowd, they went up on
the roof and let him down with his bed
through the tiles into the midst before
Jesus. 20 And when he saw their faith he
said, "Man, your sins are forgiven you."
21 And the scribes and the Pharisees be-
gan to question, saying, "Who is this that
speaks blasphemies? Who can forgive
sins but God only?" 22 When Jesus per-
ceived their questionings, he answered
them, "Why do you question in your
hearts? 23 Which is easier, to say, 'Your
sins are forgiven you,' or to say, 'Rise
and walk'? 24 But that you may know that
the Son of man has authority on earth
to forgive sins"—he said to the man
who was paralyzed—"I say to you, rise,
take up your bed and go home." 25 And
immediately he rose before them, and
took up that on which he lay, and went
home, glorifying God. 26 And amazement
seized them all, and they glorified God
and were filled with awe, saying, "We
have seen strange things today."

Jesus Calls Levi

27 After this he went out, and saw a tax
collector, named Levi, sitting at the tax
office; and he said to him, "Follow me."
28 And he left everything, and rose and
followed him.

29 And Levi made him a great feast in
his house; and there was a large com-
pany of tax collectors and others sitting
at table[s] with them. 30 And the Pharisees
and their scribes murmured against his
disciples, saying, "Why do you eat and
drink with tax collectors and sinners?"
31 And Jesus answered them, "Those
who are well have no need of a physi-
cian, but those who are sick; 32 I have not
come to call the righteous, but sinners to
repentance."

The Question about Fasting

33 And they said to him, "The disciples
of John fast often and offer prayers, and
so do the disciples of the Pharisees, but
yours eat and drink." 34 And Jesus said
to them, "Can you make wedding guests
fast while the bridegroom is with them?
35 The days will come, when the bride-
groom is taken away from them, and
then they will fast in those days." 36 He
told them a parable also: "No one tears
a piece from a new garment and puts it
upon an old garment; if he does, he will
tear the new, and the piece from the new
will not match the old. 37 And no one puts
new wine into old wineskins; if he does,
the new wine will burst the skins and
it will be spilled, and the skins will be
destroyed. 38 But new wine must be put
into fresh wineskins. 39 And no one after
drinking old wine desires new; for he
says, 'The old is good.'"[t]

The Question about the Sabbath

6 On a sabbath,[u] while he was going
through the grainfields, his disciples
plucked and ate some ears of grain, rub-
bing them in their hands. 2 But some of
the Pharisees said, "Why are you doing
what is not lawful to do on the sabbath?"
3 And Jesus answered, "Have you not read
what David did when he was hungry, he

[q] **5.17** Other ancient authorities read *was present to heal them* [r] **5.18** Greek *him* [s] **5.29** Greek *reclining* [t] **5.39** Other ancient authorities read *better* [u] **6.1** Other ancient authorities read *On the second first sabbath* (on the second sabbath after the first)

and those who were with him: [4]how he
entered the house of God, and took and
ate the bread of the Presence, which it is
not lawful for any but the priests to eat,
and also gave it to those with him?" [5]And
he said to them, "The Son of man is lord
of the sabbath."

The Man with a Withered Hand

6 On another sabbath, when he entered
the synagogue and taught, a man was
there whose right hand was withered.
[7]And the scribes and the Pharisees
watched him, to see whether he would
heal on the sabbath, so that they might
find an accusation against him. [8]But he
knew their thoughts, and he said to the
man who had the withered hand, "Come
and stand here." And he rose and stood
there. [9]And Jesus said to them, "I ask you,
is it lawful on the sabbath to do good or
to do harm, to save life or to destroy it?"
[10]And he looked around on them all, and
said to him, "Stretch out your hand." And
he did so, and his hand was restored. [11]But
they were filled with fury and discussed
with one another what they might do to
Jesus.

Jesus Chooses the Twelve Apostles

12 In these days he went out into the
hills to pray; and all night he continued
in prayer to God. [13]And when it was day,
he called his disciples, and chose from
them twelve, whom he named apostles;
[14]Simon, whom he named Peter, and An-
drew his brother, and James and John,
and Philip, and Bartholomew, [15]and Mat-
thew, and Thomas, and James the son of
Alphaeus, and Simon who was called the
Zealot, [16]and Judas the son of James, and
Judas Iscariot, who became a traitor.

Jesus Teaches and Heals

17 And he came down with them and
stood on a level place, with a great crowd
of his disciples and a great multitude of
people from all Judea and Jerusalem and
the seacoast of Tyre and Sidon, who came
to hear him and to be healed of their dis-
eases; [18]and those who were troubled
with unclean spirits were cured. [19]And
all the crowd sought to touch him, for
power came forth from him and healed
them all.

Blessings and Woes

20 And he lifted up his eyes on his disci-
ples, and said:
"Blessed are you poor, for yours is the
kingdom of God.
21 "Blessed are you that hunger now,
for you shall be satisfied.
"Blessed are you that weep now, for
you shall laugh.
22 "Blessed are you when men hate
you, and when they exclude you and re-
vile you, and cast out your name as evil,
on account of the Son of man! [23]Rejoice
in that day, and leap for joy, for behold,
your reward is great in heaven; for so
their fathers did to the prophets.
24 "But woe to you that are rich, for
you have received your consolation.
25 "Woe to you that are full now, for
you shall hunger.
"Woe to you that laugh now, for you
shall mourn and weep.
26 "Woe to you, when all men speak
well of you, for so their fathers did to the
false prophets.

Love for Enemies

27 "But I say to you that hear, Love your
enemies, do good to those who hate
you, [28]bless those who curse you, pray
for those who abuse you. [29]To him who
strikes you on the cheek, offer the other
also; and from him who takes away your
cloak do not withhold your coat as well.
[30]Give to every one who begs from you;
and of him who takes away your goods
do not ask them again. [31]And as you wish
that men would do to you, do so to them.
32 "If you love those who love you, what
credit is that to you? For even sinners

love those who love them. 33 And if you do good to those who do good to you, what credit is that to you? For even sinners do the same. 34 And if you lend to those from whom you hope to receive, what credit is that to you? Even sinners lend to sinners, to receive as much again. 35 But love your enemies, and do good, and lend, expecting nothing in return;[v] and your reward will be great, and you will be sons of the Most High; for he is kind to the ungrateful and the selfish. 36 Be merciful, even as your Father is merciful.

Judging Others

37 "Judge not, and you will not be judged; condemn not, and you will not be condemned; forgive, and you will be forgiven; 38 give, and it will be given to you; good measure, pressed down, shaken together, running over, will be put into your lap. For the measure you give will be the measure you get back."

39 He also told them a parable: "Can a blind man lead a blind man? Will they not both fall into a pit? 40 A disciple is not above his teacher, but every one when he is fully taught will be like his teacher. 41 Why do you see the speck that is in your brother's eye, but do not notice the log that is in your own eye? 42 Or how can you say to your brother, 'Brother, let me take out the speck that is in your eye,' when you yourself do not see the log that is in your own eye? You hypocrite, first take the log out of your own eye, and then you will see clearly to take out the speck that is in your brother's eye.

A Tree and Its Fruit

43 "For no good tree bears bad fruit, nor again does a bad tree bear good fruit; 44 for each tree is known by its own fruit. For figs are not gathered from thorns, nor are grapes picked from a bramble bush. 45 The good man out of the good treasure of his heart produces good, and the evil man out of his evil treasure produces evil; for out of the abundance of the heart his mouth speaks.

The Two Foundations

46 "Why do you call me 'Lord, Lord,' and not do what I tell you? 47 Every one who comes to me and hears my words and does them, I will show you what he is like: 48 he is like a man building a house, who dug deep, and laid the foundation upon rock; and when a flood arose, the stream broke against that house, and could not shake it, because it had been well built.[w] 49 But he who hears and does not do them is like a man who built a house on the ground without a foundation; against which the stream broke, and immediately it fell, and the ruin of that house was great."

Jesus Heals a Centurion's Servant

7 After he had ended all his sayings in the hearing of the people he entered Caper'na-um. 2 Now a centurion had a slave who was dear[x] to him, who was sick and at the point of death. 3 When he heard of Jesus, he sent to him elders of the Jews, asking him to come and heal his slave. 4 And when they came to Jesus, they besought him earnestly, saying, "He is worthy to have you do this for him, 5 for he loves our nation, and he built us our synagogue." 6 And Jesus went with them. When he was not far from the house, the centurion sent friends to him, saying to him, "Lord, do not trouble yourself, for I am not worthy to have you come under my roof; 7 therefore I did not presume to come to you. But say the word, and let my servant be healed. 8 For I am a man set under authority, with soldiers under me: and I say to one, 'Go,' and he goes; and to another, 'Come,' and he comes; and to my slave, 'Do this,' and he does it." 9 When Jesus heard this he marveled at him, and

[v] **6.35** Other ancient authorities read *despairing of no man*
[w] **6.48** Other ancient authorities read *founded upon the rock*
[x] **7.2** Or *valuable*

turned and said to the multitude that
followed him, “I tell you, not even in Is-
rael have I found such faith.” 10And when
those who had been sent returned to the
house, they found the slave well.

Jesus Raises the Widow’s Son at Nain

11 Soon afterward[y] he went to a city
called Na′in, and his disciples and a great
crowd went with him. 12As he drew near
to the gate of the city, behold, a man who
had died was being carried out, the only
son of his mother, and she was a widow;
and a large crowd from the city was with
her. 13And when the Lord saw her, he had
compassion on her and said to her, “Do
not weep.” 14And he came and touched
the bier, and the bearers stood still. And
he said, “Young man, I say to you, arise.”
15And the dead man sat up, and began to
speak. And he gave him to his mother.
16Fear seized them all; and they glorified
God, saying, “A great prophet has arisen
among us!” and “God has visited his peo-
ple!” 17And this report concerning him
spread through the whole of Judea and
all the surrounding country.

Messengers from John the Baptist

18 The disciples of John told him of all
these things. 19And John, calling to him
two of his disciples, sent them to the Lord,
saying, “Are you he who is to come, or
shall we look for another?” 20And when
the men had come to him, they said, “John
the Baptist has sent us to you, saying, ‘Are
you he who is to come, or shall we look
for another?’” 21In that hour he cured
many of diseases and plagues and evil
spirits, and on many that were blind he
bestowed sight. 22And he answered them,
“Go and tell John what you have seen and
heard: the blind receive their sight, the
lame walk, lepers are cleansed, and the
deaf hear, the dead are raised up, the poor
have good news preached to them. 23And
blessed is he who takes no offense at me.”

24 When the messengers of John had
gone, he began to speak to the crowds
concerning John: “What did you go out
into the wilderness to behold? A reed
shaken by the wind? 25What then did
you go out to see? A man clothed in soft
raiment? Behold, those who are gor-
geously appareled and live in luxury
are in kings’ courts. 26What then did you
go out to see? A prophet? Yes, I tell you,
and more than a prophet. 27This is he of
whom it is written,

‘Behold, I send my messenger before
thy face,
who shall prepare thy way before
thee.’

28I tell you, among those born of women
none is greater than John; yet he who is
least in the kingdom of God is greater
than he.” 29(When they heard this all the
people and the tax collectors justified
God, having been baptized with the bap-
tism of John; 30but the Pharisees and the
lawyers rejected the purpose of God for
themselves, not having been baptized by
him.)

31 “To what then shall I compare the
men of this generation, and what are
they like? 32They are like children sitting
in the market place and calling to one
another,

‘We piped to you, and you did not
dance;
we wailed, and you did not weep.’

33For John the Baptist has come eating
no bread and drinking no wine; and you
say, ‘He has a demon.’ 34The Son of man
has come eating and drinking; and you
say, ‘Behold, a glutton and a drunkard, a
friend of tax collectors and sinners!’ 35Yet
wisdom is justified by all her children.”

A Sinful Woman Forgiven

36 One of the Pharisees asked him to eat
with him, and he went into the Pharisee’s
house, and sat at table. 37And behold,
a woman of the city, who was a sinner,

[y] **7.11** Other ancient authorities read *Next day*

when she learned that he was sitting at table in the Pharisee's house, brought an alabaster flask of ointment, 38 and standing behind him at his feet, weeping, she began to wet his feet with her tears, and wiped them with the hair of her head, and kissed his feet, and anointed them with the ointment. 39 Now when the Pharisee who had invited him saw it, he said to himself, "If this man were a prophet, he would have known who and what sort of woman this is who is touching him, for she is a sinner." 40 And Jesus answering said to him, "Simon, I have something to say to you." And he answered, "What is it, Teacher?" 41 "A certain creditor had two debtors; one owed five hundred denarii, and the other fifty. 42 When they could not pay, he forgave them both. Now which of them will love him more?" 43 Simon answered, "The one, I suppose, to whom he forgave more." And he said to him, "You have judged rightly." 44 Then turning toward the woman he said to Simon, "Do you see this woman? I entered your house, you gave me no water for my feet, but she has wet my feet with her tears and wiped them with her hair. 45 You gave me no kiss, but from the time I came in she has not ceased to kiss my feet. 46 You did not anoint my head with oil, but she has anointed my feet with ointment. 47 Therefore I tell you, her sins, which are many, are forgiven, for she loved much; but he who is forgiven little, loves little." 48 And he said to her, "Your sins are forgiven." 49 Then those who were at table with him began to say among themselves, "Who is this, who even forgives sins?" 50 And he said to the woman, "Your faith has saved you; go in peace."

Some Women Accompany Jesus

8 Soon afterward he went on through cities and villages, preaching and bringing the good news of the kingdom of God. And the twelve were with him, 2 and also some women who had been healed of evil spirits and infirmities: Mary, called Mag'dalene, from whom seven demons had gone out, 3 and Jo-an'na, the wife of Chu'za, Herod's steward, and Susanna, and many others, who provided for them[z] out of their means.

The Parable of the Sower

4 And when a great crowd came together and people from town after town came to him, he said in a parable: 5 "A sower went out to sow his seed; and as he sowed, some fell along the path, and was trodden under foot, and the birds of the air devoured it. 6 And some fell on the rock; and as it grew up, it withered away, because it had no moisture. 7 And some fell among thorns; and the thorns grew with it and choked it. 8 And some fell into good soil and grew, and yielded a hundredfold." As he said this, he called out, "He who has ears to hear, let him hear."

The Purpose of the Parables

9 And when his disciples asked him what this parable meant, 10 he said, "To you it has been given to know the secrets of the kingdom of God; but for others they are in parables, so that seeing they may not see, and hearing they may not understand. 11 Now the parable is this: The seed is the word of God. 12 The ones along the path are those who have heard; then the devil comes and takes away the word from their hearts, that they may not believe and be saved. 13 And the ones on the rock are those who, when they hear the word, receive it with joy; but these have no root, they believe for a while and in time of temptation fall away. 14 And as for what fell among the thorns, they are those who hear, but as they go on their way they are choked by the cares and riches and pleasures of life, and their fruit does not mature. 15 And as for that in the good soil, they are those who, hearing the word,

[z] **8.3** Other ancient authorities read *him*

hold it fast in an honest and good heart,
and bring forth fruit with patience.

A Lamp under a Jar

16 “No one after lighting a lamp covers it
with a vessel, or puts it under a bed, but
puts it on a stand, that those who enter
may see the light. 17For nothing is hid that
shall not be made manifest, nor anything
secret that shall not be known and come
to light. 18Take heed then how you hear;
for to him who has will more be given,
and from him who has not, even what he
thinks that he has will be taken away.”

The True Kindred of Jesus

19 Then his mother and his brethren
came to him, but they could not reach
him for the crowd. 20And he was told,
“Your mother and your brethren are
standing outside, desiring to see you.”
21But he said to them, “My mother and my
brethren are those who hear the word of
God and do it.”

Jesus Calms a Storm

22 One day he got into a boat with his
disciples, and he said to them, “Let us go
across to the other side of the lake.” So
they set out, 23and as they sailed he fell
asleep. And a storm of wind came down
on the lake, and they were filling with
water, and were in danger. 24And they
went and woke him, saying, “Master,
Master, we are perishing!” And he awoke
and rebuked the wind and the raging
waves; and they ceased, and there was a
calm. 25He said to them, “Where is your
faith?” And they were afraid, and they
marveled, saying to one another, “Who
then is this, that he commands even wind
and water, and they obey him?”

Jesus Heals the Gerasene Demoniac

26 Then they arrived at the country
of the Ger′asenes,[a] which is opposite
Galilee. 27And as he stepped out on land,
there met him a man from the city who
had demons; for a long time he had
worn no clothes, and he lived not in a
house but among the tombs. 28When he
saw Jesus, he cried out and fell down
before him, and said with a loud voice,
“What have you to do with me, Jesus,
Son of the Most High God? I beseech
you, do not torment me.” 29For he had
commanded the unclean spirit to come
out of the man. (For many a time it had
seized him; he was kept under guard,
and bound with chains and fetters, but
he broke the bonds and was driven by
the demon into the desert.) 30Jesus then
asked him, “What is your name?” And he
said, “Legion”; for many demons had en-
tered him. 31And they begged him not to
command them to depart into the abyss.
32Now a large herd of swine was feeding
there on the hillside; and they begged
him to let them enter these. So he gave
them leave. 33Then the demons came out
of the man and entered the swine, and
the herd rushed down the steep bank
into the lake and were drowned.

34 When the herdsmen saw what had
happened, they fled, and told it in the city
and in the country. 35Then people went
out to see what had happened, and they
came to Jesus, and found the man from
whom the demons had gone, sitting at
the feet of Jesus, clothed and in his right
mind; and they were afraid. 36And those
who had seen it told them how he who had
been possessed with demons was healed.
37Then all the people of the surrounding
country of the Ger′asenes[b] asked him to
depart from them; for they were seized
with great fear; so he got into the boat
and returned. 38The man from whom the
demons had gone begged that he might
be with him; but he sent him away, say-
ing, 39“Return to your home, and declare
how much God has done for you.” And he

[a]**8.26** Other ancient authorities read *Gadarenes,* others *Gergesenes* [b]**8.37** Other ancient authorities read *Gadarenes,* others *Gergesenes*

went away, proclaiming throughout the whole city how much Jesus had done for him.

A Girl Restored to Life and a Woman Healed

40 Now when Jesus returned, the crowd welcomed him, for they were all waiting for him. 41 And there came a man named Ja′irus, who was a ruler of the synagogue; and falling at Jesus' feet he besought him to come to his house, 42 for he had an only daughter, about twelve years of age, and she was dying.

As he went, the people pressed round him. 43 And a woman who had had a flow of blood for twelve years and had spent all her living upon physicians[c] and could not be healed by any one, 44 came up behind him, and touched the fringe of his garment; and immediately her flow of blood ceased. 45 And Jesus said, "Who was it that touched me?" When all denied it, Peter[d] said, "Master, the multitudes surround you and press upon you!" 46 But Jesus said, "Some one touched me; for I perceive that power has gone forth from me." 47 And when the woman saw that she was not hidden, she came trembling, and falling down before him declared in the presence of all the people why she had touched him, and how she had been immediately healed. 48 And he said to her, "Daughter, your faith has made you well; go in peace."

49 While he was still speaking, a man from the ruler's house came and said, "Your daughter is dead; do not trouble the Teacher any more." 50 But Jesus on hearing this answered him, "Do not fear; only believe, and she shall be well." 51 And when he came to the house, he permitted no one to enter with him, except Peter and John and James, and the father and mother of the child. 52 And all were weeping and bewailing her; but he said, "Do not weep; for she is not dead but sleeping." 53 And they laughed at him, knowing that she was dead. 54 But taking her by the hand he called, saying, "Child, arise." 55 And her spirit returned, and she got up at once; and he directed that something should be given her to eat. 56 And her parents were amazed; but he charged them to tell no one what had happened.

The Mission of the Twelve

9 And he called the twelve together and gave them power and authority over all demons and to cure diseases, 2 and he sent them out to preach the kingdom of God and to heal. 3 And he said to them, "Take nothing for your journey, no staff, nor bag, nor bread, nor money; and do not have two tunics. 4 And whatever house you enter, stay there, and from there depart. 5 And wherever they do not receive you, when you leave that town shake off the dust from your feet as a testimony against them." 6 And they departed and went through the villages, preaching the gospel and healing everywhere.

Herod's Perplexity

7 Now Herod the tetrarch heard of all that was done, and he was perplexed, because it was said by some that John had been raised from the dead, 8 by some that Eli′jah had appeared, and by others that one of the old prophets had risen. 9 Herod said, "John I beheaded; but who is this about whom I hear such things?" And he sought to see him.

Feeding the Five Thousand

10 On their return the apostles told him what they had done. And he took them and withdrew apart to a city called Beth-sa′ida. 11 When the crowds learned it, they followed him; and he welcomed them and spoke to them of the kingdom

[c] **8.43** Other ancient authorities omit *and had spent all her living upon physicians* [d] **8.45** Other ancient authorities add *and those who were with him*

of God, and cured those who had need
of healing. [12]Now the day began to wear
away; and the twelve came and said to
him, "Send the crowd away, to go into
the villages and country round about,
to lodge and get provisions; for we are
here in a lonely place." [13]But he said to
them, "You give them something to eat."
They said, "We have no more than five
loaves and two fish—unless we are to go
and buy food for all these people." [14]For
there were about five thousand men.
And he said to his disciples, "Make them
sit down in companies, about fifty each."
[15]And they did so, and made them all sit
down. [16]And taking the five loaves and
the two fish he looked up to heaven, and
blessed and broke them, and gave them
to the disciples to set before the crowd.
[17]And all ate and were satisfied. And they
took up what was left over, twelve bas-
kets of broken pieces.

Peter's Declaration about Jesus

18 Now it happened that as he was pray-
ing alone the disciples were with him;
and he asked them, "Who do the people
say that I am?" [19]And they answered,
"John the Baptist; but others say, Eli'jah;
and others, that one of the old prophets
has risen." [20]And he said to them, "But
who do you say that I am?" And Peter
answered, "The Christ of God." [21]But
he charged and commanded them to
tell this to no one, [22]saying, "The Son of
man must suffer many things, and be re-
jected by the elders and chief priests and
scribes, and be killed, and on the third
day be raised."

23 And he said to all, "If any man
would come after me, let him deny him-
self and take up his cross daily and fol-
low me. [24]For whoever would save his
life will lose it; and whoever loses his life
for my sake, he will save it. [25]For what
does it profit a man if he gains the whole
world and loses or forfeits himself?
[26]For whoever is ashamed of me and of
my words, of him will the Son of man be
ashamed when he comes in his glory and
the glory of the Father and of the holy an-
gels. [27]But I tell you truly, there are some
standing here who will not taste death
before they see the kingdom of God."

The Transfiguration

28 Now about eight days after these say-
ings he took with him Peter and John and
James, and went up on the mountain to
pray. [29]And as he was praying, the ap-
pearance of his countenance was altered,
and his raiment became dazzling white.
[30]And behold, two men talked with him,
Moses and Eli'jah, [31]who appeared in
glory and spoke of his departure, which
he was to accomplish at Jerusalem. [32]Now
Peter and those who were with him were
heavy with sleep but kept awake, and they
saw his glory and the two men who stood
with him. [33]And as the men were parting
from him, Peter said to Jesus, "Master, it
is well that we are here; let us make three
booths, one for you and one for Moses
and one for Eli'jah"—not knowing what
he said. [34]As he said this, a cloud came
and overshadowed them; and they were
afraid as they entered the cloud. [35]And a
voice came out of the cloud, saying, "This
is my Son, my Chosen;[e] listen to him!"
[36]And when the voice had spoken, Jesus
was found alone. And they kept silence
and told no one in those days anything of
what they had seen.

Jesus Heals a Boy with a Demon

37 On the next day, when they had come
down from the mountain, a great crowd
met him. [38]And behold, a man from the
crowd cried, "Teacher, I beg you to look
upon my son, for he is my only child;
[39]and behold, a spirit seizes him, and
he suddenly cries out; it convulses him
till he foams, and shatters him, and will
hardly leave him. [40]And I begged your

[e] **9.35** Other ancient authorities read *my Beloved*

disciples to cast it out, but they could not." [41]Jesus answered, "O faithless and perverse generation, how long am I to be with you and bear with you? Bring your son here." [42]While he was coming, the demon tore him and convulsed him. But Jesus rebuked the unclean spirit, and healed the boy, and gave him back to his father. [43]And all were astonished at the majesty of God.

Jesus Again Foretells His Death

But while they were all marveling at everything he did, he said to his disciples, [44]"Let these words sink into your ears; for the Son of man is to be delivered into the hands of men." [45]But they did not understand this saying, and it was concealed from them, that they should not perceive it; and they were afraid to ask him about this saying.

True Greatness

46 And an argument arose among them as to which of them was the greatest. [47]But when Jesus perceived the thought of their hearts, he took a child and put him by his side, [48]and said to them, "Whoever receives this child in my name receives me, and whoever receives me receives him who sent me; for he who is least among you all is the one who is great."

Another Exorcist

49 John answered, "Master, we saw a man casting out demons in your name, and we forbade him, because he does not follow with us." [50]But Jesus said to him, "Do not forbid him; for he that is not against you is for you."

A Samaritan Village Refuses to Receive Jesus

51 When the days drew near for him to be received up, he set his face to go to Jerusalem. [52]And he sent messengers ahead of him, who went and entered a village of the Samaritans, to make ready for him; [53]but the people would not receive him, because his face was set toward Jerusalem. [54]And when his disciples James and John saw it, they said, "Lord, do you want us to bid fire come down from heaven and consume them?"[f] [55]But he turned and rebuked them.[g] [56]And they went on to another village.

Would-Be Followers of Jesus

57 As they were going along the road, a man said to him, "I will follow you wherever you go." [58]And Jesus said to him, "Foxes have holes, and birds of the air have nests; but the Son of man has nowhere to lay his head." [59]To another he said, "Follow me." But he said, "Lord, let me first go and bury my father." [60]But he said to him, "Leave the dead to bury their own dead; but as for you, go and proclaim the kingdom of God." [61]Another said, "I will follow you, Lord; but let me first say farewell to those at my home." [62]Jesus said to him, "No one who puts his hand to the plow and looks back is fit for the kingdom of God."

The Mission of the Seventy

10 After this the Lord appointed seventy[h] others, and sent them on ahead of him, two by two, into every town and place where he himself was about to come. [2]And he said to them, "The harvest is plentiful, but the laborers are few; pray therefore the Lord of the harvest to send out laborers into his harvest. [3]Go your way; behold, I send you out as lambs in the midst of wolves. [4]Carry no purse, no bag, no sandals; and salute no one on the road. [5]Whatever house you enter, first say, 'Peace be to this house!' [6]And if a son of peace is there, your peace shall

[f]**9.54** Other ancient authorities add *as Elijah did* [g]**9.55** Other ancient authorities add *and he said, "You do not know what manner of spirit you are of; for the Son of man came not to destroy men's lives but to save them"* [h]**10.1** Other ancient authorities read *seventy-two*

rest upon him; but if not, it shall return to
you. [7]And remain in the same house, eat-
ing and drinking what they provide, for
the laborer deserves his wages; do not
go from house to house. [8]Whenever you
enter a town and they receive you, eat
what is set before you; [9]heal the sick in it
and say to them, 'The kingdom of God has
come near to you.' [10]But whenever you
enter a town and they do not receive you,
go into its streets and say, [11]'Even the dust
of your town that clings to our feet, we
wipe off against you; nevertheless know
this, that the kingdom of God has come
near.' [12]I tell you, it shall be more tolerable
on that day for Sodom than for that town.

Woes to Unrepentant Cities

13 "Woe to you, Chora'zin! woe to you,
Beth-sa'ida! for if the mighty works done
in you had been done in Tyre and Sidon,
they would have repented long ago, sit-
ting in sackcloth and ashes. [14]But it shall be
more tolerable in the judgment for Tyre
and Sidon than for you. [15]And you, Caper'-
na-um, will you be exalted to heaven? You
shall be brought down to Hades.

16 "He who hears you hears me, and he
who rejects you rejects me, and he who
rejects me rejects him who sent me."

The Return of the Seventy

17 The seventy[i] returned with joy, say-
ing, "Lord, even the demons are sub-
ject to us in your name!" [18]And he said
to them, "I saw Satan fall like lightning
from heaven. [19]Behold, I have given you
authority to tread upon serpents and
scorpions, and over all the power of
the enemy; and nothing shall hurt you.
[20]Nevertheless do not rejoice in this, that
the spirits are subject to you; but rejoice
that your names are written in heaven."

Jesus Rejoices

21 In that same hour he rejoiced in
the Holy Spirit and said, "I thank thee,
Father, Lord of heaven and earth, that
thou hast hidden these things from the
wise and understanding and revealed
them to babes; yea, Father, for such was
thy gracious will.[j] [22]All things have been
delivered to me by my Father; and no one
knows who the Son is except the Father,
or who the Father is except the Son and
any one to whom the Son chooses to re-
veal him."

23 Then turning to the disciples he
said privately, "Blessed are the eyes
which see what you see! [24]For I tell you
that many prophets and kings desired to
see what you see, and did not see it, and
to hear what you hear, and did not hear
it."

The Parable of the Good Samaritan

25 And behold, a lawyer stood up to put
him to the test, saying, "Teacher, what
shall I do to inherit eternal life?" [26]He
said to him, "What is written in the law?
How do you read?" [27]And he answered,
"You shall love the Lord your God with
all your heart, and with all your soul,
and with all your strength, and with all
your mind; and your neighbor as your-
self." [28]And he said to him, "You have an-
swered right; do this, and you will live."

29 But he, desiring to justify himself,
said to Jesus, "And who is my neighbor?"
[30]Jesus replied, "A man was going down
from Jerusalem to Jericho, and he fell
among robbers, who stripped him and
beat him, and departed, leaving him half
dead. [31]Now by chance a priest was going
down that road; and when he saw him he
passed by on the other side. [32]So likewise
a Levite, when he came to the place and
saw him, passed by on the other side.
[33]But a Samaritan, as he journeyed, came
to where he was; and when he saw him,
he had compassion, [34]and went to him
and bound up his wounds, pouring on
oil and wine; then he set him on his own
beast and brought him to an inn, and

[i] **10.17** Other ancient authorities read *seventy-two*

[j] **10.21** Or *so it was well-pleasing before thee*

took care of him. 35 And the next day he
took out two denarii[k] and gave them to
the innkeeper, saying, 'Take care of him;
and whatever more you spend, I will re-
pay you when I come back.' 36 Which of
these three, do you think, proved neigh-
bor to the man who fell among the rob-
bers?" 37 He said, "The one who showed
mercy on him." And Jesus said to him,
"Go and do likewise."

Jesus Visits Martha and Mary

38 Now as they went on their way, he
entered a village; and a woman named
Martha received him into her house.
39 And she had a sister called Mary, who
sat at the Lord's feet and listened to his
teaching. 40 But Martha was distracted
with much serving; and she went to him
and said, "Lord, do you not care that my
sister has left me to serve alone? Tell her
then to help me." 41 But the Lord answered
her, "Martha, Martha, you are anxious
and troubled about many things; 42 one
thing is needful.[l] Mary has chosen the
good portion, which shall not be taken
away from her."

The Lord's Prayer

11 He was praying in a certain place,
and when he ceased, one of his dis-
ciples said to him, "Lord, teach us to pray,
as John taught his disciples." 2 And he
said to them, "When you pray, say:

"Father, hallowed be thy name. Thy
kingdom come. 3 Give us each day our
daily bread;[m] 4 and forgive us our sins,
for we ourselves forgive every one who
is indebted to us; and lead us not into
temptation."

Perseverance in Prayer

5 And he said to them, "Which of you
who has a friend will go to him at mid-
night and say to him, 'Friend, lend me
three loaves; 6 for a friend of mine has
arrived on a journey, and I have noth-
ing to set before him'; 7 and he will an-
swer from within, 'Do not bother me;
the door is now shut, and my children
are with me in bed; I cannot get up and
give you anything'? 8 I tell you, though he
will not get up and give him anything be-
cause he is his friend, yet because of his
importunity he will rise and give him
whatever he needs. 9 And I tell you, Ask,
and it will be given you; seek, and you
will find; knock, and it will be opened to
you. 10 For every one who asks receives,
and he who seeks finds, and to him who
knocks it will be opened. 11 What father
among you, if his son asks for[n] a fish,
will instead of a fish give him a serpent;
12 or if he asks for an egg, will give him
a scorpion? 13 If you then, who are evil,
know how to give good gifts to your chil-
dren, how much more will the heavenly
Father give the Holy Spirit to those who
ask him!"

Jesus and Beelzebul

14 Now he was casting out a demon that
was dumb; when the demon had gone
out, the dumb man spoke, and the peo-
ple marveled. 15 But some of them said,
"He casts out demons by Be-el'zebul,
the prince of demons"; 16 while others,
to test him, sought from him a sign
from heaven. 17 But he, knowing their
thoughts, said to them, "Every kingdom
divided against itself is laid waste, and
house falls upon house. 18 And if Satan
also is divided against himself, how will
his kingdom stand? For you say that I
cast out demons by Be-el'zebul. 19 And if I
cast out demons by Be-el'zebul, by whom
do your sons cast them out? Therefore
they shall be your judges. 20 But if it is by
the finger of God that I cast out demons,
then the kingdom of God has come upon

[k] **10.35** The denarius was a day's wage for a laborer [l] **10.42** Other ancient authorities read *few things are needful, or only one* [m] **11.3** Or *our bread for the morrow* [n] **11.11** Other ancient authorities insert *bread, will give him a stone; or if he asks for*

you. 21When a strong man, fully armed,
guards his own palace, his goods are in
peace; 22but when one stronger than he
assails him and overcomes him, he takes
away his armor in which he trusted, and
divides his spoil. 23He who is not with
me is against me, and he who does not
gather with me scatters.

The Return of the Unclean Spirit

24 "When the unclean spirit has gone
out of a man, he passes through water-
less places seeking rest; and finding none
he says, 'I will return to my house from
which I came.' 25And when he comes he
finds it swept and put in order. 26Then he
goes and brings seven other spirits more
evil than himself, and they enter and
dwell there; and the last state of that man
becomes worse than the first."

True Blessedness

27 As he said this, a woman in the crowd
raised her voice and said to him, "Blessed
is the womb that bore you, and the
breasts that you sucked!" 28But he said,
"Blessed rather are those who hear the
word of God and keep it!"

The Sign of Jonah

29 When the crowds were increasing,
he began to say, "This generation is an
evil generation; it seeks a sign, but no
sign shall be given to it except the sign
of Jonah. 30For as Jonah became a sign to
the men of Nin'eveh, so will the Son of
man be to this generation. 31The queen
of the South will arise at the judgment
with the men of this generation and con-
demn them; for she came from the ends
of the earth to hear the wisdom of Sol-
omon, and behold, something greater
than Solomon is here. 32The men of
Nin'eveh will arise at the judgment with
this generation and condemn it; for they
repented at the preaching of Jonah, and
behold, something greater than Jonah is
here.

The Light of the Body

33 "No one after lighting a lamp puts
it in a cellar or under a bushel, but on
a stand, that those who enter may see
the light. 34Your eye is the lamp of your
body; when your eye is sound, your
whole body is full of light; but when it
is not sound, your body is full of dark-
ness. 35Therefore be careful lest the light
in you be darkness. 36If then your whole
body is full of light, having no part dark,
it will be wholly bright, as when a lamp
with its rays gives you light."

Jesus Denounces Pharisees and Lawyers

37 While he was speaking, a Pharisee
asked him to dine with him; so he went
in and sat at table. 38The Pharisee was as-
tonished to see that he did not first wash
before dinner. 39And the Lord said to
him, "Now you Pharisees cleanse the out-
side of the cup and of the dish, but inside
you are full of extortion and wickedness.
40You fools! Did not he who made the out-
side make the inside also? 41But give for
alms those things which are within; and
behold, everything is clean for you.

42 "But woe to you Pharisees! for you
tithe mint and rue and every herb, and
neglect justice and the love of God; these
you ought to have done, without neglect-
ing the others. 43Woe to you Pharisees!
for you love the best seat in the syna-
gogues and salutations in the market
places. 44Woe to you! for you are like
graves which are not seen, and men walk
over them without knowing it."

45 One of the lawyers answered him,
"Teacher, in saying this you reproach us
also." 46And he said, "Woe to you lawyers
also! for you load men with burdens hard
to bear, and you yourselves do not touch
the burdens with one of your fingers.
47Woe to you! for you build the tombs of
the prophets whom your fathers killed.
48So you are witnesses and consent to
the deeds of your fathers; for they killed

them, and you build their tombs. 49There-
fore also the Wisdom of God said, 'I will
send them prophets and apostles, some
of whom they will kill and persecute,'
50that the blood of all the prophets, shed
from the foundation of the world, may
be required of this generation, 51from the
blood of Abel to the blood of Zechari'ah,
who perished between the altar and the
sanctuary. Yes, I tell you, it shall be re-
quired of this generation. 52Woe to you
lawyers! for you have taken away the key
of knowledge; you did not enter your-
selves, and you hindered those who were
entering."
53 As he went away from there, the
scribes and the Pharisees began to press
him hard, and to provoke him to speak of
many things, 54lying in wait for him, to
catch at something he might say.

A Warning against Hypocrisy

12 In the meantime, when so many
thousands of the multitude had
gathered together that they trod upon
one another, he began to say to his dis-
ciples first, "Beware of the leaven of the
Pharisees, which is hypocrisy. 2Nothing
is covered up that will not be revealed,
or hidden that will not be known. 3What-
ever you have said in the dark shall be
heard in the light, and what you have
whispered in private rooms shall be pro-
claimed upon the housetops.

Exhortation to Fearless Confession

4 "I tell you, my friends, do not fear those
who kill the body, and after that have no
more that they can do. 5But I will warn
you whom to fear: fear him who, after
he has killed, has power to cast into
hell;[o] yes, I tell you, fear him! 6Are not
five sparrows sold for two pennies? And
not one of them is forgotten before God.
7Why, even the hairs of your head are
all numbered. Fear not; you are of more
value than many sparrows.
8 "And I tell you, every one who ac-
knowledges me before men, the Son of
man also will acknowledge before the
angels of God; 9but he who denies me
before men will be denied before the an-
gels of God. 10And every one who speaks
a word against the Son of man will be
forgiven; but he who blasphemes against
the Holy Spirit will not be forgiven.
11And when they bring you before the
synagogues and the rulers and the au-
thorities, do not be anxious how or what
you are to answer or what you are to say;
12for the Holy Spirit will teach you in that
very hour what you ought to say."

The Parable of the Rich Fool

13 One of the multitude said to him,
"Teacher, bid my brother divide the in-
heritance with me." 14But he said to him,
"Man, who made me a judge or divider
over you?" 15And he said to them, "Take
heed, and beware of all covetousness; for
a man's life does not consist in the abun-
dance of his possessions." 16And he told
them a parable, saying, "The land of a
rich man brought forth plentifully; 17and
he thought to himself, 'What shall I do,
for I have nowhere to store my crops?'
18And he said, 'I will do this: I will pull
down my barns, and build larger ones;
and there I will store all my grain and my
goods. 19And I will say to my soul, Soul,
you have ample goods laid up for many
years; take your ease, eat, drink, be
merry.' 20But God said to him, 'Fool! This
night your soul is required of you; and
the things you have prepared, whose will
they be?' 21So is he who lays up treasure
for himself, and is not rich toward God."

Do Not Worry

22 And he said to his disciples, "There-
fore I tell you, do not be anxious about
your life, what you shall eat, nor about
your body, what you shall put on. 23For
life is more than food, and the body more

[o] **12.5** Greek *Gehenna*

than clothing. [24]Consider the ravens:
they neither sow nor reap, they have nei-
ther storehouse nor barn, and yet God
feeds them. Of how much more value are
you than the birds! [25]And which of you
by being anxious can add a cubit to his
span of life?[p] [26]If then you are not able to
do as small a thing as that, why are you
anxious about the rest? [27]Consider the
lilies, how they grow; they neither toil
nor spin;[q] yet I tell you, even Solomon
in all his glory was not arrayed like one
of these. [28]But if God so clothes the grass
which is alive in the field today and to-
morrow is thrown into the oven, how
much more will he clothe you, O men of
little faith! [29]And do not seek what you
are to eat and what you are to drink,
nor be of anxious mind. [30]For all the na-
tions of the world seek these things; and
your Father knows that you need them.
[31]Instead, seek his[r] kingdom, and these
things shall be yours as well.

32 “Fear not, little flock, for it is your
Father’s good pleasure to give you the
kingdom. [33]Sell your possessions, and
give alms; provide yourselves with
purses that do not grow old, with a trea-
sure in the heavens that does not fail,
where no thief approaches and no moth
destroys. [34]For where your treasure is,
there will your heart be also.

Watchful Slaves

35 “Let your loins be girded and your
lamps burning, [36]and be like men who
are waiting for their master to come
home from the marriage feast, so that
they may open to him at once when he
comes and knocks. [37]Blessed are those
servants whom the master finds awake
when he comes; truly, I say to you, he
will gird himself and have them sit at
table, and he will come and serve them.
[38]If he comes in the second watch, or in
the third, and finds them so, blessed are
those servants! [39]But know this, that
if the householder had known at what
hour the thief was coming, he would
have been awake and[s] would not have
left his house to be broken into. [40]You
also must be ready; for the Son of man is
coming at an hour you do not expect.”

The Faithful or the Unfaithful Slave

41 Peter said, “Lord, are you telling this
parable for us or for all?” [42]And the Lord
said, “Who then is the faithful and wise
steward, whom his master will set over
his household, to give them their portion
of food at the proper time? [43]Blessed is
that servant whom his master when he
comes will find so doing. [44]Truly, I tell
you, he will set him over all his posses-
sions. [45]But if that servant says to him-
self, ‘My master is delayed in coming,’
and begins to beat the menservants and
the maidservants, and to eat and drink
and get drunk, [46]the master of that ser-
vant will come on a day when he does
not expect him and at an hour he does
not know, and will punish[t] him, and put
him with the unfaithful. [47]And that ser-
vant who knew his master’s will, but
did not make ready or act according to
his will, shall receive a severe beating.
[48]But he who did not know, and did what
deserved a beating, shall receive a light
beating. Every one to whom much is
given, of him will much be required; and
of him to whom men commit much they
will demand the more.

Jesus the Cause of Division

49 “I came to cast fire upon the earth; and
would that it were already kindled! [50]I
have a baptism to be baptized with; and
how I am constrained until it is accom-
plished! [51]Do you think that I have come
to give peace on earth? No, I tell you,

[p] **12.25** Or *to his stature* [q] **12.27** Other ancient authorities read *Consider the lilies; they neither spin nor weave* [r] **12.31** Other ancient authorities read *God’s* [s] **12.39** Other ancient authorities omit *would have been awake and* [t] **12.46** Or *cut him in pieces*

but rather division; [52]for henceforth
in one house there will be five divided,
three against two and two against three;
[53]they will be divided, father against
son and son against father, mother
against daughter and daughter against
her mother, mother-in-law against her
daughter-in-law and daughter-in-law
against her mother-in-law."

Interpreting the Time

54 He also said to the multitudes, "When
you see a cloud rising in the west, you
say at once, 'A shower is coming'; and
so it happens. [55]And when you see the
south wind blowing, you say, 'There will
be scorching heat'; and it happens. [56]You
hypocrites! You know how to interpret
the appearance of earth and sky; but
why do you not know how to interpret
the present time?

Settling with Your Opponent

57 "And why do you not judge for your-
selves what is right? [58]As you go with
your accuser before the magistrate,
make an effort to settle with him on the
way, lest he drag you to the judge, and the
judge hand you over to the officer, and
the officer put you in prison. [59]I tell you,
you will never get out till you have paid
the very last copper."

Repent or Perish

13 There were some present at that
very time who told him of the Gal-
ileans whose blood Pilate had mingled
with their sacrifices. [2]And he answered
them, "Do you think that these Galileans
were worse sinners than all the other Gal-
ileans, because they suffered thus? [3]I tell
you, No; but unless you repent you will all
likewise perish. [4]Or those eighteen upon
whom the tower in Silo'am fell and killed
them, do you think that they were worse
offenders than all the others who dwelt in
Jerusalem? [5]I tell you, No; but unless you
repent you will all likewise perish."

The Parable of the Barren Fig Tree

6 And he told this parable: "A man had a
fig tree planted in his vineyard; and he
came seeking fruit on it and found none.
[7]And he said to the vinedresser, 'Lo, these
three years I have come seeking fruit on
this fig tree, and I find none. Cut it down;
why should it use up the ground?' [8]And
he answered him, 'Let it alone, sir, this
year also, till I dig about it and put on
manure. [9]And if it bears fruit next year,
well and good; but if not, you can cut it
down.'"

Jesus Heals a Crippled Woman

10 Now he was teaching in one of the
synagogues on the sabbath. [11]And there
was a woman who had had a spirit of in-
firmity for eighteen years; she was bent
over and could not fully straighten her-
self. [12]And when Jesus saw her, he called
her and said to her, "Woman, you are
freed from your infirmity." [13]And he laid
his hands upon her, and immediately
she was made straight, and she praised
God. [14]But the ruler of the synagogue,
indignant because Jesus had healed on
the sabbath, said to the people, "There
are six days on which work ought to be
done; come on those days and be healed,
and not on the sabbath day." [15]Then the
Lord answered him, "You hypocrites!
Does not each of you on the sabbath un-
tie his ox or his ass from the manger,
and lead it away to water it? [16]And ought
not this woman, a daughter of Abraham
whom Satan bound for eighteen years,
be loosed from this bond on the sabbath
day?" [17]As he said this, all his adversaries
were put to shame; and all the people re-
joiced at all the glorious things that were
done by him.

The Parable of the Mustard Seed

18 He said therefore, "What is the king-
dom of God like? And to what shall I
compare it? [19]It is like a grain of mustard
seed which a man took and sowed in his

garden; and it grew and became a tree,
and the birds of the air made nests in its
branches."

The Parable of the Yeast

20 And again he said, "To what shall I
compare the kingdom of God? 21It is like
leaven which a woman took and hid in
three measures of meal, till it was all
leavened."

The Narrow Door

22 He went on his way through towns
and villages, teaching, and journeying
toward Jerusalem. 23And some one said
to him, "Lord, will those who are saved
be few?" And he said to them, 24"Strive
to enter by the narrow door; for many,
I tell you, will seek to enter and will not
be able. 25When once the householder
has risen up and shut the door, you will
begin to stand outside and to knock at
the door, saying, 'Lord, open to us.' He
will answer you, 'I do not know where
you come from.' 26Then you will begin to
say, 'We ate and drank in your presence,
and you taught in our streets.' 27But he
will say, 'I tell you, I do not know where
you come from; depart from me, all you
workers of iniquity!' 28There you will
weep and gnash your teeth, when you see
Abraham and Isaac and Jacob and all the
prophets in the kingdom of God and you
yourselves thrust out. 29And men will
come from east and west, and from north
and south, and sit at table in the kingdom
of God. 30And behold, some are last who
will be first, and some are first who will
be last."

The Lament over Jerusalem

31 At that very hour some Pharisees
came, and said to him, "Get away from
here, for Herod wants to kill you." 32And
he said to them, "Go and tell that fox,
'Behold, I cast out demons and perform
cures today and tomorrow, and the third
day I finish my course. 33Nevertheless I
must go on my way today and tomorrow
and the day following; for it cannot be
that a prophet should perish away from
Jerusalem.' 34O Jerusalem, Jerusalem,
killing the prophets and stoning those
who are sent to you! How often would I
have gathered your children together
as a hen gathers her brood under her
wings, and you would not! 35Behold, your
house is forsaken. And I tell you, you
will not see me until you say, 'Blessed is
he who comes in the name of the Lord!'"

Jesus Heals the Man with Dropsy

14 One sabbath when he went to
dine at the house of a ruler who
belonged to the Pharisees, they were
watching him. 2And behold, there was a
man before him who had dropsy. 3And
Jesus spoke to the lawyers and Phari-
sees, saying, "Is it lawful to heal on the
sabbath, or not?" 4But they were silent.
Then he took him and healed him, and
let him go. 5And he said to them, "Which
of you, having an ass[u] or an ox that has
fallen into a well, will not immediately
pull him out on a sabbath day?" 6And
they could not reply to this.

Humility and Hospitality

7 Now he told a parable to those who
were invited, when he marked how they
chose the places of honor, saying to them,
8"When you are invited by any one to a
marriage feast, do not sit down in a place
of honor, lest a more eminent man than
you be invited by him; 9and he who in-
vited you both will come, and say to you,
'Give place to this man,' and then you
will begin with shame to take the lowest
place. 10But when you are invited, go and
sit in the lowest place, so that when your
host comes he may say to you, 'Friend, go
up higher'; then you will be honored in
the presence of all who sit at table with
you. 11For every one who exalts himself

[u] **14.5** Other ancient authorities read *a son*

will be humbled, and he who humbles
himself will be exalted."
12 He said also to the man who had in-
vited him, "When you give a dinner or
a banquet, do not invite your friends or
your brothers or your kinsmen or rich
neighbors, lest they also invite you in re-
turn, and you be repaid. 13But when you
give a feast, invite the poor, the maimed,
the lame, the blind, 14and you will be
blessed, because they cannot repay you.
You will be repaid at the resurrection of
the just."

The Parable of the Great Dinner

15 When one of those who sat at table with
him heard this, he said to him, "Blessed is
he who shall eat bread in the kingdom of
God!" 16But he said to him, "A man once
gave a great banquet, and invited many;
17and at the time for the banquet he sent
his servant to say to those who had been
invited, 'Come; for all is now ready.' 18But
they all alike began to make excuses. The
first said to him, 'I have bought a field,
and I must go out and see it; I pray you,
have me excused.' 19And another said, 'I
have bought five yoke of oxen, and I go
to examine them; I pray you, have me ex-
cused.' 20And another said, 'I have mar-
ried a wife, and therefore I cannot come.'
21So the servant came and reported this
to his master. Then the householder in
anger said to his servant, 'Go out quickly
to the streets and lanes of the city, and
bring in the poor and maimed and blind
and lame.' 22And the servant said, 'Sir,
what you commanded has been done,
and still there is room.' 23And the master
said to the servant, 'Go out to the high-
ways and hedges, and compel people
to come in, that my house may be filled.
24For I tell you, none of those men who
were invited shall taste my banquet.'"

The Cost of Discipleship

25 Now great multitudes accompanied
him; and he turned and said to them,
26"If any one comes to me and does not
hate his own father and mother and wife
and children and brothers and sisters,
yes, and even his own life, he cannot be
my disciple. 27Whoever does not bear
his own cross and come after me, can-
not be my disciple. 28For which of you,
desiring to build a tower, does not first
sit down and count the cost, whether he
has enough to complete it? 29Otherwise,
when he has laid a foundation, and is
not able to finish, all who see it begin to
mock him, 30saying, 'This man began to
build, and was not able to finish.' 31Or
what king, going to encounter another
king in war, will not sit down first and
take counsel whether he is able with ten
thousand to meet him who comes against
him with twenty thousand? 32And if not,
while the other is yet a great way off,
he sends an embassy and asks terms of
peace. 33So therefore, whoever of you
does not renounce all that he has cannot
be my disciple.

About Salt

34 "Salt is good; but if salt has lost its
taste, how shall its saltness be restored?
35It is fit neither for the land nor for the
dunghill; men throw it away. He who has
ears to hear, let him hear."

The Parable of the Lost Sheep

15 Now the tax collectors and sinners
were all drawing near to hear him.
2And the Pharisees and the scribes mur-
mured, saying, "This man receives sin-
ners and eats with them."
3 So he told them this parable: 4"What
man of you, having a hundred sheep, if
he has lost one of them, does not leave
the ninety-nine in the wilderness, and
go after the one which is lost, until he
finds it? 5And when he has found it, he
lays it on his shoulders, rejoicing. 6And
when he comes home, he calls together
his friends and his neighbors, saying to
them, 'Rejoice with me, for I have found

my sheep which was lost.’ 7 Just so, I tell
you, there will be more joy in heaven
over one sinner who repents than over
ninety-nine righteous persons who need
no repentance.

The Parable of the Lost Coin

8 “Or what woman, having ten silver
coins,[v] if she loses one coin, does not
light a lamp and sweep the house and
seek diligently until she finds it? 9 And
when she has found it, she calls together
her friends and neighbors, saying, ‘Re-
joice with me, for I have found the coin
which I had lost.’ 10 Just so, I tell you, there
is joy before the angels of God over one
sinner who repents.”

The Parable of the Prodigal and His Brother

11 And he said, “There was a man who
had two sons; 12 and the younger of them
said to his father, ‘Father, give me the
share of property that falls to me.’ And
he divided his living between them. 13 Not
many days later, the younger son gath-
ered all he had and took his journey into
a far country, and there he squandered
his property in loose living. 14 And when
he had spent everything, a great famine
arose in that country, and he began to be
in want. 15 So he went and joined himself
to one of the citizens of that country, who
sent him into his fields to feed swine.
16 And he would gladly have fed on[w]
the pods that the swine ate; and no one
gave him anything. 17 But when he came
to himself he said, ‘How many of my fa-
ther’s hired servants have bread enough
and to spare, but I perish here with hun-
ger! 18 I will arise and go to my father, and
I will say to him, “Father, I have sinned
against heaven and before you; 19 I am
no longer worthy to be called your son;
treat me as one of your hired servants.” ’
20 And he arose and came to his father.
But while he was yet at a distance, his
father saw him and had compassion, and
ran and embraced him and kissed him.
21 And the son said to him, ‘Father, I have
sinned against heaven and before you;
I am no longer worthy to be called your
son.’[x] 22 But the father said to his servants,
‘Bring quickly the best robe, and put it
on him; and put a ring on his hand, and
shoes on his feet; 23 and bring the fatted
calf and kill it, and let us eat and make
merry; 24 for this my son was dead, and
is alive again; he was lost, and is found.’
And they began to make merry.

25 “Now his elder son was in the field;
and as he came and drew near to the
house, he heard music and dancing.
26 And he called one of the servants and
asked what this meant. 27 And he said to
him, ‘Your brother has come, and your
father has killed the fatted calf, because
he has received him safe and sound.’ 28 But
he was angry and refused to go in. His fa-
ther came out and entreated him, 29 but
he answered his father, ‘Lo, these many
years I have served you, and I never dis-
obeyed your command; yet you never
gave me a kid, that I might make merry
with my friends. 30 But when this son of
yours came, who has devoured your liv-
ing with harlots, you killed for him the
fatted calf!’ 31 And he said to him, ‘Son, you
are always with me, and all that is mine is
yours. 32 It was fitting to make merry and
be glad, for this your brother was dead,
and is alive; he was lost, and is found.’ ”

The Parable of the Dishonest Manager

16 He also said to the disciples, “There
was a rich man who had a steward,
and charges were brought to him that
this man was wasting his goods. 2 And he
called him and said to him, ‘What is this
that I hear about you? Turn in the account

[v] **15.8** The drachma, rendered here by *silver coin,* was about a day’s wage for a laborer [w] **15.16** Other ancient authorities read *filled his belly with* [x] **15.21** Other ancient authorities add *treat me as one of your hired servants*

of your stewardship, for you can no lon-
ger be steward.' 3 And the steward said to
himself, 'What shall I do, since my master
is taking the stewardship away from me?
I am not strong enough to dig, and I am
ashamed to beg. 4 I have decided what to do,
so that people may receive me into their
houses when I am put out of the steward-
ship.' 5 So, summoning his master's debt-
ors one by one, he said to the first, 'How
much do you owe my master?' 6 He said, 'A
hundred measures of oil.' And he said to
him, 'Take your bill, and sit down quickly
and write fifty.' 7 Then he said to another,
'And how much do you owe?' He said, 'A
hundred measures of wheat.' He said to
him, 'Take your bill, and write eighty.'
8 The master commended the dishonest
steward for his prudence; for the sons of
this world[y] are wiser in their own genera-
tion than the sons of light. 9 And I tell you,
make friends for yourselves by means of
unrighteous mammon, so that when it
fails they may receive you into the eternal
habitations.

10 "He who is faithful in a very little is
faithful also in much; and he who is dis-
honest in a very little is dishonest also in
much. 11 If then you have not been faith-
ful in the unrighteous mammon, who
will entrust to you the true riches? 12 And
if you have not been faithful in that
which is another's, who will give you
that which is your own? 13 No servant can
serve two masters; for either he will hate
the one and love the other, or he will be
devoted to the one and despise the other.
You cannot serve God and mammon."

The Law and the Kingdom of God

14 The Pharisees, who were lovers of
money, heard all this, and they scoffed at
him. 15 But he said to them, "You are those
who justify yourselves before men, but
God knows your hearts; for what is ex-
alted among men is an abomination in
the sight of God.

16 "The law and the prophets were un-
til John; since then the good news of the
kingdom of God is preached, and every
one enters it violently. 17 But it is easier
for heaven and earth to pass away, than
for one dot of the law to become void.

18 "Every one who divorces his wife
and marries another commits adultery,
and he who marries a woman divorced
from her husband commits adultery.

The Rich Man and Lazarus

19 "There was a rich man, who was
clothed in purple and fine linen and who
feasted sumptuously every day. 20 And at
his gate lay a poor man named Laz'arus,
full of sores, 21 who desired to be fed with
what fell from the rich man's table; more-
over the dogs came and licked his sores.
22 The poor man died and was carried
by the angels to Abraham's bosom. The
rich man also died and was buried; 23 and
in Hades, being in torment, he lifted up
his eyes, and saw Abraham far off and
Laz'arus in his bosom. 24 And he called
out, 'Father Abraham, have mercy upon
me, and send Laz'arus to dip the end of
his finger in water and cool my tongue;
for I am in anguish in this flame.' 25 But
Abraham said, 'Son, remember that you
in your lifetime received your good
things, and Laz'arus in like manner evil
things; but now he is comforted here,
and you are in anguish. 26 And besides all
this, between us and you a great chasm
has been fixed, in order that those who
would pass from here to you may not be
able, and none may cross from there to
us.' 27 And he said, 'Then I beg you, father,
to send him to my father's house, 28 for I
have five brothers, so that he may warn
them, lest they also come into this place
of torment.' 29 But Abraham said, 'They
have Moses and the prophets; let them
hear them.' 30 And he said, 'No, father
Abraham; but if some one goes to them
from the dead, they will repent.' 31 He said

[y] **16.8** Greek *age*

to him, 'If they do not hear Moses and the
prophets, neither will they be convinced
if some one should rise from the dead.' "

Some Sayings of Jesus

17 And he said to his disciples, "Temp-
tations to sin[z] are sure to come; but
woe to him by whom they come! 2It would
be better for him if a millstone were
hung round his neck and he were cast
into the sea, than that he should cause
one of these little ones to sin.[a] 3Take heed
to yourselves; if your brother sins, re-
buke him, and if he repents, forgive him;
4and if he sins against you seven times in
the day, and turns to you seven times, and
says, 'I repent,' you must forgive him."
5 The apostles said to the Lord, "In-
crease our faith!" 6And the Lord said, "If
you had faith as a grain of mustard seed,
you could say to this sycamine tree, 'Be
rooted up, and be planted in the sea,' and
it would obey you.
7 "Will any one of you, who has a ser-
vant plowing or keeping sheep, say to
him when he has come in from the field,
'Come at once and sit down at table'?
8Will he not rather say to him, 'Prepare
supper for me, and gird yourself and
serve me, till I eat and drink; and after-
ward you shall eat and drink'? 9Does he
thank the servant because he did what
was commanded? 10So you also, when
you have done all that is commanded
you, say, 'We are unworthy servants; we
have only done what was our duty.' "

Jesus Cleanses Ten Lepers

11 On the way to Jerusalem he was pass-
ing along between Samar'ia and Galilee.
12And as he entered a village, he was
met by ten lepers, who stood at a dis-
tance 13and lifted up their voices and
said, "Jesus, Master, have mercy on us."
14When he saw them he said to them,
"Go and show yourselves to the priests."
And as they went they were cleansed.
15Then one of them, when he saw that he
was healed, turned back, praising God
with a loud voice; 16and he fell on his face
at Jesus' feet, giving him thanks. Now
he was a Samaritan. 17Then said Jesus,
"Were not ten cleansed? Where are the
nine? 18Was no one found to return and
give praise to God except this foreigner?"
19And he said to him, "Rise and go your
way; your faith has made you well."

The Coming of the Kingdom

20 Being asked by the Pharisees when
the kingdom of God was coming, he an-
swered them, "The kingdom of God is not
coming with signs to be observed; 21nor
will they say, 'Lo, here it is!' or 'There!'
for behold, the kingdom of God is in the
midst of you."[b]
22 And he said to the disciples, "The
days are coming when you will desire
to see one of the days of the Son of man,
and you will not see it. 23And they will
say to you, 'Lo, there!' or 'Lo, here!' Do
not go, do not follow them. 24For as the
lightning flashes and lights up the sky
from one side to the other, so will the Son
of man be in his day.[c] 25But first he must
suffer many things and be rejected by
this generation. 26As it was in the days of
Noah, so will it be in the days of the Son
of man. 27They ate, they drank, they mar-
ried, they were given in marriage, until
the day when Noah entered the ark, and
the flood came and destroyed them all.
28Likewise as it was in the days of Lot—
they ate, they drank, they bought, they
sold, they planted, they built, 29but on the
day when Lot went out from Sodom fire
and brimstone rained from heaven and
destroyed them all— 30so will it be on the
day when the Son of man is revealed. 31On
that day, let him who is on the housetop,
with his goods in the house, not come
down to take them away; and likewise

[z] **17.1** Greek *stumbling blocks* [a] **17.2** Greek *stumble* [b] **17.21** Or *within you* [c] **17.24** Other ancient authorities omit *in his day*

let him who is in the field not turn back.
[32]Remember Lot's wife. [33]Whoever seeks
to gain his life will lose it, but whoever
loses his life will preserve it. [34]I tell you,
in that night there will be two men in one
bed; one will be taken and the other left.
[35]There will be two women grinding to-
gether; one will be taken and the other
left."[d] [37]And they said to him, "Where,
Lord?" He said to them, "Where the body
is, there the eagles[e] will be gathered
together."

The Parable of the Widow and the Unjust Judge

18 And he told them a parable, to the
effect that they ought always to
pray and not lose heart. [2]He said, "In a
certain city there was a judge who nei-
ther feared God nor regarded man; [3]and
there was a widow in that city who kept
coming to him and saying, 'Vindicate me
against my adversary.' [4]For a while he re-
fused; but afterward he said to himself,
'Though I neither fear God nor regard
man, [5]yet because this widow bothers
me, I will vindicate her, or she will wear
me out by her continual coming.'" [6]And
the Lord said, "Hear what the unrigh-
teous judge says. [7]And will not God vin-
dicate his elect, who cry to him day and
night? Will he delay long over them? [8]I
tell you, he will vindicate them speed-
ily. Nevertheless, when the Son of man
comes, will he find faith on earth?"

The Parable of the Pharisee and the Tax Collector

9 He also told this parable to some who
trusted in themselves that they were
righteous and despised others: [10]"Two
men went up into the temple to pray, one
a Pharisee and the other a tax collector.
[11]The Pharisee stood and prayed thus
with himself, 'God, I thank thee that I am
not like other men, extortioners, unjust,
adulterers, or even like this tax collector.
[12]I fast twice a week, I give tithes of all
that I get.' [13]But the tax collector, standing
far off, would not even lift up his eyes to
heaven, but beat his breast, saying, 'God,
be merciful to me a sinner!' [14]I tell you,
this man went down to his house justi-
fied rather than the other; for every one
who exalts himself will be humbled, but
he who humbles himself will be exalted."

Jesus Blesses Little Children

15 Now they were bringing even infants
to him that he might touch them; and
when the disciples saw it, they rebuked
them. [16]But Jesus called them to him, say-
ing, "Let the children come to me, and
do not hinder them; for to such belongs
the kingdom of God. [17]Truly, I say to you,
whoever does not receive the kingdom
of God like a child shall not enter it."

The Rich Ruler

18 And a ruler asked him, "Good Teacher,
what shall I do to inherit eternal life?"
[19]And Jesus said to him, "Why do you call
me good? No one is good but God alone.
[20]You know the commandments: 'Do not
commit adultery, Do not kill, Do not steal,
Do not bear false witness, Honor your
father and mother.'" [21]And he said, "All
these I have observed from my youth."
[22]And when Jesus heard it, he said to him,
"One thing you still lack. Sell all that you
have and distribute to the poor, and you
will have treasure in heaven; and come,
follow me." [23]But when he heard this he
became sad, for he was very rich. [24]Jesus
looking at him said, "How hard it is for
those who have riches to enter the king-
dom of God! [25]For it is easier for a camel
to go through the eye of a needle than
for a rich man to enter the kingdom of
God." [26]Those who heard it said, "Then
who can be saved?" [27]But he said, "What
is impossible with men is possible with

[d]**17.35** Other ancient authorities add verse 36, *"Two men will be in the field; one will be taken and the other left"* [e]**17.37** Or *vultures*

God." 28 And Peter said, "Lo, we have left
our homes and followed you." 29 And he
said to them, "Truly, I say to you, there
is no man who has left house or wife or
brothers or parents or children, for the
sake of the kingdom of God, 30 who will
not receive manifold more in this time,
and in the age to come eternal life."

A Third Time Jesus Foretells His Death and Resurrection

31 And taking the twelve, he said to
them, "Behold, we are going up to Jeru-
salem, and everything that is written of
the Son of man by the prophets will be
accomplished. 32 For he will be delivered
to the Gentiles, and will be mocked and
shamefully treated and spit upon; 33 they
will scourge him and kill him, and on
the third day he will rise." 34 But they un-
derstood none of these things; this say-
ing was hid from them, and they did not
grasp what was said.

Jesus Heals a Blind Beggar Near Jericho

35 As he drew near to Jericho, a blind
man was sitting by the roadside beg-
ging; 36 and hearing a multitude going
by, he inquired what this meant. 37 They
told him, "Jesus of Nazareth is passing
by." 38 And he cried, "Jesus, Son of Da-
vid, have mercy on me!" 39 And those
who were in front rebuked him, telling
him to be silent; but he cried out all the
more, "Son of David, have mercy on me!"
40 And Jesus stopped, and commanded
him to be brought to him; and when he
came near, he asked him, 41 "What do you
want me to do for you?" He said, "Lord,
let me receive my sight." 42 And Jesus said
to him, "Receive your sight; your faith
has made you well." 43 And immediately
he received his sight and followed him,
glorifying God; and all the people, when
they saw it, gave praise to God.

Jesus and Zacchaeus

19 He entered Jericho and was pass-
ing through. 2 And there was a man
named Zacchae'us; he was a chief tax col-
lector, and rich. 3 And he sought to see
who Jesus was, but could not, on account
of the crowd, because he was small of
stature. 4 So he ran on ahead and climbed
up into a sycamore tree to see him, for
he was to pass that way. 5 And when Jesus
came to the place, he looked up and said
to him, "Zacchae'us, make haste and come
down; for I must stay at your house to-
day." 6 So he made haste and came down,
and received him joyfully. 7 And when
they saw it they all murmured, "He has
gone in to be the guest of a man who is
a sinner." 8 And Zacchae'us stood and said
to the Lord, "Behold, Lord, the half of my
goods I give to the poor; and if I have de-
frauded any one of anything, I restore it
fourfold." 9 And Jesus said to him, "Today
salvation has come to this house, since
he also is a son of Abraham. 10 For the Son
of man came to seek and to save the lost."

The Parable of the Ten Pounds

11 As they heard these things, he pro-
ceeded to tell a parable, because he was
near to Jerusalem, and because they
supposed that the kingdom of God was
to appear immediately. 12 He said there-
fore, "A nobleman went into a far coun-
try to receive kingly power[f] and then
return. 13 Calling ten of his servants, he
gave them ten pounds,[g] and said to them,
'Trade with these till I come.' 14 But his cit-
izens hated him and sent an embassy af-
ter him, saying, 'We do not want this man
to reign over us.' 15 When he returned,
having received the kingly power,[h] he
commanded these servants, to whom he
had given the money, to be called to him,
that he might know what they had gained
by trading. 16 The first came before him,
saying, 'Lord, your pound has made ten

[f] **19.12** Greek *a kingdom* [g] **19.13** The mina, rendered here by *pound*, was about three months' wages for a laborer [h] **19.15** Greek *a kingdom*

pounds more.' 17And he said to him, 'Well
done, good servant! Because you have
been faithful in a very little, you shall
have authority over ten cities.' 18And the
second came, saying, 'Lord, your pound
has made five pounds.' 19And he said to
him, 'And you are to be over five cities.'
20Then another came, saying, 'Lord, here
is your pound, which I kept laid away in a
napkin; 21for I was afraid of you, because
you are a severe man; you take up what
you did not lay down, and reap what you
did not sow.' 22He said to him, 'I will con-
demn you out of your own mouth, you
wicked servant! You knew that I was a
severe man, taking up what I did not lay
down and reaping what I did not sow?
23Why then did you not put my money
into the bank, and at my coming I should
have collected it with interest?' 24And
he said to those who stood by, 'Take the
pound from him, and give it to him who
has the ten pounds.' 25(And they said to
him, 'Lord, he has ten pounds!') 26'I tell
you, that to every one who has will more
be given; but from him who has not, even
what he has will be taken away. 27But as
for these enemies of mine, who did not
want me to reign over them, bring them
here and slay them before me.' "

Jesus' Triumphal Entry into Jerusalem

28 And when he had said this, he went on
ahead, going up to Jerusalem. 29When he
drew near to Beth'phage and Bethany, at
the mount that is called Olivet, he sent
two of the disciples, 30saying, "Go into the
village opposite, where on entering you
will find a colt tied, on which no one has
ever yet sat; untie it and bring it here. 31If
any one asks you, 'Why are you untying
it?' you shall say this, 'The Lord has need
of it.' " 32So those who were sent went away
and found it as he had told them. 33And as
they were untying the colt, its owners
said to them, "Why are you untying the
colt?" 34And they said, "The Lord has need
of it." 35And they brought it to Jesus, and
throwing their garments on the colt they
set Jesus upon it. 36And as he rode along,
they spread their garments on the road.
37As he was now drawing near, at the de-
scent of the Mount of Olives, the whole
multitude of the disciples began to re-
joice and praise God with a loud voice for
all the mighty works that they had seen,
38saying, "Blessed is the King who comes
in the name of the Lord! Peace in heaven
and glory in the highest!" 39And some of
the Pharisees in the multitude said to
him, "Teacher, rebuke your disciples."
40He answered, "I tell you, if these were
silent, the very stones would cry out."

Jesus Weeps over Jerusalem

41 And when he drew near and saw the
city he wept over it, 42saying, "Would
that even today you knew the things that
make for peace! But now they are hid
from your eyes. 43For the days shall come
upon you, when your enemies will cast
up a bank about you and surround you,
and hem you in on every side, 44and dash
you to the ground, you and your children
within you, and they will not leave one
stone upon another in you; because you
did not know the time of your visitation."

Jesus Cleanses the Temple

45 And he entered the temple and began
to drive out those who sold, 46saying to
them, "It is written, 'My house shall be a
house of prayer'; but you have made it a
den of robbers."

47 And he was teaching daily in the
temple. The chief priests and the scribes
and the principal men of the people
sought to destroy him; 48but they did not
find anything they could do, for all the
people hung upon his words.

The Authority of Jesus Questioned

20 One day, as he was teaching the
people in the temple and preach-
ing the gospel, the chief priests and the
scribes with the elders came up 2and said

to him, "Tell us by what authority you do these things, or who it is that gave you this authority." [3]He answered them, "I also will ask you a question; now tell me, [4]Was the baptism of John from heaven or from men?" [5]And they discussed it with one another, saying, "If we say, 'From heaven,' he will say, 'Why did you not believe him?' [6]But if we say, 'From men,' all the people will stone us; for they are convinced that John was a prophet." [7]So they answered that they did not know whence it was. [8]And Jesus said to them, "Neither will I tell you by what authority I do these things."

The Parable of the Wicked Tenants

9 And he began to tell the people this parable: "A man planted a vineyard, and let it out to tenants, and went into another country for a long while. [10]When the time came, he sent a servant to the tenants, that they should give him some of the fruit of the vineyard; but the tenants beat him, and sent him away empty-handed. [11]And he sent another servant; him also they beat and treated shamefully, and sent him away empty-handed. [12]And he sent yet a third; this one they wounded and cast out. [13]Then the owner of the vineyard said, 'What shall I do? I will send my beloved son; it may be they will respect him.' [14]But when the tenants saw him, they said to themselves, 'This is the heir; let us kill him, that the inheritance may be ours.' [15]And they cast him out of the vineyard and killed him. What then will the owner of the vineyard do to them? [16]He will come and destroy those tenants, and give the vineyard to others." When they heard this, they said, "God forbid!" [17]But he looked at them and said, "What then is this that is written:

> 'The very stone which the builders
> rejected
> has become the head of the corner'?

[18]Every one who falls on that stone will be broken to pieces; but when it falls on any one it will crush him."

The Question about Paying Taxes

19 The scribes and the chief priests tried to lay hands on him at that very hour, but they feared the people; for they perceived that he had told this parable against them. [20]So they watched him, and sent spies, who pretended to be sincere, that they might take hold of what he said, so as to deliver him up to the authority and jurisdiction of the governor. [21]They asked him, "Teacher, we know that you speak and teach rightly, and show no partiality, but truly teach the way of God. [22]Is it lawful for us to give tribute to Caesar, or not?" [23]But he perceived their craftiness, and said to them, [24]"Show me a coin.[i] Whose likeness and inscription has it?" They said, "Caesar's." [25]He said to them, "Then render to Caesar the things that are Caesar's, and to God the things that are God's." [26]And they were not able in the presence of the people to catch him by what he said; but marveling at his answer they were silent.

The Question about the Resurrection

27 There came to him some Sad′ducees, those who say that there is no resurrection, [28]and they asked him a question, saying, "Teacher, Moses wrote for us that if a man's brother dies, having a wife but no children, the man[j] must take the wife and raise up children for his brother. [29]Now there were seven brothers; the first took a wife, and died without children; [30]and the second [31]and the third took her, and likewise all seven left no children and died. [32]Afterward the woman also died. [33]In the resurrection, therefore, whose wife will the woman be? For the seven had her as wife."

34 And Jesus said to them, "The sons of this age marry and are given in marriage;

[i]**20.24** Greek *denarius* [j]**20.28** Greek *his brother*

35 but those who are accounted worthy to
attain to that age and to the resurrection
from the dead neither marry nor are
given in marriage, 36 for they cannot die
any more, because they are equal to an-
gels and are sons of God, being sons of
the resurrection. 37 But that the dead are
raised, even Moses showed, in the pas-
sage about the bush, where he calls the
Lord the God of Abraham and the God
of Isaac and the God of Jacob. 38 Now he is
not God of the dead, but of the living; for
all live to him." 39 And some of the scribes
answered, "Teacher, you have spoken
well." 40 For they no longer dared to ask
him any question.

The Question about David's Son

41 But he said to them, "How can they
say that the Christ is David's son? 42 For
David himself says in the Book of Psalms,

'The Lord said to my Lord,
Sit at my right hand,
43 till I make thy enemies a stool for
thy feet.'

44 David thus calls him Lord; so how is he
his son?"

Jesus Denounces the Scribes

45 And in the hearing of all the people
he said to his disciples, 46 "Beware of
the scribes, who like to go about in long
robes, and love salutations in the mar-
ket places and the best seats in the syna-
gogues and the places of honor at feasts,
47 who devour widows' houses and for a
pretense make long prayers. They will
receive the greater condemnation."

The Widow's Offering

21 He looked up and saw the rich put-
ting their gifts into the treasury;
2 and he saw a poor widow put in two cop-
per coins. 3 And he said, "Truly I tell you,
this poor widow has put in more than all
of them; 4 for they all contributed out of
their abundance, but she out of her pov-
erty put in all the living that she had."

The Destruction of the Temple Foretold

5 And as some spoke of the temple, how
it was adorned with noble stones and
offerings, he said, 6 "As for these things
which you see, the days will come when
there shall not be left here one stone
upon another that will not be thrown
down." 7 And they asked him, "Teacher,
when will this be, and what will be the
sign when this is about to take place?"
8 And he said, "Take heed that you are
not led astray; for many will come in my
name, saying, 'I am he!' and, 'The time
is at hand!' Do not go after them. 9 And
when you hear of wars and tumults, do
not be terrified; for this must first take
place, but the end will not be at once."

Signs and Persecutions

10 Then he said to them, "Nation will
rise against nation, and kingdom against
kingdom; 11 there will be great earth-
quakes, and in various places famines
and pestilences; and there will be terrors
and great signs from heaven. 12 But before
all this they will lay their hands on you
and persecute you, delivering you up
to the synagogues and prisons, and you
will be brought before kings and gover-
nors for my name's sake. 13 This will be a
time for you to bear testimony. 14 Settle it
therefore in your minds, not to meditate
beforehand how to answer; 15 for I will
give you a mouth and wisdom, which
none of your adversaries will be able to
withstand or contradict. 16 You will be de-
livered up even by parents and brothers
and kinsmen and friends, and some of
you they will put to death; 17 you will be
hated by all for my name's sake. 18 But not
a hair of your head will perish. 19 By your
endurance you will gain your lives.

The Destruction of Jerusalem Foretold

20 "But when you see Jerusalem sur-
rounded by armies, then know that
its desolation has come near. 21 Then
let those who are in Judea flee to the

mountains, and let those who are in-
side the city depart, and let not those
who are out in the country enter it; 22 for
these are days of vengeance, to fulfil all
that is written. 23 Alas for those who are
with child and for those who give suck
in those days! For great distress shall
be upon the earth and wrath upon this
people; 24 they will fall by the edge of
the sword, and be led captive among all
nations; and Jerusalem will be trodden
down by the Gentiles, until the times of
the Gentiles are fulfilled.

The Coming of the Son of Man

25 "And there will be signs in sun and
moon and stars, and upon the earth
distress of nations in perplexity at the
roaring of the sea and the waves, 26 men
fainting with fear and with foreboding
of what is coming on the world; for the
powers of the heavens will be shaken.
27 And then they will see the Son of man
coming in a cloud with power and great
glory. 28 Now when these things begin to
take place, look up and raise your heads,
because your redemption is drawing
near."

The Lesson of the Fig Tree

29 And he told them a parable: "Look at
the fig tree, and all the trees; 30 as soon as
they come out in leaf, you see for your-
selves and know that the summer is al-
ready near. 31 So also, when you see these
things taking place, you know that the
kingdom of God is near. 32 Truly, I say to
you, this generation will not pass away
till all has taken place. 33 Heaven and
earth will pass away, but my words will
not pass away.

Exhortation to Watch

34 "But take heed to yourselves lest your
hearts be weighed down with dissipation
and drunkenness and cares of this life,
and that day come upon you suddenly
like a snare; 35 for it will come upon all
who dwell upon the face of the whole
earth. 36 But watch at all times, praying
that you may have strength to escape all
these things that will take place, and to
stand before the Son of man."

37 And every day he was teaching in
the temple, but at night he went out and
lodged on the mount called Olivet. 38 And
early in the morning all the people came
to him in the temple to hear him.

The Plot to Kill Jesus

22 Now the feast of Unleavened
Bread drew near, which is called
the Passover. 2 And the chief priests and
the scribes were seeking how to put him
to death; for they feared the people.

3 Then Satan entered into Judas called
Iscariot, who was of the number of the
twelve; 4 he went away and conferred
with the chief priests and captains how
he might betray him to them. 5 And they
were glad, and engaged to give him
money. 6 So he agreed, and sought an op-
portunity to betray him to them in the
absence of the multitude.

The Preparation of the Passover

7 Then came the day of Unleavened
Bread, on which the passover lamb had
to be sacrificed. 8 So Jesus[k] sent Peter and
John, saying, "Go and prepare the pass-
over for us, that we may eat it." 9 They
said to him, "Where will you have us
prepare it?" 10 He said to them, "Behold,
when you have entered the city, a man
carrying a jar of water will meet you; fol-
low him into the house which he enters,
11 and tell the householder, 'The Teacher
says to you, Where is the guest room,
where I am to eat the passover with my
disciples?' 12 And he will show you a
large upper room furnished; there make
ready." 13 And they went, and found it as
he had told them; and they prepared the
passover.

[k] **22.8** Greek *he*

The Institution of the Lord's Supper

14 And when the hour came, he sat at ta-
ble, and the apostles with him. 15And he
said to them, "I have earnestly desired
to eat this passover with you before I
suffer; 16for I tell you I shall not eat it[l] un-
til it is fulfilled in the kingdom of God."
17And he took a cup, and when he had
given thanks he said, "Take this, and di-
vide it among yourselves; 18for I tell you
that from now on I shall not drink of
the fruit of the vine until the kingdom
of God comes." 19And he took bread, and
when he had given thanks he broke it
and gave it to them, saying, "This is my
body which is given for you. Do this in
remembrance of me." 20And likewise
the cup after supper, saying, "This cup
which is poured out for you is the new
covenant in my blood.[m] 21But behold the
hand of him who betrays me is with me
on the table. 22For the Son of man goes as
it has been determined; but woe to that
man by whom he is betrayed!" 23And they
began to question one another, which of
them it was that would do this.

The Dispute about Greatness

24 A dispute also arose among them,
which of them was to be regarded as the
greatest. 25And he said to them, "The
kings of the Gentiles exercise lordship
over them; and those in authority over
them are called benefactors. 26But not so
with you; rather let the greatest among
you become as the youngest, and the
leader as one who serves. 27For which is
the greater, one who sits at table, or one
who serves? Is it not the one who sits at
table? But I am among you as one who
serves.

28 "You are those who have contin-
ued with me in my trials; 29as my Father
appointed a kingdom for me, so do I
appoint for you 30that you may eat and
drink at my table in my kingdom, and sit
on thrones judging the twelve tribes of
Israel.

Jesus Predicts Peter's Denial

31 "Simon, Simon, behold, Satan de-
manded to have you,[n] that he might sift
you[o] like wheat, 32but I have prayed for
you that your faith may not fail; and
when you have turned again, strengthen
your brethren." 33And he said to him,
"Lord, I am ready to go with you to prison
and to death." 34He said, "I tell you, Peter,
the cock will not crow this day, until you
three times deny that you know me."

Purse, Bag, and Sword

35 And he said to them, "When I sent you
out with no purse or bag or sandals, did
you lack anything?" They said, "Noth-
ing." 36He said to them, "But now, let him
who has a purse take it, and likewise a
bag. And let him who has no sword sell
his mantle and buy one. 37For I tell you
that this scripture must be fulfilled in
me, 'And he was reckoned with trans-
gressors'; for what is written about
me has its fulfilment." 38And they said,
"Look, Lord, here are two swords." And
he said to them, "It is enough."

Jesus Prays on the Mount of Olives

39 And he came out, and went, as was his
custom, to the Mount of Olives; and the
disciples followed him. 40And when he
came to the place he said to them, "Pray
that you may not enter into temptation."
41And he withdrew from them about
a stone's throw, and knelt down and
prayed, 42"Father, if thou art willing, re-
move this cup from me; nevertheless not
my will, but thine, be done." 43And there
appeared to him an angel from heaven,

[l] **22.16** Other ancient authorities read *never eat it again* [m] **22.20** Other authorities omit *which is given for you. Do this in remebrance of me." 20And likewise the cup after supper, saying, "This cup which is poured out for you is the new covenant in my blood.* [n] **22.31** The Greek word for *you* here is plural; in verse 32 it is singular [o] **22.31** The Greek word for *you* here is plural; in verse 32 it is singular

strengthening him. [44]And being in an agony he prayed more earnestly; and his sweat became like great drops of blood falling down upon the ground.[p] [45]And when he rose from prayer, he came to the disciples and found them sleeping for sorrow, [46]and he said to them, "Why do you sleep? Rise and pray that you may not enter into temptation."

The Betrayal and Arrest of Jesus

47 While he was still speaking, there came a crowd, and the man called Judas, one of the twelve, was leading them. He drew near to Jesus to kiss him; [48]but Jesus said to him, "Judas, would you betray the Son of man with a kiss?" [49]And when those who were about him saw what would follow, they said, "Lord, shall we strike with the sword?" [50]And one of them struck the slave of the high priest and cut off his right ear. [51]But Jesus said, "No more of this!" And he touched his ear and healed him. [52]Then Jesus said to the chief priests and captains of the temple and elders, who had come out against him, "Have you come out as against a robber, with swords and clubs? [53]When I was with you day after day in the temple, you did not lay hands on me. But this is your hour, and the power of darkness."

Peter Denies Jesus

54 Then they seized him and led him away, bringing him into the high priest's house. Peter followed at a distance; [55]and when they had kindled a fire in the middle of the courtyard and sat down together, Peter sat among them. [56]Then a maid, seeing him as he sat in the light and gazing at him, said, "This man also was with him." [57]But he denied it, saying, "Woman, I do not know him." [58]And a little later some one else saw him and said, "You also are one of them." But Peter said, "Man, I am not." [59]And after an interval of about an hour still another insisted, saying, "Certainly this man also was with him; for he is a Galilean." [60]But Peter said, "Man, I do not know what you are saying." And immediately, while he was still speaking, the cock crowed. [61]And the Lord turned and looked at Peter. And Peter remembered the word of the Lord, how he had said to him, "Before the cock crows today, you will deny me three times." [62]And he went out and wept bitterly.

The Mocking and Beating of Jesus

63 Now the men who were holding Jesus mocked him and beat him; [64]they also blindfolded him and asked him, "Prophesy! Who is it that struck you?" [65]And they spoke many other words against him, reviling him.

Jesus before the Council

66 When day came, the assembly of the elders of the people gathered together, both chief priests and scribes; and they led him away to their council, and they said, [67]"If you are the Christ, tell us." But he said to them, "If I tell you, you will not believe; [68]and if I ask you, you will not answer. [69]But from now on the Son of man shall be seated at the right hand of the power of God." [70]And they all said, "Are you the Son of God, then?" And he said to them, "You say that I am." [71]And they said, "What further testimony do we need? We have heard it ourselves from his own lips."

Jesus before Pilate

23 Then the whole company of them arose, and brought him before Pilate. [2]And they began to accuse him, saying, "We found this man perverting our nation, and forbidding us to give tribute to Caesar, and saying that he himself is Christ a king." [3]And Pilate asked him, "Are you the King of the Jews?" And he answered him, "You have said so." [4]And Pilate said to the chief priests and the

[p]**22.44** Other ancient authorities omit verses 43 and 44.

multitudes, "I find no crime in this man."
[5]But they were urgent, saying, "He stirs
up the people, teaching throughout all
Judea, from Galilee even to this place."

Jesus before Herod

6 When Pilate heard this, he asked
whether the man was a Galilean. [7]And
when he learned that he belonged to
Herod's jurisdiction, he sent him over
to Herod, who was himself in Jerusalem
at that time. [8]When Herod saw Jesus, he
was very glad, for he had long desired
to see him, because he had heard about
him, and he was hoping to see some sign
done by him. [9]So he questioned him at
some length; but he made no answer.
[10]The chief priests and the scribes stood
by, vehemently accusing him. [11]And
Herod with his soldiers treated him with
contempt and mocked him; then, array-
ing him in gorgeous apparel, he sent him
back to Pilate. [12]And Herod and Pilate be-
came friends with each other that very
day, for before this they had been at en-
mity with each other.

Jesus Sentenced to Death

13 Pilate then called together the chief
priests and the rulers and the people,
[14]and said to them, "You brought me this
man as one who was perverting the peo-
ple; and after examining him before you,
behold, I did not find this man guilty of
any of your charges against him; [15]nei-
ther did Herod, for he sent him back to
us. Behold, nothing deserving death has
been done by him; [16]I will therefore chas-
tise him and release him."[q]

18 But they all cried out together,
"Away with this man, and release to
us Barab′bas"— [19]a man who had been
thrown into prison for an insurrection
started in the city, and for murder. [20]Pi-
late addressed them once more, desiring
to release Jesus; [21]but they shouted out,
"Crucify, crucify him!" [22]A third time
he said to them, "Why, what evil has he
done? I have found in him no crime de-
serving death; I will therefore chastise
him and release him." [23]But they were
urgent, demanding with loud cries that
he should be crucified. And their voices
prevailed. [24]So Pilate gave sentence that
their demand should be granted. [25]He
released the man who had been thrown
into prison for insurrection and mur-
der, whom they asked for; but Jesus he
delivered up to their will.

The Crucifixion of Jesus

26 And as they led him away, they seized
one Simon of Cyre′ne, who was coming
in from the country, and laid on him
the cross, to carry it behind Jesus. [27]And
there followed him a great multitude of
the people, and of women who bewailed
and lamented him. [28]But Jesus turning
to them said, "Daughters of Jerusalem,
do not weep for me, but weep for your-
selves and for your children. [29]For be-
hold, the days are coming when they
will say, 'Blessed are the barren, and the
wombs that never bore, and the breasts
that never gave suck!' [30]Then they will
begin to say to the mountains, 'Fall on us';
and to the hills, 'Cover us.' [31]For if they do
this when the wood is green, what will
happen when it is dry?"

32 Two others also, who were crim-
inals, were led away to be put to death
with him. [33]And when they came to the
place which is called The Skull, there
they crucified him, and the criminals,
one on the right and one on the left. [34]And
Jesus said, "Father, forgive them; for they
know not what they do."[r] And they cast
lots to divide his garments. [35]And the
people stood by, watching; but the rulers
scoffed at him, saying, "He saved others;

[q] **23.16** Here, or after verse 19, other ancient authorities add verse 17, *Now he was obliged to release one man to them at the festival*

[r] **23.34** Other ancient authorities omit the sentence *And Jesus . . . what they do*

let him save himself, if he is the Christ of
God, his Chosen One!" 36 The soldiers also
mocked him, coming up and offering
him vinegar, 37 and saying, "If you are the
King of the Jews, save yourself!" 38 There
was also an inscription over him,[s] "This
is the King of the Jews."

39 One of the criminals who were
hanged railed at him, saying, "Are you
not the Christ? Save yourself and us!"
40 But the other rebuked him, saying, "Do
you not fear God, since you are under
the same sentence of condemnation?
41 And we indeed justly; for we are receiv-
ing the due reward of our deeds; but this
man has done nothing wrong." 42 And
he said, "Jesus, remember me when you
come in your kingly power."[t] 43 And he
said to him, "Truly, I say to you, today
you will be with me in Paradise."

The Death of Jesus

44 It was now about the sixth hour, and
there was darkness over the whole land[u]
until the ninth hour, 45 while the sun's
light failed;[v] and the curtain of the tem-
ple was torn in two. 46 Then Jesus, crying
with a loud voice, said, "Father, into thy
hands I commit my spirit!" And hav-
ing said this he breathed his last. 47 Now
when the centurion saw what had taken
place, he praised God, and said, "Cer-
tainly this man was innocent!" 48 And
all the multitudes who assembled to see
the sight, when they saw what had taken
place, returned home beating their
breasts. 49 And all his acquaintances and
the women who had followed him from
Galilee stood at a distance and saw these
things.

The Burial of Jesus

50 Now there was a man named Joseph
from the Jewish town of Arimathe´a. He
was a member of the council, a good and
righteous man, 51 who had not consented
to their purpose and deed, and he was
looking for the kingdom of God. 52 This
man went to Pilate and asked for the
body of Jesus. 53 Then he took it down and
wrapped it in a linen shroud, and laid
him in a rock-hewn tomb, where no one
had ever yet been laid. 54 It was the day of
Preparation, and the sabbath was begin-
ning.[w] 55 The women who had come with
him from Galilee followed, and saw the
tomb, and how his body was laid; 56 then
they returned, and prepared spices and
ointments.

On the sabbath they rested according
to the commandment.

The Resurrection of Jesus

24 But on the first day of the week, at
early dawn, they went to the tomb,
taking the spices which they had pre-
pared. 2 And they found the stone rolled
away from the tomb, 3 but when they went
in they did not find the body.[x] 4 While
they were perplexed about this, behold,
two men stood by them in dazzling ap-
parel; 5 and as they were frightened and
bowed their faces to the ground, the men
said to them, "Why do you seek the liv-
ing among the dead? He is not here, but
has risen.[y] 6 Remember how he told you,
while he was still in Galilee, 7 that the Son
of man must be delivered into the hands
of sinful men, and be crucified, and on
the third day rise." 8 And they remem-
bered his words, 9 and returning from
the tomb they told all this to the eleven
and to all the rest. 10 Now it was Mary
Mag´dalene and Jo-an´na and Mary the
mother of James and the other women
with them who told this to the apostles;
11 but these words seemed to them an idle
tale, and they did not believe them. 12 But

[s] **23.38** Other ancient authorities add *in letters of Greek and Latin and Hebrew* [t] **23.42** Greek *kingdom* [u] **23.44** Or *earth* [v] **23.45** Or *the sun was eclipsed.* Other ancient authorities read *the sun was darkened* [w] **23.54** Greek *was dawning* [x] **24.3** Other ancient authorities add *of the Lord Jesus* [y] **24.5** Other ancient authorities omit *He is not here, but has risen*

Peter rose and ran to the tomb; stooping
and looking in, he saw the linen cloths by
themselves; and he went home wonder-
ing at what had happened.[z]

The Walk to Emmaus

13 That very day two of them were going
to a village named Em'ma'us, about seven
miles[a] from Jerusalem, [14]and talking with
each other about all these things that had
happened. [15]While they were talking and
discussing together, Jesus himself drew
near and went with them. [16]But their
eyes were kept from recognizing him.
[17]And he said to them, "What is this con-
versation which you are holding with
each other as you walk?" And they stood
still, looking sad. [18]Then one of them,
named Cle'opas, answered him, "Are you
the only visitor to Jerusalem who does
not know the things that have happened
there in these days?" [19]And he said to
them, "What things?" And they said to
him, "Concerning Jesus of Nazareth, who
was a prophet mighty in deed and word
before God and all the people, [20]and how
our chief priests and rulers delivered
him up to be condemned to death, and
crucified him. [21]But we had hoped that he
was the one to redeem Israel. Yes, and be-
sides all this, it is now the third day since
this happened. [22]Moreover, some women
of our company amazed us. They were at
the tomb early in the morning [23]and did
not find his body; and they came back
saying that they had even seen a vision
of angels, who said that he was alive.
[24]Some of those who were with us went to
the tomb, and found it just as the women
had said; but him they did not see." [25]And
he said to them, "O foolish men, and slow
of heart to believe all that the prophets
have spoken! [26]Was it not necessary that
the Christ should suffer these things and
enter into his glory?" [27]And beginning
with Moses and all the prophets, he in-
terpreted to them in all the scriptures
the things concerning himself.

28 So they drew near to the village to
which they were going. He appeared to
be going further, [29]but they constrained
him, saying, "Stay with us, for it is toward
evening and the day is now far spent." So
he went in to stay with them. [30]When he
was at table with them, he took the bread
and blessed, and broke it, and gave it to
them. [31]And their eyes were opened and
they recognized him; and he vanished
out of their sight. [32]They said to each
other, "Did not our hearts burn within us
while he talked to us on the road, while he
opened to us the scriptures?" [33]And they
rose that same hour and returned to Je-
rusalem; and they found the eleven gath-
ered together and those who were with
them, [34]who said, "The Lord has risen in-
deed, and has appeared to Simon!" [35]Then
they told what had happened on the road,
and how he was known to them in the
breaking of the bread.

Jesus Appears to His Disciples

36 As they were saying this, Jesus him-
self stood among them, and said to them,
"Peace to you."[b] [37]But they were startled
and frightened, and supposed that they
saw a spirit. [38]And he said to them, "Why
are you troubled, and why do question-
ings rise in your hearts? [39]See my hands
and my feet, that it is I myself; handle
me, and see; for a spirit has not flesh and
bones as you see that I have." [40]And when
he had said this, he showed them his
hands and his feet.[c] [41]And while they still
disbelieved for joy, and wondered, he
said to them, "Have you anything here to
eat?" [42]They gave him a piece of broiled
fish, [43]and he took it and ate before them.

44 Then he said to them, "These are
my words which I spoke to you, while I

[z] **24.12** Other ancient authorities omit verse 12 [a] **24.13** Greek *sixty stadia;* some ancient authorities read *a hundred and sixty stadia* [b] **24.36** Other ancient authorities omit *and said to them, "Peace to you."* [c] **24.40** Other ancient authorities omit verse 40

was still with you, that everything writ-
ten about me in the law of Moses and the
prophets and the psalms must be ful-
filled." 45 Then he opened their minds to
understand the scriptures, 46 and said to
them, "Thus it is written, that the Christ
should suffer and on the third day rise
from the dead, 47 and that repentance and
forgiveness of sins should be preached
in his name to all nations,[d] beginning
from Jerusalem. 48 You are witnesses of
these things. 49 And behold, I send the
promise of my Father upon you; but stay
in the city, until you are clothed with
power from on high."

The Ascension of Jesus

50 Then he led them out as far as Bethany,
and lifting up his hands he blessed them.
51 While he blessed them, he parted from
them and was carried up into heaven.[e]
52 And they worshiped him, and[f] returned
to Jerusalem with great joy, 53 and were
continually in the temple blessing God.

[d] **24.47** Or *nations. Beginning from Jerusalem you are witnesses* [e] **24.51** Other ancient authorities omit *and was carried up into heaven* [f] **24.52** Other ancient authorities omit *worshiped him, and*

The Gospel According to

JOHN

The Word Became Flesh

1 In the beginning was the Word, and
the Word was with God, and the Word
was God. 2He was in the beginning with
God; 3all things were made through him,
and without him was not anything made
that was made. 4In him was life,[a] and
the life was the light of men. 5The light
shines in the darkness, and the darkness
has not overcome it.

6 There was a man sent from God,
whose name was John. 7He came for tes-
timony, to bear witness to the light, that
all might believe through him. 8He was
not the light, but came to bear witness to
the light.

9 The true light that enlightens every
man was coming into the world. 10He was
in the world, and the world was made
through him, yet the world knew him
not. 11He came to his own home, and his
own people received him not. 12But to all
who received him, who believed in his
name, he gave power to become children
of God; 13who were born, not of blood nor
of the will of the flesh nor of the will of
man, but of God.

14 And the Word became flesh and
dwelt among us, full of grace and truth;
we have beheld his glory, glory as of the
only Son from the Father. 15(John bore
witness to him, and cried, "This was
he of whom I said, 'He who comes after
me ranks before me, for he was before
me.'") 16And from his fulness have we
all received, grace upon grace. 17For the
law was given through Moses; grace and
truth came through Jesus Christ. 18No one
has ever seen God; the only Son,[b] who is
in the bosom of the Father, he has made
him known.

The Testimony of John the Baptist

19 And this is the testimony of John,
when the Jews sent priests and Levites
from Jerusalem to ask him, "Who are
you?" 20He confessed, he did not deny,
but confessed, "I am not the Christ."
21And they asked him, "What then? Are
you Eli'jah?" He said, "I am not." "Are you
the prophet?" And he answered, "No."
22They said to him then, "Who are you?
Let us have an answer for those who sent
us. What do you say about yourself?"
23He said, "I am the voice of one crying in
the wilderness, 'Make straight the way of
the Lord,' as the prophet Isaiah said."

24 Now they had been sent from the
Pharisees. 25They asked him, "Then why
are you baptizing, if you are neither the
Christ, nor Eli'jah, nor the prophet?"
26John answered them, "I baptize with
water; but among you stands one whom
you do not know, 27even he who comes
after me, the thong of whose sandal I am
not worthy to untie." 28This took place in
Bethany beyond the Jordan, where John
was baptizing.

The Lamb of God

29 The next day he saw Jesus coming to-
ward him, and said, "Behold, the Lamb
of God, who takes away the sin of the
world! 30This is he of whom I said, 'After
me comes a man who ranks before me,
for he was before me.' 31I myself did not
know him; but for this I came baptizing
with water, that he might be revealed
to Israel." 32And John bore witness, "I
saw the Spirit descend as a dove from
heaven, and it remained on him. 33I my-
self did not know him; but he who sent
me to baptize with water said to me, 'He

[a] **1.4** Or *was not anything made. That which has been made was life in him* [b] **1.18** Other ancient authorities read *God*

on whom you see the Spirit descend and
remain, this is he who baptizes with the
Holy Spirit.’ 34 And I have seen and have
borne witness that this is the Son of
God.”

The First Disciples of Jesus

35 The next day again John was standing
with two of his disciples; 36 and he looked
at Jesus as he walked, and said, “Behold,
the Lamb of God!” 37 The two disciples
heard him say this, and they followed
Jesus. 38 Jesus turned, and saw them fol-
lowing, and said to them, “What do you
seek?” And they said to him, “Rabbi”
(which means Teacher), “where are you
staying?” 39 He said to them, “Come and
see.” They came and saw where he was
staying; and they stayed with him that
day, for it was about the tenth hour. 40 One
of the two who heard John speak, and fol-
lowed him, was Andrew, Simon Peter’s
brother. 41 He first found his brother Si-
mon, and said to him, “We have found
the Messiah” (which means Christ).
42 He brought him to Jesus. Jesus looked
at him, and said, “So you are Simon the
son of John? You shall be called Cephas”
(which means Peter[c]).

Jesus Calls Philip and Nathanael

43 The next day Jesus decided to go to
Galilee. And he found Philip and said to
him, “Follow me.” 44 Now Philip was from
Beth-sa′ida, the city of Andrew and Peter.
45 Philip found Nathan′a-el, and said to
him, “We have found him of whom Moses
in the law and also the prophets wrote,
Jesus of Nazareth, the son of Joseph.”
46 Nathan′a-el said to him, “Can anything
good come out of Nazareth?” Philip said
to him, “Come and see.” 47 Jesus saw Na-
than′a-el coming to him, and said of him,
“Behold, an Israelite indeed, in whom
is no guile!” 48 Nathan′a-el said to him,
“How do you know me?” Jesus answered
him, “Before Philip called you, when
you were under the fig tree, I saw you.”
49 Nathan′a-el answered him, “Rabbi, you
are the Son of God! You are the King of
Israel!” 50 Jesus answered him, “Because I
said to you, I saw you under the fig tree,
do you believe? You shall see greater
things than these.” 51 And he said to him,
“Truly, truly, I say to you, you will see
heaven opened, and the angels of God
ascending and descending upon the Son
of man.”

The Wedding at Cana

2 On the third day there was a marriage
at Cana in Galilee, and the mother
of Jesus was there; 2 Jesus also was in-
vited to the marriage, with his disciples.
3 When the wine failed, the mother of
Jesus said to him, “They have no wine.”
4 And Jesus said to her, “O woman, what
have you to do with me? My hour has
not yet come.” 5 His mother said to the
servants, “Do whatever he tells you.”
6 Now six stone jars were standing there,
for the Jewish rites of purification, each
holding twenty or thirty gallons. 7 Jesus
said to them, “Fill the jars with water.”
And they filled them up to the brim. 8 He
said to them, “Now draw some out, and
take it to the steward of the feast.” So
they took it. 9 When the steward of the
feast tasted the water now become wine,
and did not know where it came from
(though the servants who had drawn
the water knew), the steward of the feast
called the bridegroom 10 and said to him,
“Every man serves the good wine first;
and when men have drunk freely, then
the poor wine; but you have kept the
good wine until now.” 11 This, the first of
his signs, Jesus did at Cana in Galilee,
and manifested his glory; and his disci-
ples believed in him.

12 After this he went down to Caper′-
na-um, with his mother and his brethren
and his disciples; and there they stayed
for a few days.

[c] **1.42** From the word for *rock* in Aramaic and Greek, respectively

Jesus Cleanses the Temple

13 The Passover of the Jews was at hand, and Jesus went up to Jerusalem. 14 In the temple he found those who were selling oxen and sheep and pigeons, and the money-changers at their business. 15 And making a whip of cords, he drove them all, with the sheep and oxen, out of the temple; and he poured out the coins of the money-changers and overturned their tables. 16 And he told those who sold the pigeons, “Take these things away; you shall not make my Father’s house a house of trade.” 17 His disciples remembered that it was written, “Zeal for thy house will consume me.” 18 The Jews then said to him, “What sign have you to show us for doing this?” 19 Jesus answered them, “Destroy this temple, and in three days I will raise it up.” 20 The Jews then said, “It has taken forty-six years to build this temple, and will you raise it up in three days?” 21 But he spoke of the temple of his body. 22 When therefore he was raised from the dead, his disciples remembered that he had said this; and they believed the scripture and the word which Jesus had spoken.

23 Now when he was in Jerusalem at the Passover feast, many believed in his name when they saw the signs which he did; 24 but Jesus did not trust himself to them, 25 because he knew all men and needed no one to bear witness of man; for he himself knew what was in man.

Nicodemus Visits Jesus

3 Now there was a man of the Pharisees, named Nicode′mus, a ruler of the Jews. 2 This man came to Jesus[d] by night and said to him, “Rabbi, we know that you are a teacher come from God; for no one can do these signs that you do, unless God is with him.” 3 Jesus answered him, “Truly, truly, I say to you, unless one is born anew,[e] he cannot see the kingdom of God.” 4 Nicode′mus said to him, “How can a man be born when he is old? Can he enter a second time into his mother’s womb and be born?” 5 Jesus answered, “Truly, truly, I say to you, unless one is born of water and the Spirit, he cannot enter the kingdom of God. 6 That which is born of the flesh is flesh, and that which is born of the Spirit is spirit.[f] 7 Do not marvel that I said to you, ‘You must be born anew.’[g] 8 The wind[h] blows where it wills, and you hear the sound of it, but you do not know whence it comes or whither it goes; so it is with every one who is born of the Spirit.” 9 Nicode′mus said to him, “How can this be?” 10 Jesus answered him, “Are you a teacher of Israel, and yet you do not understand this? 11 Truly, truly, I say to you, we speak of what we know, and bear witness to what we have seen; but you do not receive our testimony. 12 If I have told you earthly things and you do not believe, how can you believe if I tell you heavenly things? 13 No one has ascended into heaven but he who descended from heaven, the Son of man.[i] 14 And as Moses lifted up the serpent in the wilderness, so must the Son of man be lifted up, 15 that whoever believes in him may have eternal life.”[j]

16 For God so loved the world that he gave his only Son, that whoever believes in him should not perish but have eternal life. 17 For God sent the Son into the world, not to condemn the world, but that the world might be saved through him. 18 He who believes in him is not condemned; he who does not believe is condemned already, because he has not believed in the name of the only Son of God. 19 And this is the judgment, that the light has come into the world, and men loved darkness

[d] **3.2** Greek *him* [e] **3.3** Or *from above* [f] **3.6** The same Greek word means both *wind* and *spirit* [g] **3.7** Or *from above* [h] **3.8** The same Greek word means both *wind* and *spirit* [i] **3.13** Other ancient authorities add *who is in heaven* [j] **3.15** Some interpreters hold that the quotation continues through verse 21

rather than light, because their deeds
were evil. 20For every one who does evil
hates the light, and does not come to the
light, lest his deeds should be exposed.
21But he who does what is true comes to
the light, that it may be clearly seen that
his deeds have been wrought in God.

Jesus and John the Baptist

22 After this Jesus and his disciples went
into the land of Judea; there he remained
with them and baptized. 23John also was
baptizing at Ae'non near Salim, because
there was much water there; and people
came and were baptized. 24For John had
not yet been put in prison.

25 Now a discussion arose between
John's disciples and a Jew over purifying.
26And they came to John, and said to him,
"Rabbi, he who was with you beyond the
Jordan, to whom you bore witness, here
he is, baptizing, and all are going to him."
27John answered, "No one can receive
anything except what is given him from
heaven. 28You yourselves bear me wit-
ness, that I said, I am not the Christ, but I
have been sent before him. 29He who has
the bride is the bridegroom; the friend
of the bridegroom, who stands and hears
him, rejoices greatly at the bridegroom's
voice; therefore this joy of mine is now
full. 30He must increase, but I must
decrease."[k]

The One Who Comes from Heaven

31 He who comes from above is above
all; he who is of the earth belongs to the
earth, and of the earth he speaks; he who
comes from heaven is above all. 32He
bears witness to what he has seen and
heard, yet no one receives his testimony;
33he who receives his testimony sets his
seal to this, that God is true. 34For he
whom God has sent utters the words
of God, for it is not by measure that he
gives the Spirit; 35the Father loves the
Son, and has given all things into his
hand. 36He who believes in the Son has
eternal life; he who does not obey the
Son shall not see life, but the wrath of
God rests upon him.

Jesus and the Woman of Samaria

4 Now when the Lord knew that the
Pharisees had heard that Jesus was
making and baptizing more disciples
than John 2(although Jesus himself did
not baptize, but only his disciples), 3he
left Judea and departed again to Gali-
lee. 4He had to pass through Samar'ia.
5So he came to a city of Samar'ia, called
Sy'char, near the field that Jacob gave to
his son Joseph. 6Jacob's well was there,
and so Jesus, wearied as he was with his
journey, sat down beside the well. It was
about the sixth hour.

7 There came a woman of Samar'ia to
draw water. Jesus said to her, "Give me a
drink." 8For his disciples had gone away
into the city to buy food. 9The Samaritan
woman said to him, "How is it that you,
a Jew, ask a drink of me, a woman of Sa-
mar'ia?" For Jews have no dealings with
Samaritans. 10Jesus answered her, "If you
knew the gift of God, and who it is that is
saying to you, 'Give me a drink,' you would
have asked him, and he would have given
you living water." 11The woman said to
him, "Sir, you have nothing to draw with,
and the well is deep; where do you get
that living water? 12Are you greater than
our father Jacob, who gave us the well,
and drank from it himself, and his sons,
and his cattle?" 13Jesus said to her, "Every
one who drinks of this water will thirst
again, 14but whoever drinks of the water
that I shall give him will never thirst; the
water that I shall give him will become in
him a spring of water welling up to eter-
nal life." 15The woman said to him, "Sir,
give me this water, that I may not thirst,
nor come here to draw."

16 Jesus said to her, "Go, call your
husband, and come here." 17The woman

[k] **3.30** Some interpreters hold that the quotation continues through verse 36

answered him, "I have no husband."
Jesus said to her, "You are right in say-
ing, 'I have no husband'; 18for you have
had five husbands, and he whom you
now have is not your husband; this you
said truly." 19The woman said to him,
"Sir, I perceive that you are a prophet.
20Our fathers worshiped on this moun-
tain; and you say that in Jerusalem is
the place where men ought to worship."
21Jesus said to her, "Woman, believe me,
the hour is coming when neither on this
mountain nor in Jerusalem will you wor-
ship the Father. 22You worship what you
do not know; we worship what we know,
for salvation is from the Jews. 23But the
hour is coming, and now is, when the
true worshipers will worship the Father
in spirit and truth, for such the Father
seeks to worship him. 24God is spirit, and
those who worship him must worship in
spirit and truth." 25The woman said to
him, "I know that Messiah is coming (he
who is called Christ); when he comes, he
will show us all things." 26Jesus said to
her, "I who speak to you am he."

27 Just then his disciples came. They
marveled that he was talking with a
woman, but none said, "What do you
wish?" or, "Why are you talking with
her?" 28So the woman left her water jar,
and went away into the city, and said to
the people, 29"Come, see a man who told
me all that I ever did. Can this be the
Christ?" 30They went out of the city and
were coming to him.

31 Meanwhile the disciples besought
him, saying, "Rabbi, eat." 32But he said
to them, "I have food to eat of which you
do not know." 33So the disciples said to
one another, "Has any one brought him
food?" 34Jesus said to them, "My food is
to do the will of him who sent me, and to
accomplish his work. 35Do you not say,
'There are yet four months, then comes
the harvest'? I tell you, lift up your eyes,
and see how the fields are already white
for harvest. 36He who reaps receives
wages, and gathers fruit for eternal life,
so that sower and reaper may rejoice to-
gether. 37For here the saying holds true,
'One sows and another reaps.' 38I sent
you to reap that for which you did not
labor; others have labored, and you have
entered into their labor."

39 Many Samaritans from that city
believed in him because of the woman's
testimony, "He told me all that I ever did."
40So when the Samaritans came to him,
they asked him to stay with them; and he
stayed there two days. 41And many more
believed because of his word. 42They said
to the woman, "It is no longer because of
your words that we believe, for we have
heard for ourselves, and we know that
this is indeed the Savior of the world."

Jesus Returns to Galilee

43 After the two days he departed to Gal-
ilee. 44For Jesus himself testified that a
prophet has no honor in his own coun-
try. 45So when he came to Galilee, the
Galileans welcomed him, having seen
all that he had done in Jerusalem at the
feast, for they too had gone to the feast.

Jesus Heals an Official's Son

46 So he came again to Cana in Galilee,
where he had made the water wine. And
at Caper′na-um there was an official
whose son was ill. 47When he heard that
Jesus had come from Judea to Galilee,
he went and begged him to come down
and heal his son, for he was at the point
of death. 48Jesus therefore said to him,
"Unless you see signs and wonders you
will not believe." 49The official said to
him, "Sir, come down before my child
dies." 50Jesus said to him, "Go; your son
will live." The man believed the word
that Jesus spoke to him and went his way.
51As he was going down, his servants
met him and told him that his son was
living. 52So he asked them the hour when
he began to mend, and they said to him,
"Yesterday at the seventh hour the fever

left him." 53 The father knew that was the
hour when Jesus had said to him, "Your
son will live"; and he himself believed,
and all his household. 54 This was now
the second sign that Jesus did when he
had come from Judea to Galilee.

Jesus Heals on the Sabbath

5 After this there was a feast of the
Jews, and Jesus went up to Jerusalem.
2 Now there is in Jerusalem by the
Sheep Gate a pool, in Hebrew called
Beth-za'tha,[l] which has five porticoes. 3 In
these lay a multitude of invalids, blind,
lame, paralyzed.[m] 5 One man was there,
who had been ill for thirty-eight years.
6 When Jesus saw him and knew that he
had been lying there a long time, he said
to him, "Do you want to be healed?" 7 The
sick man answered him, "Sir, I have no
man to put me into the pool when the
water is troubled, and while I am going
another steps down before me." 8 Jesus
said to him, "Rise, take up your pallet,
and walk." 9 And at once the man was
healed, and he took up his pallet and
walked.

Now that day was the sabbath. 10 So the
Jews said to the man who was cured, "It
is the sabbath, it is not lawful for you
to carry your pallet." 11 But he answered
them, "The man who healed me said to
me, 'Take up your pallet, and walk.'"
12 They asked him, "Who is the man who
said to you, 'Take up your pallet, and
walk'?" 13 Now the man who had been
healed did not know who it was, for Jesus
had withdrawn, as there was a crowd in
the place. 14 Afterward, Jesus found him
in the temple, and said to him, "See,
you are well! Sin no more, that nothing
worse befall you." 15 The man went away
and told the Jews that it was Jesus who
had healed him. 16 And this was why the
Jews persecuted Jesus, because he did
this on the sabbath. 17 But Jesus answered
them, "My Father is working still, and
I am working." 18 This was why the Jews
sought all the more to kill him, because
he not only broke the sabbath but also
called God his Father, making himself
equal with God.

The Authority of the Son

19 Jesus said to them, "Truly, truly, I say
to you, the Son can do nothing of his own
accord, but only what he sees the Father
doing; for whatever he does, that the Son
does likewise. 20 For the Father loves the
Son, and shows him all that he himself
is doing; and greater works than these
will he show him, that you may marvel.
21 For as the Father raises the dead and
gives them life, so also the Son gives life
to whom he will. 22 The Father judges no
one, but has given all judgment to the
Son, 23 that all may honor the Son, even as
they honor the Father. He who does not
honor the Son does not honor the Father
who sent him. 24 Truly, truly, I say to you,
he who hears my word and believes him
who sent me, has eternal life; he does
not come into judgment, but has passed
from death to life.

25 "Truly, truly, I say to you, the hour
is coming, and now is, when the dead
will hear the voice of the Son of God, and
those who hear will live. 26 For as the Father has life in himself, so he has granted
the Son also to have life in himself, 27 and
has given him authority to execute judgment, because he is the Son of man. 28 Do
not marvel at this; for the hour is coming
when all who are in the tombs will hear
his voice 29 and come forth, those who
have done good, to the resurrection of
life, and those who have done evil, to the
resurrection of judgment.

[l] **5.2** Other ancient authorities read *Bethesda,* others *Bethsaida* [m] **5.3** Other ancient authorities insert, wholly or in part, *waiting for the moving of the water;* [4] *for an angel of the Lord went down at certain seasons into the pool, and troubled the water: whoever stepped in first after the troubling of the water was healed of whatever disease he had*

Witnesses to Jesus

30 "I can do nothing on my own author-
ity; as I hear, I judge; and my judgment
is just, because I seek not my own will
but the will of him who sent me. 31 If I
bear witness to myself, my testimony is
not true; 32 there is another who bears
witness to me, and I know that the tes-
timony which he bears to me is true.
33 You sent to John, and he has borne
witness to the truth. 34 Not that the tes-
timony which I receive is from man;
but I say this that you may be saved.
35 He was a burning and shining lamp,
and you were willing to rejoice for a
while in his light. 36 But the testimony
which I have is greater than that of
John; for the works which the Father
has granted me to accomplish, these
very works which I am doing, bear me
witness that the Father has sent me.
37 And the Father who sent me has him-
self borne witness to me. His voice you
have never heard, his form you have
never seen; 38 and you do not have his
word abiding in you, for you do not
believe him whom he has sent. 39 You
search the scriptures, because you
think that in them you have eternal life;
and it is they that bear witness to me;
40 yet you refuse to come to me that you
may have life. 41 I do not receive glory
from men. 42 But I know that you have
not the love of God within you. 43 I have
come in my Father's name, and you do
not receive me; if another comes in his
own name, him you will receive. 44 How
can you believe, who receive glory
from one another and do not seek the
glory that comes from the only God?
45 Do not think that I shall accuse you
to the Father; it is Moses who accuses
you, on whom you set your hope. 46 If
you believed Moses, you would believe
me, for he wrote of me. 47 But if you do
not believe his writings, how will you
believe my words?"

Feeding the Five Thousand

6 After this Jesus went to the other side
of the Sea of Galilee, which is the Sea
of Tibe'ri-as. 2 And a multitude followed
him, because they saw the signs which he
did on those who were diseased. 3 Jesus
went up into the hills, and there sat
down with his disciples. 4 Now the Pass-
over, the feast of the Jews, was at hand.
5 Lifting up his eyes, then, and seeing that
a multitude was coming to him, Jesus
said to Philip, "How are we to buy bread,
so that these people may eat?" 6 This he
said to test him, for he himself knew
what he would do. 7 Philip answered him,
"Two hundred denarii[n] would not buy
enough bread for each of them to get a
little." 8 One of his disciples, Andrew, Si-
mon Peter's brother, said to him, 9 "There
is a lad here who has five barley loaves
and two fish; but what are they among
so many?" 10 Jesus said, "Make the people
sit down." Now there was much grass in
the place; so the men sat down, in num-
ber about five thousand. 11 Jesus then
took the loaves, and when he had given
thanks, he distributed them to those who
were seated; so also the fish, as much as
they wanted. 12 And when they had eaten
their fill, he told his disciples, "Gather
up the fragments left over, that nothing
may be lost." 13 So they gathered them up
and filled twelve baskets with fragments
from the five barley loaves, left by those
who had eaten. 14 When the people saw
the sign which he had done, they said,
"This is indeed the prophet who is to
come into the world!"

15 Perceiving then that they were
about to come and take him by force to
make him king, Jesus withdrew again to
the hills by himself.

Jesus Walks on the Water

16 When evening came, his disciples
went down to the sea, 17 got into a boat, and
started across the sea to Caper'na-um.

[n] **6.7** The denarius was a day's wage for a laborer

It was now dark, and Jesus had not yet
come to them. 18The sea rose because a
strong wind was blowing. 19When they
had rowed about three or four miles,[o]
they saw Jesus walking on the sea and
drawing near to the boat. They were
frightened, 20but he said to them, "It is I;
do not be afraid." 21Then they were glad
to take him into the boat, and immedi-
ately the boat was at the land to which
they were going.

The Bread from Heaven

22 On the next day the people who re-
mained on the other side of the sea saw
that there had been only one boat there,
and that Jesus had not entered the boat
with his disciples, but that his disciples
had gone away alone. 23However, boats
from Tibe'ri-as came near the place
where they ate the bread after the Lord
had given thanks. 24So when the people
saw that Jesus was not there, nor his dis-
ciples, they themselves got into the boats
and went to Caper'na-um, seeking Jesus.

25 When they found him on the other
side of the sea, they said to him, "Rabbi,
when did you come here?" 26Jesus an-
swered them, "Truly, truly, I say to you,
you seek me, not because you saw signs,
but because you ate your fill of the
loaves. 27Do not labor for the food which
perishes, but for the food which endures
to eternal life, which the Son of man will
give to you; for on him has God the Fa-
ther set his seal." 28Then they said to him,
"What must we do, to be doing the works
of God?" 29Jesus answered them, "This is
the work of God, that you believe in him
whom he has sent." 30So they said to him,
"Then what sign do you do, that we may
see, and believe you? What work do you
perform? 31Our fathers ate the manna in
the wilderness; as it is written, 'He gave
them bread from heaven to eat.'" 32Jesus
then said to them, "Truly, truly, I say to
you, it was not Moses who gave you the
bread from heaven; my Father gives you
the true bread from heaven. 33For the
bread of God is that which comes down
from heaven, and gives life to the world."
34They said to him, "Lord, give us this
bread always."

35 Jesus said to them, "I am the bread
of life; he who comes to me shall not
hunger, and he who believes in me shall
never thirst. 36But I said to you that you
have seen me and yet do not believe. 37All
that the Father gives me will come to
me; and him who comes to me I will not
cast out. 38For I have come down from
heaven, not to do my own will, but the
will of him who sent me; 39and this is the
will of him who sent me, that I should
lose nothing of all that he has given me,
but raise it up at the last day. 40For this is
the will of my Father, that every one who
sees the Son and believes in him should
have eternal life; and I will raise him up
at the last day."

41 The Jews then murmured at him,
because he said, "I am the bread which
came down from heaven." 42They said,
"Is not this Jesus, the son of Joseph,
whose father and mother we know? How
does he now say, 'I have come down from
heaven'?" 43Jesus answered them, "Do not
murmur among yourselves. 44No one can
come to me unless the Father who sent
me draws him; and I will raise him up at
the last day. 45It is written in the proph-
ets, 'And they shall all be taught by God.'
Every one who has heard and learned
from the Father comes to me. 46Not that
any one has seen the Father except him
who is from God; he has seen the Father.
47Truly, truly, I say to you, he who be-
lieves has eternal life. 48I am the bread of
life. 49Your fathers ate the manna in the
wilderness, and they died. 50This is the
bread which comes down from heaven,
that a man may eat of it and not die. 51I am
the living bread which came down from
heaven; if any one eats of this bread, he

[o]**6.19** Greek *twenty-five or thirty stadia*

will live for ever; and the bread which I
shall give for the life of the world is my
flesh."

52 The Jews then disputed among them-
selves, saying, "How can this man give us
his flesh to eat?" 53 So Jesus said to them,
"Truly, truly, I say to you, unless you eat
the flesh of the Son of man and drink his
blood, you have no life in you; 54 he who
eats my flesh and drinks my blood has
eternal life, and I will raise him up at the
last day. 55 For my flesh is food indeed,
and my blood is drink indeed. 56 He who
eats my flesh and drinks my blood abides
in me, and I in him. 57 As the living Father
sent me, and I live because of the Father,
so he who eats me will live because of
me. 58 This is the bread which came down
from heaven, not such as the fathers ate
and died; he who eats this bread will live
for ever." 59 This he said in the synagogue,
as he taught at Caper'na-um.

The Words of Eternal Life

60 Many of his disciples, when they
heard it, said, "This is a hard saying; who
can listen to it?" 61 But Jesus, knowing in
himself that his disciples murmured at
it, said to them, "Do you take offense at
this? 62 Then what if you were to see the
Son of man ascending where he was be-
fore? 63 It is the spirit that gives life, the
flesh is of no avail; the words that I have
spoken to you are spirit and life. 64 But
there are some of you that do not be-
lieve." For Jesus knew from the first who
those were that did not believe, and who
it was that should betray him. 65 And he
said, "This is why I told you that no one
can come to me unless it is granted him
by the Father."

66 After this many of his disciples drew
back and no longer went about with him.
67 Jesus said to the twelve, "Will you also
go away?" 68 Simon Peter answered him,
"Lord, to whom shall we go? You have
the words of eternal life; 69 and we have
believed, and have come to know, that you
are the Holy One of God." 70 Jesus answered
them, "Did I not choose you, the twelve,
and one of you is a devil?" 71 He spoke of Ju-
das the son of Simon Iscariot, for he, one
of the twelve, was to betray him.

The Unbelief of Jesus' Brethren

7 After this Jesus went about in Gali-
lee; he would not go about in Judea,
because the Jews[p] sought to kill him.
2 Now the Jews' feast of Tabernacles was
at hand. 3 So his brethren said to him,
"Leave here and go to Judea, that your
disciples may see the works you are do-
ing. 4 For no man works in secret if he
seeks to be known openly. If you do these
things, show yourself to the world." 5 For
even his brethren did not believe in him.
6 Jesus said to them, "My time has not yet
come, but your time is always here. 7 The
world cannot hate you, but it hates me
because I testify of it that its works are
evil. 8 Go to the feast yourselves; I am not[q]
going up to this feast, for my time has not
yet fully come." 9 So saying, he remained
in Galilee.

Jesus at the Festival of Booths

10 But after his brethren had gone up
to the feast, then he also went up, not
publicly but in private. 11 The Jews were
looking for him at the feast, and saying,
"Where is he?" 12 And there was much
muttering about him among the people.
While some said, "He is a good man,"
others said, "No, he is leading the people
astray." 13 Yet for fear of the Jews no one
spoke openly of him.

14 About the middle of the feast Jesus
went up into the temple and taught.
15 The Jews marveled at it, saying, "How
is it that this man has learning,[r] when
he has never studied?" 16 So Jesus an-
swered them, "My teaching is not mine,
but his who sent me; 17 if any man's will
is to do his will, he shall know whether

[p] **7.1** Or *Judeans* [q] **7.8** Other ancient authorities add *yet* [r] **7.15** Or *this man knows his letters*

the teaching is from God or whether I am
speaking on my own authority. [18]He who
speaks on his own authority seeks his
own glory; but he who seeks the glory
of him who sent him is true, and in him
there is no falsehood. [19]Did not Moses
give you the law? Yet none of you keeps
the law. Why do you seek to kill me?"
[20]The people answered, "You have a de-
mon! Who is seeking to kill you?" [21]Jesus
answered them, "I did one deed, and you
all marvel at it. [22]Moses gave you cir-
cumcision (not that it is from Moses, but
from the fathers), and you circumcise a
man upon the sabbath. [23]If on the sabbath
a man receives circumcision, so that the
law of Moses may not be broken, are you
angry with me because on the sabbath I
made a man's whole body well? [24]Do not
judge by appearances, but judge with
right judgment."

Is This the Christ?

25 Some of the people of Jerusalem there-
fore said, "Is not this the man whom they
seek to kill? [26]And here he is, speaking
openly, and they say nothing to him! Can
it be that the authorities really know that
this is the Christ? [27]Yet we know where
this man comes from; and when the
Christ appears, no one will know where
he comes from." [28]So Jesus proclaimed,
as he taught in the temple, "You know
me, and you know where I come from?
But I have not come of my own accord;
he who sent me is true, and him you do
not know. [29]I know him, for I come from
him, and he sent me." [30]So they sought to
arrest him; but no one laid hands on him,
because his hour had not yet come. [31]Yet
many of the people believed in him; they
said, "When the Christ appears, will he
do more signs than this man has done?"

Officers Are Sent to Arrest Jesus

32 The Pharisees heard the crowd thus
muttering about him, and the chief
priests and Pharisees sent officers to
arrest him. [33]Jesus then said, "I shall be
with you a little longer, and then I go to
him who sent me; [34]you will seek me and
you will not find me; where I am you can-
not come." [35]The Jews said to one another,
"Where does this man intend to go that
we shall not find him? Does he intend to
go to the Dispersion among the Greeks
and teach the Greeks? [36]What does he
mean by saying, 'You will seek me and
you will not find me,' and, 'Where I am
you cannot come'?"

Rivers of Living Water

37 On the last day of the feast, the great
day, Jesus stood up and proclaimed, "If
any one thirst, let him come to me and
drink. [38]He who believes in me, as[s] the
scripture has said, 'Out of his heart shall
flow rivers of living water.'" [39]Now this
he said about the Spirit, which those
who believed in him were to receive; for
as yet the Spirit had not been given, be-
cause Jesus was not yet glorified.

Division among the People

40 When they heard these words, some
of the people said, "This is really the
prophet." [41]Others said, "This is the
Christ." But some said, "Is the Christ to
come from Galilee? [42]Has not the scrip-
ture said that the Christ is descended
from David, and comes from Bethlehem,
the village where David was?" [43]So there
was a division among the people over
him. [44]Some of them wanted to arrest
him, but no one laid hands on him.

The Unbelief of Those in Authority

45 The officers then went back to the
chief priests and Pharisees, who said
to them, "Why did you not bring him?"
[46]The officers answered, "No man ever
spoke like this man!" [47]The Pharisees
answered them, "Are you led astray, you
also? [48]Have any of the authorities or of

[s] **7.38** Or *let him come to me, and let him who believes in me drink. As*

the Pharisees believed in him? 49 But this
crowd, who do not know the law, are ac-
cursed." 50 Nicode'mus, who had gone to
him before, and who was one of them,
said to them, 51 "Does our law judge a man
without first giving him a hearing and
learning what he does?" 52 They replied,
"Are you from Galilee too? Search and
you will see that no prophet is to rise
from Galilee." 53 They went each to his
8 own house, 1 but Jesus went to the
Mount of Olives. 2 Early in the morn-
ing he came again to the temple; all the
people came to him, and he sat down and
taught them. 3 The scribes and the Phar-
isees brought a woman who had been
caught in adultery, and placing her in
the midst 4 they said to him, "Teacher,
this woman has been caught in the act
of adultery. 5 Now in the law Moses com-
manded us to stone such. What do you
say about her?" 6 This they said to test
him, that they might have some charge
to bring against him. Jesus bent down
and wrote with his finger on the ground.
7 And as they continued to ask him, he
stood up and said to them, "Let him who
is without sin among you be the first to
throw a stone at her." 8 And once more he
bent down and wrote with his finger on
the ground. 9 But when they heard it, they
went away, one by one, beginning with
the eldest, and Jesus was left alone with
the woman standing before him. 10 Jesus
looked up and said to her, "Woman,
where are they? Has no one condemned
you?" 11 She said, "No one, Lord." And
Jesus said, "Neither do I condemn you;
go, and do not sin again."[t]

Jesus the Light of the World

12 Again Jesus spoke to them, saying, "I
am the light of the world; he who follows
me will not walk in darkness, but will
have the light of life." 13 The Pharisees
then said to him, "You are bearing wit-
ness to yourself; your testimony is not
true." 14 Jesus answered, "Even if I do
bear witness to myself, my testimony
is true, for I know whence I have come
and whither I am going, but you do not
know whence I come or whither I am go-
ing. 15 You judge according to the flesh,
I judge no one. 16 Yet even if I do judge,
my judgment is true, for it is not I alone
that judge, but I and he[u] who sent me.
17 In your law it is written that the testi-
mony of two men is true; 18 I bear witness
to myself, and the Father who sent me
bears witness to me." 19 They said to him
therefore, "Where is your Father?" Jesus
answered, "You know neither me nor my
Father; if you knew me, you would know
my Father also." 20 These words he spoke
in the treasury, as he taught in the tem-
ple; but no one arrested him, because his
hour had not yet come.

Jesus Foretells His Death

21 Again he said to them, "I go away, and
you will seek me and die in your sin;
where I am going, you cannot come."
22 Then said the Jews, "Will he kill him-
self, since he says, 'Where I am going, you
cannot come'?" 23 He said to them, "You
are from below, I am from above; you are
of this world, I am not of this world. 24 I
told you that you would die in your sins,
for you will die in your sins unless you
believe that I am he." 25 They said to him,
"Who are you?" Jesus said to them, "Even
what I have told you from the beginning.[v]
26 I have much to say about you and much
to judge; but he who sent me is true, and
I declare to the world what I have heard
from him." 27 They did not understand
that he spoke to them of the Father. 28 So
Jesus said, "When you have lifted up the
Son of man, then you will know that I
am he, and that I do nothing on my own

[t] **8.11** Some ancient authorities insert 7.53—8.11 either at the end of this gospel or after Luke 21.38, with variations of text. Others omit it altogether.
[u] **8.16** Other ancient authorities read *the Father*
[v] **8.25** Or *Why do I talk to you at all?*

authority but speak thus as the Father
taught me. 29 And he who sent me is with
me; he has not left me alone, for I always
do what is pleasing to him." 30 As he spoke
thus, many believed in him.

True Disciples

31 Jesus then said to the Jews who had
believed in him, "If you continue in my
word, you are truly my disciples, 32 and
you will know the truth, and the truth
will make you free." 33 They answered
him, "We are descendants of Abraham,
and have never been in bondage to any
one. How is it that you say, 'You will be
made free'?"

34 Jesus answered them, "Truly, truly,
I say to you, every one who commits sin
is a slave to sin. 35 The slave does not con-
tinue in the house for ever; the son con-
tinues for ever. 36 So if the Son makes you
free, you will be free indeed. 37 I know
that you are descendants of Abraham;
yet you seek to kill me, because my word
finds no place in you. 38 I speak of what
I have seen with my Father, and you do
what you have heard from your father."

Jesus and Abraham

39 They answered him, "Abraham is our
father." Jesus said to them, "If you were
Abraham's children, you would do what
Abraham did, 40 but now you seek to kill
me, a man who has told you the truth
which I heard from God; this is not what
Abraham did. 41 You do what your father
did." They said to him, "We were not born
of fornication; we have one Father, even
God." 42 Jesus said to them, "If God were
your Father, you would love me, for I
proceeded and came forth from God; I
came not of my own accord, but he sent
me. 43 Why do you not understand what
I say? It is because you cannot bear to
hear my word. 44 You are of your father
the devil, and your will is to do your fa-
ther's desires. He was a murderer from
the beginning, and has nothing to do
with the truth, because there is no truth
in him. When he lies, he speaks accord-
ing to his own nature, for he is a liar and
the father of lies. 45 But, because I tell the
truth, you do not believe me. 46 Which of
you convicts me of sin? If I tell the truth,
why do you not believe me? 47 He who is
of God hears the words of God; the rea-
son why you do not hear them is that you
are not of God."

48 The Jews answered him, "Are we not
right in saying that you are a Samaritan
and have a demon?" 49 Jesus answered, "I
have not a demon; but I honor my Father,
and you dishonor me. 50 Yet I do not seek
my own glory; there is One who seeks it
and he will be the judge. 51 Truly, truly, I
say to you, if any one keeps my word, he
will never see death." 52 The Jews said to
him, "Now we know that you have a de-
mon. Abraham died, as did the prophets;
and you say, 'If any one keeps my word, he
will never taste death.' 53 Are you greater
than our father Abraham, who died? And
the prophets died! Who do you claim to
be?" 54 Jesus answered, "If I glorify my-
self, my glory is nothing; it is my Father
who glorifies me, of whom you say that
he is your God. 55 But you have not known
him; I know him. If I said, I do not know
him, I should be a liar like you; but I do
know him and I keep his word. 56 Your
father Abraham rejoiced that he was to
see my day; he saw it and was glad." 57 The
Jews then said to him, "You are not yet
fifty years old, and have you seen Abra-
ham?"[w] 58 Jesus said to them, "Truly, truly,
I say to you, before Abraham was, I am."
59 So they took up stones to throw at him;
but Jesus hid himself, and went out of the
temple.

A Man Born Blind Receives Sight

9 As he passed by, he saw a man blind
from his birth. 2 And his disciples
asked him, "Rabbi, who sinned, this man

[w] **8.57** Other ancient authorities read *has Abraham seen you?*

or his parents, that he was born blind?”
[3]Jesus answered, “It was not that this
man sinned, or his parents, but that the
works of God might be made manifest
in him. [4]We must work the works of
him who sent me, while it is day; night
comes, when no one can work. [5]As long
as I am in the world, I am the light of the
world.” [6]As he said this, he spat on the
ground and made clay of the spittle and
anointed the man’s eyes with the clay,
[7]saying to him, “Go, wash in the pool of
Silo′am” (which means Sent). So he went
and washed and came back seeing. [8]The
neighbors and those who had seen him
before as a beggar, said, “Is not this the
man who used to sit and beg?” [9]Some
said, “It is he”; others said, “No, but he is
like him.” He said, “I am the man.” [10]They
said to him, “Then how were your eyes
opened?” [11]He answered, “The man called
Jesus made clay and anointed my eyes
and said to me, ‘Go to Silo′am and wash’;
so I went and washed and received my
sight.” [12]They said to him, “Where is he?”
He said, “I do not know.”

The Pharisees Investigate the Healing

13 They brought to the Pharisees the man
who had formerly been blind. [14]Now it
was a sabbath day when Jesus made the
clay and opened his eyes. [15]The Pharisees
again asked him how he had received
his sight. And he said to them, “He put
clay on my eyes, and I washed, and I see.”
[16]Some of the Pharisees said, “This man
is not from God, for he does not keep the
sabbath.” But others said, “How can a man
who is a sinner do such signs?” There was
a division among them. [17]So they again
said to the blind man, “What do you say
about him, since he has opened your
eyes?” He said, “He is a prophet.”

18 The Jews did not believe that he had
been blind and had received his sight, un-
til they called the parents of the man who
had received his sight, [19]and asked them,
“Is this your son, who you say was born
blind? How then does he now see?” [20]His
parents answered, “We know that this is
our son, and that he was born blind; [21]but
how he now sees we do not know, nor
do we know who opened his eyes. Ask
him; he is of age, he will speak for him-
self.” [22]His parents said this because they
feared the Jews, for the Jews had already
agreed that if any one should confess
him to be Christ, he was to be put out of
the synagogue. [23]Therefore his parents
said, “He is of age, ask him.”

24 So for the second time they called
the man who had been blind, and said
to him, “Give God the praise; we know
that this man is a sinner.” [25]He answered,
“Whether he is a sinner, I do not know;
one thing I know, that though I was blind,
now I see.” [26]They said to him, “What
did he do to you? How did he open your
eyes?” [27]He answered them, “I have told
you already, and you would not listen.
Why do you want to hear it again? Do
you too want to become his disciples?”
[28]And they reviled him, saying, “You
are his disciple, but we are disciples of
Moses. [29]We know that God has spoken
to Moses, but as for this man, we do not
know where he comes from.” [30]The man
answered, “Why, this is a marvel! You do
not know where he comes from, and yet
he opened my eyes. [31]We know that God
does not listen to sinners, but if any one
is a worshiper of God and does his will,
God listens to him. [32]Never since the
world began has it been heard that any
one opened the eyes of a man born blind.
[33]If this man were not from God, he could
do nothing.” [34]They answered him, “You
were born in utter sin, and would you
teach us?” And they cast him out.

Spiritual Blindness

35 Jesus heard that they had cast him
out, and having found him he said, “Do
you believe in the Son of man?”[x] [36]He

[x]**9.35** Other ancient authorities read *the Son of God*

answered, "And who is he, sir, that I may believe in him?" [37]Jesus said to him, "You have seen him, and it is he who speaks to you." [38]He said, "Lord, I believe"; and he worshiped him. [39]Jesus said, "For judgment I came into this world, that those who do not see may see, and that those who see may become blind." [40]Some of the Pharisees near him heard this, and they said to him, "Are we also blind?" [41]Jesus said to them, "If you were blind, you would have no guilt; but now that you say, 'We see,' your guilt remains.

Jesus the Good Shepherd

10 "Truly, truly, I say to you, he who does not enter the sheepfold by the door but climbs in by another way, that man is a thief and a robber; [2]but he who enters by the door is the shepherd of the sheep. [3]To him the gatekeeper opens; the sheep hear his voice, and he calls his own sheep by name and leads them out. [4]When he has brought out all his own, he goes before them, and the sheep follow him, for they know his voice. [5]A stranger they will not follow, but they will flee from him, for they do not know the voice of strangers." [6]This figure Jesus used with them, but they did not understand what he was saying to them.

7 So Jesus again said to them, "Truly, truly, I say to you, I am the door of the sheep. [8]All who came before me are thieves and robbers; but the sheep did not heed them. [9]I am the door; if any one enters by me, he will be saved, and will go in and out and find pasture. [10]The thief comes only to steal and kill and destroy; I came that they may have life, and have it abundantly. [11]I am the good shepherd. The good shepherd lays down his life for the sheep. [12]He who is a hireling and not a shepherd, whose own the sheep are not, sees the wolf coming and leaves the sheep and flees; and the wolf snatches them and scatters them. [13]He flees because he is a hireling and cares nothing for the sheep. [14]I am the good shepherd; I know my own and my own know me, [15]as the Father knows me and I know the Father; and I lay down my life for the sheep. [16]And I have other sheep, that are not of this fold; I must bring them also, and they will heed my voice. So there shall be one flock, one shepherd. [17]For this reason the Father loves me, because I lay down my life, that I may take it again. [18]No one takes it from me, but I lay it down of my own accord. I have power to lay it down, and I have power to take it again; this charge I have received from my Father."

19 There was again a division among the Jews because of these words. [20]Many of them said, "He has a demon, and he is mad; why listen to him?" [21]Others said, "These are not the sayings of one who has a demon. Can a demon open the eyes of the blind?"

Jesus Is Rejected by the Jews

22 It was the feast of the Dedication at Jerusalem; [23]it was winter, and Jesus was walking in the temple, in the portico of Solomon. [24]So the Jews gathered round him and said to him, "How long will you keep us in suspense? If you are the Christ, tell us plainly." [25]Jesus answered them, "I told you, and you do not believe. The works that I do in my Father's name, they bear witness to me; [26]but you do not believe, because you do not belong to my sheep. [27]My sheep hear my voice, and I know them, and they follow me; [28]and I give them eternal life, and they shall never perish, and no one shall snatch them out of my hand. [29]My Father, who has given them to me,[y] is greater than all, and no one is able to snatch them out of the Father's hand. [30]I and the Father are one."

31 The Jews took up stones again to stone him. [32]Jesus answered them, "I

[y] **10.29** Other ancient authorities read *What my Father has given to me*

have shown you many good works from
the Father; for which of these do you
stone me?" [33]The Jews answered him,
"We stone you for no good work but for
blasphemy; because you, being a man,
make yourself God." [34]Jesus answered
them, "Is it not written in your law, 'I
said, you are gods'? [35]If he called them
gods to whom the word of God came (and
scripture cannot be broken), [36]do you
say of him whom the Father consecrated
and sent into the world, 'You are blas-
pheming,' because I said, 'I am the Son
of God'? [37]If I am not doing the works of
my Father, then do not believe me; [38]but
if I do them, even though you do not be-
lieve me, believe the works, that you may
know and understand that the Father
is in me and I am in the Father." [39]Again
they tried to arrest him, but he escaped
from their hands.

40 He went away again across the
Jordan to the place where John at first
baptized, and there he remained. [41]And
many came to him; and they said, "John
did no sign, but everything that John said
about this man was true." [42]And many
believed in him there.

The Death of Lazarus

11 Now a certain man was ill, Laz′arus
of Bethany, the village of Mary
and her sister Martha. [2]It was Mary
who anointed the Lord with ointment
and wiped his feet with her hair, whose
brother Laz′arus was ill. [3]So the sisters
sent to him, saying, "Lord, he whom you
love is ill." [4]But when Jesus heard it he
said, "This illness is not unto death; it is
for the glory of God, so that the Son of
God may be glorified by means of it."

5 Now Jesus loved Martha and her sis-
ter and Laz′arus. [6]So when he heard that
he was ill, he stayed two days longer in
the place where he was. [7]Then after this
he said to the disciples, "Let us go into
Judea again." [8]The disciples said to him,
"Rabbi, the Jews were but now seeking
to stone you, and are you going there
again?" [9]Jesus answered, "Are there not
twelve hours in the day? If any one walks
in the day, he does not stumble, because
he sees the light of this world. [10]But if any
one walks in the night, he stumbles, be-
cause the light is not in him." [11]Thus he
spoke, and then he said to them, "Our
friend Laz′arus has fallen asleep, but I
go to awake him out of sleep." [12]The dis-
ciples said to him, "Lord, if he has fallen
asleep, he will recover." [13]Now Jesus had
spoken of his death, but they thought
that he meant taking rest in sleep. [14]Then
Jesus told them plainly, "Laz′arus is dead;
[15]and for your sake I am glad that I was
not there, so that you may believe. But let
us go to him." [16]Thomas, called the Twin,
said to his fellow disciples, "Let us also
go, that we may die with him."

Jesus the Resurrection and the Life

17 Now when Jesus came, he found that
Laz′arus[z] had already been in the tomb
four days. [18]Bethany was near Jerusalem,
about two miles[a] off, [19]and many of the
Jews had come to Martha and Mary to
console them concerning their brother.
[20]When Martha heard that Jesus was
coming, she went and met him, while
Mary sat in the house. [21]Martha said
to Jesus, "Lord, if you had been here,
my brother would not have died. [22]And
even now I know that whatever you ask
from God, God will give you." [23]Jesus said
to her, "Your brother will rise again."
[24]Martha said to him, "I know that he will
rise again in the resurrection at the last
day." [25]Jesus said to her, "I am the resur-
rection and the life;[b] he who believes in
me, though he die, yet shall he live, [26]and
whoever lives and believes in me shall
never die. Do you believe this?" [27]She
said to him, "Yes, Lord; I believe that you
are the Christ, the Son of God, he who is
coming into the world."

[z]**11.17** Greek *he* [a]**11.18** Greek *fifteen stadia* [b]**11.25** Other ancient authorities omit *and the life*

Jesus Weeps

28 When she had said this, she went and
called her sister Mary, saying quietly,
"The Teacher is here and is calling for
you." 29And when she heard it, she rose
quickly and went to him. 30Now Jesus had
not yet come to the village, but was still
in the place where Martha had met him.
31When the Jews who were with her in
the house, consoling her, saw Mary rise
quickly and go out, they followed her,
supposing that she was going to the tomb
to weep there. 32Then Mary, when she
came where Jesus was and saw him, fell
at his feet, saying to him, "Lord, if you
had been here, my brother would not
have died." 33When Jesus saw her weep-
ing, and the Jews who came with her also
weeping, he was deeply moved in spirit
and troubled; 34and he said, "Where have
you laid him?" They said to him, "Lord,
come and see." 35Jesus wept. 36So the Jews
said, "See how he loved him!" 37But some
of them said, "Could not he who opened
the eyes of the blind man have kept this
man from dying?"

Jesus Raises Lazarus to Life

38 Then Jesus, deeply moved again,
came to the tomb; it was a cave, and a
stone lay upon it. 39Jesus said, "Take
away the stone." Martha, the sister of
the dead man, said to him, "Lord, by this
time there will be an odor, for he has
been dead four days." 40Jesus said to her,
"Did I not tell you that if you would be-
lieve you would see the glory of God?"
41So they took away the stone. And Jesus
lifted up his eyes and said, "Father, I
thank thee that thou hast heard me. 42I
knew that thou hearest me always, but
I have said this on account of the peo-
ple standing by, that they may believe
that thou didst send me." 43When he
had said this, he cried with a loud voice,
"Laz'arus, come out." 44The dead man
came out, his hands and feet bound with
bandages, and his face wrapped with a
cloth. Jesus said to them, "Unbind him,
and let him go."

The Plot to Kill Jesus

45 Many of the Jews therefore, who had
come with Mary and had seen what he
did, believed in him; 46but some of them
went to the Pharisees and told them what
Jesus had done. 47So the chief priests and
the Pharisees gathered the council, and
said, "What are we to do? For this man
performs many signs. 48If we let him go
on thus, every one will believe in him,
and the Romans will come and destroy
both our holy place[c] and our nation."
49But one of them, Ca'iaphas, who was
high priest that year, said to them, "You
know nothing at all; 50you do not under-
stand that it is expedient for you that
one man should die for the people, and
that the whole nation should not per-
ish." 51He did not say this of his own ac-
cord, but being high priest that year he
prophesied that Jesus should die for the
nation, 52and not for the nation only, but
to gather into one the children of God
who are scattered abroad. 53So from that
day on they took counsel how to put him
to death.

54 Jesus therefore no longer went
about openly among the Jews, but went
from there to the country near the wil-
derness, to a town called E'phraim; and
there he stayed with the disciples.

55 Now the Passover of the Jews was
at hand, and many went up from the
country to Jerusalem before the Pass-
over, to purify themselves. 56They were
looking for Jesus and saying to one an-
other as they stood in the temple, "What
do you think? That he will not come to
the feast?" 57Now the chief priests and
the Pharisees had given orders that if
any one knew where he was, he should
let them know, so that they might arrest
him.

[c]**11.48** Greek *our place*

Mary Anoints Jesus

12 Six days before the Passover, Jesus
came to Bethany, where Laz'arus
was, whom Jesus had raised from the
dead. 2There they made him a supper;
Martha served, and Laz'arus was one
of those at table with him. 3Mary took a
pound of costly ointment of pure nard
and anointed the feet of Jesus and wiped
his feet with her hair; and the house was
filled with the fragrance of the ointment.
4But Judas Iscariot, one of his disciples
(he who was to betray him), said, 5"Why
was this ointment not sold for three hun-
dred denarii[d] and given to the poor?"
6This he said, not that he cared for the
poor but because he was a thief, and as
he had the money box he used to take
what was put into it. 7Jesus said, "Let her
alone, let her keep it for the day of my
burial. 8The poor you always have with
you, but you do not always have me."

The Plot to Kill Lazarus

9 When the great crowd of the Jews
learned that he was there, they came, not
only on account of Jesus but also to see
Laz'arus, whom he had raised from the
dead. 10So the chief priests planned to
put Laz'arus also to death, 11because on
account of him many of the Jews were
going away and believing in Jesus.

Jesus' Triumphal Entry into Jerusalem

12 The next day a great crowd who had
come to the feast heard that Jesus was
coming to Jerusalem. 13So they took
branches of palm trees and went out to
meet him, crying, "Hosanna! Blessed is
he who comes in the name of the Lord,
even the King of Israel!" 14And Jesus
found a young ass and sat upon it; as it
is written,

15 "Fear not, daughter of Zion;
behold, your king is coming,
sitting on an ass's colt!"

16His disciples did not understand this at
first; but when Jesus was glorified, then
they remembered that this had been
written of him and had been done to
him. 17The crowd that had been with him
when he called Laz'arus out of the tomb
and raised him from the dead bore wit-
ness. 18The reason why the crowd went
to meet him was that they heard he had
done this sign. 19The Pharisees then said
to one another, "You see that you can do
nothing; look, the world has gone after
him."

Some Greeks Wish to See Jesus

20 Now among those who went up to wor-
ship at the feast were some Greeks. 21So
these came to Philip, who was from Beth-
sa'ida in Galilee, and said to him, "Sir, we
wish to see Jesus." 22Philip went and told
Andrew; Andrew went with Philip and
they told Jesus. 23And Jesus answered
them, "The hour has come for the Son of
man to be glorified. 24Truly, truly, I say to
you, unless a grain of wheat falls into the
earth and dies, it remains alone; but if it
dies, it bears much fruit. 25He who loves
his life loses it, and he who hates his life
in this world will keep it for eternal life.
26If any one serves me, he must follow
me; and where I am, there shall my ser-
vant be also; if any one serves me, the Fa-
ther will honor him.

Jesus Speaks about His Death

27 "Now is my soul troubled. And what
shall I say? 'Father, save me from this
hour'? No, for this purpose I have come
to this hour. 28Father, glorify thy name."
Then a voice came from heaven, "I have
glorified it, and I will glorify it again."
29The crowd standing by heard it and
said that it had thundered. Others said,
"An angel has spoken to him." 30Jesus an-
swered, "This voice has come for your
sake, not for mine. 31Now is the judg-
ment of this world, now shall the ruler

[d] **12.5** The denarius was a day's wage for a laborer

of this world be cast out; [32]and I, when
I am lifted up from the earth, will draw
all men to myself." [33]He said this to show
by what death he was to die. [34]The crowd
answered him, "We have heard from the
law that the Christ remains for ever. How
can you say that the Son of man must
be lifted up? Who is this Son of man?"
[35]Jesus said to them, "The light is with
you for a little longer. Walk while you
have the light, lest the darkness overtake
you; he who walks in the darkness does
not know where he goes. [36]While you
have the light, believe in the light, that
you may become sons of light."

The Unbelief of the People

When Jesus had said this, he departed
and hid himself from them. [37]Though he
had done so many signs before them, yet
they did not believe in him; [38]it was that
the word spoken by the prophet Isaiah
might be fulfilled:

"Lord, who has believed our report,
and to whom has the arm of the Lord
been revealed?"

[39]Therefore they could not believe. For
Isaiah again said,

[40] "He has blinded their eyes and
hardened their heart,
lest they should see with their eyes
and perceive with their heart,
and turn for me to heal them."

[41]Isaiah said this because he saw his
glory and spoke of him. [42]Nevertheless
many even of the authorities believed
in him, but for fear of the Pharisees they
did not confess it, lest they should be put
out of the synagogue: [43]for they loved
the praise of men more than the praise
of God.

Summary of Jesus' Teaching

44 And Jesus cried out and said, "He
who believes in me, believes not in me
but in him who sent me. [45]And he who
sees me sees him who sent me. [46]I have
come as light into the world, that who-
ever believes in me may not remain in
darkness. [47]If any one hears my say-
ings and does not keep them, I do not
judge him; for I did not come to judge
the world but to save the world. [48]He
who rejects me and does not receive
my sayings has a judge; the word that I
have spoken will be his judge on the last
day. [49]For I have not spoken on my own
authority; the Father who sent me has
himself given me commandment what
to say and what to speak. [50]And I know
that his commandment is eternal life.
What I say, therefore, I say as the Father
has bidden me."

Jesus Washes the Disciples' Feet

13 Now before the feast of the Pass-
over, when Jesus knew that his
hour had come to depart out of this
world to the Father, having loved his own
who were in the world, he loved them to
the end. [2]And during supper, when the
devil had already put it into the heart
of Judas Iscariot, Simon's son, to betray
him, [3]Jesus, knowing that the Father
had given all things into his hands, and
that he had come from God and was go-
ing to God, [4]rose from supper, laid aside
his garments, and girded himself with a
towel. [5]Then he poured water into a ba-
sin, and began to wash the disciples' feet,
and to wipe them with the towel with
which he was girded. [6]He came to Simon
Peter; and Peter said to him, "Lord, do
you wash my feet?" [7]Jesus answered him,
"What I am doing you do not know now,
but afterward you will understand." [8]Pe-
ter said to him, "You shall never wash
my feet." Jesus answered him, "If I do not
wash you, you have no part in me." [9]Si-
mon Peter said to him, "Lord, not my feet
only but also my hands and my head!"
[10]Jesus said to him, "He who has bathed
does not need to wash, except for his
feet,[e] but he is clean all over; and you are

[e]**13.10** Other ancient authorities omit *except for his feet*

clean, but not all of you." [11]For he knew who was to betray him; that was why he said, "You are not all clean."

12 When he had washed their feet, and taken his garments, and resumed his place, he said to them, "Do you know what I have done to you? [13]You call me Teacher and Lord; and you are right, for so I am. [14]If I then, your Lord and Teacher, have washed your feet, you also ought to wash one another's feet. [15]For I have given you an example, that you also should do as I have done to you. [16]Truly, truly, I say to you, a servant[f] is not greater than his master; nor is he who is sent greater than he who sent him. [17]If you know these things, blessed are you if you do them. [18]I am not speaking of you all; I know whom I have chosen; it is that the scripture may be fulfilled, 'He who ate my bread has lifted his heel against me.' [19]I tell you this now, before it takes place, that when it does take place you may believe that I am he. [20]Truly, truly, I say to you, he who receives any one whom I send receives me; and he who receives me receives him who sent me."

Jesus Foretells His Betrayal

21 When Jesus had thus spoken, he was troubled in spirit, and testified, "Truly, truly, I say to you, one of you will betray me." [22]The disciples looked at one another, uncertain of whom he spoke. [23]One of his disciples, whom Jesus loved, was lying close to the breast of Jesus; [24]so Simon Peter beckoned to him and said, "Tell us who it is of whom he speaks." [25]So lying thus, close to the breast of Jesus, he said to him, "Lord, who is it?" [26]Jesus answered, "It is he to whom I shall give this morsel when I have dipped it." So when he had dipped the morsel, he gave it to Judas, the son of Simon Iscariot. [27]Then after the morsel, Satan entered into him. Jesus said to him, "What you are going to do, do quickly." [28]Now no one at the table knew why he said this to him. [29]Some thought that, because Judas had the money box, Jesus was telling him, "Buy what we need for the feast"; or, that he should give something to the poor. [30]So, after receiving the morsel, he immediately went out; and it was night.

The New Commandment

31 When he had gone out, Jesus said, "Now is the Son of man glorified, and in him God is glorified; [32]if God is glorified in him, God will also glorify him in himself, and glorify him at once. [33]Little children, yet a little while I am with you. You will seek me; and as I said to the Jews so now I say to you, 'Where I am going you cannot come.' [34]A new commandment I give to you, that you love one another; even as I have loved you, that you also love one another. [35]By this all men will know that you are my disciples, if you have love for one another."

Jesus Foretells Peter's Denial

36 Simon Peter said to him, "Lord, where are you going?" Jesus answered, "Where I am going you cannot follow me now; but you shall follow afterward." [37]Peter said to him, "Lord, why cannot I follow you now? I will lay down my life for you." [38]Jesus answered, "Will you lay down your life for me? Truly, truly, I say to you, the cock will not crow, till you have denied me three times.

Jesus the Way to the Father

14 "Let not your hearts be troubled; believe[g] in God, believe also in me. [2]In my Father's house are many rooms; if it were not so, would I have told you that I go to prepare a place for you? [3]And when I go and prepare a place for you, I will come again and will take you to myself, that where I am you may be also. [4]And you know the way where I

[f] **13.16** Or *slave* [g] **14.1** Or *you believe*

am going."[h] 5 Thomas said to him, "Lord,
we do not know where you are going;
how can we know the way?" 6 Jesus said
to him, "I am the way, and the truth, and
the life; no one comes to the Father, but
by me. 7 If you had known me, you would
have known my Father also; henceforth
you know him and have seen him."

8 Philip said to him, "Lord, show us
the Father, and we shall be satisfied."
9 Jesus said to him, "Have I been with you
so long, and yet you do not know me,
Philip? He who has seen me has seen the
Father; how can you say, 'Show us the
Father'? 10 Do you not believe that I am
in the Father and the Father in me? The
words that I say to you I do not speak on
my own authority; but the Father who
dwells in me does his works. 11 Believe me
that I am in the Father and the Father in
me; or else believe me for the sake of the
works themselves.

12 "Truly, truly, I say to you, he who be-
lieves in me will also do the works that
I do; and greater works than these will
he do, because I go to the Father. 13 What-
ever you ask in my name, I will do it, that
the Father may be glorified in the Son;
14 if you ask[i] anything in my name, I will
do it.

The Promise of the Holy Spirit

15 "If you love me, you will keep my com-
mandments. 16 And I will pray the Father,
and he will give you another Counselor,
to be with you for ever, 17 even the Spirit
of truth, whom the world cannot receive,
because it neither sees him nor knows
him; you know him, for he dwells with
you, and will be in you.

18 "I will not leave you desolate; I will
come to you. 19 Yet a little while, and the
world will see me no more, but you will
see me; because I live, you will live also.
20 In that day you will know that I am in
my Father, and you in me, and I in you.
21 He who has my commandments and
keeps them, he it is who loves me; and he
who loves me will be loved by my Father,
and I will love him and manifest myself
to him." 22 Judas (not Iscariot) said to him,
"Lord, how is it that you will manifest
yourself to us, and not to the world?"
23 Jesus answered him, "If a man loves me,
he will keep my word, and my Father will
love him, and we will come to him and
make our home with him. 24 He who does
not love me does not keep my words; and
the word which you hear is not mine but
the Father's who sent me.

25 "These things I have spoken to you,
while I am still with you. 26 But the Coun-
selor, the Holy Spirit, whom the Father
will send in my name, he will teach you
all things, and bring to your remem-
brance all that I have said to you. 27 Peace
I leave with you; my peace I give to you;
not as the world gives do I give to you.
Let not your hearts be troubled, neither
let them be afraid. 28 You heard me say to
you, 'I go away, and I will come to you.' If
you loved me, you would have rejoiced,
because I go to the Father; for the Father
is greater than I. 29 And now I have told
you before it takes place, so that when it
does take place, you may believe. 30 I will
no longer talk much with you, for the
ruler of this world is coming. He has no
power over me; 31 but I do as the Father
has commanded me, so that the world
may know that I love the Father. Rise, let
us go hence.

Jesus the True Vine

15 "I am the true vine, and my Father
is the vinedresser. 2 Every branch
of mine that bears no fruit, he takes
away, and every branch that does bear
fruit he prunes, that it may bear more
fruit. 3 You are already made clean by the
word which I have spoken to you. 4 Abide
in me, and I in you. As the branch cannot

[h] **14.4** Other ancient authorities read *where I am going you know, and the way you know*
[i] **14.14** Other ancient authorities add *me*

bear fruit by itself, unless it abides in
the vine, neither can you, unless you
abide in me. [5]I am the vine, you are the
branches. He who abides in me, and I in
him, he it is that bears much fruit, for
apart from me you can do nothing. [6]If
a man does not abide in me, he is cast
forth as a branch and withers; and the
branches are gathered, thrown into the
fire and burned. [7]If you abide in me, and
my words abide in you, ask whatever
you will, and it shall be done for you.
[8]By this my Father is glorified, that you
bear much fruit, and so prove to be my
disciples. [9]As the Father has loved me,
so have I loved you; abide in my love. [10]If
you keep my commandments, you will
abide in my love, just as I have kept my
Father's commandments and abide in his
love. [11]These things I have spoken to you,
that my joy may be in you, and that your
joy may be full.

12 “This is my commandment, that
you love one another as I have loved
you. [13]Greater love has no man than
this, that a man lay down his life for his
friends. [14]You are my friends if you do
what I command you. [15]No longer do I
call you servants,[j] for the servant[k] does
not know what his master is doing; but
I have called you friends, for all that I
have heard from my Father I have made
known to you. [16]You did not choose me,
but I chose you and appointed you that
you should go and bear fruit and that
your fruit should abide; so that whatever
you ask the Father in my name, he may
give it to you. [17]This I command you, to
love one another.

The World's Hatred

18 “If the world hates you, know that
it has hated me before it hated you. [19]If
you were of the world, the world would
love its own; but because you are not
of the world, but I chose you out of the
world, therefore the world hates you.
[20]Remember the word that I said to you,
‘A servant[l] is not greater than his mas-
ter.’ If they persecuted me, they will per-
secute you; if they kept my word, they
will keep yours also. [21]But all this they
will do to you on my account, because
they do not know him who sent me. [22]If
I had not come and spoken to them, they
would not have sin; but now they have no
excuse for their sin. [23]He who hates me
hates my Father also. [24]If I had not done
among them the works which no one else
did, they would not have sin; but now
they have seen and hated both me and
my Father. [25]It is to fulfil the word that
is written in their law, ‘They hated me
without a cause.’ [26]But when the Coun-
selor comes, whom I shall send to you
from the Father, even the Spirit of truth,
who proceeds from the Father, he will
bear witness to me; [27]and you also are
witnesses, because you have been with
me from the beginning.

16 “I have said all this to you to keep
you from falling away. [2]They will
put you out of the synagogues; indeed,
the hour is coming when whoever kills
you will think he is offering service to
God. [3]And they will do this because they
have not known the Father, nor me. [4]But
I have said these things to you, that when
their hour comes you may remember
that I told you of them.

The Work of the Spirit

“I did not say these things to you from the
beginning, because I was with you. [5]But
now I am going to him who sent me; yet
none of you asks me, ‘Where are you go-
ing?’ [6]But because I have said these things
to you, sorrow has filled your hearts.
[7]Nevertheless I tell you the truth: it is to
your advantage that I go away, for if I do
not go away, the Counselor will not come
to you; but if I go, I will send him to you.
[8]And when he comes, he will convince
the world of sin and of righteousness

[j] **15.15** Or *slaves* [k] **15.15** Or *slave* [l] **15.20** Or *slave*

and of judgment: [9]of sin, because they do
not believe in me; [10]of righteousness, be-
cause I go to the Father, and you will see
me no more; [11]of judgment, because the
ruler of this world is judged.
12 “I have yet many things to say to
you, but you cannot bear them now.
[13]When the Spirit of truth comes, he
will guide you into all the truth; for he
will not speak on his own authority, but
whatever he hears he will speak, and he
will declare to you the things that are to
come. [14]He will glorify me, for he will
take what is mine and declare it to you.
[15]All that the Father has is mine; there-
fore I said that he will take what is mine
and declare it to you.

Sorrow Will Turn into Joy

16 “A little while, and you will see me no
more; again a little while, and you will
see me.” [17]Some of his disciples said to
one another, “What is this that he says
to us, ‘A little while, and you will not see
me, and again a little while, and you will
see me’; and, ‘because I go to the Father’?”
[18]They said, “What does he mean by ‘a
little while’? We do not know what he
means.” [19]Jesus knew that they wanted to
ask him; so he said to them, “Is this what
you are asking yourselves, what I meant
by saying, ‘A little while, and you will not
see me, and again a little while, and you
will see me’? [20]Truly, truly, I say to you,
you will weep and lament, but the world
will rejoice; you will be sorrowful, but
your sorrow will turn into joy. [21]When
a woman is in travail she has sorrow,
because her hour has come; but when
she is delivered of the child, she no lon-
ger remembers the anguish, for joy that
a child[m] is born into the world. [22]So you
have sorrow now, but I will see you again
and your hearts will rejoice, and no one
will take your joy from you. [23]In that day
you will ask nothing of me. Truly, truly,
I say to you, if you ask anything of the
Father, he will give it to you in my name.
[24]Hitherto you have asked nothing in
my name; ask, and you will receive, that
your joy may be full.

Peace for the Disciples

25 “I have said this to you in figures;
the hour is coming when I shall no lon-
ger speak to you in figures but tell you
plainly of the Father. [26]In that day you
will ask in my name; and I do not say to
you that I shall pray the Father for you;
[27]for the Father himself loves you, be-
cause you have loved me and have be-
lieved that I came from the Father. [28]I
came from the Father and have come
into the world; again, I am leaving the
world and going to the Father.”
29 His disciples said, “Ah, now you
are speaking plainly, not in any figure!
[30]Now we know that you know all things,
and need none to question you; by this
we believe that you came from God.”
[31]Jesus answered them, “Do you now
believe? [32]The hour is coming, indeed it
has come, when you will be scattered, ev-
ery man to his home, and will leave me
alone; yet I am not alone, for the Father is
with me. [33]I have said this to you, that in
me you may have peace. In the world you
have tribulation; but be of good cheer, I
have overcome the world.”

Jesus Prays for His Disciples

17 When Jesus had spoken these
words, he lifted up his eyes to
heaven and said, “Father, the hour has
come; glorify thy Son that the Son may
glorify thee, [2]since thou hast given him
power over all flesh, to give eternal life
to all whom thou hast given him. [3]And
this is eternal life, that they know thee
the only true God, and Jesus Christ whom
thou hast sent. [4]I glorified thee on earth,
having accomplished the work which
thou gavest me to do; [5]and now, Father,
glorify thou me in thy own presence

[m] **16.21** Greek *a human being*

with the glory which I had with thee be-
fore the world was made.

6 "I have manifested thy name to the
men whom thou gavest me out of the
world; thine they were, and thou gav-
est them to me, and they have kept thy
word. [7]Now they know that everything
that thou hast given me is from thee;
[8]for I have given them the words which
thou gavest me, and they have received
them and know in truth that I came
from thee; and they have believed that
thou didst send me. [9]I am praying for
them; I am not praying for the world
but for those whom thou hast given me,
for they are thine; [10]all mine are thine,
and thine are mine, and I am glorified
in them. [11]And now I am no more in the
world, but they are in the world, and I am
coming to thee. Holy Father, keep them
in thy name, which thou hast given me,
that they may be one, even as we are one.
[12]While I was with them, I kept them in
thy name, which thou hast given me; I
have guarded them, and none of them
is lost but the son of perdition, that the
scripture might be fulfilled. [13]But now
I am coming to thee; and these things I
speak in the world, that they may have
my joy fulfilled in themselves. [14]I have
given them thy word; and the world has
hated them because they are not of the
world, even as I am not of the world. [15]I
do not pray that thou shouldst take them
out of the world, but that thou shouldst
keep them from the evil one.[n] [16]They are
not of the world, even as I am not of the
world. [17]Sanctify them in the truth; thy
word is truth. [18]As thou didst send me
into the world, so I have sent them into
the world. [19]And for their sake I conse-
crate myself, that they also may be conse-
crated in truth.

20 "I do not pray for these only, but
also for those who believe in me through
their word, [21]that they may all be one;
even as thou, Father, art in me, and I in
thee, that they also may be in us, so that
the world may believe that thou hast sent
me. [22]The glory which thou hast given
me I have given to them, that they may be
one even as we are one, [23]I in them and
thou in me, that they may become per-
fectly one, so that the world may know
that thou hast sent me and hast loved
them even as thou hast loved me. [24]Fa-
ther, I desire that they also, whom thou
hast given me, may be with me where I
am, to behold my glory which thou hast
given me in thy love for me before the
foundation of the world. [25]O righteous
Father, the world has not known thee,
but I have known thee; and these know
that thou hast sent me. [26]I made known to
them thy name, and I will make it known,
that the love with which thou hast loved
me may be in them, and I in them."

The Betrayal and Arrest of Jesus

18 When Jesus had spoken these
words, he went forth with his dis-
ciples across the Kidron valley, where
there was a garden, which he and his
disciples entered. [2]Now Judas, who be-
trayed him, also knew the place; for Jesus
often met there with his disciples. [3]So
Judas, procuring a band of soldiers and
some officers from the chief priests and
the Pharisees, went there with lanterns
and torches and weapons. [4]Then Jesus,
knowing all that was to befall him, came
forward and said to them, "Whom do
you seek?" [5]They answered him, "Jesus
of Nazareth." Jesus said to them, "I am
he." Judas, who betrayed him, was stand-
ing with them. [6]When he said to them,
"I am he," they drew back and fell to the
ground. [7]Again he asked them, "Whom
do you seek?" And they said, "Jesus of
Nazareth." [8]Jesus answered, "I told you
that I am he; so, if you seek me, let these
men go." [9]This was to fulfil the word
which he had spoken, "Of those whom
thou gavest me I lost not one." [10]Then

[n]**17.15** Or *from evil*

Simon Peter, having a sword, drew it and
struck the high priest's slave and cut
off his right ear. The slave's name was
Malchus. [11]Jesus said to Peter, "Put your
sword into its sheath; shall I not drink
the cup which the Father has given me?"

Jesus before the High Priest

12 So the band of soldiers and their cap-
tain and the officers of the Jews seized
Jesus and bound him. [13]First they led him
to Annas; for he was the father-in-law of
Ca'iaphas, who was high priest that year.
[14]It was Ca'iaphas who had given counsel
to the Jews that it was expedient that one
man should die for the people.

Peter Denies Jesus

15 Simon Peter followed Jesus, and so
did another disciple. As this disciple was
known to the high priest, he entered the
court of the high priest along with Jesus,
[16]while Peter stood outside at the door.
So the other disciple, who was known
to the high priest, went out and spoke to
the maid who kept the door, and brought
Peter in. [17]The maid who kept the door
said to Peter, "Are not you also one of
this man's disciples?" He said, "I am not."
[18]Now the servants[o] and officers had
made a charcoal fire, because it was cold,
and they were standing and warming
themselves; Peter also was with them,
standing and warming himself.

The High Priest Questions Jesus

19 The high priest then questioned Jesus
about his disciples and his teaching.
[20]Jesus answered him, "I have spoken
openly to the world; I have always taught
in synagogues and in the temple, where
all Jews come together; I have said noth-
ing secretly. [21]Why do you ask me? Ask
those who have heard me, what I said to
them; they know what I said." [22]When he
had said this, one of the officers standing
by struck Jesus with his hand, saying, "Is
that how you answer the high priest?"
[23]Jesus answered him, "If I have spoken
wrongly, bear witness to the wrong;
but if I have spoken rightly, why do you
strike me?" [24]Annas then sent him bound
to Ca'iaphas the high priest.

Peter Denies Jesus Again

25 Now Simon Peter was standing and
warming himself. They said to him, "Are
not you also one of his disciples?" He de-
nied it and said, "I am not." [26]One of the
servants[p] of the high priest, a kinsman
of the man whose ear Peter had cut off,
asked, "Did I not see you in the garden
with him?" [27]Peter again denied it; and at
once the cock crowed.

Jesus before Pilate

28 Then they led Jesus from the house
of Ca'iaphas to the praetorium. It was
early. They themselves did not enter the
praetorium, so that they might not be
defiled, but might eat the passover. [29]So
Pilate went out to them and said, "What
accusation do you bring against this
man?" [30]They answered him, "If this man
were not an evildoer, we would not have
handed him over." [31]Pilate said to them,
"Take him yourselves and judge him
by your own law." The Jews said to him,
"It is not lawful for us to put any man
to death." [32]This was to fulfil the word
which Jesus had spoken to show by what
death he was to die.

33 Pilate entered the praetorium
again and called Jesus, and said to him,
"Are you the King of the Jews?" [34]Jesus
answered, "Do you say this of your own
accord, or did others say it to you about
me?" [35]Pilate answered, "Am I a Jew?
Your own nation and the chief priests
have handed you over to me; what have
you done?" [36]Jesus answered, "My king-
ship is not of this world; if my kingship
were of this world, my servants would
fight, that I might not be handed over to

[o]**18.18** Or *slaves* [p]**18.26** Or *slaves*

the Jews; but my kingship is not from the
world." 37 Pilate said to him, "So you are
a king?" Jesus answered, "You say that
I am a king. For this I was born, and for
this I have come into the world, to bear
witness to the truth. Every one who is of
the truth hears my voice." 38 Pilate said to
him, "What is truth?"

Jesus Sentenced to Death

After he had said this, he went out to
the Jews again, and told them, "I find no
crime in him. 39 But you have a custom
that I should release one man for you at
the Passover; will you have me release
for you the King of the Jews?" 40 They
cried out again, "Not this man, but
Barab'bas!" Now Barab'bas was a robber.

19 Then Pilate took Jesus and
scourged him. 2 And the soldiers
plaited a crown of thorns, and put it
on his head, and arrayed him in a pur-
ple robe; 3 they came up to him, saying,
"Hail, King of the Jews!" and struck him
with their hands. 4 Pilate went out again,
and said to them, "Behold, I am bringing
him out to you, that you may know that
I find no crime in him." 5 So Jesus came
out, wearing the crown of thorns and the
purple robe. Pilate said to them, "Here
is the man!" 6 When the chief priests
and the officers saw him, they cried out,
"Crucify him, crucify him!" Pilate said to
them, "Take him yourselves and crucify
him, for I find no crime in him." 7 The Jews
answered him, "We have a law, and by
that law he ought to die, because he has
made himself the Son of God." 8 When Pi-
late heard these words, he was the more
afraid; 9 he entered the praetorium again
and said to Jesus, "Where are you from?"
But Jesus gave no answer. 10 Pilate there-
fore said to him, "You will not speak to
me? Do you not know that I have power
to release you, and power to crucify
you?" 11 Jesus answered him, "You would
have no power over me unless it had
been given you from above; therefore he
who delivered me to you has the greater
sin."

12 Upon this Pilate sought to release
him, but the Jews cried out, "If you re-
lease this man, you are not Caesar's
friend; every one who makes himself
a king sets himself against Caesar."
13 When Pilate heard these words, he
brought Jesus out and sat down on the
judgment seat at a place called The Pave-
ment, and in Hebrew, Gab'batha. 14 Now it
was the day of Preparation of the Pass-
over; it was about the sixth hour. He said
to the Jews, "Here is your King!" 15 They
cried out, "Away with him, away with
him, crucify him!" Pilate said to them,
"Shall I crucify your King?" The chief
priests answered, "We have no king but
Caesar." 16 Then he handed him over to
them to be crucified.

The Crucifixion of Jesus

17 So they took Jesus, and he went out,
bearing his own cross, to the place
called the place of a skull, which is
called in Hebrew Gol'gotha. 18 There
they crucified him, and with him two
others, one on either side, and Jesus
between them. 19 Pilate also wrote a title
and put it on the cross; it read, "Jesus of
Nazareth, the King of the Jews." 20 Many
of the Jews read this title, for the place
where Jesus was crucified was near the
city; and it was written in Hebrew, in
Latin, and in Greek. 21 The chief priests
of the Jews then said to Pilate, "Do not
write, 'The King of the Jews,' but, 'This
man said, I am King of the Jews.'" 22 Pi-
late answered, "What I have written I
have written."

23 When the soldiers had crucified
Jesus they took his garments and made
four parts, one for each soldier; also his
tunic. But the tunic was without seam,
woven from top to bottom; 24 so they said
to one another, "Let us not tear it, but
cast lots for it to see whose it shall be."
This was to fulfil the scripture,

> "They parted my garments among
> them,
> and for my clothing they cast lots."

25 So the soldiers did this. But stand-
ing by the cross of Jesus were his mother,
and his mother's sister, Mary the wife of
Clopas, and Mary Mag′dalene. [26]When
Jesus saw his mother, and the disciple
whom he loved standing near, he said to
his mother, "Woman, behold, your son!"
[27]Then he said to the disciple, "Behold,
your mother!" And from that hour the
disciple took her to his own home.

28 After this Jesus, knowing that all
was now finished, said (to fulfil the scrip-
ture), "I thirst." [29]A bowl full of vinegar
stood there; so they put a sponge full of
the vinegar on hyssop and held it to his
mouth. [30]When Jesus had received the
vinegar, he said, "It is finished"; and he
bowed his head and gave up his spirit.

Jesus' Side Is Pierced

31 Since it was the day of Preparation, in
order to prevent the bodies from remain-
ing on the cross on the sabbath (for that
sabbath was a high day), the Jews asked
Pilate that their legs might be broken,
and that they might be taken away. [32]So
the soldiers came and broke the legs of
the first, and of the other who had been
crucified with him; [33]but when they came
to Jesus and saw that he was already dead,
they did not break his legs. [34]But one of
the soldiers pierced his side with a spear,
and at once there came out blood and wa-
ter. [35]He who saw it has borne witness—
his testimony is true, and he knows that
he tells the truth—that you also may be-
lieve. [36]For these things took place that
the scripture might be fulfilled, "Not a
bone of him shall be broken." [37]And again
another scripture says, "They shall look
on him whom they have pierced."

The Burial of Jesus

38 After this Joseph of Arimathe′a, who
was a disciple of Jesus, but secretly, for
fear of the Jews, asked Pilate that he
might take away the body of Jesus, and
Pilate gave him leave. So he came and
took away his body. [39]Nicode′mus also,
who had at first come to him by night,
came bringing a mixture of myrrh and
aloes, about a hundred pounds' weight.
[40]They took the body of Jesus, and bound
it in linen cloths with the spices, as is the
burial custom of the Jews. [41]Now in the
place where he was crucified there was
a garden, and in the garden a new tomb
where no one had ever been laid. [42]So be-
cause of the Jewish day of Preparation,
as the tomb was close at hand, they laid
Jesus there.

The Resurrection of Jesus

20 Now on the first day of the week
Mary Mag′dalene came to the
tomb early, while it was still dark, and
saw that the stone had been taken away
from the tomb. [2]So she ran, and went to
Simon Peter and the other disciple, the
one whom Jesus loved, and said to them,
"They have taken the Lord out of the
tomb, and we do not know where they
have laid him." [3]Peter then came out with
the other disciple, and they went toward
the tomb. [4]They both ran, but the other
disciple outran Peter and reached the
tomb first; [5]and stooping to look in, he
saw the linen cloths lying there, but he
did not go in. [6]Then Simon Peter came,
following him, and went into the tomb;
he saw the linen cloths lying, [7]and the
napkin, which had been on his head, not
lying with the linen cloths but rolled up
in a place by itself. [8]Then the other dis-
ciple, who reached the tomb first, also
went in, and he saw and believed; [9]for as
yet they did not know the scripture, that
he must rise from the dead. [10]Then the
disciples went back to their homes.

Jesus Appears to Mary Magdalene

11 But Mary stood weeping outside the
tomb, and as she wept she stooped to

look into the tomb; 12 and she saw two an-
gels in white, sitting where the body of
Jesus had lain, one at the head and one at
the feet. 13 They said to her, "Woman, why
are you weeping?" She said to them, "Be-
cause they have taken away my Lord, and
I do not know where they have laid him."
14 Saying this, she turned round and saw
Jesus standing, but she did not know that
it was Jesus. 15 Jesus said to her, "Woman,
why are you weeping? Whom do you
seek?" Supposing him to be the gardener,
she said to him, "Sir, if you have carried
him away, tell me where you have laid
him, and I will take him away." 16 Jesus
said to her, "Mary." She turned and said
to him in Hebrew, "Rab-bo'ni!" (which
means Teacher). 17 Jesus said to her, "Do
not hold me, for I have not yet ascended
to the Father; but go to my brethren and
say to them, I am ascending to my Father
and your Father, to my God and your
God." 18 Mary Mag'dalene went and said
to the disciples, "I have seen the Lord";
and she told them that he had said these
things to her.

Jesus Appears to the Disciples

19 On the evening of that day, the first
day of the week, the doors being shut
where the disciples were, for fear of the
Jews, Jesus came and stood among them
and said to them, "Peace be with you."
20 When he had said this, he showed them
his hands and his side. Then the disci-
ples were glad when they saw the Lord.
21 Jesus said to them again, "Peace be with
you. As the Father has sent me, even so I
send you." 22 And when he had said this,
he breathed on them, and said to them,
"Receive the Holy Spirit. 23 If you forgive
the sins of any, they are forgiven; if you
retain the sins of any, they are retained."

Jesus and Thomas

24 Now Thomas, one of the twelve, called
the Twin, was not with them when Jesus
came. 25 So the other disciples told him,
"We have seen the Lord." But he said to
them, "Unless I see in his hands the print
of the nails, and place my finger in the
mark of the nails, and place my hand in
his side, I will not believe."

26 Eight days later, his disciples were
again in the house, and Thomas was with
them. The doors were shut, but Jesus
came and stood among them, and said,
"Peace be with you." 27 Then he said to
Thomas, "Put your finger here, and see
my hands; and put out your hand, and
place it in my side; do not be faithless,
but believing." 28 Thomas answered him,
"My Lord and my God!" 29 Jesus said to
him, "Have you believed because you
have seen me? Blessed are those who
have not seen and yet believe."

The Purpose of This Book

30 Now Jesus did many other signs in the
presence of the disciples, which are not
written in this book; 31 but these are writ-
ten that you may believe that Jesus is the
Christ, the Son of God, and that believing
you may have life in his name.

Jesus Appears to Seven Disciples

21 After this Jesus revealed himself
again to the disciples by the Sea
of Tibe'ri-as; and he revealed himself in
this way. 2 Simon Peter, Thomas called
the Twin, Nathan'a-el of Cana in Galilee,
the sons of Zeb'edee, and two others of
his disciples were together. 3 Simon Peter
said to them, "I am going fishing." They
said to him, "We will go with you." They
went out and got into the boat; but that
night they caught nothing.

4 Just as day was breaking, Jesus
stood on the beach; yet the disciples did
not know that it was Jesus. 5 Jesus said
to them, "Children, have you any fish?"
They answered him, "No." 6 He said to
them, "Cast the net on the right side of
the boat, and you will find some." So they
cast it, and now they were not able to
haul it in, for the quantity of fish. 7 That

disciple whom Jesus loved said to Peter,
"It is the Lord!" When Simon Peter heard
that it was the Lord, he put on his clothes,
for he was stripped for work, and sprang
into the sea. 8 But the other disciples
came in the boat, dragging the net full of
fish, for they were not far from the land,
but about a hundred yards[q] off.
9 When they got out on land, they
saw a charcoal fire there, with fish ly-
ing on it, and bread. 10 Jesus said to them,
"Bring some of the fish that you have just
caught." 11 So Simon Peter went aboard
and hauled the net ashore, full of large
fish, a hundred and fifty-three of them;
and although there were so many, the net
was not torn. 12 Jesus said to them, "Come
and have breakfast." Now none of the
disciples dared ask him, "Who are you?"
They knew it was the Lord. 13 Jesus came
and took the bread and gave it to them,
and so with the fish. 14 This was now the
third time that Jesus was revealed to the
disciples after he was raised from the
dead.

Jesus and Peter

15 When they had finished breakfast,
Jesus said to Simon Peter, "Simon, son of
John, do you love me more than these?"
He said to him, "Yes, Lord; you know
that I love you." He said to him, "Feed my
lambs." 16 A second time he said to him,
"Simon, son of John, do you love me?"
He said to him, "Yes, Lord; you know
that I love you." He said to him, "Tend my
sheep." 17 He said to him the third time,
"Simon, son of John, do you love me?"
Peter was grieved because he said to him
the third time, "Do you love me?" And he
said to him, "Lord, you know everything;
you know that I love you." Jesus said to
him, "Feed my sheep. 18 Truly, truly, I
say to you, when you were young, you
girded yourself and walked where you
would; but when you are old, you will
stretch out your hands, and another will
gird you and carry you where you do
not wish to go." 19 (This he said to show by
what death he was to glorify God.) And
after this he said to him, "Follow me."

Jesus and the Beloved Disciple

20 Peter turned and saw following them
the disciple whom Jesus loved, who had
lain close to his breast at the supper and
had said, "Lord, who is it that is going
to betray you?" 21 When Peter saw him,
he said to Jesus, "Lord, what about this
man?" 22 Jesus said to him, "If it is my will
that he remain until I come, what is that
to you? Follow me!" 23 The saying spread
abroad among the brethren that this dis-
ciple was not to die; yet Jesus did not say
to him that he was not to die, but, "If it is
my will that he remain until I come, what
is that to you?"

24 This is the disciple who is bearing witness to these things, and who has written these things; and we know that his testimony is true.

25 But there are also many other things which Jesus did; were every one of them to be written, I suppose that the world itself could not contain the books that would be written.

[q] **21.8** Greek *two hundred cubits*

The

ACTS OF THE APOSTLES

The Promise of the Holy Spirit

1 In the first book, O Theoph′ilus, I
have dealt with all that Jesus began
to do and teach, 2 until the day when he
was taken up, after he had given com-
mandment through the Holy Spirit to
the apostles whom he had chosen. 3 To
them he presented himself alive after
his passion by many proofs, appearing
to them during forty days, and speaking
of the kingdom of God. 4 And while stay-
ing[a] with them he charged them not to
depart from Jerusalem, but to wait for
the promise of the Father, which, he said,
"you heard from me, 5 for John baptized
with water, but before many days you
shall be baptized with the Holy Spirit."

The Ascension of Jesus

6 So when they had come together, they
asked him, "Lord, will you at this time
restore the kingdom to Israel?" 7 He said
to them, "It is not for you to know times
or seasons which the Father has fixed
by his own authority. 8 But you shall re-
ceive power when the Holy Spirit has
come upon you; and you shall be my
witnesses in Jerusalem and in all Judea
and Samar′ia and to the end of the earth."
9 And when he had said this, as they were
looking on, he was lifted up, and a cloud
took him out of their sight. 10 And while
they were gazing into heaven as he went,
behold, two men stood by them in white
robes, 11 and said, "Men of Galilee, why
do you stand looking into heaven? This
Jesus, who was taken up from you into
heaven, will come in the same way as you
saw him go into heaven."

Matthias Chosen to Replace Judas

12 Then they returned to Jerusalem
from the mount called Olivet, which is
near Jerusalem, a sabbath day's journey
away; 13 and when they had entered, they
went up to the upper room, where they
were staying, Peter and John and James
and Andrew, Philip and Thomas, Bar-
tholomew and Matthew, James the son of
Alphaeus and Simon the Zealot and Ju-
das the son of James. 14 All these with one
accord devoted themselves to prayer,
together with the women and Mary the
mother of Jesus, and with his brethren.

15 In those days Peter stood up among
the brethren (the company of persons
was in all about a hundred and twenty),
and said, 16 "Brethren, the scripture had
to be fulfilled, which the Holy Spirit
spoke beforehand by the mouth of Da-
vid, concerning Judas who was guide to
those who arrested Jesus. 17 For he was
numbered among us, and was allotted
his share in this ministry. 18 (Now this
man bought a field with the reward of
his wickedness; and falling headlong[b] he
burst open in the middle and all his bow-
els gushed out. 19 And it became known to
all the inhabitants of Jerusalem, so that
the field was called in their language
Akel′dama, that is, Field of Blood.) 20 For
it is written in the book of Psalms,

> 'Let his habitation become desolate,
> and let there be no one to live in it';

and

> 'His office let another take.'

21 So one of the men who have accompa-
nied us during all the time that the Lord
Jesus went in and out among us, 22 begin-
ning from the baptism of John until the
day when he was taken up from us—one
of these men must become with us a wit-
ness to his resurrection." 23 And they put
forward two, Joseph called Barsab′bas,
who was surnamed Justus, and Mat-
thi′as. 24 And they prayed and said, "Lord,

[a] **1.4** Or *eating* [b] **1.18** Or *swelling up*

who knowest the hearts of all men, show
which one of these two thou hast chosen
25 to take the place in this ministry and
apostleship from which Judas turned
aside, to go to his own place." 26 And they
cast lots for them, and the lot fell on
Matthi'as; and he was enrolled with the
eleven apostles.

The Coming of the Holy Spirit

2 When the day of Pentecost had come,
they were all together in one place.
2 And suddenly a sound came from
heaven like the rush of a mighty wind,
and it filled all the house where they
were sitting. 3 And there appeared to
them tongues as of fire, distributed and
resting on each one of them. 4 And they
were all filled with the Holy Spirit and
began to speak in other tongues, as the
Spirit gave them utterance.
5 Now there were dwelling in Jerusa-
lem Jews, devout men from every na-
tion under heaven. 6 And at this sound
the multitude came together, and they
were bewildered, because each one
heard them speaking in his own lan-
guage. 7 And they were amazed and won-
dered, saying, "Are not all these who are
speaking Galileans? 8 And how is it that
we hear, each of us in his own native
language? 9 Par'thians and Medes and
E'lamites and residents of Mesopota'mia,
Judea and Cappado'cia, Pontus and Asia,
10 Phryg'ia and Pamphyl'ia, Egypt and
the parts of Libya belonging to Cyre'ne,
and visitors from Rome, both Jews and
proselytes, 11 Cretans and Arabians, we
hear them telling in our own tongues
the mighty works of God." 12 And all were
amazed and perplexed, saying to one an-
other, "What does this mean?" 13 But oth-
ers mocking said, "They are filled with
new wine."

Peter Addresses the Crowd

14 But Peter, standing with the eleven,
lifted up his voice and addressed them,
"Men of Judea and all who dwell in Jeru-
salem, let this be known to you, and give
ear to my words. 15 For these men are not
drunk, as you suppose, since it is only
the third hour of the day; 16 but this is
what was spoken by the prophet Joel:

17 'And in the last days it shall be, God declares,
that I will pour out my Spirit upon all flesh,
and your sons and your daughters shall prophesy,
and your young men shall see visions,
and your old men shall dream dreams;
18 yea, and on my menservants and my maidservants in those days
I will pour out my Spirit; and they shall prophesy.
19 And I will show wonders in the heaven above
and signs on the earth beneath,
blood, and fire, and vapor of smoke;
20 the sun shall be turned into darkness
and the moon into blood,
before the day of the Lord comes,
the great and manifest day.
21 And it shall be that whoever calls on the name of the Lord shall be saved.'

22 "Men of Israel, hear these words:
Jesus of Nazareth, a man attested to you
by God with mighty works and wonders
and signs which God did through him in
your midst, as you yourselves know—
23 this Jesus, delivered up according to the
definite plan and foreknowledge of God,
you crucified and killed by the hands of
lawless men. 24 But God raised him up,
having loosed the pangs of death, be-
cause it was not possible for him to be
held by it. 25 For David says concerning
him,

'I saw the Lord always before me,
for he is at my right hand that I may not be shaken;

26 therefore my heart was glad, and my
tongue rejoiced;
moreover my flesh will dwell in
hope.
27 For thou wilt not abandon my soul
to Hades,
nor let thy Holy One see corruption.
28 Thou hast made known to me the
ways of life;
thou wilt make me full of gladness
with thy presence.'

29 "Brethren, I may say to you con-
fidently of the patriarch David that he
both died and was buried, and his tomb
is with us to this day. 30 Being therefore
a prophet, and knowing that God had
sworn with an oath to him that he would
set one of his descendants upon his
throne, 31 he foresaw and spoke of the res-
urrection of the Christ, that he was not
abandoned to Hades, nor did his flesh
see corruption. 32 This Jesus God raised
up, and of that we all are witnesses. 33 Be-
ing therefore exalted at the right hand
of God, and having received from the
Father the promise of the Holy Spirit, he
has poured out this which you see and
hear. 34 For David did not ascend into the
heavens; but he himself says,

'The Lord said to my Lord, Sit at my
right hand,
35 till I make thy enemies a stool for
thy feet.'

36 Let all the house of Israel therefore
know assuredly that God has made him
both Lord and Christ, this Jesus whom
you crucified."

The First Converts

37 Now when they heard this they were
cut to the heart, and said to Peter and the
rest of the apostles, "Brethren, what shall
we do?" 38 And Peter said to them, "Re-
pent, and be baptized every one of you in
the name of Jesus Christ for the forgive-
ness of your sins; and you shall receive
the gift of the Holy Spirit. 39 For the prom-
ise is to you and to your children and to
all that are far off, every one whom the
Lord our God calls to him." 40 And he
testified with many other words and ex-
horted them, saying, "Save yourselves
from this crooked generation." 41 So those
who received his word were baptized,
and there were added that day about
three thousand souls. 42 And they devoted
themselves to the apostles' teaching and
fellowship, to the breaking of bread and
the prayers.

Life among the Believers

43 And fear came upon every soul; and
many wonders and signs were done
through the apostles. 44 And all who be-
lieved were together and had all things
in common; 45 and they sold their posses-
sions and goods and distributed them to
all, as any had need. 46 And day by day, at-
tending the temple together and break-
ing bread in their homes, they partook
of food with glad and generous hearts,
47 praising God and having favor with all
the people. And the Lord added to their
number day by day those who were be-
ing saved.

Peter Heals a Crippled Beggar

3 Now Peter and John were going up to
the temple at the hour of prayer, the
ninth hour. 2 And a man lame from birth
was being carried, whom they laid daily
at that gate of the temple which is called
Beautiful to ask alms of those who en-
tered the temple. 3 Seeing Peter and John
about to go into the temple, he asked for
alms. 4 And Peter directed his gaze at him,
with John, and said, "Look at us." 5 And he
fixed his attention upon them, expecting
to receive something from them. 6 But Pe-
ter said, "I have no silver and gold, but I
give you what I have; in the name of Jesus
Christ of Nazareth, walk." 7 And he took
him by the right hand and raised him
up; and immediately his feet and ankles
were made strong. 8 And leaping up he
stood and walked and entered the temple

with them, walking and leaping and
praising God. [9]And all the people saw
him walking and praising God, [10]and rec-
ognized him as the one who sat for alms
at the Beautiful Gate of the temple; and
they were filled with wonder and amaze-
ment at what had happened to him.

Peter Speaks in Solomon's Portico

11 While he clung to Peter and John, all
the people ran together to them in the
portico called Solomon's, astounded.
[12]And when Peter saw it he addressed the
people, "Men of Israel, why do you won-
der at this, or why do you stare at us, as
though by our own power or piety we
had made him walk? [13]The God of Abra-
ham and of Isaac and of Jacob, the God of
our fathers, glorified his servant[c] Jesus,
whom you delivered up and denied in
the presence of Pilate, when he had de-
cided to release him. [14]But you denied
the Holy and Righteous One, and asked
for a murderer to be granted to you,
[15]and killed the Author of life, whom
God raised from the dead. To this we are
witnesses. [16]And his name, by faith in his
name, has made this man strong whom
you see and know; and the faith which
is through Jesus[d] has given the man this
perfect health in the presence of you all.

17 "And now, brethren, I know that
you acted in ignorance, as did also your
rulers. [18]But what God foretold by the
mouth of all the prophets, that his Christ
should suffer, he thus fulfilled. [19]Repent
therefore, and turn again, that your
sins may be blotted out, that times of re-
freshing may come from the presence
of the Lord, [20]and that he may send the
Christ appointed for you, Jesus, [21]whom
heaven must receive until the time for
establishing all that God spoke by the
mouth of his holy prophets from of old.
[22]Moses said, 'The Lord God will raise up
for you a prophet from your brethren as
he raised me up. You shall listen to him
in whatever he tells you. [23]And it shall
be that every soul that does not listen to
that prophet shall be destroyed from the
people.' [24]And all the prophets who have
spoken, from Samuel and those who
came afterwards, also proclaimed these
days. [25]You are the sons of the prophets
and of the covenant which God gave to
your fathers, saying to Abraham, 'And
in your posterity shall all the families
of the earth be blessed.' [26]God, having
raised up his servant,[e] sent him to you
first, to bless you in turning every one of
you from your wickedness."

Peter and John before the Council

4 And as they were speaking to the
people, the priests and the captain of
the temple and the Sad'ducees came upon
them, [2]annoyed because they were teach-
ing the people and proclaiming in Jesus
the resurrection from the dead. [3]And
they arrested them and put them in cus-
tody until the morrow, for it was already
evening. [4]But many of those who heard
the word believed; and the number of the
men came to about five thousand.

5 On the morrow their rulers and el-
ders and scribes were gathered together
in Jerusalem, [6]with Annas the high priest
and Ca'iaphas and John and Alexander,
and all who were of the high-priestly
family. [7]And when they had set them in
the midst, they inquired, "By what power
or by what name did you do this?" [8]Then
Peter, filled with the Holy Spirit, said to
them, "Rulers of the people and elders,
[9]if we are being examined today con-
cerning a good deed done to a cripple, by
what means this man has been healed,
[10]be it known to you all, and to all the
people of Israel, that by the name of Jesus
Christ of Nazareth, whom you crucified,
whom God raised from the dead, by him
this man is standing before you well.
[11]This is the stone which was rejected by
you builders, but which has become the

[c]**3.13** Or *child* [d]**3.16** Greek *him* [e]**3.26** Or *child*

head of the corner. [12]And there is salva-
tion in no one else, for there is no other
name under heaven given among men
by which we must be saved."
13 Now when they saw the boldness of
Peter and John, and perceived that they
were uneducated, common men, they
wondered; and they recognized that they
had been with Jesus. [14]But seeing the man
that had been healed standing beside
them, they had nothing to say in oppo-
sition. [15]But when they had commanded
them to go aside out of the council, they
conferred with one another, [16]saying,
"What shall we do with these men? For
that a notable sign has been performed
through them is manifest to all the in-
habitants of Jerusalem, and we cannot
deny it. [17]But in order that it may spread
no further among the people, let us warn
them to speak no more to any one in this
name." [18]So they called them and charged
them not to speak or teach at all in the
name of Jesus. [19]But Peter and John an-
swered them, "Whether it is right in the
sight of God to listen to you rather than to
God, you must judge; [20]for we cannot but
speak of what we have seen and heard."
[21]And when they had further threatened
them, they let them go, finding no way
to punish them, because of the people;
for all men praised God for what had
happened. [22]For the man on whom this
sign of healing was performed was more
than forty years old.

The Believers Pray for Boldness

23 When they were released they went
to their friends and reported what the
chief priests and the elders had said to
them. [24]And when they heard it, they
lifted their voices together to God and
said, "Sovereign Lord, who didst make
the heaven and the earth and the sea and
everything in them, [25]who by the mouth
of our father David, thy servant,[f] didst
say by the Holy Spirit,

'Why did the Gentiles rage,
and the peoples imagine vain
things?
26 The kings of the earth set
themselves in array,
and the rulers were gathered
together,
against the Lord and against his
Anointed'—[g]

[27]for truly in this city there were gath-
ered together against thy holy servant[h]
Jesus, whom thou didst anoint, both
Herod and Pontius Pilate, with the Gen-
tiles and the peoples of Israel, [28]to do
whatever thy hand and thy plan had
predestined to take place. [29]And now,
Lord, look upon their threats, and grant
to thy servants[i] to speak thy word with
all boldness, [30]while thou stretchest out
thy hand to heal, and signs and wonders
are performed through the name of thy
holy servant[j] Jesus." [31]And when they
had prayed, the place in which they
were gathered together was shaken;
and they were all filled with the Holy
Spirit and spoke the word of God with
boldness.

The Believers Share Their Possessions

32 Now the company of those who be-
lieved were of one heart and soul, and
no one said that any of the things which
he possessed was his own, but they had
everything in common. [33]And with great
power the apostles gave their testimony
to the resurrection of the Lord Jesus, and
great grace was upon them all. [34]There
was not a needy person among them, for
as many as were possessors of lands or
houses sold them, and brought the pro-
ceeds of what was sold [35]and laid it at
the apostles' feet; and distribution was
made to each as any had need. [36]Thus Jo-
seph who was surnamed by the apostles
Barnabas (which means, Son of encour-
agement), a Levite, a native of Cyprus,
[37]sold a field which belonged to him,

[f]**4.25** Or *child* [g]**4.26** Or *Christ* [h]**4.27** Or *child* [i]**4.29** Or *slaves* [j]**4.30** Or *child*

and brought the money and laid it at the apostles' feet.

Ananias and Sapphira

5 But a man named Anani'as with his wife Sapphi'ra sold a piece of property, [2]and with his wife's knowledge he kept back some of the proceeds, and brought only a part and laid it at the apostles' feet. [3]But Peter said, "Anani'as, why has Satan filled your heart to lie to the Holy Spirit and to keep back part of the proceeds of the land? [4]While it remained unsold, did it not remain your own? And after it was sold, was it not at your disposal? How is it that you have contrived this deed in your heart? You have not lied to men but to God." [5]When Anani'as heard these words, he fell down and died. And great fear came upon all who heard of it. [6]The young men rose and wrapped him up and carried him out and buried him.

7 After an interval of about three hours his wife came in, not knowing what had happened. [8]And Peter said to her, "Tell me whether you sold the land for so much." And she said, "Yes, for so much." [9]But Peter said to her, "How is it that you have agreed together to tempt the Spirit of the Lord? Hark, the feet of those that have buried your husband are at the door, and they will carry you out." [10]Immediately she fell down at his feet and died. When the young men came in they found her dead, and they carried her out and buried her beside her husband. [11]And great fear came upon the whole church, and upon all who heard of these things.

The Apostles Heal Many

12 Now many signs and wonders were done among the people by the hands of the apostles. And they were all together in Solomon's Portico. [13]None of the rest dared join them, but the people held them in high honor. [14]And more than ever believers were added to the Lord, multitudes both of men and women, [15]so that they even carried out the sick into the streets, and laid them on beds and pallets, that as Peter came by at least his shadow might fall on some of them. [16]The people also gathered from the towns around Jerusalem, bringing the sick and those afflicted with unclean spirits, and they were all healed.

The Apostles Are Persecuted

17 But the high priest rose up and all who were with him, that is, the party of the Sad'ducees, and filled with jealousy [18]they arrested the apostles and put them in the common prison. [19]But at night an angel of the Lord opened the prison doors and brought them out and said, [20]"Go and stand in the temple and speak to the people all the words of this Life." [21]And when they heard this, they entered the temple at daybreak and taught.

Now the high priest came and those who were with him and called together the council and all the senate of Israel, and sent to the prison to have them brought. [22]But when the officers came, they did not find them in the prison, and they returned and reported, [23]"We found the prison securely locked and the sentries standing at the doors, but when we opened it we found no one inside." [24]Now when the captain of the temple and the chief priests heard these words, they were much perplexed about them, wondering what this would come to. [25]And some one came and told them, "The men whom you put in prison are standing in the temple and teaching the people." [26]Then the captain with the officers went and brought them, but without violence, for they were afraid of being stoned by the people.

27 And when they had brought them, they set them before the council. And the high priest questioned them, [28]saying,

"We strictly charged you not to teach
in this name, yet here you have filled Je-
rusalem with your teaching and you in-
tend to bring this man's blood upon us."
29 But Peter and the apostles answered,
"We must obey God rather than men.
30 The God of our fathers raised Jesus
whom you killed by hanging him on a
tree. 31 God exalted him at his right hand
as Leader and Savior, to give repentance
to Israel and forgiveness of sins. 32 And
we are witnesses to these things, and so
is the Holy Spirit whom God has given to
those who obey him."

33 When they heard this they were
enraged and wanted to kill them. 34 But
a Pharisee in the council named Gama′-
li-el, a teacher of the law, held in honor
by all the people, stood up and ordered
the men to be put outside for a while.
35 And he said to them, "Men of Israel,
take care what you do with these men.
36 For before these days Theu′das arose,
giving himself out to be somebody, and
a number of men, about four hundred,
joined him; but he was slain and all who
followed him were dispersed and came
to nothing. 37 After him Judas the Gali-
lean arose in the days of the census and
drew away some of the people after him;
he also perished, and all who followed
him were scattered. 38 So in the present
case I tell you, keep away from these men
and let them alone; for if this plan or this
undertaking is of men, it will fail; 39 but if
it is of God, you will not be able to over-
throw them. You might even be found
opposing God!"

40 So they took his advice, and when
they had called in the apostles, they beat
them and charged them not to speak in
the name of Jesus, and let them go. 41 Then
they left the presence of the council, re-
joicing that they were counted worthy to
suffer dishonor for the name. 42 And ev-
ery day in the temple and at home they
did not cease teaching and preaching
Jesus as the Christ.

Seven Chosen to Serve

6 Now in these days when the disciples
were increasing in number, the Hel-
lenists murmured against the Hebrews
because their widows were neglected in
the daily distribution. 2 And the twelve
summoned the body of the disciples and
said, "It is not right that we should give
up preaching the word of God to serve ta-
bles. 3 Therefore, brethren, pick out from
among you seven men of good repute,
full of the Spirit and of wisdom, whom
we may appoint to this duty. 4 But we will
devote ourselves to prayer and to the
ministry of the word." 5 And what they
said pleased the whole multitude, and
they chose Stephen, a man full of faith
and of the Holy Spirit, and Philip, and
Proch′orus, and Nica′nor, and Timon,
and Par′menas, and Nicola′us, a prose-
lyte of Antioch. 6 These they set before
the apostles, and they prayed and laid
their hands upon them.

7 And the word of God increased; and
the number of the disciples multiplied
greatly in Jerusalem, and a great many
of the priests were obedient to the faith.

The Arrest of Stephen

8 And Stephen, full of grace and power,
did great wonders and signs among the
people. 9 Then some of those who be-
longed to the synagogue of the Freedmen
(as it was called), and of the Cyre′nians,
and of the Alexandrians, and of those
from Cili′cia and Asia, arose and dis-
puted with Stephen. 10 But they could not
withstand the wisdom and the Spirit with
which he spoke. 11 Then they secretly in-
stigated men, who said, "We have heard
him speak blasphemous words against
Moses and God." 12 And they stirred up
the people and the elders and the scribes,
and they came upon him and seized him
and brought him before the council,
13 and set up false witnesses who said,
"This man never ceases to speak words
against this holy place and the law; 14 for

we have heard him say that this Jesus of
Nazareth will destroy this place, and will
change the customs which Moses deliv-
ered to us." [15]And gazing at him, all who
sat in the council saw that his face was
like the face of an angel.

Stephen's Speech to the Council

7 And the high priest said, "Is this so?"
[2]And Stephen said:
"Brethren and fathers, hear me. The
God of glory appeared to our father
Abraham, when he was in Mesopota'mia,
before he lived in Haran, [3]and said to
him, 'Depart from your land and from
your kindred and go into the land which
I will show you.' [4]Then he departed from
the land of the Chalde'ans, and lived in
Haran. And after his father died, God
removed him from there into this land
in which you are now living; [5]yet he gave
him no inheritance in it, not even a foot's
length, but promised to give it to him in
possession and to his posterity after him,
though he had no child. [6]And God spoke
to this effect, that his posterity would be
aliens in a land belonging to others, who
would enslave them and ill-treat them
four hundred years. [7]'But I will judge
the nation which they serve,' said God,
'and after that they shall come out and
worship me in this place.' [8]And he gave
him the covenant of circumcision. And
so Abraham became the father of Isaac,
and circumcised him on the eighth day;
and Isaac became the father of Jacob, and
Jacob of the twelve patriarchs.
9 "And the patriarchs, jealous of Jo-
seph, sold him into Egypt; but God was
with him, [10]and rescued him out of all
his afflictions, and gave him favor and
wisdom before Pharaoh, king of Egypt,
who made him governor over Egypt
and over all his household. [11]Now there
came a famine throughout all Egypt and
Canaan, and great affliction, and our fa-
thers could find no food. [12]But when Ja-
cob heard that there was grain in Egypt,
he sent forth our fathers the first time.
[13]And at the second visit Joseph made
himself known to his brothers, and Jo-
seph's family became known to Pharaoh.
[14]And Joseph sent and called to him Jacob
his father and all his kindred, seventy-
five souls; [15]and Jacob went down into
Egypt. And he died, himself and our fa-
thers, [16]and they were carried back to
Shechem and laid in the tomb that Abra-
ham had bought for a sum of silver from
the sons of Hamor in Shechem.
17 "But as the time of the promise drew
near, which God had granted to Abra-
ham, the people grew and multiplied in
Egypt [18]till there arose over Egypt an-
other king who had not known Joseph.
[19]He dealt craftily with our race and
forced our fathers to expose their in-
fants, that they might not be kept alive.
[20]At this time Moses was born, and
was beautiful before God. And he was
brought up for three months in his fa-
ther's house; [21]and when he was exposed,
Pharaoh's daughter adopted him and
brought him up as her own son. [22]And
Moses was instructed in all the wisdom
of the Egyptians, and he was mighty in
his words and deeds.
23 "When he was forty years old, it
came into his heart to visit his breth-
ren, the sons of Israel. [24]And seeing one
of them being wronged, he defended
the oppressed man and avenged him by
striking the Egyptian. [25]He supposed
that his brethren understood that God
was giving them deliverance by his
hand, but they did not understand. [26]And
on the following day he appeared to
them as they were quarreling and would
have reconciled them, saying, 'Men, you
are brethren, why do you wrong each
other?' [27]But the man who was wronging
his neighbor thrust him aside, saying,
'Who made you a ruler and a judge over
us? [28]Do you want to kill me as you killed
the Egyptian yesterday?' [29]At this retort
Moses fled, and became an exile in the

land of Mid′ian, where he became the fa-
ther of two sons.
30 “Now when forty years had passed,
an angel appeared to him in the wilder-
ness of Mount Sinai, in a flame of fire in a
bush. [31]When Moses saw it he wondered
at the sight; and as he drew near to look,
the voice of the Lord came, [32]‘I am the God
of your fathers, the God of Abraham and
of Isaac and of Jacob.’ And Moses trem-
bled and did not dare to look. [33]And the
Lord said to him, ‘Take off the shoes from
your feet, for the place where you are
standing is holy ground. [34]I have surely
seen the ill-treatment of my people that
are in Egypt and heard their groaning,
and I have come down to deliver them.
And now come, I will send you to Egypt.’
35 “This Moses whom they refused, say-
ing, ‘Who made you a ruler and a judge?’
God sent as both ruler and deliverer by
the hand of the angel that appeared to
him in the bush. [36]He led them out, having
performed wonders and signs in Egypt
and at the Red Sea, and in the wilderness
for forty years. [37]This is the Moses who
said to the Israelites, ‘God will raise up
for you a prophet from your brethren as
he raised me up.’ [38]This is he who was in
the congregation in the wilderness with
the angel who spoke to him at Mount Si-
nai, and with our fathers; and he received
living oracles to give to us. [39]Our fathers
refused to obey him, but thrust him aside,
and in their hearts they turned to Egypt,
[40]saying to Aaron, ‘Make for us gods to go
before us; as for this Moses who led us out
from the land of Egypt, we do not know
what has become of him.’ [41]And they made
a calf in those days, and offered a sacri-
fice to the idol and rejoiced in the works
of their hands. [42]But God turned and gave
them over to worship the host of heaven,
as it is written in the book of the prophets:

‘Did you offer to me slain beasts and
sacrifices,
forty years in the wilderness,
O house of Israel?
43 And you took up the tent of Moloch,
and the star of the god Rephan,
the figures which you made to
worship;
and I will remove you beyond
Babylon.’

44 “Our fathers had the tent of witness
in the wilderness, even as he who spoke
to Moses directed him to make it, accord-
ing to the pattern that he had seen. [45]Our
fathers in turn brought it in with Joshua
when they dispossessed the nations
which God thrust out before our fathers.
So it was until the days of David, [46]who
found favor in the sight of God and asked
leave to find a habitation for the God of
Jacob. [47]But it was Solomon who built a
house for him. [48]Yet the Most High does
not dwell in houses made with hands; as
the prophet says,

49 ‘Heaven is my throne,
and earth my footstool.
What house will you build for me,
says the Lord,
or what is the place of my rest?
50 Did not my hand make all these
things?’

51 “You stiff-necked people, uncircum-
cised in heart and ears, you always resist
the Holy Spirit. As your fathers did, so
do you. [52]Which of the prophets did not
your fathers persecute? And they killed
those who announced beforehand the
coming of the Righteous One, whom you
have now betrayed and murdered, [53]you
who received the law as delivered by an-
gels and did not keep it.”

The Stoning of Stephen

54 Now when they heard these things
they were enraged, and they ground
their teeth against him. [55]But he, full of
the Holy Spirit, gazed into heaven and
saw the glory of God, and Jesus stand-
ing at the right hand of God; [56]and he
said, “Behold, I see the heavens opened,
and the Son of man standing at the right
hand of God.” [57]But they cried out with

a loud voice and stopped their ears and
rushed together upon him. 58 Then they
cast him out of the city and stoned him;
and the witnesses laid down their gar-
ments at the feet of a young man named
Saul. 59 And as they were stoning Ste-
phen, he prayed, "Lord Jesus, receive my
spirit." 60 And he knelt down and cried
with a loud voice, "Lord, do not hold this
sin against them." And when he had said
8 this, he fell asleep. 1 And Saul was con-
senting to his death.

Saul Persecutes the Church

And on that day a great persecution
arose against the church in Jerusalem;
and they were all scattered throughout
the region of Judea and Samar'ia, except
the apostles. 2 Devout men buried Ste-
phen, and made great lamentation over
him. 3 But Saul laid waste the church, and
entering house after house, he dragged
off men and women and committed them
to prison.

Philip Preaches in Samaria

4 Now those who were scattered went
about preaching the word. 5 Philip went
down to a city of Samar'ia, and pro-
claimed to them the Christ. 6 And the
multitudes with one accord gave heed
to what was said by Philip, when they
heard him and saw the signs which he
did. 7 For unclean spirits came out of
many who were possessed, crying with
a loud voice; and many who were para-
lyzed or lame were healed. 8 So there was
much joy in that city.

9 But there was a man named Simon
who had previously practiced magic
in the city and amazed the nation of Sa-
mar'ia, saying that he himself was some-
body great. 10 They all gave heed to him,
from the least to the greatest, saying,
"This man is that power of God which
is called Great." 11 And they gave heed
to him, because for a long time he had
amazed them with his magic. 12 But when
they believed Philip as he preached good
news about the kingdom of God and the
name of Jesus Christ, they were baptized,
both men and women. 13 Even Simon him-
self believed, and after being baptized he
continued with Philip. And seeing signs
and great miracles performed, he was
amazed.

14 Now when the apostles at Jerusa-
lem heard that Samar'ia had received the
word of God, they sent to them Peter and
John, 15 who came down and prayed for
them that they might receive the Holy
Spirit; 16 for it had not yet fallen on any of
them, but they had only been baptized in
the name of the Lord Jesus. 17 Then they
laid their hands on them and they re-
ceived the Holy Spirit. 18 Now when Simon
saw that the Spirit was given through the
laying on of the apostles' hands, he of-
fered them money, 19 saying, "Give me also
this power, that any one on whom I lay
my hands may receive the Holy Spirit."
20 But Peter said to him, "Your silver per-
ish with you, because you thought you
could obtain the gift of God with money!
21 You have neither part nor lot in this
matter, for your heart is not right before
God. 22 Repent therefore of this wicked-
ness of yours, and pray to the Lord that,
if possible, the intent of your heart may
be forgiven you. 23 For I see that you are
in the gall of bitterness and in the bond of
iniquity." 24 And Simon answered, "Pray
for me to the Lord, that nothing of what
you have said may come upon me."

25 Now when they had testified and
spoken the word of the Lord, they re-
turned to Jerusalem, preaching the gos-
pel to many villages of the Samaritans.

Philip and the Ethiopian Eunuch

26 But an angel of the Lord said to Philip,
"Rise and go toward the south[k] to the
road that goes down from Jerusalem to
Gaza." This is a desert road. 27 And he rose

[k] **8.26** Or *at noon*

and went. And behold, an Ethiopian, a
eunuch, a minister of the Canda'ce the
queen of the Ethiopians, in charge of all
her treasure, had come to Jerusalem to
worship [28]and was returning; seated in
his chariot, he was reading the prophet
Isaiah. [29]And the Spirit said to Philip, "Go
up and join this chariot." [30]So Philip ran
to him, and heard him reading Isaiah the
prophet, and asked, "Do you understand
what you are reading?" [31]And he said,
"How can I, unless some one guides me?"
And he invited Philip to come up and sit
with him. [32]Now the passage of the scrip-
ture which he was reading was this:

> "As a sheep led to the slaughter
> or a lamb before its shearer is dumb,
> so he opens not his mouth.
>
> 33 In his humiliation justice was
> denied him.
> Who can describe his generation?
> For his life is taken up from the
> earth."

[34]And the eunuch said to Philip, "About
whom, pray, does the prophet say this,
about himself or about some one else?"
[35]Then Philip opened his mouth, and be-
ginning with this scripture he told him
the good news of Jesus. [36]And as they
went along the road they came to some
water, and the eunuch said, "See, here is
water! What is to prevent my being bap-
tized?"[1] [38]And he commanded the chariot
to stop, and they both went down into
the water, Philip and the eunuch, and he
baptized him. [39]And when they came up
out of the water, the Spirit of the Lord
caught up Philip; and the eunuch saw
him no more, and went on his way rejoic-
ing. [40]But Philip was found at Azo'tus,
and passing on he preached the gospel to
all the towns till he came to Caesare'a.

The Conversion of Saul

9 But Saul, still breathing threats and
murder against the disciples of the
Lord, went to the high priest [2]and asked
him for letters to the synagogues at Da-
mascus, so that if he found any belong-
ing to the Way, men or women, he might
bring them bound to Jerusalem. [3]Now
as he journeyed he approached Damas-
cus, and suddenly a light from heaven
flashed about him. [4]And he fell to the
ground and heard a voice saying to him,
"Saul, Saul, why do you persecute me?"
[5]And he said, "Who are you, Lord?" And
he said, "I am Jesus, whom you are per-
secuting; [6]but rise and enter the city, and
you will be told what you are to do." [7]The
men who were traveling with him stood
speechless, hearing the voice but seeing
no one. [8]Saul arose from the ground; and
when his eyes were opened, he could see
nothing; so they led him by the hand and
brought him into Damascus. [9]And for
three days he was without sight, and nei-
ther ate nor drank.

10 Now there was a disciple at Damas-
cus named Anani'as. The Lord said to
him in a vision, "Anani'as." And he said,
"Here I am, Lord." [11]And the Lord said
to him, "Rise and go to the street called
Straight, and inquire in the house of Ju-
das for a man of Tarsus named Saul; for
behold, he is praying, [12]and he has seen a
man named Anani'as come in and lay his
hands on him so that he might regain his
sight." [13]But Anani'as answered, "Lord, I
have heard from many about this man,
how much evil he has done to thy saints
at Jerusalem; [14]and here he has author-
ity from the chief priests to bind all who
call upon thy name." [15]But the Lord said
to him, "Go, for he is a chosen instru-
ment of mine to carry my name before
the Gentiles and kings and the sons of
Israel; [16]for I will show him how much
he must suffer for the sake of my name."
[17]So Anani'as departed and entered the
house. And laying his hands on him he
said, "Brother Saul, the Lord Jesus who

[1] **8.36** Other ancient authorities add all or most of verse 37, *And Philip said, "If you believe with all your heart, you may." And he replied, "I believe that Jesus Christ is the Son of God."*

appeared to you on the road by which
you came, has sent me that you may re-
gain your sight and be filled with the
Holy Spirit." 18 And immediately some-
thing like scales fell from his eyes and
he regained his sight. Then he rose and
was baptized, 19 and took food and was
strengthened.

Saul Preaches in Damascus

For several days he was with the disciples
at Damascus. 20 And in the synagogues
immediately he proclaimed Jesus, say-
ing, "He is the Son of God." 21 And all who
heard him were amazed, and said, "Is not
this the man who made havoc in Jerusa-
lem of those who called on this name?
And he has come here for this purpose,
to bring them bound before the chief
priests." 22 But Saul increased all the
more in strength, and confounded the
Jews who lived in Damascus by proving
that Jesus was the Christ.

Saul Escapes from the Jews

23 When many days had passed, the Jews
plotted to kill him, 24 but their plot be-
came known to Saul. They were watch-
ing the gates day and night, to kill him;
25 but his disciples took him by night and
let him down over the wall, lowering
him in a basket.

Saul in Jerusalem

26 And when he had come to Jerusalem
he attempted to join the disciples; and
they were all afraid of him, for they did
not believe that he was a disciple. 27 But
Barnabas took him, and brought him to
the apostles, and declared to them how on
the road he had seen the Lord, who spoke
to him, and how at Damascus he had
preached boldly in the name of Jesus. 28 So
he went in and out among them at Jerusa-
lem, 29 preaching boldly in the name of the
Lord. And he spoke and disputed against
the Hellenists; but they were seeking to
kill him. 30 And when the brethren knew
it, they brought him down to Caesare′a,
and sent him off to Tarsus.

31 So the church throughout all Judea
and Galilee and Samar′ia had peace and
was built up; and walking in the fear of
the Lord and in the comfort of the Holy
Spirit it was multiplied.

The Healing of Aeneas

32 Now as Peter went here and there
among them all, he came down also to
the saints that lived at Lydda. 33 There
he found a man named Aene′as, who
had been bedridden for eight years and
was paralyzed. 34 And Peter said to him,
"Aene′as, Jesus Christ heals you; rise and
make your bed." And immediately he
rose. 35 And all the residents of Lydda and
Sharon saw him, and they turned to the
Lord.

Peter in Lydda and Joppa

36 Now there was at Joppa a disciple
named Tabitha, which means Dorcas or
Gazelle. She was full of good works and
acts of charity. 37 In those days she fell
sick and died; and when they had washed
her, they laid her in an upper room.
38 Since Lydda was near Joppa, the disci-
ples, hearing that Peter was there, sent
two men to him entreating him, "Please
come to us without delay." 39 So Peter rose
and went with them. And when he had
come, they took him to the upper room.
All the widows stood beside him weep-
ing, and showing coats and garments
which Dorcas made while she was with
them. 40 But Peter put them all outside
and knelt down and prayed; then turn-
ing to the body he said, "Tabitha, rise."
And she opened her eyes, and when she
saw Peter she sat up. 41 And he gave her
his hand and lifted her up. Then calling
the saints and widows he presented her
alive. 42 And it became known through-
out all Joppa, and many believed in the
Lord. 43 And he stayed in Joppa for many
days with one Simon, a tanner.

Peter and Cornelius

10 At Caesare'a there was a man
named Cornelius, a centurion of
what was known as the Italian Cohort,
[2]a devout man who feared God with all
his household, gave alms liberally to the
people, and prayed constantly to God.
[3]About the ninth hour of the day he saw
clearly in a vision an angel of God com-
ing in and saying to him, "Cornelius."
[4]And he stared at him in terror, and said,
"What is it, Lord?" And he said to him,
"Your prayers and your alms have as-
cended as a memorial before God. [5]And
now send men to Joppa, and bring one
Simon who is called Peter; [6]he is lodging
with Simon, a tanner, whose house is by
the seaside." [7]When the angel who spoke
to him had departed, he called two of
his servants and a devout soldier from
among those that waited on him, [8]and
having related everything to them, he
sent them to Joppa.

9 The next day, as they were on their
journey and coming near the city, Peter
went up on the housetop to pray, about
the sixth hour. [10]And he became hungry
and desired something to eat; but while
they were preparing it, he fell into a
trance [11]and saw the heaven opened,
and something descending, like a great
sheet, let down by four corners upon
the earth. [12]In it were all kinds of ani-
mals and reptiles and birds of the air.
[13]And there came a voice to him, "Rise,
Peter; kill and eat." [14]But Peter said, "No,
Lord; for I have never eaten anything
that is common or unclean." [15]And the
voice came to him again a second time,
"What God has cleansed, you must not
call common." [16]This happened three
times, and the thing was taken up at
once to heaven.

17 Now while Peter was inwardly per-
plexed as to what the vision which he had
seen might mean, behold, the men that
were sent by Cornelius, having made
inquiry for Simon's house, stood before
the gate [18]and called out to ask whether
Simon who was called Peter was lodging
there. [19]And while Peter was pondering
the vision, the Spirit said to him, "Behold,
three men are looking for you. [20]Rise and
go down, and accompany them without
hesitation; for I have sent them." [21]And
Peter went down to the men and said, "I
am the one you are looking for; what is
the reason for your coming?" [22]And they
said, "Cornelius, a centurion, an upright
and God-fearing man, who is well spo-
ken of by the whole Jewish nation, was
directed by a holy angel to send for you
to come to his house, and to hear what
you have to say." [23]So he called them in to
be his guests.

The next day he rose and went off with
them, and some of the brethren from
Joppa accompanied him. [24]And on the
following day they entered Caesare'a.
Cornelius was expecting them and had
called together his kinsmen and close
friends. [25]When Peter entered, Corne-
lius met him and fell down at his feet and
worshiped him. [26]But Peter lifted him up,
saying, "Stand up; I too am a man." [27]And
as he talked with him, he went in and
found many persons gathered; [28]and he
said to them, "You yourselves know how
unlawful it is for a Jew to associate with
or to visit any one of another nation; but
God has shown me that I should not call
any man common or unclean. [29]So when
I was sent for, I came without objection. I
ask then why you sent for me."

30 And Cornelius said, "Four days ago,
about this hour, I was keeping the ninth
hour of prayer in my house; and behold,
a man stood before me in bright apparel,
[31]saying, 'Cornelius, your prayer has
been heard and your alms have been
remembered before God. [32]Send there-
fore to Joppa and ask for Simon who is
called Peter; he is lodging in the house
of Simon, a tanner, by the seaside.' [33]So
I sent to you at once, and you have been
kind enough to come. Now therefore we

are all here present in the sight of God, to
hear all that you have been commanded
by the Lord."

Gentiles Hear the Good News

34 And Peter opened his mouth and
said: "Truly I perceive that God shows no
partiality, 35 but in every nation any one
who fears him and does what is right is
acceptable to him. 36 You know the word
which he sent to Israel, preaching good
news of peace by Jesus Christ (he is Lord
of all), 37 the word which was proclaimed
throughout all Judea, beginning from
Galilee after the baptism which John
preached: 38 how God anointed Jesus of
Nazareth with the Holy Spirit and with
power; how he went about doing good
and healing all that were oppressed by
the devil, for God was with him. 39 And
we are witnesses to all that he did both in
the country of the Jews and in Jerusalem.
They put him to death by hanging him on
a tree; 40 but God raised him on the third
day and made him manifest; 41 not to all
the people but to us who were chosen by
God as witnesses, who ate and drank with
him after he rose from the dead. 42 And he
commanded us to preach to the people,
and to testify that he is the one ordained
by God to be judge of the living and the
dead. 43 To him all the prophets bear wit-
ness that every one who believes in him
receives forgiveness of sins through his
name."

Gentiles Receive the Holy Spirit

44 While Peter was still saying this,
the Holy Spirit fell on all who heard the
word. 45 And the believers from among
the circumcised who came with Peter
were amazed, because the gift of the
Holy Spirit had been poured out even
on the Gentiles. 46 For they heard them
speaking in tongues and extolling God.
Then Peter declared, 47 "Can any one
forbid water for baptizing these people
who have received the Holy Spirit just as
we have?" 48 And he commanded them to
be baptized in the name of Jesus Christ.
Then they asked him to remain for some
days.

Peter's Report to the Church at Jerusalem

11 Now the apostles and the brethren
who were in Judea heard that the
Gentiles also had received the word of
God. 2 So when Peter went up to Jerusa-
lem, the circumcision party criticized
him, 3 saying, "Why did you go to uncir-
cumcised men and eat with them?" 4 But
Peter began and explained to them in or-
der: 5 "I was in the city of Joppa praying;
and in a trance I saw a vision, something
descending, like a great sheet, let down
from heaven by four corners; and it
came down to me. 6 Looking at it closely I
observed animals and beasts of prey and
reptiles and birds of the air. 7 And I heard
a voice saying to me, 'Rise, Peter; kill and
eat.' 8 But I said, 'No, Lord; for nothing
common or unclean has ever entered
my mouth.' 9 But the voice answered a
second time from heaven, 'What God
has cleansed you must not call com-
mon.' 10 This happened three times, and
all was drawn up again into heaven. 11 At
that very moment three men arrived at
the house in which we were, sent to me
from Caesare'a. 12 And the Spirit told me
to go with them, making no distinction.
These six brethren also accompanied
me, and we entered the man's house.
13 And he told us how he had seen the
angel standing in his house and saying,
'Send to Joppa and bring Simon called
Peter; 14 he will declare to you a message
by which you will be saved, you and all
your household.' 15 As I began to speak,
the Holy Spirit fell on them just as on us
at the beginning. 16 And I remembered
the word of the Lord, how he said, 'John
baptized with water, but you shall be
baptized with the Holy Spirit.' 17 If then
God gave the same gift to them as he gave

to us when we believed in the Lord Jesus
Christ, who was I that I could withstand
God?" 18 When they heard this they were
silenced. And they glorified God, say-
ing, "Then to the Gentiles also God has
granted repentance unto life."

The Church in Antioch

19 Now those who were scattered be-
cause of the persecution that arose
over Stephen traveled as far as Phoe-
ni'cia and Cyprus and Antioch, speak-
ing the word to none except Jews.
20 But there were some of them, men of
Cyprus and Cyre'ne, who on coming
to Antioch spoke to the Greeks[m] also,
preaching the Lord Jesus. 21 And the
hand of the Lord was with them, and
a great number that believed turned
to the Lord. 22 News of this came to the
ears of the church in Jerusalem, and
they sent Barnabas to Antioch. 23 When
he came and saw the grace of God, he
was glad; and he exhorted them all to
remain faithful to the Lord with stead-
fast purpose; 24 for he was a good man,
full of the Holy Spirit and of faith. And
a large company was added to the Lord.
25 So Barnabas went to Tarsus to look
for Saul; 26 and when he had found him,
he brought him to Antioch. For a whole
year they met with[n] the church, and
taught a large company of people; and
in Antioch the disciples were for the
first time called Christians.

27 Now in these days prophets came
down from Jerusalem to Antioch. 28 And
one of them named Ag'abus stood up
and foretold by the Spirit that there
would be a great famine over all the
world; and this took place in the days
of Claudius. 29 And the disciples deter-
mined, every one according to his abil-
ity, to send relief to the brethren who
lived in Judea; 30 and they did so, send-
ing it to the elders by the hand of Barn-
abas and Saul.

James Killed and Peter Imprisoned

12 About that time Herod the king
laid violent hands upon some who
belonged to the church. 2 He killed James
the brother of John with the sword; 3 and
when he saw that it pleased the Jews, he
proceeded to arrest Peter also. This was
during the days of Unleavened Bread.
4 And when he had seized him, he put
him in prison, and delivered him to four
squads of soldiers to guard him, intend-
ing after the Passover to bring him out to
the people. 5 So Peter was kept in prison;
but earnest prayer for him was made to
God by the church.

Peter Delivered from Prison

6 The very night when Herod was about
to bring him out, Peter was sleeping
between two soldiers, bound with two
chains, and sentries before the door
were guarding the prison; 7 and behold,
an angel of the Lord appeared, and a
light shone in the cell; and he struck
Peter on the side and woke him, saying,
"Get up quickly." And the chains fell off
his hands. 8 And the angel said to him,
"Dress yourself and put on your san-
dals." And he did so. And he said to him,
"Wrap your mantle around you and fol-
low me." 9 And he went out and followed
him; he did not know that what was done
by the angel was real, but thought he was
seeing a vision. 10 When they had passed
the first and the second guard, they came
to the iron gate leading into the city. It
opened to them of its own accord, and
they went out and passed on through
one street; and immediately the angel
left him. 11 And Peter came to himself, and
said, "Now I am sure that the Lord has
sent his angel and rescued me from the
hand of Herod and from all that the Jew-
ish people were expecting."

12 When he realized this, he went to
the house of Mary, the mother of John
whose other name was Mark, where

[m] **11.20** Other ancient authorities read *Hellenists*

[n] **11.26** Or *were guests of*

many were gathered together and were
praying. 13 And when he knocked at the
door of the gateway, a maid named Rhoda
came to answer. 14 Recognizing Peter's
voice, in her joy she did not open the gate
but ran in and told that Peter was stand-
ing at the gate. 15 They said to her, "You
are mad." But she insisted that it was
so. They said, "It is his angel!" 16 But Pe-
ter continued knocking; and when they
opened, they saw him and were amazed.
17 But motioning to them with his hand to
be silent, he described to them how the
Lord had brought him out of the prison.
And he said, "Tell this to James and to the
brethren." Then he departed and went to
another place.

18 Now when day came, there was no
small stir among the soldiers over what
had become of Peter. 19 And when Herod
had sought for him and could not find
him, he examined the sentries and or-
dered that they should be put to death.
Then he went down from Judea to Cae-
sare'a, and remained there.

The Death of Herod

20 Now Herod was angry with the people
of Tyre and Sidon; and they came to him
in a body, and having persuaded Blastus,
the king's chamberlain, they asked for
peace, because their country depended
on the king's country for food. 21 On an
appointed day Herod put on his royal
robes, took his seat upon the throne,
and made an oration to them. 22 And the
people shouted, "The voice of a god, and
not of man!" 23 Immediately an angel of
the Lord smote him, because he did not
give God the glory; and he was eaten by
worms and died.

24 But the word of God grew and
multiplied.

25 And Barnabas and Saul returned
from° Jerusalem when they had fulfilled
their mission, bringing with them John
whose other name was Mark.

Barnabas and Saul Commissioned

13 Now in the church at Antioch
there were prophets and teachers,
Barnabas, Symeon who was called Ni-
ger, Lucius of Cyre'ne, Man'a-en a mem-
ber of the court of Herod the tetrarch,
and Saul. 2 While they were worshiping
the Lord and fasting, the Holy Spirit
said, "Set apart for me Barnabas and
Saul for the work to which I have called
them." 3 Then after fasting and praying
they laid their hands on them and sent
them off.

The Apostles Preach in Cyprus

4 So, being sent out by the Holy Spirit,
they went down to Seleu'cia; and from
there they sailed to Cyprus. 5 When they
arrived at Sal'amis, they proclaimed
the word of God in the synagogues of
the Jews. And they had John to assist
them. 6 When they had gone through the
whole island as far as Paphos, they came
upon a certain magician, a Jewish false
prophet, named Bar-Jesus. 7 He was with
the proconsul, Sergius Paulus, a man of
intelligence, who summoned Barnabas
and Saul and sought to hear the word of
God. 8 But El'ymas the magician (for that
is the meaning of his name) withstood
them, seeking to turn away the procon-
sul from the faith. 9 But Saul, who is also
called Paul, filled with the Holy Spirit,
looked intently at him 10 and said, "You
son of the devil, you enemy of all righ-
teousness, full of all deceit and villainy,
will you not stop making crooked the
straight paths of the Lord? 11 And now,
behold, the hand of the Lord is upon
you, and you shall be blind and unable
to see the sun for a time." Immediately
mist and darkness fell upon him and he
went about seeking people to lead him
by the hand. 12 Then the proconsul be-
lieved, when he saw what had occurred,
for he was astonished at the teaching of
the Lord.

°**12.25** Other ancient authorities read *to*

Paul and Barnabas in Antioch of Pisidia

13 Now Paul and his company set sail from Paphos, and came to Perga in Pamphyl′ia. And John left them and returned to Jerusalem; [14]but they passed on from Perga and came to Antioch of Pisid′ia. And on the sabbath day they went into the synagogue and sat down. [15]After the reading of the law and the prophets, the rulers of the synagogue sent to them, saying, "Brethren, if you have any word of exhortation for the people, say it." [16]So Paul stood up, and motioning with his hand said:

"Men of Israel, and you that fear God, listen. [17]The God of this people Israel chose our fathers and made the people great during their stay in the land of Egypt, and with uplifted arm he led them out of it. [18]And for about forty years he bore with[p] them in the wilderness. [19]And when he had destroyed seven nations in the land of Canaan, he gave them their land as an inheritance, for about four hundred and fifty years. [20]And after that he gave them judges until Samuel the prophet. [21]Then they asked for a king; and God gave them Saul the son of Kish, a man of the tribe of Benjamin, for forty years. [22]And when he had removed him, he raised up David to be their king; of whom he testified and said, 'I have found in David the son of Jesse a man after my heart, who will do all my will.' [23]Of this man's posterity God has brought to Israel a Savior, Jesus, as he promised. [24]Before his coming John had preached a baptism of repentance to all the people of Israel. [25]And as John was finishing his course, he said, 'What do you suppose that I am? I am not he. No, but after me one is coming, the sandals of whose feet I am not worthy to untie.'

26 "Brethren, sons of the family of Abraham, and those among you that fear God, to us has been sent the message of this salvation. [27]For those who live in Jerusalem and their rulers, because they did not recognize him nor understand the utterances of the prophets which are read every sabbath, fulfilled these by condemning him. [28]Though they could charge him with nothing deserving death, yet they asked Pilate to have him killed. [29]And when they had fulfilled all that was written of him, they took him down from the tree, and laid him in a tomb. [30]But God raised him from the dead; [31]and for many days he appeared to those who came up with him from Galilee to Jerusalem, who are now his witnesses to the people. [32]And we bring you the good news that what God promised to the fathers, [33]this he has fulfilled to us their children by raising Jesus; as also it is written in the second psalm,

'Thou art my Son,
today I have begotten thee.'

[34]And as for the fact that he raised him from the dead, no more to return to corruption, he spoke in this way,

'I will give you the holy and sure
blessings of David.'

[35]Therefore he says also in another psalm,

'Thou wilt not let thy Holy One see
corruption.'

[36]For David, after he had served the counsel of God in his own generation, fell asleep, and was laid with his fathers, and saw corruption; [37]but he whom God raised up saw no corruption. [38]Let it be known to you therefore, brethren, that through this man forgiveness of sins is proclaimed to you, [39]and by him every one that believes is freed from everything from which you could not be freed by the law of Moses. [40]Beware, therefore, lest there come upon you what is said in the prophets:

41 'Behold, you scoffers, and wonder,
and perish;
for I do a deed in your days,
a deed you will never believe, if one
declares it to you.'"

[p] **13.18** Other ancient authorities read *cared for* (Deut 1.31)

42 As they went out, the people begged
that these things might be told them the
next sabbath. 43And when the meeting
of the synagogue broke up, many Jews
and devout converts to Judaism followed
Paul and Barnabas, who spoke to them
and urged them to continue in the grace
of God.

44 The next sabbath almost the whole
city gathered together to hear the word
of God. 45But when the Jews saw the mul-
titudes, they were filled with jealousy,
and contradicted what was spoken by
Paul, and reviled him. 46And Paul and
Barnabas spoke out boldly, saying, "It
was necessary that the word of God
should be spoken first to you. Since you
thrust it from you, and judge yourselves
unworthy of eternal life, behold, we turn
to the Gentiles. 47For so the Lord has com-
manded us, saying,

'I have set you to be a light for the
Gentiles,
that you may bring salvation to the
uttermost parts of the earth.'"

48 And when the Gentiles heard this,
they were glad and glorified the word
of God; and as many as were ordained
to eternal life believed. 49And the word
of the Lord spread throughout all the
region. 50But the Jews incited the de-
vout women of high standing and the
leading men of the city, and stirred up
persecution against Paul and Barnabas,
and drove them out of their district.
51But they shook off the dust from their
feet against them, and went to Ico'nium.
52And the disciples were filled with joy
and with the Holy Spirit.

Paul and Barnabas in Iconium

14 Now at Ico'nium they entered to-
gether into the Jewish synagogue,
and so spoke that a great company be-
lieved, both of Jews and of Greeks. 2But
the unbelieving Jews stirred up the Gen-
tiles and poisoned their minds against
the brethren. 3So they remained for a
long time, speaking boldly for the Lord,
who bore witness to the word of his grace,
granting signs and wonders to be done
by their hands. 4But the people of the city
were divided; some sided with the Jews,
and some with the apostles. 5When an
attempt was made by both Gentiles and
Jews, with their rulers, to molest them
and to stone them, 6they learned of it and
fled to Lystra and Derbe, cities of Lyc-
ao'nia, and to the surrounding country;
7and there they preached the gospel.

Paul and Barnabas in Lystra and Derbe

8 Now at Lystra there was a man sitting,
who could not use his feet; he was a crip-
ple from birth, who had never walked.
9He listened to Paul speaking; and Paul,
looking intently at him and seeing that
he had faith to be made well, 10said in
a loud voice, "Stand upright on your
feet." And he sprang up and walked.
11And when the crowds saw what Paul
had done, they lifted up their voices,
saying in Lycao'nian, "The gods have
come down to us in the likeness of men!"
12Barnabas they called Zeus, and Paul,
because he was the chief speaker, they
called Hermes. 13And the priest of Zeus,
whose temple was in front of the city,
brought oxen and garlands to the gates
and wanted to offer sacrifice with the
people. 14But when the apostles Barna-
bas and Paul heard of it, they tore their
garments and rushed out among the
multitude, crying, 15"Men, why are you
doing this? We also are men, of like na-
ture with you, and bring you good news,
that you should turn from these vain
things to a living God who made the
heaven and the earth and the sea and all
that is in them. 16In past generations he
allowed all the nations to walk in their
own ways; 17yet he did not leave himself
without witness, for he did good and
gave you from heaven rains and fruit-
ful seasons, satisfying your hearts with

food and gladness." 18 With these words
they scarcely restrained the people from
offering sacrifice to them.

The Return to Antioch in Syria

19 But Jews came there from Antioch
and Ico'nium; and having persuaded the
people, they stoned Paul and dragged
him out of the city, supposing that he
was dead. 20 But when the disciples gath-
ered about him, he rose up and entered
the city; and on the next day he went on
with Barnabas to Derbe. 21 When they
had preached the gospel to that city and
had made many disciples, they returned
to Lystra and to Ico'nium and to Antioch,
22 strengthening the souls of the disci-
ples, exhorting them to continue in the
faith, and saying that through many
tribulations we must enter the kingdom
of God. 23 And when they had appointed
elders for them in every church, with
prayer and fasting, they committed them
to the Lord in whom they believed.

24 Then they passed through Pisid'ia,
and came to Pamphyl'ia. 25 And when
they had spoken the word in Perga, they
went down to Attali'a; 26 and from there
they sailed to Antioch, where they had
been commended to the grace of God
for the work which they had fulfilled.
27 And when they arrived, they gathered
the church together and declared all that
God had done with them, and how he had
opened a door of faith to the Gentiles.
28 And they remained no little time with
the disciples.

The Council at Jerusalem

15 But some men came down from
Judea and were teaching the breth-
ren, "Unless you are circumcised accord-
ing to the custom of Moses, you cannot
be saved." 2 And when Paul and Barnabas
had no small dissension and debate with
them, Paul and Barnabas and some of the
others were appointed to go up to Jerusa-
lem to the apostles and the elders about
this question. 3 So, being sent on their
way by the church, they passed through
both Phoeni'cia and Samar'ia, reporting
the conversion of the Gentiles, and they
gave great joy to all the brethren. 4 When
they came to Jerusalem, they were wel-
comed by the church and the apostles
and the elders, and they declared all that
God had done with them. 5 But some be-
lievers who belonged to the party of the
Pharisees rose up, and said, "It is neces-
sary to circumcise them, and to charge
them to keep the law of Moses."

6 The apostles and the elders were
gathered together to consider this mat-
ter. 7 And after there had been much
debate, Peter rose and said to them,
"Brethren, you know that in the early
days God made choice among you, that
by my mouth the Gentiles should hear
the word of the gospel and believe. 8 And
God who knows the heart bore witness to
them, giving them the Holy Spirit just as
he did to us; 9 and he made no distinction
between us and them, but cleansed their
hearts by faith. 10 Now therefore why do
you make trial of God by putting a yoke
upon the neck of the disciples which nei-
ther our fathers nor we have been able
to bear? 11 But we believe that we shall
be saved through the grace of the Lord
Jesus, just as they will."

12 And all the assembly kept silence;
and they listened to Barnabas and Paul
as they related what signs and wonders
God had done through them among the
Gentiles. 13 After they finished speak-
ing, James replied, "Brethren, listen to
me. 14 Symeon has related how God first
visited the Gentiles, to take out of them
a people for his name. 15 And with this
the words of the prophets agree, as it is
written,

16 'After this I will return,
and I will rebuild the dwelling of
David, which has fallen;
I will rebuild its ruins,
and I will set it up,

17 that the rest of men may seek the
Lord,
and all the Gentiles who are called
by my name,
18 says the Lord, who has made these
things known from of old.'
19 Therefore my judgment is that we
should not trouble those of the Gentiles
who turn to God, 20 but should write to
them to abstain from the pollutions of
idols and from unchastity and from what
is strangled[q] and from blood. 21 For from
early generations Moses has had in ev-
ery city those who preach him, for he is
read every sabbath in the synagogues."

The Council's Letter to Gentile Believers

22 Then it seemed good to the apostles
and the elders, with the whole church, to
choose men from among them and send
them to Antioch with Paul and Barnabas.
They sent Judas called Barsab'bas, and
Silas, leading men among the brethren,
23 with the following letter: "The breth-
ren, both the apostles and the elders, to
the brethren who are of the Gentiles in
Antioch and Syria and Cili'cia, greeting.
24 Since we have heard that some persons
from us have troubled you with words,
unsettling your minds, although we gave
them no instructions, 25 it has seemed
good to us in assembly to choose men and
send them to you with our beloved Barn-
abas and Paul, 26 men who have risked
their lives for the sake of our Lord Jesus
Christ. 27 We have therefore sent Judas
and Silas, who themselves will tell you
the same things by word of mouth. 28 For
it has seemed good to the Holy Spirit and
to us to lay upon you no greater burden
than these necessary things: 29 that you
abstain from what has been sacrificed
to idols and from blood and from what
is strangled[r] and from unchastity. If you
keep yourselves from these, you will do
well. Farewell."

30 So when they were sent off, they
went down to Antioch; and having gath-
ered the congregation together, they de-
livered the letter. 31 And when they read
it, they rejoiced at the exhortation. 32 And
Judas and Silas, who were themselves
prophets, exhorted the brethren with
many words and strengthened them.
33 And after they had spent some time,
they were sent off in peace by the breth-
ren to those who had sent them.[s] 35 But
Paul and Barnabas remained in Antioch,
teaching and preaching the word of the
Lord, with many others also.

Paul and Barnabas Separate

36 And after some days Paul said to
Barnabas, "Come, let us return and visit
the brethren in every city where we pro-
claimed the word of the Lord, and see
how they are." 37 And Barnabas wanted
to take with them John called Mark. 38 But
Paul thought best not to take with them
one who had withdrawn from them in
Pamphyl'ia, and had not gone with them
to the work. 39 And there arose a sharp
contention, so that they separated from
each other; Barnabas took Mark with
him and sailed away to Cyprus, 40 but
Paul chose Silas and departed, being
commended by the brethren to the grace
of the Lord. 41 And he went through Syria
and Cili'cia, strengthening the churches.

Timothy Joins Paul and Silas

16 And he came also to Derbe and to
Lystra. A disciple was there, named
Timothy, the son of a Jewish woman
who was a believer; but his father was
a Greek. 2 He was well spoken of by the
brethren at Lystra and Ico'nium. 3 Paul
wanted Timothy to accompany him;
and he took him and circumcised him

[q] **15.20** Other early authorities omit *and from what is strangled* [r] **15.29** Other early authorities omit *and from what is strangled* [s] **15.33** Other ancient authorities insert verse 34, *But it seemed good to Silas to remain there*

because of the Jews that were in those
places, for they all knew that his father
was a Greek. 4As they went on their way
through the cities, they delivered to them
for observance the decisions which had
been reached by the apostles and elders
who were at Jerusalem. 5So the churches
were strengthened in the faith, and they
increased in numbers daily.

Paul's Vision of the Man of Macedonia

6 And they went through the region of
Phry'gia and Galatia, having been for-
bidden by the Holy Spirit to speak the
word in Asia. 7And when they had come
opposite My'sia, they attempted to go
into Bithyn'ia, but the Spirit of Jesus did
not allow them; 8so, passing by My'sia,
they went down to Tro'as. 9And a vision
appeared to Paul in the night: a man of
Macedo'nia was standing beseeching
him and saying, "Come over to Mace-
do'nia and help us." 10And when he had
seen the vision, immediately we sought
to go on into Macedo'nia, concluding that
God had called us to preach the gospel to
them.

The Conversion of Lydia

11 Setting sail therefore from Tro'as, we
made a direct voyage to Sam'othrace,
and the following day to Ne-ap'olis, 12and
from there to Philippi, which is the lead-
ing city of the district[t] of Macedo'nia,
and a Roman colony. We remained in
this city some days; 13and on the sabbath
day we went outside the gate to the riv-
erside, where we supposed there was
a place of prayer; and we sat down and
spoke to the women who had come to-
gether. 14One who heard us was a woman
named Lydia, from the city of Thyat-
i'ra, a seller of purple goods, who was a
worshiper of God. The Lord opened her
heart to give heed to what was said by
Paul. 15And when she was baptized, with
her household, she besought us, saying,
"If you have judged me to be faithful to
the Lord, come to my house and stay."
And she prevailed upon us.

Paul and Silas in Prison

16 As we were going to the place of
prayer, we were met by a slave girl who
had a spirit of divination and brought
her owners much gain by soothsay-
ing. 17She followed Paul and us, crying,
"These men are servants of the Most
High God, who proclaim to you the way
of salvation." 18And this she did for many
days. But Paul was annoyed, and turned
and said to the spirit, "I charge you in the
name of Jesus Christ to come out of her."
And it came out that very hour.

19 But when her owners saw that their
hope of gain was gone, they seized Paul
and Silas and dragged them into the mar-
ket place before the rulers; 20and when
they had brought them to the magis-
trates they said, "These men are Jews and
they are disturbing our city. 21They advo-
cate customs which it is not lawful for
us Romans to accept or practice." 22The
crowd joined in attacking them; and the
magistrates tore the garments off them
and gave orders to beat them with rods.
23And when they had inflicted many
blows upon them, they threw them into
prison, charging the jailer to keep them
safely. 24Having received this charge, he
put them into the inner prison and fas-
tened their feet in the stocks.

25 But about midnight Paul and Silas
were praying and singing hymns to God,
and the prisoners were listening to them,
26and suddenly there was a great earth-
quake, so that the foundations of the
prison were shaken; and immediately all
the doors were opened and every one's
fetters were unfastened. 27When the
jailer woke and saw that the prison doors
were open, he drew his sword and was
about to kill himself, supposing that the
prisoners had escaped. 28But Paul cried

[t]**16.12** The Greek text is uncertain

with a loud voice, "Do not harm yourself,
for we are all here." 29 And he called for
lights and rushed in, and trembling with
fear he fell down before Paul and Silas,
30 and brought them out and said, "Men,
what must I do to be saved?" 31 And they
said, "Believe in the Lord Jesus, and you
will be saved, you and your household."
32 And they spoke the word of the Lord
to him and to all that were in his house.
33 And he took them the same hour of the
night, and washed their wounds, and he
was baptized at once, with all his fam-
ily. 34 Then he brought them up into his
house, and set food before them; and he
rejoiced with all his household that he
had believed in God.

35 But when it was day, the magistrates
sent the police, saying, "Let those men
go." 36 And the jailer reported the words
to Paul, saying, "The magistrates have
sent to let you go; now therefore come
out and go in peace." 37 But Paul said to
them, "They have beaten us publicly,
uncondemned, men who are Roman cit-
izens, and have thrown us into prison;
and do they now cast us out secretly? No!
let them come themselves and take us
out." 38 The police reported these words
to the magistrates, and they were afraid
when they heard that they were Roman
citizens; 39 so they came and apologized
to them. And they took them out and
asked them to leave the city. 40 So they
went out of the prison, and visited Lydia;
and when they had seen the brethren,
they exhorted them and departed.

The Uproar in Thessalonica

17 Now when they had passed
through Amphip'olis and Apol-
lo'nia, they came to Thessaloni'ca, where
there was a synagogue of the Jews. 2 And
Paul went in, as was his custom, and for
three weeks[u] he argued with them from
the scriptures, 3 explaining and proving
that it was necessary for the Christ to
suffer and to rise from the dead, and say-
ing, "This Jesus, whom I proclaim to you,
is the Christ." 4 And some of them were
persuaded, and joined Paul and Silas; as
did a great many of the devout Greeks
and not a few of the leading women. 5 But
the Jews were jealous, and taking some
wicked fellows of the rabble, they gath-
ered a crowd, set the city in an uproar,
and attacked the house of Jason, seeking
to bring them out to the people. 6 And
when they could not find them, they
dragged Jason and some of the breth-
ren before the city authorities, crying,
"These men who have turned the world
upside down have come here also, 7 and
Jason has received them; and they are
all acting against the decrees of Caesar,
saying that there is another king, Jesus."
8 And the people and the city authorities
were disturbed when they heard this.
9 And when they had taken security from
Jason and the rest, they let them go.

Paul and Silas in Beroea

10 The brethren immediately sent Paul
and Silas away by night to Beroe'a; and
when they arrived they went into the
Jewish synagogue. 11 Now these Jews
were more noble than those in Thessa-
loni'ca, for they received the word with
all eagerness, examining the scriptures
daily to see if these things were so.
12 Many of them therefore believed, with
not a few Greek women of high standing
as well as men. 13 But when the Jews of
Thessaloni'ca learned that the word of
God was proclaimed by Paul at Beroe'a
also, they came there too, stirring up
and inciting the crowds. 14 Then the
brethren immediately sent Paul off on
his way to the sea, but Silas and Timothy
remained there. 15 Those who conducted
Paul brought him as far as Athens; and
receiving a command for Silas and Tim-
othy to come to him as soon as possible,
they departed.

[u] **17.2** Or *sabbaths*

Paul in Athens

16 Now while Paul was waiting for
them at Athens, his spirit was provoked
within him as he saw that the city was
full of idols. 17So he argued in the syn-
agogue with the Jews and the devout
persons, and in the market place every
day with those who chanced to be there.
18Some also of the Epicurean and Stoic
philosophers met him. And some said,
"What would this babbler say?" Others
said, "He seems to be a preacher of for-
eign divinities"—because he preached
Jesus and the resurrection. 19And they
took hold of him and brought him to the
Are-op'agus, saying, "May we know what
this new teaching is which you present?
20For you bring some strange things to
our ears; we wish to know therefore
what these things mean." 21Now all the
Athenians and the foreigners who lived
there spent their time in nothing except
telling or hearing something new.

22 So Paul, standing in the middle of
the Are-op'agus, said: "Men of Athens, I
perceive that in every way you are very
religious. 23For as I passed along, and
observed the objects of your worship, I
found also an altar with this inscription,
'To an unknown god.' What therefore
you worship as unknown, this I pro-
claim to you. 24The God who made the
world and everything in it, being Lord
of heaven and earth, does not live in
shrines made by man, 25nor is he served
by human hands, as though he needed
anything, since he himself gives to all
men life and breath and everything.
26And he made from one every nation of
men to live on all the face of the earth,
having determined allotted periods and
the boundaries of their habitation, 27that
they should seek God, in the hope that
they might feel after him and find him.
Yet he is not far from each one of us, 28for

'In him we live and move and have
our being';

as even some of your poets have said,

'For we are indeed his offspring.'

29Being then God's offspring, we ought
not to think that the Deity is like gold,
or silver, or stone, a representation by
the art and imagination of man. 30The
times of ignorance God overlooked,
but now he commands all men every-
where to repent, 31because he has fixed
a day on which he will judge the world
in righteousness by a man whom he has
appointed, and of this he has given as-
surance to all men by raising him from
the dead."

32 Now when they heard of the resur-
rection of the dead, some mocked; but
others said, "We will hear you again
about this." 33So Paul went out from
among them. 34But some men joined him
and believed, among them Dionys'ius
the Are-op'agite and a woman named
Dam'aris and others with them.

Paul in Corinth

18 After this he left Athens and went
to Corinth. 2And he found a Jew
named Aquila, a native of Pontus, lately
come from Italy with his wife Priscilla,
because Claudius had commanded all
the Jews to leave Rome. And he went
to see them; 3and because he was of the
same trade he stayed with them, and they
worked, for by trade they were tentmak-
ers. 4And he argued in the synagogue
every sabbath, and persuaded Jews and
Greeks.

5 When Silas and Timothy arrived
from Macedo'nia, Paul was occupied
with preaching, testifying to the Jews
that the Christ was Jesus. 6And when
they opposed and reviled him, he shook
out his garments and said to them, "Your
blood be upon your heads! I am inno-
cent. From now on I will go to the Gen-
tiles." 7And he left there and went to the
house of a man named Titius[v] Justus, a
worshiper of God; his house was next

[v] **18.7** Other early authorities read *Titus*

door to the synagogue. 8Crispus, the
ruler of the synagogue, believed in the
Lord, together with all his household;
and many of the Corinthians hearing
Paul believed and were baptized. 9And
the Lord said to Paul one night in a vi-
sion, "Do not be afraid, but speak and do
not be silent; 10for I am with you, and no
man shall attack you to harm you; for I
have many people in this city." 11And he
stayed a year and six months, teaching
the word of God among them.
12 But when Gallio was proconsul of
Acha'ia, the Jews made a united attack
upon Paul and brought him before the
tribunal, 13saying, "This man is persuad-
ing men to worship God contrary to the
law." 14But when Paul was about to open
his mouth, Gallio said to the Jews, "If it
were a matter of wrongdoing or vicious
crime, I should have reason to bear with
you, O Jews; 15but since it is a matter of
questions about words and names and
your own law, see to it yourselves; I re-
fuse to be a judge of these things." 16And
he drove them from the tribunal. 17And
they all seized Sos'thenes, the ruler of
the synagogue, and beat him in front of
the tribunal. But Gallio paid no attention
to this.

Paul's Return to Antioch

18 After this Paul stayed many days lon-
ger, and then took leave of the brethren
and sailed for Syria, and with him Pris-
cilla and Aquila. At Cen'chre-ae he cut
his hair, for he had a vow. 19And they
came to Ephesus, and he left them there;
but he himself went into the synagogue
and argued with the Jews. 20When they
asked him to stay for a longer period, he
declined; 21but on taking leave of them
he said, "I will return to you if God wills,"
and he set sail from Ephesus.
22 When he had landed at Caesare'a,
he went up and greeted the church,
and then went down to Antioch. 23After
spending some time there he departed
and went from place to place through the
region of Galatia and Phryg'ia, strength-
ening all the disciples.

Ministry of Apollos

24 Now a Jew named Apol'los, a native of
Alexandria, came to Ephesus. He was an
eloquent man, well versed in the scrip-
tures. 25He had been instructed in the
way of the Lord; and being fervent in
spirit, he spoke and taught accurately
the things concerning Jesus, though he
knew only the baptism of John. 26He be-
gan to speak boldly in the synagogue;
but when Priscilla and Aquila heard
him, they took him and expounded to
him the way of God more accurately.
27And when he wished to cross to Acha'ia,
the brethren encouraged him, and wrote
to the disciples to receive him. When
he arrived, he greatly helped those who
through grace had believed, 28for he
powerfully confuted the Jews in public,
showing by the scriptures that the Christ
was Jesus.

Paul in Ephesus

19 While Apol'los was at Corinth,
Paul passed through the upper
country and came to Ephesus. There he
found some disciples. 2And he said to
them, "Did you receive the Holy Spirit
when you believed?" And they said, "No,
we have never even heard that there is
a Holy Spirit." 3And he said, "Into what
then were you baptized?" They said,
"Into John's baptism." 4And Paul said,
"John baptized with the baptism of re-
pentance, telling the people to believe in
the one who was to come after him, that
is, Jesus." 5On hearing this, they were
baptized in the name of the Lord Jesus.
6And when Paul had laid his hands upon
them, the Holy Spirit came on them; and
they spoke with tongues and prophesied.
7There were about twelve of them in all.
8 And he entered the synagogue and
for three months spoke boldly, arguing

and pleading about the kingdom of God;
9but when some were stubborn and dis-
believed, speaking evil of the Way be-
fore the congregation, he withdrew from
them, taking the disciples with him, and
argued daily in the hall of Tyran'nus.[w]
10This continued for two years, so that all
the residents of Asia heard the word of
the Lord, both Jews and Greeks.

The Sons of Sceva

11 And God did extraordinary miracles
by the hands of Paul, 12so that handker-
chiefs or aprons were carried away from
his body to the sick, and diseases left them
and the evil spirits came out of them.
13Then some of the itinerant Jewish exor-
cists undertook to pronounce the name
of the Lord Jesus over those who had evil
spirits, saying, "I adjure you by the Jesus
whom Paul preaches." 14Seven sons of
a Jewish high priest named Sceva were
doing this. 15But the evil spirit answered
them, "Jesus I know, and Paul I know; but
who are you?" 16And the man in whom
the evil spirit was leaped on them, mas-
tered all of them, and overpowered them,
so that they fled out of that house naked
and wounded. 17And this became known
to all residents of Ephesus, both Jews and
Greeks; and fear fell upon them all; and
the name of the Lord Jesus was extolled.
18Many also of those who were now be-
lievers came, confessing and divulging
their practices. 19And a number of those
who practiced magic arts brought their
books together and burned them in the
sight of all; and they counted the value of
them and found it came to fifty thousand
pieces of silver. 20So the word of the Lord
grew and prevailed mightily.

The Riot in Ephesus

21 Now after these events Paul resolved
in the Spirit to pass through Macedo'nia
and Acha'ia and go to Jerusalem, saying,
"After I have been there, I must also see
Rome." 22And having sent into Mace-
do'nia two of his helpers, Timothy and
Eras'tus, he himself stayed in Asia for a
while.

23 About that time there arose no
little stir concerning the Way. 24For a
man named Deme'trius, a silversmith,
who made silver shrines of Ar'temis,
brought no little business to the crafts-
men. 25These he gathered together, with
the workmen of like occupation, and
said, "Men, you know that from this
business we have our wealth. 26And you
see and hear that not only at Ephesus but
almost throughout all Asia this Paul has
persuaded and turned away a consider-
able company of people, saying that gods
made with hands are not gods. 27And
there is danger not only that this trade
of ours may come into disrepute but
also that the temple of the great goddess
Ar'temis may count for nothing, and
that she may even be deposed from her
magnificence, she whom all Asia and the
world worship."

28 When they heard this they were en-
raged, and cried out, "Great is Ar'temis
of the Ephesians!" 29So the city was filled
with the confusion; and they rushed to-
gether into the theater, dragging with
them Ga'ius and Aristar'chus, Mace-
do'nians who were Paul's companions
in travel. 30Paul wished to go in among
the crowd, but the disciples would not
let him; 31some of the A'si-archs also,
who were friends of his, sent to him and
begged him not to venture into the the-
ater. 32Now some cried one thing, some
another; for the assembly was in con-
fusion, and most of them did not know
why they had come together. 33Some of
the crowd prompted Alexander, whom
the Jews had put forward. And Alexan-
der motioned with his hand, wishing
to make a defense to the people. 34But
when they recognized that he was a Jew,
for about two hours they all with one

[w] **19.9** Other ancient authorities add *from the fifth hour to the tenth*

voice cried out, "Great is Ar′temis of the
Ephesians!" [35]And when the town clerk
had quieted the crowd, he said, "Men of
Ephesus, what man is there who does
not know that the city of the Ephesians
is temple keeper of the great Ar′temis,
and of the sacred stone that fell from
the sky?[x] [36]Seeing then that these things
cannot be contradicted, you ought to be
quiet and do nothing rash. [37]For you have
brought these men here who are neither
sacrilegious nor blasphemers of our
goddess. [38]If therefore Deme′trius and
the craftsmen with him have a complaint
against any one, the courts are open,
and there are proconsuls; let them bring
charges against one another. [39]But if you
seek anything further,[y] it shall be settled
in the regular assembly. [40]For we are in
danger of being charged with rioting
today, there being no cause that we can
give to justify this commotion." [41]And
when he had said this, he dismissed the
assembly.

Paul Goes to Macedonia and Greece

20 After the uproar ceased, Paul
sent for the disciples and having
exhorted them took leave of them and
departed for Macedo′nia. [2]When he had
gone through these parts and had given
them much encouragement, he came to
Greece. [3]There he spent three months,
and when a plot was made against him
by the Jews as he was about to set sail for
Syria, he determined to return through
Macedo′nia. [4]Sop′ater of Beroe′a, the son
of Pyrrhus, accompanied him; and of the
Thessalo′nians, Aristar′chus and Secun′-
dus; and Ga′ius of Derbe, and Timothy;
and the Asians, Tych′icus and Troph′i-
mus. [5]These went on and were waiting
for us at Tro′as, [6]but we sailed away from
Philippi after the days of Unleavened
Bread, and in five days we came to them
at Tro′as, where we stayed for seven days.

Paul's Farewell Visit to Troas

7 On the first day of the week, when we
were gathered together to break bread,
Paul talked with them, intending to de-
part on the morrow; and he prolonged his
speech until midnight. [8]There were many
lights in the upper chamber where we
were gathered. [9]And a young man named
Eu′tychus was sitting in the window. He
sank into a deep sleep as Paul talked still
longer; and being overcome by sleep, he
fell down from the third story and was
taken up dead. [10]But Paul went down and
bent over him, and embracing him said,
"Do not be alarmed, for his life is in him."
[11]And when Paul had gone up and had bro-
ken bread and eaten, he conversed with
them a long while, until daybreak, and
so departed. [12]And they took the lad away
alive, and were not a little comforted.

The Voyage from Troas to Miletus

13 But going ahead to the ship, we set sail
for Assos, intending to take Paul aboard
there; for so he had arranged, intending
himself to go by land. [14]And when he met
us at Assos, we took him on board and
came to Mityle′ne. [15]And sailing from
there we came the following day oppo-
site Chi′os; the next day we touched at
Samos; and[z] the day after that we came
to Mile′tus. [16]For Paul had decided to sail
past Ephesus, so that he might not have
to spend time in Asia; for he was hasten-
ing to be at Jerusalem, if possible, on the
day of Pentecost.

Paul Speaks to the Ephesian Elders

17 And from Mile′tus he sent to Ephe-
sus and called to him the elders of the
church. [18]And when they came to him, he
said to them:

Paul's Journey to Jerusalem

"You yourselves know how I lived
among you all the time from the first day

[x] **19.35** The meaning of the Greek is uncertain [y] **19.39** Other ancient authorities read *about other matters* [z] **20.15** Other ancient authorities add *after remaining at Trogyllium*

that I set foot in Asia, [19]serving the Lord
with all humility and with tears and with
trials which befell me through the plots
of the Jews; [20]how I did not shrink from
declaring to you anything that was prof-
itable, and teaching you in public and
from house to house, [21]testifying both
to Jews and to Greeks of repentance to
God and of faith in our Lord Jesus Christ.
[22]And now, behold, I am going to Jerusa-
lem, bound in the Spirit, not knowing
what shall befall me there; [23]except that
the Holy Spirit testifies to me in every
city that imprisonment and afflictions
await me. [24]But I do not account my life
of any value nor as precious to myself, if
only I may accomplish my course and the
ministry which I received from the Lord
Jesus, to testify to the gospel of the grace
of God. [25]And now, behold, I know that
all you among whom I have gone about
preaching the kingdom will see my face
no more. [26]Therefore I testify to you this
day that I am innocent of the blood of
all of you, [27]for I did not shrink from de-
claring to you the whole counsel of God.
[28]Take heed to yourselves and to all the
flock, in which the Holy Spirit has made
you guardians, to feed the church of the
Lord[a] which he obtained with his own
blood.[b] [29]I know that after my departure
fierce wolves will come in among you,
not sparing the flock; [30]and from among
your own selves will arise men speaking
perverse things, to draw away the dis-
ciples after them. [31]Therefore be alert,
remembering that for three years I did
not cease night or day to admonish every
one with tears. [32]And now I commend
you to God and to the word of his grace,
which is able to build you up and to give
you the inheritance among all those who
are sanctified. [33]I coveted no one's sil-
ver or gold or apparel. [34]You yourselves
know that these hands ministered to my
necessities, and to those who were with
me. [35]In all things I have shown you that
by so toiling one must help the weak, re-
membering the words of the Lord Jesus,
how he said, 'It is more blessed to give
than to receive.'"

36 And when he had spoken thus, he
knelt down and prayed with them all.
[37]And they all wept and embraced Paul
and kissed him, [38]sorrowing most of all
because of the word he had spoken, that
they should see his face no more. And
they brought him to the ship.

21 And when we had parted from
them and set sail, we came by a
straight course to Cos, and the next day to
Rhodes, and from there to Pat′ara.[c] [2]And
having found a ship crossing to Phoeni′-
cia, we went aboard, and set sail. [3]When
we had come in sight of Cyprus, leaving it
on the left we sailed to Syria, and landed
at Tyre; for there the ship was to unload
its cargo. [4]And having sought out the
disciples, we stayed there for seven days.
Through the Spirit they told Paul not to
go on to Jerusalem. [5]And when our days
there were ended, we departed and went
on our journey; and they all, with wives
and children, brought us on our way till
we were outside the city; and kneeling
down on the beach we prayed and bade
one another farewell. [6]Then we went on
board the ship, and they returned home.

7 When we had finished the voyage
from Tyre, we arrived at Ptolema′is; and
we greeted the brethren and stayed with
them for one day. [8]On the morrow we
departed and came to Caesare′a; and we
entered the house of Philip the evange-
list, who was one of the seven, and stayed
with him. [9]And he had four unmarried
daughters, who prophesied. [10]While we
were staying for some days, a prophet
named Ag′abus came down from Judea.
[11]And coming to us he took Paul's girdle
and bound his own feet and hands, and
said, "Thus says the Holy Spirit, 'So shall

[a]**20.28** Other ancient authorities read *of God* [b]**20.28** Or *with the blood of his Own* [c]**21.1** Other ancient authorities add *and Myra*

the Jews at Jerusalem bind the man who
owns this girdle and deliver him into the
hands of the Gentiles.' " [12]When we heard
this, we and the people there begged him
not to go up to Jerusalem. [13]Then Paul an-
swered, "What are you doing, weeping
and breaking my heart? For I am ready
not only to be imprisoned but even to
die at Jerusalem for the name of the Lord
Jesus." [14]And when he would not be per-
suaded, we ceased and said, "The will of
the Lord be done."

15 After these days we made ready and
went up to Jerusalem. [16]And some of the
disciples from Caesare′a went with us,
bringing us to the house of Mnason of
Cyprus, an early disciple, with whom we
should lodge.

Paul Visits James at Jerusalem

17 When we had come to Jerusalem, the
brethren received us gladly. [18]On the
following day Paul went in with us to
James; and all the elders were present.
[19]After greeting them, he related one by
one the things that God had done among
the Gentiles through his ministry. [20]And
when they heard it, they glorified God.
And they said to him, "You see, brother,
how many thousands there are among
the Jews of those who have believed; they
are all zealous for the law, [21]and they
have been told about you that you teach
all the Jews who are among the Gentiles
to forsake Moses, telling them not to cir-
cumcise their children or observe the
customs. [22]What then is to be done? They
will certainly hear that you have come.
[23]Do therefore what we tell you. We have
four men who are under a vow; [24]take
these men and purify yourself along with
them and pay their expenses, so that they
may shave their heads. Thus all will know
that there is nothing in what they have
been told about you but that you yourself
live in observance of the law. [25]But as for
the Gentiles who have believed, we have
sent a letter with our judgment that they
should abstain from what has been sac-
rificed to idols and from blood and from
what is strangled[d] and from unchastity."
[26]Then Paul took the men, and the next
day he purified himself with them and
went into the temple, to give notice when
the days of purification would be fulfilled
and the offering presented for every one
of them.

Paul Arrested in the Temple

27 When the seven days were almost
completed, the Jews from Asia, who had
seen him in the temple, stirred up all the
crowd, and laid hands on him, [28]crying
out, "Men of Israel, help! This is the man
who is teaching men everywhere against
the people and the law and this place;
moreover he also brought Greeks into
the temple, and he has defiled this holy
place." [29]For they had previously seen
Troph′imus the Ephesian with him in
the city, and they supposed that Paul had
brought him into the temple. [30]Then all
the city was aroused, and the people ran
together; they seized Paul and dragged
him out of the temple, and at once the
gates were shut. [31]And as they were try-
ing to kill him, word came to the tribune
of the cohort that all Jerusalem was in
confusion. [32]He at once took soldiers and
centurions, and ran down to them; and
when they saw the tribune and the sol-
diers, they stopped beating Paul. [33]Then
the tribune came up and arrested him,
and ordered him to be bound with two
chains. He inquired who he was and
what he had done. [34]Some in the crowd
shouted one thing, some another; and as
he could not learn the facts because of
the uproar, he ordered him to be brought
into the barracks. [35]And when he came to
the steps, he was actually carried by the
soldiers because of the violence of the
crowd; [36]for the mob of the people fol-
lowed, crying, "Away with him!"

[d]**21.25** Other early authorities omit *and from what is strangled*

Paul Defends Himself

37 As Paul was about to be brought into
the barracks, he said to the tribune,
"May I say something to you?" And he
said, "Do you know Greek? 38 Are you not
the Egyptian, then, who recently stirred
up a revolt and led the four thousand
men of the Assassins out into the wilder-
ness?" 39 Paul replied, "I am a Jew, from
Tarsus in Cili′cia, a citizen of no mean
city; I beg you, let me speak to the peo-
ple." 40 And when he had given him leave,
Paul, standing on the steps, motioned
with his hand to the people; and when
there was a great hush, he spoke to them
in the Hebrew language, saying:

22 "Brethren and fathers, hear the
defense which I now make before
you."

2 And when they heard that he ad-
dressed them in the Hebrew language,
they were the more quiet. And he said:

3 "I am a Jew, born at Tarsus in Cili′cia,
but brought up in this city at the feet of
Gama′li-el, educated according to the
strict manner of the law of our fathers,
being zealous for God as you all are this
day. 4 I persecuted this Way to the death,
binding and delivering to prison both
men and women, 5 as the high priest and
the whole council of elders bear me wit-
ness. From them I received letters to the
brethren, and I journeyed to Damascus
to take those also who were there and
bring them in bonds to Jerusalem to be
punished.

Paul Tells of His Conversion

6 "As I made my journey and drew near
to Damascus, about noon a great light
from heaven suddenly shone about me.
7 And I fell to the ground and heard a
voice saying to me, 'Saul, Saul, why do
you persecute me?' 8 And I answered,
'Who are you, Lord?' And he said to me, 'I
am Jesus of Nazareth whom you are per-
secuting.' 9 Now those who were with me
saw the light but did not hear the voice of
the one who was speaking to me. 10 And I
said, 'What shall I do, Lord?' And the Lord
said to me, 'Rise, and go into Damascus,
and there you will be told all that is ap-
pointed for you to do.' 11 And when I could
not see because of the brightness of that
light, I was led by the hand by those who
were with me, and came into Damascus.

12 "And one Anani′as, a devout man ac-
cording to the law, well spoken of by all
the Jews who lived there, 13 came to me,
and standing by me said to me, 'Brother
Saul, receive your sight.' And in that
very hour I received my sight and saw
him. 14 And he said, 'The God of our fa-
thers appointed you to know his will, to
see the Just One and to hear a voice from
his mouth; 15 for you will be a witness for
him to all men of what you have seen and
heard. 16 And now why do you wait? Rise
and be baptized, and wash away your
sins, calling on his name.'

Paul Sent to the Gentiles

17 "When I had returned to Jerusalem
and was praying in the temple, I fell into
a trance 18 and saw him saying to me,
'Make haste and get quickly out of Jeru-
salem, because they will not accept your
testimony about me.' 19 And I said, 'Lord,
they themselves know that in every syn-
agogue I imprisoned and beat those who
believed in thee. 20 And when the blood of
Stephen thy witness was shed, I also was
standing by and approving, and keeping
the garments of those who killed him.'
21 And he said to me, 'Depart; for I will
send you far away to the Gentiles.'"

Paul and the Roman Tribune

22 Up to this word they listened to him;
then they lifted up their voices and
said, "Away with such a fellow from the
earth! For he ought not to live." 23 And
as they cried out and waved their gar-
ments and threw dust into the air, 24 the
tribune commanded him to be brought
into the barracks, and ordered him to

be examined by scourging, to find out
why they shouted thus against him.
25But when they had tied him up with the
thongs, Paul said to the centurion who
was standing by, "Is it lawful for you to
scourge a man who is a Roman citizen,
and uncondemned?" 26When the centu-
rion heard that, he went to the tribune
and said to him, "What are you about
to do? For this man is a Roman citizen."
27So the tribune came and said to him,
"Tell me, are you a Roman citizen?" And
he said, "Yes." 28The tribune answered, "I
bought this citizenship for a large sum."
Paul said, "But I was born a citizen." 29So
those who were about to examine him
withdrew from him instantly; and the
tribune also was afraid, for he realized
that Paul was a Roman citizen and that
he had bound him.

Paul before the Council

30 But on the morrow, desiring to know
the real reason why the Jews accused
him, he unbound him, and commanded
the chief priests and all the council to
meet, and he brought Paul down and set
him before them.

23 And Paul, looking intently at the
council, said, "Brethren, I have
lived before God in all good conscience
up to this day." 2And the high priest
Anani'as commanded those who stood
by him to strike him on the mouth. 3Then
Paul said to him, "God shall strike you,
you whitewashed wall! Are you sitting
to judge me according to the law, and
yet contrary to the law you order me to
be struck?" 4Those who stood by said,
"Would you revile God's high priest?"
5And Paul said, "I did not know, breth-
ren, that he was the high priest; for it
is written, 'You shall not speak evil of a
ruler of your people.'"

6 But when Paul perceived that one
part were Sad'ducees and the other Phar-
isees, he cried out in the council, "Breth-
ren, I am a Pharisee, a son of Pharisees;
with respect to the hope and the resur-
rection of the dead I am on trial." 7And
when he had said this, a dissension arose
between the Pharisees and the Sad'du-
cees; and the assembly was divided.
8For the Sad'ducees say that there is no
resurrection, nor angel, nor spirit; but
the Pharisees acknowledge them all.
9Then a great clamor arose; and some of
the scribes of the Pharisees' party stood
up and contended, "We find nothing
wrong in this man. What if a spirit or
an angel spoke to him?" 10And when the
dissension became violent, the tribune,
afraid that Paul would be torn in pieces
by them, commanded the soldiers to go
down and take him by force from among
them and bring him into the barracks.

11 The following night the Lord stood
by him and said, "Take courage, for as
you have testified about me at Jerusalem,
so you must bear witness also at Rome."

The Plot to Kill Paul

12 When it was day, the Jews made a plot
and bound themselves by an oath neither
to eat nor drink till they had killed Paul.
13There were more than forty who made
this conspiracy. 14And they went to the
chief priests and elders, and said, "We
have strictly bound ourselves by an oath
to taste no food till we have killed Paul.
15You therefore, along with the council,
give notice now to the tribune to bring
him down to you, as though you were go-
ing to determine his case more exactly.
And we are ready to kill him before he
comes near."

16 Now the son of Paul's sister heard
of their ambush; so he went and entered
the barracks and told Paul. 17And Paul
called one of the centurions and said,
"Bring this young man to the tribune;
for he has something to tell him." 18So he
took him and brought him to the tribune
and said, "Paul the prisoner called me
and asked me to bring this young man to
you, as he has something to say to you."

[19]The tribune took him by the hand, and
going aside asked him privately, "What
is it that you have to tell me?" [20]And he
said, "The Jews have agreed to ask you
to bring Paul down to the council tomor-
row, as though they were going to in-
quire somewhat more closely about him.
[21]But do not yield to them; for more than
forty of their men lie in ambush for him,
having bound themselves by an oath nei-
ther to eat nor drink till they have killed
him; and now they are ready, waiting for
the promise from you." [22]So the tribune
dismissed the young man, charging him,
"Tell no one that you have informed me
of this."

Paul Sent to Felix the Governor

23 Then he called two of the centurions
and said, "At the third hour of the night
get ready two hundred soldiers with
seventy horsemen and two hundred
spearmen to go as far as Caesare'a. [24]Also
provide mounts for Paul to ride, and
bring him safely to Felix the governor."
[25]And he wrote a letter to this effect:

26 "Claudius Lys'ias to his Excellency
the governor Felix, greeting. [27]This man
was seized by the Jews, and was about
to be killed by them, when I came upon
them with the soldiers and rescued him,
having learned that he was a Roman cit-
izen. [28]And desiring to know the charge
on which they accused him, I brought
him down to their council. [29]I found that
he was accused about questions of their
law, but charged with nothing deserving
death or imprisonment. [30]And when it
was disclosed to me that there would be a
plot against the man, I sent him to you at
once, ordering his accusers also to state
before you what they have against him."

31 So the soldiers, according to their
instructions, took Paul and brought
him by night to Antip'atris. [32]And on the
morrow they returned to the barracks,
leaving the horsemen to go on with him.
[33]When they came to Caesare'a and de-
livered the letter to the governor, they
presented Paul also before him. [34]On
reading the letter, he asked to what prov-
ince he belonged. When he learned that
he was from Cili'cia [35]he said, "I will hear
you when your accusers arrive." And
he commanded him to be guarded in
Herod's praetorium.

Paul before Felix at Caesarea

24 And after five days the high priest
Anani'as came down with some
elders and a spokesman, one Tertul'lus.
They laid before the governor their case
against Paul; [2]and when he was called,
Tertul'lus began to accuse him, saying:

"Since through you we enjoy much
peace, and since by your provision, most
excellent Felix, reforms are introduced
on behalf of this nation, [3]in every way
and everywhere we accept this with all
gratitude. [4]But, to detain you no fur-
ther, I beg you in your kindness to hear
us briefly. [5]For we have found this man
a pestilent fellow, an agitator among all
the Jews throughout the world, and a
ringleader of the sect of the Nazarenes.
[6]He even tried to profane the temple, but
we seized him.[e] [8]By examining him your-
self you will be able to learn from him
about everything of which we accuse
him."

9 The Jews also joined in the charge,
affirming that all this was so.

Paul's Defense before Felix

10 And when the governor had motioned
to him to speak, Paul replied:

"Realizing that for many years you
have been judge over this nation, I cheer-
fully make my defense. [11]As you may as-
certain, it is not more than twelve days

[e]**24.6** Other ancient authorities add *and we would have judged him according to our law. [7]But the chief captain Lysias came and with great violence took him out of our hands, [8]commanding his accusers to come before you.*

since I went up to worship at Jerusalem;
12and they did not find me disputing with
any one or stirring up a crowd, either in
the temple or in the synagogues, or in
the city. 13Neither can they prove to you
what they now bring up against me. 14But
this I admit to you, that according to the
Way, which they call a sect, I worship the
God of our fathers, believing everything
laid down by the law or written in the
prophets, 15having a hope in God which
these themselves accept, that there will
be a resurrection of both the just and the
unjust. 16So I always take pains to have a
clear conscience toward God and toward
men. 17Now after some years I came to
bring to my nation alms and offerings.
18As I was doing this, they found me puri-
fied in the temple, without any crowd or
tumult. But some Jews from Asia— 19they
ought to be here before you and to make
an accusation, if they have anything
against me. 20Or else let these men them-
selves say what wrongdoing they found
when I stood before the council, 21except
this one thing which I cried out while
standing among them, 'With respect to
the resurrection of the dead I am on trial
before you this day.'"

22 But Felix, having a rather accurate
knowledge of the Way, put them off, say-
ing, "When Lys'ias the tribune comes
down, I will decide your case." 23Then
he gave orders to the centurion that he
should be kept in custody but should
have some liberty, and that none of his
friends should be prevented from at-
tending to his needs.

Paul Held in Custody

24 After some days Felix came with his
wife Drusil'la, who was a Jewess; and he
sent for Paul and heard him speak upon
faith in Christ Jesus. 25And as he argued
about justice and self-control and future
judgment, Felix was alarmed and said,
"Go away for the present; when I have
an opportunity I will summon you."
26At the same time he hoped that money
would be given him by Paul. So he sent
for him often and conversed with him.
27But when two years had elapsed, Felix
was succeeded by Porcius Festus; and
desiring to do the Jews a favor, Felix left
Paul in prison.

Paul Appeals to the Emperor

25 Now when Festus had come into
his province, after three days he
went up to Jerusalem from Caesare'a.
2And the chief priests and the principal
men of the Jews informed him against
Paul; and they urged him, 3asking as a
favor to have the man sent to Jerusalem,
planning an ambush to kill him on the
way. 4Festus replied that Paul was being
kept at Caesare'a, and that he himself in-
tended to go there shortly. 5"So," said he,
"let the men of authority among you go
down with me, and if there is anything
wrong about the man, let them accuse
him."

6 When he had stayed among them
not more than eight or ten days, he went
down to Caesare'a; and the next day he
took his seat on the tribunal and ordered
Paul to be brought. 7And when he had
come, the Jews who had gone down from
Jerusalem stood about him, bringing
against him many serious charges which
they could not prove. 8Paul said in his
defense, "Neither against the law of the
Jews, nor against the temple, nor against
Caesar have I offended at all." 9But Fes-
tus, wishing to do the Jews a favor, said to
Paul, "Do you wish to go up to Jerusalem,
and there be tried on these charges be-
fore me?" 10But Paul said, "I am standing
before Caesar's tribunal, where I ought
to be tried; to the Jews I have done no
wrong, as you know very well. 11If then
I am a wrongdoer, and have committed
anything for which I deserve to die, I do
not seek to escape death; but if there is
nothing in their charges against me, no
one can give me up to them. I appeal to

Caesar." 12Then Festus, when he had con-
ferred with his council, answered, "You
have appealed to Caesar; to Caesar you
shall go."

Festus Consults King Agrippa

13 Now when some days had passed,
Agrippa the king and Berni′ce arrived
at Caesare′a to welcome Festus. 14And
as they stayed there many days, Festus
laid Paul's case before the king, saying,
"There is a man left prisoner by Felix;
15and when I was at Jerusalem, the chief
priests and the elders of the Jews gave
information about him, asking for sen-
tence against him. 16I answered them
that it was not the custom of the Romans
to give up any one before the accused
met the accusers face to face, and had op-
portunity to make his defense concern-
ing the charge laid against him. 17When
therefore they came together here, I
made no delay, but on the next day took
my seat on the tribunal and ordered the
man to be brought in. 18When the accus-
ers stood up, they brought no charge
in his case of such evils as I supposed;
19but they had certain points of dispute
with him about their own superstition
and about one Jesus, who was dead, but
whom Paul asserted to be alive. 20Being
at a loss how to investigate these ques-
tions, I asked whether he wished to go to
Jerusalem and be tried there regarding
them. 21But when Paul had appealed to
be kept in custody for the decision of the
emperor, I commanded him to be held
until I could send him to Caesar." 22And
Agrippa said to Festus, "I should like to
hear the man myself." "Tomorrow," said
he, "you shall hear him."

Paul Brought before Agrippa

23 So on the morrow Agrippa and Ber-
ni′ce came with great pomp, and they
entered the audience hall with the mil-
itary tribunes and the prominent men
of the city. Then by command of Festus
Paul was brought in. 24And Festus said,
"King Agrippa and all who are present
with us, you see this man about whom
the whole Jewish people petitioned me,
both at Jerusalem and here, shouting
that he ought not to live any longer. 25But
I found that he had done nothing deserv-
ing death; and as he himself appealed to
the emperor, I decided to send him. 26But
I have nothing definite to write to my
lord about him. Therefore I have brought
him before you, and, especially before
you, King Agrippa, that, after we have
examined him, I may have something to
write. 27For it seems to me unreasonable,
in sending a prisoner, not to indicate the
charges against him."

Paul Defends Himself before Agrippa

26 Agrippa said to Paul, "You have
permission to speak for yourself."
Then Paul stretched out his hand and
made his defense:

2 "I think myself fortunate that it is be-
fore you, King Agrippa, I am to make my
defense today against all the accusations
of the Jews, 3because you are especially
familiar with all customs and controver-
sies of the Jews; therefore I beg you to lis-
ten to me patiently.

4 "My manner of life from my youth,
spent from the beginning among my own
nation and at Jerusalem, is known by all
the Jews. 5They have known for a long
time, if they are willing to testify, that
according to the strictest party of our
religion I have lived as a Pharisee. 6And
now I stand here on trial for hope in the
promise made by God to our fathers, 7to
which our twelve tribes hope to attain,
as they earnestly worship night and day.
And for this hope I am accused by Jews,
O king! 8Why is it thought incredible by
any of you that God raises the dead?

9 "I myself was convinced that I ought
to do many things in opposing the name
of Jesus of Nazareth. 10And I did so in Je-
rusalem; I not only shut up many of the

saints in prison, by authority from the
chief priests, but when they were put
to death I cast my vote against them.
11And I punished them often in all the
synagogues and tried to make them blas-
pheme; and in raging fury against them,
I persecuted them even to foreign cities.

Paul Tells of His Conversion

12 "Thus I journeyed to Damascus with
the authority and commission of the
chief priests. 13At midday, O king, I saw
on the way a light from heaven, brighter
than the sun, shining round me and
those who journeyed with me. 14And
when we had all fallen to the ground, I
heard a voice saying to me in the Hebrew
language, 'Saul, Saul, why do you perse-
cute me? It hurts you to kick against the
goads.' 15And I said, 'Who are you, Lord?'
And the Lord said, 'I am Jesus whom you
are persecuting. 16But rise and stand
upon your feet; for I have appeared to
you for this purpose, to appoint you to
serve and bear witness to the things in
which you have seen me and to those in
which I will appear to you, 17delivering
you from the people and from the Gen-
tiles—to whom I send you 18to open their
eyes, that they may turn from darkness
to light and from the power of Satan to
God, that they may receive forgiveness
of sins and a place among those who are
sanctified by faith in me.'

Paul Tells of His Preaching

19 "Wherefore, O King Agrippa, I was
not disobedient to the heavenly vision,
20but declared first to those at Damas-
cus, then at Jerusalem and throughout
all the country of Judea, and also to the
Gentiles, that they should repent and
turn to God and perform deeds worthy
of their repentance. 21For this reason the
Jews seized me in the temple and tried
to kill me. 22To this day I have had the
help that comes from God, and so I stand
here testifying both to small and great,
saying nothing but what the prophets
and Moses said would come to pass:
23that the Christ must suffer, and that, by
being the first to rise from the dead, he
would proclaim light both to the people
and to the Gentiles."

Paul Appeals to Agrippa to Believe

24 And as he thus made his defense,
Festus said with a loud voice, "Paul, you
are mad; your great learning is turning
you mad." 25But Paul said, "I am not mad,
most excellent Festus, but I am speaking
the sober truth. 26For the king knows
about these things, and to him I speak
freely; for I am persuaded that none of
these things has escaped his notice, for
this was not done in a corner. 27King
Agrippa, do you believe the prophets? I
know that you believe." 28And Agrippa
said to Paul, "In a short time you think
to make me a Christian!" 29And Paul said,
"Whether short or long, I would to God
that not only you but also all who hear
me this day might become such as I am—
except for these chains."

30 Then the king rose, and the gover-
nor and Berni'ce and those who were
sitting with them; 31and when they had
withdrawn, they said to one another,
"This man is doing nothing to deserve
death or imprisonment." 32And Agrippa
said to Festus, "This man could have been
set free if he had not appealed to Caesar."

Paul Sails for Rome

27 And when it was decided that we
should sail for Italy, they deliv-
ered Paul and some other prisoners to
a centurion of the Augustan Cohort,
named Julius. 2And embarking in a ship
of Adramyt'tium, which was about to sail
to the ports along the coast of Asia, we
put to sea, accompanied by Aristar'chus,
a Macedo'nian from Thessaloni'ca. 3The
next day we put in at Sidon; and Ju-
lius treated Paul kindly, and gave him
leave to go to his friends and be cared

for. [4]And putting to sea from there we sailed under the lee of Cyprus, because the winds were against us. [5]And when we had sailed across the sea which is off Cili′cia and Pamphyl′ia, we came to Myra in Ly′cia. [6]There the centurion found a ship of Alexandria sailing for Italy, and put us on board. [7]We sailed slowly for a number of days, and arrived with difficulty off Cni′dus, and as the wind did not allow us to go on, we sailed under the lee of Crete off Salmo′ne. [8]Coasting along it with difficulty, we came to a place called Fair Havens, near which was the city of Lase′a.

9 As much time had been lost, and the voyage was already dangerous because the fast had already gone by, Paul advised them, [10]saying, "Sirs, I perceive that the voyage will be with injury and much loss, not only of the cargo and the ship, but also of our lives." [11]But the centurion paid more attention to the captain and to the owner of the ship than to what Paul said. [12]And because the harbor was not suitable to winter in, the majority advised to put to sea from there, on the chance that somehow they could reach Phoenix, a harbor of Crete, looking northeast and southeast,[f] and winter there.

The Storm at Sea

13 And when the south wind blew gently, supposing that they had obtained their purpose, they weighed anchor and sailed along Crete, close inshore. [14]But soon a tempestuous wind, called the northeaster, struck down from the land; [15]and when the ship was caught and could not face the wind, we gave way to it and were driven. [16]And running under the lee of a small island called Cauda,[g] we managed with difficulty to secure the boat; [17]after hoisting it up, they took measures[h] to undergird the ship; then, fearing that they should run on the Syr′tis, they lowered the gear, and so were driven. [18]As we were violently storm-tossed, they began next day to throw the cargo overboard; [19]and the third day they cast out with their own hands the tackle of the ship. [20]And when neither sun nor stars appeared for many a day, and no small tempest lay on us, all hope of our being saved was at last abandoned.

21 As they had been long without food, Paul then came forward among them and said, "Men, you should have listened to me, and should not have set sail from Crete and incurred this injury and loss. [22]I now bid you take heart; for there will be no loss of life among you, but only of the ship. [23]For this very night there stood by me an angel of the God to whom I belong and whom I worship, [24]and he said, 'Do not be afraid, Paul; you must stand before Caesar; and lo, God has granted you all those who sail with you.' [25]So take heart, men, for I have faith in God that it will be exactly as I have been told. [26]But we shall have to run on some island."

27 When the fourteenth night had come, as we were drifting across the sea of A′dria, about midnight the sailors suspected that they were nearing land. [28]So they sounded and found twenty fathoms; a little farther on they sounded again and found fifteen fathoms. [29]And fearing that we might run on the rocks, they let out four anchors from the stern, and prayed for day to come. [30]And as the sailors were seeking to escape from the ship, and had lowered the boat into the sea, under pretense of laying out anchors from the bow, [31]Paul said to the centurion and the soldiers, "Unless these men stay in the ship, you cannot be saved." [32]Then the soldiers cut away the ropes of the boat, and let it go.

33 As day was about to dawn, Paul urged them all to take some food, saying,

[f]**27.12** Or *southwest and northwest*
[g]**27.16** Other ancient authorities read *Clauda*
[h]**27.17** Greek *helps*

"Today is the fourteenth day that you have continued in suspense and without food, having taken nothing. [34]Therefore I urge you to take some food; it will give you strength, since not a hair is to perish from the head of any of you." [35]And when he had said this, he took bread, and giving thanks to God in the presence of all he broke it and began to eat. [36]Then they all were encouraged and ate some food themselves. [37](We were in all two hundred and seventy-six[i] persons in the ship.) [38]And when they had eaten enough, they lightened the ship, throwing out the wheat into the sea.

The Shipwreck

39 Now when it was day, they did not recognize the land, but they noticed a bay with a beach, on which they planned if possible to bring the ship ashore. [40]So they cast off the anchors and left them in the sea, at the same time loosening the ropes that tied the rudders; then hoisting the foresail to the wind they made for the beach. [41]But striking a shoal[j] they ran the vessel aground; the bow stuck and remained immovable, and the stern was broken up by the surf. [42]The soldiers' plan was to kill the prisoners, lest any should swim away and escape; [43]but the centurion, wishing to save Paul, kept them from carrying out their purpose. He ordered those who could swim to throw themselves overboard first and make for the land, [44]and the rest on planks or on pieces of the ship. And so it was that all escaped to land.

Paul on the Island of Malta

28 After we had escaped, we then learned that the island was called Malta. [2]And the natives showed us unusual kindness, for they kindled a fire and welcomed us all, because it had begun to rain and was cold. [3]Paul had gathered a bundle of sticks and put them on the fire, when a viper came out because of the heat and fastened on his hand. [4]When the natives saw the creature hanging from his hand, they said to one another, "No doubt this man is a murderer. Though he has escaped from the sea, justice has not allowed him to live." [5]He, however, shook off the creature into the fire and suffered no harm. [6]They waited, expecting him to swell up or suddenly fall down dead; but when they had waited a long time and saw no misfortune come to him, they changed their minds and said that he was a god.

7 Now in the neighborhood of that place were lands belonging to the chief man of the island, named Publius, who received us and entertained us hospitably for three days. [8]It happened that the father of Publius lay sick with fever and dysentery; and Paul visited him and prayed, and putting his hands on him healed him. [9]And when this had taken place, the rest of the people on the island who had diseases also came and were cured. [10]They presented many gifts to us;[k] and when we sailed, they put on board whatever we needed.

Paul Arrives at Rome

11 After three months we set sail in a ship which had wintered in the island, a ship of Alexandria, with the Twin Brothers as figurehead. [12]Putting in at Syracuse, we stayed there for three days. [13]And from there we made a circuit and arrived at Rhe'gium; and after one day a south wind sprang up, and on the second day we came to Pute'oli. [14]There we found brethren, and were invited to stay with them for seven days. And so we came to Rome. [15]And the brethren there, when they heard of us, came as far as the Forum of Ap'pius and Three Taverns to meet us. On seeing them Paul thanked God and

[i]**27.37** Other ancient authorities read *seventy-six* or *about seventy-six*
[j]**27.41** Greek *place of two seas*
[k]**28.10** Or *honored us with many honors*

took courage. [16]And when we came into Rome, Paul was allowed to stay by himself, with the soldier that guarded him.

Paul and Jewish Leaders in Rome

17 After three days he called together the local leaders of the Jews; and when they had gathered, he said to them, "Brethren, though I had done nothing against the people or the customs of our fathers, yet I was delivered prisoner from Jerusalem into the hands of the Romans. [18]When they had examined me, they wished to set me at liberty, because there was no reason for the death penalty in my case. [19]But when the Jews objected, I was compelled to appeal to Caesar—though I had no charge to bring against my nation. [20]For this reason therefore I have asked to see you and speak with you, since it is because of the hope of Israel that I am bound with this chain." [21]And they said to him, "We have received no letters from Judea about you, and none of the brethren coming here has reported or spoken any evil about you. [22]But we desire to hear from you what your views are; for with regard to this sect we know that everywhere it is spoken against."

Paul Preaches in Rome

23 When they had appointed a day for him, they came to him at his lodging in great numbers. And he expounded the matter to them from morning till evening, testifying to the kingdom of God and trying to convince them about Jesus both from the law of Moses and from the prophets. [24]And some were convinced by what he said, while others disbelieved. [25]So, as they disagreed among themselves, they departed, after Paul had made one statement: "The Holy Spirit was right in saying to your fathers through Isaiah the prophet:

26 'Go to this people, and say,
You shall indeed hear but never understand,
and you shall indeed see but never perceive.
27 For this people's heart has grown dull,
and their ears are heavy of hearing,
and their eyes they have closed;
lest they should perceive with their eyes,
and hear with their ears,
and understand with their heart,
and turn for me to heal them.'

[28]Let it be known to you then that this salvation of God has been sent to the Gentiles; they will listen."[l]

30 And he lived there two whole years at his own expense,[m] and welcomed all who came to him, [31]preaching the kingdom of God and teaching about the Lord Jesus Christ quite openly and unhindered.

[l] **28.28** Other ancient authorities add verse 29, *And when he had said these words, the Jews departed, holding much dispute among themselves* [m] **28.30** Or *in his own hired dwelling*

The Letter of Paul to the

ROMANS

Salutation

1 Paul, a servant[a] of Jesus Christ, called
to be an apostle, set apart for the gos-
pel of God [2]which he promised before-
hand through his prophets in the holy
scriptures, [3]the gospel concerning his
Son, who was descended from David
according to the flesh [4]and designated[b]
Son of God in power according to the
Spirit of holiness by his resurrection
from the dead, Jesus Christ our Lord,
[5]through whom we have received grace
and apostleship to bring about the obe-
dience of faith for the sake of his name
among all the nations, [6]including your-
selves who are called to belong to Jesus
Christ;

7 To all God's beloved in Rome, who are
called to be saints:

Grace to you and peace from God our
Father and the Lord Jesus Christ.

Prayer of Thanksgiving

8 First, I thank my God through Jesus
Christ for all of you, because your faith
is proclaimed in all the world. [9]For
God is my witness, whom I serve with
my spirit in the gospel of his Son, that
without ceasing I mention you always
in my prayers, [10]asking that somehow
by God's will I may now at last succeed
in coming to you. [11]For I long to see you,
that I may impart to you some spiritual
gift to strengthen you, [12]that is, that we
may be mutually encouraged by each
other's faith, both yours and mine. [13]I
want you to know, brethren, that I have
often intended to come to you (but thus
far have been prevented), in order that
I may reap some harvest among you as
well as among the rest of the Gentiles. [14]I
am under obligation both to Greeks and
to barbarians, both to the wise and to the
foolish: [15]so I am eager to preach the gos-
pel to you also who are in Rome.

The Power of the Gospel

16 For I am not ashamed of the gospel:
it is the power of God for salvation to
every one who has faith, to the Jew first
and also to the Greek. [17]For in it the righ-
teousness of God is revealed through
faith for faith; as it is written, "He who
through faith is righteous shall live."[c]

The Guilt of Mankind

18 For the wrath of God is revealed from
heaven against all ungodliness and
wickedness of men who by their wicked-
ness suppress the truth. [19]For what can
be known about God is plain to them,
because God has shown it to them. [20]Ever
since the creation of the world his invis-
ible nature, namely, his eternal power
and deity, has been clearly perceived in
the things that have been made. So they
are without excuse; [21]for although they
knew God they did not honor him as God
or give thanks to him, but they became
futile in their thinking and their sense-
less minds were darkened. [22]Claiming
to be wise, they became fools, [23]and ex-
changed the glory of the immortal God
for images resembling mortal man or
birds or animals or reptiles.

24 Therefore God gave them up in
the lusts of their hearts to impurity, to
the dishonoring of their bodies among
themselves, [25]because they exchanged
the truth about God for a lie and wor-
shiped and served the creature rather
than the Creator, who is blessed for ever!
Amen.

26 For this reason God gave them up to
dishonorable passions. Their women ex-
changed natural relations for unnatural,

[a]**1.1** Or *slave* [b]**1.4** Or *constituted* [c]**1.17** Or *The righteous shall live by faith*

27 and the men likewise gave up natural
relations with women and were con-
sumed with passion for one another,
men committing shameless acts with
men and receiving in their own persons
the due penalty for their error.
28 And since they did not see fit to ac-
knowledge God, God gave them up to
a base mind and to improper conduct.
29 They were filled with all manner of
wickedness, evil, covetousness, malice.
Full of envy, murder, strife, deceit, malig-
nity, they are gossips, 30 slanderers, hat-
ers of God, insolent, haughty, boastful,
inventors of evil, disobedient to parents,
31 foolish, faithless, heartless, ruthless.
32 Though they know God's decree that
those who do such things deserve to die,
they not only do them but approve those
who practice them.

The Righteous Judgment of God

2 Therefore you have no excuse,
O man, whoever you are, when you
judge another; for in passing judgment
upon him you condemn yourself, be-
cause you, the judge, are doing the very
same things. 2 We know that the judg-
ment of God rightly falls upon those who
do such things. 3 Do you suppose, O man,
that when you judge those who do such
things and yet do them yourself, you will
escape the judgment of God? 4 Or do you
presume upon the riches of his kindness
and forbearance and patience? Do you
not know that God's kindness is meant
to lead you to repentance? 5 But by your
hard and impenitent heart you are stor-
ing up wrath for yourself on the day of
wrath when God's righteous judgment
will be revealed. 6 For he will render to
every man according to his works: 7 to
those who by patience in well-doing seek
for glory and honor and immortality, he
will give eternal life; 8 but for those who
are factious and do not obey the truth,
but obey wickedness, there will be wrath
and fury. 9 There will be tribulation and
distress for every human being who does
evil, the Jew first and also the Greek, 10 but
glory and honor and peace for every one
who does good, the Jew first and also the
Greek. 11 For God shows no partiality.
12 All who have sinned without the law
will also perish without the law, and all
who have sinned under the law will be
judged by the law. 13 For it is not the hear-
ers of the law who are righteous before
God, but the doers of the law who will
be justified. 14 When Gentiles who have
not the law do by nature what the law
requires, they are a law to themselves,
even though they do not have the law.
15 They show that what the law requires
is written on their hearts, while their
conscience also bears witness and their
conflicting thoughts accuse or perhaps
excuse them 16 on that day when, accord-
ing to my gospel, God judges the secrets
of men by Christ Jesus.

The Jews and the Law

17 But if you call yourself a Jew and rely
upon the law and boast of your relation
to God 18 and know his will and approve
what is excellent, because you are in-
structed in the law, 19 and if you are sure
that you are a guide to the blind, a light to
those who are in darkness, 20 a corrector
of the foolish, a teacher of children, hav-
ing in the law the embodiment of knowl-
edge and truth— 21 you then who teach
others, will you not teach yourself?
While you preach against stealing, do
you steal? 22 You who say that one must
not commit adultery, do you commit
adultery? You who abhor idols, do you
rob temples? 23 You who boast in the law,
do you dishonor God by breaking the
law? 24 For, as it is written, "The name of
God is blasphemed among the Gentiles
because of you."
25 Circumcision indeed is of value if
you obey the law; but if you break the law,
your circumcision becomes uncircumci-
sion. 26 So, if a man who is uncircumcised

keeps the precepts of the law, will not his
uncircumcision be regarded as circum-
cision? [27]Then those who are physically
uncircumcised but keep the law will con-
demn you who have the written code and
circumcision but break the law. [28]For he
is not a real Jew who is one outwardly,
nor is true circumcision something ex-
ternal and physical. [29]He is a Jew who is
one inwardly, and real circumcision is a
matter of the heart, spiritual and not lit-
eral. His praise is not from men but from
God.

3 Then what advantage has the Jew?
Or what is the value of circumcision?
[2]Much in every way. To begin with, the
Jews are entrusted with the oracles of
God. [3]What if some were unfaithful?
Does their faithlessness nullify the faith-
fulness of God? [4]By no means! Let God be
true though every man be false, as it is
written,

> "That thou mayest be justified in thy
> words,
> and prevail when thou art judged."

[5]But if our wickedness serves to show
the justice of God, what shall we say?
That God is unjust to inflict wrath on
us? (I speak in a human way.) [6]By no
means! For then how could God judge
the world? [7]But if through my falsehood
God's truthfulness abounds to his glory,
why am I still being condemned as a sin-
ner? [8]And why not do evil that good may
come?—as some people slanderously
charge us with saying. Their condemna-
tion is just.

None Is Righteous

9 What then? Are we Jews any better
off?[d] No, not at all; for I[e] have already
charged that all men, both Jews and
Greeks, are under the power of sin, [10]as
it is written:

> "None is righteous, no, not one;
> 11 no one understands, no one seeks
> for God.
> 12 All have turned aside, together they
> have gone wrong;
> no one does good, not even one."
> 13 "Their throat is an open grave,
> they use their tongues to deceive."
> "The venom of asps is under their
> lips."
> 14 "Their mouth is full of curses and
> bitterness."
> 15 "Their feet are swift to shed blood,
> 16 in their paths are ruin and misery,
> 17 and the way of peace they do not
> know."
> 18 "There is no fear of God before their
> eyes."

19 Now we know that whatever the law
says it speaks to those who are under the
law, so that every mouth may be stopped,
and the whole world may be held ac-
countable to God. [20]For no human being
will be justified in his sight by works
of the law, since through the law comes
knowledge of sin.

Righteousness through Faith

21 But now the righteousness of God
has been manifested apart from law, al-
though the law and the prophets bear
witness to it, [22]the righteousness of
God through faith in Jesus Christ for all
who believe. For there is no distinction;
[23]since all have sinned and fall short of
the glory of God, [24]they are justified by
his grace as a gift, through the redemp-
tion which is in Christ Jesus, [25]whom God
put forward as an expiation by his blood,
to be received by faith. This was to show
God's righteousness, because in his di-
vine forbearance he had passed over for-
mer sins; [26]it was to prove at the present
time that he himself is righteous and that
he justifies him who has faith in Jesus.

27 Then what becomes of our boast-
ing? It is excluded. On what principle?
On the principle of works? No, but on
the principle of faith. [28]For we hold that
a man is justified by faith apart from

[d] **3.9** Or *at any disadvantage?*
[e] **3.9** Greek *we*

works of law. [29]Or is God the God of Jews
only? Is he not the God of Gentiles also?
Yes, of Gentiles also, [30]since God is one;
and he will justify the circumcised on
the ground of their faith and the uncir-
cumcised through their faith. [31]Do we
then overthrow the law by this faith? By
no means! On the contrary, we uphold
the law.

The Example of Abraham

4 What then shall we say about[f] Abra-
ham, our forefather according to the
flesh? [2]For if Abraham was justified by
works, he has something to boast about,
but not before God. [3]For what does the
scripture say? "Abraham believed God,
and it was reckoned to him as righteous-
ness." [4]Now to one who works, his wages
are not reckoned as a gift but as his due.
[5]And to one who does not work but trusts
him who justifies the ungodly, his faith is
reckoned as righteousness. [6]So also Da-
vid pronounces a blessing upon the man
to whom God reckons righteousness
apart from works:

7 "Blessed are those whose iniquities
are forgiven, and whose sins are
covered;
8 blessed is the man against whom the
Lord will not reckon his sin."

9 Is this blessing pronounced only
upon the circumcised, or also upon the
uncircumcised? We say that faith was
reckoned to Abraham as righteousness.
[10]How then was it reckoned to him? Was
it before or after he had been circum-
cised? It was not after, but before he was
circumcised. [11]He received circumcision
as a sign or seal of the righteousness
which he had by faith while he was still
uncircumcised. The purpose was to
make him the father of all who believe
without being circumcised and who thus
have righteousness reckoned to them,
[12]and likewise the father of the circum-
cised who are not merely circumcised
but also follow the example of the faith
which our father Abraham had before
he was circumcised.

God's Promise Realized through Faith

13 The promise to Abraham and his de-
scendants, that they should inherit the
world, did not come through the law but
through the righteousness of faith. [14]If
it is the adherents of the law who are to
be the heirs, faith is null and the prom-
ise is void. [15]For the law brings wrath,
but where there is no law there is no
transgression.

16 That is why it depends on faith,
in order that the promise may rest
on grace and be guaranteed to all his
descendants—not only to the adherents
of the law but also to those who share
the faith of Abraham, for he is the father
of us all, [17]as it is written, "I have made
you the father of many nations"—in
the presence of the God in whom he
believed, who gives life to the dead and
calls into existence the things that do
not exist. [18]In hope he believed against
hope, that he should become the father
of many nations; as he had been told, "So
shall your descendants be." [19]He did not
weaken in faith when he considered his
own body, which was as good as dead be-
cause he was about a hundred years old,
or when he considered the barrenness
of Sarah's womb. [20]No distrust made
him waver concerning the promise of
God, but he grew strong in his faith as he
gave glory to God, [21]fully convinced that
God was able to do what he had prom-
ised. [22]That is why his faith was "reck-
oned to him as righteousness." [23]But the
words, "it was reckoned to him," were
written not for his sake alone, [24]but for
ours also. It will be reckoned to us who
believe in him that raised from the dead
Jesus our Lord, [25]who was put to death
for our trespasses and raised for our
justification.

[f]**4.1** Other ancient authorities read *was gained by*

Results of Justification

5 Therefore, since we are justified
by faith, we[g] have peace with God
through our Lord Jesus Christ. 2 Through
him we have obtained access[h] to this
grace in which we stand, and we[i] re-
joice in our hope of sharing the glory of
God. 3 More than that, we[j] rejoice in our
sufferings, knowing that suffering pro-
duces endurance, 4 and endurance pro-
duces character, and character produces
hope, 5 and hope does not disappoint us,
because God's love has been poured into
our hearts through the Holy Spirit who
has been given to us.
6 While we were yet helpless, at the
right time Christ died for the ungodly.
7 Why, one will hardly die for a righteous
man—though perhaps for a good man
one will dare even to die. 8 But God shows
his love for us in that while we were yet
sinners Christ died for us. 9 Since, there-
fore, we are now justified by his blood,
much more shall we be saved by him
from the wrath of God. 10 For if while we
were enemies we were reconciled to God
by the death of his Son, much more, now
that we are reconciled, shall we be saved
by his life. 11 Not only so, but we also re-
joice in God through our Lord Jesus
Christ, through whom we have now re-
ceived our reconciliation.

Adam and Christ

12 Therefore as sin came into the world
through one man and death through sin,
and so death spread to all men because
all men sinned— 13 sin indeed was in the
world before the law was given, but sin is
not counted where there is no law. 14 Yet
death reigned from Adam to Moses, even
over those whose sins were not like the
transgression of Adam, who was a type
of the one who was to come.
15 But the free gift is not like the tres-
pass. For if many died through one man's
trespass, much more have the grace
of God and the free gift in the grace of
that one man Jesus Christ abounded for
many. 16 And the free gift is not like the
effect of that one man's sin. For the judg-
ment following one trespass brought
condemnation, but the free gift follow-
ing many trespasses brings justification.
17 If, because of one man's trespass, death
reigned through that one man, much
more will those who receive the abun-
dance of grace and the free gift of righ-
teousness reign in life through the one
man Jesus Christ.
18 Then as one man's trespass led to
condemnation for all men, so one man's
act of righteousness leads to acquittal
and life for all men. 19 For as by one man's
disobedience many were made sinners,
so by one man's obedience many will
be made righteous. 20 Law came in, to
increase the trespass; but where sin in-
creased, grace abounded all the more,
21 so that, as sin reigned in death, grace
also might reign through righteousness
to eternal life through Jesus Christ our
Lord.

Dying and Rising with Christ

6 What shall we say then? Are we
to continue in sin that grace may
abound? 2 By no means! How can we who
died to sin still live in it? 3 Do you not
know that all of us who have been bap-
tized into Christ Jesus were baptized
into his death? 4 We were buried there-
fore with him by baptism into death, so
that as Christ was raised from the dead
by the glory of the Father, we too might
walk in newness of life.
5 For if we have been united with him
in a death like his, we shall certainly be
united with him in a resurrection like
his. 6 We know that our old self was cru-
cified with him so that the sinful body
might be destroyed, and we might no

[g] **5.1** Other ancient authorities read *let us* [h] **5.2** Other ancient authorities add *by faith* [i] **5.2** Or *let us* [j] **5.3** Or *let us*

longer be enslaved to sin. [7]For he who
has died is freed from sin. [8]But if we
have died with Christ, we believe that we
shall also live with him. [9]For we know
that Christ being raised from the dead
will never die again; death no longer has
dominion over him. [10]The death he died
he died to sin, once for all, but the life he
lives he lives to God. [11]So you also must
consider yourselves dead to sin and
alive to God in Christ Jesus.
12 Let not sin therefore reign in your
mortal bodies, to make you obey their
passions. [13]Do not yield your members
to sin as instruments of wickedness, but
yield yourselves to God as men who have
been brought from death to life, and
your members to God as instruments of
righteousness. [14]For sin will have no do-
minion over you, since you are not un-
der law but under grace.

Slaves of Righteousness

15 What then? Are we to sin because
we are not under law but under grace?
By no means! [16]Do you not know that if
you yield yourselves to any one as obe-
dient slaves, you are slaves of the one
whom you obey, either of sin, which
leads to death, or of obedience, which
leads to righteousness? [17]But thanks be
to God, that you who were once slaves
of sin have become obedient from the
heart to the standard of teaching to
which you were committed, [18]and, hav-
ing been set free from sin, have become
slaves of righteousness. [19]I am speaking
in human terms, because of your nat-
ural limitations. For just as you once
yielded your members to impurity and
to greater and greater iniquity, so now
yield your members to righteousness
for sanctification.
20 When you were slaves of sin, you
were free in regard to righteousness.
[21]But then what return did you get
from the things of which you are now
ashamed? The end of those things is
death. [22]But now that you have been set
free from sin and have become slaves of
God, the return you get is sanctification
and its end, eternal life. [23]For the wages
of sin is death, but the free gift of God is
eternal life in Christ Jesus our Lord.

An Analogy from Marriage

7 Do you not know, brethren—for I am
speaking to those who know the law—
that the law is binding on a person only
during his life? [2]Thus a married woman
is bound by law to her husband as long
as he lives; but if her husband dies she is
discharged from the law concerning the
husband. [3]Accordingly, she will be called
an adulteress if she lives with another
man while her husband is alive. But if
her husband dies she is free from that
law, and if she marries another man she
is not an adulteress.
4 Likewise, my brethren, you have died
to the law through the body of Christ, so
that you may belong to another, to him
who has been raised from the dead in
order that we may bear fruit for God.
[5]While we were living in the flesh, our
sinful passions, aroused by the law, were
at work in our members to bear fruit for
death. [6]But now we are discharged from
the law, dead to that which held us cap-
tive, so that we serve not under the old
written code but in the new life of the
Spirit.

The Law and Sin

7 What then shall we say? That the law is
sin? By no means! Yet, if it had not been
for the law, I should not have known sin.
I should not have known what it is to
covet if the law had not said, "You shall
not covet." [8]But sin, finding opportunity
in the commandment, wrought in me all
kinds of covetousness. Apart from the
law sin lies dead. [9]I was once alive apart
from the law, but when the command-
ment came, sin revived and I died; [10]the
very commandment which promised life

proved to be death to me. [11]For sin, find-
ing opportunity in the commandment,
deceived me and by it killed me. [12]So the
law is holy, and the commandment is
holy and just and good.

The Inner Conflict

13 Did that which is good, then, bring
death to me? By no means! It was sin,
working death in me through what is
good, in order that sin might be shown
to be sin, and through the command-
ment might become sinful beyond mea-
sure. [14]We know that the law is spiritual;
but I am carnal, sold under sin. [15]I do not
understand my own actions. For I do not
do what I want, but I do the very thing
I hate. [16]Now if I do what I do not want,
I agree that the law is good. [17]So then it
is no longer I that do it, but sin which
dwells within me. [18]For I know that
nothing good dwells within me, that is,
in my flesh. I can will what is right, but
I cannot do it. [19]For I do not do the good
I want, but the evil I do not want is what
I do. [20]Now if I do what I do not want, it
is no longer I that do it, but sin which
dwells within me.

21 So I find it to be a law that when I
want to do right, evil lies close at hand.
[22]For I delight in the law of God, in my
inmost self, [23]but I see in my members
another law at war with the law of my
mind and making me captive to the law
of sin which dwells in my members.
[24]Wretched man that I am! Who will
deliver me from this body of death?
[25]Thanks be to God through Jesus Christ
our Lord! So then, I of myself serve the
law of God with my mind, but with my
flesh I serve the law of sin.

Life in the Spirit

8 There is therefore now no condem-
nation for those who are in Christ
Jesus. [2]For the law of the Spirit of life
in Christ Jesus has set me free from the
law of sin and death. [3]For God has done
what the law, weakened by the flesh,
could not do: sending his own Son in
the likeness of sinful flesh and for sin,[k]
he condemned sin in the flesh, [4]in or-
der that the just requirement of the law
might be fulfilled in us, who walk not
according to the flesh but according to
the Spirit. [5]For those who live according
to the flesh set their minds on the things
of the flesh, but those who live accord-
ing to the Spirit set their minds on the
things of the Spirit. [6]To set the mind on
the flesh is death, but to set the mind on
the Spirit is life and peace. [7]For the mind
that is set on the flesh is hostile to God;
it does not submit to God's law, indeed it
cannot; [8]and those who are in the flesh
cannot please God.

9 But you are not in the flesh, you are
in the Spirit, if the Spirit of God really
dwells in you. Any one who does not
have the Spirit of Christ does not be-
long to him. [10]But if Christ is in you, al-
though your bodies are dead because
of sin, your spirits are alive because of
righteousness. [11]If the Spirit of him who
raised Jesus from the dead dwells in
you, he who raised Christ Jesus from the
dead will give life to your mortal bodies
also through his Spirit who dwells in
you.

12 So then, brethren, we are debtors,
not to the flesh, to live according to the
flesh— [13]for if you live according to the
flesh you will die, but if by the Spirit
you put to death the deeds of the body
you will live. [14]For all who are led by
the Spirit of God are sons of God. [15]For
you did not receive the spirit of slavery
to fall back into fear, but you have re-
ceived the spirit of sonship. When we
cry, "Abba! Father!" [16]it is the Spirit him-
self bearing witness with our spirit that
we are children of God, [17]and if children,
then heirs, heirs of God and fellow heirs
with Christ, provided we suffer with

[k] **8.3** Or *and as a sin offering*

him in order that we may also be glori-
fied with him.

Future Glory

18 I consider that the sufferings of this
present time are not worth comparing
with the glory that is to be revealed to
us. 19 For the creation waits with eager
longing for the revealing of the sons of
God; 20 for the creation was subjected
to futility, not of its own will but by the
will of him who subjected it in hope; 21 be-
cause the creation itself will be set free
from its bondage to decay and obtain the
glorious liberty of the children of God.
22 We know that the whole creation has
been groaning in travail together until
now; 23 and not only the creation, but we
ourselves, who have the first fruits of
the Spirit, groan inwardly as we wait for
adoption as sons, the redemption of our
bodies. 24 For in this hope we were saved.
Now hope that is seen is not hope. For
who hopes for what he sees? 25 But if we
hope for what we do not see, we wait for
it with patience.

26 Likewise the Spirit helps us in our
weakness; for we do not know how to
pray as we ought, but the Spirit himself
intercedes for us with sighs too deep for
words. 27 And he who searches the hearts
of men knows what is the mind of the
Spirit, because[l] the Spirit intercedes for
the saints according to the will of God.

28 We know that in everything God
works for good[m] with those who love
him,[n] who are called according to his
purpose. 29 For those whom he foreknew
he also predestined to be conformed to
the image of his Son, in order that he
might be the first-born among many
brethren. 30 And those whom he predes-
tined he also called; and those whom he
called he also justified; and those whom
he justified he also glorified.

God's Love in Christ Jesus

31 What then shall we say to this? If God
is for us, who is against us? 32 He who
did not spare his own Son but gave him
up for us all, will he not also give us all
things with him? 33 Who shall bring any
charge against God's elect? It is God
who justifies; 34 who is to condemn? Is
it Christ Jesus, who died, yes, who was
raised from the dead, who is at the right
hand of God, who indeed intercedes
for us?[o] 35 Who shall separate us from
the love of Christ? Shall tribulation, or
distress, or persecution, or famine, or
nakedness, or peril, or sword? 36 As it is
written,

> "For thy sake we are being killed all
> the day long;
> we are regarded as sheep to be
> slaughtered."

37 No, in all these things we are more than
conquerors through him who loved us.
38 For I am sure that neither death, nor life,
nor angels, nor principalities, nor things
present, nor things to come, nor powers,
39 nor height, nor depth, nor anything else
in all creation, will be able to separate us
from the love of God in Christ Jesus our
Lord.

God's Election of Israel

9 I am speaking the truth in Christ, I
am not lying; my conscience bears
me witness in the Holy Spirit, 2 that I have
great sorrow and unceasing anguish in
my heart. 3 For I could wish that I myself
were accursed and cut off from Christ
for the sake of my brethren, my kinsmen
by race. 4 They are Israelites, and to them
belong the sonship, the glory, the cove-
nants, the giving of the law, the worship,
and the promises; 5 to them belong the pa-
triarchs, and of their race, according to
the flesh, is the Christ, who is God over
all, blessed for ever.[p] Amen.

[l] **8.27** Or *that* [m] **8.28** Other ancient authorities read *in everything he works for good*, or *everything works for good* [n] **8.28** Greek *God* [o] **8.34** Or *It is Christ Jesus . . . for us* [p] **9.5** Or *Christ. God who is over all be blessed for ever*

6 But it is not as though the word of God
had failed. For not all who are descended
from Israel belong to Israel, [7]and not all
are children of Abraham because they are
his descendants; but "Through Isaac shall
your descendants be named." [8]This means
that it is not the children of the flesh who
are the children of God, but the children
of the promise are reckoned as descen-
dants. [9]For this is what the promise said,
"About this time I will return and Sarah
shall have a son." [10]And not only so, but
also when Rebecca had conceived chil-
dren by one man, our forefather Isaac,
[11]though they were not yet born and had
done nothing either good or bad, in order
that God's purpose of election might con-
tinue, not because of works but because
of his call, [12]she was told, "The elder will
serve the younger." [13]As it is written, "Ja-
cob I loved, but Esau I hated."

14 What shall we say then? Is there in-
justice on God's part? By no means! [15]For
he says to Moses, "I will have mercy on
whom I have mercy, and I will have com-
passion on whom I have compassion."
[16]So it depends not upon man's will or
exertion, but upon God's mercy. [17]For the
scripture says to Pharaoh, "I have raised
you up for the very purpose of showing
my power in you, so that my name may
be proclaimed in all the earth." [18]So then
he has mercy upon whomever he wills,
and he hardens the heart of whomever
he wills.

God's Wrath and Mercy

19 You will say to me then, "Why does
he still find fault? For who can resist his
will?" [20]But who are you, a man, to an-
swer back to God? Will what is molded
say to its molder, "Why have you made
me thus?" [21]Has the potter no right over
the clay, to make out of the same lump one
vessel for beauty and another for menial
use? [22]What if God, desiring to show his
wrath and to make known his power, has
endured with much patience the vessels
of wrath made for destruction, [23]in order
to make known the riches of his glory
for the vessels of mercy, which he has
prepared beforehand for glory, [24]even
us whom he has called, not from the Jews
only but also from the Gentiles?

25 As indeed he says in Hose'a,

"Those who were not my people
I will call 'my people,'
and her who was not beloved
I will call 'my beloved.'"
26 "And in the very place where it was
said to them, 'You are not my
people,'
they will be called 'sons of the living
God.'"

27 And Isaiah cries out concerning
Israel: "Though the number of the sons
of Israel be as the sand of the sea, only a
remnant of them will be saved; [28]for the
Lord will execute his sentence upon the
earth with rigor and dispatch." [29]And as
Isaiah predicted,

"If the Lord of hosts had not left us
children,
we would have fared like Sodom and
been made like Gomor'rah."

Israel's Unbelief

30 What shall we say, then? That Gen-
tiles who did not pursue righteousness
have attained it, that is, righteousness
through faith; [31]but that Israel who pur-
sued the righteousness which is based
on law did not succeed in fulfilling that
law. [32]Why? Because they did not pursue
it through faith, but as if it were based
on works. They have stumbled over the
stumbling stone, [33]as it is written,

"Behold, I am laying in Zion a stone
that will make men stumble,
a rock that will make them fall;
and he who believes in him will not
be put to shame."

10 Brethren, my heart's desire and
prayer to God for them is that they
may be saved. [2]I bear them witness that

they have a zeal for God, but it is not
enlightened. 3For, being ignorant of the
righteousness that comes from God, and
seeking to establish their own, they did
not submit to God's righteousness. 4For
Christ is the end of the law, that every
one who has faith may be justified.

Salvation Is for All

5 Moses writes that the man who prac-
tices the righteousness which is based
on the law shall live by it. 6But the righ-
teousness based on faith says, Do not
say in your heart, "Who will ascend into
heaven?" (that is, to bring Christ down)
7or "Who will descend into the abyss?"
(that is, to bring Christ up from the
dead). 8But what does it say? The word
is near you, on your lips and in your
heart (that is, the word of faith which we
preach); 9because, if you confess with
your lips that Jesus is Lord and believe
in your heart that God raised him from
the dead, you will be saved. 10For man be-
lieves with his heart and so is justified,
and he confesses with his lips and so is
saved. 11The scripture says, "No one who
believes in him will be put to shame."
12For there is no distinction between
Jew and Greek; the same Lord is Lord of
all and bestows his riches upon all who
call upon him. 13For, "every one who calls
upon the name of the Lord will be saved."

14 But how are men to call upon him in
whom they have not believed? And how
are they to believe in him of whom they
have never heard? And how are they to
hear without a preacher? 15And how can
men preach unless they are sent? As it
is written, "How beautiful are the feet
of those who preach good news!" 16But
they have not all heeded the gospel; for
Isaiah says, "Lord, who has believed what
he has heard from us?" 17So faith comes
from what is heard, and what is heard
comes by the preaching of Christ.

18 But I ask, have they not heard? In-
deed they have; for

> "Their voice has gone out to all the
> earth,
> and their words to the ends of the
> world."

19Again I ask, did Israel not understand?
First Moses says,

> "I will make you jealous of those
> who are not a nation;
> with a foolish nation I will make you
> angry."

20Then Isaiah is so bold as to say,

> "I have been found by those who did
> not seek me;
> I have shown myself to those who
> did not ask for me."

21But of Israel he says, "All day long I
have held out my hands to a disobedient
and contrary people."

Israel's Rejection Is Not Final

11 I ask, then, has God rejected his
people? By no means! I myself am
an Israelite, a descendant of Abraham, a
member of the tribe of Benjamin. 2God
has not rejected his people whom he fore-
knew. Do you not know what the scripture
says of Eli'jah, how he pleads with God
against Israel? 3"Lord, they have killed
thy prophets, they have demolished thy
altars, and I alone am left, and they seek
my life." 4But what is God's reply to him? "I
have kept for myself seven thousand men
who have not bowed the knee to Ba'al." 5So
too at the present time there is a remnant,
chosen by grace. 6But if it is by grace, it is
no longer on the basis of works; otherwise
grace would no longer be grace.

7 What then? Israel failed to obtain
what it sought. The elect obtained it, but
the rest were hardened, 8as it is written,

> "God gave them a spirit of stupor,
> eyes that should not see and ears
> that should not hear,
> down to this very day."

9And David says,

> "Let their feast become a snare and
> a trap,
> a pitfall and a retribution for them;

10 let their eyes be darkened so that
they cannot see,
and bend their backs for ever."

The Salvation of the Gentiles

11 So I ask, have they stumbled so as to
fall? By no means! But through their
trespass salvation has come to the Gen-
tiles, so as to make Israel jealous. 12 Now
if their trespass means riches for the
world, and if their failure means riches
for the Gentiles, how much more will
their full inclusion mean!

13 Now I am speaking to you Gentiles.
Inasmuch then as I am an apostle to the
Gentiles, I magnify my ministry 14 in or-
der to make my fellow Jews jealous, and
thus save some of them. 15 For if their re-
jection means the reconciliation of the
world, what will their acceptance mean
but life from the dead? 16 If the dough of-
fered as first fruits is holy, so is the whole
lump; and if the root is holy, so are the
branches.

17 But if some of the branches were
broken off, and you, a wild olive shoot,
were grafted in their place to share the
richness[q] of the olive tree, 18 do not boast
over the branches. If you do boast, re-
member it is not you that support the
root, but the root that supports you.
19 You will say, "Branches were broken
off so that I might be grafted in." 20 That
is true. They were broken off because
of their unbelief, but you stand fast only
through faith. So do not become proud,
but stand in awe. 21 For if God did not
spare the natural branches, neither will
he spare you. 22 Note then the kindness
and the severity of God: severity toward
those who have fallen, but God's kind-
ness to you, provided you continue in his
kindness; otherwise you too will be cut
off. 23 And even the others, if they do not
persist in their unbelief, will be grafted
in, for God has the power to graft them
in again. 24 For if you have been cut from
what is by nature a wild olive tree, and
grafted, contrary to nature, into a cul-
tivated olive tree, how much more will
these natural branches be grafted back
into their own olive tree.

All Israel Will Be Saved

25 Lest you be wise in your own conceits,
I want you to understand this mystery,
brethren: a hardening has come upon
part of Israel, until the full number of
the Gentiles come in, 26 and so all Israel
will be saved; as it is written,

"The Deliverer will come from Zion,
he will banish ungodliness from
Jacob";
27 "and this will be my covenant with
them
when I take away their sins."

28 As regards the gospel they are enemies
of God, for your sake; but as regards elec-
tion they are beloved for the sake of their
forefathers. 29 For the gifts and the call of
God are irrevocable. 30 Just as you were
once disobedient to God but now have
received mercy because of their disobe-
dience, 31 so they have now been disobedi-
ent in order that by the mercy shown to
you they also may[r] receive mercy. 32 For
God has consigned all men to disobedi-
ence, that he may have mercy upon all.

33 O the depth of the riches and wis-
dom and knowledge of God! How un-
searchable are his judgments and how
inscrutable his ways!

34 "For who has known the mind of the
Lord,
or who has been his counselor?"
35 "Or who has given a gift to him
that he might be repaid?"

36 For from him and through him and to
him are all things. To him be glory for
ever. Amen.

The New Life in Christ

12 I appeal to you therefore, brethren,
by the mercies of God, to present

[q] **11.17** Other ancient authorities read *rich root*

[r] **11.31** Other ancient authorities add *now*

your bodies as a living sacrifice, holy and
acceptable to God, which is your spiri-
tual worship. 2 Do not be conformed to
this world[s] but be transformed by the re-
newal of your mind, that you may prove
what is the will of God, what is good and
acceptable and perfect.[t]
3 For by the grace given to me I bid ev-
ery one among you not to think of him-
self more highly than he ought to think,
but to think with sober judgment, each
according to the measure of faith which
God has assigned him. 4 For as in one
body we have many members, and all
the members do not have the same func-
tion, 5 so we, though many, are one body
in Christ, and individually members
one of another. 6 Having gifts that differ
according to the grace given to us, let us
use them: if prophecy, in proportion to
our faith; 7 if service, in our serving; he
who teaches, in his teaching; 8 he who
exhorts, in his exhortation; he who con-
tributes, in liberality; he who gives aid,
with zeal; he who does acts of mercy,
with cheerfulness.

Marks of the True Christian

9 Let love be genuine; hate what is evil,
hold fast to what is good; 10 love one an-
other with brotherly affection; outdo
one another in showing honor. 11 Never
flag in zeal, be aglow with the Spirit,
serve the Lord. 12 Rejoice in your hope,
be patient in tribulation, be constant in
prayer. 13 Contribute to the needs of the
saints, practice hospitality.
14 Bless those who persecute you;
bless and do not curse them. 15 Rejoice
with those who rejoice, weep with those
who weep. 16 Live in harmony with one
another; do not be haughty, but associate
with the lowly;[u] never be conceited. 17 Re-
pay no one evil for evil, but take thought
for what is noble in the sight of all. 18 If
possible, so far as it depends upon you,
live peaceably with all. 19 Beloved, never
avenge yourselves, but leave it[v] to the
wrath of God; for it is written, "Ven-
geance is mine, I will repay, says the
Lord." 20 No, "if your enemy is hungry,
feed him; if he is thirsty, give him drink;
for by so doing you will heap burning
coals upon his head." 21 Do not be over-
come by evil, but overcome evil with
good.

Being Subject to Authorities

13 Let every person be subject to the
governing authorities. For there is
no authority except from God, and those
that exist have been instituted by God.
2 Therefore he who resists the authori-
ties resists what God has appointed, and
those who resist will incur judgment.
3 For rulers are not a terror to good con-
duct, but to bad. Would you have no
fear of him who is in authority? Then do
what is good, and you will receive his ap-
proval, 4 for he is God's servant for your
good. But if you do wrong, be afraid, for
he does not bear the sword in vain; he is
the servant of God to execute his wrath
on the wrongdoer. 5 Therefore one must
be subject, not only to avoid God's wrath
but also for the sake of conscience. 6 For
the same reason you also pay taxes, for
the authorities are ministers of God,
attending to this very thing. 7 Pay all of
them their dues, taxes to whom taxes are
due, revenue to whom revenue is due,
respect to whom respect is due, honor to
whom honor is due.

Love for One Another

8 Owe no one anything, except to love
one another; for he who loves his neigh-
bor has fulfilled the law. 9 The command-
ments, "You shall not commit adultery,
You shall not kill, You shall not steal, You
shall not covet," and any other command-
ment, are summed up in this sentence,

[s] **12.2** Greek *age* [t] **12.2** Or *what is the good and acceptable and perfect will of God* [u] **12.16** Or *give yourselves to humble tasks* [v] **12.19** Greek *give place*

"You shall love your neighbor as your-
self." [10]Love does no wrong to a neighbor;
therefore love is the fulfilling of the law.

An Urgent Appeal

11 Besides this you know what hour it is,
how it is full time now for you to wake
from sleep. For salvation is nearer to us
now than when we first believed; [12]the
night is far gone, the day is at hand. Let
us then cast off the works of darkness
and put on the armor of light; [13]let us con-
duct ourselves becomingly as in the day,
not in reveling and drunkenness, not
in debauchery and licentiousness, not
in quarreling and jealousy. [14]But put on
the Lord Jesus Christ, and make no pro-
vision for the flesh, to gratify its desires.

Do Not Judge Another

14 As for the man who is weak in faith,
welcome him, but not for disputes
over opinions. [2]One believes he may eat
anything, while the weak man eats only
vegetables. [3]Let not him who eats despise
him who abstains, and let not him who
abstains pass judgment on him who eats;
for God has welcomed him. [4]Who are
you to pass judgment on the servant of
another? It is before his own master that
he stands or falls. And he will be upheld,
for the Master is able to make him stand.

5 One man esteems one day as bet-
ter than another, while another man
esteems all days alike. Let every one
be fully convinced in his own mind.
[6]He who observes the day, observes it
in honor of the Lord. He also who eats,
eats in honor of the Lord, since he gives
thanks to God; while he who abstains,
abstains in honor of the Lord and gives
thanks to God. [7]None of us lives to him-
self, and none of us dies to himself. [8]If
we live, we live to the Lord, and if we die,
we die to the Lord; so then, whether we
live or whether we die, we are the Lord's.
[9]For to this end Christ died and lived
again, that he might be Lord both of the
dead and of the living.

10 Why do you pass judgment on your
brother? Or you, why do you despise your
brother? For we shall all stand before the
judgment seat of God; [11]for it is written,

> "As I live, says the Lord, every knee
> shall bow to me,
> and every tongue shall give praise[w]
> to God."

[12]So each of us shall give account of him-
self to God.

Do Not Make Another Stumble

13 Then let us no more pass judgment
on one another, but rather decide never
to put a stumbling block or hindrance
in the way of a brother. [14]I know and am
persuaded in the Lord Jesus that nothing
is unclean in itself; but it is unclean for
any one who thinks it unclean. [15]If your
brother is being injured by what you eat,
you are no longer walking in love. Do not
let what you eat cause the ruin of one for
whom Christ died. [16]So do not let what
is good to you be spoken of as evil. [17]For
the kingdom of God does not mean food
and drink but righteousness and peace
and joy in the Holy Spirit; [18]he who thus
serves Christ is acceptable to God and
approved by men. [19]Let us then pursue
what makes for peace and for mutual up-
building. [20]Do not, for the sake of food,
destroy the work of God. Everything is
indeed clean, but it is wrong for any one
to make others fall by what he eats; [21]it is
right not to eat meat or drink wine or do
anything that makes your brother stum-
ble.[x] [22]The faith that you have, keep be-
tween yourself and God; happy is he who
has no reason to judge himself for what
he approves. [23]But he who has doubts is
condemned, if he eats, because he does
not act from faith; for whatever does not
proceed from faith is sin.[y]

[w] **14.11** Or *confess* [x] **14.21** Other ancient authorities add *or be upset or be weakened*
[y] **14.23** Other authorities, some ancient, insert here Ch 16.25–27

Please Others, Not Yourselves

15 We who are strong ought to bear
with the failings of the weak, and
not to please ourselves; [2]let each of us
please his neighbor for his good, to
edify him. [3]For Christ did not please
himself; but, as it is written, "The re-
proaches of those who reproached thee
fell on me." [4]For whatever was written
in former days was written for our in-
struction, that by steadfastness and by
the encouragement of the scriptures
we might have hope. [5]May the God
of steadfastness and encouragement
grant you to live in such harmony with
one another, in accord with Christ
Jesus, [6]that together you may with one
voice glorify the God and Father of our
Lord Jesus Christ.

The Gospel for Jews and Gentiles Alike

7 Welcome one another, therefore, as
Christ has welcomed you, for the glory
of God. [8]For I tell you that Christ be-
came a servant to the circumcised to
show God's truthfulness, in order to
confirm the promises given to the pa-
triarchs, [9]and in order that the Gentiles
might glorify God for his mercy. As it is
written,

"Therefore I will praise thee among
the Gentiles,
and sing to thy name";

[10]and again it is said,

"Rejoice, O Gentiles, with his
people";

[11]and again,

"Praise the Lord, all Gentiles,
and let all the peoples praise
him";

[12]and further Isaiah says,

"The root of Jesse shall come,
he who rises to rule the
Gentiles;
in him shall the Gentiles hope."

[13]May the God of hope fill you with all
joy and peace in believing, so that by the
power of the Holy Spirit you may abound
in hope.

Paul's Reason for Writing So Boldly

14 I myself am satisfied about you, my
brethren, that you yourselves are full
of goodness, filled with all knowledge,
and able to instruct one another. [15]But on
some points I have written to you very
boldly by way of reminder, because of
the grace given me by God [16]to be a min-
ister of Christ Jesus to the Gentiles in the
priestly service of the gospel of God, so
that the offering of the Gentiles may be
acceptable, sanctified by the Holy Spirit.
[17]In Christ Jesus, then, I have reason to
be proud of my work for God. [18]For I will
not venture to speak of anything except
what Christ has wrought through me
to win obedience from the Gentiles, by
word and deed, [19]by the power of signs
and wonders, by the power of the Holy
Spirit, so that from Jerusalem and as far
round as Illyr′icum I have fully preached
the gospel of Christ, [20]thus making it my
ambition to preach the gospel, not where
Christ has already been named, lest I
build on another man's foundation, [21]but
as it is written,

"They shall see who have never been
told of him,
and they shall understand who have
never heard of him."

Paul's Plan to Visit Rome

22 This is the reason why I have so often
been hindered from coming to you. [23]But
now, since I no longer have any room
for work in these regions, and since I
have longed for many years to come to
you, [24]I hope to see you in passing as I go
to Spain, and to be sped on my journey
there by you, once I have enjoyed your
company for a little. [25]At present, how-
ever, I am going to Jerusalem with aid for
the saints. [26]For Macedo′nia and Acha′ia
have been pleased to make some con-
tribution for the poor among the saints

at Jerusalem; 27 they were pleased to do
it, and indeed they are in debt to them,
for if the Gentiles have come to share in
their spiritual blessings, they ought also
to be of service to them in material bless-
ings. 28 When therefore I have completed
this, and have delivered to them what has
been raised,[z] I shall go on by way of you
to Spain; 29 and I know that when I come
to you I shall come in the fulness of the
blessing[a] of Christ.

30 I appeal to you, brethren, by our
Lord Jesus Christ and by the love of the
Spirit, to strive together with me in
your prayers to God on my behalf, 31 that
I may be delivered from the unbelievers
in Judea, and that my service for Jeru-
salem may be acceptable to the saints,
32 so that by God's will I may come to you
with joy and be refreshed in your com-
pany. 33 The God of peace be with you all.
Amen.

Personal Greetings

16 I commend to you our sister
Phoebe, a deaconess of the church
at Cen′chre-ae, 2 that you may receive her
in the Lord as befits the saints, and help
her in whatever she may require from
you, for she has been a helper of many
and of myself as well.

3 Greet Prisca and Aq′uila, my fellow
workers in Christ Jesus, 4 who risked
their necks for my life, to whom not
only I but also all the churches of the
Gentiles give thanks; 5 greet also the
church in their house. Greet my beloved
Epae′netus, who was the first convert in
Asia for Christ. 6 Greet Mary, who has
worked hard among you. 7 Greet An-
droni′cus and Ju′nias, my kinsmen and
my fellow prisoners; they are men of
note among the apostles, and they were
in Christ before me. 8 Greet Amplia′tus,
my beloved in the Lord. 9 Greet Urba′nus,
our fellow worker in Christ, and my
beloved Stachys. 10 Greet Apel′les, who
is approved in Christ. Greet those who
belong to the family of Aristobu′lus.
11 Greet my kinsman Hero′dion. Greet
those in the Lord who belong to the fam-
ily of Narcis′sus. 12 Greet those workers
in the Lord, Tryphae′na and Trypho′sa.
Greet the beloved Persis, who has
worked hard in the Lord. 13 Greet Rufus,
eminent in the Lord, also his mother
and mine. 14 Greet Asyn′critus, Phlegon,
Hermes, Pat′robas, Hermas, and the
brethren who are with them. 15 Greet
Philol′ogus, Julia, Nereus and his sister,
and Olym′pas, and all the saints who are
with them. 16 Greet one another with a
holy kiss. All the churches of Christ
greet you.

Final Instructions

17 I appeal to you, brethren, to take note
of those who create dissensions and dif-
ficulties, in opposition to the doctrine
which you have been taught; avoid them.
18 For such persons do not serve our Lord
Christ, but their own appetites,[b] and by
fair and flattering words they deceive
the hearts of the simple-minded. 19 For
while your obedience is known to all, so
that I rejoice over you, I would have you
wise as to what is good and guileless as to
what is evil; 20 then the God of peace will
soon crush Satan under your feet. The
grace of our Lord Jesus Christ be with
you.[c]

21 Timothy, my fellow worker, greets
you; so do Lucius and Jason and So-
sip′ater, my kinsmen.

22 I Tertius, the writer of this letter,
greet you in the Lord.

23 Ga′ius, who is host to me and to the
whole church, greets you. Eras′tus, the
city treasurer, and our brother Quartus,
greet you.[d]

[z] **15.28** Greek *sealed to them this fruit* [a] **15.29** Other ancient authorities insert *of the gospel*
[b] **16.18** Greek *their own belly* (Phil 3.19) [c] **16.20** Other ancient authorities omit this sentence
[d] **16.23** Other ancient authorities insert verse 24, *The grace of our Lord Jesus Christ be with you all. Amen*

Final Doxology

25 Now to him who is able to strengthen
you according to my gospel and the
preaching of Jesus Christ, according to
the revelation of the mystery which was
kept secret for long ages [26]but is now
disclosed and through the prophetic
writings is made known to all nations,
according to the command of the eter-
nal God, to bring about the obedience of
faith— [27]to the only wise God be glory for
evermore through Jesus Christ! Amen.

The First Letter of Paul to the

CORINTHIANS

Salutation

1 Paul, called by the will of God to be
an apostle of Christ Jesus, and our
brother Sos′thenes,
2 To the church of God which is at
Corinth, to those sanctified in Christ
Jesus, called to be saints together with
all those who in every place call on the
name of our Lord Jesus Christ, both their
Lord and ours:
3 Grace to you and peace from God our
Father and the Lord Jesus Christ.

4 I give thanks to God[a] always for you
because of the grace of God which was
given you in Christ Jesus, [5]that in ev-
ery way you were enriched in him with
all speech and all knowledge— [6]even as
the testimony to Christ was confirmed
among you— [7]so that you are not lacking
in any spiritual gift, as you wait for the
revealing of our Lord Jesus Christ; [8]who
will sustain you to the end, guiltless in
the day of our Lord Jesus Christ. [9]God is
faithful, by whom you were called into
the fellowship of his Son, Jesus Christ
our Lord.

Divisions in the Church

10 I appeal to you, brethren, by the name
of our Lord Jesus Christ, that all of you
agree and that there be no dissensions
among you, but that you be united in the
same mind and the same judgment. [11]For
it has been reported to me by Chlo′e's
people that there is quarreling among
you, my brethren. [12]What I mean is that
each one of you says, “I belong to Paul,”
or “I belong to Apol′los,” or “I belong to
Cephas,” or “I belong to Christ.” [13]Is Christ
divided? Was Paul crucified for you? Or
were you baptized in the name of Paul?
[14]I am thankful[b] that I baptized none of
you except Crispus and Ga′ius; [15]lest any
one should say that you were baptized in
my name. [16](I did baptize also the house-
hold of Steph′anas. Beyond that, I do not
know whether I baptized any one else.)
[17]For Christ did not send me to baptize
but to preach the gospel, and not with
eloquent wisdom, lest the cross of Christ
be emptied of its power.

Christ the Power and Wisdom of God

18 For the word of the cross is folly to
those who are perishing, but to us who
are being saved it is the power of God.
[19]For it is written,

“I will destroy the wisdom of the
wise,
and the cleverness of the clever I
will thwart.”

[20]Where is the wise man? Where is the
scribe? Where is the debater of this age?
Has not God made foolish the wisdom
of the world? [21]For since, in the wisdom
of God, the world did not know God
through wisdom, it pleased God through
the folly of what we preach to save
those who believe. [22]For Jews demand
signs and Greeks seek wisdom, [23]but
we preach Christ crucified, a stumbling
block to Jews and folly to Gentiles, [24]but
to those who are called, both Jews and
Greeks, Christ the power of God and the
wisdom of God. [25]For the foolishness of
God is wiser than men, and the weakness
of God is stronger than men.
26 For consider your call, brethren;
not many of you were wise according to
worldly standards, not many were pow-
erful, not many were of noble birth; [27]but
God chose what is foolish in the world to
shame the wise, God chose what is weak
in the world to shame the strong, [28]God
chose what is low and despised in the

[a]**1.4** Other ancient authorities read *my God*

[b]**1.14** Other ancient authorities read *I thank God*

world, even things that are not, to bring
to nothing things that are, 29so that no
human being might boast in the pres-
ence of God. 30He is the source of your
life in Christ Jesus, whom God made our
wisdom, our righteousness and sanctifi-
cation and redemption; 31therefore, as it
is written, "Let him who boasts, boast of
the Lord."

Proclaiming Christ Crucified

2 When I came to you, brethren, I did
not come proclaiming to you the tes-
timony[c] of God in lofty words or wisdom.
2For I decided to know nothing among
you except Jesus Christ and him cruci-
fied. 3And I was with you in weakness
and in much fear and trembling; 4and my
speech and my message were not in plau-
sible words of wisdom, but in demon-
stration of the Spirit and power, 5that
your faith might not rest in the wisdom
of men but in the power of God.

The True Wisdom of God

6 Yet among the mature we do impart
wisdom, although it is not a wisdom of
this age or of the rulers of this age, who
are doomed to pass away. 7But we im-
part a secret and hidden wisdom of God,
which God decreed before the ages for
our glorification. 8None of the rulers of
this age understood this; for if they had,
they would not have crucified the Lord of
glory. 9But, as it is written,

> "What no eye has seen, nor ear
> heard,
> nor the heart of man conceived,
> what God has prepared for those
> who love him,"

10God has revealed to us through the
Spirit. For the Spirit searches every-
thing, even the depths of God. 11For what
person knows a man's thoughts except
the spirit of the man which is in him? So
also no one comprehends the thoughts
of God except the Spirit of God. 12Now we
have received not the spirit of the world,
but the Spirit which is from God, that we
might understand the gifts bestowed on
us by God. 13And we impart this in words
not taught by human wisdom but taught
by the Spirit, interpreting spiritual
truths to those who possess the Spirit.[d]
14 The unspiritual[e] man does not re-
ceive the gifts of the Spirit of God, for
they are folly to him, and he is not able to
understand them because they are spir-
itually discerned. 15The spiritual man
judges all things, but is himself to be
judged by no one. 16"For who has known
the mind of the Lord so as to instruct
him?" But we have the mind of Christ.

On Divisions in the Corinthian Church

3 But I, brethren, could not address
you as spiritual men, but as men of
the flesh, as babes in Christ. 2I fed you
with milk, not solid food; for you were
not ready for it; and even yet you are not
ready, 3for you are still of the flesh. For
while there is jealousy and strife among
you, are you not of the flesh, and behav-
ing like ordinary men? 4For when one
says, "I belong to Paul," and another, "I
belong to Apol'los," are you not merely
men?
5 What then is Apol'los? What is Paul?
Servants through whom you believed,
as the Lord assigned to each. 6I planted,
Apol'los watered, but God gave the
growth. 7So neither he who plants nor
he who waters is anything, but only God
who gives the growth. 8He who plants
and he who waters are equal, and each
shall receive his wages according to his
labor. 9For we are God's fellow workers;[f]
you are God's field, God's building.
10 According to the commission of
God given to me, like a skilled master

[c] **2.1** Other ancient authorities read *mystery* (or *secret*) [d] **2.13** Or *interpreting spiritual truths in spiritual language;* or *comparing spiritual things with spiritual* [e] **2.14** Or *natural* [f] **3.9** Or *fellow workers for God*

builder I laid a foundation, and another
man is building upon it. Let each man
take care how he builds upon it. 11For no
other foundation can any one lay than
that which is laid, which is Jesus Christ.
12Now if any one builds on the founda-
tion with gold, silver, precious stones,
wood, hay, stubble— 13each man's work
will become manifest; for the Day will
disclose it, because it will be revealed
with fire, and the fire will test what sort
of work each one has done. 14If the work
which any man has built on the founda-
tion survives, he will receive a reward.
15If any man's work is burned up, he will
suffer loss, though he himself will be
saved, but only as through fire.

16 Do you not know that you are God's
temple and that God's Spirit dwells in
you? 17If any one destroys God's temple,
God will destroy him. For God's temple is
holy, and that temple you are.

18 Let no one deceive himself. If any
one among you thinks that he is wise in
this age, let him become a fool that he
may become wise. 19For the wisdom of
this world is folly with God. For it is writ-
ten, "He catches the wise in their crafti-
ness," 20and again, "The Lord knows that
the thoughts of the wise are futile." 21So
let no one boast of men. For all things
are yours, 22whether Paul or Apol'los or
Cephas or the world or life or death or
the present or the future, all are yours;
23and you are Christ's; and Christ is
God's.

The Ministry of the Apostles

4 This is how one should regard us,
as servants of Christ and stewards
of the mysteries of God. 2Moreover it is
required of stewards that they be found
trustworthy. 3But with me it is a very
small thing that I should be judged by
you or by any human court. I do not even
judge myself. 4I am not aware of anything
against myself, but I am not thereby
acquitted. It is the Lord who judges me.
5Therefore do not pronounce judgment
before the time, before the Lord comes,
who will bring to light the things now
hidden in darkness and will disclose the
purposes of the heart. Then every man
will receive his commendation from
God.

6 I have applied all this to myself and
Apol'los for your benefit, brethren, that
you may learn by us not to go beyond
what is written, that none of you may
be puffed up in favor of one against an-
other. 7For who sees anything different
in you? What have you that you did not
receive? If then you received it, why do
you boast as if it were not a gift?

8 Already you are filled! Already you
have become rich! Without us you have
become kings! And would that you did
reign, so that we might share the rule
with you! 9For I think that God has ex-
hibited us apostles as last of all, like men
sentenced to death; because we have be-
come a spectacle to the world, to angels
and to men. 10We are fools for Christ's
sake, but you are wise in Christ. We are
weak, but you are strong. You are held in
honor, but we in disrepute. 11To the pres-
ent hour we hunger and thirst, we are
ill-clad and buffeted and homeless, 12and
we labor, working with our own hands.
When reviled, we bless; when perse-
cuted, we endure; 13when slandered, we
try to conciliate; we have become, and
are now, as the refuse of the world, the
offscouring of all things.

Fatherly Admonition

14 I do not write this to make you
ashamed, but to admonish you as my
beloved children. 15For though you have
countless guides in Christ, you do not
have many fathers. For I became your
father in Christ Jesus through the gos-
pel. 16I urge you, then, be imitators of me.
17Therefore I sent[g] to you Timothy, my

[g] **4.17** Or *am sending*

beloved and faithful child in the Lord,
to remind you of my ways in Christ, as I
teach them everywhere in every church.
18 Some are arrogant, as though I were
not coming to you. 19 But I will come to
you soon, if the Lord wills, and I will find
out not the talk of these arrogant peo-
ple but their power. 20 For the kingdom
of God does not consist in talk but in
power. 21 What do you wish? Shall I come
to you with a rod, or with love in a spirit
of gentleness?

Sexual Immorality Defiles the Church

5 It is actually reported that there is
immorality among you, and of a kind
that is not found even among pagans;
for a man is living with his father's wife.
2 And you are arrogant! Ought you not
rather to mourn? Let him who has done
this be removed from among you.

3 For though absent in body I am pres-
ent in spirit, and as if present, I have
already pronounced judgment 4 in the
name of the Lord Jesus on the man who
has done such a thing. When you are as-
sembled, and my spirit is present, with
the power of our Lord Jesus, 5 you are to
deliver this man to Satan for the destruc-
tion of the flesh, that his spirit may be
saved in the day of the Lord Jesus.[h]

6 Your boasting is not good. Do you
not know that a little leaven leavens the
whole lump? 7 Cleanse out the old leaven
that you may be a new lump, as you re-
ally are unleavened. For Christ, our pas-
chal lamb, has been sacrificed. 8 Let us,
therefore, celebrate the festival, not with
the old leaven, the leaven of malice and
evil, but with the unleavened bread of
sincerity and truth.

Sexual Immorality Must Be Judged

9 I wrote to you in my letter not to as-
sociate with immoral men; 10 not at all
meaning the immoral of this world, or
the greedy and robbers, or idolaters,
since then you would need to go out of
the world. 11 But rather I wrote[i] to you not
to associate with any one who bears the
name of brother if he is guilty of immo-
rality or greed, or is an idolater, reviler,
drunkard, or robber—not even to eat
with such a one. 12 For what have I to do
with judging outsiders? Is it not those in-
side the church whom you are to judge?
13 God judges those outside. "Drive out
the wicked person from among you."

Lawsuits among Believers

6 When one of you has a grievance
against a brother, does he dare go to
law before the unrighteous instead of
the saints? 2 Do you not know that the
saints will judge the world? And if the
world is to be judged by you, are you in-
competent to try trivial cases? 3 Do you
not know that we are to judge angels?
How much more, matters pertaining to
this life! 4 If then you have such cases,
why do you lay them before those who
are least esteemed by the church? 5 I say
this to your shame. Can it be that there
is no man among you wise enough to
decide between members of the broth-
erhood, 6 but brother goes to law against
brother, and that before unbelievers?

7 To have lawsuits at all with one an-
other is defeat for you. Why not rather
suffer wrong? Why not rather be de-
frauded? 8 But you yourselves wrong
and defraud, and that even your own
brethren.

9 Do you not know that the unrigh-
teous will not inherit the kingdom of
God? Do not be deceived; neither the
immoral, nor idolaters, nor adulterers,
nor homosexuals,[j] 10 nor thieves, nor the
greedy, nor drunkards, nor revilers, nor
robbers will inherit the kingdom of God.
11 And such were some of you. But you
were washed, you were sanctified, you

[h] **5.5** Other ancient authorities omit *Jesus*
[i] **5.11** Or *now I write*
[j] **6.9** Two Greek words are rendered by this expression

were justified in the name of the Lord
Jesus Christ and in the Spirit of our God.

Glorify God in Body and Spirit

12 “All things are lawful for me,” but not
all things are helpful. “All things are law-
ful for me,” but I will not be enslaved by
anything. 13 “Food is meant for the stom-
ach and the stomach for food”—and God
will destroy both one and the other. The
body is not meant for immorality, but for
the Lord, and the Lord for the body. 14 And
God raised the Lord and will also raise us
up by his power. 15 Do you not know that
your bodies are members of Christ? Shall
I therefore take the members of Christ
and make them members of a prostitute?
Never! 16 Do you not know that he who
joins himself to a prostitute becomes
one body with her? For, as it is written,
“The two shall become one.”[k] 17 But he
who is united to the Lord becomes one
spirit with him. 18 Shun immorality. Ev-
ery other sin which a man commits is
outside the body; but the immoral man
sins against his own body. 19 Do you not
know that your body is a temple of the
Holy Spirit within you, which you have
from God? You are not your own; 20 you
were bought with a price. So glorify God
in your body.

Directions concerning Marriage

7 Now concerning the matters about
which you wrote. It is well for a man
not to touch a woman. 2 But because
of the temptation to immorality, each
man should have his own wife and each
woman her own husband. 3 The husband
should give to his wife her conjugal
rights, and likewise the wife to her hus-
band. 4 For the wife does not rule over
her own body, but the husband does;
likewise the husband does not rule over
his own body, but the wife does. 5 Do not
refuse one another except perhaps by
agreement for a season, that you may
devote yourselves to prayer; but then
come together again, lest Satan tempt
you through lack of self-control. 6 I say
this by way of concession, not of com-
mand. 7 I wish that all were as I myself am.
But each has his own special gift from
God, one of one kind and one of another.

8 To the unmarried and the widows I
say that it is well for them to remain sin-
gle as I do. 9 But if they cannot exercise
self-control, they should marry. For it is
better to marry than to be aflame with
passion.

10 To the married I give charge, not I
but the Lord, that the wife should not
separate from her husband 11 (but if she
does, let her remain single or else be rec-
onciled to her husband)—and that the
husband should not divorce his wife.

12 To the rest I say, not the Lord, that if
any brother has a wife who is an unbe-
liever, and she consents to live with him,
he should not divorce her. 13 If any woman
has a husband who is an unbeliever, and
he consents to live with her, she should
not divorce him. 14 For the unbelieving
husband is consecrated through his
wife, and the unbelieving wife is conse-
crated through her husband. Otherwise,
your children would be unclean, but as
it is they are holy. 15 But if the unbelieving
partner desires to separate, let it be so;
in such a case the brother or sister is not
bound. For God has called us[l] to peace.
16 Wife, how do you know whether you
will save your husband? Husband, how
do you know whether you will save your
wife?

The Life That the Lord Has Assigned

17 Only, let every one lead the life which
the Lord has assigned to him, and in
which God has called him. This is my
rule in all the churches. 18 Was any one at
the time of his call already circumcised?
Let him not seek to remove the marks of
circumcision. Was any one at the time of

[k] **6.16** Greek *one flesh* [l] **7.15** Other ancient authorities read *you*

his call uncircumcised? Let him not seek circumcision. [19]For neither circumcision counts for anything nor uncircumcision, but keeping the commandments of God. [20]Every one should remain in the state in which he was called. [21]Were you a slave when called? Never mind. But if you can gain your freedom, avail yourself of the opportunity.[m] [22]For he who was called in the Lord as a slave is a freedman of the Lord. Likewise he who was free when called is a slave of Christ. [23]You were bought with a price; do not become slaves of men. [24]So, brethren, in whatever state each was called, there let him remain with God.

The Unmarried and the Widows

25 Now concerning the unmarried,[n] I have no command of the Lord, but I give my opinion as one who by the Lord's mercy is trustworthy. [26]I think that in view of the impending[o] distress it is well for a person to remain as he is. [27]Are you bound to a wife? Do not seek to be free. Are you free from a wife? Do not seek marriage. [28]But if you marry, you do not sin, and if a girl[p] marries she does not sin. Yet those who marry will have worldly troubles, and I would spare you that. [29]I mean, brethren, the appointed time has grown very short; from now on, let those who have wives live as though they had none, [30]and those who mourn as though they were not mourning, and those who rejoice as though they were not rejoicing, and those who buy as though they had no goods, [31]and those who deal with the world as though they had no dealings with it. For the form of this world is passing away.

32 I want you to be free from anxieties. The unmarried man is anxious about the affairs of the Lord, how to please the Lord; [33]but the married man is anxious about worldly affairs, how to please his wife, [34]and his interests are divided. And the unmarried woman or girl[q] is anxious about the affairs of the Lord, how to be holy in body and spirit; but the married woman is anxious about worldly affairs, how to please her husband. [35]I say this for your own benefit, not to lay any restraint upon you, but to promote good order and to secure your undivided devotion to the Lord.

36 If any one thinks that he is not behaving properly toward his betrothed,[r] if his passions are strong, and it has to be, let him do as he wishes: let them marry—it is no sin. [37]But whoever is firmly established in his heart, being under no necessity but having his desire under control, and has determined this in his heart, to keep her as his betrothed,[s] he will do well. [38]So that he who marries his betrothed[t] does well; and he who refrains from marriage will do better.

39 A wife is bound to her husband as long as he lives. If the husband dies, she is free to be married to whom she wishes, only in the Lord. [40]But in my judgment she is happier if she remains as she is. And I think that I have the Spirit of God.

Food Offered to Idols

8 Now concerning food offered to idols: we know that "all of us possess knowledge." "Knowledge" puffs up, but love builds up. [2]If any one imagines that he knows something, he does not yet know as he ought to know. [3]But if one loves God, one is known by him.

4 Hence, as to the eating of food offered to idols, we know that "an idol has no real existence," and that "there is no God but one." [5]For although there may be so-called gods in heaven or on earth—as indeed there are many "gods" and many "lords"— [6]yet for us there is one God, the

[m]**7.21** Or *make use of your present condition instead* [n]**7.25** Greek *virgins* [o]**7.26** Or *present*
[p]**7.28** Greek *virgin* [q]**7.34** Greek *virgin* [r]**7.36** Greek *virgin* [s]**7.37** Greek *virgin*
[t]**7.38** Greek *virgin*

Father, from whom are all things and
for whom we exist, and one Lord, Jesus
Christ, through whom are all things and
through whom we exist.
7 However, not all possess this knowl-
edge. But some, through being hitherto
accustomed to idols, eat food as really
offered to an idol; and their conscience,
being weak, is defiled. [8]Food will not
commend us to God. We are no worse off
if we do not eat, and no better off if we do.
[9]Only take care lest this liberty of yours
somehow become a stumbling block to
the weak. [10]For if any one sees you, a man
of knowledge, at table in an idol's tem-
ple, might he not be encouraged, if his
conscience is weak, to eat food offered
to idols? [11]And so by your knowledge
this weak man is destroyed, the brother
for whom Christ died. [12]Thus, sinning
against your brethren and wounding
their conscience when it is weak, you sin
against Christ. [13]Therefore, if food is a
cause of my brother's falling, I will never
eat meat, lest I cause my brother to fall.

The Rights of an Apostle

9 Am I not free? Am I not an apostle?
Have I not seen Jesus our Lord? Are
not you my workmanship in the Lord? [2]If
to others I am not an apostle, at least I am
to you; for you are the seal of my apostle-
ship in the Lord.
3 This is my defense to those who
would examine me. [4]Do we not have
the right to our food and drink? [5]Do we
not have the right to be accompanied
by a wife,[u] as the other apostles and the
brethren of the Lord and Cephas? [6]Or is
it only Barnabas and I who have no right
to refrain from working for a living?
[7]Who serves as a soldier at his own ex-
pense? Who plants a vineyard without
eating any of its fruit? Who tends a flock
without getting some of the milk?
8 Do I say this on human authority?
Does not the law say the same? [9]For it is
written in the law of Moses, "You shall
not muzzle an ox when it is treading out
the grain." Is it for oxen that God is con-
cerned? [10]Does he not speak entirely for
our sake? It was written for our sake,
because the plowman should plow in
hope and the thresher thresh in hope of a
share in the crop. [11]If we have sown spiri-
tual good among you, is it too much if we
reap your material benefits? [12]If others
share this rightful claim upon you, do
not we still more?
Nevertheless, we have not made use
of this right, but we endure anything
rather than put an obstacle in the way of
the gospel of Christ. [13]Do you not know
that those who are employed in the tem-
ple service get their food from the tem-
ple, and those who serve at the altar
share in the sacrificial offerings? [14]In
the same way, the Lord commanded that
those who proclaim the gospel should
get their living by the gospel.
15 But I have made no use of any of
these rights, nor am I writing this to
secure any such provision. For I would
rather die than have any one deprive
me of my ground for boasting. [16]For if
I preach the gospel, that gives me no
ground for boasting. For necessity is laid
upon me. Woe to me if I do not preach the
gospel! [17]For if I do this of my own will, I
have a reward; but if not of my own will, I
am entrusted with a commission. [18]What
then is my reward? Just this: that in my
preaching I may make the gospel free of
charge, not making full use of my right
in the gospel.
19 For though I am free from all men,
I have made myself a slave to all, that I
might win the more. [20]To the Jews I be-
came as a Jew, in order to win Jews; to
those under the law I became as one un-
der the law—though not being myself
under the law—that I might win those
under the law. [21]To those outside the law
I became as one outside the law—not

[u] **9.5** Greek *woman, sister*

being without law toward God but under
the law of Christ—that I might win those
outside the law. [22]To the weak I became
weak, that I might win the weak. I have
become all things to all men, that I might
by all means save some. [23]I do it all for the
sake of the gospel, that I may share in its
blessings.

24 Do you not know that in a race all
the runners compete, but only one re-
ceives the prize? So run that you may
obtain it. [25]Every athlete exercises self-
control in all things. They do it to receive
a perishable wreath, but we an imper-
ishable. [26]Well, I do not run aimlessly, I
do not box as one beating the air; [27]but I
pommel my body and subdue it, lest af-
ter preaching to others I myself should
be disqualified.

Warnings from Israel's History

10 I want you to know, brethren, that
our fathers were all under the
cloud, and all passed through the sea,
[2]and all were baptized into Moses in
the cloud and in the sea, [3]and all ate the
same supernatural[v] food [4]and all drank
the same supernatural[w] drink. For they
drank from the supernatural[x] Rock
which followed them, and the Rock was
Christ. [5]Nevertheless with most of them
God was not pleased; for they were over-
thrown in the wilderness.

6 Now these things are warnings for
us, not to desire evil as they did. [7]Do not
be idolaters as some of them were; as it
is written, "The people sat down to eat
and drink and rose up to dance." [8]We
must not indulge in immorality as some
of them did, and twenty-three thousand
fell in a single day. [9]We must not put the
Lord[y] to the test, as some of them did
and were destroyed by serpents; [10]nor
grumble, as some of them did and were
destroyed by the Destroyer. [11]Now these
things happened to them as a warning,
but they were written down for our in-
struction, upon whom the end of the
ages has come. [12]Therefore let any one
who thinks that he stands take heed lest
he fall. [13]No temptation has overtaken
you that is not common to man. God
is faithful, and he will not let you be
tempted beyond your strength, but with
the temptation will also provide the way
of escape, that you may be able to endure
it.

14 Therefore, my beloved, shun the
worship of idols. [15]I speak as to sensible
men; judge for yourselves what I say.
[16]The cup of blessing which we bless,
is it not a participation[z] in the blood
of Christ? The bread which we break,
is it not a participation[a] in the body of
Christ? [17]Because there is one bread,
we who are many are one body, for we
all partake of the one bread. [18]Consider
the practice of Israel; are not those who
eat the sacrifices partners in the altar?
[19]What do I imply then? That food of-
fered to idols is anything, or that an idol
is anything? [20]No, I imply that what pa-
gans sacrifice they offer to demons and
not to God. I do not want you to be part-
ners with demons. [21]You cannot drink
the cup of the Lord and the cup of de-
mons. You cannot partake of the table of
the Lord and the table of demons. [22]Shall
we provoke the Lord to jealousy? Are
we stronger than he?

Do All to the Glory of God

23 "All things are lawful," but not all
things are helpful. "All things are law-
ful," but not all things build up. [24]Let
no one seek his own good, but the good
of his neighbor. [25]Eat whatever is sold
in the meat market without raising any
question on the ground of conscience.
[26]For "the earth is the Lord's, and ev-
erything in it." [27]If one of the unbeliev-
ers invites you to dinner and you are

[v]**10.3** Greek *spiritual* [w]**10.4** Greek *spiritual* [x]**10.4** Greek *spiritual* [y]**10.9** Other ancient authorities read *Christ* [z]**10.16** Or *communion* [a]**10.16** Or *communion*

disposed to go, eat whatever is set before
you without raising any question on the
ground of conscience. 28(But if some one
says to you, "This has been offered in
sacrifice," then out of consideration for
the man who informed you, and for con-
science' sake— 29I mean his conscience,
not yours—do not eat it.) For why should
my liberty be determined by another
man's scruples? 30If I partake with thank-
fulness, why am I denounced because of
that for which I give thanks?

31 So, whether you eat or drink, or
whatever you do, do all to the glory
of God. 32Give no offense to Jews or to
Greeks or to the church of God, 33just as
I try to please all men in everything I do,
not seeking my own advantage, but that
11 of many, that they may be saved. 1Be
imitators of me, as I am of Christ.

Head Coverings

2 I commend you because you remember
me in everything and maintain the tra-
ditions even as I have delivered them to
you. 3But I want you to understand that
the head of every man is Christ, the head
of a woman is her husband, and the head
of Christ is God. 4Any man who prays or
prophesies with his head covered dishon-
ors his head, 5but any woman who prays
or prophesies with her head unveiled
dishonors her head—it is the same as if
her head were shaven. 6For if a woman
will not veil herself, then she should cut
off her hair; but if it is disgraceful for
a woman to be shorn or shaven, let her
wear a veil. 7For a man ought not to cover
his head, since he is the image and glory
of God; but woman is the glory of man.
8(For man was not made from woman,
but woman from man. 9Neither was man
created for woman, but woman for man.)
10That is why a woman ought to have a
veil[b] on her head, because of the angels.
11(Nevertheless, in the Lord woman is not
independent of man nor man of woman;
12for as woman was made from man,
so man is now born of woman. And all
things are from God.) 13Judge for your-
selves; is it proper for a woman to pray
to God with her head uncovered? 14Does
not nature itself teach you that for a man
to wear long hair is degrading to him,
15but if a woman has long hair, it is her
pride? For her hair is given to her for a
covering. 16If any one is disposed to be
contentious, we recognize no other prac-
tice, nor do the churches of God.

Abuses at the Lord's Supper

17 But in the following instructions I do
not commend you, because when you
come together it is not for the better but
for the worse. 18For, in the first place,
when you assemble as a church, I hear
that there are divisions among you; and
I partly believe it, 19for there must be
factions among you in order that those
who are genuine among you may be rec-
ognized. 20When you meet together, it is
not the Lord's supper that you eat. 21For
in eating, each one goes ahead with his
own meal, and one is hungry and an-
other is drunk. 22What! Do you not have
houses to eat and drink in? Or do you
despise the church of God and humiliate
those who have nothing? What shall I say
to you? Shall I commend you in this? No,
I will not.

The Institution of the Lord's Supper

23 For I received from the Lord what I
also delivered to you, that the Lord Jesus
on the night when he was betrayed took
bread, 24and when he had given thanks,
he broke it, and said, "This is my body
which is for[c] you. Do this in remem-
brance of me." 25In the same way also the
cup, after supper, saying, "This cup is
the new covenant in my blood. Do this, as
often as you drink it, in remembrance of

[b] **11.10** Greek *authority* (the veil being a symbol of this)

[c] **11.24** Other ancient authorities read *broken for*

me." [26]For as often as you eat this bread
and drink the cup, you proclaim the
Lord's death until he comes.

Partaking of the Supper Unworthily

27 Whoever, therefore, eats the bread or
drinks the cup of the Lord in an unwor-
thy manner will be guilty of profaning
the body and blood of the Lord. [28]Let a
man examine himself, and so eat of the
bread and drink of the cup. [29]For any one
who eats and drinks without discerning
the body eats and drinks judgment upon
himself. [30]That is why many of you are
weak and ill, and some have died.[d] [31]But
if we judged ourselves truly, we should
not be judged. [32]But when we are judged
by the Lord, we are chastened[e] so that we
may not be condemned along with the
world.

33 So then, my brethren, when you come
together to eat, wait for one another—
[34]if any one is hungry, let him eat at
home—lest you come together to be con-
demned. About the other things I will
give directions when I come.

Spiritual Gifts

12 Now concerning spiritual gifts,
brethren, I do not want you to be
uninformed. [2]You know that when you
were heathen, you were led astray to
dumb idols, however you may have been
moved. [3]Therefore I want you to under-
stand that no one speaking by the Spirit
of God ever says "Jesus be cursed!" and
no one can say "Jesus is Lord" except by
the Holy Spirit.

4 Now there are varieties of gifts, but
the same Spirit; [5]and there are variet-
ies of service, but the same Lord; [6]and
there are varieties of working, but it is
the same God who inspires them all in
every one. [7]To each is given the mani-
festation of the Spirit for the common
good. [8]To one is given through the Spirit
the utterance of wisdom, and to another
the utterance of knowledge according to
the same Spirit, [9]to another faith by the
same Spirit, to another gifts of healing
by the one Spirit, [10]to another the work-
ing of miracles, to another prophecy, to
another the ability to distinguish be-
tween spirits, to another various kinds
of tongues, to another the interpretation
of tongues. [11]All these are inspired by
one and the same Spirit, who apportions
to each one individually as he wills.

One Body with Many Members

12 For just as the body is one and has
many members, and all the members of
the body, though many, are one body, so
it is with Christ. [13]For by one Spirit we
were all baptized into one body—Jews
or Greeks, slaves or free—and all were
made to drink of one Spirit.

14 For the body does not consist of one
member but of many. [15]If the foot should
say, "Because I am not a hand, I do not
belong to the body," that would not make
it any less a part of the body. [16]And if the
ear should say, "Because I am not an eye, I
do not belong to the body," that would not
make it any less a part of the body. [17]If the
whole body were an eye, where would be
the hearing? If the whole body were an
ear, where would be the sense of smell?
[18]But as it is, God arranged the organs in
the body, each one of them, as he chose.
[19]If all were a single organ, where would
the body be? [20]As it is, there are many
parts, yet one body. [21]The eye cannot say
to the hand, "I have no need of you," nor
again the head to the feet, "I have no need
of you." [22]On the contrary, the parts of the
body which seem to be weaker are indis-
pensable, [23]and those parts of the body
which we think less honorable we invest
with the greater honor, and our unpre-
sentable parts are treated with greater
modesty, [24]which our more presentable

[d]**11.30** Greek *have fallen asleep* (as in 15.6, 20)

[e]**11.32** Or *when we are judged we are being chastened by the Lord*

parts do not require. But God has so ad-
justed the body, giving the greater honor
to the inferior part, 25 that there may be
no discord in the body, but that the mem-
bers may have the same care for one an-
other. 26 If one member suffers, all suffer
together; if one member is honored, all
rejoice together.

27 Now you are the body of Christ and
individually members of it. 28 And God
has appointed in the church first apos-
tles, second prophets, third teachers,
then workers of miracles, then healers,
helpers, administrators, speakers in var-
ious kinds of tongues. 29 Are all apostles?
Are all prophets? Are all teachers? Do all
work miracles? 30 Do all possess gifts of
healing? Do all speak with tongues? Do
all interpret? 31 But earnestly desire the
higher gifts.

And I will show you a still more excel-
lent way.

The Gift of Love

13 If I speak in the tongues of men
and of angels, but have not love, I
am a noisy gong or a clanging cymbal.
2 And if I have prophetic powers, and
understand all mysteries and all knowl-
edge, and if I have all faith, so as to re-
move mountains, but have not love, I am
nothing. 3 If I give away all I have, and if I
deliver my body to be burned,[f] but have
not love, I gain nothing.

4 Love is patient and kind; love is not
jealous or boastful; 5 it is not arrogant
or rude. Love does not insist on its own
way; it is not irritable or resentful; 6 it
does not rejoice at wrong, but rejoices in
the right. 7 Love bears all things, believes
all things, hopes all things, endures all
things.

8 Love never ends; as for prophecies,
they will pass away; as for tongues, they
will cease; as for knowledge, it will pass
away. 9 For our knowledge is imperfect
and our prophecy is imperfect; 10 but
when the perfect comes, the imperfect
will pass away. 11 When I was a child, I
spoke like a child, I thought like a child,
I reasoned like a child; when I became a
man, I gave up childish ways. 12 For now
we see in a mirror dimly, but then face to
face. Now I know in part; then I shall un-
derstand fully, even as I have been fully
understood. 13 So faith, hope, love abide,
these three; but the greatest of these is
love.

Gifts of Prophecy and Tongues

14 Make love your aim, and ear-
nestly desire the spiritual gifts,
especially that you may prophesy. 2 For
one who speaks in a tongue speaks not
to men but to God; for no one under-
stands him, but he utters mysteries in
the Spirit. 3 On the other hand, he who
prophesies speaks to men for their up-
building and encouragement and con-
solation. 4 He who speaks in a tongue
edifies himself, but he who prophesies
edifies the church. 5 Now I want you all
to speak in tongues, but even more to
prophesy. He who prophesies is greater
than he who speaks in tongues, unless
some one interprets, so that the church
may be edified.

6 Now, brethren, if I come to you
speaking in tongues, how shall I benefit
you unless I bring you some revelation
or knowledge or prophecy or teaching?
7 If even lifeless instruments, such as the
flute or the harp, do not give distinct
notes, how will any one know what is
played? 8 And if the bugle gives an in-
distinct sound, who will get ready for
battle? 9 So with yourselves; if you in a
tongue utter speech that is not intelli-
gible, how will any one know what is
said? For you will be speaking into the
air. 10 There are doubtless many differ-
ent languages in the world, and none is
without meaning; 11 but if I do not know
the meaning of the language, I shall be a

[f] **13.3** Other ancient authorities read *body that I may glory*

foreigner to the speaker and the speaker
a foreigner to me. 12 So with yourselves;
since you are eager for manifestations
of the Spirit, strive to excel in building
up the church.

13 Therefore, he who speaks in a
tongue should pray for the power to in-
terpret. 14 For if I pray in a tongue, my
spirit prays but my mind is unfruit-
ful. 15 What am I to do? I will pray with
the spirit and I will pray with the mind
also; I will sing with the spirit and I will
sing with the mind also. 16 Otherwise, if
you bless[g] with the spirit, how can any
one in the position of an outsider[h] say
the "Amen" to your thanksgiving when
he does not know what you are saying?
17 For you may give thanks well enough,
but the other man is not edified. 18 I thank
God that I speak in tongues more than
you all; 19 nevertheless, in church I would
rather speak five words with my mind, in
order to instruct others, than ten thou-
sand words in a tongue.

20 Brethren, do not be children in your
thinking; be babes in evil, but in think-
ing be mature. 21 In the law it is written,
"By men of strange tongues and by the
lips of foreigners will I speak to this peo-
ple, and even then they will not listen to
me, says the Lord." 22 Thus, tongues are a
sign not for believers but for unbeliev-
ers, while prophecy is not for unbeliev-
ers but for believers. 23 If, therefore, the
whole church assembles and all speak in
tongues, and outsiders or unbelievers
enter, will they not say that you are mad?
24 But if all prophesy, and an unbeliever
or outsider enters, he is convicted by all,
he is called to account by all, 25 the secrets
of his heart are disclosed; and so, falling
on his face, he will worship God and de-
clare that God is really among you.

Orderly Worship

26 What then, brethren? When you
come together, each one has a hymn, a
lesson, a revelation, a tongue, or an in-
terpretation. Let all things be done for
edification. 27 If any speak in a tongue, let
there be only two or at most three, and
each in turn; and let one interpret. 28 But
if there is no one to interpret, let each of
them keep silence in church and speak
to himself and to God. 29 Let two or three
prophets speak, and let the others weigh
what is said. 30 If a revelation is made to
another sitting by, let the first be silent.
31 For you can all prophesy one by one, so
that all may learn and all be encouraged;
32 and the spirits of prophets are subject
to prophets. 33 For God is not a God of con-
fusion but of peace.

As in all the churches of the saints,
34 the women should keep silence in the
churches. For they are not permitted
to speak, but should be subordinate, as
even the law says. 35 If there is anything
they desire to know, let them ask their
husbands at home. For it is shameful for
a woman to speak in church. 36 What! Did
the word of God originate with you, or
are you the only ones it has reached?

37 If any one thinks that he is a prophet,
or spiritual, he should acknowledge that
what I am writing to you is a command
of the Lord. 38 If any one does not recog-
nize this, he is not recognized. 39 So, my
brethren, earnestly desire to prophesy,
and do not forbid speaking in tongues;
40 but all things should be done decently
and in order.

The Resurrection of Christ

15 Now I would remind you, breth-
ren, in what terms I preached to
you the gospel, which you received,
in which you stand, 2 by which you are
saved, if you hold it fast—unless you be-
lieved in vain.

3 For I delivered to you as of first
importance what I also received, that
Christ died for our sins in accordance
with the scriptures, 4 that he was buried,

[g] **14.16** That is, *give thanks to God* [h] **14.16** Or *him that is without gifts*

that he was raised on the third day in accordance with the scriptures, 5 and that he appeared to Cephas, then to the twelve. 6 Then he appeared to more than five hundred brethren at one time, most of whom are still alive, though some have fallen asleep. 7 Then he appeared to James, then to all the apostles. 8 Last of all, as to one untimely born, he appeared also to me. 9 For I am the least of the apostles, unfit to be called an apostle, because I persecuted the church of God. 10 But by the grace of God I am what I am, and his grace toward me was not in vain. On the contrary, I worked harder than any of them, though it was not I, but the grace of God which is with me. 11 Whether then it was I or they, so we preach and so you believed.

The Resurrection of the Dead

12 Now if Christ is preached as raised from the dead, how can some of you say that there is no resurrection of the dead? 13 But if there is no resurrection of the dead, then Christ has not been raised; 14 if Christ has not been raised, then our preaching is in vain and your faith is in vain. 15 We are even found to be misrepresenting God, because we testified of God that he raised Christ, whom he did not raise if it is true that the dead are not raised. 16 For if the dead are not raised, then Christ has not been raised. 17 If Christ has not been raised, your faith is futile and you are still in your sins. 18 Then those also who have fallen asleep in Christ have perished. 19 If for this life only we have hoped in Christ, we are of all men most to be pitied.

20 But in fact Christ has been raised from the dead, the first fruits of those who have fallen asleep. 21 For as by a man came death, by a man has come also the resurrection of the dead. 22 For as in Adam all die, so also in Christ shall all be made alive. 23 But each in his own order: Christ the first fruits, then at his coming those who belong to Christ. 24 Then comes the end, when he delivers the kingdom to God the Father after destroying every rule and every authority and power. 25 For he must reign until he has put all his enemies under his feet. 26 The last enemy to be destroyed is death. 27 "For God[i] has put all things in subjection under his feet." But when it says, "All things are put in subjection under him," it is plain that he is excepted who put all things under him. 28 When all things are subjected to him, then the Son himself will also be subjected to him who put all things under him, that God may be everything to every one.

29 Otherwise, what do people mean by being baptized on behalf of the dead? If the dead are not raised at all, why are people baptized on their behalf? 30 Why am I in peril every hour? 31 I protest, brethren, by my pride in you which I have in Christ Jesus our Lord, I die every day! 32 What do I gain if, humanly speaking, I fought with beasts at Ephesus? If the dead are not raised, "Let us eat and drink, for tomorrow we die." 33 Do not be deceived: "Bad company ruins good morals." 34 Come to your right mind, and sin no more. For some have no knowledge of God. I say this to your shame.

The Resurrection Body

35 But some one will ask, "How are the dead raised? With what kind of body do they come?" 36 You foolish man! What you sow does not come to life unless it dies. 37 And what you sow is not the body which is to be, but a bare kernel, perhaps of wheat or of some other grain. 38 But God gives it a body as he has chosen, and to each kind of seed its own body. 39 For not all flesh is alike, but there is one kind for men, another for animals, another for birds, and another for fish. 40 There

[i] **15.27** Greek *he*

are celestial bodies and there are terres-
trial bodies; but the glory of the celestial
is one, and the glory of the terrestrial is
another. 41 There is one glory of the sun,
and another glory of the moon, and an-
other glory of the stars; for star differs
from star in glory.
42 So is it with the resurrection of the
dead. What is sown is perishable, what
is raised is imperishable. 43 It is sown in
dishonor, it is raised in glory. It is sown
in weakness, it is raised in power. 44 It is
sown a physical body, it is raised a spir-
itual body. If there is a physical body,
there is also a spiritual body. 45 Thus it
is written, “The first man Adam became
a living being”; the last Adam became a
life-giving spirit. 46 But it is not the spir-
itual which is first but the physical, and
then the spiritual. 47 The first man was
from the earth, a man of dust; the second
man is from heaven. 48 As was the man
of dust, so are those who are of the dust;
and as is the man of heaven, so are those
who are of heaven. 49 Just as we have
borne the image of the man of dust, we
shall[j] also bear the image of the man of
heaven. 50 I tell you this, brethren: flesh
and blood cannot inherit the kingdom of
God, nor does the perishable inherit the
imperishable.
51 Lo! I tell you a mystery. We shall not
all sleep, but we shall all be changed, 52 in
a moment, in the twinkling of an eye, at
the last trumpet. For the trumpet will
sound, and the dead will be raised im-
perishable, and we shall be changed.
53 For this perishable nature must put
on the imperishable, and this mortal na-
ture must put on immortality. 54 When
the perishable puts on the imperishable,
and the mortal puts on immortality,
then shall come to pass the saying that is
written:

> “Death is swallowed up in victory.”
> 55 “O death, where is thy victory?
> O death, where is thy sting?”

56 The sting of death is sin, and the power
of sin is the law. 57 But thanks be to God,
who gives us the victory through our
Lord Jesus Christ.
58 Therefore, my beloved brethren, be
steadfast, immovable, always abounding
in the work of the Lord, knowing that in
the Lord your labor is not in vain.

The Collection for the Saints

16 Now concerning the contribution
for the saints: as I directed the
churches of Galatia, so you also are to do.
2 On the first day of every week, each of
you is to put something aside and store
it up, as he may prosper, so that contri-
butions need not be made when I come.
3 And when I arrive, I will send those
whom you accredit by letter to carry
your gift to Jerusalem. 4 If it seems ad-
visable that I should go also, they will
accompany me.

Plans for Travel

5 I will visit you after passing through
Macedo′nia, for I intend to pass through
Macedo′nia, 6 and perhaps I will stay
with you or even spend the winter, so
that you may speed me on my journey,
wherever I go. 7 For I do not want to see
you now just in passing; I hope to spend
some time with you, if the Lord permits.
8 But I will stay in Ephesus until Pente-
cost, 9 for a wide door for effective work
has opened to me, and there are many
adversaries.
10 When Timothy comes, see that you
put him at ease among you, for he is do-
ing the work of the Lord, as I am. 11 So let
no one despise him. Speed him on his
way in peace, that he may return to me;
for I am expecting him with the brethren.
12 As for our brother Apol′los, I
strongly urged him to visit you with the
other brethren, but it was not at all his
will[k] to come now. He will come when he
has opportunity.

[j] **15.49** Other ancient authorities read *let us*

[k] **16.12** Or *God’s will for him*

Final Messages and Greetings
13 Be watchful, stand firm in your faith,
be courageous, be strong. 14 Let all that
you do be done in love.
15 Now, brethren, you know that
the household of Steph′anas were the
first converts in Acha′ia, and they have
devoted themselves to the service of
the saints; 16 I urge you to be subject to
such men and to every fellow worker
and laborer. 17 I rejoice at the coming of
Steph′anas and Fortuna′tus and Acha′i-
cus, because they have made up for your
absence; 18 for they refreshed my spirit
as well as yours. Give recognition to
such men.
19 The churches of Asia send greetings.
Aq′uila and Prisca, together with the church
in their house, send you hearty greetings in
the Lord. 20 All the brethren send greetings.
Greet one another with a holy kiss.

21 I, Paul, write this greeting with my
own hand. 22 If any one has no love for
the Lord, let him be accursed. Our Lord,
come![l] 23 The grace of the Lord Jesus be
with you. 24 My love be with you all in
Christ Jesus. Amen.

[l] **16.22** Greek *Maranatha*

The Second Letter of Paul to the

CORINTHIANS

Salutation

1 Paul, an apostle of Christ Jesus by
the will of God, and Timothy our
brother.

To the church of God which is at
Corinth, with all the saints who are in the
whole of Acha'ia:

2 Grace to you and peace from God our
Father and the Lord Jesus Christ.

Paul's Thanksgiving after Affliction

3 Blessed be the God and Father of our
Lord Jesus Christ, the Father of mercies
and God of all comfort, 4 who comforts
us in all our affliction, so that we may
be able to comfort those who are in any
affliction, with the comfort with which
we ourselves are comforted by God.
5 For as we share abundantly in Christ's
sufferings, so through Christ we share
abundantly in comfort too.[a] 6 If we are
afflicted, it is for your comfort and sal-
vation; and if we are comforted, it is for
your comfort, which you experience
when you patiently endure the same
sufferings that we suffer. 7 Our hope for
you is unshaken; for we know that as
you share in our sufferings, you will also
share in our comfort.

8 For we do not want you to be igno-
rant, brethren, of the affliction we expe-
rienced in Asia; for we were so utterly,
unbearably crushed that we despaired
of life itself. 9 Why, we felt that we had
received the sentence of death; but that
was to make us rely not on ourselves
but on God who raises the dead; 10 he de-
livered us from so deadly a peril, and he
will deliver us; on him we have set our
hope that he will deliver us again. 11 You
also must help us by prayer, so that many
will give thanks on our behalf for the
blessing granted us in answer to many
prayers.

The Postponement of Paul's Visit

12 For our boast is this, the testimony
of our conscience that we have behaved
in the world, and still more toward you,
with holiness and godly sincerity, not by
earthly wisdom but by the grace of God.
13 For we write you nothing but what you
can read and understand; I hope you will
understand fully, 14 as you have under-
stood in part, that you can be proud of
us as we can be of you, on the day of the
Lord Jesus.

15 Because I was sure of this, I wanted
to come to you first, so that you might
have a double pleasure;[b] 16 I wanted to
visit you on my way to Macedo'nia, and
to come back to you from Macedo'nia
and have you send me on my way to Ju-
dea. 17 Was I vacillating when I wanted
to do this? Do I make my plans like a
worldly man, ready to say Yes and No at
once? 18 As surely as God is faithful, our
word to you has not been Yes and No.
19 For the Son of God, Jesus Christ, whom
we preached among you, Silva'nus and
Timothy and I, was not Yes and No; but
in him it is always Yes. 20 For all the prom-
ises of God find their Yes in him. That is
why we utter the Amen through him, to
the glory of God. 21 But it is God who es-
tablishes us with you in Christ, and has
commissioned us; 22 he has put his seal
upon us and given us his Spirit in our
hearts as a guarantee.

23 But I call God to witness against
me—it was to spare you that I refrained
from coming to Corinth. 24 Not that we
lord it over your faith; we work with you
for your joy, for you stand firm in your

[a] **1.5** Or *For as the sufferings of Christ abound for us, so also our comfort abounds through Christ*
[b] **1.15** Other ancient authorities read *favor*

2 faith. [1]For I made up my mind not to
make you another painful visit. [2]For
if I cause you pain, who is there to make
me glad but the one whom I have pained?
[3]And I wrote as I did, so that when I
came I might not be pained by those who
should have made me rejoice, for I felt
sure of all of you, that my joy would be
the joy of you all. [4]For I wrote you out of
much affliction and anguish of heart and
with many tears, not to cause you pain
but to let you know the abundant love
that I have for you.

Forgiveness for the Offender

5 But if any one has caused pain, he
has caused it not to me, but in some
measure—not to put it too severely—to
you all. [6]For such a one this punishment
by the majority is enough; [7]so you should
rather turn to forgive and comfort him,
or he may be overwhelmed by excessive
sorrow. [8]So I beg you to reaffirm your
love for him. [9]For this is why I wrote,
that I might test you and know whether
you are obedient in everything. [10]Any
one whom you forgive, I also forgive.
What I have forgiven, if I have forgiven
anything, has been for your sake in the
presence of Christ, [11]to keep Satan from
gaining the advantage over us; for we
are not ignorant of his designs.

Paul's Anxiety in Troas

12 When I came to Tro'as to preach the
gospel of Christ, a door was opened for
me in the Lord; [13]but my mind could not
rest because I did not find my brother
Titus there. So I took leave of them and
went on to Macedo'nia.

14 But thanks be to God, who in Christ
always leads us in triumph, and through
us spreads the fragrance of the knowl-
edge of him everywhere. [15]For we are
the aroma of Christ to God among those
who are being saved and among those
who are perishing, [16]to one a fragrance
from death to death, to the other a fra-
grance from life to life. Who is sufficient
for these things? [17]For we are not, like so
many, peddlers of God's word; but as men
of sincerity, as commissioned by God, in
the sight of God we speak in Christ.

Ministers of the New Covenant

3 Are we beginning to commend our-
selves again? Or do we need, as some
do, letters of recommendation to you, or
from you? [2]You yourselves are our letter
of recommendation, written on your[c]
hearts, to be known and read by all men;
[3]and you show that you are a letter from
Christ delivered by us, written not with
ink but with the Spirit of the living God,
not on tablets of stone but on tablets of
human hearts.

4 Such is the confidence that we have
through Christ toward God. [5]Not that we
are sufficient of ourselves to claim any-
thing as coming from us; our sufficiency
is from God, [6]who has qualified us to be
ministers of a new covenant, not in a
written code but in the Spirit; for the
written code kills, but the Spirit gives
life.

7 Now if the dispensation of death,
carved in letters on stone, came with
such splendor that the Israelites could
not look at Moses' face because of its
brightness, fading as this was, [8]will not
the dispensation of the Spirit be attended
with greater splendor? [9]For if there was
splendor in the dispensation of condem-
nation, the dispensation of righteous-
ness must far exceed it in splendor.
[10]Indeed, in this case, what once had
splendor has come to have no splendor
at all, because of the splendor that sur-
passes it. [11]For if what faded away came
with splendor, what is permanent must
have much more splendor.

12 Since we have such a hope, we are
very bold, [13]not like Moses, who put a veil
over his face so that the Israelites might

[c] **3.2** Other ancient authorities read *our*

not see the end of the fading splendor. 14But their minds were hardened; for to this day, when they read the old covenant, that same veil remains unlifted, because only through Christ is it taken away. 15Yes, to this day whenever Moses is read a veil lies over their minds; 16but when a man turns to the Lord the veil is removed. 17Now the Lord is the Spirit, and where the Spirit of the Lord is, there is freedom. 18And we all, with unveiled face, beholding[d] the glory of the Lord, are being changed into his likeness from one degree of glory to another; for this comes from the Lord who is the Spirit.

Treasure in Clay Jars

4 Therefore, having this ministry by the mercy of God,[e] we do not lose heart. 2We have renounced disgraceful, underhanded ways; we refuse to practice cunning or to tamper with God's word, but by the open statement of the truth we would commend ourselves to every man's conscience in the sight of God. 3And even if our gospel is veiled, it is veiled only to those who are perishing. 4In their case the god of this world has blinded the minds of the unbelievers, to keep them from seeing the light of the gospel of the glory of Christ, who is the likeness of God. 5For what we preach is not ourselves, but Jesus Christ as Lord, with ourselves as your servants[f] for Jesus' sake. 6For it is the God who said, "Let light shine out of darkness," who has shone in our hearts to give the light of the knowledge of the glory of God in the face of Christ.

7 But we have this treasure in earthen vessels, to show that the transcendent power belongs to God and not to us. 8We are afflicted in every way, but not crushed; perplexed, but not driven to despair; 9persecuted, but not forsaken; struck down, but not destroyed; 10always carrying in the body the death of Jesus, so that the life of Jesus may also be manifested in our bodies. 11For while we live we are always being given up to death for Jesus' sake, so that the life of Jesus may be manifested in our mortal flesh. 12So death is at work in us, but life in you.

13 Since we have the same spirit of faith as he had who wrote, "I believed, and so I spoke," we too believe, and so we speak, 14knowing that he who raised the Lord Jesus will raise us also with Jesus and bring us with you into his presence. 15For it is all for your sake, so that as grace extends to more and more people it may increase thanksgiving, to the glory of God.

Living by Faith

16 So we do not lose heart. Though our outer nature is wasting away, our inner nature is being renewed every day. 17For this slight momentary affliction is preparing for us an eternal weight of glory beyond all comparison, 18because we look not to the things that are seen but to the things that are unseen; for the things that are seen are transient, but the things that are unseen are eternal.

5 For we know that if the earthly tent we live in is destroyed, we have a building from God, a house not made with hands, eternal in the heavens. 2Here indeed we groan, and long to put on our heavenly dwelling, 3so that by putting it on we may not be found naked. 4For while we are still in this tent, we sigh with anxiety; not that we would be unclothed, but that we would be further clothed, so that what is mortal may be swallowed up by life. 5He who has prepared us for this very thing is God, who has given us the Spirit as a guarantee.

6 So we are always of good courage; we know that while we are at home in the body we are away from the Lord, 7for we walk by faith, not by sight. 8We are of good courage, and we would rather be

[d]**3.18** Or *reflecting* [e]**4.1** Greek *as we have received mercy* [f]**4.5** Or *slaves*

away from the body and at home with
the Lord. 9So whether we are at home or
away, we make it our aim to please him.
10For we must all appear before the judg-
ment seat of Christ, so that each one may
receive good or evil, according to what
he has done in the body.

The Ministry of Reconciliation

11 Therefore, knowing the fear of the
Lord, we persuade men; but what we are
is known to God, and I hope it is known
also to your conscience. 12We are not
commending ourselves to you again
but giving you cause to be proud of us,
so that you may be able to answer those
who pride themselves on a man's posi-
tion and not on his heart. 13For if we are
beside ourselves, it is for God; if we are
in our right mind, it is for you. 14For the
love of Christ controls us, because we
are convinced that one has died for all;
therefore all have died. 15And he died for
all, that those who live might live no lon-
ger for themselves but for him who for
their sake died and was raised.

16 From now on, therefore, we regard
no one from a human point of view;
even though we once regarded Christ
from a human point of view, we regard
him thus no longer. 17Therefore, if any
one is in Christ, he is a new creation;[g]
the old has passed away, behold, the
new has come. 18All this is from God,
who through Christ reconciled us to
himself and gave us the ministry of rec-
onciliation; 19that is, God was in Christ
reconciling[h] the world to himself, not
counting their trespasses against them,
and entrusting to us the message of rec-
onciliation. 20So we are ambassadors for
Christ, God making his appeal through
us. We beseech you on behalf of Christ,
be reconciled to God. 21For our sake he
made him to be sin who knew no sin, so
that in him we might become the righ-
teousness of God.

6 Working together with him, then, we
entreat you not to accept the grace of
God in vain. 2For he says,

> "At the acceptable time I have
> listened to you,
> and helped you on the day of
> salvation."

Behold, now is the acceptable time; be-
hold, now is the day of salvation. 3We
put no obstacle in any one's way, so
that no fault may be found with our
ministry, 4but as servants of God we
commend ourselves in every way:
through great endurance, in afflictions,
hardships, calamities, 5beatings, im-
prisonments, tumults, labors, watch-
ing, hunger; 6by purity, knowledge,
forbearance, kindness, the Holy Spirit,
genuine love, 7truthful speech, and
the power of God; with the weapons of
righteousness for the right hand and
for the left; 8in honor and dishonor,
in ill repute and good repute. We are
treated as impostors, and yet are true;
9as unknown, and yet well known; as
dying, and behold we live; as punished,
and yet not killed; 10as sorrowful, yet
always rejoicing; as poor, yet making
many rich; as having nothing, and yet
possessing everything.

11 Our mouth is open to you, Corin-
thians; our heart is wide. 12You are not
restricted by us, but you are restricted
in your own affections. 13In return—I
speak as to children—widen your hearts
also.

The Temple of the Living God

14 Do not be mismated with unbelievers.
For what partnership have righteous-
ness and iniquity? Or what fellowship
has light with darkness? 15What accord
has Christ with Be'lial?[i] Or what has a
believer in common with an unbeliever?
16What agreement has the temple of God
with idols? For we are the temple of the
living God; as God said,

[g] **5.17** Or *creature*
[h] **5.19** Or *in Christ God was reconciling*
[i] **6.15** Greek *Beliar*

"I will live in them and move among them,
and I will be their God,
and they shall be my people.
17 Therefore come out from them,
and be separate from them, says the Lord,
and touch nothing unclean;
then I will welcome you,
18 and I will be a father to you,
and you shall be my sons and daughters,
says the Lord Almighty."

7 Since we have these promises, beloved, let us cleanse ourselves from every defilement of body and spirit, and make holiness perfect in the fear of God.

Paul's Joy at the Church's Repentance

2 Open your hearts to us; we have wronged no one, we have corrupted no one, we have taken advantage of no one. [3]I do not say this to condemn you, for I said before that you are in our hearts, to die together and to live together. [4]I have great confidence in you; I have great pride in you; I am filled with comfort. With all our affliction, I am overjoyed.

5 For even when we came into Macedo'nia, our bodies had no rest but we were afflicted at every turn—fighting without and fear within. [6]But God, who comforts the downcast, comforted us by the coming of Titus, [7]and not only by his coming but also by the comfort with which he was comforted in you, as he told us of your longing, your mourning, your zeal for me, so that I rejoiced still more. [8]For even if I made you sorry with my letter, I do not regret it (though I did regret it), for I see that that letter grieved you, though only for a while. [9]As it is, I rejoice, not because you were grieved, but because you were grieved into repenting; for you felt a godly grief, so that you suffered no loss through us. [10]For godly grief produces a repentance that leads to salvation and brings no regret, but worldly grief produces death. [11]For see what earnestness this godly grief has produced in you, what eagerness to clear yourselves, what indignation, what alarm, what longing, what zeal, what punishment! At every point you have proved yourselves guiltless in the matter. [12]So although I wrote to you, it was not on account of the one who did the wrong, nor on account of the one who suffered the wrong, but in order that your zeal for us might be revealed to you in the sight of God. [13]Therefore we are comforted.

And besides our own comfort we rejoiced still more at the joy of Titus, because his mind has been set at rest by you all. [14]For if I have expressed to him some pride in you, I was not put to shame; but just as everything we said to you was true, so our boasting before Titus has proved true. [15]And his heart goes out all the more to you, as he remembers the obedience of you all, and the fear and trembling with which you received him. [16]I rejoice, because I have perfect confidence in you.

Encouragement to Be Generous

8 We want you to know, brethren, about the grace of God which has been shown in the churches of Macedo'nia, [2]for in a severe test of affliction, their abundance of joy and their extreme poverty have overflowed in a wealth of liberality on their part. [3]For they gave according to their means, as I can testify, and beyond their means, of their own free will, [4]begging us earnestly for the favor of taking part in the relief of the saints— [5]and this, not as we expected, but first they gave themselves to the Lord and to us by the will of God. [6]Accordingly we have urged Titus that as he had already made a beginning, he should also complete among you this gracious work. [7]Now as you excel in everything—in faith, in utterance, in knowledge, in all

earnestness, and in your love for us—see
that you excel in this gracious work also.
8 I say this not as a command, but to
prove by the earnestness of others that
your love also is genuine. 9For you know
the grace of our Lord Jesus Christ, that
though he was rich, yet for your sake he
became poor, so that by his poverty you
might become rich. 10And in this matter
I give my advice: it is best for you now
to complete what a year ago you began
not only to do but to desire, 11so that your
readiness in desiring it may be matched
by your completing it out of what you
have. 12For if the readiness is there, it is
acceptable according to what a man has,
not according to what he has not. 13I do
not mean that others should be eased
and you burdened, 14but that as a matter
of equality your abundance at the pres-
ent time should supply their want, so
that their abundance may supply your
want, that there may be equality. 15As it
is written, "He who gathered much had
nothing over, and he who gathered little
had no lack."

Commendation of Titus

16 But thanks be to God who puts the
same earnest care for you into the heart
of Titus. 17For he not only accepted our
appeal, but being himself very earnest
he is going to you of his own accord.
18With him we are sending the brother
who is famous among all the churches
for his preaching of the gospel; 19and not
only that, but he has been appointed by
the churches to travel with us in this gra-
cious work which we are carrying on,
for the glory of the Lord and to show our
good will. 20We intend that no one should
blame us about this liberal gift which we
are administering, 21for we aim at what
is honorable not only in the Lord's sight
but also in the sight of men. 22And with
them we are sending our brother whom
we have often tested and found earnest
in many matters, but who is now more
earnest than ever because of his great
confidence in you. 23As for Titus, he is
my partner and fellow worker in your
service; and as for our brethren, they are
messengers[j] of the churches, the glory
of Christ. 24So give proof, before the
churches, of your love and of our boast-
ing about you to these men.

The Collection for Christians at Jerusalem

9 Now it is superfluous for me to write
to you about the offering for the
saints, 2for I know your readiness, of
which I boast about you to the people
of Macedo'nia, saying that Acha'ia has
been ready since last year; and your
zeal has stirred up most of them. 3But
I am sending the brethren so that our
boasting about you may not prove vain
in this case, so that you may be ready, as
I said you would be; 4lest if some Mace-
do'nians come with me and find that you
are not ready, we be humiliated—to say
nothing of you—for being so confident.
5So I thought it necessary to urge the
brethren to go on to you before me, and
arrange in advance for this gift you have
promised, so that it may be ready not as
an exaction but as a willing gift.
6 The point is this: he who sows spar-
ingly will also reap sparingly, and he
who sows bountifully will also reap
bountifully. 7Each one must do as he has
made up his mind, not reluctantly or un-
der compulsion, for God loves a cheer-
ful giver. 8And God is able to provide
you with every blessing in abundance,
so that you may always have enough of
everything and may provide in abun-
dance for every good work. 9As it is
written,

> "He scatters abroad, he gives to the poor;
> his righteousness[k] endures for ever."

[j] **8.23** Greek *apostles*

[k] **9.9** Or *benevolence*

10 He who supplies seed to the sower and bread for food will supply and multiply your resources[l] and increase the harvest of your righteousness.[m] 11 You will be enriched in every way for great generosity, which through us will produce thanksgiving to God; 12 for the rendering of this service not only supplies the wants of the saints but also overflows in many thanksgivings to God. 13 Under the test of this service, you[n] will glorify God by your obedience in acknowledging the gospel of Christ, and by the generosity of your contribution for them and for all others; 14 while they long for you and pray for you, because of the surpassing grace of God in you. 15 Thanks be to God for his inexpressible gift!

Paul Defends His Ministry

10 I, Paul, myself entreat you, by the meekness and gentleness of Christ—I who am humble when face to face with you, but bold to you when I am away!— 2 I beg of you that when I am present I may not have to show boldness with such confidence as I count on showing against some who suspect us of acting in worldly fashion. 3 For though we live in the world we are not carrying on a worldly war, 4 for the weapons of our warfare are not worldly but have divine power to destroy strongholds. 5 We destroy arguments and every proud obstacle to the knowledge of God, and take every thought captive to obey Christ, 6 being ready to punish every disobedience, when your obedience is complete.

7 Look at what is before your eyes. If any one is confident that he is Christ's, let him remind himself that as he is Christ's, so are we. 8 For even if I boast a little too much of our authority, which the Lord gave for building you up and not for destroying you, I shall not be put to shame. 9 I would not seem to be frightening you with letters. 10 For they say, "His letters are weighty and strong, but his bodily presence is weak, and his speech of no account." 11 Let such people understand that what we say by letter when absent, we do when present. 12 Not that we venture to class or compare ourselves with some of those who commend themselves. But when they measure themselves by one another, and compare themselves with one another, they are without understanding.

13 But we will not boast beyond limit, but will keep to the limits God has apportioned us, to reach even to you. 14 For we are not overextending ourselves, as though we did not reach you; we were the first to come all the way to you with the gospel of Christ. 15 We do not boast beyond limit, in other men's labors; but our hope is that as your faith increases, our field among you may be greatly enlarged, 16 so that we may preach the gospel in lands beyond you, without boasting of work already done in another's field. 17 "Let him who boasts, boast of the Lord." 18 For it is not the man who commends himself that is accepted, but the man whom the Lord commends.

Paul and the False Apostles

11 I wish you would bear with me in a little foolishness. Do bear with me! 2 I feel a divine jealousy for you, for I betrothed you to Christ to present you as a pure bride to her one husband. 3 But I am afraid that as the serpent deceived Eve by his cunning, your thoughts will be led astray from a sincere and pure devotion to Christ. 4 For if some one comes and preaches another Jesus than the one we preached, or if you receive a different spirit from the one you received, or if you accept a different gospel from the one you accepted, you submit to it readily enough. 5 I think that I am not in the least inferior to these superlative apostles. 6 Even if I am unskilled in speaking,

[l] **9.10** Greek *sowing* [m] **9.10** Or *benevolence* [n] **9.13** Or *they*

I am not in knowledge; in every way we
have made this plain to you in all things.
7 Did I commit a sin in abasing myself
so that you might be exalted, because I
preached God's gospel without cost to
you? [8]I robbed other churches by accept-
ing support from them in order to serve
you. [9]And when I was with you and was
in want, I did not burden any one, for
my needs were supplied by the breth-
ren who came from Macedo′nia. So I re-
frained and will refrain from burdening
you in any way. [10]As the truth of Christ
is in me, this boast of mine shall not be
silenced in the regions of Acha′ia. [11]And
why? Because I do not love you? God
knows I do!
12 And what I do I will continue to
do, in order to undermine the claim of
those who would like to claim that in
their boasted mission they work on the
same terms as we do. [13]For such men
are false apostles, deceitful workmen,
disguising themselves as apostles of
Christ. [14]And no wonder, for even Satan
disguises himself as an angel of light.
[15]So it is not strange if his servants also
disguise themselves as servants of righ-
teousness. Their end will correspond to
their deeds.

Paul's Sufferings as an Apostle

16 I repeat, let no one think me foolish;
but even if you do, accept me as a fool, so
that I too may boast a little. [17](What I am
saying I say not with the Lord's authority
but as a fool, in this boastful confidence;
[18]since many boast of worldly things,
I too will boast.) [19]For you gladly bear
with fools, being wise yourselves! [20]For
you bear it if a man makes slaves of you,
or preys upon you, or takes advantage of
you, or puts on airs, or strikes you in the
face. [21]To my shame, I must say, we were
too weak for that!
But whatever any one dares to boast
of—I am speaking as a fool—I also dare
to boast of that. [22]Are they Hebrews?
So am I. Are they Israelites? So am I.
Are they descendants of Abraham? So
am I. [23]Are they servants of Christ? I
am a better one—I am talking like a
madman—with far greater labors, far
more imprisonments, with countless
beatings, and often near death. [24]Five
times I have received at the hands of the
Jews the forty lashes less one. [25]Three
times I have been beaten with rods;
once I was stoned. Three times I have
been shipwrecked; a night and a day I
have been adrift at sea; [26]on frequent
journeys, in danger from rivers, danger
from robbers, danger from my own peo-
ple, danger from Gentiles, danger in the
city, danger in the wilderness, danger at
sea, danger from false brethren; [27]in toil
and hardship, through many a sleepless
night, in hunger and thirst, often with-
out food, in cold and exposure. [28]And,
apart from other things, there is the
daily pressure upon me of my anxiety
for all the churches. [29]Who is weak, and
I am not weak? Who is made to fall, and I
am not indignant?
30 If I must boast, I will boast of the
things that show my weakness. [31]The God
and Father of the Lord Jesus, he who is
blessed for ever, knows that I do not lie.
[32]At Damascus, the governor under King
Ar′etas guarded the city of Damascus in
order to seize me, [33]but I was let down in
a basket through a window in the wall,
and escaped his hands.

Paul's Visions and Revelations

12 I must boast; there is nothing to
be gained by it, but I will go on
to visions and revelations of the Lord.
[2]I know a man in Christ who fourteen
years ago was caught up to the third
heaven—whether in the body or out of
the body I do not know, God knows. [3]And
I know that this man was caught up into
Paradise—whether in the body or out
of the body I do not know, God knows—
[4]and he heard things that cannot be told,

which man may not utter. [5]On behalf of
this man I will boast, but on my own be-
half I will not boast, except of my weak-
nesses. [6]Though if I wish to boast, I shall
not be a fool, for I shall be speaking the
truth. But I refrain from it, so that no
one may think more of me than he sees
in me or hears from me. [7]And to keep
me from being too elated by the abun-
dance of revelations, a thorn was given
me in the flesh, a messenger of Satan,
to harass me, to keep me from being too
elated. [8]Three times I besought the Lord
about this, that it should leave me; [9]but
he said to me, "My grace is sufficient
for you, for my power is made perfect
in weakness." I will all the more gladly
boast of my weaknesses, that the power
of Christ may rest upon me. [10]For the
sake of Christ, then, I am content with
weaknesses, insults, hardships, perse-
cutions, and calamities; for when I am
weak, then I am strong.

Paul's Concern for the Corinthian Church

11 I have been a fool! You forced me to
it, for I ought to have been commended
by you. For I am not at all inferior to
these superlative apostles, even though
I am nothing. [12]The signs of a true apos-
tle were performed among you in all
patience, with signs and wonders and
mighty works. [13]For in what were you
less favored than the rest of the churches,
except that I myself did not burden you?
Forgive me this wrong!

14 Here for the third time I am ready
to come to you. And I will not be a bur-
den, for I seek not what is yours but you;
for children ought not to lay up for their
parents, but parents for their children.
[15]I will most gladly spend and be spent
for your souls. If I love you the more,
am I to be loved the less? [16]But granting
that I myself did not burden you, I was
crafty, you say, and got the better of you
by guile. [17]Did I take advantage of you
through any of those whom I sent to you?
[18]I urged Titus to go, and sent the brother
with him. Did Titus take advantage of
you? Did we not act in the same spirit?
Did we not take the same steps?

19 Have you been thinking all along
that we have been defending ourselves
before you? It is in the sight of God that
we have been speaking in Christ, and
all for your upbuilding, beloved. [20]For
I fear that perhaps I may come and find
you not what I wish, and that you may
find me not what you wish; that perhaps
there may be quarreling, jealousy, an-
ger, selfishness, slander, gossip, conceit,
and disorder. [21]I fear that when I come
again my God may humble me before
you, and I may have to mourn over many
of those who sinned before and have
not repented of the impurity, immoral-
ity, and licentiousness which they have
practiced.

Further Warning

13 This is the third time I am coming
to you. Any charge must be sus-
tained by the evidence of two or three
witnesses. [2]I warned those who sinned
before and all the others, and I warn
them now while absent, as I did when
present on my second visit, that if I come
again I will not spare them— [3]since you
desire proof that Christ is speaking in
me. He is not weak in dealing with you,
but is powerful in you. [4]For he was cruci-
fied in weakness, but lives by the power
of God. For we are weak in him, but in
dealing with you we shall live with him
by the power of God.

5 Examine yourselves, to see whether
you are holding to your faith. Test your-
selves. Do you not realize that Jesus
Christ is in you?—unless indeed you fail
to meet the test! [6]I hope you will find out
that we have not failed. [7]But we pray God
that you may not do wrong—not that we
may appear to have met the test, but that
you may do what is right, though we may

seem to have failed. [8]For we cannot do anything against the truth, but only for the truth. [9]For we are glad when we are weak and you are strong. What we pray for is your improvement. [10]I write this while I am away from you, in order that when I come I may not have to be severe in my use of the authority which the Lord has given me for building up and not for tearing down.

Final Greetings and Benediction

11 Finally, brethren, farewell. Mend your ways, heed my appeal, agree with one another, live in peace, and the God of love and peace will be with you. [12]Greet one another with a holy kiss. [13]All the saints greet you.

14 The grace of the Lord Jesus Christ and the love of God and the fellowship of[o] the Holy Spirit be with you all.

[o]**13.14** Or *and participation in*

The Letter of Paul to the

GALATIANS

Salutation

1 Paul an apostle—not from men nor
through man, but through Jesus
Christ and God the Father, who raised
him from the dead— [2]and all the breth-
ren who are with me,
To the churches of Galatia:
3 Grace to you and peace from God the
Father and our Lord Jesus Christ, [4]who
gave himself for our sins to deliver us
from the present evil age, according to
the will of our God and Father; [5]to whom
be the glory for ever and ever. Amen.

There Is No Other Gospel

6 I am astonished that you are so quickly
deserting him who called you in the
grace of Christ and turning to a different
gospel— [7]not that there is another gos-
pel, but there are some who trouble you
and want to pervert the gospel of Christ.
[8]But even if we, or an angel from heaven,
should preach to you a gospel contrary
to that which we preached to you, let him
be accursed. [9]As we have said before, so
now I say again, If any one is preaching
to you a gospel contrary to that which
you received, let him be accursed.
10 Am I now seeking the favor of men,
or of God? Or am I trying to please men?
If I were still pleasing men, I should not
be a servant[a] of Christ.

Paul's Vindication of His Apostleship

11 For I would have you know, brethren,
that the gospel which was preached by
me is not man's[b] gospel. [12]For I did not
receive it from man, nor was I taught it,
but it came through a revelation of Jesus
Christ. [13]For you have heard of my for-
mer life in Judaism, how I persecuted
the church of God violently and tried to
destroy it; [14]and I advanced in Judaism
beyond many of my own age among my
people, so extremely zealous was I for
the traditions of my fathers. [15]But when
he who had set me apart before I was
born, and had called me through his
grace, [16]was pleased to reveal his Son
to[c] me, in order that I might preach him
among the Gentiles, I did not confer with
flesh and blood, [17]nor did I go up to Jeru-
salem to those who were apostles before
me, but I went away into Arabia; and
again I returned to Damascus.
18 Then after three years I went up to
Jerusalem to visit Cephas, and remained
with him fifteen days. [19]But I saw none
of the other apostles except James the
Lord's brother. [20](In what I am writing
to you, before God, I do not lie!) [21]Then I
went into the regions of Syria and Cili′-
cia. [22]And I was still not known by sight
to the churches of Christ in Judea; [23]they
only heard it said, "He who once perse-
cuted us is now preaching the faith he
once tried to destroy." [24]And they glori-
fied God because of me.

Paul and the Other Apostles

2 Then after fourteen years I went up
again to Jerusalem with Barnabas,
taking Titus along with me. [2]I went up
by revelation; and I laid before them (but
privately before those who were of re-
pute) the gospel which I preach among
the Gentiles, lest somehow I should be
running or had run in vain. [3]But even Ti-
tus, who was with me, was not compelled
to be circumcised, though he was a
Greek. [4]But because of false brethren se-
cretly brought in, who slipped in to spy
out our freedom which we have in Christ
Jesus, that they might bring us into bond-
age— [5]to them we did not yield submis-
sion even for a moment, that the truth of

[a]**1.10** Or *slave* [b]**1.11** Greek *according to man* [c]**1.16** Greek *in*

the gospel might be preserved for you.
6 And from those who were reputed to be
something (what they were makes no dif-
ference to me; God shows no partiality)—
those, I say, who were of repute added
nothing to me; 7 but on the contrary,
when they saw that I had been entrusted
with the gospel to the uncircumcised,
just as Peter had been entrusted with the
gospel to the circumcised 8 (for he who
worked through Peter for the mission
to the circumcised worked through me
also for the Gentiles), 9 and when they
perceived the grace that was given to me,
James and Cephas and John, who were re-
puted to be pillars, gave to me and Barna-
bas the right hand of fellowship, that we
should go to the Gentiles and they to the
circumcised; 10 only they would have us
remember the poor, which very thing I
was eager to do.

Paul Rebukes Peter at Antioch

11 But when Cephas came to Antioch
I opposed him to his face, because he
stood condemned. 12 For before certain
men came from James, he ate with the
Gentiles; but when they came he drew
back and separated himself, fearing the
circumcision party. 13 And with him the
rest of the Jews acted insincerely, so
that even Barnabas was carried away by
their insincerity. 14 But when I saw that
they were not straightforward about
the truth of the gospel, I said to Cephas
before them all, "If you, though a Jew,
live like a Gentile and not like a Jew,
how can you compel the Gentiles to live
like Jews?" 15 We ourselves, who are Jews
by birth and not Gentile sinners, 16 yet
who know that a man is not justified[d]
by works of the law but through faith in
Jesus Christ, even we have believed in
Christ Jesus, in order to be justified by
faith in Christ, and not by works of the
law, because by works of the law shall no
one be justified. 17 But if, in our endeavor
to be justified in Christ, we ourselves
were found to be sinners, is Christ then
an agent of sin? Certainly not! 18 But if
I build up again those things which I
tore down, then I prove myself a trans-
gressor. 19 For I through the law died to
the law, that I might live to God. 20 I have
been crucified with Christ; it is no lon-
ger I who live, but Christ who lives in
me; and the life I now live in the flesh I
live by faith in the Son of God, who loved
me and gave himself for me. 21 I do not
nullify the grace of God; for if justifica-
tion[e] were through the law, then Christ
died to no purpose.

Law or Faith

3 O foolish Galatians! Who has be-
witched you, before whose eyes Jesus
Christ was publicly portrayed as cruci-
fied? 2 Let me ask you only this: Did you
receive the Spirit by works of the law, or
by hearing with faith? 3 Are you so fool-
ish? Having begun with the Spirit, are
you now ending with the flesh? 4 Did you
experience so many things in vain?—if it
really is in vain. 5 Does he who supplies
the Spirit to you and works miracles
among you do so by works of the law, or
by hearing with faith?

6 Thus Abraham "believed God, and it
was reckoned to him as righteousness."
7 So you see that it is men of faith who are
the sons of Abraham. 8 And the scripture,
foreseeing that God would justify the
Gentiles by faith, preached the gospel
beforehand to Abraham, saying, "In you
shall all the nations be blessed." 9 So then,
those who are men of faith are blessed
with Abraham who had faith.

10 For all who rely on works of the
law are under a curse; for it is written,
"Cursed be every one who does not abide
by all things written in the book of the
law, and do them." 11 Now it is evident that
no man is justified before God by the law;
for "He who through faith is righteous

[d] **2.16** Or *reckoned righteous;* and so elsewhere [e] **2.21** Or *righteousness*

shall live";[f] [12]but the law does not rest on
faith, for "He who does them shall live
by them." [13]Christ redeemed us from the
curse of the law, having become a curse
for us—for it is written, "Cursed be ev-
ery one who hangs on a tree"— [14]that in
Christ Jesus the blessing of Abraham
might come upon the Gentiles, that we
might receive the promise of the Spirit
through faith.

The Promise to Abraham

15 To give a human example, brethren:
no one annuls even a man's will,[g] or adds
to it, once it has been ratified. [16]Now the
promises were made to Abraham and
to his offspring. It does not say, "And to
offsprings," referring to many; but, re-
ferring to one, "And to your offspring,"
which is Christ. [17]This is what I mean:
the law, which came four hundred and
thirty years afterward, does not annul a
covenant previously ratified by God, so
as to make the promise void. [18]For if the
inheritance is by the law, it is no longer
by promise; but God gave it to Abraham
by a promise.

The Purpose of the Law

19 Why then the law? It was added be-
cause of transgressions, till the offspring
should come to whom the promise had
been made; and it was ordained by an-
gels through an intermediary. [20]Now an
intermediary implies more than one;
but God is one.

21 Is the law then against the prom-
ises of God? Certainly not; for if a law
had been given which could make alive,
then righteousness would indeed be by
the law. [22]But the scripture consigned
all things to sin, that what was promised
to faith in Jesus Christ might be given to
those who believe.

23 Now before faith came, we were con-
fined under the law, kept under restraint
until faith should be revealed. [24]So that
the law was our custodian until Christ
came, that we might be justified by faith.
[25]But now that faith has come, we are no
longer under a custodian; [26]for in Christ
Jesus you are all sons of God, through
faith. [27]For as many of you as were bap-
tized into Christ have put on Christ.
[28]There is neither Jew nor Greek, there
is neither slave nor free, there is neither
male nor female; for you are all one in
Christ Jesus. [29]And if you are Christ's,
then you are Abraham's offspring, heirs
according to promise.

4 I mean that the heir, as long as he is a
child, is no better than a slave, though
he is the owner of all the estate; [2]but he is
under guardians and trustees until the
date set by the father. [3]So with us; when
we were children, we were slaves to the
elemental spirits of the universe. [4]But
when the time had fully come, God sent
forth his Son, born of woman, born un-
der the law, [5]to redeem those who were
under the law, so that we might receive
adoption as sons. [6]And because you are
sons, God has sent the Spirit of his Son
into our hearts, crying, "Abba! Father!"
[7]So through God you are no longer a
slave but a son, and if a son then an heir.

Paul Reproves the Galatians

8 Formerly, when you did not know God,
you were in bondage to beings that by
nature are no gods; [9]but now that you
have come to know God, or rather to be
known by God, how can you turn back
again to the weak and beggarly elemen-
tal spirits, whose slaves you want to
be once more? [10]You observe days, and
months, and seasons, and years! [11]I am
afraid I have labored over you in vain.

12 Brethren, I beseech you, become
as I am, for I also have become as you
are. You did me no wrong; [13]you know
it was because of a bodily ailment that I
preached the gospel to you at first; [14]and
though my condition was a trial to you,

[f]**3.11** Or *the righteous shall live by faith*   [g]**3.15** Or *covenant* (as in verse 17)

you did not scorn or despise me, but re-
ceived me as an angel of God, as Christ
Jesus. [15]What has become of the satisfac-
tion you felt? For I bear you witness that,
if possible, you would have plucked out
your eyes and given them to me. [16]Have I
then become your enemy by telling you
the truth?[h] [17]They make much of you,
but for no good purpose; they want to
shut you out, that you may make much
of them. [18]For a good purpose it is al-
ways good to be made much of, and not
only when I am present with you. [19]My
little children, with whom I am again in
travail until Christ be formed in you! [20]I
could wish to be present with you now
and to change my tone, for I am per-
plexed about you.

The Allegory of Hagar and Sarah

21 Tell me, you who desire to be under
law, do you not hear the law? [22]For it
is written that Abraham had two sons,
one by a slave and one by a free woman.
[23]But the son of the slave was born ac-
cording to the flesh, the son of the free
woman through promise. [24]Now this is
an allegory: these women are two cove-
nants. One is from Mount Sinai, bearing
children for slavery; she is Hagar. [25]Now
Hagar is Mount Sinai in Arabia;[i] she cor-
responds to the present Jerusalem, for
she is in slavery with her children. [26]But
the Jerusalem above is free, and she is
our mother. [27]For it is written,

> "Rejoice, O barren one that dost not
> bear;
> break forth and shout, thou who art
> not in travail;
> for the desolate hath more children
> than she who hath a husband."

[28]Now we,[j] brethren, like Isaac, are chil-
dren of promise. [29]But as at that time he
who was born according to the flesh per-
secuted him who was born according to
the Spirit, so it is now. [30]But what does
the scripture say? "Cast out the slave and
her son; for the son of the slave shall not
inherit with the son of the free woman."
[31]So, brethren, we are not children of the
slave but of the free woman.

5 For freedom Christ has set us free;
stand fast therefore, and do not sub-
mit again to a yoke of slavery.

The Nature of Christian Freedom

2 Now I, Paul, say to you that if you re-
ceive circumcision, Christ will be of
no advantage to you. [3]I testify again to
every man who receives circumcision
that he is bound to keep the whole law.
[4]You are severed from Christ, you who
would be justified by the law; you have
fallen away from grace. [5]For through
the Spirit, by faith, we wait for the hope
of righteousness. [6]For in Christ Jesus
neither circumcision nor uncircumci-
sion is of any avail, but faith working
through love. [7]You were running well;
who hindered you from obeying the
truth? [8]This persuasion is not from
him who called you. [9]A little leaven
leavens the whole lump. [10]I have confi-
dence in the Lord that you will take no
other view than mine; and he who is
troubling you will bear his judgment,
whoever he is. [11]But if I, brethren, still
preach circumcision, why am I still
persecuted? In that case the stumbling
block of the cross has been removed. [12]I
wish those who unsettle you would mu-
tilate themselves!

13 For you were called to freedom,
brethren; only do not use your free-
dom as an opportunity for the flesh, but
through love be servants of one another.
[14]For the whole law is fulfilled in one
word, "You shall love your neighbor as
yourself." [15]But if you bite and devour
one another take heed that you are not
consumed by one another.

[h]**4.16** Or *by dealing truly with you* [i]**4.25** Other ancient authorities read *For Sinai is a mountain in Arabia* [j]**4.28** Other ancient authorities read *you*

The Works of the Flesh and the Fruit of the Spirit

16 But I say, walk by the Spirit, and do not
gratify the desires of the flesh. [17]For the
desires of the flesh are against the Spirit,
and the desires of the Spirit are against
the flesh; for these are opposed to each
other, to prevent you from doing what
you would. [18]But if you are led by the
Spirit you are not under the law. [19]Now
the works of the flesh are plain: immoral-
ity, impurity, licentiousness, [20]idolatry,
sorcery, enmity, strife, jealousy, anger,
selfishness, dissension, party spirit,
[21]envy,[k] drunkenness, carousing, and
the like. I warn you, as I warned you be-
fore, that those who do such things shall
not inherit the kingdom of God. [22]But the
fruit of the Spirit is love, joy, peace, pa-
tience, kindness, goodness, faithfulness,
[23]gentleness, self-control; against such
there is no law. [24]And those who belong
to Christ Jesus have crucified the flesh
with its passions and desires.

25 If we live by the Spirit, let us also
walk by the Spirit. [26]Let us have no self-
conceit, no provoking of one another, no
envy of one another.

Bear One Another's Burdens

6 Brethren, if a man is overtaken in
any trespass, you who are spiritual
should restore him in a spirit of gentle-
ness. Look to yourself, lest you too be
tempted. [2]Bear one another's burdens,
and so fulfil the law of Christ. [3]For if any
one thinks he is something, when he is
nothing, he deceives himself. [4]But let
each one test his own work, and then his
reason to boast will be in himself alone
and not in his neighbor. [5]For each man
will have to bear his own load.

6 Let him who is taught the word share
all good things with him who teaches.

7 Do not be deceived; God is not
mocked, for whatever a man sows, that
he will also reap. [8]For he who sows to
his own flesh will from the flesh reap
corruption; but he who sows to the
Spirit will from the Spirit reap eternal
life. [9]And let us not grow weary in well-
doing, for in due season we shall reap,
if we do not lose heart. [10]So then, as we
have opportunity, let us do good to all
men, and especially to those who are of
the household of faith.

Final Admonitions and Benediction

11 See with what large letters I am writ-
ing to you with my own hand. [12]It is those
who want to make a good showing in the
flesh that would compel you to be cir-
cumcised, and only in order that they
may not be persecuted for the cross of
Christ. [13]For even those who receive cir-
cumcision do not themselves keep the
law, but they desire to have you circum-
cised that they may glory in your flesh.
[14]But far be it from me to glory except
in the cross of our Lord Jesus Christ, by
which[l] the world has been crucified to
me, and I to the world. [15]For neither cir-
cumcision counts for anything, nor un-
circumcision, but a new creation. [16]Peace
and mercy be upon all who walk by this
rule, upon the Israel of God.

17 Henceforth let no man trouble me;
for I bear on my body the marks of Jesus.

18 The grace of our Lord Jesus Christ
be with your spirit, brethren. Amen.

[k] **5.21** Other ancient authorities add *murder*
[l] **6.14** Or *through whom*

The Letter of Paul to the

EPHESIANS

Salutation

1 Paul, an apostle of Christ Jesus by the
will of God,
To the saints who are also faithful[a] in
Christ Jesus:
2 Grace to you and peace from God our
Father and the Lord Jesus Christ.

Spiritual Blessings in Christ

3 Blessed be the God and Father of our
Lord Jesus Christ, who has blessed us in
Christ with every spiritual blessing in
the heavenly places, [4]even as he chose
us in him before the foundation of the
world, that we should be holy and blame-
less before him. [5]He destined us in love[b]
to be his sons through Jesus Christ, ac-
cording to the purpose of his will, [6]to
the praise of his glorious grace which
he freely bestowed on us in the Beloved.
[7]In him we have redemption through his
blood, the forgiveness of our trespasses,
according to the riches of his grace
[8]which he lavished upon us. [9]For he has
made known to us in all wisdom and in-
sight the mystery of his will, according to
his purpose which he set forth in Christ
[10]as a plan for the fulness of time, to unite
all things in him, things in heaven and
things on earth.
11 In him, according to the purpose of
him who accomplishes all things accord-
ing to the counsel of his will, [12]we who
first hoped in Christ have been destined
and appointed to live for the praise of his
glory. [13]In him you also, who have heard
the word of truth, the gospel of your sal-
vation, and have believed in him, were
sealed with the promised Holy Spirit,
[14]who is the guarantee of our inheri-
tance until we acquire possession of it,
to the praise of his glory.

Paul's Prayer

15 For this reason, because I have heard
of your faith in the Lord Jesus and your
love[c] toward all the saints, [16]I do not cease
to give thanks for you, remembering you
in my prayers, [17]that the God of our Lord
Jesus Christ, the Father of glory, may
give you a spirit of wisdom and of reve-
lation in the knowledge of him, [18]having
the eyes of your hearts enlightened, that
you may know what is the hope to which
he has called you, what are the riches of
his glorious inheritance in the saints,
[19]and what is the immeasurable great-
ness of his power in us who believe, ac-
cording to the working of his great might
[20]which he accomplished in Christ when
he raised him from the dead and made
him sit at his right hand in the heavenly
places, [21]far above all rule and author-
ity and power and dominion, and above
every name that is named, not only in
this age but also in that which is to come;
[22]and he has put all things under his
feet and has made him the head over all
things for the church, [23]which is his body,
the fulness of him who fills all in all.

From Death to Life

2 And you he made alive, when you
were dead through the trespasses
and sins [2]in which you once walked, fol-
lowing the course of this world, follow-
ing the prince of the power of the air, the
spirit that is now at work in the sons of
disobedience. [3]Among these we all once
lived in the passions of our flesh, follow-
ing the desires of body and mind, and
so we were by nature children of wrath,
like the rest of mankind. [4]But God, who
is rich in mercy, out of the great love
with which he loved us, [5]even when we

[a] **1.1** Other ancient authorities read *who are at Ephesus and faithful* [b] **1.5** Or *before him in love, having destined us* [c] **1.15** Other ancient authorities omit *your love*

were dead through our trespasses, made
us alive together with Christ (by grace
you have been saved), [6]and raised us up
with him, and made us sit with him in the
heavenly places in Christ Jesus, [7]that in
the coming ages he might show the im-
measurable riches of his grace in kind-
ness toward us in Christ Jesus. [8]For by
grace you have been saved through faith;
and this is not your own doing, it is the
gift of God— [9]not because of works, lest
any man should boast. [10]For we are his
workmanship, created in Christ Jesus
for good works, which God prepared be-
forehand, that we should walk in them.

One in Christ

11 Therefore remember that at one time
you Gentiles in the flesh, called the un-
circumcision by what is called the cir-
cumcision, which is made in the flesh
by hands— [12]remember that you were at
that time separated from Christ, alien-
ated from the commonwealth of Israel,
and strangers to the covenants of prom-
ise, having no hope and without God in
the world. [13]But now in Christ Jesus you
who once were far off have been brought
near in the blood of Christ. [14]For he is our
peace, who has made us both one, and has
broken down the dividing wall of hostil-
ity, [15]by abolishing in his flesh the law of
commandments and ordinances, that he
might create in himself one new man in
place of the two, so making peace, [16]and
might reconcile us both to God in one
body through the cross, thereby bring-
ing the hostility to an end. [17]And he came
and preached peace to you who were far
off and peace to those who were near;
[18]for through him we both have access in
one Spirit to the Father. [19]So then you are
no longer strangers and sojourners, but
you are fellow citizens with the saints
and members of the household of God,
[20]built upon the foundation of the apos-
tles and prophets, Christ Jesus himself
being the cornerstone, [21]in whom the
whole structure is joined together and
grows into a holy temple in the Lord;
[22]in whom you also are built into it for a
dwelling place of God in the Spirit.

Paul's Ministry to the Gentiles

3 For this reason I, Paul, a prisoner for
Christ Jesus on behalf of you Gen-
tiles— [2]assuming that you have heard of
the stewardship of God's grace that was
given to me for you, [3]how the mystery
was made known to me by revelation, as
I have written briefly. [4]When you read
this you can perceive my insight into
the mystery of Christ, [5]which was not
made known to the sons of men in other
generations as it has now been revealed
to his holy apostles and prophets by the
Spirit; [6]that is, how the Gentiles are fel-
low heirs, members of the same body,
and partakers of the promise in Christ
Jesus through the gospel.

7 Of this gospel I was made a minister
according to the gift of God's grace which
was given me by the working of his
power. [8]To me, though I am the very least
of all the saints, this grace was given, to
preach to the Gentiles the unsearchable
riches of Christ, [9]and to make all men see
what is the plan of the mystery hidden
for ages in[d] God who created all things;
[10]that through the church the manifold
wisdom of God might now be made
known to the principalities and powers
in the heavenly places. [11]This was accord-
ing to the eternal purpose which he has
realized in Christ Jesus our Lord, [12]in
whom we have boldness and confidence
of access through our faith in him. [13]So I
ask you not to[e] lose heart over what I am
suffering for you, which is your glory.

Prayer for the Readers

14 For this reason I bow my knees before
the Father, [15]from whom every family
in heaven and on earth is named, [16]that

[d] **3.9** Or *by* [e] **3.13** Or *I ask that I may not*

according to the riches of his glory he
may grant you to be strengthened with
might through his Spirit in the inner
man, [17]and that Christ may dwell in
your hearts through faith; that you, be-
ing rooted and grounded in love, [18]may
have power to comprehend with all the
saints what is the breadth and length and
height and depth, [19]and to know the love
of Christ which surpasses knowledge,
that you may be filled with all the fulness
of God.

20 Now to him who by the power at
work within us is able to do far more
abundantly than all that we ask or think,
[21]to him be glory in the church and in
Christ Jesus to all generations, for ever
and ever. Amen.

Unity in the Body of Christ

4 I therefore, a prisoner for the Lord,
beg you to lead a life worthy of the
calling to which you have been called,
[2]with all lowliness and meekness, with
patience, forbearing one another in love,
[3]eager to maintain the unity of the Spirit
in the bond of peace. [4]There is one body
and one Spirit, just as you were called to
the one hope that belongs to your call,
[5]one Lord, one faith, one baptism, [6]one
God and Father of us all, who is above all
and through all and in all. [7]But grace was
given to each of us according to the mea-
sure of Christ's gift. [8]Therefore it is said,

> "When he ascended on high he led a
> host of captives,
> and he gave gifts to men."

[9](In saying, "He ascended," what does it
mean but that he had also descended into
the lower parts of the earth? [10]He who
descended is he who also ascended far
above all the heavens, that he might fill
all things.) [11]And his gifts were that some
should be apostles, some prophets, some
evangelists, some pastors and teachers,
[12]for the equipment of the saints, for the
work of ministry, for building up the
body of Christ, [13]until we all attain to the
unity of the faith and of the knowledge
of the Son of God, to mature manhood, to
the measure of the stature of the fulness
of Christ; [14]so that we may no longer be
children, tossed to and fro and carried
about with every wind of doctrine, by
the cunning of men, by their craftiness
in deceitful wiles. [15]Rather, speaking the
truth in love, we are to grow up in every
way into him who is the head, into Christ,
[16]from whom the whole body, joined and
knit together by every joint with which
it is supplied, when each part is working
properly, makes bodily growth and up-
builds itself in love.

The Old Life and the New

17 Now this I affirm and testify in the
Lord, that you must no longer live as the
Gentiles do, in the futility of their minds;
[18]they are darkened in their understand-
ing, alienated from the life of God be-
cause of the ignorance that is in them,
due to their hardness of heart; [19]they
have become callous and have given
themselves up to licentiousness, greedy
to practice every kind of uncleanness.
[20]You did not so learn Christ!— [21]assum-
ing that you have heard about him and
were taught in him, as the truth is in
Jesus. [22]Put off your old nature which be-
longs to your former manner of life and
is corrupt through deceitful lusts, [23]and
be renewed in the spirit of your minds,
[24]and put on the new nature, created af-
ter the likeness of God in true righteous-
ness and holiness.

Rules for the New Life

25 Therefore, putting away falsehood, let
every one speak the truth with his neigh-
bor, for we are members one of another.
[26]Be angry but do not sin; do not let the
sun go down on your anger, [27]and give no
opportunity to the devil. [28]Let the thief no
longer steal, but rather let him labor, do-
ing honest work with his hands, so that he
may be able to give to those in need. [29]Let

no evil talk come out of your mouths, but
only such as is good for edifying, as fits
the occasion, that it may impart grace to
those who hear. [30]And do not grieve the
Holy Spirit of God, in whom you were
sealed for the day of redemption. [31]Let
all bitterness and wrath and anger and
clamor and slander be put away from
you, with all malice, [32]and be kind to one
another, tenderhearted, forgiving one
another, as God in Christ forgave you.
5 Therefore be imitators of God, as be-
loved children. [2]And walk in love, as
Christ loved us and gave himself up for us,
a fragrant offering and sacrifice to God.

Renounce Pagan Ways

3 But immorality and all impurity or
covetousness must not even be named
among you, as is fitting among saints.
[4]Let there be no filthiness, nor silly talk,
nor levity, which are not fitting; but in-
stead let there be thanksgiving. [5]Be sure
of this, that no immoral or impure man,
or one who is covetous (that is, an idola-
ter), has any inheritance in the kingdom
of Christ and of God. [6]Let no one deceive
you with empty words, for it is because
of these things that the wrath of God
comes upon the sons of disobedience.
[7]Therefore do not associate with them,
[8]for once you were darkness, but now
you are light in the Lord; walk as children
of light [9](for the fruit of light is found in
all that is good and right and true), [10]and
try to learn what is pleasing to the Lord.
[11]Take no part in the unfruitful works of
darkness, but instead expose them. [12]For
it is a shame even to speak of the things
that they do in secret; [13]but when any-
thing is exposed by the light it becomes
visible, for anything that becomes visi-
ble is light. [14]Therefore it is said,

> "Awake, O sleeper, and arise from
> the dead,
> and Christ shall give you light."

15 Look carefully then how you walk,
not as unwise men but as wise, [16]making
the most of the time, because the days
are evil. [17]Therefore do not be foolish,
but understand what the will of the Lord
is. [18]And do not get drunk with wine, for
that is debauchery; but be filled with
the Spirit, [19]addressing one another in
psalms and hymns and spiritual songs,
singing and making melody to the Lord
with all your heart, [20]always and for
everything giving thanks in the name of
our Lord Jesus Christ to God the Father.

The Christian Household

21 Be subject to one another out of rev-
erence for Christ. [22]Wives, be subject to
your husbands, as to the Lord. [23]For the
husband is the head of the wife as Christ
is the head of the church, his body, and
is himself its Savior. [24]As the church is
subject to Christ, so let wives also be
subject in everything to their husbands.
[25]Husbands, love your wives, as Christ
loved the church and gave himself up for
her, [26]that he might sanctify her, having
cleansed her by the washing of water
with the word, [27]that he might present
the church to himself in splendor, with-
out spot or wrinkle or any such thing,
that she might be holy and without blem-
ish. [28]Even so husbands should love their
wives as their own bodies. He who loves
his wife loves himself. [29]For no man ever
hates his own flesh, but nourishes and
cherishes it, as Christ does the church,
[30]because we are members of his body.
[31]"For this reason a man shall leave his
father and mother and be joined to his
wife, and the two shall become one flesh."
[32]This is a great mystery, and I mean in
reference to Christ and the church;
[33]however, let each one of you love his
wife as himself, and let the wife see that
she respects her husband.

Children and Parents

6 Children, obey your parents in the
Lord, for this is right. [2]"Honor your
father and mother" (this is the first

commandment with a promise), [3]“that it
may be well with you and that you may
live long on the earth.” [4]Fathers, do not
provoke your children to anger, but
bring them up in the discipline and in-
struction of the Lord.

Slaves and Masters

5 Slaves, be obedient to those who are
your earthly masters, with fear and
trembling, in singleness of heart, as to
Christ; [6]not in the way of eye-service, as
men-pleasers, but as servants[f] of Christ,
doing the will of God from the heart,
[7]rendering service with a good will as
to the Lord and not to men, [8]knowing
that whatever good any one does, he will
receive the same again from the Lord,
whether he is a slave or free. [9]Masters,
do the same to them, and forbear threat-
ening, knowing that he who is both their
Master and yours is in heaven, and that
there is no partiality with him.

The Whole Armor of God

10 Finally, be strong in the Lord and in
the strength of his might. [11]Put on the
whole armor of God, that you may be able
to stand against the wiles of the devil.
[12]For we are not contending against flesh
and blood, but against the principalities,
against the powers, against the world
rulers of this present darkness, against
the spiritual hosts of wickedness in the
heavenly places. [13]Therefore take the
whole armor of God, that you may be
able to withstand in the evil day, and hav-
ing done all, to stand. [14]Stand therefore,
having girded your loins with truth,
and having put on the breastplate of
righteousness, [15]and having shod your
feet with the equipment of the gospel
of peace; [16]above all taking the shield of
faith, with which you can quench all the
flaming darts of the evil one. [17]And take
the helmet of salvation, and the sword
of the Spirit, which is the word of God.
[18]Pray at all times in the Spirit, with all
prayer and supplication. To that end
keep alert with all perseverance, making
supplication for all the saints, [19]and also
for me, that utterance may be given me
in opening my mouth boldly to proclaim
the mystery of the gospel, [20]for which I
am an ambassador in chains; that I may
declare it boldly, as I ought to speak.

Personal Matters and Benediction

21 Now that you also may know how I
am and what I am doing, Tych′icus the
beloved brother and faithful minister in
the Lord will tell you everything. [22]I have
sent him to you for this very purpose,
that you may know how we are, and that
he may encourage your hearts.

23 Peace be to the brethren, and love
with faith, from God the Father and the
Lord Jesus Christ. [24]Grace be with all
who love our Lord Jesus Christ with love
undying.

[f]**6.6** Or *slaves*

The Letter of Paul to the

PHILIPPIANS

Salutation

1 Paul and Timothy, servants[a] of Christ
Jesus,
To all the saints in Christ Jesus who
are at Philippi, with the bishops[b] and
deacons:
2 Grace to you and peace from God our
Father and the Lord Jesus Christ.

Paul's Prayer for the Philippians

3 I thank my God in all my remembrance
of you, [4]always in every prayer of mine
for you all making my prayer with joy,
[5]thankful for your partnership in the
gospel from the first day until now.
[6]And I am sure that he who began a good
work in you will bring it to completion
at the day of Jesus Christ. [7]It is right for
me to feel thus about you all, because
I hold you in my heart, for you are all
partakers with me of grace, both in my
imprisonment and in the defense and
confirmation of the gospel. [8]For God is
my witness, how I yearn for you all with
the affection of Christ Jesus. [9]And it is
my prayer that your love may abound
more and more, with knowledge and all
discernment, [10]so that you may approve
what is excellent, and may be pure and
blameless for the day of Christ, [11]filled
with the fruits of righteousness which
come through Jesus Christ, to the glory
and praise of God.

Paul's Present Circumstances

12 I want you to know, brethren, that
what has happened to me has really
served to advance the gospel, [13]so that
it has become known throughout the
whole praetorian guard[c] and to all the
rest that my imprisonment is for Christ;
[14]and most of the brethren have been
made confident in the Lord because of
my imprisonment, and are much more
bold to speak the word of God without
fear.
15 Some indeed preach Christ from
envy and rivalry, but others from good
will. [16]The latter do it out of love, know-
ing that I am put here for the defense of
the gospel; [17]the former proclaim Christ
out of partisanship, not sincerely but
thinking to afflict me in my imprison-
ment. [18]What then? Only that in every
way, whether in pretense or in truth,
Christ is proclaimed; and in that I rejoice.
19 Yes, and I shall rejoice. For I know
that through your prayers and the help
of the Spirit of Jesus Christ this will turn
out for my deliverance, [20]as it is my eager
expectation and hope that I shall not be
at all ashamed, but that with full courage
now as always Christ will be honored
in my body, whether by life or by death.
[21]For to me to live is Christ, and to die is
gain. [22]If it is to be life in the flesh, that
means fruitful labor for me. Yet which
I shall choose I cannot tell. [23]I am hard
pressed between the two. My desire is
to depart and be with Christ, for that is
far better. [24]But to remain in the flesh is
more necessary on your account. [25]Con-
vinced of this, I know that I shall remain
and continue with you all, for your prog-
ress and joy in the faith, [26]so that in me
you may have ample cause to glory in
Christ Jesus, because of my coming to
you again.
27 Only let your manner of life be
worthy of the gospel of Christ, so that
whether I come and see you or am ab-
sent, I may hear of you that you stand
firm in one spirit, with one mind striv-
ing side by side for the faith of the gos-
pel, [28]and not frightened in anything by
your opponents. This is a clear omen to

[a]**1.1** Or *slaves* [b]**1.1** Or *overseers* [c]**1.13** Greek *in the whole praetorium*

them of their destruction, but of your salvation, and that from God. 29 For it has been granted to you that for the sake of Christ you should not only believe in him but also suffer for his sake, 30 engaged in the same conflict which you saw and now hear to be mine.

Imitating Christ's Humility

2 So if there is any encouragement in Christ, any incentive of love, any participation in the Spirit, any affection and sympathy, 2 complete my joy by being of the same mind, having the same love, being in full accord and of one mind. 3 Do nothing from selfishness or conceit, but in humility count others better than yourselves. 4 Let each of you look not only to his own interests, but also to the interests of others. 5 Have this mind among yourselves, which was in Christ Jesus, 6 who, though he was in the form of God, did not count equality with God a thing to be grasped, 7 but emptied himself, taking the form of a servant,[d] being born in the likeness of men. 8 And being found in human form he humbled himself and became obedient unto death, even death on a cross. 9 Therefore God has highly exalted him and bestowed on him the name which is above every name, 10 that at the name of Jesus every knee should bow, in heaven and on earth and under the earth, 11 and every tongue confess that Jesus Christ is Lord, to the glory of God the Father.

Shining as Lights in the World

12 Therefore, my beloved, as you have always obeyed, so now, not only as in my presence but much more in my absence, work out your own salvation with fear and trembling; 13 for God is at work in you, both to will and to work for his good pleasure.

14 Do all things without grumbling or questioning, 15 that you may be blameless and innocent, children of God without blemish in the midst of a crooked and perverse generation, among whom you shine as lights in the world, 16 holding fast the word of life, so that in the day of Christ I may be proud that I did not run in vain or labor in vain. 17 Even if I am to be poured as a libation upon the sacrificial offering of your faith, I am glad and rejoice with you all. 18 Likewise you also should be glad and rejoice with me.

Timothy and Epaphroditus

19 I hope in the Lord Jesus to send Timothy to you soon, so that I may be cheered by news of you. 20 I have no one like him, who will be genuinely anxious for your welfare. 21 They all look after their own interests, not those of Jesus Christ. 22 But Timothy's worth you know, how as a son with a father he has served with me in the gospel. 23 I hope therefore to send him just as soon as I see how it will go with me; 24 and I trust in the Lord that shortly I myself shall come also.

25 I have thought it necessary to send to you Epaphrodi'tus my brother and fellow worker and fellow soldier, and your messenger and minister to my need, 26 for he has been longing for you all, and has been distressed because you heard that he was ill. 27 Indeed he was ill, near to death. But God had mercy on him, and not only on him but on me also, lest I should have sorrow upon sorrow. 28 I am the more eager to send him, therefore, that you may rejoice at seeing him again, and that I may be less anxious. 29 So receive him in the Lord with all joy; and honor such men, 30 for he nearly died for the work of Christ, risking his life to complete your service to me.

Breaking with the Past

3 Finally, my brethren, rejoice in the Lord. To write the same things to you is not irksome to me, and is safe for you.

[d] **2.7** Or *slave*

2 Look out for the dogs, look out for
the evil-workers, look out for those
who mutilate the flesh. 3For we are the
true circumcision, who worship God in
spirit,[e] and glory in Christ Jesus, and
put no confidence in the flesh. 4Though
I myself have reason for confidence in
the flesh also. If any other man thinks he
has reason for confidence in the flesh, I
have more: 5circumcised on the eighth
day, of the people of Israel, of the tribe of
Benjamin, a Hebrew born of Hebrews; as
to the law a Pharisee, 6as to zeal a perse-
cutor of the church, as to righteousness
under the law blameless. 7But whatever
gain I had, I counted as loss for the sake
of Christ. 8Indeed I count everything as
loss because of the surpassing worth of
knowing Christ Jesus my Lord. For his
sake I have suffered the loss of all things,
and count them as refuse, in order that
I may gain Christ 9and be found in him,
not having a righteousness of my own,
based on law, but that which is through
faith in Christ, the righteousness from
God that depends on faith; 10that I may
know him and the power of his resur-
rection, and may share his sufferings,
becoming like him in his death, 11that if
possible I may attain the resurrection
from the dead.

Pressing toward the Goal

12 Not that I have already obtained this
or am already perfect; but I press on to
make it my own, because Christ Jesus
has made me his own. 13Brethren, I do
not consider that I have made it my own;
but one thing I do, forgetting what lies
behind and straining forward to what
lies ahead, 14I press on toward the goal
for the prize of the upward call of God in
Christ Jesus. 15Let those of us who are ma-
ture be thus minded; and if in anything
you are otherwise minded, God will re-
veal that also to you. 16Only let us hold
true to what we have attained.

17 Brethren, join in imitating me, and
mark those who so live as you have an
example in us. 18For many, of whom I
have often told you and now tell you
even with tears, live as enemies of the
cross of Christ. 19Their end is destruc-
tion, their god is the belly, and they
glory in their shame, with minds set
on earthly things. 20But our common-
wealth is in heaven, and from it we
await a Savior, the Lord Jesus Christ,
21who will change our lowly body to
be like his glorious body, by the power
which enables him even to subject all
things to himself.

4 Therefore, my brethren, whom I
love and long for, my joy and crown,
stand firm thus in the Lord, my beloved.

Exhortations

2 I entreat Eu-o′dia and I entreat Syn′ty-
che to agree in the Lord. 3And I ask you
also, true yokefellow, help these women,
for they have labored side by side with
me in the gospel together with Clement
and the rest of my fellow workers, whose
names are in the book of life.

4 Rejoice in the Lord always; again I
will say, Rejoice. 5Let all men know your
forbearance. The Lord is at hand. 6Have
no anxiety about anything, but in ev-
erything by prayer and supplication
with thanksgiving let your requests be
made known to God. 7And the peace of
God, which passes all understanding,
will keep your hearts and your minds in
Christ Jesus.

8 Finally, brethren, whatever is true,
whatever is honorable, whatever is just,
whatever is pure, whatever is lovely,
whatever is gracious, if there is any ex-
cellence, if there is anything worthy of
praise, think about these things. 9What
you have learned and received and heard
and seen in me, do; and the God of peace
will be with you.

[e] **3.3** Other ancient authorities read *worship by the Spirit of God*

Acknowledgment of the Philippians' Gift

10 I rejoice in the Lord greatly that now
at length you have revived your con-
cern for me; you were indeed concerned
for me, but you had no opportunity.
11 Not that I complain of want; for I have
learned, in whatever state I am, to be
content. 12 I know how to be abased, and
I know how to abound; in any and all
circumstances I have learned the secret
of facing plenty and hunger, abundance
and want. 13 I can do all things in him who
strengthens me.

14 Yet it was kind of you to share my
trouble. 15 And you Philippians your-
selves know that in the beginning of the
gospel, when I left Macedo'nia, no church
entered into partnership with me in giv-
ing and receiving except you only; 16 for
even in Thessaloni'ca you sent me help[f]
once and again. 17 Not that I seek the gift;
but I seek the fruit which increases to
your credit. 18 I have received full pay-
ment, and more; I am filled, having re-
ceived from Epaphrodi'tus the gifts you
sent, a fragrant offering, a sacrifice ac-
ceptable and pleasing to God. 19 And my
God will supply every need of yours ac-
cording to his riches in glory in Christ
Jesus. 20 To our God and Father be glory
for ever and ever. Amen.

Final Greetings and Benediction

21 Greet every saint in Christ Jesus. The
brethren who are with me greet you.
22 All the saints greet you, especially
those of Caesar's household.

23 The grace of the Lord Jesus Christ
be with your spirit.

[f] **4.16** Other ancient authorities read *money for my needs*

The Letter of Paul to the

COLOSSIANS

Salutation

1 Paul, an apostle of Christ Jesus by the will of God, and Timothy our brother,

2 To the saints and faithful brethren in Christ at Colos′sae:

Grace to you and peace from God our Father.

Paul Thanks God for the Colossians

3 We always thank God, the Father of our Lord Jesus Christ, when we pray for you, [4]because we have heard of your faith in Christ Jesus and of the love which you have for all the saints, [5]because of the hope laid up for you in heaven. Of this you have heard before in the word of the truth, the gospel [6]which has come to you, as indeed in the whole world it is bearing fruit and growing—so among yourselves, from the day you heard and understood the grace of God in truth, [7]as you learned it from Ep′aphras our beloved fellow servant. He is a faithful minister of Christ on our[a] behalf [8]and has made known to us your love in the Spirit.

9 And so, from the day we heard of it, we have not ceased to pray for you, asking that you may be filled with the knowledge of his will in all spiritual wisdom and understanding, [10]to lead a life worthy of the Lord, fully pleasing to him, bearing fruit in every good work and increasing in the knowledge of God. [11]May you be strengthened with all power, according to his glorious might, for all endurance and patience with joy, [12]giving thanks to the Father, who has qualified us[b] to share in the inheritance of the saints in light. [13]He has delivered us from the dominion of darkness and transferred us to the kingdom of his beloved Son, [14]in whom we have redemption, the forgiveness of sins.

The Supremacy of Christ

15 He is the image of the invisible God, the first-born of all creation; [16]for in him all things were created, in heaven and on earth, visible and invisible, whether thrones or dominions or principalities or authorities—all things were created through him and for him. [17]He is before all things, and in him all things hold together. [18]He is the head of the body, the church; he is the beginning, the first-born from the dead, that in everything he might be pre-eminent. [19]For in him all the fulness of God was pleased to dwell, [20]and through him to reconcile to himself all things, whether on earth or in heaven, making peace by the blood of his cross.

21 And you, who once were estranged and hostile in mind, doing evil deeds, [22]he has now reconciled in his body of flesh by his death, in order to present you holy and blameless and irreproachable before him, [23]provided that you continue in the faith, stable and steadfast, not shifting from the hope of the gospel which you heard, which has been preached to every creature under heaven, and of which I, Paul, became a minister.

Paul's Interest in the Colossians

24 Now I rejoice in my sufferings for your sake, and in my flesh I complete what is lacking in Christ's afflictions for the sake of his body, that is, the church, [25]of which I became a minister according to the divine office which was given to me for you, to make the word of God fully known, [26]the mystery hidden for ages and generations[c] but now made

[a] **1.7** Other ancient authorities read *your* [b] **1.12** Other ancient authorities read *you* [c] **1.26** Or *from angels and men*

manifest to his saints. [27]To them God
chose to make known how great among
the Gentiles are the riches of the glory
of this mystery, which is Christ in you,
the hope of glory. [28]Him we proclaim,
warning every man and teaching every
man in all wisdom, that we may present
every man mature in Christ. [29]For this I
toil, striving with all the energy which
he mightily inspires within me.

2 For I want you to know how greatly
I strive for you, and for those at La-
odice'a, and for all who have not seen my
face, [2]that their hearts may be encour-
aged as they are knit together in love,
to have all the riches of assured under-
standing and the knowledge of God's
mystery, of Christ, [3]in whom are hid all
the treasures of wisdom and knowledge.
[4]I say this in order that no one may de-
lude you with beguiling speech. [5]For
though I am absent in body, yet I am with
you in spirit, rejoicing to see your good
order and the firmness of your faith in
Christ.

Fullness of Life in Christ

6 As therefore you received Christ Jesus
the Lord, so live in him, [7]rooted and built
up in him and established in the faith,
just as you were taught, abounding in
thanksgiving.

8 See to it that no one makes a prey of
you by philosophy and empty deceit, ac-
cording to human tradition, according
to the elemental spirits of the universe,
and not according to Christ. [9]For in him
the whole fulness of deity dwells bodily,
[10]and you have come to fulness of life in
him, who is the head of all rule and au-
thority. [11]In him also you were circum-
cised with a circumcision made without
hands, by putting off the body of flesh
in the circumcision of Christ; [12]and you
were buried with him in baptism, in
which you were also raised with him
through faith in the working of God, who
raised him from the dead. [13]And you,
who were dead in trespasses and the
uncircumcision of your flesh, God made
alive together with him, having forgiven
us all our trespasses, [14]having canceled
the bond which stood against us with its
legal demands; this he set aside, nailing
it to the cross. [15]He disarmed the princi-
palities and powers and made a public
example of them, triumphing over them
in him.[d]

16 Therefore let no one pass judgment
on you in questions of food and drink or
with regard to a festival or a new moon
or a sabbath. [17]These are only a shadow
of what is to come; but the substance
belongs to Christ. [18]Let no one disqual-
ify you, insisting on self-abasement and
worship of angels, taking his stand on
visions, puffed up without reason by his
sensuous mind, [19]and not holding fast to
the Head, from whom the whole body,
nourished and knit together through
its joints and ligaments, grows with a
growth that is from God.

Warnings against False Teachers

20 If with Christ you died to the elemen-
tal spirits of the universe, why do you
live as if you still belonged to the world?
Why do you submit to regulations, [21]"Do
not handle, Do not taste, Do not touch"
[22](referring to things which all perish as
they are used), according to human pre-
cepts and doctrines? [23]These have indeed
an appearance of wisdom in promoting
rigor of devotion and self-abasement
and severity to the body, but they are of
no value in checking the indulgence of
the flesh.[e]

The New Life in Christ

3 If then you have been raised with
Christ, seek the things that are above,
where Christ is, seated at the right hand
of God. [2]Set your minds on things that

[d]**2.15** Or *in it* (that is, the cross)

[e]**2.23** Or *are of no value, serving only to indulge the flesh*

are above, not on things that are on
earth. [3]For you have died, and your life
is hid with Christ in God. [4]When Christ
who is our life appears, then you also
will appear with him in glory.
5 Put to death therefore what is earthly
in you: immorality, impurity, passion,
evil desire, and covetousness, which is
idolatry. [6]On account of these the wrath
of God is coming.[f] [7]In these you once
walked, when you lived in them. [8]But
now put them all away: anger, wrath,
malice, slander, and foul talk from your
mouth. [9]Do not lie to one another, see-
ing that you have put off the old nature
with its practices [10]and have put on the
new nature, which is being renewed in
knowledge after the image of its creator.
[11]Here there cannot be Greek and Jew,
circumcised and uncircumcised, barbar-
ian, Scyth′ian, slave, free man, but Christ
is all, and in all.
12 Put on then, as God's chosen ones,
holy and beloved, compassion, kind-
ness, lowliness, meekness, and patience,
[13]forbearing one another and, if one has
a complaint against another, forgiving
each other; as the Lord has forgiven you,
so you also must forgive. [14]And above
all these put on love, which binds ev-
erything together in perfect harmony.
[15]And let the peace of Christ rule in your
hearts, to which indeed you were called
in the one body. And be thankful. [16]Let
the word of Christ dwell in you richly, as
you teach and admonish one another in
all wisdom, and as you sing psalms and
hymns and spiritual songs with thank-
fulness in your hearts to God. [17]And
whatever you do, in word or deed, do
everything in the name of the Lord Jesus,
giving thanks to God the Father through
him.

Rules for Christian Households

18 Wives, be subject to your husbands,
as is fitting in the Lord. [19]Husbands, love
your wives, and do not be harsh with
them. [20]Children, obey your parents in
everything, for this pleases the Lord.
[21]Fathers, do not provoke your children,
lest they become discouraged. [22]Slaves,
obey in everything those who are your
earthly masters, not with eyeservice, as
men-pleasers, but in singleness of heart,
fearing the Lord. [23]Whatever your task,
work heartily, as serving the Lord and
not men, [24]knowing that from the Lord
you will receive the inheritance as your
reward; you are serving the Lord Christ.
[25]For the wrongdoer will be paid back
for the wrong he has done, and there is
no partiality.

4 Masters, treat your slaves justly and
fairly, knowing that you also have a
Master in heaven.

Further Instructions

2 Continue steadfastly in prayer, being
watchful in it with thanksgiving; [3]and
pray for us also, that God may open to us
a door for the word, to declare the mys-
tery of Christ, on account of which I am
in prison, [4]that I may make it clear, as I
ought to speak.
5 Conduct yourselves wisely toward
outsiders, making the most of the time.
[6]Let your speech always be gracious,
seasoned with salt, so that you may know
how you ought to answer every one.

Final Greetings and Benediction

7 Tych′icus will tell you all about my af-
fairs; he is a beloved brother and faithful
minister and fellow servant in the Lord.
[8]I have sent him to you for this very pur-
pose, that you may know how we are and
that he may encourage your hearts, [9]and
with him One′simus, the faithful and be-
loved brother, who is one of yourselves.
They will tell you of everything that has
taken place here.
10 Aristar′chus my fellow prisoner
greets you, and Mark the cousin of

[f] **3.6** Other ancient authorities add *upon the sons of disobedience*

Barnabas (concerning whom you have
received instructions—if he comes to
you, receive him), [11]and Jesus who is
called Justus. These are the only men of
the circumcision among my fellow work-
ers for the kingdom of God, and they
have been a comfort to me. [12]Ep'aphras,
who is one of yourselves, a servant[g] of
Christ Jesus, greets you, always remem-
bering you earnestly in his prayers, that
you may stand mature and fully assured
in all the will of God. [13]For I bear him wit-
ness that he has worked hard for you and
for those in La-odice'a and in Hi-erap'olis.
[14]Luke the beloved physician and Demas
greet you. [15]Give my greetings to the
brethren at La-odice'a, and to Nympha
and the church in her house. [16]And when
this letter has been read among you,
have it read also in the church of the La-
odice'ans; and see that you read also the
letter from La-odice'a. [17]And say to Ar-
chip'pus, "See that you fulfil the ministry
which you have received in the Lord."

18 I, Paul, write this greeting with my own hand. Remember my fetters. Grace be with you.

[g] **4.12** Or *slave*

The First Letter of Paul to the

THESSALONIANS

Salutation

1 Paul, Silva'nus, and Timothy,
To the church of the Thessalo'nians
in God the Father and the Lord Jesus
Christ:
Grace to you and peace.

The Thessalonians' Faith and Example

2 We give thanks to God always for you
all, constantly mentioning you in our
prayers, [3]remembering before our God
and Father your work of faith and labor
of love and steadfastness of hope in our
Lord Jesus Christ. [4]For we know, breth-
ren beloved by God, that he has chosen
you; [5]for our gospel came to you not
only in word, but also in power and in
the Holy Spirit and with full conviction.
You know what kind of men we proved
to be among you for your sake. [6]And you
became imitators of us and of the Lord,
for you received the word in much afflic-
tion, with joy inspired by the Holy Spirit;
[7]so that you became an example to all the
believers in Macedo'nia and in Acha'ia.
[8]For not only has the word of the Lord
sounded forth from you in Macedo'nia
and Acha'ia, but your faith in God has
gone forth everywhere, so that we need
not say anything. [9]For they themselves
report concerning us what a welcome
we had among you, and how you turned
to God from idols, to serve a living and
true God, [10]and to wait for his Son from
heaven, whom he raised from the dead,
Jesus who delivers us from the wrath to
come.

Paul's Ministry in Thessalonica

2 For you yourselves know, brethren,
that our visit to you was not in vain;
[2]but though we had already suffered and
been shamefully treated at Philippi, as
you know, we had courage in our God to
declare to you the gospel of God in the
face of great opposition. [3]For our appeal
does not spring from error or unclean-
ness, nor is it made with guile; [4]but just
as we have been approved by God to be
entrusted with the gospel, so we speak,
not to please men, but to please God who
tests our hearts. [5]For we never used ei-
ther words of flattery, as you know, or a
cloak for greed, as God is witness; [6]nor
did we seek glory from men, whether
from you or from others, though we
might have made demands as apostles of
Christ. [7]But we were gentle[a] among you,
like a nurse taking care of her children.
[8]So, being affectionately desirous of you,
we were ready to share with you not only
the gospel of God but also our own selves,
because you had become very dear to us.
9 For you remember our labor and toil,
brethren; we worked night and day, that
we might not burden any of you, while
we preached to you the gospel of God.
[10]You are witnesses, and God also, how
holy and righteous and blameless was
our behavior to you believers; [11]for you
know how, like a father with his chil-
dren, we exhorted each one of you and
encouraged you and charged you [12]to
lead a life worthy of God, who calls you
into his own kingdom and glory.
13 And we also thank God constantly
for this, that when you received the
word of God which you heard from us,
you accepted it not as the word of men
but as what it really is, the word of God,
which is at work in you believers. [14]For
you, brethren, became imitators of the
churches of God in Christ Jesus which
are in Judea; for you suffered the same
things from your own countrymen
as they did from the Jews, [15]who killed

[a] **2.7** Other ancient authorities read *babes*

both the Lord Jesus and the prophets,
and drove us out, and displease God and
oppose all men [16]by hindering us from
speaking to the Gentiles that they may
be saved—so as always to fill up the mea-
sure of their sins. But God's wrath has
come upon them at last![b]

Paul's Desire to Visit the Thessalonians Again

17 But since we were bereft of you, breth-
ren, for a short time, in person not in
heart, we endeavored the more eagerly
and with great desire to see you face to
face; [18]because we wanted to come to
you—I, Paul, again and again—but Satan
hindered us. [19]For what is our hope or
joy or crown of boasting before our Lord
Jesus at his coming? Is it not you? [20]For
you are our glory and joy.

3 Therefore when we could bear it no
longer, we were willing to be left be-
hind at Athens alone, [2]and we sent Tim-
othy, our brother and God's servant in
the gospel of Christ, to establish you in
your faith and to exhort you, [3]that no
one be moved by these afflictions. You
yourselves know that this is to be our
lot. [4]For when we were with you, we told
you beforehand that we were to suffer af-
fliction; just as it has come to pass, and as
you know. [5]For this reason, when I could
bear it no longer, I sent that I might know
your faith, for fear that somehow the
tempter had tempted you and that our
labor would be in vain.

Timothy's Encouraging Report

6 But now that Timothy has come to us
from you, and has brought us the good
news of your faith and love and reported
that you always remember us kindly and
long to see us, as we long to see you— [7]for
this reason, brethren, in all our distress
and affliction we have been comforted
about you through your faith; [8]for now
we live, if you stand fast in the Lord. [9]For
what thanksgiving can we render to God
for you, for all the joy which we feel for
your sake before our God, [10]praying ear-
nestly night and day that we may see you
face to face and supply what is lacking in
your faith?

11 Now may our God and Father him-
self, and our Lord Jesus, direct our way
to you; [12]and may the Lord make you in-
crease and abound in love to one another
and to all men, as we do to you, [13]so that
he may establish your hearts unblam-
able in holiness before our God and Fa-
ther, at the coming of our Lord Jesus with
all his saints.

A Life Pleasing to God

4 Finally, brethren, we beseech and
exhort you in the Lord Jesus, that as
you learned from us how you ought to
live and to please God, just as you are
doing, you do so more and more. [2]For
you know what instructions we gave
you through the Lord Jesus. [3]For this is
the will of God, your sanctification: that
you abstain from immorality; [4]that each
one of you know how to control his own
body in holiness and honor, [5]not in the
passion of lust like heathen who do not
know God; [6]that no man transgress, and
wrong his brother in this matter,[c] be-
cause the Lord is an avenger in all these
things, as we solemnly forewarned you.
[7]For God has not called us for unclean-
ness, but in holiness. [8]Therefore who-
ever disregards this, disregards not man
but God, who gives his Holy Spirit to you.

9 But concerning love of the breth-
ren you have no need to have any one
write to you, for you yourselves have
been taught by God to love one another;
[10]and indeed you do love all the breth-
ren throughout Macedo'nia. But we ex-
hort you, brethren, to do so more and
more, [11]to aspire to live quietly, to mind
your own affairs, and to work with your
hands, as we charged you; [12]so that you

[b] **2.16** Or *completely*, or *for ever*

[c] **4.6** Or *defraud his brother in business*

may command the respect of outsiders,
and be dependent on nobody.

The Coming of the Lord

13 But we would not have you ignorant,
brethren, concerning those who are
asleep, that you may not grieve as others
do who have no hope. [14]For since we be-
lieve that Jesus died and rose again, even
so, through Jesus, God will bring with
him those who have fallen asleep. [15]For
this we declare to you by the word of the
Lord, that we who are alive, who are left
until the coming of the Lord, shall not
precede those who have fallen asleep.
[16]For the Lord himself will descend from
heaven with a cry of command, with
the archangel's call, and with the sound
of the trumpet of God. And the dead in
Christ will rise first; [17]then we who are
alive, who are left, shall be caught up to-
gether with them in the clouds to meet
the Lord in the air; and so we shall al-
ways be with the Lord. [18]Therefore com-
fort one another with these words.

5 But as to the times and the seasons,
brethren, you have no need to have
anything written to you. [2]For you your-
selves know well that the day of the Lord
will come like a thief in the night. [3]When
people say, "There is peace and security,"
then sudden destruction will come upon
them as travail comes upon a woman
with child, and there will be no escape.
[4]But you are not in darkness, brethren,
for that day to surprise you like a thief.
[5]For you are all sons of light and sons of
the day; we are not of the night or of dark-
ness. [6]So then let us not sleep, as others
do, but let us keep awake and be sober.
[7]For those who sleep sleep at night, and
those who get drunk are drunk at night.
[8]But, since we belong to the day, let us be
sober, and put on the breastplate of faith
and love, and for a helmet the hope of sal-
vation. [9]For God has not destined us for
wrath, but to obtain salvation through
our Lord Jesus Christ, [10]who died for
us so that whether we wake or sleep we
might live with him. [11]Therefore encour-
age one another and build one another
up, just as you are doing.

Final Exhortations, Greetings, and Benediction

12 But we beseech you, brethren, to re-
spect those who labor among you and
are over you in the Lord and admonish
you, [13]and to esteem them very highly in
love because of their work. Be at peace
among yourselves.[d] [14]And we exhort
you, brethren, admonish the idle, en-
courage the fainthearted, help the weak,
be patient with them all. [15]See that none
of you repays evil for evil, but always
seek to do good to one another and to all.
[16]Rejoice always, [17]pray constantly, [18]give
thanks in all circumstances; for this is
the will of God in Christ Jesus for you.
[19]Do not quench the Spirit, [20]do not de-
spise prophesying, [21]but test everything;
hold fast what is good, [22]abstain from ev-
ery form of evil.

23 May the God of peace himself sanc-
tify you wholly; and may your spirit and
soul and body be kept sound and blame-
less at the coming of our Lord Jesus
Christ. [24]He who calls you is faithful, and
he will do it.

25 Brethren, pray for us.

26 Greet all the brethren with a holy kiss.

27 I adjure you by the Lord that this letter be read to all the brethren.

28 The grace of our Lord Jesus Christ be with you.

[d] **5.13** Or *with them*

The Second Letter of Paul to the

THESSALONIANS

Salutation

1 Paul, Silva'nus, and Timothy,
To the church of the Thessalo'nians
in God our Father and the Lord Jesus
Christ:
2 Grace to you and peace from God the
Father and the Lord Jesus Christ.

Thanksgiving

3 We are bound to give thanks to God al-
ways for you, brethren, as is fitting, be-
cause your faith is growing abundantly,
and the love of every one of you for one
another is increasing. [4]Therefore we
ourselves boast of you in the churches
of God for your steadfastness and faith
in all your persecutions and in the afflic-
tions which you are enduring.

The Judgment at Christ's Coming

5 This is evidence of the righteous judg-
ment of God, that you may be made wor-
thy of the kingdom of God, for which you
are suffering— [6]since indeed God deems
it just to repay with affliction those who
afflict you, [7]and to grant rest with us to
you who are afflicted, when the Lord
Jesus is revealed from heaven with his
mighty angels in flaming fire, [8]inflicting
vengeance upon those who do not know
God and upon those who do not obey the
gospel of our Lord Jesus. [9]They shall suf-
fer the punishment of eternal destruc-
tion and exclusion from the presence of
the Lord and from the glory of his might,
[10]when he comes on that day to be glori-
fied in his saints, and to be marveled at
in all who have believed, because our
testimony to you was believed. [11]To this
end we always pray for you, that our
God may make you worthy of his call,
and may fulfil every good resolve and
work of faith by his power, [12]so that the
name of our Lord Jesus may be glori-
fied in you, and you in him, according to
the grace of our God and the Lord Jesus
Christ.

The Man of Lawlessness

2 Now concerning the coming of our
Lord Jesus Christ and our assem-
bling to meet him, we beg you, brethren,
[2]not to be quickly shaken in mind or ex-
cited, either by spirit or by word, or by
letter purporting to be from us, to the
effect that the day of the Lord has come.
[3]Let no one deceive you in any way; for
that day will not come, unless the rebel-
lion comes first, and the man of lawless-
ness[a] is revealed, the son of perdition,
[4]who opposes and exalts himself against
every so-called god or object of worship,
so that he takes his seat in the temple
of God, proclaiming himself to be God.
[5]Do you not remember that when I was
still with you I told you this? [6]And you
know what is restraining him now so
that he may be revealed in his time. [7]For
the mystery of lawlessness is already at
work; only he who now restrains it will
do so until he is out of the way. [8]And
then the lawless one will be revealed,
and the Lord Jesus will slay him with
the breath of his mouth and destroy
him by his appearing and his coming.
[9]The coming of the lawless one by the
activity of Satan will be with all power
and with pretended signs and wonders,
[10]and with all wicked deception for those
who are to perish, because they refused
to love the truth and so be saved. [11]There-
fore God sends upon them a strong delu-
sion, to make them believe what is false,
[12]so that all may be condemned who did
not believe the truth but had pleasure in
unrighteousness.

[a] **2.3** Other ancient authorities read *sin*

Chosen for Salvation

13 But we are bound to give thanks to
God always for you, brethren beloved by
the Lord, because God chose you from
the beginning[b] to be saved, through sanc-
tification by the Spirit[c] and belief in the
truth. 14 To this he called you through our
gospel, so that you may obtain the glory
of our Lord Jesus Christ. 15 So then, breth-
ren, stand firm and hold to the traditions
which you were taught by us, either by
word of mouth or by letter.
16 Now may our Lord Jesus Christ him-
self, and God our Father, who loved us
and gave us eternal comfort and good
hope through grace, 17 comfort your
hearts and establish them in every good
work and word.

Request for Prayer

3 Finally, brethren, pray for us, that
the word of the Lord may speed on
and triumph, as it did among you, 2 and
that we may be delivered from wicked
and evil men; for not all have faith. 3 But
the Lord is faithful; he will strengthen
you and guard you from evil.[d] 4 And we
have confidence in the Lord about you,
that you are doing and will do the things
which we command. 5 May the Lord di-
rect your hearts to the love of God and to
the steadfastness of Christ.

Warning against Idleness

6 Now we command you, brethren, in the
name of our Lord Jesus Christ, that you
keep away from any brother who is living
in idleness and not in accord with the tra-
dition that you received from us. 7 For you
yourselves know how you ought to im-
itate us; we were not idle when we were
with you, 8 we did not eat any one's bread
without paying, but with toil and labor we
worked night and day, that we might not
burden any of you. 9 It was not because we
have not that right, but to give you in our
conduct an example to imitate. 10 For even
when we were with you, we gave you this
command: If any one will not work, let
him not eat. 11 For we hear that some of
you are living in idleness, mere busybod-
ies, not doing any work. 12 Now such per-
sons we command and exhort in the Lord
Jesus Christ to do their work in quietness
and to earn their own living. 13 Brethren,
do not be weary in well-doing.
14 If any one refuses to obey what we
say in this letter, note that man, and have
nothing to do with him, that he may be
ashamed. 15 Do not look on him as an en-
emy, but warn him as a brother.

Final Greetings and Benediction

16 Now may the Lord of peace himself
give you peace at all times in all ways.
The Lord be with you all.

17 I, Paul, write this greeting with my
own hand. This is the mark in every let-
ter of mine; it is the way I write. 18 The
grace of our Lord Jesus Christ be with
you all.

[b] **2.13** Other ancient authorities read *as the first converts* [c] **2.13** Or *of spirit* [d] **3.3** Or *the evil one*

The First Letter of Paul to

TIMOTHY

Salutation

1 Paul, an apostle of Christ Jesus by
command of God our Savior and of
Christ Jesus our hope,
2 To Timothy, my true child in the
faith:
Grace, mercy, and peace from God the
Father and Christ Jesus our Lord.

Warning against False Teachers

3 As I urged you when I was going to
Macedo'nia, remain at Ephesus that you
may charge certain persons not to teach
any different doctrine, 4 nor to occupy
themselves with myths and endless ge-
nealogies which promote speculations
rather than the divine training[a] that is in
faith; 5 whereas the aim of our charge is
love that issues from a pure heart and a
good conscience and sincere faith. 6 Cer-
tain persons by swerving from these
have wandered away into vain discus-
sion, 7 desiring to be teachers of the law,
without understanding either what they
are saying or the things about which
they make assertions.
8 Now we know that the law is good,
if any one uses it lawfully, 9 understand-
ing this, that the law is not laid down for
the just but for the lawless and disobe-
dient, for the ungodly and sinners, for
the unholy and profane, for murderers
of fathers and murderers of mothers,
for manslayers, 10 immoral persons, sod-
omites, kidnapers, liars, perjurers, and
whatever else is contrary to sound doc-
trine, 11 in accordance with the glorious
gospel of the blessed God with which I
have been entrusted.

Gratitude for Mercy

12 I thank him who has given me strength
for this, Christ Jesus our Lord, because
he judged me faithful by appointing me
to his service, 13 though I formerly blas-
phemed and persecuted and insulted
him; but I received mercy because I had
acted ignorantly in unbelief, 14 and the
grace of our Lord overflowed for me
with the faith and love that are in Christ
Jesus. 15 The saying is sure and worthy of
full acceptance, that Christ Jesus came
into the world to save sinners. And I am
the foremost of sinners; 16 but I received
mercy for this reason, that in me, as the
foremost, Jesus Christ might display his
perfect patience for an example to those
who were to believe in him for eternal
life. 17 To the King of ages, immortal, in-
visible, the only God, be honor and glory
for ever and ever.[b] Amen.
18 This charge I commit to you, Timo-
thy, my son, in accordance with the pro-
phetic utterances which pointed to you,
that inspired by them you may wage the
good warfare, 19 holding faith and a good
conscience. By rejecting conscience, cer-
tain persons have made shipwreck of
their faith, 20 among them Hymenae'us
and Alexander, whom I have deliv-
ered to Satan that they may learn not to
blaspheme.

Instructions concerning Prayer

2 First of all, then, I urge that suppli-
cations, prayers, intercessions, and
thanksgivings be made for all men, 2 for
kings and all who are in high positions,
that we may lead a quiet and peaceable
life, godly and respectful in every way.
3 This is good, and it is acceptable in the
sight of God our Savior, 4 who desires
all men to be saved and to come to the
knowledge of the truth. 5 For there is one
God, and there is one mediator between
God and men, the man Christ Jesus,

[a] **1.4** Or *stewardship*, or *order* [b] **1.17** Greek *to the ages of ages*

[6]who gave himself as a ransom for all, the testimony to which was borne at the proper time. [7]For this I was appointed a preacher and apostle (I am telling the truth, I am not lying), a teacher of the Gentiles in faith and truth.

8 I desire then that in every place the men should pray, lifting holy hands without anger or quarreling; [9]also that women should adorn themselves modestly and sensibly in seemly apparel, not with braided hair or gold or pearls or costly attire [10]but by good deeds, as befits women who profess religion. [11]Let a woman learn in silence with all submissiveness. [12]I permit no woman to teach or to have authority over men; she is to keep silent. [13]For Adam was formed first, then Eve; [14]and Adam was not deceived, but the woman was deceived and became a transgressor. [15]Yet woman will be saved through bearing children,[c] if she continues[d] in faith and love and holiness, with modesty.

Qualifications of Bishops

3 The saying is sure: If any one aspires to the office of bishop, he desires a noble task. [2]Now a bishop must be above reproach, the husband of one wife, temperate, sensible, dignified, hospitable, an apt teacher, [3]no drunkard, not violent but gentle, not quarrelsome, and no lover of money. [4]He must manage his own household well, keeping his children submissive and respectful in every way; [5]for if a man does not know how to manage his own household, how can he care for God's church? [6]He must not be a recent convert, or he may be puffed up with conceit and fall into the condemnation of the devil;[e] [7]moreover he must be well thought of by outsiders, or he may fall into reproach and the snare of the devil.[f]

Qualifications of Deacons

8 Deacons likewise must be serious, not double-tongued, not addicted to much wine, not greedy for gain; [9]they must hold the mystery of the faith with a clear conscience. [10]And let them also be tested first; then if they prove themselves blameless let them serve as deacons. [11]The women likewise must be serious, no slanderers, but temperate, faithful in all things. [12]Let deacons be the husband of one wife, and let them manage their children and their households well; [13]for those who serve well as deacons gain a good standing for themselves and also great confidence in the faith which is in Christ Jesus.

The Mystery of Our Religion

14 I hope to come to you soon, but I am writing these instructions to you so that, [15]if I am delayed, you may know how one ought to behave in the household of God, which is the church of the living God, the pillar and bulwark of the truth. [16]Great indeed, we confess, is the mystery of our religion:

He[g] was manifested in the flesh,
vindicated[h] in the Spirit,
  seen by angels,
preached among the nations,
believed on in the world,
  taken up in glory.

False Asceticism

4 Now the Spirit expressly says that in later times some will depart from the faith by giving heed to deceitful spirits and doctrines of demons, [2]through the pretensions of liars whose consciences are seared, [3]who forbid marriage and enjoin abstinence from foods which God created to be received with thanksgiving by those who believe and know the truth. [4]For everything created by God is

[c] **2.15** Or *by the birth of the child* [d] **2.15** Greek *they continue* [e] **3.6** Or *slanderer*
[f] **3.7** Or *slanderer* [g] **3.16** Greek *Who;* other ancient authorities read *God;* others, *Which*
[h] **3.16** Or *justified*

good, and nothing is to be rejected if it
is received with thanksgiving; 5 for then
it is consecrated by the word of God and
prayer.

A Good Minister of Jesus Christ

6 If you put these instructions before
the brethren, you will be a good min-
ister of Christ Jesus, nourished on the
words of the faith and of the good doc-
trine which you have followed. 7 Have
nothing to do with godless and silly
myths. Train yourself in godliness; 8 for
while bodily training is of some value,
godliness is of value in every way, as it
holds promise for the present life and
also for the life to come. 9 The saying is
sure and worthy of full acceptance. 10 For
to this end we toil and strive,[i] because
we have our hope set on the living God,
who is the Savior of all men, especially
of those who believe.

11 Command and teach these things.
12 Let no one despise your youth, but set
the believers an example in speech and
conduct, in love, in faith, in purity. 13 Till
I come, attend to the public reading of
scripture, to preaching, to teaching. 14 Do
not neglect the gift you have, which was
given you by prophetic utterance when
the elders laid their hands upon you.
15 Practice these duties, devote yourself to
them, so that all may see your progress.
16 Take heed to yourself and to your teach-
ing; hold to that, for by so doing you will
save both yourself and your hearers.

Duties toward Believers

5 Do not rebuke an older man but
exhort him as you would a father;
treat younger men like brothers, 2 older
women like mothers, younger women
like sisters, in all purity.

3 Honor widows who are real widows.
4 If a widow has children or grandchil-
dren, let them first learn their religious
duty to their own family and make some
return to their parents; for this is ac-
ceptable in the sight of God. 5 She who
is a real widow, and is left all alone, has
set her hope on God and continues in
supplications and prayers night and
day; 6 whereas she who is self-indulgent
is dead even while she lives. 7 Command
this, so that they may be without re-
proach. 8 If any one does not provide for
his relatives, and especially for his own
family, he has disowned the faith and is
worse than an unbeliever.

9 Let a widow be enrolled if she is not
less than sixty years of age, having been
the wife of one husband; 10 and she must
be well attested for her good deeds, as
one who has brought up children, shown
hospitality, washed the feet of the saints,
relieved the afflicted, and devoted herself
to doing good in every way. 11 But refuse
to enrol younger widows; for when they
grow wanton against Christ they desire
to marry, 12 and so they incur condemna-
tion for having violated their first pledge.
13 Besides that, they learn to be idlers, gad-
ding about from house to house, and not
only idlers but gossips and busybodies,
saying what they should not. 14 So I would
have younger widows marry, bear chil-
dren, rule their households, and give
the enemy no occasion to revile us. 15 For
some have already strayed after Satan.
16 If any believing woman[j] has relatives
who are widows, let her assist them; let
the church not be burdened, so that it
may assist those who are real widows.

17 Let the elders who rule well be con-
sidered worthy of double honor, espe-
cially those who labor in preaching and
teaching; 18 for the scripture says, "You
shall not muzzle an ox when it is tread-
ing out the grain," and, "The laborer
deserves his wages." 19 Never admit any
charge against an elder except on the ev-
idence of two or three witnesses. 20 As for

[i] **4.10** Other ancient authorities read *suffer reproach*

[j] **5.16** Other ancient authorities read *man or woman;* others, simply *man*

those who persist in sin, rebuke them in
the presence of all, so that the rest may
stand in fear. [21]In the presence of God
and of Christ Jesus and of the elect angels
I charge you to keep these rules with-
out favor, doing nothing from partial-
ity. [22]Do not be hasty in the laying on of
hands, nor participate in another man's
sins; keep yourself pure.
23 No longer drink only water, but use
a little wine for the sake of your stomach
and your frequent ailments.
24 The sins of some men are conspicu-
ous, pointing to judgment, but the sins of
others appear later. [25]So also good deeds
are conspicuous; and even when they
are not, they cannot remain hidden.

6 Let all who are under the yoke of slav-
ery regard their masters as worthy
of all honor, so that the name of God and
the teaching may not be defamed. [2]Those
who have believing masters must not be
disrespectful on the ground that they are
brethren; rather they must serve all the
better since those who benefit by their
service are believers and beloved.

False Teaching and True Riches

Teach and urge these duties. [3]If any one
teaches otherwise and does not agree
with the sound words of our Lord Jesus
Christ and the teaching which accords
with godliness, [4]he is puffed up with
conceit, he knows nothing; he has a mor-
bid craving for controversy and for dis-
putes about words, which produce envy,
dissension, slander, base suspicions,
[5]and wrangling among men who are de-
praved in mind and bereft of the truth,
imagining that godliness is a means of
gain. [6]There is great gain in godliness
with contentment; [7]for we brought noth-
ing into the world, and[k] we cannot take
anything out of the world; [8]but if we have
food and clothing, with these we shall be
content. [9]But those who desire to be rich
fall into temptation, into a snare, into
many senseless and hurtful desires that
plunge men into ruin and destruction.
[10]For the love of money is the root of all
evils; it is through this craving that some
have wandered away from the faith and
pierced their hearts with many pangs.

The Good Fight of Faith

11 But as for you, man of God, shun all
this; aim at righteousness, godliness,
faith, love, steadfastness, gentleness.
[12]Fight the good fight of the faith; take
hold of the eternal life to which you were
called when you made the good confes-
sion in the presence of many witnesses.
[13]In the presence of God who gives life to
all things, and of Christ Jesus who in his
testimony before Pontius Pilate made
the good confession, [14]I charge you to
keep the commandment unstained and
free from reproach until the appearing
of our Lord Jesus Christ; [15]and this will be
made manifest at the proper time by the
blessed and only Sovereign, the King of
kings and Lord of lords, [16]who alone has
immortality and dwells in unapproach-
able light, whom no man has ever seen
or can see. To him be honor and eternal
dominion. Amen.
17 As for the rich in this world, charge
them not to be haughty, nor to set their
hopes on uncertain riches but on God
who richly furnishes us with everything
to enjoy. [18]They are to do good, to be rich
in good deeds, liberal and generous, [19]thus
laying up for themselves a good founda-
tion for the future, so that they may take
hold of the life which is life indeed.

Personal Instructions and Benediction

20 O Timothy, guard what has been en-
trusted to you. Avoid the godless chat-
ter and contradictions of what is falsely
called knowledge, [21]for by professing it
some have missed the mark as regards
the faith.

Grace be with you.

[k]**6.7** Other ancient authorities insert *it is certain that*

The Second Letter of Paul to

TIMOTHY

Salutation

1 Paul, an apostle of Christ Jesus by the
will of God according to the promise
of the life which is in Christ Jesus,
2 To Timothy, my beloved child:
Grace, mercy, and peace from God the
Father and Christ Jesus our Lord.

Thanksgiving and Encouragement

3 I thank God whom I serve with a clear
conscience, as did my fathers, when I re-
member you constantly in my prayers.
4As I remember your tears, I long night
and day to see you, that I may be filled
with joy. 5I am reminded of your sin-
cere faith, a faith that dwelt first in your
grandmother Lo′is and your mother Eu-
nice and now, I am sure, dwells in you.
6Hence I remind you to rekindle the gift
of God that is within you through the
laying on of my hands; 7for God did not
give us a spirit of timidity but a spirit of
power and love and self-control.
8 Do not be ashamed then of testifying
to our Lord, nor of me his prisoner, but
take your share of suffering for the gos-
pel in the power of God, 9who saved us
and called us with a holy calling, not in
virtue of our works but in virtue of his
own purpose and the grace which he gave
us in Christ Jesus ages ago, 10and now has
manifested through the appearing of
our Savior Christ Jesus, who abolished
death and brought life and immortality
to light through the gospel. 11For this gos-
pel I was appointed a preacher and apos-
tle and teacher, 12and therefore I suffer
as I do. But I am not ashamed, for I know
whom I have believed, and I am sure that
he is able to guard until that Day what
has been entrusted to me.[a] 13Follow the
pattern of the sound words which you
have heard from me, in the faith and love
which are in Christ Jesus; 14guard the
truth that has been entrusted to you by
the Holy Spirit who dwells within us.
15 You are aware that all who are in
Asia turned away from me, and among
them Phy′gelus and Hermog′enes. 16May
the Lord grant mercy to the household of
Onesiph′orus, for he often refreshed me;
he was not ashamed of my chains, 17but
when he arrived in Rome he searched
for me eagerly and found me— 18may the
Lord grant him to find mercy from the
Lord on that Day—and you well know all
the service he rendered at Ephesus.

A Good Soldier of Christ Jesus

2 You then, my son, be strong in the
grace that is in Christ Jesus, 2and what
you have heard from me before many
witnesses entrust to faithful men who
will be able to teach others also. 3Take
your share of suffering as a good soldier
of Christ Jesus. 4No soldier on service
gets entangled in civilian pursuits, since
his aim is to satisfy the one who enlisted
him. 5An athlete is not crowned unless
he competes according to the rules. 6It is
the hard-working farmer who ought to
have the first share of the crops. 7Think
over what I say, for the Lord will grant
you understanding in everything.
8 Remember Jesus Christ, risen from
the dead, descended from David, as
preached in my gospel, 9the gospel for
which I am suffering and wearing fet-
ters like a criminal. But the word of God
is not fettered. 10Therefore I endure ev-
erything for the sake of the elect, that
they also may obtain the salvation which
in Christ Jesus goes with eternal glory.
11The saying is sure:

If we have died with him, we shall
also live with him;

[a] **1.12** Or *what I have entrusted to him*

12 if we endure, we shall also reign
with him;
if we deny him, he also will deny us;
13 if we are faithless, he remains
faithful—
for he cannot deny himself.

A Worker Approved by God

14 Remind them of this, and charge them
before the Lord[b] to avoid disputing about
words, which does no good, but only ru-
ins the hearers. 15 Do your best to present
yourself to God as one approved, a work-
man who has no need to be ashamed,
rightly handling the word of truth.
16 Avoid such godless chatter, for it will
lead people into more and more ungodli-
ness, 17 and their talk will eat its way like
gangrene. Among them are Hymenae'us
and Phile'tus, 18 who have swerved from
the truth by holding that the resurrec-
tion is past already. They are upsetting
the faith of some. 19 But God's firm foun-
dation stands, bearing this seal: "The
Lord knows those who are his," and, "Let
every one who names the name of the
Lord depart from iniquity."

20 In a great house there are not only
vessels of gold and silver but also of
wood and earthenware, and some for
noble use, some for ignoble. 21 If any one
purifies himself from what is ignoble,
then he will be a vessel for noble use,
consecrated and useful to the master of
the house, ready for any good work. 22 So
shun youthful passions and aim at righ-
teousness, faith, love, and peace, along
with those who call upon the Lord from
a pure heart. 23 Have nothing to do with
stupid, senseless controversies; you
know that they breed quarrels. 24 And the
Lord's servant must not be quarrelsome
but kindly to every one, an apt teacher,
forbearing, 25 correcting his opponents
with gentleness. God may perhaps grant
that they will repent and come to know
the truth, 26 and they may escape from
the snare of the devil, after being cap-
tured by him to do his will.[c]

Godlessness in the Last Days

3 But understand this, that in the last
days there will come times of stress.
2 For men will be lovers of self, lovers of
money, proud, arrogant, abusive, dis-
obedient to their parents, ungrateful,
unholy, 3 inhuman, implacable, slander-
ers, profligates, fierce, haters of good,
4 treacherous, reckless, swollen with
conceit, lovers of pleasure rather than
lovers of God, 5 holding the form of reli-
gion but denying the power of it. Avoid
such people. 6 For among them are those
who make their way into households and
capture weak women, burdened with
sins and swayed by various impulses,
7 who will listen to anybody and can
never arrive at a knowledge of the truth.
8 As Jannes and Jambres opposed Moses,
so these men also oppose the truth, men
of corrupt mind and counterfeit faith;
9 but they will not get very far, for their
folly will be plain to all, as was that of
those two men.

Paul's Charge to Timothy

10 Now you have observed my teaching,
my conduct, my aim in life, my faith,
my patience, my love, my steadfastness,
11 my persecutions, my sufferings, what
befell me at Antioch, at Ico'nium, and at
Lystra, what persecutions I endured; yet
from them all the Lord rescued me. 12 In-
deed all who desire to live a godly life in
Christ Jesus will be persecuted, 13 while
evil men and impostors will go on from
bad to worse, deceivers and deceived.
14 But as for you, continue in what you
have learned and have firmly believed,
knowing from whom you learned it
15 and how from childhood you have been
acquainted with the sacred writings
which are able to instruct you for salva-
tion through faith in Christ Jesus. 16 All

[b] **2.14** Other ancient authorities read *God*

[c] **2.26** Or *by him, to do his* (that is, God's) *will*

scripture is inspired by God and[d] profit-
able for teaching, for reproof, for correc-
tion, and for training in righteousness,
[17]that the man of God may be complete,
equipped for every good work.

4 I charge you in the presence of God
and of Christ Jesus who is to judge the
living and the dead, and by his appear-
ing and his kingdom: [2]preach the word,
be urgent in season and out of season,
convince, rebuke, and exhort, be unfail-
ing in patience and in teaching. [3]For the
time is coming when people will not en-
dure sound teaching, but having itching
ears they will accumulate for themselves
teachers to suit their own likings, [4]and
will turn away from listening to the truth
and wander into myths. [5]As for you, al-
ways be steady, endure suffering, do the
work of an evangelist, fulfil your ministry.

6 For I am already on the point of be-
ing sacrificed; the time of my departure
has come. [7]I have fought the good fight,
I have finished the race, I have kept the
faith. [8]Henceforth there is laid up for me
the crown of righteousness, which the
Lord, the righteous judge, will award to
me on that Day, and not only to me but
also to all who have loved his appearing.

Personal Instructions

9 Do your best to come to me soon. [10]For
Demas, in love with this present world,
has deserted me and gone to Thessa-
loni′ca; Crescens has gone to Galatia,[e] Ti-
tus to Dalmatia. [11]Luke alone is with me.
Get Mark and bring him with you; for he
is very useful in serving me. [12]Tych′icus I
have sent to Ephesus. [13]When you come,
bring the cloak that I left with Carpus at
Tro′as, also the books, and above all the
parchments. [14]Alexander the copper-
smith did me great harm; the Lord will
requite him for his deeds. [15]Beware of
him yourself, for he strongly opposed
our message. [16]At my first defense no one
took my part; all deserted me. May it not
be charged against them! [17]But the Lord
stood by me and gave me strength to pro-
claim the word fully, that all the Gentiles
might hear it. So I was rescued from the
lion's mouth. [18]The Lord will rescue me
from every evil and save me for his heav-
enly kingdom. To him be the glory for
ever and ever. Amen.

Final Greetings and Benediction

19 Greet Prisca and Aq′uila, and the
household of Onesiph′orus. [20]Eras′tus
remained at Corinth; Troph′imus I left ill
at Mile′tus. [21]Do your best to come before
winter. Eubu′lus sends greetings to you,
as do Pudens and Linus and Claudia and
all the brethren.

22 The Lord be with your spirit. Grace
be with you.

[d] **3.16** Or *Every scripture inspired by God is also*

[e] **4.10** Other ancient authorities read *Gaul*

The Letter of Paul to

TITUS

Salutation

1 Paul, a servant[a] of God and an apostle
of Jesus Christ, to further the faith
of God's elect and their knowledge of
the truth which accords with godliness,
2 in hope of eternal life which God, who
never lies, promised ages ago 3 and at
the proper time manifested in his word
through the preaching with which I have
been entrusted by command of God our
Savior;

4 To Titus, my true child in a common
faith:

Grace and peace from God the Father
and Christ Jesus our Savior.

Titus in Crete

5 This is why I left you in Crete, that you
might amend what was defective, and ap-
point elders in every town as I directed
you, 6 if any man is blameless, the hus-
band of one wife, and his children are
believers and not open to the charge of
being profligate or insubordinate. 7 For a
bishop, as God's steward, must be blame-
less; he must not be arrogant or quick-
tempered or a drunkard or violent or
greedy for gain, 8 but hospitable, a lover
of goodness, master of himself, upright,
holy, and self-controlled; 9 he must hold
firm to the sure word as taught, so that
he may be able to give instruction in
sound doctrine and also to confute those
who contradict it. 10 For there are many
insubordinate men, empty talkers and
deceivers, especially the circumcision
party; 11 they must be silenced, since they
are upsetting whole families by teaching
for base gain what they have no right to
teach. 12 One of themselves, a prophet of
their own, said, "Cretans are always li-
ars, evil beasts, lazy gluttons." 13 This tes-
timony is true. Therefore rebuke them
sharply, that they may be sound in the
faith, 14 instead of giving heed to Jewish
myths or to commands of men who re-
ject the truth. 15 To the pure all things are
pure, but to the corrupt and unbelieving
nothing is pure; their very minds and
consciences are corrupted. 16 They pro-
fess to know God, but they deny him by
their deeds; they are detestable, disobe-
dient, unfit for any good deed.

Teach Sound Doctrine

2 But as for you, teach what befits
sound doctrine. 2 Bid the older men
be temperate, serious, sensible, sound in
faith, in love, and in steadfastness. 3 Bid
the older women likewise to be rever-
ent in behavior, not to be slanderers or
slaves to drink; they are to teach what is
good, 4 and so train the young women to
love their husbands and children, 5 to be
sensible, chaste, domestic, kind, and sub-
missive to their husbands, that the word
of God may not be discredited. 6 Likewise
urge the younger men to control them-
selves. 7 Show yourself in all respects a
model of good deeds, and in your teach-
ing show integrity, gravity, 8 and sound
speech that cannot be censured, so that
an opponent may be put to shame, hav-
ing nothing evil to say of us. 9 Bid slaves
to be submissive to their masters and to
give satisfaction in every respect; they
are not to be refractory, 10 nor to pilfer,
but to show entire and true fidelity, so
that in everything they may adorn the
doctrine of God our Savior.

11 For the grace of God has appeared
for the salvation of all men, 12 training
us to renounce irreligion and worldly
passions, and to live sober, upright,
and godly lives in this world, 13 awaiting
our blessed hope, the appearing of the

[a] **1.1** Or *slave*

glory of our great God and Savior[b] Jesus
Christ, [14]who gave himself for us to re-
deem us from all iniquity and to purify
for himself a people of his own who are
zealous for good deeds.
15 Declare these things; exhort and re-
prove with all authority. Let no one dis-
regard you.

Maintain Good Deeds

3 Remind them to be submissive to
rulers and authorities, to be obedi-
ent, to be ready for any honest work,
[2]to speak evil of no one, to avoid quar-
reling, to be gentle, and to show perfect
courtesy toward all men. [3]For we our-
selves were once foolish, disobedient,
led astray, slaves to various passions
and pleasures, passing our days in mal-
ice and envy, hated by men and hating
one another; [4]but when the goodness
and loving kindness of God our Savior
appeared, [5]he saved us, not because of
deeds done by us in righteousness, but
in virtue of his own mercy, by the wash-
ing of regeneration and renewal in the
Holy Spirit, [6]which he poured out upon
us richly through Jesus Christ our Sav-
ior, [7]so that we might be justified by his
grace and become heirs in hope of eter-
nal life. [8]The saying is sure.
I desire you to insist on these things,
so that those who have believed in God
may be careful to apply themselves to
good deeds;[c] these are excellent and prof-
itable to men. [9]But avoid stupid contro-
versies, genealogies, dissensions, and
quarrels over the law, for they are un-
profitable and futile. [10]As for a man who
is factious, after admonishing him once
or twice, have nothing more to do with
him, [11]knowing that such a person is per-
verted and sinful; he is self-condemned.

Final Messages and Benediction

12 When I send Ar′temas or Tych′icus
to you, do your best to come to me at
Nicop′olis, for I have decided to spend
the winter there. [13]Do your best to speed
Zenas the lawyer and Apol′los on their
way; see that they lack nothing. [14]And let
our people learn to apply themselves to
good deeds,[d] so as to help cases of urgent
need, and not to be unfruitful.
15 All who are with me send greetings
to you. Greet those who love us in the
faith.

Grace be with you all.

[b] **2.13** Or *of the great God and our Savior* [c] **3.8** Or *enter honorable occupations* [d] **3.14** Or *enter honorable occupations*

The Letter of Paul to

PHILEMON

Salutation

1 Paul, a prisoner for Christ Jesus, and
Timothy our brother,
To Phile'mon our beloved fellow
worker [2]and Apph'ia our sister and
Archip'pus our fellow soldier, and the
church in your house:
3 Grace to you and peace from God our
Father and the Lord Jesus Christ.

Philemon's Love and Faith

4 I thank my God always when I remem-
ber you in my prayers, [5]because I hear of
your love and of the faith which you have
toward the Lord Jesus and all the saints,
[6]and I pray that the sharing of your faith
may promote the knowledge of all the
good that is ours in Christ. [7]For I have de-
rived much joy and comfort from your
love, my brother, because the hearts of
the saints have been refreshed through
you.

Paul's Plea for Onesimus

8 Accordingly, though I am bold enough
in Christ to command you to do what is
required, [9]yet for love's sake I prefer
to appeal to you—I, Paul, an ambassa-
dor[a] and now a prisoner also for Christ
Jesus— [10]I appeal to you for my child,
One'simus, whose father I have become
in my imprisonment. [11](Formerly he was
useless to you, but now he is indeed use-
ful[b] to you and to me.) [12]I am sending him
back to you, sending my very heart. [13]I
would have been glad to keep him with
me, in order that he might serve me on
your behalf during my imprisonment
for the gospel; [14]but I preferred to do
nothing without your consent in order
that your goodness might not be by com-
pulsion but of your own free will.
15 Perhaps this is why he was parted
from you for a while, that you might
have him back for ever, [16]no longer as a
slave but more than a slave, as a beloved
brother, especially to me but how much
more to you, both in the flesh and in the
Lord. [17]So if you consider me your part-
ner, receive him as you would receive
me. [18]If he has wronged you at all, or
owes you anything, charge that to my
account. [19]I, Paul, write this with my
own hand, I will repay it—to say noth-
ing of your owing me even your own
self. [20]Yes, brother, I want some benefit
from you in the Lord. Refresh my heart
in Christ.
21 Confident of your obedience, I write
to you, knowing that you will do even
more than I say. [22]At the same time, pre-
pare a guest room for me, for I am hop-
ing through your prayers to be granted
to you.

Final Greetings and Benediction

23 Ep'aphras, my fellow prisoner in
Christ Jesus, sends greetings to you,
[24]and so do Mark, Aristar'chus, Demas,
and Luke, my fellow workers.
25 The grace of the Lord Jesus Christ
be with your spirit.

[a] **1.9** Or *an old man*
[b] **1.11** The name Onesimus means *useful* or (compare verse 20) *beneficial*

The Letter to the

HEBREWS

God Has Spoken by His Son

1 In many and various ways God spoke
of old to our fathers by the prophets;
2but in these last days he has spoken to us
by a Son, whom he appointed the heir of
all things, through whom also he created
the world. 3He reflects the glory of God
and bears the very stamp of his nature,
upholding the universe by his word of
power. When he had made purification
for sins, he sat down at the right hand
of the Majesty on high, 4having become
as much superior to angels as the name
he has obtained is more excellent than
theirs.

The Son Is Superior to Angels

5 For to what angel did God ever say,
"Thou art my Son,
today I have begotten thee"?
Or again,
"I will be to him a father,
and he shall be to me a son"?
6And again, when he brings the first-
born into the world, he says,
"Let all God's angels worship
him."
7Of the angels he says,
"Who makes his angels winds,
and his servants flames of fire."
8But of the Son he says,
"Thy throne, O God,[a] is for ever and
ever,
the righteous scepter is the scepter
of thy[b] kingdom.
9 Thou hast loved righteousness and
hated lawlessness;
therefore God, thy God, has
anointed thee
with the oil of gladness beyond thy
comrades."
10And,
"Thou, Lord, didst found the earth
in the beginning,
and the heavens are the work of thy
hands;
11 they will perish, but thou remainest;
they will all grow old like a garment,
12 like a mantle thou wilt roll them up,
and they will be changed.[c]
But thou art the same,
and thy years will never end."
13 But to what angel has he ever said,
"Sit at my right hand,
till I make thy enemies
a stool for thy feet"?
14Are they not all ministering spirits
sent forth to serve, for the sake of those
who are to obtain salvation?

Warning to Pay Attention

2 Therefore we must pay the closer at-
tention to what we have heard, lest
we drift away from it. 2For if the message
declared by angels was valid and every
transgression or disobedience received
a just retribution, 3how shall we escape if
we neglect such a great salvation? It was
declared at first by the Lord, and it was
attested to us by those who heard him,
4while God also bore witness by signs
and wonders and various miracles and
by gifts of the Holy Spirit distributed ac-
cording to his own will.

Exaltation through Abasement

5 For it was not to angels that God sub-
jected the world to come, of which we
are speaking. 6It has been testified
somewhere,
"What is man that thou art mindful
of him,
or the son of man, that thou carest
for him?

[a]**1.8** Or *God is thy throne* [b]**1.8** Other ancient authorities read *his* [c]**1.12** Other ancient authorities add *like a garment*

7 Thou didst make him for a little
while lower than the angels,
thou hast crowned him with glory
and honor,[d]
8 putting everything in subjection
under his feet."
Now in putting everything in subjection
to him, he left nothing outside his con-
trol. As it is, we do not yet see everything
in subjection to him. 9But we see Jesus,
who for a little while was made lower
than the angels, crowned with glory and
honor because of the suffering of death,
so that by the grace of God he might taste
death for every one.
10 For it was fitting that he, for whom
and by whom all things exist, in bringing
many sons to glory, should make the pi-
oneer of their salvation perfect through
suffering. 11For he who sanctifies and
those who are sanctified have all one ori-
gin. That is why he is not ashamed to call
them brethren, 12saying,
"I will proclaim thy name to my
brethren,
in the midst of the congregation I
will praise thee."
13And again,
"I will put my trust in him."
And again,
"Here am I, and the children God has
given me."
14 Since therefore the children share
in flesh and blood, he himself likewise
partook of the same nature, that through
death he might destroy him who has the
power of death, that is, the devil, 15and
deliver all those who through fear of
death were subject to lifelong bondage.
16For surely it is not with angels that he
is concerned but with the descendants of
Abraham. 17Therefore he had to be made
like his brethren in every respect, so that
he might become a merciful and faithful
high priest in the service of God, to make
expiation for the sins of the people. 18For
because he himself has suffered and
been tempted, he is able to help those
who are tempted.

Moses a Servant, Christ a Son

3 Therefore, holy brethren, who share
in a heavenly call, consider Jesus,
the apostle and high priest of our con-
fession. 2He was faithful to him who
appointed him, just as Moses also was
faithful in[e] God's house. 3Yet Jesus has
been counted worthy of as much more
glory than Moses as the builder of a
house has more honor than the house.
4(For every house is built by some one,
but the builder of all things is God.) 5Now
Moses was faithful in all God's house as
a servant, to testify to the things that
were to be spoken later, 6but Christ was
faithful over God's[f] house as a son. And
we are his house if we hold fast our con-
fidence and pride in our hope.[g]

Warning against Unbelief

7 Therefore, as the Holy Spirit says,
"Today, when you hear his voice,
8 do not harden your hearts as in the
rebellion,
on the day of testing in the
wilderness,
9 where your fathers put me to the
test
and saw my works for forty years.
10 Therefore I was provoked with that
generation,
and said, 'They always go astray in
their hearts;
they have not known my ways.'
11 As I swore in my wrath,
'They shall never enter my rest.'"
12Take care, brethren, lest there be in
any of you an evil, unbelieving heart,
leading you to fall away from the living
God. 13But exhort one another every day,

[d] **2.7** Other ancient authorities insert *and didst set him over the works of thy hands* [e] **3.2** Other ancient authorities insert *all* [f] **3.6** Greek *his* [g] **3.6** Other ancient authorities insert *firm to the end*

as long as it is called "today," that none of
you may be hardened by the deceitful-
ness of sin. 14 For we share in Christ, if
only we hold our first confidence firm to
the end, 15 while it is said,

"Today, when you hear his voice,
do not harden your hearts as in the
rebellion."

16 Who were they that heard and yet were
rebellious? Was it not all those who left
Egypt under the leadership of Moses?
17 And with whom was he provoked forty
years? Was it not with those who sinned,
whose bodies fell in the wilderness?
18 And to whom did he swear that they
should never enter his rest, but to those
who were disobedient? 19 So we see that
they were unable to enter because of
unbelief.

The Rest That God Promised

4 Therefore, while the promise of en-
tering his rest remains, let us fear
lest any of you be judged to have failed to
reach it. 2 For good news came to us just
as to them; but the message which they
heard did not benefit them, because it
did not meet with faith in the hearers.[h]
3 For we who have believed enter that
rest, as he has said,

"As I swore in my wrath,
'They shall never enter my
rest,'"

although his works were finished from
the foundation of the world. 4 For he has
somewhere spoken of the seventh day in
this way, "And God rested on the seventh
day from all his works." 5 And again in
this place he said,

"They shall never enter my rest."

6 Since therefore it remains for some
to enter it, and those who formerly re-
ceived the good news failed to enter
because of disobedience, 7 again he sets
a certain day, "Today," saying through
David so long afterward, in the words al-
ready quoted,

"Today, when you hear his voice,
do not harden your hearts."

8 For if Joshua had given them rest, God[i]
would not speak later of another day. 9 So
then, there remains a sabbath rest for
the people of God; 10 for whoever enters
God's rest also ceases from his labors as
God did from his.

11 Let us therefore strive to enter that
rest, that no one fall by the same sort of
disobedience. 12 For the word of God is
living and active, sharper than any two-
edged sword, piercing to the division of
soul and spirit, of joints and marrow,
and discerning the thoughts and inten-
tions of the heart. 13 And before him no
creature is hidden, but all are open and
laid bare to the eyes of him with whom
we have to do.

Jesus the Great High Priest

14 Since then we have a great high
priest who has passed through the
heavens, Jesus, the Son of God, let us
hold fast our confession. 15 For we have
not a high priest who is unable to sym-
pathize with our weaknesses, but one
who in every respect has been tempted
as we are, yet without sinning. 16 Let us
then with confidence draw near to the
throne of grace, that we may receive
mercy and find grace to help in time of
need.

5 For every high priest chosen from
among men is appointed to act on
behalf of men in relation to God, to offer
gifts and sacrifices for sins. 2 He can deal
gently with the ignorant and wayward,
since he himself is beset with weakness.
3 Because of this he is bound to offer sac-
rifice for his own sins as well as for those
of the people. 4 And one does not take the
honor upon himself, but he is called by
God, just as Aaron was.

5 So also Christ did not exalt himself to
be made a high priest, but was appointed
by him who said to him,

[h] **4.2** Other manuscripts read *they were not united in faith with the hearers*

[i] **4.8** Greek *he*

"Thou art my Son,
today I have begotten thee";
[6]as he says also in another place,
"Thou art a priest for ever,
after the order of Melchiz'edek."
7 In the days of his flesh, Jesus[j] offered
up prayers and supplications, with loud
cries and tears, to him who was able to
save him from death, and he was heard
for his godly fear. [8]Although he was a
Son, he learned obedience through what
he suffered; [9]and being made perfect he
became the source of eternal salvation
to all who obey him, [10]being designated
by God a high priest after the order of
Melchiz'edek.

Warning against Falling Away

11 About this we have much to say which
is hard to explain, since you have be-
come dull of hearing. [12]For though by
this time you ought to be teachers, you
need some one to teach you again the
first principles of God's word. You need
milk, not solid food; [13]for every one who
lives on milk is unskilled in the word
of righteousness, for he is a child. [14]But
solid food is for the mature, for those
who have their faculties trained by prac-
tice to distinguish good from evil.

The Peril of Falling Away

6 Therefore let us leave the elemen-
tary doctrines of Christ and go on to
maturity, not laying again a foundation
of repentance from dead works and of
faith toward God, [2]with instruction[k]
about ablutions, the laying on of hands,
the resurrection of the dead, and eter-
nal judgment. [3]And this we will do if
God permits.[l] [4]For it is impossible to
restore again to repentance those who
have once been enlightened, who have
tasted the heavenly gift, and have be-
come partakers of the Holy Spirit, [5]and
have tasted the goodness of the word of
God and the powers of the age to come,
[6]if they then commit apostasy, since they
crucify the Son of God on their own ac-
count and hold him up to contempt. [7]For
land which has drunk the rain that often
falls upon it, and brings forth vegetation
useful to those for whose sake it is culti-
vated, receives a blessing from God. [8]But
if it bears thorns and thistles, it is worth-
less and near to being cursed; its end is
to be burned.
9 Though we speak thus, yet in your
case, beloved, we feel sure of better
things that belong to salvation. [10]For God
is not so unjust as to overlook your work
and the love which you showed for his
sake in serving the saints, as you still do.
[11]And we desire each one of you to show
the same earnestness in realizing the
full assurance of hope until the end, [12]so
that you may not be sluggish, but imita-
tors of those who through faith and pa-
tience inherit the promises.

The Certainty of God's Promise

13 For when God made a promise to
Abraham, since he had no one greater
by whom to swear, he swore by himself,
[14]saying, "Surely I will bless you and mul-
tiply you." [15]And thus Abraham,[m] having
patiently endured, obtained the prom-
ise. [16]Men indeed swear by a greater than
themselves, and in all their disputes an
oath is final for confirmation. [17]So when
God desired to show more convincingly
to the heirs of the promise the unchange-
able character of his purpose, he inter-
posed with an oath, [18]so that through
two unchangeable things, in which it is
impossible that God should prove false,
we who have fled for refuge might have
strong encouragement to seize the hope
set before us. [19]We have this as a sure
and steadfast anchor of the soul, a hope
that enters into the inner shrine behind
the curtain, [20]where Jesus has gone as a

[j] **5.7** Greek *he* [k] **6.2** Other ancient manuscripts read *of instruction* [l] **6.3** Other ancient manuscripts read *let us do this if God permits* [m] **6.15** Greek *he*

forerunner on our behalf, having be-
come a high priest for ever after the or-
der of Melchiz′edek.

The Priestly Order of Melchizedek

7 For this Melchiz′edek, king of Salem,
priest of the Most High God, met
Abraham returning from the slaughter
of the kings and blessed him; [2]and to him
Abraham apportioned a tenth part of ev-
erything. He is first, by translation of his
name, king of righteousness, and then
he is also king of Salem, that is, king of
peace. [3]He is without father or mother
or genealogy, and has neither beginning
of days nor end of life, but resembling
the Son of God he continues a priest for
ever.

4 See how great he is! Abraham the
patriarch gave him a tithe of the spoils.
[5]And those descendants of Levi who
receive the priestly office have a com-
mandment in the law to take tithes from
the people, that is, from their brethren,
though these also are descended from
Abraham. [6]But this man who has not
their genealogy received tithes from
Abraham and blessed him who had the
promises. [7]It is beyond dispute that
the inferior is blessed by the superior.
[8]Here tithes are received by mortal men;
there, by one of whom it is testified that
he lives. [9]One might even say that Levi
himself, who receives tithes, paid tithes
through Abraham, [10]for he was still in
the loins of his ancestor when Melchiz′e-
dek met him.

Another Priest, Like Melchizedek

11 Now if perfection had been attainable
through the Levit′ical priesthood (for un-
der it the people received the law), what
further need would there have been for
another priest to arise after the order of
Melchiz′edek, rather than one named af-
ter the order of Aaron? [12]For when there
is a change in the priesthood, there is
necessarily a change in the law as well.
[13]For the one of whom these things are
spoken belonged to another tribe, from
which no one has ever served at the altar.
[14]For it is evident that our Lord was de-
scended from Judah, and in connection
with that tribe Moses said nothing about
priests.

15 This becomes even more evident
when another priest arises in the like-
ness of Melchiz′edek, [16]who has become
a priest, not according to a legal require-
ment concerning bodily descent but by
the power of an indestructible life. [17]For
it is witnessed of him,

> "Thou art a priest for ever,
> after the order of Melchiz′edek."

[18]On the one hand, a former command-
ment is set aside because of its weakness
and uselessness [19](for the law made noth-
ing perfect); on the other hand, a better
hope is introduced, through which we
draw near to God.

20 And it was not without an oath.
[21]Those who formerly became priests
took their office without an oath, but this
one was addressed with an oath,

> "The Lord has sworn
> and will not change his mind,
> 'Thou art a priest for ever.'"

[22]This makes Jesus the surety of a better
covenant.

23 The former priests were many in
number, because they were prevented
by death from continuing in office; [24]but
he holds his priesthood permanently,
because he continues for ever. [25]Con-
sequently he is able for all time to save
those who draw near to God through
him, since he always lives to make inter-
cession for them.

26 For it was fitting that we should
have such a high priest, holy, blameless,
unstained, separated from sinners, ex-
alted above the heavens. [27]He has no
need, like those high priests, to offer
sacrifices daily, first for his own sins and
then for those of the people; he did this
once for all when he offered up himself.

[28]Indeed, the law appoints men in their weakness as high priests, but the word of the oath, which came later than the law, appoints a Son who has been made perfect for ever.

Mediator of a Better Covenant

8 Now the point in what we are saying is this: we have such a high priest, one who is seated at the right hand of the throne of the Majesty in heaven, [2]a minister in the sanctuary and the true tent[n] which is set up not by man but by the Lord. [3]For every high priest is appointed to offer gifts and sacrifices; hence it is necessary for this priest also to have something to offer. [4]Now if he were on earth, he would not be a priest at all, since there are priests who offer gifts according to the law. [5]They serve a copy and shadow of the heavenly sanctuary; for when Moses was about to erect the tent,[o] he was instructed by God, saying, "See that you make everything according to the pattern which was shown you on the mountain." [6]But as it is, Christ[p] has obtained a ministry which is as much more excellent than the old as the covenant he mediates is better, since it is enacted on better promises. [7]For if that first covenant had been faultless, there would have been no occasion for a second.

8 For he finds fault with them when he says:

"The days will come, says the Lord,
when I will establish a new
covenant with the house of
Israel
and with the house of Judah;
9 not like the covenant that I made
with their fathers
on the day when I took them by the
hand
to lead them out of the land of
Egypt;
for they did not continue in my
covenant,
and so I paid no heed to them, says
the Lord.
10 This is the covenant that I will make
with the house of Israel
after those days, says the Lord:
I will put my laws into their
minds,
and write them on their hearts,
and I will be their God,
and they shall be my people.
11 And they shall not teach every one
his fellow
or every one his brother, saying,
'Know the Lord,'
for all shall know me,
from the least of them to the
greatest.
12 For I will be merciful toward their
iniquities,
and I will remember their sins no
more."

[13]In speaking of a new covenant he treats the first as obsolete. And what is becoming obsolete and growing old is ready to vanish away.

The Earthly and the Heavenly Sanctuaries

9 Now even the first covenant had regulations for worship and an earthly sanctuary. [2]For a tent[q] was prepared, the outer one, in which were the lampstand and the table and the bread of the Presence;[r] it is called the Holy Place. [3]Behind the second curtain stood a tent[s] called the Holy of Holies, [4]having the golden altar of incense and the ark of the covenant covered on all sides with gold, which contained a golden urn holding the manna, and Aaron's rod that budded, and the tables of the covenant; [5]above it were the cherubim of glory overshadowing the mercy seat. Of these things we cannot now speak in detail.

[n]**8.2** Or *tabernacle* [o]**8.5** Or *tabernacle* [p]**8.6** Greek *he* [q]**9.2** Or *tabernacle*
[r]**9.2** Greek *the presentation of the loaves* [s]**9.3** Or *tabernacle*

6 These preparations having thus been
made, the priests go continually into the
outer tent,[t] performing their ritual du-
ties; 7but into the second only the high
priest goes, and he but once a year, and
not without taking blood which he of-
fers for himself and for the errors of the
people. 8By this the Holy Spirit indicates
that the way into the sanctuary is not
yet opened as long as the outer tent[u] is
still standing 9(which is symbolic for the
present age). According to this arrange-
ment, gifts and sacrifices are offered
which cannot perfect the conscience of
the worshiper, 10but deal only with food
and drink and various ablutions, regula-
tions for the body imposed until the time
of reformation.

11 But when Christ appeared as a high
priest of the good things that have come,[v]
then through the greater and more per-
fect tent[w] (not made with hands, that is,
not of this creation) 12he entered once
for all into the Holy Place, taking[x] not
the blood of goats and calves but his own
blood, thus securing an eternal redemp-
tion. 13For if the sprinkling of defiled
persons with the blood of goats and bulls
and with the ashes of a heifer sanctifies
for the purification of the flesh, 14how
much more shall the blood of Christ,
who through the eternal Spirit offered
himself without blemish to God, purify
your[y] conscience from dead works to
serve the living God.

15 Therefore he is the mediator of a
new covenant, so that those who are
called may receive the promised eternal
inheritance, since a death has occurred
which redeems them from the transgres-
sions under the first covenant.[z] 16For
where a will[a] is involved, the death of
the one who made it must be established.
17For a will[b] takes effect only at death,
since it is not in force as long as the one
who made it is alive. 18Hence even the
first covenant was not ratified without
blood. 19For when every commandment
of the law had been declared by Moses
to all the people, he took the blood of
calves and goats, with water and scarlet
wool and hyssop, and sprinkled both the
book itself and all the people, 20saying,
"This is the blood of the covenant which
God commanded you." 21And in the same
way he sprinkled with the blood both the
tent[c] and all the vessels used in worship.
22Indeed, under the law almost every-
thing is purified with blood, and without
the shedding of blood there is no forgive-
ness of sins.

Christ's Sacrifice Takes Away Sin

23 Thus it was necessary for the cop-
ies of the heavenly things to be puri-
fied with these rites, but the heavenly
things themselves with better sacrifices
than these. 24For Christ has entered,
not into a sanctuary made with hands,
a copy of the true one, but into heaven
itself, now to appear in the presence of
God on our behalf. 25Nor was it to offer
himself repeatedly, as the high priest
enters the Holy Place yearly with blood
not his own; 26for then he would have
had to suffer repeatedly since the foun-
dation of the world. But as it is, he has
appeared once for all at the end of the
age to put away sin by the sacrifice of
himself. 27And just as it is appointed for
men to die once, and after that comes
judgment, 28so Christ, having been of-
fered once to bear the sins of many, will
appear a second time, not to deal with
sin but to save those who are eagerly
waiting for him.

[t]**9.6** Or *tabernacle* [u]**9.8** Or *tabernacle* [v]**9.11** Other manuscripts read *good things to come*
[w]**9.11** Or *tabernacle* [x]**9.12** Greek *through* [y]**9.14** Other manuscripts read *our*
[z]**9.15** The Greek word here used means both *covenant* and *will* [a]**9.16** The Greek word here used means both *covenant* and *will* [b]**9.17** The Greek word here used means both *covenant* and *will*
[c]**9.21** Or *tabernacle*

Christ's Sacrifice Once for All

10 For since the law has but a shadow
of the good things to come instead
of the true form of these realities, it
can never, by the same sacrifices which
are continually offered year after year,
make perfect those who draw near.
2 Otherwise, would they not have ceased
to be offered? If the worshipers had
once been cleansed, they would no lon-
ger have any consciousness of sin. 3 But
in these sacrifices there is a reminder of
sin year after year. 4 For it is impossible
that the blood of bulls and goats should
take away sins.

5 Consequently, when Christ[d] came
into the world, he said,

"Sacrifices and offerings thou hast
not desired,
but a body hast thou prepared for
me;
6 in burnt offerings and sin offerings
thou hast taken no pleasure.
7 Then I said, 'Lo, I have come to do
thy will, O God,'
as it is written of me in the roll of
the book."

8 When he said above, "Thou hast neither
desired nor taken pleasure in sacrifices
and offerings and burnt offerings and
sin offerings" (these are offered accord-
ing to the law), 9 then he added, "Lo, I
have come to do thy will." He abolishes
the first in order to establish the second.
10 And by that will we have been sancti-
fied through the offering of the body of
Jesus Christ once for all.

11 And every priest stands daily at his
service, offering repeatedly the same
sacrifices, which can never take away
sins. 12 But when Christ[e] had offered for
all time a single sacrifice for sins, he sat
down at the right hand of God, 13 then to
wait until his enemies should be made
a stool for his feet. 14 For by a single of-
fering he has perfected for all time
those who are sanctified. 15 And the Holy
Spirit also bears witness to us; for after
saying,

16 "This is the covenant that I will
make with them
after those days, says the Lord:
I will put my laws on their hearts,
and write them on their minds,"
17 then he adds,
"I will remember their sins and
their misdeeds no more."
18 Where there is forgiveness of these,
there is no longer any offering for sin.

A Call to Persevere

19 Therefore, brethren, since we have
confidence to enter the sanctuary by the
blood of Jesus, 20 by the new and living
way which he opened for us through the
curtain, that is, through his flesh, 21 and
since we have a great priest over the
house of God, 22 let us draw near with a
true heart in full assurance of faith, with
our hearts sprinkled clean from an evil
conscience and our bodies washed with
pure water. 23 Let us hold fast the confes-
sion of our hope without wavering, for
he who promised is faithful; 24 and let us
consider how to stir up one another to
love and good works, 25 not neglecting
to meet together, as is the habit of some,
but encouraging one another, and all the
more as you see the Day drawing near.

26 For if we sin deliberately after re-
ceiving the knowledge of the truth, there
no longer remains a sacrifice for sins,
27 but a fearful prospect of judgment, and
a fury of fire which will consume the
adversaries. 28 A man who has violated
the law of Moses dies without mercy at
the testimony of two or three witnesses.
29 How much worse punishment do you
think will be deserved by the man who
has spurned the Son of God, and pro-
faned the blood of the covenant by which
he was sanctified, and outraged the
Spirit of grace? 30 For we know him who
said, "Vengeance is mine, I will repay."

[d] **10.5** Greek *he* [e] **10.12** Greek *this one*

And again, "The Lord will judge his peo-
ple." 31 It is a fearful thing to fall into the
hands of the living God.

32 But recall the former days when, af-
ter you were enlightened, you endured
a hard struggle with sufferings, 33 some-
times being publicly exposed to abuse
and affliction, and sometimes being
partners with those so treated. 34 For you
had compassion on the prisoners, and
you joyfully accepted the plundering of
your property, since you knew that you
yourselves had a better possession and
an abiding one. 35 Therefore do not throw
away your confidence, which has a great
reward. 36 For you have need of endur-
ance, so that you may do the will of God
and receive what is promised.

37 "For yet a little while,
and the coming one shall come and
shall not tarry;
38 but my righteous one shall live by
faith,
and if he shrinks back,
my soul has no pleasure in him."

39 But we are not of those who shrink
back and are destroyed, but of those who
have faith and keep their souls.

The Meaning of Faith

11 Now faith is the assurance of things
hoped for, the conviction of things
not seen. 2 For by it the men of old re-
ceived divine approval. 3 By faith we un-
derstand that the world was created by
the word of God, so that what is seen was
made out of things which do not appear.

The Examples of Abel, Enoch, and Noah

4 By faith Abel offered to God a more
acceptable sacrifice than Cain, through
which he received approval as righ-
teous, God bearing witness by accepting
his gifts; he died, but through his faith
he is still speaking. 5 By faith Enoch was
taken up so that he should not see death;
and he was not found, because God had
taken him. Now before he was taken he
was attested as having pleased God. 6 And
without faith it is impossible to please
him. For whoever would draw near to
God must believe that he exists and that
he rewards those who seek him. 7 By faith
Noah, being warned by God concern-
ing events as yet unseen, took heed and
constructed an ark for the saving of his
household; by this he condemned the
world and became an heir of the righ-
teousness which comes by faith.

The Faith of Abraham

8 By faith Abraham obeyed when he
was called to go out to a place which he
was to receive as an inheritance; and he
went out, not knowing where he was to
go. 9 By faith he sojourned in the land of
promise, as in a foreign land, living in
tents with Isaac and Jacob, heirs with
him of the same promise. 10 For he looked
forward to the city which has founda-
tions, whose builder and maker is God.
11 By faith Sarah herself received power
to conceive, even when she was past the
age, since she considered him faithful
who had promised. 12 Therefore from
one man, and him as good as dead, were
born descendants as many as the stars of
heaven and as the innumerable grains of
sand by the seashore.

13 These all died in faith, not having
received what was promised, but having
seen it and greeted it from afar, and hav-
ing acknowledged that they were strang-
ers and exiles on the earth. 14 For people
who speak thus make it clear that they
are seeking a homeland. 15 If they had
been thinking of that land from which
they had gone out, they would have had
opportunity to return. 16 But as it is, they
desire a better country, that is, a heav-
enly one. Therefore God is not ashamed
to be called their God, for he has pre-
pared for them a city.

17 By faith Abraham, when he was
tested, offered up Isaac, and he who had

received the promises was ready to offer
up his only son, [18]of whom it was said,
"Through Isaac shall your descendants
be named." [19]He considered that God was
able to raise men even from the dead;
hence he did receive him back, and this
was a symbol. [20]By faith Isaac invoked
future blessings on Jacob and Esau. [21]By
faith Jacob, when dying, blessed each of
the sons of Joseph, bowing in worship
over the head of his staff. [22]By faith Jo-
seph, at the end of his life, made mention
of the exodus of the Israelites and gave
directions concerning his burial.[f]

The Faith of Moses

23 By faith Moses, when he was born, was
hid for three months by his parents, be-
cause they saw that the child was beauti-
ful; and they were not afraid of the king's
edict. [24]By faith Moses, when he was
grown up, refused to be called the son
of Pharaoh's daughter, [25]choosing rather
to share ill-treatment with the people of
God than to enjoy the fleeting pleasures
of sin. [26]He considered abuse suffered
for the Christ greater wealth than the
treasures of Egypt, for he looked to the
reward. [27]By faith he left Egypt, not be-
ing afraid of the anger of the king; for he
endured as seeing him who is invisible.
[28]By faith he kept the Passover and sprin-
kled the blood, so that the Destroyer of
the first-born might not touch them.

The Faith of Other Israelite Heroes

29 By faith the people crossed the Red
Sea as if on dry land; but the Egyptians,
when they attempted to do the same,
were drowned. [30]By faith the walls of
Jericho fell down after they had been en-
circled for seven days. [31]By faith Rahab
the harlot did not perish with those who
were disobedient, because she had given
friendly welcome to the spies.

32 And what more shall I say? For time
would fail me to tell of Gideon, Barak,
Samson, Jephthah, of David and Samuel
and the prophets— [33]who through faith
conquered kingdoms, enforced justice,
received promises, stopped the mouths
of lions, [34]quenched raging fire, escaped
the edge of the sword, won strength out
of weakness, became mighty in war,
put foreign armies to flight. [35]Women
received their dead by resurrection.
Some were tortured, refusing to accept
release, that they might rise again to a
better life. [36]Others suffered mocking
and scourging, and even chains and im-
prisonment. [37]They were stoned, they
were sawn in two,[g] they were killed with
the sword; they went about in skins of
sheep and goats, destitute, afflicted, ill-
treated— [38]of whom the world was not
worthy—wandering over deserts and
mountains, and in dens and caves of the
earth.

39 And all these, though well attested
by their faith, did not receive what was
promised, [40]since God had foreseen
something better for us, that apart from
us they should not be made perfect.

The Example of Jesus

12 Therefore, since we are sur-
rounded by so great a cloud of wit-
nesses, let us also lay aside every weight,
and sin which clings so closely, and let
us run with perseverance the race that
is set before us, [2]looking to Jesus the pi-
oneer and perfecter of our faith, who for
the joy that was set before him endured
the cross, despising the shame, and is
seated at the right hand of the throne of
God.

3 Consider him who endured from
sinners such hostility against himself,
so that you may not grow weary or faint-
hearted. [4]In your struggle against sin
you have not yet resisted to the point of
shedding your blood. [5]And have you for-
gotten the exhortation which addresses
you as sons?—

[f]**11.22** Greek *bones* [g]**11.37** Other manuscripts add *they were tempted*

"My son, do not regard lightly the
discipline of the Lord,
nor lose courage when you are
punished by him.
6 For the Lord disciplines him whom
he loves,
and chastises every son whom he
receives."

[7]It is for discipline that you have to en-
dure. God is treating you as sons; for
what son is there whom his father does
not discipline? [8]If you are left without
discipline, in which all have partici-
pated, then you are illegitimate children
and not sons. [9]Besides this, we have had
earthly fathers to discipline us and we
respected them. Shall we not much more
be subject to the Father of spirits and
live? [10]For they disciplined us for a short
time at their pleasure, but he disciplines
us for our good, that we may share his
holiness. [11]For the moment all discipline
seems painful rather than pleasant; later
it yields the peaceful fruit of righteous-
ness to those who have been trained by it.

Warnings against Rejecting God's Grace

12 Therefore lift your drooping hands
and strengthen your weak knees, [13]and
make straight paths for your feet, so that
what is lame may not be put out of joint
but rather be healed. [14]Strive for peace
with all men, and for the holiness with-
out which no one will see the Lord. [15]See
to it that no one fail to obtain the grace of
God; that no "root of bitterness" spring
up and cause trouble, and by it the many
become defiled; [16]that no one be immoral
or irreligious like Esau, who sold his
birthright for a single meal. [17]For you
know that afterward, when he desired to
inherit the blessing, he was rejected, for
he found no chance to repent, though he
sought it with tears.

18 For you have not come to what may
be touched, a blazing fire, and darkness,
and gloom, and a tempest, [19]and the
sound of a trumpet, and a voice whose
words made the hearers entreat that no
further messages be spoken to them.
[20]For they could not endure the order
that was given, "If even a beast touches
the mountain, it shall be stoned." [21]In-
deed, so terrifying was the sight that
Moses said, "I tremble with fear." [22]But
you have come to Mount Zion and to
the city of the living God, the heavenly
Jerusalem, and to innumerable angels
in festal gathering, [23]and to the assem-
bly[h] of the first-born who are enrolled in
heaven, and to a judge who is God of all,
and to the spirits of just men made per-
fect, [24]and to Jesus, the mediator of a new
covenant, and to the sprinkled blood that
speaks more graciously than the blood of
Abel.

25 See that you do not refuse him who
is speaking. For if they did not escape
when they refused him who warned
them on earth, much less shall we escape
if we reject him who warns from heaven.
[26]His voice then shook the earth; but now
he has promised, "Yet once more I will
shake not only the earth but also the
heaven." [27]This phrase, "Yet once more,"
indicates the removal of what is shaken,
as of what has been made, in order that
what cannot be shaken may remain.
[28]Therefore let us be grateful for receiv-
ing a kingdom that cannot be shaken,
and thus let us offer to God acceptable
worship, with reverence and awe; [29]for
our God is a consuming fire.

Service Well-Pleasing to God

13 Let brotherly love continue. [2]Do
not neglect to show hospitality
to strangers, for thereby some have en-
tertained angels unawares. [3]Remember
those who are in prison, as though in
prison with them; and those who are ill-
treated, since you also are in the body.
[4]Let marriage be held in honor among

[h] **12.23** Or *angels, and to the festal gathering and assembly*

all, and let the marriage bed be unde-
filed; for God will judge the immoral and
adulterous. [5]Keep your life free from
love of money, and be content with what
you have; for he has said, "I will never
fail you nor forsake you." [6]Hence we can
confidently say,

> "The Lord is my helper,
> I will not be afraid;
> what can man do to me?"

7 Remember your leaders, those who
spoke to you the word of God; consider
the outcome of their life, and imitate
their faith. [8]Jesus Christ is the same
yesterday and today and for ever. [9]Do
not be led away by diverse and strange
teachings; for it is well that the heart
be strengthened by grace, not by foods,
which have not benefited their adher-
ents. [10]We have an altar from which
those who serve the tent[i] have no right
to eat. [11]For the bodies of those animals
whose blood is brought into the sanctu-
ary by the high priest as a sacrifice for
sin are burned outside the camp. [12]So
Jesus also suffered outside the gate in
order to sanctify the people through his
own blood. [13]Therefore let us go forth to
him outside the camp, bearing abuse for
him. [14]For here we have no lasting city,
but we seek the city which is to come.
[15]Through him then let us continually
offer up a sacrifice of praise to God, that
is, the fruit of lips that acknowledge his
name. [16]Do not neglect to do good and to
share what you have, for such sacrifices
are pleasing to God.

17 Obey your leaders and submit to
them; for they are keeping watch over
your souls, as men who will have to give
account. Let them do this joyfully, and
not sadly, for that would be of no advan-
tage to you.

18 Pray for us, for we are sure that we
have a clear conscience, desiring to act
honorably in all things. [19]I urge you the
more earnestly to do this in order that I
may be restored to you the sooner.

Benediction

20 Now may the God of peace who
brought again from the dead our Lord
Jesus, the great shepherd of the sheep, by
the blood of the eternal covenant, [21]equip
you with everything good that you may
do his will, working in you[j] that which
is pleasing in his sight, through Jesus
Christ; to whom be glory for ever and
ever. Amen.

Final Exhortation and Greetings

22 I appeal to you, brethren, bear with
my word of exhortation, for I have writ-
ten to you briefly. [23]You should under-
stand that our brother Timothy has been
released, with whom I shall see you if he
comes soon. [24]Greet all your leaders and
all the saints. Those who come from Italy
send you greetings. [25]Grace be with all of
you. Amen.

[i] **13.10** Or *tabernacle* [j] **13.21** Other ancient authorities read *us*

The Letter of

JAMES

Salutation

1 James, a servant of God and of the
Lord Jesus Christ,
To the twelve tribes in the Dispersion:
Greeting.

Faith and Wisdom

2 Count it all joy, my brethren, when you
meet various trials, 3for you know that
the testing of your faith produces stead-
fastness. 4And let steadfastness have its
full effect, that you may be perfect and
complete, lacking in nothing.
5 If any of you lacks wisdom, let him
ask God, who gives to all men generously
and without reproaching, and it will be
given him. 6But let him ask in faith, with
no doubting, for he who doubts is like a
wave of the sea that is driven and tossed
by the wind. 7,8For that person must not
suppose that a double-minded man, un-
stable in all his ways, will receive any-
thing from the Lord.

Poverty and Riches

9 Let the lowly brother boast in his exal-
tation, 10and the rich in his humiliation,
because like the flower of the grass he
will pass away. 11For the sun rises with its
scorching heat and withers the grass; its
flower falls, and its beauty perishes. So
will the rich man fade away in the midst
of his pursuits.

Trial and Temptation

12 Blessed is the man who endures
trial, for when he has stood the test he
will receive the crown of life which God
has promised to those who love him.
13Let no one say when he is tempted, "I
am tempted by God"; for God cannot
be tempted with evil and he himself
tempts no one; 14but each person is
tempted when he is lured and enticed
by his own desire. 15Then desire when
it has conceived gives birth to sin; and
sin when it is full-grown brings forth
death.
16 Do not be deceived, my beloved
brethren. 17Every good endowment and
every perfect gift is from above, com-
ing down from the Father of lights with
whom there is no variation or shadow
due to change.[a] 18Of his own will he
brought us forth by the word of truth
that we should be a kind of first fruits of
his creatures.

Hearing and Doing the Word

19 Know this, my beloved brethren.
Let every man be quick to hear, slow to
speak, slow to anger, 20for the anger of
man does not work the righteousness
of God. 21Therefore put away all filthi-
ness and rank growth of wickedness and
receive with meekness the implanted
word, which is able to save your souls.
22 But be doers of the word, and not
hearers only, deceiving yourselves.
23For if any one is a hearer of the word
and not a doer, he is like a man who ob-
serves his natural face in a mirror; 24for
he observes himself and goes away and
at once forgets what he was like. 25But he
who looks into the perfect law, the law of
liberty, and perseveres, being no hearer
that forgets but a doer that acts, he shall
be blessed in his doing.
26 If any one thinks he is religious, and
does not bridle his tongue but deceives
his heart, this man's religion is vain.
27Religion that is pure and undefiled be-
fore God and the Father is this: to visit
orphans and widows in their affliction,
and to keep oneself unstained from the
world.

[a] **1.17** Other ancient authorities read *variation due to a shadow of turning*

Warning against Partiality

2 My brethren, show no partiality as
you hold the faith of our Lord Jesus
Christ, the Lord of glory. 2For if a man
with gold rings and in fine clothing
comes into your assembly, and a poor
man in shabby clothing also comes in,
3and you pay attention to the one who
wears the fine clothing and say, "Have a
seat here, please," while you say to the
poor man, "Stand there," or, "Sit at my
feet," 4have you not made distinctions
among yourselves, and become judges
with evil thoughts? 5Listen, my beloved
brethren. Has not God chosen those who
are poor in the world to be rich in faith
and heirs of the kingdom which he has
promised to those who love him? 6But
you have dishonored the poor man. Is
it not the rich who oppress you, is it
not they who drag you into court? 7Is it
not they who blaspheme that honorable
name by which you are called?

8 If you really fulfil the royal law, ac-
cording to the scripture, "You shall love
your neighbor as yourself," you do well.
9But if you show partiality, you commit
sin, and are convicted by the law as trans-
gressors. 10For whoever keeps the whole
law but fails in one point has become
guilty of all of it. 11For he who said, "Do
not commit adultery," said also, "Do not
kill." If you do not commit adultery but
do kill, you have become a transgressor
of the law. 12So speak and so act as those
who are to be judged under the law of lib-
erty. 13For judgment is without mercy to
one who has shown no mercy; yet mercy
triumphs over judgment.

Faith without Works Is Dead

14 What does it profit, my brethren, if a
man says he has faith but has not works?
Can his faith save him? 15If a brother
or sister is ill-clad and in lack of daily
food, 16and one of you says to them, "Go
in peace, be warmed and filled," without
giving them the things needed for the
body, what does it profit? 17So faith by it-
self, if it has no works, is dead.

18 But some one will say, "You have
faith and I have works." Show me your
faith apart from your works, and I by my
works will show you my faith. 19You be-
lieve that God is one; you do well. Even
the demons believe—and shudder. 20Do
you want to be shown, you foolish fellow,
that faith apart from works is barren?
21Was not Abraham our father justified
by works, when he offered his son Isaac
upon the altar? 22You see that faith was
active along with his works, and faith
was completed by works, 23and the scrip-
ture was fulfilled which says, "Abraham
believed God, and it was reckoned to him
as righteousness"; and he was called the
friend of God. 24You see that a man is jus-
tified by works and not by faith alone.
25And in the same way was not also Ra-
hab the harlot justified by works when
she received the messengers and sent
them out another way? 26For as the body
apart from the spirit is dead, so faith
apart from works is dead.

Taming the Tongue

3 Let not many of you become teach-
ers, my brethren, for you know
that we who teach shall be judged with
greater strictness. 2For we all make
many mistakes, and if any one makes
no mistakes in what he says he is a per-
fect man, able to bridle the whole body
also. 3If we put bits into the mouths of
horses that they may obey us, we guide
their whole bodies. 4Look at the ships
also; though they are so great and are
driven by strong winds, they are guided
by a very small rudder wherever the
will of the pilot directs. 5So the tongue
is a little member and boasts of great
things. How great a forest is set ablaze
by a small fire!

6 And the tongue is a fire. The tongue is
an unrighteous world among our mem-
bers, staining the whole body, setting on

fire the cycle of nature,[b] and set on fire by
hell.[c] 7 For every kind of beast and bird,
of reptile and sea creature, can be tamed
and has been tamed by humankind, 8 but
no human being can tame the tongue—a
restless evil, full of deadly poison. 9 With
it we bless the Lord and Father, and with
it we curse men, who are made in the
likeness of God. 10 From the same mouth
come blessing and cursing. My brethren,
this ought not to be so. 11 Does a spring
pour forth from the same opening fresh
water and brackish? 12 Can a fig tree, my
brethren, yield olives, or a grapevine
figs? No more can salt water yield fresh.

Two Kinds of Wisdom

13 Who is wise and understanding
among you? By his good life let him show
his works in the meekness of wisdom.
14 But if you have bitter jealousy and self-
ish ambition in your hearts, do not boast
and be false to the truth. 15 This wisdom
is not such as comes down from above,
but is earthly, unspiritual, devilish. 16 For
where jealousy and selfish ambition ex-
ist, there will be disorder and every vile
practice. 17 But the wisdom from above
is first pure, then peaceable, gentle,
open to reason, full of mercy and good
fruits, without uncertainty or insincer-
ity. 18 And the harvest of righteousness is
sown in peace by those who make peace.

Friendship with the World

4 What causes wars, and what causes
fightings among you? Is it not your
passions that are at war in your mem-
bers? 2 You desire and do not have; so
you kill. And you covet[d] and cannot ob-
tain; so you fight and wage war. You do
not have, because you do not ask. 3 You
ask and do not receive, because you ask
wrongly, to spend it on your passions.
4 Unfaithful creatures! Do you not know
that friendship with the world is enmity
with God? Therefore whoever wishes to
be a friend of the world makes himself
an enemy of God. 5 Or do you suppose
it is in vain that the scripture says, "He
yearns jealously over the spirit which he
has made to dwell in us"? 6 But he gives
more grace; therefore it says, "God op-
poses the proud, but gives grace to the
humble." 7 Submit yourselves therefore
to God. Resist the devil and he will flee
from you. 8 Draw near to God and he will
draw near to you. Cleanse your hands,
you sinners, and purify your hearts, you
men of double mind. 9 Be wretched and
mourn and weep. Let your laughter be
turned to mourning and your joy to de-
jection. 10 Humble yourselves before the
Lord and he will exalt you.

Warning against Judging Another

11 Do not speak evil against one another,
brethren. He that speaks evil against a
brother or judges his brother, speaks
evil against the law and judges the law.
But if you judge the law, you are not a
doer of the law but a judge. 12 There is
one lawgiver and judge, he who is able to
save and to destroy. But who are you that
you judge your neighbor?

Boasting about Tomorrow

13 Come now, you who say, "Today or to-
morrow we will go into such and such a
town and spend a year there and trade
and get gain"; 14 whereas you do not know
about tomorrow. What is your life? For
you are a mist that appears for a little time
and then vanishes. 15 Instead you ought to
say, "If the Lord wills, we shall live and we
shall do this or that." 16 As it is, you boast in
your arrogance. All such boasting is evil.
17 Whoever knows what is right to do and
fails to do it, for him it is sin.

Warning to Rich Oppressors

5 Come now, you rich, weep and howl
for the miseries that are coming upon
you. 2 Your riches have rotted and your

[b] **3.6** Or *wheel of birth* [c] **3.6** Greek *Gehenna* [d] **4.2** Or *you kill and you covet*

garments are moth-eaten. 3Your gold
and silver have rusted, and their rust
will be evidence against you and will
eat your flesh like fire. You have laid up
treasure[e] for the last days. 4Behold, the
wages of the laborers who mowed your
fields, which you kept back by fraud, cry
out; and the cries of the harvesters have
reached the ears of the Lord of hosts.
5You have lived on the earth in luxury
and in pleasure; you have fattened your
hearts in a day of slaughter. 6You have
condemned, you have killed the righ-
teous man; he does not resist you.

Patience in Suffering

7 Be patient, therefore, brethren, un-
til the coming of the Lord. Behold, the
farmer waits for the precious fruit of
the earth, being patient over it until it
receives the early and the late rain. 8You
also be patient. Establish your hearts, for
the coming of the Lord is at hand. 9Do not
grumble, brethren, against one another,
that you may not be judged; behold, the
Judge is standing at the doors. 10As an ex-
ample of suffering and patience, breth-
ren, take the prophets who spoke in the
name of the Lord. 11Behold, we call those
happy who were steadfast. You have
heard of the steadfastness of Job, and you
have seen the purpose of the Lord, how
the Lord is compassionate and merciful.

12 But above all, my brethren, do not
swear, either by heaven or by earth or
with any other oath, but let your yes be
yes and your no be no, that you may not
fall under condemnation.

The Prayer of Faith

13 Is any one among you suffering? Let
him pray. Is any cheerful? Let him sing
praise. 14Is any among you sick? Let him
call for the elders of the church, and let
them pray over him, anointing him with
oil in the name of the Lord; 15and the
prayer of faith will save the sick man,
and the Lord will raise him up; and if he
has committed sins, he will be forgiven.
16Therefore confess your sins to one
another, and pray for one another, that
you may be healed. The prayer of a righ-
teous man has great power in its effects.
17Eli′jah was a man of like nature with
ourselves and he prayed fervently that it
might not rain, and for three years and
six months it did not rain on the earth.
18Then he prayed again and the heaven
gave rain, and the earth brought forth its
fruit.

19 My brethren, if any one among you
wanders from the truth and some one
brings him back, 20let him know that
whoever brings back a sinner from the
error of his way will save his soul from
death and will cover a multitude of sins.

[e] **5.3** Or *will eat your flesh, since you have stored up fire*

The First Letter of

PETER

Salutation

1 Peter, an apostle of Jesus Christ,

To the exiles of the Dispersion in Pontus, Galatia, Cappado′cia, Asia, and Bithyn′ia, [2]chosen and destined by God the Father and sanctified by the Spirit for obedience to Jesus Christ and for sprinkling with his blood:

May grace and peace be multiplied to you.

A Living Hope

3 Blessed be the God and Father of our Lord Jesus Christ! By his great mercy we have been born anew to a living hope through the resurrection of Jesus Christ from the dead, [4]and to an inheritance which is imperishable, undefiled, and unfading, kept in heaven for you, [5]who by God's power are guarded through faith for a salvation ready to be revealed in the last time. [6]In this you rejoice,[a] though now for a little while you may have to suffer various trials, [7]so that the genuineness of your faith, more precious than gold which though perishable is tested by fire, may redound to praise and glory and honor at the revelation of Jesus Christ. [8]Without having seen[b] him you[c] love him; though you do not now see him you[d] believe in him and rejoice with unutterable and exalted joy. [9]As the outcome of your faith you obtain the salvation of your souls.

10 The prophets who prophesied of the grace that was to be yours searched and inquired about this salvation; [11]they inquired what person or time was indicated by the Spirit of Christ within them when predicting the sufferings of Christ and the subsequent glory. [12]It was revealed to them that they were serving not themselves but you, in the things which have now been announced to you by those who preached the good news to you through the Holy Spirit sent from heaven, things into which angels long to look.

A Call to Holy Living

13 Therefore gird up your minds, be sober, set your hope fully upon the grace that is coming to you at the revelation of Jesus Christ. [14]As obedient children, do not be conformed to the passions of your former ignorance, [15]but as he who called you is holy, be holy yourselves in all your conduct; [16]since it is written, "You shall be holy, for I am holy." [17]And if you invoke as Father him who judges each one impartially according to his deeds, conduct yourselves with fear throughout the time of your exile. [18]You know that you were ransomed from the futile ways inherited from your fathers, not with perishable things such as silver or gold, [19]but with the precious blood of Christ, like that of a lamb without blemish or spot. [20]He was destined before the foundation of the world but was made manifest at the end of the times for your sake. [21]Through him you have confidence in God, who raised him from the dead and gave him glory, so that your faith and hope are in God.[e]

22 Having purified your souls by your obedience to the truth for a sincere love of the brethren, love one another earnestly from the heart. [23]You have been born anew, not of perishable seed but of imperishable, through the living and abiding word of God; [24]for

[a] **1.6** Or *Rejoice in this* [b] **1.8** Other ancient authorities read *known* [c] **1.8** Or omit *you*
[d] **1.8** Or omit *you* [e] **1.21** Or *so that your faith is hope in God*

"All flesh is like grass
and all its glory like the flower of grass.
The grass withers, and the flower falls,
25 but the word of the Lord abides for ever."

That word is the good news which was preached to you.

The Living Stone and a Chosen People

2 So put away all malice and all guile and insincerity and envy and all slander. [2]Like newborn babes, long for the pure spiritual milk, that by it you may grow up to salvation; [3]for you have tasted the kindness of the Lord.

4 Come to him, to that living stone, rejected by men but in God's sight chosen and precious; [5]and like living stones be yourselves built into a spiritual house, to be a holy priesthood, to offer spiritual sacrifices acceptable to God through Jesus Christ. [6]For it stands in scripture:

"Behold, I am laying in Zion a stone,
a cornerstone chosen and precious,
and he who believes in him will not be put to shame."

[7]To you therefore who believe, he is precious, but for those who do not believe,

"The very stone which the builders rejected
has become the head of the corner,"

[8]and

"A stone that will make men stumble,
a rock that will make them fall";

for they stumble because they disobey the word, as they were destined to do.

9 But you are a chosen race, a royal priesthood, a holy nation, God's own people,[f] that you may declare the wonderful deeds of him who called you out of darkness into his marvelous light. [10]Once you were no people but now you are God's people; once you had not received mercy but now you have received mercy.

Live as Servants of God

11 Beloved, I beseech you as aliens and exiles to abstain from the passions of the flesh that wage war against your soul. [12]Maintain good conduct among the Gentiles, so that in case they speak against you as wrongdoers, they may see your good deeds and glorify God on the day of visitation.

13 Be subject for the Lord's sake to every human institution,[g] whether it be to the emperor as supreme, [14]or to governors as sent by him to punish those who do wrong and to praise those who do right. [15]For it is God's will that by doing right you should put to silence the ignorance of foolish men. [16]Live as free men, yet without using your freedom as a pretext for evil; but live as servants of God. [17]Honor all men. Love the brotherhood. Fear God. Honor the emperor.

The Example of Christ's Suffering

18 Servants, be submissive to your masters with all respect, not only to the kind and gentle but also to the overbearing. [19]For one is approved if, mindful of God, he endures pain while suffering unjustly. [20]For what credit is it, if when you do wrong and are beaten for it you take it patiently? But if when you do right and suffer for it you take it patiently, you have God's approval. [21]For to this you have been called, because Christ also suffered for you, leaving you an example, that you should follow in his steps. [22]He committed no sin; no guile was found on his lips. [23]When he was reviled, he did not revile in return; when he suffered, he did not threaten; but he trusted to him who judges justly. [24]He himself bore our sins in his body on the tree,[h] that we might die to sin and live to

[f] **2.9** Greek *a people for his possession* [g] **2.13** Or *every institution ordained for men* [h] **2.24** Or *carried up . . . to the tree*

righteousness. By his wounds you have
been healed. 25For you were straying
like sheep, but have now returned to the
Shepherd and Guardian of your souls.

Wives and Husbands

3 Likewise you wives, be submissive to
your husbands, so that some, though
they do not obey the word, may be won
without a word by the behavior of their
wives, 2when they see your reverent
and chaste behavior. 3Let not yours be
the outward adorning with braiding of
hair, decoration of gold, and wearing
of robes, 4but let it be the hidden per-
son of the heart with the imperishable
jewel of a gentle and quiet spirit, which
in God's sight is very precious. 5So once
the holy women who hoped in God used
to adorn themselves and were submis-
sive to their husbands, 6as Sarah obeyed
Abraham, calling him lord. And you are
now her children if you do right and let
nothing terrify you.
7 Likewise you husbands, live con-
siderately with your wives, bestowing
honor on the woman as the weaker sex,
since you are joint heirs of the grace of
life, in order that your prayers may not
be hindered.

Suffering for Doing Right

8 Finally, all of you, have unity of spirit,
sympathy, love of the brethren, a tender
heart and a humble mind. 9Do not return
evil for evil or reviling for reviling; but
on the contrary bless, for to this you
have been called, that you may obtain a
blessing. 10For

"He that would love life
and see good days,
let him keep his tongue from evil
and his lips from speaking guile;
11 let him turn away from evil and do
right;
let him seek peace and pursue it.
12 For the eyes of the Lord are upon the
righteous,
and his ears are open to their
prayer.
But the face of the Lord is against
those that do evil."

13 Now who is there to harm you if you
are zealous for what is right? 14But even
if you do suffer for righteousness' sake,
you will be blessed. Have no fear of them,
nor be troubled, 15but in your hearts rev-
erence Christ as Lord. Always be pre-
pared to make a defense to any one who
calls you to account for the hope that
is in you, yet do it with gentleness and
reverence; 16and keep your conscience
clear, so that, when you are abused, those
who revile your good behavior in Christ
may be put to shame. 17For it is better to
suffer for doing right, if that should be
God's will, than for doing wrong. 18For
Christ also died[i] for sins once for all, the
righteous for the unrighteous, that he
might bring us to God, being put to death
in the flesh but made alive in the spirit;
19in which he went and preached to the
spirits in prison, 20who formerly did not
obey, when God's patience waited in the
days of Noah, during the building of the
ark, in which a few, that is, eight persons,
were saved through water. 21Baptism,
which corresponds to this, now saves
you, not as a removal of dirt from the
body but as an appeal to God for a clear
conscience, through the resurrection of
Jesus Christ, 22who has gone into heaven
and is at the right hand of God, with an-
gels, authorities, and powers subject to
him.

Good Stewards of God's Grace

4 Since therefore Christ suffered in the
flesh,[j] arm yourselves with the same
thought, for whoever has suffered in the
flesh has ceased from sin, 2so as to live for
the rest of the time in the flesh no longer

[i] **3.18** Other ancient authorities read *suffered for you*

[j] **4.1** Other ancient authorities add *for us;* some

by human passions but by the will of God.
3 Let the time that is past suffice for doing
what the Gentiles like to do, living in li-
centiousness, passions, drunkenness,
revels, carousing, and lawless idolatry.
4 They are surprised that you do not now
join them in the same wild profligacy,
and they abuse you; 5 but they will give
account to him who is ready to judge the
living and the dead. 6 For this is why the
gospel was preached even to the dead,
that though judged in the flesh like men,
they might live in the spirit like God.
7 The end of all things is at hand;
therefore keep sane and sober for your
prayers. 8 Above all hold unfailing your
love for one another, since love covers
a multitude of sins. 9 Practice hospitality
ungrudgingly to one another. 10 As each
has received a gift, employ it for one
another, as good stewards of God's var-
ied grace: 11 whoever speaks, as one who
utters oracles of God; whoever renders
service, as one who renders it by the
strength which God supplies; in order
that in everything God may be glorified
through Jesus Christ. To him belong
glory and dominion for ever and ever.
Amen.

Suffering as a Christian

12 Beloved, do not be surprised at the
fiery ordeal which comes upon you to
prove you, as though something strange
were happening to you. 13 But rejoice in
so far as you share Christ's sufferings,
that you may also rejoice and be glad
when his glory is revealed. 14 If you are
reproached for the name of Christ, you
are blessed, because the spirit of glory[k]
and of God rests upon you. 15 But let none
of you suffer as a murderer, or a thief, or
a wrongdoer, or a mischief-maker; 16 yet
if one suffers as a Christian, let him not
be ashamed, but under that name let him
glorify God. 17 For the time has come for
judgment to begin with the household of
God; and if it begins with us, what will be
the end of those who do not obey the gos-
pel of God? 18 And

"If the righteous man is scarcely
saved,
where will the impious and sinner
appear?"

19 Therefore let those who suffer accord-
ing to God's will do right and entrust
their souls to a faithful Creator.

Tending the Flock of God

5 So I exhort the elders among you, as a
fellow elder and a witness of the suf-
ferings of Christ as well as a partaker in
the glory that is to be revealed. 2 Tend the
flock of God that is your charge,[l] not by
constraint but willingly,[m] not for shame-
ful gain but eagerly, 3 not as domineering
over those in your charge but being ex-
amples to the flock. 4 And when the chief
Shepherd is manifested you will obtain
the unfading crown of glory. 5 Likewise
you that are younger be subject to the el-
ders. Clothe yourselves, all of you, with
humility toward one another, for "God
opposes the proud, but gives grace to the
humble."
6 Humble yourselves therefore un-
der the mighty hand of God, that in due
time he may exalt you. 7 Cast all your
anxieties on him, for he cares about
you. 8 Be sober, be watchful. Your ad-
versary the devil prowls around like a
roaring lion, seeking some one to de-
vour. 9 Resist him, firm in your faith,
knowing that the same experience of
suffering is required of your brother-
hood throughout the world. 10 And af-
ter you have suffered a little while, the
God of all grace, who has called you to
his eternal glory in Christ, will himself
restore, establish, and strengthen[n] you.

[k] **4.14** Other ancient authorities insert *and of power* [l] **5.2** Other ancient authorities add *exercising the oversight* [m] **5.2** Other ancient authorities add *as God would have you* [n] **5.10** Other ancient authorities read *restore, establish, strengthen and settle*

[11]To him be the dominion for ever and ever. Amen.

Final Greetings and Benediction

12 By Silva'nus, a faithful brother as I regard him, I have written briefly to you, exhorting and declaring that this is the true grace of God; stand fast in it. [13]She who is at Babylon, who is likewise chosen, sends you greetings; and so does my son Mark. [14]Greet one another with the kiss of love.

Peace to all of you that are in Christ.

The Second Letter of

PETER

Salutation

1 Simon Peter, a servant and apostle of
Jesus Christ,
To those who have obtained a faith of
equal standing with ours in the righ-
teousness of our God and Savior Jesus
Christ:[a]
2 May grace and peace be multiplied to
you in the knowledge of God and of Jesus
our Lord.

The Christian's Call and Election

3 His divine power has granted to us
all things that pertain to life and godli-
ness, through the knowledge of him who
called us to[b] his own glory and excel-
lence, 4 by which he has granted to us his
precious and very great promises, that
through these you may escape from the
corruption that is in the world because
of passion, and become partakers of
the divine nature. 5 For this very reason
make every effort to supplement your
faith with virtue, and virtue with knowl-
edge, 6 and knowledge with self-control,
and self-control with steadfastness, and
steadfastness with godliness, 7 and godli-
ness with brotherly affection, and broth-
erly affection with love. 8 For if these
things are yours and abound, they keep
you from being ineffective or unfruit-
ful in the knowledge of our Lord Jesus
Christ. 9 For whoever lacks these things
is blind and shortsighted and has for-
gotten that he was cleansed from his old
sins. 10 Therefore, brethren, be the more
zealous to confirm your call and elec-
tion, for if you do this you will never fall;
11 so there will be richly provided for you
an entrance into the eternal kingdom of
our Lord and Savior Jesus Christ.
12 Therefore I intend always to remind
you of these things, though you know
them and are established in the truth
that you have. 13 I think it right, as long as
I am in this body,[c] to arouse you by way
of reminder, 14 since I know that the put-
ting off of my body[d] will be soon, as our
Lord Jesus Christ showed me. 15 And I will
see to it that after my departure you may
be able at any time to recall these things.

Eyewitnesses of Christ's Glory

16 For we did not follow cleverly devised
myths when we made known to you the
power and coming of our Lord Jesus
Christ, but we were eyewitnesses of his
majesty. 17 For when he received honor
and glory from God the Father and the
voice was borne to him by the Majestic
Glory, "This is my beloved Son,[e] with
whom I am well pleased," 18 we heard
this voice borne from heaven, for we
were with him on the holy mountain.
19 And we have the prophetic word made
more sure. You will do well to pay at-
tention to this as to a lamp shining in a
dark place, until the day dawns and the
morning star rises in your hearts. 20 First
of all you must understand this, that no
prophecy of scripture is a matter of one's
own interpretation, 21 because no proph-
ecy ever came by the impulse of man,
but men moved by the Holy Spirit spoke
from God.[f]

False Prophets and Their Punishment

2 But false prophets also arose among
the people, just as there will be false
teachers among you, who will secretly
bring in destructive heresies, even de-
nying the Master who bought them,

[a] **1.1** Or *of our God and the Savior Jesus Christ* [b] **1.3** Or *by* [c] **1.13** Greek *tent* [d] **1.14** Greek *tent* [e] **1.17** Or *my Son, my* (or *the*) *Beloved* [f] **1.21** Other authorities read *moved by the Holy Spirit holy men of God spoke*

bringing upon themselves swift destruction. 2 And many will follow their licentiousness, and because of them the way of truth will be reviled. 3 And in their greed they will exploit you with false words; from of old their condemnation has not been idle, and their destruction has not been asleep.

4 For if God did not spare the angels when they sinned, but cast them into hell[g] and committed them to pits of nether gloom to be kept until the judgment; 5 if he did not spare the ancient world, but preserved Noah, a herald of righteousness, with seven other persons, when he brought a flood upon the world of the ungodly; 6 if by turning the cities of Sodom and Gomor′rah to ashes he condemned them to extinction and made them an example to those who were to be ungodly; 7 and if he rescued righteous Lot, greatly distressed by the licentiousness of the wicked 8 (for by what that righteous man saw and heard as he lived among them, he was vexed in his righteous soul day after day with their lawless deeds), 9 then the Lord knows how to rescue the godly from trial, and to keep the unrighteous under punishment until the day of judgment, 10 and especially those who indulge in the lust of defiling passion and despise authority.

Bold and wilful, they are not afraid to revile the glorious ones, 11 whereas angels, though greater in might and power, do not pronounce a reviling judgment upon them before the Lord. 12 But these, like irrational animals, creatures of instinct, born to be caught and killed, reviling in matters of which they are ignorant, will be destroyed in the same destruction with them, 13 suffering wrong for their wrongdoing. They count it pleasure to revel in the daytime. They are blots and blemishes, reveling in their dissipation,[h] carousing with you. 14 They have eyes full of adultery, insatiable for sin. They entice unsteady souls. They have hearts trained in greed. Accursed children! 15 Forsaking the right way they have gone astray; they have followed the way of Balaam, the son of Be′or, who loved gain from wrongdoing, 16 but was rebuked for his own transgression; a dumb ass spoke with human voice and restrained the prophet's madness.

17 These are waterless springs and mists driven by a storm; for them the nether gloom of darkness has been reserved. 18 For, uttering loud boasts of folly, they entice with licentious passions of the flesh men who have barely escaped from those who live in error. 19 They promise them freedom, but they themselves are slaves of corruption; for whatever overcomes a man, to that he is enslaved. 20 For if, after they have escaped the defilements of the world through the knowledge of our Lord and Savior Jesus Christ, they are again entangled in them and overpowered, the last state has become worse for them than the first. 21 For it would have been better for them never to have known the way of righteousness than after knowing it to turn back from the holy commandment delivered to them. 22 It has happened to them according to the true proverb, The dog turns back to his own vomit, and the sow is washed only to wallow in the mire.

The Promise of the Lord's Coming

3 This is now the second letter that I have written to you, beloved, and in both of them I have aroused your sincere mind by way of reminder; 2 that you should remember the predictions of the holy prophets and the commandment of the Lord and Savior through your apostles. 3 First of all you must understand this, that scoffers will come in the last days with scoffing, following their own passions 4 and saying, "Where

[g] **2.4** Greek *Tartarus*   [h] **2.13** Other ancient authorities read *love feasts*

is the promise of his coming? For ever
since the fathers fell asleep, all things
have continued as they were from the
beginning of creation." 5They deliber-
ately ignore this fact, that by the word
of God heavens existed long ago, and an
earth formed out of water and by means
of water, 6through which the world that
then existed was deluged with water
and perished. 7But by the same word the
heavens and earth that now exist have
been stored up for fire, being kept until
the day of judgment and destruction of
ungodly men.

8 But do not ignore this one fact, be-
loved, that with the Lord one day is as a
thousand years, and a thousand years
as one day. 9The Lord is not slow about
his promise as some count slowness,
but is forbearing toward you,[i] not wish-
ing that any should perish, but that all
should reach repentance. 10But the day of
the Lord will come like a thief, and then
the heavens will pass away with a loud
noise, and the elements will be dissolved
with fire, and the earth and the works
that are upon it will be burned up.

11 Since all these things are thus to be
dissolved, what sort of persons ought
you to be in lives of holiness and godli-
ness, 12waiting for and hastening[j] the
coming of the day of God, because of
which the heavens will be kindled and
dissolved, and the elements will melt
with fire! 13But according to his promise
we wait for new heavens and a new earth
in which righteousness dwells.

Final Exhortation and Doxology

14 Therefore, beloved, since you wait for
these, be zealous to be found by him with-
out spot or blemish, and at peace. 15And
count the forbearance of our Lord as sal-
vation. So also our beloved brother Paul
wrote to you according to the wisdom
given him, 16speaking of this as he does
in all his letters. There are some things
in them hard to understand, which the
ignorant and unstable twist to their own
destruction, as they do the other scrip-
tures. 17You therefore, beloved, knowing
this beforehand, beware lest you be car-
ried away with the error of lawless men
and lose your own stability. 18But grow
in the grace and knowledge of our Lord
and Savior Jesus Christ. To him be the
glory both now and to the day of eternity.
Amen.

[i] **3.9** Other ancient authorities read *on your account*

[j] **3.12** Or *earnestly desiring*

The First Letter of

JOHN

The Word of Life

1 That which was from the beginning, which we have heard, which we have seen with our eyes, which we have looked upon and touched with our hands, concerning the word of life— 2the life was made manifest, and we saw it, and testify to it, and proclaim to you the eternal life which was with the Father and was made manifest to us— 3that which we have seen and heard we proclaim also to you, so that you may have fellowship with us; and our fellowship is with the Father and with his Son Jesus Christ. 4And we are writing this that our[a] joy may be complete.

God Is Light

5 This is the message we have heard from him and proclaim to you, that God is light and in him is no darkness at all. 6If we say we have fellowship with him while we walk in darkness, we lie and do not live according to the truth; 7but if we walk in the light, as he is in the light, we have fellowship with one another, and the blood of Jesus his Son cleanses us from all sin. 8If we say we have no sin, we deceive ourselves, and the truth is not in us. 9If we confess our sins, he is faithful and just, and will forgive our sins and cleanse us from all unrighteousness. 10If we say we have not sinned, we make him a liar, and his word is not in us.

Christ Our Advocate

2 My little children, I am writing this to you so that you may not sin; but if any one does sin, we have an advocate with the Father, Jesus Christ the righteous; 2and he is the expiation for our sins, and not for ours only but also for the sins of the whole world. 3And by this we may be sure that we know him, if we keep his commandments. 4He who says "I know him" but disobeys his commandments is a liar, and the truth is not in him; 5but whoever keeps his word, in him truly love for God is perfected. By this we may be sure that we are in him: 6he who says he abides in him ought to walk in the same way in which he walked.

A New Commandment

7 Beloved, I am writing you no new commandment, but an old commandment which you had from the beginning; the old commandment is the word which you have heard. 8Yet I am writing you a new commandment, which is true in him and in you, because[b] the darkness is passing away and the true light is already shining. 9He who says he is in the light and hates his brother is in the darkness still. 10He who loves his brother abides in the light, and in it[c] there is no cause for stumbling. 11But he who hates his brother is in the darkness and walks in the darkness, and does not know where he is going, because the darkness has blinded his eyes.

12 I am writing to you, little children, because your sins are forgiven for his sake. 13I am writing to you, fathers, because you know him who is from the beginning. I am writing to you, young men, because you have overcome the evil one. I write to you, children, because you know the Father. 14I write to you, fathers, because you know him who is from the beginning. I write to you, young men, because you are strong, and the word of God abides in you, and you have overcome the evil one.

15 Do not love the world or the things in the world. If any one loves the world, love for the Father is not in him. 16For all

[a] **1.4** Other ancient authorities read *your* [b] **2.8** Or *that* [c] **2.10** Or *him*

that is in the world, the lust of the flesh
and the lust of the eyes and the pride
of life, is not of the Father but is of the
world. [17]And the world passes away, and
the lust of it; but he who does the will of
God abides for ever.

Warning against Antichrists

18 Children, it is the last hour; and as
you have heard that antichrist is com-
ing, so now many antichrists have come;
therefore we know that it is the last
hour. [19]They went out from us, but they
were not of us; for if they had been of
us, they would have continued with us;
but they went out, that it might be plain
that they all are not of us. [20]But you have
been anointed by the Holy One, and you
all know.[d] [21]I write to you, not because
you do not know the truth, but because
you know it, and know that no lie is of
the truth. [22]Who is the liar but he who
denies that Jesus is the Christ? This is
the antichrist, he who denies the Father
and the Son. [23]No one who denies the Son
has the Father. He who confesses the Son
has the Father also. [24]Let what you heard
from the beginning abide in you. If what
you heard from the beginning abides in
you, then you will abide in the Son and
in the Father. [25]And this is what he has
promised us,[e] eternal life.

26 I write this to you about those who
would deceive you; [27]but the anointing
which you received from him abides
in you, and you have no need that any
one should teach you; as his anointing
teaches you about everything, and is
true, and is no lie, just as it has taught
you, abide in him.

Children of God

28 And now, little children, abide in him,
so that when he appears we may have
confidence and not shrink from him in
shame at his coming. [29]If you know that
he is righteous, you may be sure that ev-
ery one who does right is born of him.

3 See what love the Father has given us,
that we should be called children of
God; and so we are. The reason why the
world does not know us is that it did not
know him. [2]Beloved, we are God's chil-
dren now; it does not yet appear what
we shall be, but we know that when he
appears we shall be like him, for we shall
see him as he is. [3]And every one who
thus hopes in him purifies himself as he
is pure.

4 Every one who commits sin is guilty
of lawlessness; sin is lawlessness. [5]You
know that he appeared to take away
sins, and in him there is no sin. [6]No one
who abides in him sins; no one who
sins has either seen him or known him.
[7]Little children, let no one deceive you.
He who does right is righteous, as he is
righteous. [8]He who commits sin is of the
devil; for the devil has sinned from the
beginning. The reason the Son of God
appeared was to destroy the works of
the devil. [9]No one born of God commits
sin; for God's[f] nature abides in him, and
he cannot sin because he is[g] born of God.
[10]By this it may be seen who are the chil-
dren of God, and who are the children of
the devil: whoever does not do right is
not of God, nor he who does not love his
brother.

Love One Another

11 For this is the message which you
have heard from the beginning, that we
should love one another, [12]and not be like
Cain who was of the evil one and mur-
dered his brother. And why did he mur-
der him? Because his own deeds were
evil and his brother's righteous. [13]Do not
wonder, brethren, that the world hates

[d]**2.20** Other ancient authorities read *you know everything* [e]**2.25** Other ancient authorities read *you* [f]**3.9** Greek *his* [g]**3.9** Or *for the offspring of God abide in him, and they cannot sin because they are*

you. [14]We know that we have passed out
of death into life, because we love the
brethren. He who does not love remains
in death. [15]Any one who hates his brother
is a murderer, and you know that no
murderer has eternal life abiding in
him. [16]By this we know love, that he laid
down his life for us; and we ought to lay
down our lives for the brethren. [17]But if
any one has the world's goods and sees
his brother in need, yet closes his heart
against him, how does God's love abide
in him? [18]Little children, let us not love in
word or speech but in deed and in truth.
19 By this we shall know that we are of
the truth, and reassure our hearts before
him [20]whenever our hearts condemn us;
for God is greater than our hearts, and
he knows everything. [21]Beloved, if our
hearts do not condemn us, we have confi-
dence before God; [22]and we receive from
him whatever we ask, because we keep
his commandments and do what pleases
him. [23]And this is his commandment,
that we should believe in the name of his
Son Jesus Christ and love one another,
just as he has commanded us. [24]All who
keep his commandments abide in him,
and he in them. And by this we know
that he abides in us, by the Spirit which
he has given us.

Testing the Spirits

4 Beloved, do not believe every spirit,
but test the spirits to see whether
they are of God; for many false prophets
have gone out into the world. [2]By this
you know the Spirit of God: every spirit
which confesses that Jesus Christ has
come in the flesh is of God, [3]and every
spirit which does not confess Jesus is not
of God. This is the spirit of antichrist, of
which you heard that it was coming, and
now it is in the world already. [4]Little chil-
dren, you are of God, and have overcome
them; for he who is in you is greater than
he who is in the world. [5]They are of the
world, therefore what they say is of the
world, and the world listens to them. [6]We
are of God. Whoever knows God listens
to us, and he who is not of God does not
listen to us. By this we know the spirit of
truth and the spirit of error.

God Is Love

7 Beloved, let us love one another; for
love is of God, and he who loves is born
of God and knows God. [8]He who does not
love does not know God; for God is love.
[9]In this the love of God was made man-
ifest among us, that God sent his only
Son into the world, so that we might live
through him. [10]In this is love, not that
we loved God but that he loved us and
sent his Son to be the expiation for our
sins. [11]Beloved, if God so loved us, we also
ought to love one another. [12]No man has
ever seen God; if we love one another,
God abides in us and his love is perfected
in us.
13 By this we know that we abide in him
and he in us, because he has given us of
his own Spirit. [14]And we have seen and
testify that the Father has sent his Son
as the Savior of the world. [15]Whoever
confesses that Jesus is the Son of God,
God abides in him, and he in God. [16]So we
know and believe the love God has for
us. God is love, and he who abides in love
abides in God, and God abides in him. [17]In
this is love perfected with us, that we may
have confidence for the day of judgment,
because as he is so are we in this world.
[18]There is no fear in love, but perfect love
casts out fear. For fear has to do with
punishment, and he who fears is not per-
fected in love. [19]We love, because he first
loved us. [20]If any one says, "I love God,"
and hates his brother, he is a liar; for he
who does not love his brother whom he
has seen, cannot[h] love God whom he has
not seen. [21]And this commandment we
have from him, that he who loves God
should love his brother also.

[h] **4.20** Other ancient authorities read *how can he*

Faith Conquers the World
5 Every one who believes that Jesus is
the Christ is a child of God, and every
one who loves the parent loves the child.
2 By this we know that we love the chil-
dren of God, when we love God and obey
his commandments. 3 For this is the love
of God, that we keep his commandments.
And his commandments are not burden-
some. 4 For whatever is born of God over-
comes the world; and this is the victory
that overcomes the world, our faith. 5 Who
is it that overcomes the world but he who
believes that Jesus is the Son of God?

Testimony concerning the Son of God
6 This is he who came by water and blood,
Jesus Christ, not with the water only but
with the water and the blood. 7 And the
Spirit is the witness, because the Spirit
is the truth. 8 There are three witnesses,
the Spirit, the water, and the blood; and
these three agree. 9 If we receive the tes-
timony of men, the testimony of God is
greater; for this is the testimony of God
that he has borne witness to his Son. 10 He
who believes in the Son of God has the
testimony in himself. He who does not
believe God has made him a liar, because
he has not believed in the testimony that
God has borne to his Son. 11 And this is the
testimony, that God gave us eternal life,
and this life is in his Son. 12 He who has
the Son has life; he who has not the Son
of God has not life.

Epilogue
13 I write this to you who believe in the
name of the Son of God, that you may
know that you have eternal life. 14 And
this is the confidence which we have in
him, that if we ask anything according
to his will he hears us. 15 And if we know
that he hears us in whatever we ask, we
know that we have obtained the requests
made of him. 16 If any one sees his brother
committing what is not a mortal sin, he
will ask, and God[i] will give him life for
those whose sin is not mortal. There is
sin which is mortal; I do not say that one
is to pray for that. 17 All wrongdoing is
sin, but there is sin which is not mortal.

18 We know that any one born of God
does not sin, but He who was born of
God keeps him, and the evil one does not
touch him.

19 We know that we are of God, and the
whole world is in the power of the evil
one.

20 And we know that the Son of God
has come and has given us understand-
ing, to know him who is true; and we
are in him who is true, in his Son Jesus
Christ. This is the true God and eternal
life. 21 Little children, keep yourselves
from idols.

[i] **5.16** Greek *he*

The Second Letter of

JOHN

Salutation

1 The elder to the elect lady and her chil-
dren, whom I love in the truth, and not
only I but also all who know the truth,
2 because of the truth which abides in us
and will be with us for ever:

3 Grace, mercy, and peace will be with
us, from God the Father and from Jesus
Christ the Father's Son, in truth and love.

Truth and Love

4 I rejoiced greatly to find some of your
children following the truth, just as we
have been commanded by the Father.
5 And now I beg you, lady, not as though
I were writing you a new command-
ment, but the one we have had from the
beginning, that we love one another.
6 And this is love, that we follow his com-
mandments; this is the commandment,
as you have heard from the beginning,
that you follow love. 7 For many deceiv-
ers have gone out into the world, men
who will not acknowledge the coming
of Jesus Christ in the flesh; such a one is
the deceiver and the antichrist. 8 Look to
yourselves, that you may not lose what
you[a] have worked for, but may win a
full reward. 9 Any one who goes ahead
and does not abide in the doctrine of
Christ does not have God; he who abides
in the doctrine has both the Father and
the Son. 10 If any one comes to you and
does not bring this doctrine, do not re-
ceive him into the house or give him any
greeting; 11 for he who greets him shares
his wicked work.

Final Greetings

12 Though I have much to write to you, I
would rather not use paper and ink, but
I hope to come to see you and talk with
you face to face, so that our joy may be
complete.

13 The children of your elect sister
greet you.

[a] **1.8** Other ancient authorities read *we*

The Third Letter of

JOHN

Salutation

1 The elder to the beloved Ga′ius, whom I
love in the truth.

Gaius Commended for His Hospitality

2 Beloved, I pray that all may go well
with you and that you may be in health; I
know that it is well with your soul. [3]For I
greatly rejoiced when some of the breth-
ren arrived and testified to the truth of
your life, as indeed you do follow the
truth. [4]No greater joy can I have than
this, to hear that my children follow the
truth.

5 Beloved, it is a loyal thing you do
when you render any service to the
brethren, especially to strangers, [6]who
have testified to your love before the
church. You will do well to send them
on their journey as befits God's service.
[7]For they have set out for his sake and
have accepted nothing from the heathen.
[8]So we ought to support such men, that
we may be fellow workers in the truth.

Diotrephes and Demetrius

9 I have written something to the church;
but Diot′rephes, who likes to put himself
first, does not acknowledge my authority.
[10]So if I come, I will bring up what he is do-
ing, prating against me with evil words.
And not content with that, he refuses
himself to welcome the brethren, and
also stops those who want to welcome
them and puts them out of the church.

11 Beloved, do not imitate evil but im-
itate good. He who does good is of God;
he who does evil has not seen God. [12]De-
me′trius has testimony from every one,
and from the truth itself; I testify to him
too, and you know my testimony is true.

Final Greetings

13 I had much to write to you, but I would
rather not write with pen and ink; [14]I
hope to see you soon, and we will talk to-
gether face to face.

15 Peace be to you. The friends greet
you. Greet the friends, every one of them.

The Letter of

JUDE

Salutation

1 Jude, a servant of Jesus Christ and
brother of James,
To those who are called, beloved
in God the Father and kept for Jesus
Christ:
2 May mercy, peace, and love be multi-
plied to you.

Occasion of the Letter

3 Beloved, being very eager to write to
you of our common salvation, I found
it necessary to write appealing to you
to contend for the faith which was once
for all delivered to the saints. 4For admis-
sion has been secretly gained by some
who long ago were designated for this
condemnation, ungodly persons who
pervert the grace of our God into licen-
tiousness and deny our only Master and
Lord, Jesus Christ.[a]

Judgment on False Teachers

5 Now I desire to remind you, though you
were once for all fully informed, that he[b]
who saved a people out of the land of
Egypt, afterward destroyed those who
did not believe. 6And the angels that did
not keep their own position but left their
proper dwelling have been kept by him
in eternal chains in the nether gloom
until the judgment of the great day; 7just
as Sodom and Gomor'rah and the sur-
rounding cities, which likewise acted
immorally and indulged in unnatural
lust, serve as an example by undergoing
a punishment of eternal fire.
8 Yet in like manner these men in
their dreamings defile the flesh, reject
authority, and revile the glorious ones.[c]
9But when the archangel Michael, con-
tending with the devil, disputed about
the body of Moses, he did not presume
to pronounce a reviling judgment upon
him, but said, "The Lord rebuke you."
10But these men revile whatever they
do not understand, and by those things
that they know by instinct as irrational
animals do, they are destroyed. 11Woe to
them! For they walk in the way of Cain,
and abandon themselves for the sake
of gain to Balaam's error, and perish in
Korah's rebellion. 12These are blemish-
es[d] on your love feasts, as they boldly
carouse together, looking after them-
selves; waterless clouds, carried along
by winds; fruitless trees in late autumn,
twice dead, uprooted; 13wild waves of
the sea, casting up the foam of their own
shame; wandering stars for whom the
nether gloom of darkness has been re-
served for ever.
14 It was of these also that Enoch in the
seventh generation from Adam prophe-
sied, saying, "Behold, the Lord came with
his holy myriads, 15to execute judgment
on all, and to convict all the ungodly of
all their deeds of ungodliness which they
have committed in such an ungodly way,
and of all the harsh things which un-
godly sinners have spoken against him."
16These are grumblers, malcontents,
following their own passions, loud-
mouthed boasters, flattering people to
gain advantage.

Warnings and Exhortations

17 But you must remember, beloved, the
predictions of the apostles of our Lord
Jesus Christ; 18they said to you, "In the
last time there will be scoffers, following
their own ungodly passions." 19It is these
who set up divisions, worldly people,
devoid of the Spirit. 20But you, beloved,

[a] **1.4** Or *the only Master and our Lord Jesus Christ God* [c] **1.8** Greek *glories* [d] **1.12** Or *reefs* [b] **1.5** Ancient authorities read *Jesus* or *the Lord* or

build yourselves up on your most holy faith; pray in the Holy Spirit; [21]keep yourselves in the love of God; wait for the mercy of our Lord Jesus Christ unto eternal life. [22]And convince some, who doubt; [23]save some, by snatching them out of the fire; on some have mercy with fear, hating even the garment spotted by the flesh.[e]

Benediction

24 Now to him who is able to keep you from falling and to present you without blemish before the presence of his glory with rejoicing, [25]to the only God, our Savior through Jesus Christ our Lord, be glory, majesty, dominion, and authority, before all time and now and for ever. Amen.

[e] **1.23** The Greek text in this sentence is uncertain at several points

The

REVELATION TO JOHN

(The Apocalypse)

Introduction and Salutation

1 The revelation of Jesus Christ, which
God gave him to show to his ser-
vants what must soon take place; and
he made it known by sending his angel
to his servant John, 2 who bore witness
to the word of God and to the testimony
of Jesus Christ, even to all that he saw.
3 Blessed is he who reads aloud the words
of the prophecy, and blessed are those
who hear, and who keep what is written
therein; for the time is near.

4 John to the seven churches that are in
Asia:
Grace to you and peace from him who
is and who was and who is to come, and
from the seven spirits who are before his
throne, 5 and from Jesus Christ the faith-
ful witness, the first-born of the dead,
and the ruler of kings on earth.
To him who loves us and has freed us
from our sins by his blood 6 and made us
a kingdom, priests to his God and Father,
to him be glory and dominion for ever
and ever. Amen. 7 Behold, he is coming
with the clouds, and every eye will see
him, every one who pierced him; and all
tribes of the earth will wail on account of
him. Even so. Amen.
8 "I am the Alpha and the Omega," says
the Lord God, who is and who was and
who is to come, the Almighty.

A Vision of Christ

9 I John, your brother, who share with
you in Jesus the tribulation and the king-
dom and the patient endurance, was on
the island called Patmos on account of
the word of God and the testimony of
Jesus. 10 I was in the Spirit on the Lord's
day, and I heard behind me a loud voice
like a trumpet 11 saying, "Write what you
see in a book and send it to the seven
churches, to Ephesus and to Smyrna
and to Per'gamum and to Thyati'ra and
to Sardis and to Philadelphia and to
La-odice'a."
12 Then I turned to see the voice that
was speaking to me, and on turning I saw
seven golden lampstands, 13 and in the
midst of the lampstands one like a son of
man, clothed with a long robe and with
a golden girdle round his breast; 14 his
head and his hair were white as white
wool, white as snow; his eyes were like
a flame of fire, 15 his feet were like bur-
nished bronze, refined as in a furnace,
and his voice was like the sound of many
waters; 16 in his right hand he held seven
stars, from his mouth issued a sharp
two-edged sword, and his face was like
the sun shining in full strength.
17 When I saw him, I fell at his feet as
though dead. But he laid his right hand
upon me, saying, "Fear not, I am the first
and the last, 18 and the living one; I died,
and behold I am alive for evermore, and I
have the keys of Death and Hades. 19 Now
write what you see, what is and what is to
take place hereafter. 20 As for the mystery
of the seven stars which you saw in my
right hand, and the seven golden lamp-
stands, the seven stars are the angels of
the seven churches and the seven lamp-
stands are the seven churches.

The Message to Ephesus

2 "To the angel of the church in Ephe-
sus write: 'The words of him who
holds the seven stars in his right hand,
who walks among the seven golden
lampstands.
2 "'I know your works, your toil and
your patient endurance, and how you
cannot bear evil men but have tested
those who call themselves apostles but
are not, and found them to be false; 3 I

know you are enduring patiently and
bearing up for my name's sake, and you
have not grown weary. 4But I have this
against you, that you have abandoned
the love you had at first. 5Remember
then from what you have fallen, repent
and do the works you did at first. If not, I
will come to you and remove your lamp-
stand from its place, unless you repent.
6Yet this you have, you hate the works
of the Nicola'itans, which I also hate. 7He
who has an ear, let him hear what the
Spirit says to the churches. To him who
conquers I will grant to eat of the tree of
life, which is in the paradise of God.'

The Message to Smyrna

8 "And to the angel of the church in
Smyrna write: 'The words of the first and
the last, who died and came to life.

9 "'I know your tribulation and your
poverty (but you are rich) and the slan-
der of those who say that they are Jews
and are not, but are a synagogue of Sa-
tan. 10Do not fear what you are about to
suffer. Behold, the devil is about to throw
some of you into prison, that you may
be tested, and for ten days you will have
tribulation. Be faithful unto death, and I
will give you the crown of life. 11He who
has an ear, let him hear what the Spirit
says to the churches. He who conquers
shall not be hurt by the second death.'

The Message to Pergamum

12 "And to the angel of the church in
Per'gamum write: 'The words of him who
has the sharp two-edged sword.

13 "'I know where you dwell, where
Satan's throne is; you hold fast my name
and you did not deny my faith even in the
days of An'tipas my witness, my faithful
one, who was killed among you, where
Satan dwells. 14But I have a few things
against you: you have some there who
hold the teaching of Balaam, who taught
Balak to put a stumbling block before the
sons of Israel, that they might eat food
sacrificed to idols and practice immo-
rality. 15So you also have some who hold
the teaching of the Nicola'itans. 16Repent
then. If not, I will come to you soon and
war against them with the sword of my
mouth. 17He who has an ear, let him hear
what the Spirit says to the churches. To
him who conquers I will give some of
the hidden manna, and I will give him
a white stone, with a new name written
on the stone which no one knows except
him who receives it.'

The Message to Thyatira

18 "And to the angel of the church in
Thyati'ra write: 'The words of the Son of
God, who has eyes like a flame of fire, and
whose feet are like burnished bronze.

19 "'I know your works, your love and
faith and service and patient endurance,
and that your latter works exceed the
first. 20But I have this against you, that
you tolerate the woman Jez'ebel, who
calls herself a prophetess and is teaching
and beguiling my servants to practice
immorality and to eat food sacrificed to
idols. 21I gave her time to repent, but
she refuses to repent of her immorality.
22Behold, I will throw her on a sickbed,
and those who commit adultery with
her I will throw into great tribulation,
unless they repent of her doings; 23and I
will strike her children dead. And all the
churches shall know that I am he who
searches mind and heart, and I will give
to each of you as your works deserve.
24But to the rest of you in Thyati'ra, who
do not hold this teaching, who have not
learned what some call the deep things
of Satan, to you I say, I do not lay upon
you any other burden; 25only hold fast
what you have, until I come. 26He who
conquers and who keeps my works until
the end, I will give him power over the
nations, 27and he shall rule them with
a rod of iron, as when earthen pots are
broken in pieces, even as I myself have
received power from my Father; 28and I

will give him the morning star. [29]He who
has an ear, let him hear what the Spirit
says to the churches.'

The Message to Sardis

3 "And to the angel of the church in
Sardis write: 'The words of him who
has the seven spirits of God and the
seven stars.
"'I know your works; you have the
name of being alive, and you are dead.
[2]Awake, and strengthen what remains
and is on the point of death, for I have
not found your works perfect in the
sight of my God. [3]Remember then what
you received and heard; keep that, and
repent. If you will not awake, I will come
like a thief, and you will not know at
what hour I will come upon you. [4]Yet
you have still a few names in Sardis, peo-
ple who have not soiled their garments;
and they shall walk with me in white, for
they are worthy. [5]He who conquers shall
be clad thus in white garments, and I will
not blot his name out of the book of life;
I will confess his name before my Father
and before his angels. [6]He who has an
ear, let him hear what the Spirit says to
the churches.'

The Message to Philadelphia

7 "And to the angel of the church in Phil-
adelphia write: 'The words of the holy
one, the true one, who has the key of
David, who opens and no one shall shut,
who shuts and no one opens.
8 "'I know your works. Behold, I have
set before you an open door, which no
one is able to shut; I know that you have
but little power, and yet you have kept
my word and have not denied my name.
[9]Behold, I will make those of the syn-
agogue of Satan who say that they are
Jews and are not, but lie—behold, I will
make them come and bow down before
your feet, and learn that I have loved
you. [10]Because you have kept my word of
patient endurance, I will keep you from
the hour of trial which is coming on
the whole world, to try those who dwell
upon the earth. [11]I am coming soon; hold
fast what you have, so that no one may
seize your crown. [12]He who conquers, I
will make him a pillar in the temple of
my God; never shall he go out of it, and
I will write on him the name of my God,
and the name of the city of my God, the
new Jerusalem which comes down from
my God out of heaven, and my own new
name. [13]He who has an ear, let him hear
what the Spirit says to the churches.'

The Message to Laodicea

14 "And to the angel of the church in La-
odice'a write: 'The words of the Amen,
the faithful and true witness, the begin-
ning of God's creation.
15 "'I know your works: you are nei-
ther cold nor hot. Would that you were
cold or hot! [16]So, because you are luke-
warm, and neither cold nor hot, I will
spew you out of my mouth. [17]For you
say, I am rich, I have prospered, and I
need nothing; not knowing that you
are wretched, pitiable, poor, blind, and
naked. [18]Therefore I counsel you to buy
from me gold refined by fire, that you
may be rich, and white garments to
clothe you and to keep the shame of your
nakedness from being seen, and salve
to anoint your eyes, that you may see.
[19]Those whom I love, I reprove and chas-
ten; so be zealous and repent. [20]Behold, I
stand at the door and knock; if any one
hears my voice and opens the door, I will
come in to him and eat with him, and he
with me. [21]He who conquers, I will grant
him to sit with me on my throne, as I my-
self conquered and sat down with my Fa-
ther on his throne. [22]He who has an ear,
let him hear what the Spirit says to the
churches.'"

The Heavenly Worship

4 After this I looked, and lo, in heaven
an open door! And the first voice,

which I had heard speaking to me like
a trumpet, said, "Come up hither, and
I will show you what must take place
after this." [2]At once I was in the Spirit,
and lo, a throne stood in heaven, with
one seated on the throne! [3]And he who
sat there appeared like jasper and car-
nelian, and round the throne was a rain-
bow that looked like an emerald. [4]Round
the throne were twenty-four thrones,
and seated on the thrones were twenty-
four elders, clad in white garments, with
golden crowns upon their heads. [5]From
the throne issue flashes of lightning, and
voices and peals of thunder, and before
the throne burn seven torches of fire,
which are the seven spirits of God; [6]and
before the throne there is as it were a sea
of glass, like crystal.

And round the throne, on each side
of the throne, are four living creatures,
full of eyes in front and behind: [7]the first
living creature like a lion, the second liv-
ing creature like an ox, the third living
creature with the face of a man, and the
fourth living creature like a flying ea-
gle. [8]And the four living creatures, each
of them with six wings, are full of eyes
all round and within, and day and night
they never cease to sing,

"Holy, holy, holy, is the Lord God
Almighty,
who was and is and is to come!"

[9]And whenever the living creatures give
glory and honor and thanks to him who
is seated on the throne, who lives for
ever and ever, [10]the twenty-four elders
fall down before him who is seated on
the throne and worship him who lives
for ever and ever; they cast their crowns
before the throne, singing,

11 "Worthy art thou, our Lord and
God,
to receive glory and honor and
power,
for thou didst create all things,
and by thy will they existed and
were created."

The Scroll and the Lamb

5 And I saw in the right hand of him
who was seated on the throne a scroll
written within and on the back, sealed
with seven seals; [2]and I saw a strong an-
gel proclaiming with a loud voice, "Who
is worthy to open the scroll and break its
seals?" [3]And no one in heaven or on earth
or under the earth was able to open the
scroll or to look into it, [4]and I wept much
that no one was found worthy to open
the scroll or to look into it. [5]Then one of
the elders said to me, "Weep not; lo, the
Lion of the tribe of Judah, the Root of Da-
vid, has conquered, so that he can open
the scroll and its seven seals."

6 And between the throne and the
four living creatures and among the el-
ders, I saw a Lamb standing, as though
it had been slain, with seven horns and
with seven eyes, which are the seven
spirits of God sent out into all the earth;
[7]and he went and took the scroll from
the right hand of him who was seated
on the throne. [8]And when he had taken
the scroll, the four living creatures and
the twenty-four elders fell down before
the Lamb, each holding a harp, and with
golden bowls full of incense, which are
the prayers of the saints; [9]and they sang
a new song, saying,

"Worthy art thou to take the scroll
and to open its seals,
for thou wast slain and by thy blood
didst ransom men for God
from every tribe and tongue and
people and nation,
10 and hast made them a kingdom and
priests to our God,
and they shall reign on earth."

[11]Then I looked, and I heard around the
throne and the living creatures and the
elders the voice of many angels, num-
bering myriads of myriads and thou-
sands of thousands, [12]saying with a loud
voice, "Worthy is the Lamb who was
slain, to receive power and wealth and
wisdom and might and honor and glory

and blessing!" 13And I heard every crea-
ture in heaven and on earth and under
the earth and in the sea, and all therein,
saying, "To him who sits upon the throne
and to the Lamb be blessing and honor
and glory and might for ever and ever!"
14And the four living creatures said,
"Amen!" and the elders fell down and
worshiped.

The Seven Seals

6 Now I saw when the Lamb opened one
of the seven seals, and I heard one of
the four living creatures say, as with a
voice of thunder, "Come!" 2And I saw, and
behold, a white horse, and its rider had a
bow; and a crown was given to him, and
he went out conquering and to conquer.
3 When he opened the second seal,
I heard the second living creature say,
"Come!" 4And out came another horse,
bright red; its rider was permitted to
take peace from the earth, so that men
should slay one another; and he was
given a great sword.
5 When he opened the third seal,
I heard the third living creature say,
"Come!" And I saw, and behold, a black
horse, and its rider had a balance in his
hand; 6and I heard what seemed to be a
voice in the midst of the four living crea-
tures saying, "A quart of wheat for a de-
narius,[a] and three quarts of barley for a
denarius;[b] but do not harm oil and wine!"
7 When he opened the fourth seal, I
heard the voice of the fourth living crea-
ture say, "Come!" 8And I saw, and behold,
a pale horse, and its rider's name was
Death, and Hades followed him; and they
were given power over a fourth of the
earth, to kill with sword and with famine
and with pestilence and by wild beasts of
the earth.
9 When he opened the fifth seal, I saw
under the altar the souls of those who
had been slain for the word of God and
for the witness they had borne; 10they
cried out with a loud voice, "O Sovereign
Lord, holy and true, how long before
thou wilt judge and avenge our blood on
those who dwell upon the earth?" 11Then
they were each given a white robe and
told to rest a little longer, until the num-
ber of their fellow servants and their
brethren should be complete, who were
to be killed as they themselves had been.
12 When he opened the sixth seal, I
looked, and behold, there was a great
earthquake; and the sun became black
as sackcloth, the full moon became like
blood, 13and the stars of the sky fell to the
earth as the fig tree sheds its winter fruit
when shaken by a gale; 14the sky van-
ished like a scroll that is rolled up, and
every mountain and island was removed
from its place. 15Then the kings of the
earth and the great men and the generals
and the rich and the strong, and every
one, slave and free, hid in the caves and
among the rocks of the mountains, 16call-
ing to the mountains and rocks, "Fall on
us and hide us from the face of him who
is seated on the throne, and from the
wrath of the Lamb; 17for the great day of
their wrath has come, and who can stand
before it?"

The 144,000 of Israel Sealed

7 After this I saw four angels standing
at the four corners of the earth, hold-
ing back the four winds of the earth, that
no wind might blow on earth or sea or
against any tree. 2Then I saw another
angel ascend from the rising of the sun,
with the seal of the living God, and he
called with a loud voice to the four angels
who had been given power to harm earth
and sea, 3saying, "Do not harm the earth
or the sea or the trees, till we have sealed
the servants of our God upon their
foreheads." 4And I heard the number
of the sealed, a hundred and forty-four

[a] **6.6** The denarius was a day's wage for a laborer

[b] **6.6** The denarius was a day's wage for a laborer

thousand sealed, out of every tribe of the
sons of Israel, 5 twelve thousand sealed
out of the tribe of Judah, twelve thousand
of the tribe of Reuben, twelve thousand
of the tribe of Gad, 6 twelve thousand of
the tribe of Asher, twelve thousand of
the tribe of Naph'tali, twelve thousand of
the tribe of Manas'seh, 7 twelve thousand
of the tribe of Simeon, twelve thousand
of the tribe of Levi, twelve thousand of
the tribe of Is'sachar, 8 twelve thousand
of the tribe of Zeb'ulun, twelve thousand
of the tribe of Joseph, twelve thousand
sealed out of the tribe of Benjamin.

The Multitude from Every Nation

9 After this I looked, and behold, a great
multitude which no man could number,
from every nation, from all tribes and
peoples and tongues, standing before the
throne and before the Lamb, clothed in
white robes, with palm branches in their
hands, 10 and crying out with a loud voice,
"Salvation belongs to our God who sits
upon the throne, and to the Lamb!" 11 And
all the angels stood round the throne and
round the elders and the four living crea-
tures, and they fell on their faces before
the throne and worshiped God, 12 saying,
"Amen! Blessing and glory and wisdom
and thanksgiving and honor and power
and might be to our God for ever and
ever! Amen."

13 Then one of the elders addressed
me, saying, "Who are these, clothed
in white robes, and whence have they
come?" 14 I said to him, "Sir, you know."
And he said to me, "These are they who
have come out of the great tribulation;
they have washed their robes and made
them white in the blood of the Lamb.

15 Therefore are they before the
throne of God,
and serve him day and night
within his temple;
and he who sits upon the throne
will shelter them with his
presence.

16 They shall hunger no more, neither
thirst any more;
the sun shall not strike them, nor
any scorching heat.

17 For the Lamb in the midst of the
throne will be their shepherd,
and he will guide them to springs
of living water;
and God will wipe away every tear
from their eyes."

The Seventh Seal and the Golden Censer

8 When the Lamb opened the seventh
seal, there was silence in heaven for
about half an hour. 2 Then I saw the seven
angels who stand before God, and seven
trumpets were given to them. 3 And an-
other angel came and stood at the altar
with a golden censer; and he was given
much incense to mingle with the prayers
of all the saints upon the golden altar be-
fore the throne; 4 and the smoke of the in-
cense rose with the prayers of the saints
from the hand of the angel before God.
5 Then the angel took the censer and filled
it with fire from the altar and threw it on
the earth; and there were peals of thun-
der, loud noises, flashes of lightning, and
an earthquake.

The Seven Trumpets

6 Now the seven angels who had the
seven trumpets made ready to blow
them.

7 The first angel blew his trumpet, and
there followed hail and fire, mixed with
blood, which fell on the earth; and a third
of the earth was burnt up, and a third of
the trees were burnt up, and all green
grass was burnt up.

8 The second angel blew his trumpet,
and something like a great mountain,
burning with fire, was thrown into the
sea; 9 and a third of the sea became blood,
a third of the living creatures in the
sea died, and a third of the ships were
destroyed.

10 The third angel blew his trumpet,
and a great star fell from heaven, blaz-
ing like a torch, and it fell on a third of
the rivers and on the fountains of water.
11 The name of the star is Wormwood. A
third of the waters became wormwood,
and many men died of the water, because
it was made bitter.

12 The fourth angel blew his trumpet,
and a third of the sun was struck, and
a third of the moon, and a third of the
stars, so that a third of their light was
darkened; a third of the day was kept
from shining, and likewise a third of the
night.

13 Then I looked, and I heard an eagle
crying with a loud voice, as it flew in
midheaven, "Woe, woe, woe to those who
dwell on the earth, at the blasts of the
other trumpets which the three angels
are about to blow!"

9 And the fifth angel blew his trumpet,
and I saw a star fallen from heaven
to earth, and he was given the key of the
shaft of the bottomless pit; 2 he opened
the shaft of the bottomless pit, and from
the shaft rose smoke like the smoke of a
great furnace, and the sun and the air
were darkened with the smoke from the
shaft. 3 Then from the smoke came lo-
custs on the earth, and they were given
power like the power of scorpions of the
earth; 4 they were told not to harm the
grass of the earth or any green growth
or any tree, but only those of mankind
who have not the seal of God upon their
foreheads; 5 they were allowed to tor-
ture them for five months, but not to kill
them, and their torture was like the tor-
ture of a scorpion, when it stings a man.
6 And in those days men will seek death
and will not find it; they will long to die,
and death will fly from them.

7 In appearance the locusts were like
horses arrayed for battle; on their heads
were what looked like crowns of gold;
their faces were like human faces, 8 their
hair like women's hair, and their teeth
like lions' teeth; 9 they had scales like iron
breastplates, and the noise of their wings
was like the noise of many chariots with
horses rushing into battle. 10 They have
tails like scorpions, and stings, and their
power of hurting men for five months
lies in their tails. 11 They have as king
over them the angel of the bottomless
pit; his name in Hebrew is Abad'don, and
in Greek he is called Apol'lyon.[c]

12 The first woe has passed; behold,
two woes are still to come.

13 Then the sixth angel blew his trum-
pet, and I heard a voice from the four
horns of the golden altar before God,
14 saying to the sixth angel who had the
trumpet, "Release the four angels who
are bound at the great river Euphra'tes."
15 So the four angels were released, who
had been held ready for the hour, the day,
the month, and the year, to kill a third of
mankind. 16 The number of the troops of
cavalry was twice ten thousand times
ten thousand; I heard their number.
17 And this was how I saw the horses in
my vision: the riders wore breastplates
the color of fire and of sapphire[d] and
of sulphur, and the heads of the horses
were like lions' heads, and fire and smoke
and sulphur issued from their mouths.
18 By these three plagues a third of man-
kind was killed, by the fire and smoke
and sulphur issuing from their mouths.
19 For the power of the horses is in their
mouths and in their tails; their tails are
like serpents, with heads, and by means
of them they wound.

20 The rest of mankind, who were not
killed by these plagues, did not repent
of the works of their hands nor give up
worshiping demons and idols of gold and
silver and bronze and stone and wood,
which cannot either see or hear or walk;
21 nor did they repent of their murders or
their sorceries or their immorality or
their thefts.

[c] **9.11** Or *Destroyer* [d] **9.17** Greek *hyacinth*

The Angel with the Little Scroll

10 Then I saw another mighty an-
gel coming down from heaven,
wrapped in a cloud, with a rainbow over
his head, and his face was like the sun,
and his legs like pillars of fire. 2 He had a
little scroll open in his hand. And he set
his right foot on the sea, and his left foot
on the land, 3 and called out with a loud
voice, like a lion roaring; when he called
out, the seven thunders sounded. 4 And
when the seven thunders had sounded,
I was about to write, but I heard a voice
from heaven saying, "Seal up what the
seven thunders have said, and do not
write it down." 5 And the angel whom I
saw standing on sea and land lifted up
his right hand to heaven 6 and swore by
him who lives for ever and ever, who cre-
ated heaven and what is in it, the earth
and what is in it, and the sea and what
is in it, that there should be no more de-
lay, 7 but that in the days of the trumpet
call to be sounded by the seventh angel,
the mystery of God, as he announced
to his servants the prophets, should be
fulfilled.
8 Then the voice which I had heard
from heaven spoke to me again, saying,
"Go, take the scroll which is open in the
hand of the angel who is standing on the
sea and on the land." 9 So I went to the an-
gel and told him to give me the little scroll;
and he said to me, "Take it and eat; it will
be bitter to your stomach, but sweet as
honey in your mouth." 10 And I took the lit-
tle scroll from the hand of the angel and
ate it; it was sweet as honey in my mouth,
but when I had eaten it my stomach was
made bitter. 11 And I was told, "You must
again prophesy about many peoples and
nations and tongues and kings."

The Two Witnesses

11 Then I was given a measuring rod
like a staff, and I was told: "Rise and
measure the temple of God and the altar
and those who worship there, 2 but do not
measure the court outside the temple;
leave that out, for it is given over to the
nations, and they will trample over the
holy city for forty-two months. 3 And I
will grant my two witnesses power to
prophesy for one thousand two hundred
and sixty days, clothed in sackcloth."
4 These are the two olive trees and
the two lampstands which stand before
the Lord of the earth. 5 And if any one
would harm them, fire pours from their
mouth and consumes their foes; if any
one would harm them, thus he is doomed
to be killed. 6 They have power to shut
the sky, that no rain may fall during the
days of their prophesying, and they have
power over the waters to turn them into
blood, and to smite the earth with ev-
ery plague, as often as they desire. 7 And
when they have finished their testimony,
the beast that ascends from the bottom-
less pit will make war upon them and
conquer them and kill them, 8 and their
dead bodies will lie in the street of the
great city which is allegorically[e] called
Sodom and Egypt, where their Lord
was crucified. 9 For three days and a half
men from the peoples and tribes and
tongues and nations gaze at their dead
bodies and refuse to let them be placed
in a tomb, 10 and those who dwell on the
earth will rejoice over them and make
merry and exchange presents, because
these two prophets had been a torment
to those who dwell on the earth. 11 But
after the three and a half days a breath
of life from God entered them, and they
stood up on their feet, and great fear
fell on those who saw them. 12 Then they
heard a loud voice from heaven saying to
them, "Come up hither!" And in the sight
of their foes they went up to heaven in
a cloud. 13 And at that hour there was a
great earthquake, and a tenth of the city
fell; seven thousand people were killed
in the earthquake, and the rest were

[e] **11.8** Greek *spiritually*

terrified and gave glory to the God of
heaven.
14 The second woe has passed; behold,
the third woe is soon to come.

The Seventh Trumpet

15 Then the seventh angel blew his
trumpet, and there were loud voices
in heaven, saying, "The kingdom of the
world has become the kingdom of our
Lord and of his Christ, and he shall reign
for ever and ever." 16 And the twenty-four
elders who sit on their thrones before
God fell on their faces and worshiped
God, 17 saying,

"We give thanks to thee, Lord God
Almighty, who art and who
wast,
that thou hast taken thy great
power and begun to reign.
18 The nations raged, but thy wrath
came,
and the time for the dead to be
judged,
for rewarding thy servants, the
prophets and saints,
and those who fear thy name, both
small and great,
and for destroying the destroyers of
the earth."

19 Then God's temple in heaven was
opened, and the ark of his covenant was
seen within his temple; and there were
flashes of lightning, loud noises, peals of
thunder, an earthquake, and heavy hail.

The Woman and the Dragon

12 And a great portent appeared in
heaven, a woman clothed with the
sun, with the moon under her feet, and
on her head a crown of twelve stars;
2 she was with child and she cried out in
her pangs of birth, in anguish for deliv-
ery. 3 And another portent appeared in
heaven; behold, a great red dragon, with
seven heads and ten horns, and seven
diadems upon his heads. 4 His tail swept
down a third of the stars of heaven, and
cast them to the earth. And the dragon
stood before the woman who was about
to bear a child, that he might devour her
child when she brought it forth; 5 she
brought forth a male child, one who is to
rule all the nations with a rod of iron, but
her child was caught up to God and to his
throne, 6 and the woman fled into the wil-
derness, where she has a place prepared
by God, in which to be nourished for one
thousand two hundred and sixty days.

Michael Defeats the Dragon

7 Now war arose in heaven, Michael and
his angels fighting against the dragon;
and the dragon and his angels fought,
8 but they were defeated and there was
no longer any place for them in heaven.
9 And the great dragon was thrown
down, that ancient serpent, who is called
the Devil and Satan, the deceiver of the
whole world—he was thrown down to
the earth, and his angels were thrown
down with him. 10 And I heard a loud
voice in heaven, saying, "Now the salva-
tion and the power and the kingdom of
our God and the authority of his Christ
have come, for the accuser of our breth-
ren has been thrown down, who accuses
them day and night before our God. 11 And
they have conquered him by the blood of
the Lamb and by the word of their testi-
mony, for they loved not their lives even
unto death. 12 Rejoice then, O heaven and
you that dwell therein! But woe to you,
O earth and sea, for the devil has come
down to you in great wrath, because he
knows that his time is short!"

The Dragon Fights Again on Earth

13 And when the dragon saw that he had
been thrown down to the earth, he pur-
sued the woman who had borne the male
child. 14 But the woman was given the two
wings of the great eagle that she might fly
from the serpent into the wilderness, to
the place where she is to be nourished for
a time, and times, and half a time. 15 The

serpent poured water like a river out of
his mouth after the woman, to sweep her
away with the flood. [16]But the earth came
to the help of the woman, and the earth
opened its mouth and swallowed the
river which the dragon had poured from
his mouth. [17]Then the dragon was angry
with the woman, and went off to make
war on the rest of her offspring, on those
who keep the commandments of God and
bear testimony to Jesus. And he stood[f] on
the sand of the sea.

The First Beast

13 And I saw a beast rising out of
the sea, with ten horns and seven
heads, with ten diadems upon its horns
and a blasphemous name upon its heads.
[2]And the beast that I saw was like a leop-
ard, its feet were like a bear's, and its
mouth was like a lion's mouth. And to
it the dragon gave his power and his
throne and great authority. [3]One of its
heads seemed to have a mortal wound,
but its mortal wound was healed, and
the whole earth followed the beast with
wonder. [4]Men worshiped the dragon, for
he had given his authority to the beast,
and they worshiped the beast, saying,
"Who is like the beast, and who can fight
against it?"

5 And the beast was given a mouth ut-
tering haughty and blasphemous words,
and it was allowed to exercise author-
ity for forty-two months; [6]it opened its
mouth to utter blasphemies against God,
blaspheming his name and his dwelling,
that is, those who dwell in heaven. [7]Also
it was allowed to make war on the saints
and to conquer them.[g] And authority
was given it over every tribe and peo-
ple and tongue and nation, [8]and all who
dwell on earth will worship it, every one
whose name has not been written before
the foundation of the world in the book
of life of the Lamb that was slain. [9]If any
one has an ear, let him hear:

10 If any one is to be taken captive,
to captivity he goes;
if any one slays with the sword,
with the sword must he be slain.

Here is a call for the endurance and faith
of the saints.

The Second Beast

11 Then I saw another beast which rose
out of the earth; it had two horns like a
lamb and it spoke like a dragon. [12]It exer-
cises all the authority of the first beast
in its presence, and makes the earth
and its inhabitants worship the first
beast, whose mortal wound was healed.
[13]It works great signs, even making fire
come down from heaven to earth in the
sight of men; [14]and by the signs which
it is allowed to work in the presence of
the beast, it deceives those who dwell
on earth, bidding them make an image
for the beast which was wounded by the
sword and yet lived; [15]and it was allowed
to give breath to the image of the beast so
that the image of the beast should even
speak, and to cause those who would not
worship the image of the beast to be slain.
[16]Also it causes all, both small and great,
both rich and poor, both free and slave,
to be marked on the right hand or the
forehead, [17]so that no one can buy or sell
unless he has the mark, that is, the name
of the beast or the number of its name.
[18]This calls for wisdom: let him who has
understanding reckon the number of the
beast, for it is a human number, its num-
ber is six hundred and sixty-six.[h]

The Lamb and the 144,000

14 Then I looked, and lo, on Mount
Zion stood the Lamb, and with
him a hundred and forty-four thousand
who had his name and his Father's name

[f] **12.17** Other ancient authorities read *And I stood,* connecting the sentence with 13.1
[g] **13.7** Other ancient authorities omit this sentence
[h] **13.18** Other ancient authorities read *six hundred and sixteen*

written on their foreheads. 2And I heard a
voice from heaven like the sound of many
waters and like the sound of loud thun-
der; the voice I heard was like the sound
of harpers playing on their harps, 3and
they sing a new song before the throne
and before the four living creatures and
before the elders. No one could learn that
song except the hundred and forty-four
thousand who had been redeemed from
the earth. 4It is these who have not defiled
themselves with women, for they are
chaste;[i] it is these who follow the Lamb
wherever he goes; these have been re-
deemed from mankind as first fruits for
God and the Lamb, 5and in their mouth no
lie was found, for they are spotless.

The Messages of the Three Angels

6 Then I saw another angel flying in
midheaven, with an eternal gospel to
proclaim to those who dwell on earth, to
every nation and tribe and tongue and
people; 7and he said with a loud voice,
"Fear God and give him glory, for the
hour of his judgment has come; and wor-
ship him who made heaven and earth,
the sea and the fountains of water."

8 Another angel, a second, followed,
saying, "Fallen, fallen is Babylon the
great, she who made all nations drink
the wine of her impure passion."

9 And another angel, a third, followed
them, saying with a loud voice, "If any
one worships the beast and its image,
and receives a mark on his forehead
or on his hand, 10he also shall drink the
wine of God's wrath, poured unmixed
into the cup of his anger, and he shall
be tormented with fire and brimstone
in the presence of the holy angels and
in the presence of the Lamb. 11And the
smoke of their torment goes up for ever
and ever; and they have no rest, day or
night, these worshipers of the beast
and its image, and whoever receives the
mark of its name."

12 Here is a call for the endurance of
the saints, those who keep the command-
ments of God and the faith of Jesus.

13 And I heard a voice from heaven
saying, "Write this: Blessed are the dead
who die in the Lord henceforth." "Blessed
indeed," says the Spirit, "that they may
rest from their labors, for their deeds
follow them!"

Reaping the Earth's Harvest

14 Then I looked, and lo, a white cloud,
and seated on the cloud one like a son of
man, with a golden crown on his head,
and a sharp sickle in his hand. 15And an-
other angel came out of the temple, call-
ing with a loud voice to him who sat upon
the cloud, "Put in your sickle, and reap,
for the hour to reap has come, for the
harvest of the earth is fully ripe." 16So he
who sat upon the cloud swung his sickle
on the earth, and the earth was reaped.

17 And another angel came out of the
temple in heaven, and he too had a sharp
sickle. 18Then another angel came out
from the altar, the angel who has power
over fire, and he called with a loud voice
to him who had the sharp sickle, "Put in
your sickle, and gather the clusters of
the vine of the earth, for its grapes are
ripe." 19So the angel swung his sickle
on the earth and gathered the vintage
of the earth, and threw it into the great
wine press of the wrath of God; 20and the
wine press was trodden outside the city,
and blood flowed from the wine press,
as high as a horse's bridle, for one thou-
sand six hundred stadia.[j]

The Angels with the Seven Last Plagues

15 Then I saw another portent in
heaven, great and wonderful, seven
angels with seven plagues, which are the
last, for with them the wrath of God is
ended.

[i] **14.4** Greek *virgins* [j] **14.20** About two hundred miles

2 And I saw what appeared to be a sea
of glass mingled with fire, and those who
had conquered the beast and its image
and the number of its name, standing
beside the sea of glass with harps of God
in their hands. [3]And they sing the song of
Moses, the servant of God, and the song
of the Lamb, saying,

"Great and wonderful are thy deeds,
O Lord God the Almighty!
Just and true are thy ways,
O King of the ages![k]
4 Who shall not fear and glorify thy
name, O Lord?
For thou alone art holy.
All nations shall come and worship
thee,
for thy judgments have been
revealed."

5 After this I looked, and the temple
of the tent of witness in heaven was
opened, [6]and out of the temple came the
seven angels with the seven plagues,
robed in pure bright linen, and their
breasts girded with golden girdles. [7]And
one of the four living creatures gave the
seven angels seven golden bowls full of
the wrath of God who lives for ever and
ever; [8]and the temple was filled with
smoke from the glory of God and from
his power, and no one could enter the
temple until the seven plagues of the
seven angels were ended.

The Bowls of God's Wrath

16 Then I heard a loud voice from the
temple telling the seven angels,
"Go and pour out on the earth the seven
bowls of the wrath of God."

2 So the first angel went and poured his
bowl on the earth, and foul and evil sores
came upon the men who bore the mark
of the beast and worshiped its image.

3 The second angel poured his bowl
into the sea, and it became like the blood
of a dead man, and every living thing
died that was in the sea.

4 The third angel poured his bowl into
the rivers and the fountains of water,
and they became blood. [5]And I heard the
angel of water say,

"Just art thou in these thy
judgments,
thou who art and wast, O Holy
One.
6 For men have shed the blood of
saints and prophets,
and thou hast given them blood to
drink.
It is their due!"

[7]And I heard the altar cry,

"Yea, Lord God the Almighty,
true and just are thy judgments!"

8 The fourth angel poured his bowl on
the sun, and it was allowed to scorch men
with fire; [9]men were scorched by the
fierce heat, and they cursed the name of
God who had power over these plagues,
and they did not repent and give him
glory.

10 The fifth angel poured his bowl on
the throne of the beast, and its kingdom
was in darkness; men gnawed their
tongues in anguish [11]and cursed the God
of heaven for their pain and sores, and
did not repent of their deeds.

12 The sixth angel poured his bowl
on the great river Euphra'tes, and its
water was dried up, to prepare the way
for the kings from the east. [13]And I saw,
issuing from the mouth of the dragon
and from the mouth of the beast and
from the mouth of the false prophet,
three foul spirits like frogs; [14]for they
are demonic spirits, performing signs,
who go abroad to the kings of the whole
world, to assemble them for battle on
the great day of God the Almighty.
[15]("Lo, I am coming like a thief! Blessed
is he who is awake, keeping his gar-
ments that he may not go naked and be
seen exposed!") [16]And they assembled
them at the place which is called in He-
brew Armaged'don.

[k] **15.3** Other ancient authorities read *the nations*

17 The seventh angel poured his bowl
into the air, and a great voice came out of
the temple, from the throne, saying, "It is
done!" [18]And there were flashes of light-
ning, loud noises, peals of thunder, and a
great earthquake such as had never been
since men were on the earth, so great
was that earthquake. [19]The great city was
split into three parts, and the cities of the
nations fell, and God remembered great
Babylon, to make her drain the cup of
the fury of his wrath. [20]And every island
fled away, and no mountains were to
be found; [21]and great hailstones, heavy
as a hundredweight, dropped on men
from heaven, till men cursed God for
the plague of the hail, so fearful was that
plague.

The Great Whore and the Beast

17 Then one of the seven angels who
had the seven bowls came and said
to me, "Come, I will show you the judg-
ment of the great harlot who is seated
upon many waters, [2]with whom the
kings of the earth have committed for-
nication, and with the wine of whose
fornication the dwellers on earth have
become drunk." [3]And he carried me
away in the Spirit into a wilderness, and
I saw a woman sitting on a scarlet beast
which was full of blasphemous names,
and it had seven heads and ten horns.
[4]The woman was arrayed in purple and
scarlet, and bedecked with gold and
jewels and pearls, holding in her hand a
golden cup full of abominations and the
impurities of her fornication; [5]and on
her forehead was written a name of mys-
tery: "Babylon the great, mother of har-
lots and of earth's abominations." [6]And I
saw the woman, drunk with the blood of
the saints and the blood of the martyrs of
Jesus.

When I saw her I marveled greatly. [7]But
the angel said to me, "Why marvel? I will
tell you the mystery of the woman, and of
the beast with seven heads and ten horns
that carries her. [8]The beast that you saw
was, and is not, and is to ascend from the
bottomless pit and go to perdition; and
the dwellers on earth whose names have
not been written in the book of life from
the foundation of the world, will marvel
to behold the beast, because it was and is
not and is to come. [9]This calls for a mind
with wisdom: the seven heads are seven
hills on which the woman is seated;
[10]they are also seven kings, five of whom
have fallen, one is, the other has not yet
come, and when he comes he must re-
main only a little while. [11]As for the beast
that was and is not, it is an eighth but it
belongs to the seven, and it goes to per-
dition. [12]And the ten horns that you saw
are ten kings who have not yet received
royal power, but they are to receive au-
thority as kings for one hour, together
with the beast. [13]These are of one mind
and give over their power and authority
to the beast; [14]they will make war on the
Lamb, and the Lamb will conquer them,
for he is Lord of lords and King of kings,
and those with him are called and chosen
and faithful."

15 And he said to me, "The waters that
you saw, where the harlot is seated, are
peoples and multitudes and nations and
tongues. [16]And the ten horns that you
saw, they and the beast will hate the har-
lot; they will make her desolate and na-
ked, and devour her flesh and burn her
up with fire, [17]for God has put it into their
hearts to carry out his purpose by being
of one mind and giving over their royal
power to the beast, until the words of
God shall be fulfilled. [18]And the woman
that you saw is the great city which has
dominion over the kings of the earth."

The Fall of Babylon

18 After this I saw another angel com-
ing down from heaven, having
great authority; and the earth was made
bright with his splendor. [2]And he called
out with a mighty voice,

"Fallen, fallen is Babylon the great!
It has become a dwelling place of
demons,
a haunt of every foul spirit,
a haunt of every foul and hateful
bird;
3 for all nations have drunk[1] the wine
of her impure passion,
and the kings of the earth have
committed fornication with her,
and the merchants of the earth have
grown rich with the wealth of
her wantonness."
4Then I heard another voice from heaven
saying,
"Come out of her, my people,
lest you take part in her sins,
lest you share in her plagues;
5 for her sins are heaped high as
heaven,
and God has remembered her
iniquities.
6 Render to her as she herself has
rendered,
and repay her double for her
deeds;
mix a double draught for her in the
cup she mixed.
7 As she glorified herself and played
the wanton,
so give her a like measure of
torment and mourning.
Since in her heart she says, 'A queen
I sit,
I am no widow, mourning I shall
never see,'
8 so shall her plagues come in a single
day,
pestilence and mourning and
famine,
and she shall be burned with fire;
for mighty is the Lord God who
judges her."
9 And the kings of the earth, who com-
mitted fornication and were wanton
with her, will weep and wail over her
when they see the smoke of her burning;
10they will stand far off, in fear of her tor-
ment, and say,
"Alas! alas! thou great city,
thou mighty city, Babylon!
In one hour has thy judgment come."
11 And the merchants of the earth weep
and mourn for her, since no one buys
their cargo any more, 12cargo of gold,
silver, jewels and pearls, fine linen, pur-
ple, silk and scarlet, all kinds of scented
wood, all articles of ivory, all articles
of costly wood, bronze, iron and mar-
ble, 13cinnamon, spice, incense, myrrh,
frankincense, wine, oil, fine flour and
wheat, cattle and sheep, horses and char-
iots, and slaves, that is, human souls.
14 "The fruit for which thy soul longed
has gone from thee,
and all thy dainties and thy splendor
are lost to thee, never to be
found again!"
15The merchants of these wares, who
gained wealth from her, will stand far
off, in fear of her torment, weeping and
mourning aloud,
16 "Alas, alas, for the great city
that was clothed in fine linen, in
purple and scarlet,
bedecked with gold, with jewels, and
with pearls!
17 In one hour all this wealth has been
laid waste."
And all shipmasters and seafaring
men, sailors and all whose trade is on the
sea, stood far off 18and cried out as they
saw the smoke of her burning,
"What city was like the great city?"
19And they threw dust on their heads, as
they wept and mourned, crying out,
"Alas, alas, for the great city
where all who had ships at sea grew
rich by her wealth!
In one hour she has been laid waste.
20 Rejoice over her, O heaven,
O saints and apostles and prophets,
for God has given judgment for you
against her!"

[1] **18.3** Other ancient authorities read *fallen by*

21 Then a mighty angel took up a stone
like a great millstone and threw it into
the sea, saying,
"So shall Babylon the great city
be thrown down with violence,
and shall be found no more;
22 and the sound of harpers and
minstrels, of flute players and
trumpeters,
shall be heard in thee no more;
and a craftsman of any craft
shall be found in thee no more;
and the sound of the millstone
shall be heard in thee no more;
23 and the light of a lamp
shall shine in thee no more;
and the voice of bridegroom and
bride
shall be heard in thee no more;
for thy merchants were the great
men of the earth,
and all nations were deceived by
thy sorcery.
24 And in her was found the blood of
prophets and of saints,
and of all who have been slain on
earth."

The Rejoicing in Heaven

19 After this I heard what seemed to
be the mighty voice of a great mul-
titude in heaven, crying,
"Hallelujah! Salvation and glory and
power belong to our God,
2 for his judgments are true and
just;
he has judged the great harlot who
corrupted the earth with her
fornication,
and he has avenged on her the blood
of his servants."
3 Once more they cried,
"Hallelujah! The smoke from her
goes up for ever and ever."
4 And the twenty-four elders and the
four living creatures fell down and wor-
shiped God who is seated on the throne,
saying, "Amen. Hallelujah!" 5 And from
the throne came a voice crying,
"Praise our God, all you his
servants,
you who fear him, small and great."
6 Then I heard what seemed to be the
voice of a great multitude, like the sound
of many waters and like the sound of
mighty thunderpeals, crying,
"Hallelujah! For the Lord our God
the Almighty reigns.
7 Let us rejoice and exult and give
him the glory,
for the marriage of the Lamb has
come,
and his Bride has made herself
ready;
8 it was granted her to be clothed with
fine linen, bright and pure"—
for the fine linen is the righteous deeds
of the saints.
9 And the angel said[m] to me, "Write
this: Blessed are those who are invited
to the marriage supper of the Lamb."
And he said to me, "These are true words
of God." 10 Then I fell down at his feet to
worship him, but he said to me, "You
must not do that! I am a fellow servant
with you and your brethren who hold
the testimony of Jesus. Worship God."
For the testimony of Jesus is the spirit of
prophecy.

The Rider on the White Horse

11 Then I saw heaven opened, and be-
hold, a white horse! He who sat upon it
is called Faithful and True, and in righ-
teousness he judges and makes war.
12 His eyes are like a flame of fire, and on
his head are many diadems; and he has a
name inscribed which no one knows but
himself. 13 He is clad in a robe dipped in[n]
blood, and the name by which he is called
is The Word of God. 14 And the armies of
heaven, arrayed in fine linen, white and
pure, followed him on white horses.
15 From his mouth issues a sharp sword

[m] **19.9** Greek *he said* [n] **19.13** Other ancient authorities read *sprinkled with*

with which to smite the nations, and he
will rule them with a rod of iron; he will
tread the wine press of the fury of the
wrath of God the Almighty. [16]On his robe
and on his thigh he has a name inscribed,
King of kings and Lord of lords.

The Beast and Its Armies Defeated

17 Then I saw an angel standing in the
sun, and with a loud voice he called to all
the birds that fly in midheaven, "Come,
gather for the great supper of God, [18]to
eat the flesh of kings, the flesh of cap-
tains, the flesh of mighty men, the flesh
of horses and their riders, and the flesh
of all men, both free and slave, both small
and great." [19]And I saw the beast and the
kings of the earth with their armies
gathered to make war against him who
sits upon the horse and against his army.
[20]And the beast was captured, and with
it the false prophet who in its presence
had worked the signs by which he de-
ceived those who had received the mark
of the beast and those who worshiped
its image. These two were thrown alive
into the lake of fire that burns with brim-
stone. [21]And the rest were slain by the
sword of him who sits upon the horse,
the sword that issues from his mouth;
and all the birds were gorged with their
flesh.

The Thousand Years

20 Then I saw an angel coming down
from heaven, holding in his hand
the key of the bottomless pit and a great
chain. [2]And he seized the dragon, that
ancient serpent, who is the Devil and Sa-
tan, and bound him for a thousand years,
[3]and threw him into the pit, and shut it
and sealed it over him, that he should de-
ceive the nations no more, till the thou-
sand years were ended. After that he
must be loosed for a little while.

4 Then I saw thrones, and seated on
them were those to whom judgment was
committed. Also I saw the souls of those
who had been beheaded for their testi-
mony to Jesus and for the word of God,
and who had not worshiped the beast or
its image and had not received its mark
on their foreheads or their hands. They
came to life, and reigned with Christ a
thousand years. [5]The rest of the dead
did not come to life until the thousand
years were ended. This is the first res-
urrection. [6]Blessed and holy is he who
shares in the first resurrection! Over
such the second death has no power, but
they shall be priests of God and of Christ,
and they shall reign with him a thousand
years.

Satan's Doom

7 And when the thousand years are
ended, Satan will be loosed from his
prison [8]and will come out to deceive the
nations which are at the four corners
of the earth, that is, Gog and Magog, to
gather them for battle; their number
is like the sand of the sea. [9]And they
marched up over the broad earth and
surrounded the camp of the saints and
the beloved city; but fire came down from
heaven[o] and consumed them, [10]and the
devil who had deceived them was thrown
into the lake of fire and brimstone where
the beast and the false prophet were, and
they will be tormented day and night for
ever and ever.

The Dead Are Judged

11 Then I saw a great white throne and
him who sat upon it; from his presence
earth and sky fled away, and no place
was found for them. [12]And I saw the
dead, great and small, standing before
the throne, and books were opened. Also
another book was opened, which is the
book of life. And the dead were judged
by what was written in the books, by
what they had done. [13]And the sea gave
up the dead in it, Death and Hades gave

[o]**20.9** Other ancient authorities read *from God, out of heaven,* or *out of heaven from God*

up the dead in them, and all were judged
by what they had done. [14]Then Death and
Hades were thrown into the lake of fire.
This is the second death, the lake of fire;
[15]and if any one's name was not found
written in the book of life, he was thrown
into the lake of fire.

The New Heaven and the New Earth

21 Then I saw a new heaven and a new
earth; for the first heaven and the
first earth had passed away, and the sea
was no more. [2]And I saw the holy city,
new Jerusalem, coming down out of
heaven from God, prepared as a bride
adorned for her husband; [3]and I heard a
great voice from the throne saying, "Be-
hold, the dwelling of God is with men. He
will dwell with them, and they shall be
his people,[p] and God himself will be with
them;[q] [4]he will wipe away every tear
from their eyes, and death shall be no
more, neither shall there be mourning
nor crying nor pain any more, for the
former things have passed away."

5 And he who sat upon the throne said,
"Behold, I make all things new." Also he
said, "Write this, for these words are
trustworthy and true." [6]And he said to
me, "It is done! I am the Alpha and the
Omega, the beginning and the end. To the
thirsty I will give water without price
from the fountain of the water of life.
[7]He who conquers shall have this her-
itage, and I will be his God and he shall
be my son. [8]But as for the cowardly, the
faithless, the polluted, as for murderers,
fornicators, sorcerers, idolaters, and all
liars, their lot shall be in the lake that
burns with fire and brimstone, which is
the second death."

Vision of the New Jerusalem

9 Then came one of the seven angels who
had the seven bowls full of the seven last
plagues, and spoke to me, saying, "Come,
I will show you the Bride, the wife of the
Lamb." [10]And in the Spirit he carried
me away to a great, high mountain, and
showed me the holy city Jerusalem com-
ing down out of heaven from God, [11]hav-
ing the glory of God, its radiance like
a most rare jewel, like a jasper, clear as
crystal. [12]It had a great, high wall, with
twelve gates, and at the gates twelve an-
gels, and on the gates the names of the
twelve tribes of the sons of Israel were
inscribed; [13]on the east three gates, on
the north three gates, on the south three
gates, and on the west three gates. [14]And
the wall of the city had twelve founda-
tions, and on them the twelve names of
the twelve apostles of the Lamb.

15 And he who talked to me had a
measuring rod of gold to measure the
city and its gates and walls. [16]The city
lies foursquare, its length the same as
its breadth; and he measured the city
with his rod, twelve thousand stadia;[r] its
length and breadth and height are equal.
[17]He also measured its wall, a hundred
and forty-four cubits by a man's mea-
sure, that is, an angel's. [18]The wall was
built of jasper, while the city was pure
gold, clear as glass. [19]The foundations of
the wall of the city were adorned with
every jewel; the first was jasper, the sec-
ond sapphire, the third agate, the fourth
emerald, [20]the fifth onyx, the sixth carne-
lian, the seventh chrysolite, the eighth
beryl, the ninth topaz, the tenth chrys-
oprase, the eleventh jacinth, the twelfth
amethyst. [21]And the twelve gates were
twelve pearls, each of the gates made of
a single pearl, and the street of the city
was pure gold, transparent as glass.

22 And I saw no temple in the city, for
its temple is the Lord God the Almighty
and the Lamb. [23]And the city has no need
of sun or moon to shine upon it, for the
glory of God is its light, and its lamp is
the Lamb. [24]By its light shall the nations

[p]**21.3** Other ancient authorities read *peoples*
[q]**21.3** Other ancient authorities add *and be their God*
[r]**21.16** About fifteen hundred miles

walk; and the kings of the earth shall bring their glory into it, 25 and its gates shall never be shut by day—and there shall be no night there; 26 they shall bring into it the glory and the honor of the nations. 27 But nothing unclean shall enter it, nor any one who practices abomination or falsehood, but only those who are written in the Lamb's book of life.

The River of Life

22 Then he showed me the river of the water of life, bright as crystal, flowing from the throne of God and of the Lamb 2 through the middle of the street of the city; also, on either side of the river, the tree of life[s] with its twelve kinds of fruit, yielding its fruit each month; and the leaves of the tree were for the healing of the nations. 3 There shall no more be anything accursed, but the throne of God and of the Lamb shall be in it, and his servants shall worship him; 4 they shall see his face, and his name shall be on their foreheads. 5 And night shall be no more; they need no light of lamp or sun, for the Lord God will be their light, and they shall reign for ever and ever.

6 And he said to me, "These words are trustworthy and true. And the Lord, the God of the spirits of the prophets, has sent his angel to show his servants what must soon take place. 7 And behold, I am coming soon."

Blessed is he who keeps the words of the prophecy of this book.

Epilogue and Benediction

8 I John am he who heard and saw these things. And when I heard and saw them, I fell down to worship at the feet of the angel who showed them to me; 9 but he said to me, "You must not do that! I am a fellow servant with you and your brethren the prophets, and with those who keep the words of this book. Worship God."

10 And he said to me, "Do not seal up the words of the prophecy of this book, for the time is near. 11 Let the evildoer still do evil, and the filthy still be filthy, and the righteous still do right, and the holy still be holy."

12 "Behold, I am coming soon, bringing my recompense, to repay every one for what he has done. 13 I am the Alpha and the Omega, the first and the last, the beginning and the end."

14 Blessed are those who wash their robes,[t] that they may have the right to the tree of life and that they may enter the city by the gates. 15 Outside are the dogs and sorcerers and fornicators and murderers and idolaters, and every one who loves and practices falsehood.

16 "I Jesus have sent my angel to you with this testimony for the churches. I am the root and the offspring of David, the bright morning star."

17 The Spirit and the Bride say, "Come." And let him who hears say, "Come." And let him who is thirsty come, let him who desires take the water of life without price.

18 I warn every one who hears the words of the prophecy of this book: if any one adds to them, God will add to him the plagues described in this book, 19 and if any one takes away from the words of the book of this prophecy, God will take away his share in the tree of life and in the holy city, which are described in this book.

20 He who testifies to these things says, "Surely I am coming soon." Amen. Come, Lord Jesus!

21 The grace of the Lord Jesus be with all the saints.[u] Amen.

[s] **22.2** Or *the Lamb. In the midst of the street of the city, and on either side of the river, was the tree of life,* etc.
[t] **22.14** Other ancient authorities read *do his commandments*
[u] **22.21** Other ancient authorities omit *all;* others omit *the saints*

NOTES

NOTES

NOTES

NOTES

NOTES

NOTES

NOTES

NOTES

www.SeeMessiah.com

About Cenacle

Cenacle is a new media company telling the stories of the Bible, Church history, and the lives of the saints. Cenacle is known for *Messiah*, an 8 part series on the Bible and early Church history released September 2019.

Hosted by Leonardo Defilippis and filmed at nearly 30 locations in the US, Holy Land, and Rome, *Messiah* explores the messianic prophecies of the Bible and how they were fulfilled by Jesus and the Church. Learn more at SeeMessiah.com.

CPSIA information can be obtained
at www.ICGtesting.com
Printed in the USA
BVHW050944270623
666404BV00016B/62

9 781951 739065